International Dimensions of Educational Leadership and Management for Economic Growth

Icarbord Tshabangu
https://orcid.org/0000-0003-4875-9369
Leeds Trinity University, UK

IGI Global
Scientific Publishing
Publishing Tomorrow's Research Today

Vice President of Editorial Melissa Wagner
Director of Acquisitions Mikaela Felty
Director of Book Development Jocelynn Hessler
Production Manager Mike Brehm
Cover Design Jose Rosado

Published in the United States of America by
IGI Global Scientific Publishing
701 East Chocolate Avenue
Hershey, PA, 17033, USA
Tel: 717-533-8845 | Fax: 717-533-7115
Website: https://www.igi-global.com E-mail: cust@igi-global.com

Library of Congress Cataloging-in-Publication Data

Names: Tshabangu, Icarbord, 1968- editor
Title: International dimensions of educational leadership and management for economic growth / Icarbord Tshabangu.
Description: Hershey, PA : IGI Global Scientific Publishing, [2026] | Includes bibliographical references and index. | Summary: "This book aims to address the subject of leadership and management in education by providing international dimensions and understanding in the field"-- Provided by publisher.
Identifiers: LCCN 2025021285 (print) | LCCN 2025021286 (ebook) | ISBN 9798337336169 hardcover | ISBN 9798337336176 paperback | ISBN 9798337336183 ebook
Subjects: LCSH: Educational leadership--Cross-cultural studies | Education--Economic aspects--Cross-cultural studies | School management and organization--Cross-cultural studies
Classification: LCC LB2806 .I5265 2026 (print) | LCC LB2806 (ebook)
LC record available at https://lccn.loc.gov/2025021285
LC ebook record available at https://lccn.loc.gov/2025021286

British Cataloguing in Publication Data
A Cataloguing in Publication record for this book is available from the British Library.

Table of Contents

Detailed Table of Contents

Educational leadership is no longer confined to national boundaries. It is a global endeavour shaped by diverse ideologies, cultural paradigms, and socio-economic imperatives. This chapter traces the evolution of key leadership theories—from transactional and transformational models to distributed and servant leadership—through the lens of international experiences. Drawing on comparative insights, it examines how cultural, political, and economic contexts influence leadership practices in education systems worldwide. The chapter critically examines how leadership influences institutional effectiveness, equity, and innovation, ultimately contributing to economic development. By weaving together theory and practice, it invites readers to reconsider what it means to lead in an interconnected, multicultural educational landscape. In doing so, it aims not merely to inform but to provoke a reimagining of leadership that is as ethical, inclusive, effective, and visionary.

This chapter explores the pivotal role of transformational educational leadership in fostering economic resilience across global contexts. It examines how visionary, adaptive, and inclusive leadership practices in educational institutions contribute to sustainable economic development, workforce preparedness, and social stability. By integrating global perspectives, the chapter highlights best practices, policy innovations, and leadership models that address contemporary challenges such as technological disruption, inequality, and socioeconomic shocks. Case studies from various regions are presented to illustrate strategic frameworks that leverage education as a driver for economic recovery and long-term resilience. The chapter also emphasises the significance of collaborative networks, digital transformation, and capacity-building initiatives in enhancing institutional adaptability and societal well-being.

This study examines the comparative dynamics of educational leadership and management in the European Union (EU) and the South Asian Association for Regional Cooperation (SAARC) regions, with a focus on their roles in promoting economic growth. Through a qualitative analysis, the research examines key aspects, including educational integration, human capital development, innovation capacity, and labour market alignment. The EU's cohesive, innovation-driven educational system, along with its alignment with economic goals, provides a model of success. In contrast, the SAARC region faces challenges related to fragmented educational systems and insufficient leadership. The study emphasises the importance of regional collaboration, inclusive education, vocational training, and policy harmonisation for unlocking the economic potential of the SAARC region. Recommendations are made for both areas to enhance educational leadership, promote innovation, and align education with labour market needs, thereby driving sustainable economic development.

This chapter explores the relationship between educational leadership, management, and economic growth in the BRICS nations (Brazil, Russia, India, China, and South Africa). By analysing educational policies, labour market demands, and educational outputs, the research investigates how educational disparities impact economic development. The study highlights the challenges faced by countries such as Brazil, India, and South Africa, where inequalities in access, quality, and skills mismatches hinder economic growth. In contrast, China and Russia have effectively aligned their education systems with industrial and technological goals, fostering economic

peacebuilding mechanisms, promoting a sense of civic responsibility and active citizenship, amidst diversity.

This chapter examines the pivotal role that community involvement plays in shaping educational leadership that promotes sustainable growth. It suggests that relying solely on top-down leadership is no longer enough to address the complex challenges facing education today. Instead, meaningful participation from communities is shown to improve accountability, relevance, and fairness within schools. Using a mix of theoretical insights and examples from different countries, the chapter explores various ways communities engage, the institutional structures that support this involvement, and approaches to building local capacity. Challenges such as decentralisation issues, power imbalances, and cultural barriers are also considered. The chapter concludes by emphasising that including community voices in educational decisions not only enhances learning but also supports broader social and economic progress, which is crucial for the future of education.

In an era defined by complexity, uncertainty, and rapid change, traditional management approaches in education often fall short in delivering quality outcomes. This chapter explores innovative management strategies that reimagine how educational institutions can lead with vision, agility, and inclusivity. Drawing on global examples and evidence-informed practices, the chapter examines how educational leaders can foster a culture of continuous improvement, embed innovation into strategic planning, and leverage data to make context-sensitive decisions. It also emphasises the role of inclusive governance and stakeholder collaboration in sustaining quality across diverse educational landscapes. Rather than offering a one-size-fits-all solution, the chapter highlights the necessity of adapting strategies to local needs while maintaining a global awareness. In doing so, it argues for a reframing of leadership—one that is proactive, reflective, and deeply committed to the human dimensions of education as a lever for economic and societal growth.

Foreword

The effectiveness of education systems is closely tied to the quality of their leaders and managers. However, the responsibilities of these professionals are becoming increasingly complex. Not only must they respond to growing demands driven by national socio-economic, cultural, and political needs and pressures, but they are also called to address global challenges, including economic instability, technological disruption, social inequality, and environmental sustainability, among others. Educators also work within the context of ongoing national and international debates, including those around: the purposes of education; the efficacy of the many theories and models of leadership; how best to ensure equity and social justice in diverse settings; and how to adapt to the rise of digital technologies and their practical and ethical implications. Of course, there is no consensus around, and no simple solutions to these types of issues. The pace of change in the world feels faster than ever before, demanding agility and adaptability from professionals and systems alike. How then can leaders and managers begin to tackle them?

Education systems are shaped by unique historical, political, and socio-economic conditions, which means that leadership models and management strategies often reflect local priorities, enablers and constraints. While not all national educational practices are transferable to different cultural contexts, there is nonetheless significant value in studying and learning from the approaches adopted by other countries. Such diversity presents a rich opportunity for cross-cultural learning and innovation. Insights arising from them can broaden perspectives, which can encourage adapting behaviours that are sensitive to local needs while being informed by global best practices.

Moreover, cross-cultural dialogue in educational leadership fosters a spirit of collaboration and shared responsibility for improving learning outcomes worldwide, collectively thinking beyond national borders and considering how education can contribute to meeting goals such as economic development, social cohesion, and sustainability. This book, with its inclusion of comparative approaches, facilitates this way of thinking.

As the title of this volume indicates, the focus is on international education systems' leadership and management for economic growth – a key political global aim. Importantly, the authors draw attention to the human dimension involved in this endeavour: the need for communities' voices, students' holistic development, and the contributions of peace education, for example. These authors remind us that leaders and managers can only achieve their aims by remaining aware of, and genuinely valuing, the human perspectives that make and shape educational environments.

This book offers a timely and insightful exploration of how educational leadership can serve as a strategic driver of economic development in ways that are sustainable and equitable. It brings together an array of authors from different continents with varied conceptual, theoretical, and practical frameworks that reflect the global and cultural diversity of educational leadership. The contributors draw on their expertise across a range of areas, including digital technology, artificial intelligence, business, national security, economics and social media, highlighting how these and other forces are part of a wider reshaping of the expectations and capacities of educational leaders. At the same time, the book remains grounded in core concerns such as quality management, organisational culture, and sustainable development, offering a balanced view of both innovation and continuity.

This edited collection, therefore, invites readers to explore the transformative power of educational leadership in a globalised world. By drawing on exemplary practices, theoretical insights, and comparative perspectives, it challenges us to broaden our horizons - encouraging us to think globally, act locally, and lead with the best interests of our learners at heart for a more equitable world.

Kate Adams (PhD) is Professor of Education in the School of Education and Childhood at Leeds Trinity University, UK. She is a former primary school teacher and a long-standing researcher of children's inner worlds and the implications for holistic approaches to education. Kate has held several leadership roles. These include a current position as Deputy Director of Postgraduate Research, and former roles of institutional Director of Research at two other UK universities. She is on the Executive Committee of the International Association for Children's Spirituality and serves on the international advisory boards for three peer-reviewed journals

Kate Adams
Leeds Trinity University, UK

Preface

Educational management and leadership are a discipline focused on developing skills and policies for the effective management of educational institutions. Management is the utilisation of physical and human resources through cooperative efforts. It is a process of working with and through individuals and groups of people to accomplish organisational goals. On the other hand, leadership is about influencing others' actions to achieve desirable ends, and leaders shape organisational goals through motivating others. In education, there has been a gradual shift from educational management and administration towards an emphasis on educational leadership, which is seen as an exercise of influence rather than authority. This notion is linked to contemporary epistemologies, such as distributed leadership, where there is a loosening of formal roles within an organisation, thereby allowing those below the hierarchy, such as teachers and students, to exercise some power and influence. (Spillane & Diamond, 2007; Harris, 2008; Wise, 2011; Bush, Bell & Middlewood, 2019; Bush, 2020). Both leadership and management continue to be vital functions that help maximise efficiency in organisations, such as the provision of quality education, managing performance, and strategic planning, ultimately leading to national economic growth.

The key facets in fostering economic growth include the following: ***human capital development,*** which relies on effective educational leadership to ensure that educational systems and institutions effectively equip their workforce, their learners and infrastructure. Ultimately, this enhances staff productivity and outcomes, a key driver for economic growth. ***Strategic alignment*** requires educational leaders to align educational outcomes with the needs of the industry. Such an alignment requires educational institutions to design and adapt curricula to ensure relevant skills, for improved employment rates and productivity. There is also a need for partnerships, work placements, apprenticeships and internships between education and industry, as a vital cog in economic development. ***Fostering Innovation*** requires educational leaders to cultivate learning spaces that promote creativity and entrepreneurialism. Through the integration of relevant academic content and industrial opportunities, we aim to produce graduates capable of innovations in business and technology, which is critical for driving economic growth. ***Efficient and Equitable Resource Provision*** involves strategically allocating human, material and financial resources for optimum outcomes, which involves directly funding frontline services and areas that bring high returns on investment, such as quality infrastructure and service delivery, to optimise positive impact on the broader economy, thus reducing educational and other inequalities, fostering greater social mobility, inclusiveness and sustainable economic growth in the long term (UNECE, 2013; Quamrul H. Ashraf, David N. Weil (2024; Missaglia & Vaggi, 2025). Research indicates that for every $1 invested in education, the returns generated in economic growth could be as much as 15 times (UNESCO, 2015). Effective educational leadership and management are therefore essential for translating educational investment into tangible economic benefits for a nation.

Centuries ago, citizens were largely uneducated. Rulers often had a monopoly of information, and thus Tolstoy (1894) records that rulers often demanded or enforced obedience without question. In the 21st century, where the media and technology have revolutionised modern democracy, such forms of leadership at every level, including education, have become obsolete, and a greater demand for shared leadership has taken root. It is now unthinkable that the role of educational employees, students and parents can only be limited to mere deference towards the institutional leaders. It is because of such a factor that educational leaders ought to consider more and more leadership approaches that are transformational, democratic, and distributed in nature.

Cloke and Goldsmith (2002: 37) note that while leadership is consensual, management tends to be coercive, and the difference is clearly revealed in what happens when employees disagree with management. As opposed to a manager, the leader has a long-range perspective. By its nature, management is linear, logical and fails to satisfactorily attend to most educational concerns, which are dynamic and dialectical. It is not surprising, therefore, that in the academic arena there have been recent moves to calibrate management courses to include leadership aspects (Harber, 1999; Cloke & Goldsmith, 2002).

This book advances a search for a transformational as opposed to transactional form of leadership or management. Transformational leadership is collaborative, consultative and consensus-seeking. On the contrary, transactional leadership tends to confine itself to a managerial level, relying more on hierarchy and the power of organisational position, thriving on formal authority and the ability to reward and punish performance (Markham, 1998). This scenario is typical of the Performance appraisal system in some educational institutions, hence the reluctance, at times, by some employees to fully cooperate with its implementation. Transformational leadership offers a humanistic approach defined by an open and empowering culture where communication, strong values and mutual respect are the norm (Clegg, 2000). At a global level, the gatekeepers of most educational institutions often operate between these two registers: transformational and transactional leadership and management. Tavca (2000, cited in Stronach, Sirca and Dimc, 2000: 51) bemoans the fact that some educational leaders will only consider themselves to be administrators and managers and thus fail to tap into,

> *The whole knowledge patrimony, which has been accumulated through centuries by capable others, this knowledge formalised in the organisational theory, the theory of leadership and the theory of management, must be considered valuable in educational institutions.*

The way heads of educational institutions understand the nexus and significance between education and economic growth through human capital in their organisation, and can succeed, will often depend on whether they gravitate more towards being leaders or managers, transactional or transformational.

The objective of this publication has been to explore the subject of leadership and management in education, offering international perspectives and insights into the field. The publication contributes to a knowledge base relevant to the training of educational leaders and educators in leadership roles. Leadership and management roles are key in communicating organisational policies and plans to ensure competitiveness and the attainment of institutional goals. The book should prompt practitioners to reflect on issues and factors that impact their practice, educational governance, and the role this plays in human and economic development. It has been noted above that education and economic growth are inextricably linked, with education serving as a catalyst for human capital and productivity, which ultimately leads to a stronger economy. Effective educational management and leadership are, therefore, key to ensuring the economic growth of any nation.

The targeted audience for this book is educational policymakers, teachers, educational leaders, and educational researchers. The book chapters provide conceptual, practical, and theoretical frameworks in the field, exploring different cultural practices in educational leadership and management. They also offer readers and practitioners an international dimension, allowing them to learn from other relevant experiences, cultural practices, and contexts that are suitable for academic management and leadership.

INSIDE THIS BOOK

This book has thirteen chapters on educational leadership and management, focused on theoretical and strategic models of leadership, varied case studies and analyses on countries and regions and discusses multidisciplinary approaches and institutional strategies necessary for economic growth.

Chapter 1 asserts that educational leadership is no longer confined to national boundaries. It is a global endeavour shaped by diverse ideologies, cultural paradigms, and socioeconomic imperatives. This chapter traces the evolution of key leadership theories—from transactional and transformational models to distributed and servant leadership—through the lens of international experiences. Drawing on comparative insights, it examines how cultural, political, and economic contexts influence leadership practices in education systems worldwide. The chapter critically examines how leadership influences institutional effectiveness, equity, and innovation, ultimately contributing to economic development. By weaving together theory and practice, it invites readers to reconsider what it means to lead in an interconnected, multicultural educational landscape. In doing so, it aims not merely to inform but to provoke a reimagining of leadership that is as ethical, inclusive, practical, and visionary.

Chapter 2 explores the pivotal role of transformational educational leadership in fostering economic resilience across global contexts. It examines how visionary, adaptive, and inclusive leadership practices in educational institutions contribute to sustainable economic development, workforce preparedness, and social stability. By integrating global perspectives, the chapter highlights best practices, policy innovations, and leadership models that address contemporary challenges such as technological disruption, inequality, and socioeconomic shocks. Case studies from various regions are presented to illustrate strategic frameworks that leverage education as a driver for economic recovery and long-term resilience. The chapter also emphasises the significance of collaborative networks, digital transformation, and capacity-building initiatives in enhancing institutional adaptability and societal well-being.

Chapter 3 examines the comparative dynamics of educational leadership and management in the European Union (EU) and the South Asian Association for Regional Cooperation (SAARC) regions, with a focus on their roles in promoting economic growth. Through a qualitative analysis, the research examines key aspects, including educational integration, human capital development, innovation capacity, and labour market alignment. The EU's cohesive, innovation-driven educational system, along with its alignment with economic goals, provides a model of success. In contrast, the SAARC region faces challenges related to fragmented educational systems and insufficient leadership. The study emphasises the importance of regional collaboration, inclusive education, vocational training, and policy harmonisation for unlocking the economic potential of the SAARC region. Recommendations are made for both areas to enhance educational leadership, promote innovation, and align education with labour market needs, thereby driving sustainable economic development.

Chapter 4 explores the relationship between educational leadership, management, and economic growth in the BRICS nations (Brazil, Russia, India, China, and South Africa). By analysing educational policies, labour market demands, and educational outputs, the research investigates how educational disparities impact economic development. The study highlights the challenges faced by countries such as Brazil, India, and South Africa, where inequalities in access, quality, and skills mismatches hinder economic growth. In contrast, China and Russia have effectively aligned their education systems with industrial and technological goals, fostering economic competitiveness. Using a mixed-methods approach, which combines quantitative data analysis with qualitative case studies, the research provides insights into how educational reforms can drive economic integration and sustainable growth. Findings emphasise the need for systemic educational reforms to address inequality and improve workforce readiness, contributing to SDG 4 (Quality Education) and SDG 8 (Decent Work and Economic Growth).

Chapter 5 posits that education is essential for society's growth and economic development. From the UDHR, all international conventions, national constitutions, and enactments have prioritised education for transforming society. This became more explicit with the SDG4 (quality education). Based on the UDHR and SDG4 guidelines, India also prioritises augmenting the educational sector in its policies and programs. The national education policies provide a foundational framework for this effort. Although many researchers praise the 'Kerala model' of education, several others sharply criticise it as not aligning with the demands of quality and job market requirements. In 2023, almost 250000 students emigrated from Kerala for educational purposes. The student emigration constitutes nearly 11.3% of the state's total emigration, raising serious concerns about the quality of education. From this perspective, this chapter critically examines sustainable education and economic development aspirations, evaluating the educational landscape of the most literate state in India, Kerala.

Chapter 6 asserts that leadership and management in developing countries operate amid volatility, policy drift, and thin infrastructure. Inside those frictions sits a growth engine. Effective educational leadership is an economic capability: it compounds human capital, improves allocative efficiency in local labour markets, professionalises routines that firms later mimic, and thickens the trust investors watch before they commit. Read this as an economics of leadership. We trace context-sensitive models and inclusive management that translate into development signals: higher retention and completion, faster school-to-work transitions, rising female labour-force participation, microenterprise formation, and multiplier effects. The claim is not romantic; it is empirical. Growth here is not only capital and technology. It is mediated by place-literate leadership that reduces wastage, compresses delays, and aligns schools with value chains, while holding equity, sustainability, and fiscal prudence together.

Chapter 7 argues that educational institutions should embrace democratic leadership styles to enhance organisational commitment and a cooperative working culture. Evidence clearly demonstrates the importance of democratic educational reform in promoting economic development in Ethiopia. With the application of participatory approaches to leadership, schools can become both child and staff-centred, which manifests in improved educational outcomes and economic growth. Study results suggest that democratic educational leadership creates the right environment that leads to enhanced OCB in teachers. KMO value was used to ensure that the analytical sample is suitable, whereas CFA was used to determine the reliability and validity of the measurement model. SEM analysis showed that democratic leadership may improve OCB indirectly and directly, through encouraging greater participation and engagement of teachers. This study proposes a policy change that is consistent with the democratic school practices to promote excellence in education as well as ensure socioeconomic development.

Chapter 8 analyses how Nigeria faces persistent challenges to national security, arising from ethnic and religious conflicts, terrorism and widespread violence. These occurrences highlight the importance of both critical political and educational leadership and effective peace education. Peace education aims to equip individuals with the skills and knowledge to resolve conflicts peacefully, promote tolerance, political accountability and build inclusive societies. Leadership, particularly educational leadership that is focused on peace education, would prioritise adequate funding, educational quality and curricula reform, which will lead to innovation and human capital development that can foster environments where open dialogue and diverse viewpoints are valued, thus providing an opportunity for effective peacebuilding and meaningful economic growth in various spheres. Through the nation's educational curriculum and willing educational leaders, there is great potential for ensuring national security through peacebuilding mechanisms, promoting a sense of civic responsibility and active citizenship, amidst diversity.

Chapter 9 examines the pivotal role that community involvement plays in shaping educational leadership that promotes sustainable growth. It suggests that relying solely on top-down leadership is no longer enough to address the complex challenges facing education today. Instead, meaningful participation from communities is shown to improve accountability, relevance, and fairness within schools. Using a mix of theoretical insights and examples from different countries, the chapter explores various ways communities engage, the institutional structures that support this involvement, and approaches to building local capacity. Challenges such as decentralisation issues, power imbalances, and cultural barriers are also considered. The chapter concludes by emphasising that including community voices in educational decisions not only enhances learning but also supports broader social and economic progress, which is crucial for the future of education.

Chapter 10 asserts that in an era defined by complexity, uncertainty, and rapid change, traditional management approaches in education often fall short in delivering quality outcomes. This chapter explores innovative management strategies that reimagine how educational institutions can lead with vision, agility, and inclusivity. Drawing on global examples and evidence-informed practices, the chapter examines how educational leaders can foster a culture of continuous improvement, embed innovation into strategic planning, and leverage data to make context-sensitive decisions. It also emphasises the role of inclusive governance and stakeholder collaboration in sustaining quality across diverse educational landscapes. Rather than offering a one-size-fits-all solution, the chapter highlights the necessity of adapting strategies to local needs while maintaining a global awareness. In doing so, it argues for a reframing of leadership—one that is proactive, reflective, and deeply committed to the human dimensions of education as a lever for economic and societal growth.

Chapter 11 takes a closer look at the decisive role that artificial intelligence (AI) and social media can play in shaping sustainable and inclusive education systems. It focuses on how educational leaders are essential in managing the tricky balance between embracing new technologies and addressing ethical concerns, especially around fairness and human values. Through several cross-cultural examples, the chapter shows how different regions approach AI integration, highlighting common challenges like digital gaps and biases in algorithms. It also explores how these technologies impact human capital growth, economic sustainability, and policy-making. By offering practical advice for policymakers and education leaders, the chapter encourages leadership that is flexible, collaborative, and ethically aware, aiming to use AI and social media as tools to promote fair and meaningful change in education today.

Chapter 12 explores the vital role of disciplinary networks in fostering positive behavioural management through a global leadership lens. It examines how distributed and transformational leadership theories, combined with social learning and systems thinking, provide a robust framework for understanding and improving behaviour governance in schools. Drawing on diverse international case studies from Finland's collaborative culture to Bangladesh's community engagement, the chapter highlights culturally responsive strategies that empower educators, students, and stakeholders. It underscores the impact of inclusive leadership on school climate, equity, and academic outcomes, while offering policy recommendations to align disciplinary practices with broader social and economic goals. Finally, the chapter argues that strategic leadership, rooted in collaborative networks, is essential for creating sustainable, equitable, and effective behavioural management systems across varied educational contexts worldwide.

Chapter 13 examines the role of academic heads in accounting departments, as endorsed by the South African Institute of Chartered Accountants, with a focus on Historically Disadvantaged Institutions. Drawing on the author's ten years of experience as Academic Head of the Accounting Department, combined with document analysis and an integrated theoretical framework, the chapter offers a holistic lens for understanding lived academic leadership in accounting education in South Africa. The chapter outlines the academic head's role, responsibilities, and expectations, as well as the challenges, opportunities, and core competencies required to fulfil their roles. Additionally, the chapter outlines the key outcomes of the SAICA endorsement journey, including the formal endorsement of the BCom programme, staff capacity development, and improvements in students' performance. It concludes by emphasising the need for a more strategic and integrated approach to leadership development for academic heads of accounting departments.

CONCLUSION

Educational leadership and management are critical drivers of economic growth, primarily through the development of human capital, which includes skills, knowledge, and competencies necessary for national economic needs. Effective and efficient education leadership undergirds the creation of educational systems that are responsive to the labour market, opportunities for innovation, and equity. Educational leadership has a duty to create a satisfactory educational environment upon which a conducive culture and environment for socioeconomic growth can be founded and nurtured.

Icarbord Tshabangu
Leeds Trinity University, United Kingdom

Acknowledgment

The editor would like to acknowledge the help of all the people involved in this project and, more specifically, the chapter authors who took part in both the review process and chapter contribution, respectively. Without their support, this book would not have become a reality.

Our sincere gratitude also goes to the main reviewers who helped assess and/or review most chapters for approval. Their contribution, time and expertise proved invaluable to this book project, particularly in raising the quality of the chapters and the book overall.

Icarbord Tshabangu
Leeds Trinity University, UK

Chapter 1
Theories of Educational Leadership:
A Global Perspective

Mustafa Kayyali
https://orcid.org/0000-0003-3300-262X
Maaref University of Applied Sciences, Syria

ABSTRACT

Educational leadership is no longer confined to national boundaries. It is a global endeavour shaped by diverse ideologies, cultural paradigms, and socio-economic imperatives. This chapter traces the evolution of key leadership theories—from transactional and transformational models to distributed and servant leadership—through the lens of international experiences. Drawing on comparative insights, it examines how cultural, political, and economic contexts influence leadership practices in education systems worldwide. The chapter critically examines how leadership influences institutional effectiveness, equity, and innovation, ultimately contributing to economic development. By weaving together theory and practice, it invites readers to reconsider what it means to lead in an interconnected, multicultural educational landscape. In doing so, it aims not merely to inform but to provoke a reimagining of leadership that is as ethical, inclusive, effective, and visionary.

INTRODUCTION

Educational leadership has been a site of rich theoretical exploration and practical urgency, and more so, in the current era of global transformation (Kezar, 2023). Across continents and cultures, educational systems are being reimagined in response to economic volatility, demographic shifts, technological disruption,

DOI: 10.4018/979-8-3373-3616-9.ch001

and the call for greater equity and inclusion. Amid these pressures, one constant remains: the centrality of effective leadership in shaping educational outcomes. Whether in a rural school in Sub-Saharan Africa or a sprawling university in East Asia, academic leaders are being asked not only to manage, but to lead—to inspire change, cultivate resilience, and drive innovation (Makoe, 2023). However, what kind of leadership is needed in such a complex and interconnected world? What theories can help us understand the multifaceted roles that leaders play in diverse educational contexts? Moreover, how do these theories translate across cultures, economies, and political systems?

This chapter aims to address these questions by providing a comprehensive and comparative exploration of the major theories of educational leadership. It is not merely a catalogue of ideas, but a critical reflection on how these theories interact with the global realities of schooling and higher education. While leadership is often framed as a universal competency, it is deeply influenced by the values, histories, and institutional structures within which it is practised. Western-centric paradigms, while influential, are increasingly being challenged and enriched by leadership models emerging from the Global South, indigenous communities, and post-conflict societies. In an era where international benchmarks and rankings dominate the discourse, there is a growing need to question whose leadership is being valued, whose knowledge is being recognised, and whose voices are shaping the future of education.

To understand educational leadership today, one must begin with its theoretical foundations (Mazurkiewicz, 2021). The roots of contemporary practice can be traced through a diverse intellectual lineage, ranging from early behavioural and trait theories of leadership to transformational and transactional approaches, and more recent models such as distributed, instructional, and ethical leadership. Each of these theories provides a distinct perspective through which to view the challenges and opportunities facing educational leaders. However, theories do not exist in a vacuum. They are adopted, adapted, and contested in local contexts—where policy agendas, cultural expectations, and social inequalities intersect in unpredictable ways.

This chapter does not seek to prescribe a single best model of leadership. Instead, it aims to create a space for dialogue—between theory and practice, between the local and the global, and between traditional paradigms and emerging perspectives. It is an invitation to rethink what leadership means in education, and how it can be exercised in ways that are both contextually relevant and globally informed.

The discussion unfolds in five parts. It begins by revisiting foundational leadership theories and their influence on educational leadership discourse. It then examines how these theories have been reinterpreted and contested across various cultural and economic contexts. A section on global models of leadership examines how varied nations have translated theory into policy and practice. The fourth section focuses on leadership as a catalyst for economic and social development, particularly in under-resourced and postcolonial contexts. Finally, the chapter concludes by proposing a synthesis of insights, advocating for a globally responsive and ethically grounded vision of leadership that recognises diversity not as a challenge, but as a powerful resource. In traversing these themes, this chapter positions educational leadership as both an intellectual endeavour and a moral responsibility. It argues that understanding and applying leadership theories with cultural sensitivity and global awareness is not merely an academic exercise but a practical imperative in an increasingly interconnected world.

BACKGROUND - CLASSIC AND CONTEMPORARY LEADERSHIP THEORIES

Educational leadership theory, like the winding course of a river through uneven terrain, has never moved in a straight line (Verwolf, 2025). It bends and shifts, carving new directions as it encounters cultural contours, historical upheavals, and ideological stones. To revisit the foundations of leadership theory is not to walk backwards in time with nostalgia, but to pause long enough to listen to the echoes that still reverberate in today's school corridors and university halls. The past does not merely lie behind us—it hums beneath our feet, unsettled and persistent.

There is a strange comfort in the early theories of leadership—perhaps because they offer the illusion of clarity. The so-called "Great Man" theory, one of the earliest conceptualisations of leadership, painted it as something innate, as if greatness were a birthright. Leadership, in this frame, was not learned; it was bestowed, inherited, almost divine. One thinks of it now with a mixture of amusement and unease. The implicit gender bias, the elitism, the blind spot for context—it is all there, transparent in hindsight. However, its legacy still lingers. Even now, some educational institutions continue to lionise charismatic figures, prioritising personality over purpose, and elevating strong voices while silencing collaborative ones.

Trait theories soon followed, still holding onto the idea that specific personal characteristics—such as confidence, intelligence, and sociability—predicted leadership success (Ionela, 2021). On the surface, it seemed rational: identify the traits, cultivate them, and leadership would follow. However, this approach also had its blind spots. It overlooked the relational, the dynamic, the contextual. Leadership was reduced to a checklist, a set of attributes detached from the actual terrain of schools grappling with inequality or universities caught between tradition and transformation (Kayyali, 2025).

Table 1. Leadership Theory Alignment Matrix

Theory/model	Core emphasis	Strengths for learning	Risks if misapplied	Best-fit contexts
Transformational	Inspire, set moral/visionary direction	Energy; shared purpose; culture shift	Hero-model drift; charisma over context	System reform; crisis recovery
Transactional	Clear goals, incentives, and monitoring	Predictability; accountability	Compliance culture; narrow metrics	High-stakes testing; turnaround ops
Distributed	Agency shared across roles	Ownership; innovation at edges	Role ambiguity; diffusion of responsibility	Trusted teams; PLC cultures
Instructional	Pedagogy, coaching, assessment	Learning-centered focus	Narrowing to test prep; neglect of context	Closing achievement gaps
Servant/Ethical	Care, dignity, justice orientation	Trust; inclusion; community legitimacy	Decision paralysis occurs when too much consultation occurs	Diverse communities; faith/values
Culturally responsive	Honour local knowledges; anti-deficit	Belonging; relevance	Tokenism is superficial	Multilingual/indigenous settings
Systems/ Contingency	Fit leadership to context constraints	Adaptivity; realism	Fragmentation without core values	Volatile or resource-scarce systems

It was the behavioural theorists who shifted the focus from *who* a leader is to *what* a leader does. In the mid-20th century, models such as Ohio State's Leadership Behaviour Description Questionnaire and the University of Michigan studies reframed leadership around observable actions, including initiating structure, showing consideration, managing production, and facilitating relationships (Van Wart et al., 2023). Theories like these laid the groundwork for understanding leadership not as a static trait, but as an interplay of patterns, habits, and choices. Suddenly, leadership felt learnable, teachable. A quiet revolution, even if it did not yet have the vocabulary for inclusion, ethics, or cultural fluency.

Then came the contingency thinkers. Fiedler's Contingency Theory, House's Path-Goal Theory, and Hersey and Blanchard's Situational Leadership—all of them pushed the field forward by insisting that leadership effectiveness depends on fit. The leader is no longer an abstract constant; they must adapt to context, shape-shift to meet the demands of time, task, and temperament (Cairney & Toomey, 2025). The logic resonated—especially in education, where no two classrooms are identical, and where a principal's tone on a rainy Monday morning might matter as much as their five-year strategic plan. However, contingency models often assumed that leaders had both the self-awareness and the institutional freedom to adapt. That assumption is still prevalent and can sometimes feel painfully naïve.

Figure 1. Global Emphasis on Leadership Models

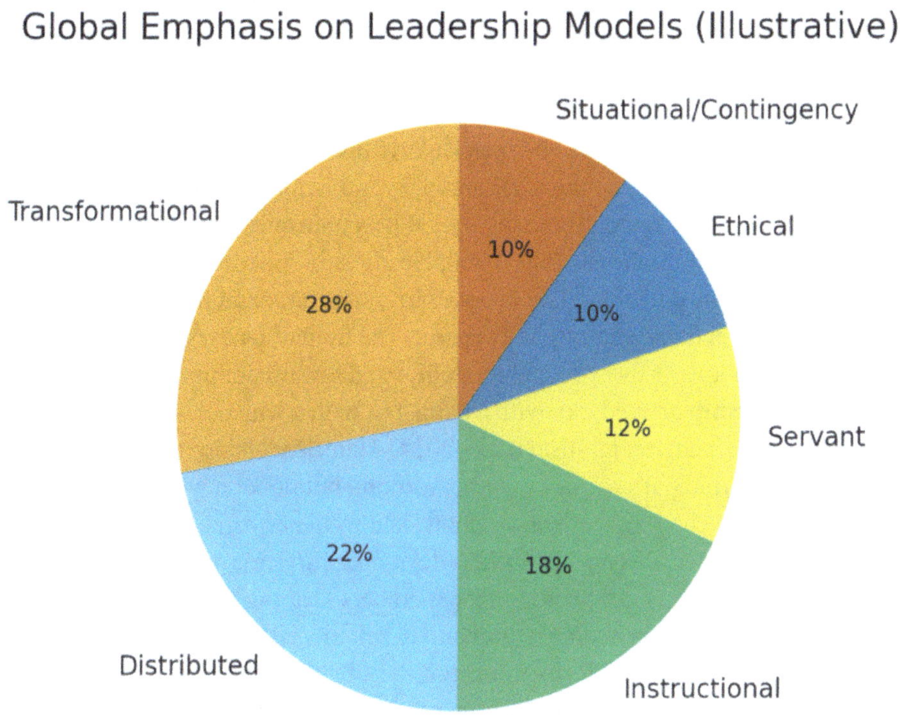

The **transformational leadership model,** arguably one of the most influential in educational literature, burst onto the scene with a kind of evangelical fervour (Bryant & Bryant, 2023). Developed by Burns and further developed by Bass, it asked leaders to inspire, elevate, and motivate through vision and moral clarity. The transformational leader was not just efficient—they were emotionally intelligent, ethically grounded, and future-oriented. In the context of education, this model gained significant traction. Schools and universities, after all, are places built on aspiration. The idea that leaders could be catalysts for profound change resonated deeply, particularly in times of systemic upheaval or reform.

However, as this model gained popularity, cracks began to appear. The emphasis on vision and charisma sometimes veered dangerously close to a return of the Great

Man archetype—albeit repackaged in modern language. Critics questioned its practicality, arguing that not every school needed a visionary; some required stability, accountability, and a steady hand (Poole & Todd-Diaz, 2022). Others pointed out that transformational leadership, when applied without cultural sensitivity, could feel colonial, imposing "change" where communities might have needed listening, not leading. Thereafter, **transactional leadership** emerged, often portrayed as the less glamorous sibling. Where transformational leadership soared on ideals, transactional leadership managed the ground game through rewards, consequences, and measurable goals. In many ways, it reflected the managerialism creeping into education systems across the globe, particularly under neoliberal regimes. Performance metrics, standardised testing, rankings, and audits—all of these fit neatly into the transactional mould. Some dismissed it as uninspiring, even authoritarian. However, for all its limitations, transactional leadership spoke a language that many educational systems understood: accountability, structure, and predictability.

Then, quietly and insistently, came a pivot. The field of leadership began to look downward and outward, away from hierarchies and toward communities; thus, **distributed leadership** arrived, not with a bang, but with a whisper —an invitation to share, collaborate, and decentralise (Blain, 2024). Here, leadership is not the exclusive property of the principal's office or the boardroom, but rather a web of interactions that flow through teachers, students, parents, and local networks—the school as an ecosystem. In practice, this meant teachers designing curricula collectively, students having a voice in policy, and community members shaping school culture. It was messy, yes—but also democratic, human. It acknowledged something previous models had not: that leadership does not require a title to be exercised, but influence.

Understandably, with democratisation came dilemmas. If everyone leads, who is responsible? If decision-making is shared, who bears the consequences when things fall apart? Distributed leadership walked a tightrope between empowerment and diffusion, collaboration and chaos (Ansell et al, 2022). However, its appeal endured, especially in cultures with strong collectivist traditions or in post-conflict contexts where hierarchical models had failed.

Then, **Instructional leadership** also carved out its niche, especially in systems focused on student outcomes and teacher effectiveness. This model brought leadership into the heart of the classroom, framing the principal not as an administrator, but as an instructional coach —a pedagogical guide (Voelkel Jr., 2023). It re-centred the learning process, positioning leadership as inherently tied to the quality of teaching. In contexts where achievement gaps were widening, this approach felt pragmatic and urgent. However, it also risked narrowing the leader's role to that of a curriculum technician, sidestepping the broader socio-political challenges that schools must contend with—such as poverty, trauma, and cultural erasure.

More recently, the conversation has turned toward ethical and culturally responsive leadership—perhaps in response to a growing recognition that education is not neutral, and neither is leadership (Banwo et al, 2022). **The ethical leader** leads with justice in mind—not just legal or procedural justice, but moral justice as well. They interrogate their own biases, engage with diverse epistemologies, and take a stand when silence would be more comfortable. This kind of leadership does not sit easily within spreadsheets or strategic frameworks. It is slow, reflective, and often uncomfortable. However, it is also essential—particularly in divided societies where schools are often the frontline of social cohesion or fracture.

Culturally responsive leadership, too, has demanded attention. As classrooms become more diverse—linguistically, racially, socioeconomically—leaders are called to move beyond tokenism and toward genuine inclusion (Lopez, 2025). This means more than celebrating holidays or translating newsletters. It means engaging deeply with the cultural assets of communities, resisting deficit thinking, and shaping policies that affirm rather than assimilate. It also means recognising when dominant leadership theories—especially those rooted in Western individualism—fall short in capturing the relational, collective, and intergenerational values that animate many communities worldwide.

What is striking is how rarely these models exist in isolation. In the real world of education, leadership is a hybrid, fluid concept. A principal may act as a transformational leader when rallying staff behind a new vision, a transactional leader when managing performance reviews, a distributed leader when facilitating departmental collaboration, and an ethical leader when confronting systemic racism (Sharma & Adeoye, 2024). The dance between these roles is constant—and rarely choreographed. Theory offers language, categories, and tools. However, life in educational institutions resists being put into tidy boxes.

Thus, the question arises: What do we do with this theoretical abundance? Are we richer for having so many models, or are we drowning in complexity? The answer lies in how we use them. Theories are not blueprints. They are lenses—some sharp, others distorted. They help us notice patterns, frame questions, and anticipate tensions. However, they are only as useful as our capacity to wield them with humility, curiosity, and context-awareness.

What becomes increasingly clear is that leadership is not a fixed identity, nor a static practice (Fry & Vu, 2024). It is an evolving relationship—between people, between ideas, between aspirations and constraints. It is as much about presence as it is about power. The best theories, then, are those that leave room for breath—for ambiguity, contradiction, learning.

As we revisit the foundations of educational leadership, we must also confront their silences (Wilkinson, 2021). Whose voices are absent in the canonical theories? Whose leadership practices remain undocumented because they do not fit established frames? What might we learn from the headteacher in Nairobi who weaves conflict resolution into morning assemblies? Or from the community organiser in Bogotá who teaches teenagers to lead without ever stepping into a school? Leadership is everywhere, but theory often struggles to identify it.

Moreover, maybe that is the most urgent task before us—not to chase the next trend, but to pause long enough to see what is already unfolding in the quiet corners of our institutions. To recognise leadership not as something to impose, but as something to uncover. In doing so, we do not abandon the foundations—we illuminate them with new light, new questions, new voices.

CONTEXTUALISING LEADERSHIP: THE CULTURAL, ECONOMIC, AND POLITICAL

Educational leadership, despite its theoretical scaffolding and scholarly refinement, cannot be meaningfully understood outside of its context (Jimerson & Myers, 2024). Theories shimmer in journals and textbooks, neat and self-assured. However, in practice, leadership is invariably entangled in the complex, multifaceted realities of culture, economy, and politics. It is easy to speak of "best practices" in abstraction—far harder when the school roof leaks, the ministry rotates leadership every six months, and teachers have not been paid in weeks. Context does not just shape leadership; it defines it, sometimes in visible ways, sometimes imperceptibly. However, there is a tendency—especially in global discourse—to chase after universals, to flatten difference into digestible models, to translate leadership into rubrics with little regard for the 'soil' in which it is meant to grow.

Culture is a slippery word. It stretches far beyond language, dress, or food—it pulses through values, norms, and unspoken assumptions. It whispers in the pauses between words, in the gestures leaders do or do not make, in what is considered respectful, rebellious, wise, or weak. A leadership style that's celebrated in one country may feel intrusive or alienating in another (Ghaleb, 2024). In collectivist cultures, for instance, leadership often leans toward consensus, harmony, and indirectness. In highly individualistic settings, assertiveness and personal vision are often highly valued. However, these are not binary opposites—there is always nuance. Take Japan's senpai–kohai dynamic, for instance. Leadership is deeply relational, rooted in age, experience, and obligation (Jian, 2022). Authority is earned through time and service, not flair or rhetoric. In contrast, consider some Western models that valorise disruptive innovation, where a young, bold leader can overturn systems overnight and be lauded for it (Kayyali, 2023).

What happens, then, when educational leadership frameworks—often birthed in Euro-American academic enclaves—are exported wholesale into such settings?

Often, there is friction. Sometimes compliance. Occasionally, outright resistance. But more often, quiet adaptation. Leaders learn to speak two dialects at once—the local and the imported (Leu Bonanno, 2023). They nod at the language of strategic plans and SMART goals while tending to the more delicate, slow-burning work of building trust, preserving face, navigating family networks, or honouring ancestral wisdom. What leadership truly looks like is what it needs to look like to survive and serve. And that shape changes.

In **economics,** the rhetoric of leadership—transformational, visionary, empowering—often presumes a kind of abundance (El Hawi, 2021). Time to reflect. Resources to implement. Staff to delegate to. However, in many corners of the world, educational leaders are operating under conditions of scarcity so severe that survival becomes the primary mode of leadership. In such contexts, leadership becomes improvisational, resourceful, almost alchemical. A school head in rural Kenya repurposes chalkboard wood to build benches. A district supervisor in Venezuela juggles three currencies to keep the lights on. The word "strategic" feels almost laughable in such situations. However, leadership persists, even thrives in unexpected ways.

It is in these spaces that the neat boundaries of leadership theory begin to fray. What does instructional leadership mean when textbooks arrive six months late? How do you enact distributed leadership when staff turnover is so high that continuity is a luxury? Moreover, what of ethical leadership when leaders must choose between obeying budget directives or feeding their students? The economic frame forces a reckoning—not just with inequity, but with the moral complexity of decision-making in constrained environments. It challenges the assumption that leadership is always about scaling up, improving metrics, and achieving growth. Sometimes, it is about protecting what little remains. Sometimes, it is just about staying open for one more week.

Politics is an ever-present undertow. No educational leader, no matter how skilled or insulated, escapes it. Sometimes it is overt—a new minister with a pet reform, a reshuffling of district leadership, a crackdown on "non-aligned" schools. At other times, it is more insidious—a whispered pressure to toe the party line, to suppress dissent, and to reward loyalty over competence. In some regimes, principals are little more than political appointees. In others, leadership requires subtle forms of resistance, coded language, or strategic silence.

In politically volatile contexts, leadership becomes performance—simultaneously signalling compliance while quietly carving out spaces for autonomy (Nurohman, 2025). A university dean in Turkey might navigate shifting ideological boundaries to preserve academic freedom. A school director in Myanmar might cloak civic education in the language of "values" to avoid government scrutiny. Here, leadership is a dance, a balancing act on a wire stretched between conviction and survival. It is not the grand gestures that define such leaders, but the quiet choices, the subversions hidden in plain sight.

Even in so-called stable democracies, politics seeps into the daily life of educational leadership. School board elections. Union negotiations. Curriculum wars. The sudden pivot toward "accountability" or "21st-century skills." These are not neutral shifts—they are deeply political acts, reflecting whose voices are centred and whose values are prioritised. Educational leaders, whether they admit it or not, are political actors. They interpret policy, allocate resources, mediate conflict, and shape narratives. Some wield that power knowingly; others stumble into it. However, none are exempt.

Too often, leadership training and theory sidestep these realities (Dugan, 2024). They teach how to lead change but rarely how to survive it. They coach on innovation but not on dissent. They emphasise communication but overlook the cost of speaking the truth. This is where context matters most—not as an add-on, but as the frame through which leadership must be understood and enacted.

There is also a danger in romanticising the idea of "contextual" leadership—as though every local practice is inherently noble, or every global influence inherently corrupt. Context, too, can conceal hierarchies, perpetuate discrimination, and justify inertia. A leader invoking "culture" to exclude girls from science education is not exercising contextual sensitivity; they are wielding power in regressive ways. Recognising context does not mean surrendering to it. It means reading it carefully, critically, and with an eye for both what must be preserved and what must be challenged (Gordon, 2023).

There is no universal template for this approach. Some leaders build coalitions across cultural divides, slowly shifting norms through dialogue and example. Others work within religious frameworks to expand rather than restrict possibilities—finding in scripture not constraint, but inspiration for inclusion. Still others operate from the margins, drawing on community wisdom, oral traditions, or grassroots activism to reshape what leadership looks like.

Moreover, most people tend to do a small quantity of everything. They improvise. They negotiate. They contradict themselves. They fail and recalibrate. What makes their leadership meaningful is not adherence to any one theory, but the grace with which they navigate their circumstances, the courage with which they make decisions whose impact they may never fully see.

Take, for example, the experience of a headmistress in a conflict-affected region of northern Nigeria. Faced with the constant threat of violence, low attendance, and community scepticism, she has to make choices daily that defy policy but preserve safety. She shortens the school day, hires local elders as peace mediators, and integrates trauma support into morning routines—not because any manual told her to, but because the context demands it. Her leadership would never score highly on a

Western framework focused on instructional coaching or data-driven results. However, it is profoundly effective in its own way, deeply attuned to her community's rhythms and wounds.

Alternatively, consider a rector in Chile, who must navigate between state directives, activist student movements, and international funding expectations. Their leadership is less about vision than translation—taking the demands of one group and rendering them palatable to another, without betraying either group's interests. It is messy work. Thankless, often. But absolutely vital.

These are not edge cases. They are, in many parts of the world, the norm. They demand a reframing of how leadership is conceptualised, taught, and supported. Rather than asking leaders to conform to models, the field should ask what models can do to reflect the fundamental dilemmas of practice. Rather than importing solutions, the global North could start listening more deeply to the ingenuity of leaders working in constraint (Arora, 2024). What would happen if leadership theory emerged from the margins—from refugee schools, from indigenous education networks, from under-resourced teacher collectives—rather than from elite research institutions?

There is a quiet revolution waiting in that question. One that does not reject theory, but grounds it. One that does not idolise context, but engages with it seriously. One that sees leadership not as a ladder to climb, but as a terrain to navigate—with humility, courage, and a fierce commitment to justice.

Ultimately, educational leadership is not an abstract concept. It is embodied work, relational labour, a daily reckoning with forces far larger than the individual. Culture, economy, politics—they are not the background; they are the stage, the script, the audience, and sometimes the storm. To lead in education is to be vulnerable to these winds, and yet still find a way to anchor—to chart direction, however uncertain, toward something better than what came before.

GLOBAL MODELS IN MOTION: COMPARATIVE INSIGHTS ACROSS CONTINENTS

Educational leadership travels. It migrates across borders not just in policies and academic journals, but also in whispers between ministries, in consultant memos, and in professional development workshops attended by school leaders halfway around the globe from where the original theory originated (Marginson, 2024). What is curious, almost ironic, is how leadership models—often imagined as reflections of deeply rooted local values—so easily extend into contexts for which they were not designed. It is like watching a play in translation: the actors perform with conviction, but the script was written for another stage, another audience, another kind of silence.

However, the play continues. Educational systems borrow, mimic, adapt, resist, and repurpose leadership frameworks with a kind of uneven rhythm (Hood, 2024). Sometimes it is driven by aspiration—an eagerness to join the global conversation, to not be left behind. Sometimes it is mandated, usually by international agencies tying funding to reform. Moreover, it is sometimes genuinely collaborative, marked by a mutual curiosity that transcends cultural boundaries. However, the transfer of leadership models—whether from North to South, East to West, or any direction in between—is never just about ideas. It is about power, interpretation, and fit. The same model, planted in different soil, grows differently. Alternatively, does not grow at all.

Consider the case of *instructional leadership*, widely championed in the United States and Australia during the accountability movement (Simon et al, 2021). It posited that school leaders should spend less time on bureaucracy and more time in classrooms, coaching teachers, analysing student data, and improving pedagogy. In systems where resources allowed for assistant principals, curriculum specialists, and data analysts, this model gained traction. However, when exported to contexts like sub-Saharan Africa or Southeast Asia, the model encountered friction—not because its core was flawed, but because the infrastructure to support it often did not exist. A principal juggling multiple roles—disciplinarian, financial officer, counsellor, custodian—cannot feasibly carve out hours to observe instruction or debrief lesson plans (Chairez, 2022). So what happens? Either the model is adopted superficially—merely ticking the box without the substance—or it is quietly modified. Some find workarounds, embedding instructional leadership in staff meetings or informal peer mentoring (Kayyali, 2026). Others abandon it altogether, prioritising relational leadership or community engagement instead. The theory remains, but the practice morphs.

Now shift to *distributed leadership*, a model whose appeal lies in its democratic promise: power shared across the school community, not hoarded at the top. In Finland, often cited as an educational utopia, distributed leadership is woven into the fabric of schooling—not because it was imported, but because it has grown from a cultural soil that values autonomy, trust, and collegiality. Teachers in Finnish schools routinely shape curriculum, policy, and professional development (Heikkilä, 2021). Principals serve more as facilitators than commanders. The system works, in part, because the social contract supports it—teachers are respected, trained extensively, and given space to lead without micromanagement.

When this same model is introduced in contexts where hierarchies are rigid or where trust between staff and administration is thin, results vary. In many East Asian systems, where leadership often carries Confucian undertones of respect for authority and social harmony, distributed leadership sometimes clashes with unspoken expectations (Deng, 2021). Teachers may hesitate to voice dissent, even when invited to do so. Leaders may feel they are relinquishing control. Nevertheless, adaptation happens. In Singapore, for example, distributed leadership has been adopted not as a flat hierarchy, but as a structured delegation approach. Teacher leaders are appointed formally, roles are clearly defined, and collaboration occurs within culturally appropriate bounds. It is not a replication of the Finnish model—it is an interpretation shaped by Singapore's own bureaucratic precision and commitment to centralised excellence.

Compare that with parts of sub-Saharan Africa, where distributed leadership may resemble strategic delegation less and more like survival. In regions where school leaders face chronic shortages of staff, supplies, and infrastructure, leadership is necessarily shared, not because of ideology, but because there is simply no other choice. Teachers step in to manage operations. Parents take on roles in decision-making (Putri et al, 2024). Students themselves become informal leaders, organising study circles or mediating peer conflicts. Here, distributed leadership emerges organically, not from policy documents but from necessity. However, ironically, such contexts are rarely recognised in the global literature as sites of leadership innovation (Kayyali, 2025). The language used is often deficit-based, referring to "lack of capacity," "resource-strapped," and "fragile systems." However, what is really lacking is recognition of the forms of leadership that do not fit neatly into Western theoretical boxes.

And then there is *transformational leadership*, arguably the most romanticised of all models (Eaton et al, 2024). The idea of a visionary, change-driving, morally anchored leader resonates globally. It taps into archetypes—the reformer, the saviour, the charismatic principal who turns a failing school around with sheer will and vision. In the United States, this model aligned well with movements for school turnaround and equity-focused reform. Leaders were encouraged to "inspire," "disrupt," and "raise expectations." However, when exported to more collectivist societies, this emphasis on individual charisma sometimes feels discordant. In many Pacific Island cultures, for instance, leadership is expected to be humble, non-confrontational, and embedded within the community. The loudest voice in the room is not automatically the most respected.

Table 2. Global Leadership Implementation KPIs

KPI	Definition	Baseline (2024)	Target (2027)	Owner
Teacher agency index (1–5)	Perceived ability to lead improvements	3.2	4.2	School leadership team
Instructional coaching coverage (%)	Teachers receiving cycles per term	28	60	T&L office
Cultural partnership breadth (#/yr)	Ties with community/ indigenous orgs	6	18	Community liaison
Ethical disclosure rate (%)	Transparent rationale on major decisions	35	85	Principal/Board
Student belonging (1–5)	Survey composite of belonging/safety	3.4	4.3	Student affairs
Distributed leadership roles (#)	Recognised teacher/staff leadership roles	12	35	HR/Principal
Policy navigation wins (#/qtr)	Issues resolved w/o harming learning	3	10	Principal/Cluster Lead

Still, transformational leadership is not rejected outright. It is reframed. In Bhutan, for instance, school leadership has been influenced by the national philosophy of Gross National Happiness, which emphasises holistic well-being, environmental stewardship, and cultural preservation. Transformational leadership is less about high-stakes reform and more about nurturing harmony, resilience, and spiritual growth. A principal may be transformational not by being disruptive, but by being deeply attuned to the emotional and ethical development of their students and staff. The model travels, yes—but it wears new clothes.

The *servant leadership* model—originating in part from religious and philosophical traditions—has found particular resonance in contexts where education is closely tied to moral or spiritual development (Von Behren, 2025). In many Latin American and African countries, where faith-based schooling is prevalent, leadership as service aligns naturally with community expectations and values. The principal is not a distant figure issuing directives, but a caretaker, a moral exemplar, a mediator. However, even here, interpretations vary. In Catholic schools in the Philippines, servant leadership may blend with institutional hierarchy. In Tanzanian schools influenced by indigenous traditions, service may be less about religious humility and more about communal responsibility. The ethos is shared; the expression diverges.

What is clear in all these examples is that leadership models do not land in a vacuum (Kayyali & Christiansen, 2024). They arrive in history. Into memories of colonisation, liberation, dictatorship, and migration. Into systems still healing from trauma or still shaped by pride. Into places where the chalkboards may be new, but the ghosts on the walls are old. A leadership model, no matter how evidence-based or elegantly articulated, will always be read through these local lenses.

Even within continents, variation runs deep. Compare two systems often mentioned in the same breath: China and South Korea. Both have high-performing education systems, Confucian heritage, and competitive academic cultures. However, leadership plays out differently. In China, educational leadership is tightly interwoven with state ideology (Lin, 2024). School principals are party appointees, expected to enforce policy and promote national priorities. In South Korea, while centralisation remains strong, there is more room for school-level innovation. Principals often serve as mediators between the pressures of high-stakes testing and the growing demand for student well-being. Both systems are results-driven, but different relationships with the state, civil society, and international discourse shape their leadership landscapes.

Alternatively, consider how Indigenous communities worldwide have responded to mainstream models of leadership. In parts of Canada, Australia, and New Zealand, Indigenous educators have pushed back against imported leadership paradigms that ignore their worldviews. Instead, they have reclaimed traditional leadership forms rooted in collective memory, land-based knowledge, and spiritual guidance. Elders, rather than administrators, may be the true leaders. Decision-making is often a consensual, cyclical, and relational process. These models defy neat categorisation. They challenge the very idea that leadership can be taught in modules or measured by rubrics. However, they lead. Powerfully.

So, what does all this mean? That leadership theory is not universal. That its mobility is real, but its transformation in transit is even more real. That models must be held lightly—used as tools, not templates. That comparison should never slide into competition. That we must ask not "What works?" but "What works *where*, *why*, and *for whom*?"

The real work of comparative leadership studies, then, is not just to map differences, but to learn from them—deeply, humbly, and with a willingness to be changed (Mudd-Fegett & Mudd, 2024). It is about acknowledging that the Nigerian principal and the Finnish headteacher are not operating on the same playing field, yet both are leaders in their own right. It is about refusing the impulse to rank and instead choosing to understand. It is about honouring leadership not just as action, but as a process of adaptation.

Global models in motion are messy. They collide with context. They get bent, bruised, reshaped. Moreover, that is not a failure, but a feature. Because in those moments of friction—when theory meets reality, when imported ideas are remade in the local idiom—something new emerges. Not a perfect model. But a living, breathing practice. Moreover, that is what educational leadership must ultimately be, more than any chart or checklist.

LEADERSHIP FOR CHANGE: INNOVATION, EQUITY, AND INCLUSIVE GROWTH

Leadership, at its most alive, is not simply about navigating what *is*. It is about imagining—and then stubbornly, courageously inching toward—what *could be*. Educational leaders who aspire to be agents of change do not merely manage institutions; they disrupt inertia, expose flaws in unjust systems, and create openings through which light can pour into learning spaces that have been too long darkened by indifference, exclusion, or routine (Acton, 2021). However, let us not romanticise this. Leading for change—especially change grounded in equity and inclusion—is not some glossy motivational campaign. It is rarely clean. Often lonely. Frequently misunderstood. However, it may be the only kind of leadership worth aspiring to.

The call for innovation in education is everywhere now—buzzing through policy documents, TED talks, tech expos, and donor-funded pilot projects. However, when stripped of substance, the word becomes a catch-all, diluted to the point of meaninglessness. What does it actually mean to lead for innovation? Is it about gadgets in classrooms, or about shifting the fundamental relationships between teachers, students, and knowledge? Is it innovation when a school swaps textbooks for tablets, but keeps the same outdated curriculum? Is it innovation to gamify lessons, yet fail to question the structural inequities that keep some children perpetually behind?

True innovation in education does not start with technology (Facer & Selwyn, 2021). It begins with the disruption of assumptions. It begins when a leader looks at a school timetable and sees not efficiency, but an architecture of control, when they question why classrooms still operate like factories, built for standardisation rather than discovery. When they resist the seduction of global rankings and instead ask: who is this system working *for*, and who is it quietly leaving behind?

The most radical innovations in education often do not make headlines. They look like a principal rearranging the school calendar to accommodate agricultural seasons in a rural farming community. Alternatively, a headteacher in a refugee camp establishes multilingual instruction so that no child is shamed for the language they dream in. Alternatively, a dean who reimagines assessment in a way that measures not just cognitive performance, but collaborative growth, ethical reasoning, or resilience. Innovation like this is not flashy. It is purposeful. It is deeply contextual. Moreover, it is driven by leaders who understand that doing things differently only matters if it helps more students belong, succeed, and thrive.

Equity, then, is the heartbeat of any real change. Moreover, that is where things get messy. Because equity asks leaders not just to tinker with tools, but to interrogate power, it asks them to notice patterns—who gets tracked into advanced programs, who is punished more harshly, who gets to speak in meetings, who does not. It requires discomfort. It demands that leaders question not only *others'* practices, but their own. Moreover, while many may nod in agreement with the language of equity, far fewer are ready for the upheaval it brings.

To lead for equity is to live in the grey. It means being misunderstood, accused of favouritism, or even of lowering standards. It means balancing urgency with patience—knowing that systems resist change, but students cannot wait. It means saying no to well-intentioned reforms that benefit the privileged and calling out traditions that masquerade as merit. It means rethinking everything: admissions policies, disciplinary codes, grading systems, hiring practices. It is leadership as excavation—digging deep into the roots of inequality, even when those roots are uncomfortable to name. And then there is inclusive growth—the phrase sounds like it belongs in a World Bank report, abstract and sanitised. However, in the hands of a thoughtful leader, it becomes something real. It means not just expanding access, but transforming the educational experience for those who have been historically excluded. It means asking not only "how many are enrolled?" but "what happens once they arrive?" Do they feel seen? Are their identities affirmed? Are their voices shaping the culture, or just tolerated at its margins?

Figure 2. Leadership Levers vs. Student Outcome Gains

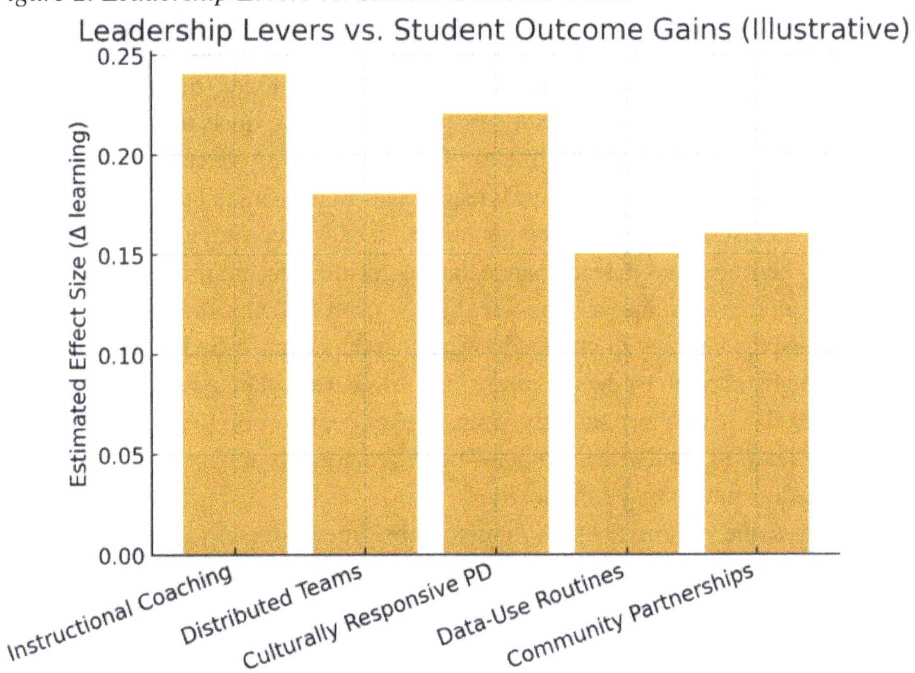

Inclusion is often mistaken for mere presence. However, presence is not equivalent to participation (Tripp & Waight, 2024). Participation is not power. Moreover, power without justice is not inclusion—it is assimilation. Leaders who truly commit to inclusive growth understand this. They move beyond symbolic gestures. They confront the barriers—physical, pedagogical, cultural—that keep some students always one step behind. They create spaces where difference is not just accepted but celebrated, where policies are rewritten with those most impacted by them, where growth is not measured by GDP analogies but by how deeply the institution becomes a place where all learners—regardless of race, class, gender, ability, or background—can flourish.

It is tempting to believe that such leadership requires heroic personalities—visionary figures who sweep into broken systems and rescue them (Allison & Goethals, 2024). However, the truth is more grounded and perhaps more hopeful. Leadership for innovation, equity, and inclusion is often found in the quiet, persistent work of people who never see themselves as heroes. It is the teacher who pushes back against a biased curriculum. The administrator who mentors first-generation students navigating unfamiliar academic terrain. The district leader who decentralises budgeting, allowing marginalised schools to have more autonomy. Change does not always come in waves. Sometimes, it arrives as ripples—subtle, patient, steady.

Still, let us not downplay the resistance. Every change threatens someone's comfort. Leaders advocating for innovation and equity often face backlash—from parents clinging to nostalgia, from staff resistant to critique, from policymakers obsessed with metrics. The pressure to perform—to produce neat data, glossy reports, improvement graphs—is intense. However, leading for real change means accepting that progress is not always linear. It may take years to build trust, to shift culture, to see results that cannot be quantified in exam scores. However, there are strategies. There are ways to lead change that do not alienate, but invite. Storytelling, for one. Leaders who centre stories—real ones, from students and communities—can humanise the urgency of change in ways that data cannot. Shared leadership is also key. Change driven by decree rarely lasts. However, when educators, students, and families co-create the vision, the change takes deeper root. Reflective practice, continuous learning, and vulnerability—these are not soft skills; they are survival tools for leaders navigating complexity.

Globally, some systems are beginning to reimagine leadership development with this ethos in mind (Singh et al, 2021). In New Zealand, for example, the focus on culturally responsive leadership has reoriented professional learning toward bicultural competence and partnerships with Māori communities (Ide & Beddoe, 2022). In parts of South Africa, post-apartheid education reforms have spurred leaders to confront systemic legacies head-on, embedding equity in everything from language policy to teacher training. In Canada, inclusive education initiatives have prompted school leaders to rethink special education as a system-wide responsibility, not a siloed program.

These examples do not offer blueprints—they offer proof. Proof that it is possible to lead for change in bold ways without being reckless, compassionate without being passive, and grounded without being stagnant. They remind us that innovation is not the enemy of tradition, that equity is not at odds with excellence, that inclusion is not a burden but a blessing. However, they also remind us that none of this happens accidentally. It takes will. And stamina. And sometimes, a little rebellion. Thus, the question returns: What does it really take to lead for change?

Not a flawless plan. Not a perfect pedigree. But clarity of purpose. A willingness to name what is not working. A refusal to settle for polite reforms when profound transformation is required. Moreover, above all, a belief—quiet or loud—that schools and universities can be places not just of learning, but of justice. Places where innovation does not widen the gap, but bridges it, where equity is not an afterthought, but the foundation, where growth includes everyone—not just the ones who have always had a seat at the table.

SYNTHESISING THEORIES FOR A GLOBAL SHARED FUTURE

If there is one thing the past century of educational leadership theory has taught us, it is that no single model holds the key (Jain et al, 2022). No framework, no matter how elegantly theorised or widely endorsed, can claim universal truth. However, there is a lingering temptation—particularly in an era of international benchmarks and cross-border rankings—to search for that elusive one-size-fits-all formula. The illusion of a global standard underlies the surface of reform efforts, data dashboards, and professional development packages disseminated from one continent to another. However, authentic leadership —the kind that lives and breathes inside schools and universities—refuses to be boxed up and exported wholesale. It resists being standardised. It insists on context, demands complexity, and thrives in contradiction.

Still, as fractured as the landscape may appear—transformational here, instructional there, distributed in one setting, authoritarian in another—there is something quietly forming beneath the cacophony. Not a new theory, exactly. Not even a hybrid. But a rhythm. A pulse. A willingness, perhaps, to move beyond the either-or logic that has long pitted models against each other. The future of educational leadership may not lie in choosing sides but in learning to synthesise across them—discerning what serves, discarding what constrains, and reshaping what remains.

This synthesis is not mechanical. It is not a tidy fusion of bullet points pulled from competing theories. It is more like composing a piece of music. Specific motifs—values, principles, practices—recur across geographies, albeit in different keys. Leadership that inspires without dominating. Leadership that listens deeply and acts decisively (Nurohman, 2025). Leadership that holds space for ambiguity yet refuses to abandon moral clarity. These are not traits tied to any one framework; they are threads that appear in various forms across the spectrum. The challenge, then, is not to reinvent leadership every time we cross a border, but to cultivate the discernment needed to know which elements to carry forward, which to adapt, and which to release altogether.

Consider this: transformational leadership brings vision and energy. Instructional leadership focuses on and brings precision to elevate teaching and learning. Distributed leadership spreads agency, decentralises control, and breathes democracy into the institution. Servant leadership centres on humility and human connection. Ethical leadership compels leaders to act with integrity in the face of injustice (Hernandez, 2022). Culturally responsive leadership calls leaders to name the historical wounds their institutions may carry and to move toward healing. All of these have value. However, the real artistry lies in knowing when and how to draw from each without falling into incoherence or contradiction.

This is what leadership already looks like in practice, at least among those who resist being boxed in. A headteacher in São Paulo may start her week navigating a municipal directive with bureaucratic precision, then spend an afternoon in the favelas listening to families whose lived realities do not align with official data. She invokes policy language when she must, but leads through presence and trust when the forms fall short. The theory she practices is not drawn from one book, but from necessity, memory, intuition—and yes, from theory too, but refracted through lived complexity.

This kind of synthesis, however, is not instinctual for everyone. It requires a different kind of preparation—one that goes beyond mastery of isolated models and teaches leaders to think relationally. To hold paradox without flinching. To understand that leadership, like culture, is not static. It shifts in response to time, pressure, people, and place. Moreover, it must be taught in this manner. Leadership development, if it is to be meaningful in a global frame, must stop asking, "Which model is best?" and start asking, "Which combination of approaches best honours the community this leader serves?"

However, here is where things get trickier. Synthesising across theories presumes an openness to learning from the unfamiliar. Moreover, that is not always easy, especially in a field still shaped by colonial inheritances, Eurocentric norms, and neoliberal pressures. The global South has often been on the receiving end of leadership frameworks developed in the North—packaged with funding incentives, accreditation checklists, and claims of "evidence-based practice" (Abouzeid et al, 2022). However, what if the synthesis required for a shared future means turning that flow around—or at the very least, making it bidirectional? What if wisdom about leadership is just as likely to come from a community school in rural Uganda or a Māori-led initiative in New Zealand as from a prestigious policy institute in London or Washington?

To take this seriously would mean re-centring the margins. It would mean inviting voices that have been historically excluded from theory-making to co-author the future of leadership thought. It would also mean relinquishing the need to measure everything by the same yardstick. A shared future in leadership theory cannot mean uniformity; it must mean interdependence—a mutual acknowledgement of differences as strengths, not problems to be solved.

Synthesis also requires leaders to cultivate moral imagination. That is, the ability to envision systems not only as they are, but as they could be if justice, dignity, and belonging were the starting point—not the outcome, which is perhaps the most overlooked dimension of global leadership discourse. Much is said about scaling innovation, building capacity, and fostering excellence. Far less is said about dreaming. However, dreamers are the ones who build new paradigms. Who asks, "What if school did not replicate the inequalities of society but actively worked against them?" Alternatively, "What if we redefined success to include healing, joy, or solidarity?" These are not naïve questions. They are courageous ones. Moreover, they demand a leadership practice capacious enough to hold them.

In this way, synthesis is not only intellectual—it is ethical. It is not just about borrowing techniques or blending ideas. It is about recognising that every theory of leadership carries with it a set of values, a worldview, a hidden politics. To synthesise responsibly, one must critically examine these. Not all leadership practices, after all, are worth preserving. Some carry legacies of exclusion, coercion, or compliance (Votto, 2025). Some prioritise outputs over people. Others disguise elitism as meritocracy. Part of the task, then, is to sift. To ask which aspects of each theory elevate human flourishing and which reinforce systems that stifle it.

There is also a temporal dimension to consider. Theories are not fixed in time. They emerge in response to particular historical conditions and tend to reflect the anxieties of their moment. The rise of instructional leadership, for instance, corresponded with the accountability era, characterised by an obsession with test scores and measurable gains (Theoharis, 2024). The popularity of distributed leadership mirrored democratic aspirations in the post-industrial world. Recognising these genealogies helps leaders avoid reifying theories as eternal truths. It reminds us that the leadership theories of tomorrow may not yet exist—that part of the synthesis we seek might involve crafting entirely new vocabularies. Moreover, maybe that is the most exciting part. A shared future does not require convergence, but rather co-creation. Instead of exporting "best practices," we might create spaces—both literal and discursive—for educators across contexts to share what works, what does not, and what remains a question mark. That global application is not about stamping the same model everywhere, but about cultivating the kind of dialogical practice that allows leaders to speak across difference without erasing it.

Some are already doing this work. Transnational leadership networks, collaborative action research across borders, culturally grounded professional learning communities—these are not just projects; they are prototypes for a new way of thinking (Johannesson, 2022). A way that resists both the false comfort of homogeneity and the paralysis of relativism. A way that says: yes, leadership must be rooted in place, but also in shared commitments—to dignity, to access, to transformation.

Ultimately, synthesising theories for global application is not about neutralising context—it is about holding it sacred. It is about building a field that's less about exporting solutions and more about exchanging possibilities. A field that allows a leader in Cairo to learn from one in Helsinki, not by mimicking, but by translating—with care, with nuance, and with an ear for what resonates. A field that takes seriously the idea that every school, every classroom, every community is both utterly unique and deeply connected to the rest. This is not easy work. It is not algorithmic or efficient. However, it is necessary. Because education, at its core, is about human development. Moreover, leadership, in that context, cannot be reduced to strategy. It must be relational. Ethical. Creative. Moreover, above all, humble enough to admit that no one theory will ever be enough—but all of them, in conversation, just might be.

CONCLUSION

As this chapter has illustrated, the theories of educational leadership—while initially forged in specific social and intellectual traditions—have evolved into a kaleidoscope of frameworks that are constantly being reinterpreted considering global realities. From the foundational paradigms of transformational and transactional leadership to more participatory and culturally nuanced approaches, such as distributed and servant leadership, the field has grown increasingly complex, diverse, and dialogic. However, this diversity is not a sign of theoretical fragmentation; rather, it reflects the multiplicity of contexts in which educational leaders operate. Education leadership is, fundamentally, a situated practice. It is shaped by history, culture, politics, and economics—and it cannot be fully understood without considering the lived realities of those who lead and those who are led.

What emerges from a global perspective is a sobering but empowering insight: there is no one-size-fits-all model of leadership. The most effective leaders are not those who implement predefined strategies, but those who can interpret and navigate their environments with emotional intelligence, political acuity, and ethical clarity. The challenge is not merely technical—it is moral. Educational leadership in the

21st century must confront issues of inequality, marginalisation, and exclusion. It must ask not only how to improve learning outcomes, but also whose outcomes are being prioritised and whose needs are being neglected. Theories of leadership must therefore evolve from abstract blueprints into adaptable frameworks that empower leaders to respond authentically to the complexities of their communities.

Moreover, the global exchange of leadership models must be approached with humility and a critical eye. The export of Western theories to non-Western contexts often risks reinforcing neo-colonial assumptions about what constitutes good leadership. Instead, we must advocate for a pluralistic understanding of leadership—one that values indigenous knowledge systems, local innovations, and culturally rooted forms of authority. This is not to suggest that we abandon global benchmarks or cross-cultural collaboration, but that we engage with them more reflexively, recognising the limits of universality and the power of context.

Another critical dimension is the role of leadership in driving economic and social transformation. As education systems are increasingly positioned as engines of national development, the link between educational leadership and economic growth becomes more pronounced. However, this instrumental view must be balanced with a more profound commitment to human development, democratic participation, and social justice. Leaders must be held accountable not only for efficiency and performance but also for fostering inclusive, safe, and empowering learning environments.

In conclusion, this chapter calls for a reimagining of educational leadership that is both grounded in robust theoretical knowledge and attuned to the messy, moral, and multicultural realities of practice. Leadership is not a static role, but a dynamic and evolving process—one that must be continuously informed by reflection, inquiry, and dialogue. A global perspective on leadership does not seek to erase differences, but to learn from them. It asks us to see beyond the binaries of theory and practice, as well as global and local, tradition and innovation. It urges us to envision leadership as a shared journey, not a fixed destination.

Ultimately, educational leadership must be redefined as an act of service—one that nurtures potential, challenges injustice, and cultivates the collective capacity of communities to learn, grow, and thrive. In an age of uncertainty, this kind of leadership is not just desirable; it is indispensable.

REFERENCES

Abouzeid, M., Muthanna, A., Nuwayhid, I., El-Jardali, F., Connors, P., Habib, R. R., Akbarzadeh, S., & Jabbour, S. (2022). Barriers to sustainable health research leadership in the Global South: Time for a Grand Bargain on localisation of research leadership? *Health Research Policy and Systems*, *20*(1), 136. DOI: 10.1186/s12961-022-00910-6

Acton, K. S. (2021). School leaders as change agents: Do principals have the tools they need? *Management in Education*, *35*(1), 43–51. DOI: 10.1177/0892020620927415

Allison, S. T., & Goethals, G. R. (2024). *Heroic leadership: An influence taxonomy of 100 exceptional individuals*. Routledge. DOI: 10.4324/9781003328681

Ansell, C., Sørensen, E., & Torfing, J. (2022). *Co-creation for sustainability: the UN SDGs and the power of local partnerships*. Emerald Publishing. DOI: 10.1108/9781800437982

Arora, P. (2024). *From pessimism to promise: Lessons from the Global South on designing inclusive tech*. MIT Press.

Banwo, B. O., Khalifa, M., & Seashore Louis, K. (2022). Exploring trust: Culturally responsive and positive school leadership. *Journal of Educational Administration*, *60*(3), 323–339. DOI: 10.1108/JEA-03-2021-0065

Blain, J. (2024). *Unleash the Inner CEO: Make Distributed Leadership a Reality*. Jaico Publishing House.

Bryant, W., & Bryant, C. (2023). *Leadership Practices: A Global and Biblical Perspective*. Christian Faith Publishing, Inc.

Cairney, P., & Toomey, C. (2025). Systems Leadership: A qualitative systematic review of advice for policymakers. *Open Research Europe*, *5*, 6. DOI: 10.12688/openreseurope.18982.1

Chairez, C. C. (2022). Principal perspectives on the dual roles of manager and instructional leader (Doctoral dissertation, Walden University).

Deng, W. (2021). Impact of the Western Developed Leadership Theories on the Promotion of Confucian Asian into Administrative Position (Doctoral dissertation, South University).

Dugan, J. P. (2024). *Leadership theory: Cultivating critical perspectives*. John Wiley & Sons.

Eaton, L., Bridgman, T., & Cummings, S. (2024). Advancing the democratisation of work: A new intellectual history of transformational leadership theory. *Leadership, 20*(3), 125–143. DOI: 10.1177/17427150241232705

El Hawi, R. (2021). Transformational leadership and rhetoric competencies for organisational success: Analysis of Jack's rhetoric. *International Journal of Recent Technology and Engineering, 8*, 892–896.

Facer, K., & Selwyn, N. (2021). *Digital technology and the futures of education: Towards 'Non-Stupid'optimism. Futures of Education initiative*. UNESCO.

Fry, L. W., & Vu, M. C. (2024). Leading without a self: Implications of buddhist practices for pseudo-spiritual leadership. *Journal of Business Ethics, 190*(1), 41–57. DOI: 10.1007/s10551-023-05416-x

Ghaleb, B. (2024). The concept of alienation and alienation in organisations. *Pancasila International Journal of Applied Social Science, 2*(2), 206–223. DOI: 10.59653/pancasila.v2i02.714

Gordon, C. (2023). Reading literature in/against the digital age: Shallow assumptions, deep problems, expectant pedagogies. *Convergence (London), 29*(1), 28–46. DOI: 10.1177/13548565221148105

Heikkilä, M. (2021). Finnish teachers' participation in local curriculum development: A study of processes in five school contexts. *Policy Futures in Education, 19*(7), 752–769. DOI: 10.1177/1478210320967816

Hernandez, J. O. S. É. (2022). *Servant-leadership as a cornerstone for restoration of human dignity. Servant-Leadership, Feminism, and Gender Well-Being: How Leaders Transcend Global Inequities through Hope*. Unity, and Love.

Hood, M. K. (2024). *Improvisation and Creativity in Educational Leadership*. Gwynedd Mercy University.

Ide, Y., & Beddoe, L. (2022). Attitude or skills?: Cultural competence development within an Aotearoa New Zealand bicultural framework. *Aotearoa New Zealand Social Work, 34*(4), 47–60. DOI: 10.11157/anzswj-vol34iss4id954

Ionela, S. (2021). Leadership: from classic theories to the 21th century's challenges. In SHS Web of Conferences (Vol. 120, p. 02023). EDP Sciences.

Jain, V., Gupta, S. S., Shankar, K. T., & Bagaria, K. R. (2022). A study on leadership management, principles, theories, and educational management. *World Journal of English Language, 12*(3), 203–211. DOI: 10.5430/wjel.v12n3p203

Jian, G. (2022). From empathic leader to empathic leadership practice: An extension to relational leadership theory. *Human Relations, 75*(5), 931–955. DOI: 10.1177/0018726721998450

Jimerson, J. B., & Myers, R. D. (2024). Scaffolding Criticality: Iterations of Theory in Principal Preparation. *Education Sciences, 14*(12), 1298. DOI: 10.3390/educsci14121298

Johannesson, P. (2022). Development of professional learning communities through action research: Understanding professional learning in practice. *Educational Action Research, 30*(3), 411–426. DOI: 10.1080/09650792.2020.1854100

Kayyali, M. (2023). Promoting Entrepreneurship and Innovation in Higher Education. *Online Submission, 2*(1), 1–26.

Kayyali, M. (2025). A). Leadership's Role in Fostering a Resilient Organizational Culture. In *Enhancing Resilience in Business Continuity Management* (pp. 267–294). IGI Global Scientific Publishing. DOI: 10.4018/979-8-3693-8809-9.ch009

Kayyali, M. (2025 B). Understanding Innovation in Higher Education: Challenges and Future Directions. In Cultivating Creativity and Navigating Talent Management in Academia (pp. 117-138). IGI Global Scientific Publishing.

Kayyali, M. (2026). Agile Leadership and Labor Dynamics: Navigating Organisational Change in the Digital Era. In Leading Inclusive Workplaces Through Digital Transformation and Organizational Change (pp. 1-36). IGI Global Scientific Publishing.

Kayyali, M., & Christiansen, B. (Eds.). (2024). *Insights Into International Higher Education Leadership and the Skills Gap*. IGI Global. DOI: 10.4018/979-8-3693-3443-0

Kezar, A. J. (Ed.). (2023). *Rethinking leadership in a complex, multicultural, and global environment: New concepts and models for higher education*. Taylor & Francis. DOI: 10.4324/9781003446842

Leu Bonanno, S. (2023). Examining the foundations of culturally and linguistically sustaining school leadership: Towards a democratic project of schooling in dual language bilingual education. *Educational Administration Quarterly, 59*(1), 72–111. DOI: 10.1177/0013161X221106972

Lin, P. (2024). Investigating leadership in formal school clusters: The case of Education Collectives in China (Doctoral dissertation, Institute of Education).

Lopez, L. (2025). Culturally Responsive Leadership: Shaping Inclusive Classrooms For Diverse Learners.

Makoe, M. (2023). Resilient leadership in time of crisis in distance education institutions in Sub-Saharan Africa. In *Handbook of Open, Distance and Digital Education* (pp. 547–561). Springer Nature Singapore. DOI: 10.1007/978-981-19-2080-6_30

Marginson, S. (2024). The new geo-politics of higher education 2: Between nationalism and globalism.

Mazurkiewicz, G. (2021). Educational leadership in times of crisis. *Risks*, *9*(5), 90. DOI: 10.3390/risks9050090

Mudd-Fegett, K., & Mudd, H. K. (2024). Transformational Leadership. In Transformational Learning in Social Work and Human Services Education (pp. 63-83). IGI Global. DOI: 10.4018/979-8-3693-2407-3.ch004

Nurohman, D. A. (2025). *SILENT INFLUENCE: How Great Leaders Lead Without Shouting Preface*. PT Indonesia Delapan Kreasi Nusa.

Poole, A. H., & Todd-Diaz, A. (2022). 'I'm not a very good visionary': Challenge and change in twenty-first century North American archival education. *Archival Science*, *22*(4), 585–616. DOI: 10.1007/s10502-022-09389-0

Putri, H. A., Pisriwati, S. A., & Siswanto, D. H. (2024). Leadership strategies in decision-making for senior high school principals. *Journal of Organizational and Human Resource Development Strategies*, *1*(02), 104–111. DOI: 10.56741/ohds.v1i02.707

Sharma, S. N., & Adeoye, M. A. (2024). *New perspectives on transformative leadership in education*. EduPedia Publications Pvt Ltd.

Simon, S., Heck, D., Christie, M., & Farragher, Y. (2021). Leading pedagogical reform: Australian principals tell their stories. *International Journal of Leadership in Education*, *24*(2), 266–289. DOI: 10.1080/13603124.2019.1613566

Singh, D. P., Thompson, R. J., & Curran, K. A. (Eds.). (2021). *Reimagining leadership on the commons: Shifting the paradigm for a more ethical, equitable, and just world*. Emerald Publishing Limited. DOI: 10.1108/S2058-8801202101

Theoharis, G. (2024). *The school leaders our children deserve: Seven keys to equity, social justice, and school reform*. Teachers College Press.

Tripp, J. N., & Waight, N. (2024). Co-creating a community of belonging and presence: Multilingual learners' experiences of science and language learning at an urban, inclusive STEM-focused high school. *Science Education*, *108*(1), 25–62. DOI: 10.1002/sce.21827

Van Wart, M., Suino, P., & Medina, P. S. (2023). *Leadership in public and nonprofit organisations: an introduction*. Routledge. DOI: 10.4324/9781003261896

Verwolf, B. (2025). Stepping into Leadership: Addressing the Transition for New Heads of School (Doctoral dissertation, Baylor University).

Voelkel, R. H.Jr, Fiori, C., & van Tassell, F. (2023). District leadership in redefining roles of instructional coaches to guide professional learning communities through systemic change. *Leadership and Policy in Schools*, *22*(1), 141–160. DOI: 10.1080/15700763.2021.1917622

Von Behren, M. T. (2025). Servants of the Times: A Phenomenological, Critical Realist, and Servant-Leadership Study of the Lived Experience of Five People Who Started New Non-Profit Organizations to Serve People in Intercultural Settings (Doctoral dissertation, Gonzaga University).

Votto, R. (2025). *Navigating Ethical Friction: From Coercion to Connection in Organizational Lifea Paired Case Study of Leadership, Trust, and Power*. Trust, and Power.

Wilkinson, J. (2021). *Educational leadership through a practice lens*. Springer Singapore. DOI: 10.1007/978-981-16-7629-1

KEY TERMS AND DEFINITIONS

Culturally responsive leadership: honouring local knowledges and resisting deficit frames to ensure relevance and belonging.

Distributed leadership: shared agency and decision-making across teachers, students, and community networks.

Instructional leadership: leadership centred on pedagogy, assessment, and coaching to raise learning quality.

Servant/ethical leadership: service, dignity, and justice as the basis for trust, inclusion, and legitimate authority.

Systems/contingency leadership: adapting leadership style to contextual constraints, politics, and resource conditions.

Transactional leadership: goal-and-incentive management emphasising structure, accountability, and predictable performance.

Transformational leadership: vision-led influence that elevates motivation, culture, and moral purpose across the institution.

Chapter 2

Transformational Educational Leadership for Economic Resilience: Global Perspectives and Strategic Models

Rishikaysh Marotrao Kaakandikar
https://orcid.org/0000-0003-0349-6788
SaiBalaji International Institute of Management Sciences, India

Tejashree Soni
SaiBalaji International Institute of Management Sciences, India

ABSTRACT

This chapter explores the pivotal role of transformational educational leadership in fostering economic resilience across global contexts. It examines how visionary, adaptive, and inclusive leadership practices in educational institutions contribute to sustainable economic development, workforce preparedness, and social stability. By integrating global perspectives, the chapter highlights best practices, policy innovations, and leadership models that address contemporary challenges such as technological disruption, inequality, and socioeconomic shocks. Case studies from various regions are presented to illustrate strategic frameworks that leverage education as a driver for economic recovery and long-term resilience. The chapter also emphasises the significance of collaborative networks, digital transformation, and capacity-building initiatives in enhancing institutional adaptability and societal well-being.

DOI: 10.4018/979-8-3373-3616-9.ch002

INTRODUCTION

Transformational educational leadership is a dynamic and forward-thinking approach that seeks to inspire and empower stakeholders in the education system to exceed expectations and drive meaningful change. At its core, this leadership model emphasises vision, motivation, and collaboration over command and control. Rather than focusing solely on short-term outcomes or routine administrative tasks, transformational leaders in education aim to reshape institutional culture, inspire innovation, and foster holistic development for both educators and learners. Transformational educational leadership has emerged as a crucial catalyst for fostering economic resilience across global contexts. Leadership styles that emphasise vision, inclusivity, and adaptability enable educational institutions to address socioeconomic challenges and technological disruptions effectively (Bass, 1985; Avolio et al., 1999). Transformational leaders in education drive innovation, enhance institutional agility, and build future-ready human capital essential for sustainable development (Yukl, 1999; García-Morales et al., 2008). Studies highlight that visionary leadership helps bridge gaps in workforce preparedness, particularly by equipping learners with skills suited for rapidly evolving economies (Chen et al., 2022; Copp et al., 2021).

Key principles of transformational leadership in education include:

- **Inspirational Motivation**: Leaders articulate a compelling vision of the future, encouraging all stakeholders to strive toward shared goals with purpose and enthusiasm.
- **Idealised Influence**: They serve as role models, demonstrating ethical behaviour, commitment, and integrity that others aspire to emulate.
- **Individualised Consideration**: Transformational leaders recognise the unique needs and potential of each staff member or student, offering mentorship and support to foster growth.
- **Intellectual Stimulation**: They promote creativity and critical thinking by challenging traditional norms and encouraging innovative solutions.

Globally, educational leaders are increasingly adopting **strategic frameworks** focused on capacity-building, knowledge transfer, and digital transformation to foster resilience (Tao et al., 2024; Tsiotas, 2022). Transformational leadership in higher education, often termed "Education 4.0 Leadership," has been linked to institutional resilience through technological integration, digital literacy, and adaptive learning environments (Güçlü, 2024; Ronksley-, Pavia, & Neumann, 2022). Case studies demonstrate that such leadership approaches enhance institutional performance during crises, driving long-term sustainability and social equity (Odeh et al., 2023; Waidyaratne, 2022).

This model is particularly suited to the evolving demands of modern education, where adaptability, inclusiveness, and strategic foresight are essential. It transcends conventional top-down hierarchies, embracing collaboration, distributed leadership, and stakeholder engagement. Ultimately, transformational educational leadership seeks not only to improve academic outcomes but to nurture a learning environment that prepares students for lifelong success in a complex, changing world.

DIFFERENCES BETWEEN TRANSACTIONAL AND TRANSFORMATIONAL LEADERSHIP

Transactional and transformational leadership represent two distinct paradigms within educational leadership, each with its own focus, methods, and outcomes.

Transactional leadership is primarily based on a system of rewards and penalties. It emphasises order, structure, and the completion of specific tasks. Transactional leaders maintain the status quo, focus on performance metrics, and ensure that rules and procedures are followed. In an educational context, this might involve managing attendance, enforcing discipline, or implementing standardised testing with little deviation from set norms. This model is effective for short-term goals and routine operations but often lacks the vision necessary to respond to complex, systemic challenges.

Transformational leadership, by contrast, goes beyond transactional exchanges. It is proactive, purpose-driven, and oriented toward long-term change. Rather than merely managing existing systems, transformational leaders seek to transform them. They invest in people, encourage innovation, and promote a shared vision for continuous improvement. For instance, a transformational educational leader might introduce project-based learning to enhance engagement or integrate technology to support personalised education.

The significant distinctions can be summarised as:

- **Focus**: Transactional leaders focus on tasks and outcomes; transformational leaders focus on vision and development.
- **Motivation**: Transactional leaders use extrinsic motivators; transformational leaders cultivate intrinsic motivation.
- **Change**: Transactional leadership maintains systems; transformational leadership evolves them.

While both styles have their place, transformational leadership is increasingly essential in education, where complexity and rapid change demand a more adaptive and visionary approach.

THE POST-PANDEMIC AND RAPIDLY EVOLVING GLOBAL ECONOMY

The COVID-19 pandemic marked a watershed moment in global education, exposing vulnerabilities, deepening inequalities, and forcing institutions to adapt almost overnight. In this context, transformational educational leadership has emerged as a vital force in navigating uncertainty, driving resilience, and shaping a future-ready educational ecosystem.

During the crisis, schools and universities had to pivot to online learning, redesign curricula, and provide socio-emotional support to students and teachers alike. Transformational leaders proved instrumental in this transition, not only by implementing technological solutions but by maintaining morale, fostering a sense of community, and reimagining what learning could look like in a digital world. Their ability to inspire, empathise, and lead with clarity amid chaos underscored the profound need for visionary leadership.

In the post-pandemic era, as countries rebuild and economies evolve, educational institutions must respond to new realities. **Rapid technological advancements**, including AI, automation, and the digital economy, are reshaping the job market. **Workforce demands** now emphasise critical thinking, adaptability, emotional intelligence, and lifelong learning. **Global interconnectedness** requires cultural competence and collaboration across borders.

Transformational leaders play a key role in addressing these shifts by:

- **Aligning education with future skills** through curriculum reform and cross-disciplinary learning.
- **Fostering equity and inclusion**, especially for marginalised learners affected disproportionately by the pandemic.
- **Building resilient learning environments** that can adapt to future disruptions, whether social, economic, or environmental.

The Role of Education in Workforce Development

Education serves as the cornerstone of workforce development by equipping individuals with the knowledge, skills, and competencies needed to participate in the economy. In a rapidly transforming global landscape—driven by digitisation, climate change, and globalisation—educational institutions must go beyond basic literacy and numeracy to prepare learners for dynamic labour markets. This requires a forward-thinking and strategic leadership approach in education.

Transformational educational leaders play a pivotal role in aligning educational goals with economic development. By fostering partnerships with industry, government bodies, and community stakeholders, they ensure that academic institutions do not operate in isolation but are responsive to real-world needs. This helps in identifying skill gaps, introducing relevant vocational training, and promoting practical exposure through internships, apprenticeships, and project-based learning.

Furthermore, workforce development is not only about preparing students for current jobs but also about cultivating a mindset of lifelong learning. In an age where technological advancements render many skills obsolete within years, transformational leaders must champion continuous education, professional development, and upskilling programs. This is particularly important for sectors like healthcare, manufacturing, IT, agriculture, and clean energy, where job profiles are rapidly evolving.

Another crucial aspect is bridging the urban-rural and digital divide. In many developing regions, access to quality education remains unequal, affecting employability and economic participation. Educational leaders must advocate for inclusive strategies—such as mobile learning units, community-based learning hubs, and digital infrastructure—to ensure equitable access to education and skills training.

Ultimately, when education systems are strategically aligned with national development goals and future economic needs, they contribute significantly to sustainable economic resilience. A well-educated, adaptable, and skilled workforce is better equipped to withstand economic shocks, drive innovation, and support inclusive growth. Educational leadership is thus not just about academic outcomes—it is an investment in human capital and the socioeconomic fabric of the nation.

LEADERS SHAPING CURRICULA TO ALIGN WITH FUTURE JOB MARKETS

As the global economy becomes increasingly knowledge-driven and technology-centric, educational leaders must take an active role in shaping curricula that prepare students not just for the jobs of today but for the emerging careers of tomorrow. This involves a shift from rigid, subject-specific learning to flexible, interdisciplinary, and skills-oriented frameworks.

Transformational leaders anticipate trends—such as the rise of artificial intelligence, machine learning, renewable energy, green jobs, and digital services—and integrate these into curriculum planning. By engaging with industry experts, labour market analysts, and technological innovators, they co-design curricula that include both technical competencies and soft skills like communication, collaboration, adaptability, and emotional intelligence.

Modern curriculum development is no longer confined to national academic boards; it is an ongoing, participatory process that requires stakeholder input. Educational leaders must facilitate curriculum reforms that include:

- STEM and STEAM education with hands-on learning
- Entrepreneurship and innovation modules
- Digital literacy as a foundational skill across disciplines
- Environmental education aligned with sustainable development goals
- Work-integrated learning, such as case studies, simulations, and real-world projects

In addition, transformational leaders must create mechanisms to update curricula regularly, ensuring they remain relevant in the face of rapid change. This may involve annual reviews, pilot testing new content, and integrating feedback from employers and alums.

Another key aspect is promoting student agency—allowing students to personalise their learning paths through electives, digital courses, and internships. Leaders who empower teachers to become co-creators of knowledge and encourage interdisciplinary teaching practices can create a more dynamic and responsive curriculum.

In the long run, aligning curricula with job market trends enhances employability, reduces skill mismatches, and fosters entrepreneurial thinking. It also ensures that education systems become drivers of innovation and competitiveness, rather than reactive institutions. Through visionary curriculum leadership, educational institutions can shape not just individual futures but the future of economies.

CREATING INCLUSIVE AND ADAPTIVE EDUCATIONAL ECOSYSTEMS

Economic resilience is not possible without inclusive education systems that serve diverse learners equitably. Transformational leaders in education understand that inclusion and adaptability are foundational to creating robust learning ecosystems that support social mobility, reduce inequality, and unlock the full potential of every learner.

Inclusivity begins with recognising diversity—in language, ability, socioeconomic background, gender, culture, and learning style. Educational leaders must design systems that accommodate this diversity rather than force conformity. This may involve:

- Implementing multilingual education policies in linguistically diverse regions
- Ensuring disability-friendly infrastructure and resources
- Supporting gender-sensitive pedagogy and leadership development
- Addressing rural-urban disparities in access to quality education

An inclusive educational ecosystem also promotes equity in digital access, especially in a post-pandemic world where remote learning has become more common. Leaders must work to close the digital divide by investing in affordable internet, devices, and teacher training—ensuring that no student is left behind in the digital transition.

Adaptability is equally crucial in an era defined by rapid technological, environmental, and socio-political change. Adaptive education systems are characterised by:

- Flexible learning pathways (e.g., online, hybrid, self-paced modules)
- Rapid response capabilities to crises (e.g., pandemic-safe policies, learning continuity plans)
- Data-driven decision-making to monitor progress and intervene effectively

Transformational leaders foster such adaptability by building a culture of collaboration, where educators, students, policymakers, and communities co-create and co-own educational change. They encourage innovation, tolerate failure, and celebrate experimentation. Leadership development programs, peer learning networks, and participatory governance structures further enable schools and colleges to evolve with changing demands.

By creating inclusive and adaptive ecosystems, educational leaders ensure that systems are resilient to shocks and responsive to future challenges. This not only strengthens individual learner outcomes but also enhances national capacity to withstand economic disruptions, reduce unemployment, and promote inclusive growth.

GLOBAL PERSPECTIVES AND BEST PRACTICES

Finland – a model for equity and innovation in education

Finland consistently ranks among the top performers in global education assessments. The country's success is deeply rooted in its transformational approach to education leadership. Finnish educational leaders prioritise trust, autonomy, and equity, allowing teachers significant freedom in curriculum design and classroom management. Rather than focusing on high-stakes testing, Finland emphasises holistic development, creativity, and collaborative learning.

Leadership at the school level in Finland is often distributed, where principals serve more as facilitators than authoritarian figures. The national policy framework supports inclusion, with free access to education, meals, transportation, and health services. Additionally, teacher education in Finland is highly rigorous, ensuring that leaders and educators are well-prepared for evolving pedagogical needs.

Post-pandemic, Finnish leaders have doubled down on digital transformation and student well-being, showcasing how adaptability and empathy can build resilient systems.

Singapore – strategic alignment between education and economy

Singapore offers another compelling case where transformational leadership aligns education with national economic strategies. Educational leaders in Singapore work closely with ministries and industry stakeholders to forecast labour demands and develop forward-looking curricula. Programs such as Skills Future allow citizens to upskill continuously, demonstrating the country's commitment to lifelong learning.

School leaders are rigorously trained through leadership academies and expected to innovate while adhering to a strong governance framework. The integration of AI and digital tools into classrooms, combined with teacher-led action research, has fostered an ecosystem of continuous improvement.

Singapore's model exemplifies how strategic leadership, rooted in national vision and policy coherence, drives educational excellence and economic resilience.

Rwanda – rebuilding through visionary leadership

Following its traumatic history, Rwanda has made remarkable strides in reconstructing its education system. Transformational leadership at the national and local levels has played a pivotal role. Rwanda's Vision 2050 positions education as a driver of socioeconomic development, with a focus on ICT and entrepreneurship.

School leaders are trained not just in administration but in community engagement and peacebuilding. The government promotes inclusive education through national policies that support girls' education, refugee integration, and digital literacy.

Rwanda's success lies in mobilising communities, investing in local leadership, and embedding values of resilience, unity, and innovation in its education system. It is a powerful example of how developing countries can lead transformational change with limited resources.

India – decentralisation and innovation in diverse contexts

India presents a complex landscape with vast regional disparities, but it also showcases promising leadership models at both grassroots and institutional levels.

Programs like Samagra Shiksha aim to strengthen school leadership by integrating data-driven planning, gender equity, and digital education.

State-level innovations—for instance, Delhi's Happiness Curriculum and Andhra Pradesh's School Leadership Training—reflect how localised leadership can influence student engagement, emotional intelligence, and performance. Indian leaders are also navigating challenges like the digital divide and low teacher-pupil ratios through adaptive, community-based strategies.

The National Education Policy (NEP) 2020 empowers educational leaders to focus on holistic development, flexibility in curriculum, and vocational integration, signalling a move towards transformational thinking at a systemic level.

CROSS-CULTURAL LEADERSHIP STYLES AND THEIR IMPACT

Understanding cross-cultural leadership styles is critical for building globally relevant education systems. Culture profoundly influences how leadership is perceived, practised, and accepted in different regions.

Leadership in Individualistic vs. Collectivist Cultures

In individualistic societies (e.g., the U.S., U.K.), leadership tends to emphasise personal initiative, accountability, and self-expression. Educational leaders often encourage innovation, critical thinking, and individual achievement. In contrast, collectivist cultures (e.g., Japan, China, and parts of Africa) emphasise group harmony, consensus, and shared responsibility. Leaders in these systems may adopt a more consensus-driven, hierarchical style.

These cultural nuances impact how change is introduced. In individualistic settings, leaders may encourage bottom-up innovation. In collectivist contexts, change is often negotiated with multiple stakeholders to maintain social balance.

For example, in Japan, school leaders are expected to model humility and consensus-building. Teachers work in tight-knit communities called "lesson study groups," promoting peer collaboration. In South Korea, despite hierarchical traditions, school principals are increasingly adopting transformational practices like shared decision-making and emotional intelligence training.

Role of gender and diversity in leadership

Gender plays a significant role in cross-cultural leadership. In many societies, female leadership in education is rising, but it is often met with structural or cultural barriers. Nordic countries lead in gender equality, with strong representation of women in top educational leadership roles. Their policies ensure work-life balance, parental leave, and leadership development pathways for women.

Conversely, in some developing countries, patriarchal norms limit women's leadership potential. However, transformational female leaders are emerging as change agents. For instance, in Uganda and Kenya, women-led community schools have significantly improved girls' enrollment and learning outcomes. Cultural acceptance is shifting through persistent advocacy and mentorship networks.

ADAPTIVE AND CULTURALLY COMPETENT LEADERSHIP

Cross-cultural leadership also involves cultural intelligence (CQ)—the ability to understand and adapt across different cultural settings. Leaders with high CQ build inclusive schools that respect multilingualism, indigenous knowledge systems, and diverse religious or ethnic backgrounds.

Culturally competent leaders are better equipped to:

- Navigate sensitive issues (e.g., caste, ethnicity, gender)
- Promote inclusive curricula
- Build trust with marginalised communities

An example is New Zealand's educational leadership that integrates Māori values and pedagogy into mainstream education, promoting bicultural harmony.

Ultimately, effective cross-cultural leadership recognises that no one-size-fits-all model works globally. Instead, success lies in contextualisation—balancing global best practices with local realities.

Lessons from international organisations (e.g., UNESCO, OECD)

International organisations like UNESCO, OECD, UNICEF, and the World Bank play an instrumental role in shaping global educational policy, leadership training, and resilience frameworks. Their research, toolkits, and capacity-building programs guide national strategies and local interventions.

UNESCO – transforming education for sustainable futures

UNESCO advocates for inclusive, equitable, and quality education for all, aligned with Sustainable Development Goal 4 (SDG4). It emphasises leadership in building systems that promote human rights, gender equity, environmental sustainability, and lifelong learning.

Key contributions include:

- Global Education Monitoring (GEM) reports that highlight disparities and recommend policy reforms.
- UNESCO International Institute for Educational Planning (IIEP), which offers leadership training, planning tools, and crisis-response frameworks.
- The Futures of Education initiative, which invites leaders to reimagine education beyond 2050, incorporates climate change, AI, and ethics.

UNESCO's role in post-crisis contexts—such as Syria, Ukraine, and Haiti—demonstrates how global coordination and leadership training can support fragile states in rebuilding education systems.

OECD – Leadership and Skills for the Future

The Organisation for Economic Co-operation and Development (OECD) provides high-impact data and comparative policy analysis through programs like:

- PISA (Programme for International Student Assessment), which informs global education benchmarking.
- The Education 2030 framework outlines the skills, values, and attitudes needed for future readiness.

OECD encourages leadership models that are visionary, adaptive, and evidence-based. For example, OECD findings helped Finland and Canada reform leadership training and assessment strategies to improve learning equity and innovation.

UNICEF and The World Bank – Bridging Equity Gaps

UNICEF focuses on education for vulnerable children—especially in conflict zones, low-income countries, and disaster-affected areas. It promotes school leadership that fosters safe learning environments, psychosocial support, and inclusive education.

The World Bank, through its Education Global Practice, supports systemic reform in over 100 countries. It funds leadership development programs, digital transformation, and governance improvement. Its SABER (Systems Approach for Better Education Results) tool enables countries to assess and improve leadership practices.

For instance, in Bangladesh and Ethiopia, World Bank-supported programs have trained thousands of school heads in instructional leadership and data use to improve student outcomes.

Across organisations, common leadership lessons include:

- **Equity and inclusion** must guide every educational policy.
- **Data and evidence** are crucial for effective decision-making.
- **Capacity-building and professional development** are long-term investments.
- **Resilience planning** must be institutionalised to prepare for future disruptions.

By integrating these global lessons into national strategies, educational leaders can build systems that are not only high-performing but also equitable, inclusive, and future-ready.

Strategic Models of Transformational Leadership

A. Vision-Driven Leadership Models (e.g., Fullan's Change Theory)

Vision-driven leadership in education refers to the ability of leaders to craft, communicate, and implement a compelling, shared vision that guides the actions and attitudes of all stakeholders. It is central to transformational leadership, especially in times of rapid change. A clearly defined vision aligns institutional goals with broader educational, economic, and social outcomes. Visionary leaders look beyond day-to-day operations and strive to create purposeful, future-oriented education systems. They foster a culture of possibility, ownership, and engagement that motivates teachers, students, and communities to participate in sustained, meaningful change.

One of the most widely studied and influential vision-driven frameworks in educational leadership is Michael Fullan's Change Theory.

FULLAN'S CHANGE THEORY: A FRAMEWORK FOR EDUCATIONAL TRANSFORMATION

Michael Fullan, a leading expert in educational reform, developed a comprehensive framework for managing change in schools and educational systems. His Change Theory identifies critical components that leaders must consider to implement sustainable transformation successfully.

Key principles include:

Moral purpose

Fullan emphasises that educational change must be guided by a moral purpose—improving the lives of students through equitable and practical learning. Leaders must ensure that decisions are grounded in values such as inclusion, justice, and lifelong learning.

For example, in a school implementing reforms to close achievement gaps, the leader's vision is centred around creating equal learning opportunities for all. This moral clarity builds trust and motivation among teachers and communities.

Understanding change

Change is complex, nonlinear, and often resisted. Visionary leaders must understand that successful change requires a profound grasp of people's motivations, institutional culture, and the dynamics of innovation adoption. Fullan argues that leaders must create conditions where people can learn and adapt, not just comply.

Capacity building

Leaders must invest in developing the skills, knowledge, and confidence of educators to carry out change. This includes professional development, peer learning, mentorship, and providing the resources needed to innovate. Vision without capacity is futile.

Coherence making

One of the most challenging tasks in systemic reform is aligning multiple initiatives, stakeholders, and levels of leadership. Fullan emphasises the need for coherence—ensuring that every action connects back to the larger vision. Fragmentation, he warns, leads to reform fatigue.

A successful leader articulates how classroom practices, school policies, and community engagement all fit together in achieving long-term goals.

Cultivating collaborative cultures

Effective change cannot happen in isolation. Vision-driven leaders promote collaboration among teachers, schools, districts, and even across nations. They use data, dialogue, and shared inquiry to build collective ownership of the vision.

Applying Fullan's theory in real educational contexts: Canada's Ontario school reform

Fullan served as an advisor to Ontario's Ministry of Education during its major reforms in the early 2000s. The strategy included:

- Clear vision: improving literacy, numeracy, and graduation rates.
- Building capacity: large-scale professional learning for teachers and principals.
- Collaborative networks: school-to-school mentoring and knowledge sharing.

Outcomes included improved test scores, reduced dropout rates, and increased public trust in education. This success illustrates how vision, coherence, and collaboration can drive sustained change.

India's NEP 2020 alignment

Fullan's framework is also reflected in India's National Education Policy 2020, which envisions holistic, multidisciplinary, and flexible education. The policy focuses on moral development, teacher empowerment, and systemic alignment—all elements of Fullan's model.

Implementing NEP across such a vast and diverse country requires leaders at every level to embody vision-driven leadership—linking local practices with national goals and adapting reforms to context.

Conclusion: Fullan's legacy and the way forward

Fullan's Change Theory continues to inspire educational leaders worldwide. It provides a roadmap for embedding moral purpose, coherence, and capacity-building into leadership practice. As education systems navigate challenges like technological disruption, climate change, and post-pandemic recovery, visionary leadership grounded in ethical and systemic thinking is more critical than ever.

In essence, vision-driven leadership is not about personal ambition—it is about collective upliftment, creating learning environments where all students thrive, and education becomes a valid instrument of social and economic transformation.

COLLABORATIVE AND DISTRIBUTED LEADERSHIP

Transformational leadership in education increasingly emphasises collaboration and distribution of leadership responsibilities rather than traditional hierarchical models. In a world where change is constant, no single leader can address every challenge alone. Instead, empowering multiple actors within the system ensures resilience, innovation, and shared accountability.

Collaborative leadership involves building strong professional relationships, fostering mutual respect, and co-creating solutions with various stakeholders. Distributed leadership, on the other hand, decentralises authority, enabling teachers, students, parents, and administrators to play leadership roles in decision-making and implementation.

Together, these approaches shift the focus from "leader as commander" to "leader as facilitator of collective purpose."

Principles of collaborative and distributed leadership

I. shared vision and values

Leaders foster a common understanding of goals and values, ensuring all stakeholders are aligned and motivated. This shared purpose promotes ownership and coherence in practice.

ii. Empowerment and trust

Distributed leadership depends on a foundation of trust. Leaders must delegate responsibilities and trust their teams to act in the best interest of students. Empowerment leads to greater initiative, creativity, and accountability.

III. collaborative professional culture

Transformational leaders create cultures where teachers learn from each other through peer coaching, learning communities, and shared planning time. This builds collective capacity.

IV. student and community involvement

Modern educational leadership extends beyond staff. Students contribute through councils and feedback loops; communities shape policies through participatory governance. These voices enrich decisions and ensure cultural relevance.

benefits of collaborative and distributed leadership

- **Improved Innovation**: Multiple perspectives foster more creative solutions.
- **Sustainability of Reforms**: Leadership continuity is ensured when many people are invested.
- **Higher Staff Morale and Retention**: Empowered staff feel valued and stay engaged.
- **Better Student Outcomes**: Schools with collaborative leadership often show improved academic and emotional performance.
- **Real-World Examples**

England – leadership in multi-academy trusts (MATs)

In the U.K., multi-academy trusts are networks of schools led by central teams. They practice distributed leadership by involving department heads, middle leaders, and even students in strategic planning. Schools that distribute leadership tend to be more innovative and resilient to staff turnover.

south africa – teacher leadership in under-resourced schools

In South Africa, the "Teachers Leading Change" initiative empowers teachers in rural areas to take leadership in curriculum design, pedagogy, and parent engagement. Even without formal titles, these teachers drive significant improvements in school culture and learner outcomes.

New Zealand – whānau-based leadership

Māori educational philosophy encourages collective responsibility and familial (whānau) leadership. Principals work with elders, families, and local leaders to embed cultural values and create inclusive schools. This distributed model enhances equity and cultural pride.

- **Leadership Tools and Structures**
- **Instructional Leadership Teams (ILTs)**: Groups of teachers and administrators who analyse data, design interventions, and monitor progress.
- **Professional Learning Communities (PLCs)**: Teacher-driven groups that engage in ongoing collaborative inquiry.
- **Distributed Decision-Making Boards**: Committees involving teachers, students, and parents to oversee school improvement plans.

challenges in implementation

Despite its benefits, collaborative leadership faces several hurdles:

- **Time constraints**: Collaboration requires time for dialogue and coordination.
- **Role confusion**: Clear boundaries must be set to avoid duplication or conflict.
- **Power dynamics**: Leaders must manage egos and ensure all voices are valued equally.
- **Training needs**: Not all educators are equipped for leadership roles without proper development.

Transformational leaders must address these proactively through training, transparent communication, and inclusive practices.

policy frameworks and institutional strategies

Educational policy is a powerful lever for national development and economic resilience. In the 21st century, countries are recognising that education is not just a social investment but a strategic economic asset. Visionary policies align education with labour market demands, foster lifelong learning, and create inclusive systems that prepare citizens to navigate disruptions, from pandemics to technological shifts.

Transformational leadership in policy-making ensures that reforms are context-sensitive, future-oriented, and inclusive, especially in low-resource settings or volatile environments.

CASE STUDIES OF NATIONAL POLICIES

India – National Education Policy (NEP) 2020

India's NEP 2020 marks a paradigm shift from rote learning to competency-based education. Key policy features enhancing economic resilience include:

- Multidisciplinary education and flexibility in subject choices
- Vocational training from Grade 6 onwards
- Digital infrastructure and online learning platforms
- Local language integration for equity
- Promotion of entrepreneurship, innovation, and skill development

By fostering creativity, critical thinking, and employability, the NEP aims to create a workforce ready for the Fourth Industrial Revolution, particularly in AI, data science, and green technologies.

Germany – dual vocational training system

Germany's **dual education model** combines classroom instruction with apprenticeships in industry. It has long been hailed as a blueprint for aligning education with economic needs.

Supported by robust policy frameworks and industry collaboration, the system:

- Reduces youth unemployment
- Provides a smooth school-to-work transition
- Strengthens productivity in SMEs and large corporations alike

This model underlines how policy-driven integration of education and labour can build long-term resilience.

Rwanda – vision 2050 and education reform

Post-genocide Rwanda has rebuilt its education system around technology, equity, and resilience. Under Vision 2050, national policies prioritise:

- Digital literacy and ICT integration
- Gender equity and inclusive access
- Partnerships with NGOs and edtech providers

Transformational leadership at the ministerial level has turned Rwanda into a leader in ICT-driven learning in East Africa, despite limited resources.

Standard Policy Themes Driving Economic Resilience

- Curriculum Alignment with Market Trends: Policies are increasingly focusing on STEM, environmental sustainability, and soft skills.
- National Skills Development Plans: Countries like Australia, Kenya, and Malaysia have launched skill councils and industry-academia collaboration platforms.
- Universal Access and Equity: Ensuring that rural, marginalised, and disabled learners have access to quality education is a resilience strategy in itself.

- Flexible Learning Models: Blended, hybrid, and online learning modalities are now built into policy frameworks to ensure continuity during crises.
- Emphasis on Research and Innovation: Investment in R&D, higher education institutions, and incubators strengthens national problem-solving capacities.

Role of Leadership in Policy Execution

Policy success depends on implementation leadership. Visionary policymakers ensure:

- Stakeholder participation in policy design
- Devolution of authority to local bodies for contextual execution
- Continuous feedback mechanisms for real-time adjustment
- Strong emphasis on capacity-building for school heads, administrators, and teachers

Policies can only achieve economic resilience when translated into meaningful, measurable action—something only possible through committed leadership at all levels.

Public-Private Partnerships and Their Role in Strategic Reforms

Public-Private Partnerships (PPPs) have become a critical strategy for achieving educational reform, especially in contexts where public systems face resource constraints. Well-designed PPPs leverage the efficiency, innovation, and investment capacity of the private sector while ensuring that public goals of equity, access, and accountability remain intact.

In transformational leadership models, PPPs are not merely contractual arrangements—they are strategic alliances that contribute to system-wide change, skill development, and economic readiness.

Forms of Educational PPPs

Infrastructure and Facilities

- Private partners build or maintain school infrastructure under long-term contracts.
- Example: The Build-Operate-Transfer (BOT) model in the Philippines' school building program.

EdTech and Digital Platforms

- o Governments partner with private firms to offer scalable digital learning.
- o Example: India's DIKSHA platform was co-created with private edtech and IT firms.

Curriculum and Skill Development

- o Industry leaders co-design curriculum and training for employability.
- o Example: IBM's P-TECH model in the U.S. integrates high school, college, and industry certifications.

School Management

- Public-funded schools are run by private organisations under strict accountability frameworks.
- Example: Charter Schools in the U.S. or Concessional Schools in Colombia.

Assessment and Quality Assurance

- NGOs and private firms assist in learning outcome measurement, policy evaluation, and teacher training.
- Example: ASER Centre in India conducts national learning surveys used by policymakers.

Advantages of PPPs in Strategic Reform

- Resource Efficiency: Reduces government financial burden
- Innovation and Flexibility: Faster adoption of new models, technologies, and teaching methods
- Industry Relevance: Better alignment with labour market needs
- Scalability: Ability to reach underserved areas quickly
- Accountability through Performance-Based Contracts

Challenges and Critiques

- Equity Concerns: Risk of focusing on profitable regions or groups
- Quality Control: Lack of regulatory oversight may lead to inconsistent standards

- Sustainability: Short-term contracts may not ensure long-term systemic change
- Privatisation Risks: May undermine the public good ethos of education

To mitigate these issues, governments must adopt clear policy guidelines, evaluation frameworks, and equity mandates when engaging private actors.

CASE EXAMPLE: BRIDGE INTERNATIONAL ACADEMIES IN AFRICA

Bridge International operates low-cost private schools in Kenya, Nigeria, and Uganda. Using standardised content and tech-enabled teaching, it offers scalable, data-driven education.

While praised for expanding access, Bridge has also faced criticism over teacher autonomy and regulation compliance. The case underscores the importance of balanced, well-regulated PPP models that safeguard quality and equity.

Leadership Considerations in PPPs

Transformational leaders ensure that PPPs:

- Align with national education goals
- Promote inclusivity and ethics
- Include robust monitoring and evaluation tools
- Foster transparency and community engagement

They build trust among stakeholders, ensure mutual accountability, and institutionalise learning from pilot projects into broader systems.

Governance and Accountability in Education Leadership

Governance and accountability are the backbone of effective educational leadership. Strong governance ensures that vision, policy, and practices align. Accountability ensures that decisions lead to measurable impact and that institutions remain responsive to students, teachers, and the public.

In transformational leadership models, governance is not merely about control—it is about empowerment, transparency, and stewardship of shared goals.

Dimensions of governance in education: institutional governance

- School boards, councils, and academic senates play key roles in strategic decisions.
- Decentralised governance enables local problem-solving and innovation.

Administrative and Financial Governance

- Budget planning, fund allocation, and resource management must be transparent and need-based.
- Example: School-Based Management (SBM) models in the Philippines and Indonesia increase principal autonomy with clear financial accountability.

Data-Driven Governance

- Use of education management information systems (EMIS) to track attendance, performance, dropout rates, etc.
- Enables evidence-based decision-making and timely interventions.

Accountability Mechanisms

- Performance Reviews: Annual evaluations of school heads and teachers based on set KPIs
- Learning Outcomes Monitoring: Regular assessments to gauge student progress
- Audits and Compliance Checks: Especially in PPP models or donor-funded programs
- Community Oversight: Parent-teacher associations and local committees improve transparency
- Grievance Redressal Systems: Empower students, parents, and staff to report issues

Accountability must be formative—focused on improvement—not just punitive.

International Good Practices

- Chile's National Quality Assurance System evaluates schools and supports underperforming ones.
- Finland's Trust-Based Accountability replaces high-stakes testing with professional evaluation and collaboration.

- Uganda's Scorecard Approach allows communities to rate public services, including schools, and send feedback to decision-makers.

Leadership Role in Strengthening Governance

Transformational leaders promote good governance by:

- Ensuring stakeholder representation in governance bodies
- Demanding transparency in data and budgets
- Setting high ethical standards and modelling accountability
- Creating a culture of self-evaluation and peer review
- Empowering others to lead and own their responsibilities

CHALLENGES AND BARRIERS

Resource limitations and funding gaps:

Despite the ambitious goals of transformational educational leadership, one of the most significant barriers to its success remains resource limitations and persistent funding gaps. These constraints are particularly acute in low-income and developing countries, but are also evident in underfunded regions within wealthier nations.

Lack of adequate funding affects nearly every aspect of the education system:

- Infrastructure: Schools operate without proper classrooms, sanitation, libraries, or digital access.
- Teacher shortages and training: Inadequate salaries, insufficient professional development, and high attrition rates compromise quality.
- Learning materials: A lack of up-to-date textbooks, laboratory equipment, or educational technologies impairs curriculum delivery.

In many regions, budgetary allocation to education falls below global benchmarks. The UNESCO recommendation of allocating at least 4–6% of GDP or 15–20% of national budgets to education is not met in dozens of countries. Even when funding is allocated, inefficiencies in procurement, leakage, and corruption can erode its impact.

The digital divide further magnifies inequality. Schools without internet, devices, or reliable electricity were left behind during the COVID-19 pandemic. Transformational leadership that depends on innovation, digital learning, and systemic reform cannot flourish without a minimum resource threshold.

Leaders face the dilemma of vision without means. In such scenarios, they must:

- Prioritise resource allocation for maximum impact
- Forge partnerships with the private sector and international donors
- Advocate for sustained investment in education as a national priority
- Innovate with low-cost, high-impact solutions (e.g., open educational resources, solar-powered devices)

While lack of funds is a severe constraint, strategic leadership and community mobilisation can bridge some gaps until systemic solutions are achieved.

RESISTANCE TO CHANGE AND INSTITUTIONAL INERTIA

Educational institutions are historically conservative by design—built to maintain societal structures and pass down cultural values. Consequently, resistance to change is a deeply embedded barrier to transformational leadership.

Table 1: Classification of Resistance to Educational Change and Leadership Strategies

Type of Resistance	Source	Impact	Recommended Leadership Response
Passive Resistance	Teachers and mid-level staff	Low engagement, lack of initiative	Build trust, provide clear communication, and be involved in decision-making.
Active Resistance	Teacher unions, bureaucrats, and senior staff	Public criticism, work slowdowns, policy blocks	Engage in dialogue, negotiate collaboratively, and share evidence
Cultural or Ideological Resistance	Communities, religious groups, and school boards	Rejection of new content (e.g., gender, science)	Contextualise reforms, involve community leaders, and use inclusive language.
Systemic/Bureaucratic Resistance	Education ministries, regulatory bodies	Delays, procedural hurdles, misalignment	Streamline processes, create reform champions within the system
Psychological/Emotional Resistance	Individual educators	Fear, burnout, nostalgia for the status quo	Offer counselling, peer mentorship, and celebrate small wins

This resistance arises from multiple sources:

- **Teachers and Administrators:** Many educators feel overwhelmed by constant policy changes, reform fatigue, or fear that new approaches may threaten their roles or expose skill deficits. Without adequate support and participation, teachers may disengage from reform efforts.

- **Institutional Inertia: Lon:** Standing systems and bureaucratic cultures can be slow, inflexible, and bound by rigid hierarchies. Even when visionary leaders are appointed, the legacy systems they inherit, outdated assessment frameworks, rigid curricula, and fragmented governance act as barriers to swift innovation.
- **Leadership Hierarchies:** Often, leadership is top-down, leaving little room for distributed decision-making. This disempowers local leaders, teachers, and students from contributing meaningfully to the change process.
- **Mistrust and Lack of Ownership:** When reforms are perceived as externally imposed (e.g., by global agencies or central governments), they often lack local legitimacy. Teachers and parents may resist changes that do not align with cultural expectations or ground realities.

Strategies to Overcome Resistance

Transformational leaders must be adept change agents, equipped with:

- Emotional intelligence to understand fears and motivations
- Communication skills to build buy-in and co-create vision
- Incremental strategies that introduce change progressively
- Capacity-building initiatives that prepare staff for new roles
- Recognition and rewards for innovation and effort

Leadership is not just about vision—it is about managing transitions compassionately and collaboratively. Sustainable change occurs not through imposition, but through collective engagement and mutual respect.

FUTURE DIRECTIONS AND RECOMMENDATIONS

Table 2. classification of leadership development models for resilient education systems

Type of Leadership Development Model	Key Features	Examples	Impact on Resilience
Mentorship-Based Model	One-on-one guidance from experienced leaders; personalised support	Principal mentorship in Ontario schools	Builds confidence, transfers tacit knowledge
Professional Learning Communities (PLCs)	Group learning among educators to share practice and solve problems	PLCs in U.S. and Finnish schools	Encourages collaboration, decentralises expertise
Fellowship/Leadership Academies	Intensive training and networking for emerging leaders	Teach For All, Australia's Bastow Institute	Builds next-gen leadership pipeline with systemic focus
Decentralised School-Based Training	Training programs led by local school or district leaders	School-Based Management in the Philippines	Empowers local decision-making, aligns with context
International Exposure Programs	Cross-cultural and global best practice exchanges	Fulbright Fellowships, UNESCO IIEP programs	Promotes global thinking, adaptability, and innovation

Embracing Lifelong Learning and Upskilling

As economies evolve and automation transforms the world of work, the concept of education as a one-time event is no longer sufficient. Lifelong learning and continuous upskilling are now essential for individual adaptability and national competitiveness. Transformational educational leadership must champion systems that facilitate learning beyond traditional age brackets, institutions, and qualifications.

From Rigid Pathways to Flexible Ecosystems

Educational institutions must evolve from being degree-centric to skill- and competency-based. This includes:

- Recognising informal and experiential learning
- Providing modular learning opportunities (e.g., micro-credentials, MOOCs)

- Facilitating stackable qualifications that allow learners to build skills over time

Such systems ensure that individuals can pivot between careers and remain relevant in dynamic economies.

Integrating Lifelong Learning Into National Policies

Countries like Singapore and Finland are global leaders in embedding lifelong learning into national strategy. Singapore's Skills Future Initiative, for example, provides citizens with credits to pursue new courses at any stage of life.

In India, the National Skills Development Mission and NEP 2020 emphasise vocational integration, entrepreneurship, and flexibility, reflecting a growing shift toward continuous skilling.

Role of Leaders in Promoting Lifelong Learning

Transformational leaders in education must:

- Encourage cross-sector collaborations between universities, industries, and community organisations.
- Ensure digital access and inclusion for all age groups
- Promote a culture of curiosity and continuous self-improvement
- Guide policy to support re-skilling amid technological disruption

Lifelong learning is not just about employability—it is about empowerment, resilience, and the right to evolve throughout one's life.

Building Resilient Education Systems through Leadership Development)

The COVID-19 pandemic revealed the fragility of global education systems. Schools closed, digital divides widened, and inequalities deepened. The path forward demands not just improved infrastructure or content, but firm, agile leadership capable of guiding institutions through uncertainty.

The need for leadership at all levels

Systemic resilience requires leaders at:

- National level (policy and strategic planning)
- Institutional level (school or university management)
- Classroom level (teacher-leaders and student mentors)

These leaders must be trained not only in administrative functions but in change management, crisis response, emotional intelligence, and innovation.

Leadership development models

Effective leadership development includes:

- Mentorship and coaching programs for emerging leaders
- Fellowships and international exposure to broaden global understanding
- Professional learning communities for peer-to-peer knowledge exchange
- Decentralised leadership structures to empower frontline educators

Organisations like Teach for All, UNESCO's IIEP, and Harvard's Graduate School of Education have launched global leadership programs focused on sustainability, equity, and innovation.

Embedding Resilience into Leadership Training

Training programs must equip leaders with the ability to:

- Plan for continuity during disruptions
- Use data and foresight tools to anticipate risks
- Cultivate empathy and adaptability
- Mobilise communities and partners during emergencies

Leaders should be prepared not only for growth but for shock absorption, making education systems more proactive, inclusive, and responsive.

Investing in Leadership is Investing in the System

Studies consistently show that schools with empowered leaders outperform others in academic outcomes, teacher retention, and student well-being. Thus, leadership is not an administrative add-on—it is the core engine of resilience in education.

Global Collaboration for Sustainable Educational Transformation

In a hyper-connected world, educational challenges—like climate change, digital inequality, migration, and conflict—are transnational. Addressing them requires global cooperation, shared knowledge, and unified action. Transformational leaders must increasingly think beyond borders.

Why Global Collaboration Matters

No country has all the answers. By collaborating internationally, education systems can:

- Share best practices and innovations
- Leverage global research and technology
- Develop joint programs to solve cross-border challenges (e.g., refugee education)
- Benchmark progress using global standards (e.g., SDG 4, PISA assessments)

Role of International Organisations

Institutions like UNESCO, OECD, UNICEF, and the World Bank facilitate:

- Technical assistance to developing nations
- Research dissemination and global monitoring
- Collaborative frameworks (e.g., Education2030, Global Education Monitoring Report)

Their role is not to dictate but to support localised solutions through global dialogue.

South-South and Triangular Cooperation

Collaboration is not limited to wealthy nations supporting developing ones. Increasingly, South-South cooperation (e.g., India-Brazil-South Africa) and triangular partnerships (public-private-NGO alliances) are yielding innovative, scalable models suited to similar contexts.

Digital Collaboration and Open Resources

Technology enables global classrooms through platforms like Coursera, Edmodo, or the Khan Academy. Open Educational Resources (OERs) and digital forums allow educators to co-create, adapt, and scale teaching materials without borders.

Global Citizenship as a Learning Outcome

Global collaboration is not just about systems—it is about values. Educators must embed global citizenship education (GCED), sustainability, and peace-building into curricula. Students must learn to be not just national contributors, but planetary stewards.

Transformational leadership today is global in vision and collaborative in approach—building bridges, not silos. Ultimately, transformational educational leadership offers a strategic model for achieving both economic resilience and inclusive growth by fostering collaboration across education systems, industries, and communities (García-Morales et al., 2008; Tao et al., 2024). By focusing on adaptive leadership practices and innovation-driven learning environments, educational institutions can serve as engines of social stability and economic recovery worldwide (Tsiotas, 2022; Avolio et al., 1999). This chapter consolidates global insights, theoretical models, and practical examples to guide policymakers, researchers, and practitioners in leveraging educational leadership for economic resilience.

CONCLUSION

In the face of unprecedented challenges and opportunities, educational leadership has never been more crucial. It is the driving force that transforms vision into reality, policies into practice, and institutions into engines of growth and inclusion.

Strategic, transformational leaders:

- Navigate complex socioeconomic landscapes with agility
- Align education with the future of work and sustainability
- Foster inclusive cultures that leave no learner behind
- Leverage technology and innovation to expand access and impact
- Build resilient systems capable of enduring and evolving

Their role extends beyond school walls—they are nation builders, culture shapers, and future designers. As the world continues to confront uncertainty, the education sector must invest in leadership not just as a role, but as a system-wide capability.

Empowering current and future leaders—at every level—is essential to build education systems that are equitable, adaptive, and globally relevant.

The future of education is not just in textbooks or classrooms—it lies in the hands of those bold enough to lead transformation with courage, clarity, and compassion.

REFERENCES

Avolio, B. J., Bass, B. M., & Jung, D. I. (1999). Reexamining the components of transformational and transactional leadership using the multifactor leadership questionnaire. *Journal of Occupational and Organizational Psychology*, *72*(4), 441–462. DOI: 10.1348/096317999166789

Bass, B. M. (1985). *Leadership and performance beyond expectations*. Free Press.

Chen, J., Ghardallou, W., Comite, U., Ahmad, N., Ryu, H. B., Ariza-Montes, A., & Han, H. (2022). Managing hospital employees' burnout through transformational leadership: The role of resilience, role clarity, and intrinsic motivation. *International Journal of Environmental Research and Public Health*, *19*(17), 10941. DOI: 10.3390/ijerph191710941 PMID: 36078657

Copp, S., Olorunsola, V. O., & Alola, U. V. (2021). Achieving environmental sustainability through green transformational leadership policy: Can green team resilience help? *Business Strategy and the Environment*, *30*(1), 671–682. DOI: 10.1002/bse.2646

Fullan, M. (2001). *Leading in a culture of change*. Jossey-Bass.

Fullan, M. (2011). *The moral imperative realised*. Corwin Press.

García-Morales, V. J., Lloréns-Montes, F. J., & Verdú-Jover, A. J. (2008). The effects of transformational leadership on organisational performance through knowledge and innovation. *British Journal of Management*, *19*(4), 299–317. DOI: 10.1111/j.1467-8551.2007.00547.x

Güçlü, H. (2024). Transformational educational leadership for shaping Education 4.0 in higher education. *Journal of Innovation in Practice and Development*, *4*(1), 4900. Advance online publication. DOI: 10.57237/jipd.2024.4900

Odeh, M. R. B. S., Obeidat, B. Y., Jaradat, M. O., Masa'deh, R., & Alshurideh, M. T. (2023). The transformational leadership role in achieving organisational resilience through adaptive cultures: The case of Dubai service sector. *International Journal of Productivity and Performance Management*, *72*(2), 440–468. DOI: 10.1108/IJPPM-02-2021-0093

OECD. (2019). *OECD future of education and skills 2030: OECD learning compass 2030*. OECD Publishing. https://www.oecd.org/education/2030-project/

Ronksley-Pavia, M., & Neumann, M. M. (2022). Exploring educator leadership practices in gifted education to facilitate online learning experiences for (re)engaging gifted students. *Education Sciences*, *12*(2), 99. Advance online publication. DOI: 10.3390/educsci12020099

Tao, Y., He, J. X., Liu, H., & Zhang, Z. Y. (2024). Strategy configurations and competitive advantage, organisational resilience: Research based on Chinese manufacturing firms. *Guanli Gongcheng Xuebao*, *38*(5), 1–21. DOI: 10.1234/jiieem.2024.38501

Tsiotas, D. (2022). A 3D index for measuring economic resilience with application to the modern international and global financial crises. *arXiv*. https://doi.org//arXiv.2202.08564DOI: 10.48550

UNESCO. (2021). *Reimagining our futures together: A new social contract for education.* UNESCO Publishing. https://unesdoc.unesco.org/ark:/48223/pf0000379707

UNICEF. (2021). *Reimagining education: Learning in a post-COVID-19 world.* UNICEF. https://www.unicef.org/reports/reimagining-education-learning-post-covid-19-world

Waidyaratne, S. M. (2022). Impact of transformational leadership on employee resilience during a crisis. *Sri Lanka Journal of Management Studies*, *4*(1), 147–162. DOI: 10.4038/sljms.v4i1.92

World Bank. (2020). *The World Bank education strategy 2020: Learning for all – Investing in people's knowledge and skills to promote development.* World Bank. https://www.worldbank.org/en/topic/education/publication/education-strategy-2020

Yukl, G. (1999). An evaluation of conceptual weaknesses in transformational and charismatic leadership theories. *The Leadership Quarterly*, *10*(2), 285–305. DOI: 10.1016/S1048-9843(99)00013-2

KEY TERMS AND DEFINITIONS

Accountability in Leadership: The responsibility of leaders to ensure that educational practices and policies lead to measurable outcomes while maintaining transparency and ethical standards.

Adaptive Educational Ecosystem: An education system designed with flexibility and resilience to respond to rapid technological, social, or environmental changes.

Collaborative Leadership: An approach where leaders co-create strategies and solutions with staff, students, and communities through mutual respect and shared responsibility.

Distributed Leadership: A decentralised leadership model where decision-making is shared across different levels—teachers, students, parents, and administrators—rather than concentrated in a single authority figure.

Economic Resilience: The capacity of educational systems to contribute to national and global economies by building a skilled, adaptable workforce capable of withstanding disruptions.

Education 4.0 Leadership: A form of transformational leadership that integrates digital technologies, adaptive learning, and innovation into education to align with the demands of the Fourth Industrial Revolution.

Fullan's Change Theory: An educational leadership framework emphasising moral purpose, capacity building, collaboration, and systemic coherence as foundations for sustainable change.

Global Collaboration in Education: Cross-border cooperation among institutions, policymakers, and organisations (e.g., UNESCO, OECD, UNICEF, World Bank) to share best practices, innovations, and solutions to educational challenges.

Governance in Education: Structures and processes that ensure transparency, accountability, and stakeholder participation in decision-making at institutional and policy levels.

Idealised Influence: When leaders act as ethical role models, demonstrating integrity, responsibility, and dedication, which encourages others to emulate them.

Inclusive Education: A principle ensuring that diverse learners (across gender, socioeconomic status, language, or disability) have equitable access to quality learning opportunities.

Individualised Consideration: Personalised attention and mentorship provided by leaders to recognise and nurture the unique strengths, needs, and aspirations of each individual.

Inspirational Motivation: The ability of leaders to articulate a compelling and meaningful vision of the future, motivating stakeholders to pursue shared goals with enthusiasm and commitment.

Intellectual Stimulation: Encouragement of critical thinking, problem-solving, and creativity by challenging existing assumptions and promoting innovative solutions.

Lifelong Learning: An approach to continuous education and skills development across all life stages, enabling individuals to remain adaptable in changing economies.

Public–Private Partnerships (PPPs): Collaborations between governments and private organisations aimed at enhancing educational access, infrastructure, technology, and workforce readiness.

Transactional Leadership: A leadership style based on systems of rewards and punishments, emphasising compliance, structure, and short-term task completion rather than long-term vision.

Transformational Educational Leadership: A leadership approach that inspires and empowers educators, students, and stakeholders to achieve beyond expectations by fostering vision, innovation, inclusivity, and collaboration, rather than relying on control and compliance.

Vision-Driven Leadership: Leadership that centres on creating and communicating a shared long-term vision, aligning institutional goals with broader social and economic outcomes.

Chapter 3 Educational Leadership for Economic Growth: A Study of the EU and SAARC Regions

Sabina Sehajpal
https://orcid.org/0009-0004-6655-6279
Chandigarh University, India

Priyanka Malhotra
Noida Institute of Engineering and Technology, India

Sanjeev Jain
https://orcid.org/0009-0005-0905-6304
Chandigarh University, India

ABSTRACT

This study examines the comparative dynamics of educational leadership and management in the European Union (EU) and the South Asian Association for Regional Cooperation (SAARC) regions, with a focus on their roles in promoting economic growth. Through a qualitative analysis, the research examines key aspects, including educational integration, human capital development, innovation capacity, and labour market alignment. The EU's cohesive, innovation-driven educational system, along with its alignment with economic goals, provides a model of success. In contrast, the SAARC region faces challenges related to fragmented educational systems and insufficient leadership. The study emphasises the importance of regional collaboration, inclusive education, vocational training, and policy harmonisation for unlocking the economic potential of the SAARC region. Recommendations are

DOI: 10.4018/979-8-3373-3616-9.ch003

made for both areas to enhance educational leadership, promote innovation, and align education with labour market needs, thereby driving sustainable economic development.

INTRODUCTION

In the contemporary global landscape, the interplay between education and economic growth has become a focal point of discourse, particularly within the context of regional development. The nexus between educational leadership, management, and economic prosperity remains central to the sustainable growth of nations. Within this framework, the European Union (EU) and the South Asian Association for Regional Cooperation (SAARC) emerge as two distinct, yet increasingly interconnected, regional entities with unique educational ecosystems. This study aims to undertake a comparative analysis of educational leadership and management within the EU and SAARC regions, with a particular emphasis on their roles in fostering economic growth. While both areas are inextricably tied to the global economic order, their educational frameworks and institutional models diverge significantly, reflecting disparate socio-political contexts, historical trajectories, and economic priorities (Srinivasan et al., 2024). The juxtaposition of these regions presents a compelling opportunity to examine how educational governance structures, leadership paradigms, and management practices influence or hinder economic progress, ultimately shaping the broader developmental prospects of their respective nations. The global importance of this discourse resides in its capacity to illuminate how differentiated architectures of educational leadership and governance function as cardinal determinants of transnational economic competitiveness, sociocultural resilience, and innovation capacity, thereby rendering the EU–SAARC comparative prism not merely a regional interrogation but a paradigmatic exemplar for understanding the universal imperative of aligning human capital formation with the exigencies of an interdependent, knowledge-driven global economy.

At the core of this inquiry is the understanding that economic growth, in its most robust form, is a multifaceted phenomenon influenced by an array of determinants, one of the most pivotal being human capital development. The nexus between human capital—the collective knowledge, skills, and abilities of the populace—and economic productivity has been well-documented in the literature, underscoring the importance of an efficient educational system in equipping individuals with the requisite competencies for participation in the labour market. The European Union, a conglomerate of economically advanced nations, has long been regarded as a global leader in the realms of educational excellence and economic competitiveness. With its established educational governance structures, a highly coordinated policy framework, and an emphasis on research and innovation, the EU represents a benchmark of success in integrating educational leadership and economic growth (Sridharan & Srinivasa-Raghavan, 2007). In contrast, SAARC, a regional cooperative body comprising South Asian nations, presents a different narrative—one marked by diverse educational challenges, socioeconomic disparities, and varying degrees of political stability. While the region has made notable strides in expanding access to education, the disparities in educational quality, infrastructure, and leadership capabilities present significant impediments to harnessing the full potential of education for economic transformation. The practical challenges coalescing around this nexus are manifest in the entrenched disjunctions between policy rhetoric and systemic enactment, including fiscal insufficiencies, infrastructural deficits, pedagogical obsolescence, governance fragmentation, and the perennial misalignment of curricular architectures with volatile labor market imperatives, all of which collectively engender a labyrinthine milieu wherein the translation of educational leadership into sustainable economic dividends remains persistently precarious and uneven.

The European Union's education system is underpinned by a well-organised framework that promotes a high degree of integration across member states. The Bologna Process, for instance, has been instrumental in harmonising higher education standards across Europe, facilitating mobility, and ensuring that educational qualifications are recognised and valued across borders. The EU's focus on research and innovation, through initiatives like Horizon Europe, has spurred economic growth by fostering an environment conducive to knowledge creation, technological advancement, and the commercialisation of research. In terms of leadership, the EU places a premium on collaborative decision-making, where a confluence of national governments, academic institutions, and civil society organisations influences educational policy development. This participatory model has enabled the region to develop a cohesive educational system that aligns closely with its economic and social objectives (Dinda, 2014). Furthermore, the EU's emphasis on inclusive education and lifelong learning has ensured that its citizens are equipped to navigate the rapidly changing global economy, thus contributing to the region's economic resilience and competitiveness.

By contrast, the SAARC region presents a more heterogeneous educational landscape, characterised by significant disparities in educational attainment, infrastructure, and governance. The region's educational systems are shaped by historical legacies of colonialism, political instability, and socio-economic inequality, all of which have contributed to persistent challenges in educational access and quality. Despite significant strides made in recent years to expand educational access, particularly at the primary and secondary levels, disparities in educational outcomes remain pervasive across the region. Factors such as inadequate funding, poor infrastructure, and the lack of trained educators continue to hamper the effectiveness of educational systems in many SAARC countries (Mehanna, 2008). Furthermore, the absence of cohesive leadership structures and management practices at the regional level exacerbates these challenges, preventing the effective implementation of policies that could promote educational reform and economic development.

Notwithstanding these challenges, the SAARC region has shown remarkable potential for growth, driven in part by its young and dynamic population. With a burgeoning workforce, the area holds immense promise for economic development, provided that it can fully leverage the potential of its human capital. However, this potential remains largely untapped due to the limitations of educational leadership and management systems. For instance, in many SAARC countries, the decentralisation of education has led to fragmented and inconsistent policy implementation, hindering efforts to standardise educational quality and align curricula with the needs of the labour market (Soni & Sahoo, 2021). Additionally, the lack of institutional collaboration across countries has resulted in missed opportunities for knowledge exchange and joint initiatives aimed at enhancing educational outcomes.

In examining the comparative dynamics of educational leadership and management between the EU and SAARC regions, it is crucial to consider the varying models of governance and their implications for economic growth. The EU's centralised approach to educational policy, characterised by mechanisms like Erasmus+ and the European Education Area, contrasts sharply with SAARC's more fragmented approach, where educational policy is often subject to national agendas and priorities (I. Ahmed, 2010). This divergence reflects broader differences in regional integration and political cohesion, with the EU's highly coordinated governance structures providing a clear advantage in terms of policy alignment and the strategic deployment of educational resources. In contrast, SAARC's diverse political landscapes, compounded by varying levels of regional cooperation, present significant barriers to the development of a unified educational strategy that can propel economic growth across the region (S. Kumar, 2024).

This chapter, therefore, seeks to illuminate the critical role of educational leadership and management in shaping economic outcomes within both the EU and SAARC regions. By examining the structural, cultural, and political factors that influence educational policy and practice, the research will offer insights into how educational systems in both regions can be reformed and aligned with broader economic objectives. It will also explore the potential for cross-regional learning, identifying best practices from the EU that could be adapted to the specific context of the SAARC region to drive economic growth. Ultimately, this comparative analysis aims to contribute to a deeper understanding of how educational leadership and management can be optimised to foster sustainable economic development in diverse regional settings. The findings of this study hold significant implications for policymakers, educators, and development practitioners seeking to harness the transformative power of education in the pursuit of economic growth.

BACKGROUND

The background of this study is rooted in the recognition that education, long acknowledged as the cornerstone of human capital development, serves as a primary driver of economic growth. However, its translation into tangible developmental outcomes is profoundly contingent on the quality of leadership, governance, and management systems that underpin its implementation. Across the globe, the dichotomy between regions with robust, cohesive, and innovation-driven educational ecosystems and those constrained by fragmentation, underfunding, and socio-political volatility offers a compelling lens through which to analyse the determinants of economic resilience. The European Union exemplifies a paradigm where strategic initiatives, such as the Bologna Process, Erasmus+, and Horizon Europe, have successfully harmonised higher education standards, fostered cross-border student mobility, and catalysed research-driven innovation, thereby producing a workforce aligned with the imperatives of a globalised, knowledge-intensive economy. For instance, the integration of Germany's dual education system—combining vocational training with formal education—has been instrumental in ensuring exceptionally low youth unemployment rates, demonstrating the practical dividends of well-governed educational leadership. In stark contrast, the South Asian Association for Regional Cooperation (SAARC) illustrates the challenges of implementing comparable frameworks in contexts marked by resource asymmetries, political instability, and infrastructural deficits. Case studies from India and Nepal, for example, reveal that while India's National Education Policy (2020) ambitiously aims to align curricula with global labor market needs and foster digital literacy, the practical implementation has been hindered by uneven technological penetration, disparities between urban and rural institutions, and inadequate teacher training; similarly, in Nepal, efforts to decentralise education governance have often resulted in policy incoherence and inequitable distribution of resources, exacerbating educational inequality. These practical impediments underscore the persistent disjuncture between policy ambition and ground-level execution, highlighting the urgent need for frameworks that bridge the gap between conceptual ideals of educational leadership and the contextual realities of governance, infrastructure, and societal constraints. It is within this juxtaposition that the present study situates itself, seeking to unravel how leadership paradigms and governance architectures either facilitate or obstruct the transformative potential of education as a vehicle of sustainable economic growth.

The problem at the heart of this study emanates from the persistent contradiction between the widely celebrated ideal state of education as the cornerstone of human capital formation and economic progress, and the empirical realities that reveal deep disparities in leadership, governance, and systemic implementation across different regional contexts. Theoretically, education is envisioned as a universal equaliser capable of producing skilled, adaptable, and innovative labor forces that drive sustained economic growth; however, contradictory evidence from global and regional analyses demonstrates that while the European Union (EU) has managed to institutionalise highly integrated educational governance models aligned with labor market needs, the South Asian Association for Regional Cooperation (SAARC) remains beset by fragmentation, underfunding, weak leadership capacity, and misaligned curricula, resulting in inconclusive outcomes regarding the extent to which education truly serves as an economic catalyst in diverse contexts. Within the scholarly corpus, theoretical gaps persist in explicitly linking governance paradigms of education to economic transformation, as existing frameworks often isolate education from the structural and political conditions that shape its efficacy. Simultaneously, knowledge gaps are evident in the comparative literature, as much of the discourse remains Eurocentric, underexploring the nuanced challenges and contextual contingencies of the Global South, particularly in regions like SAARC. Contextual gaps also loom large, given that most analyses fail to situate educational leadership within the specific socio-political complexities of fragile democracies, economic inequities, and cultural heterogeneities that characterise South Asia, thereby limiting the transferability of existing models. At the practical level, the implementation of reformist policies, such as India's National Education Policy (2020) or Nepal's decentralisation efforts, reveals challenges including infrastructural inadequacy, insufficient digital readiness, poor teacher training, and regional disparities, which undermine the operationalisation of ambitious frameworks. This study aims to address these multi-layered gaps by adopting a cross-regional comparative approach that highlights the successes of the EU's collaborative, innovation-driven educational governance, while critically examining the constraints and missed opportunities in SAARC. By situating educational leadership as a mediating variable between education systems and economic growth, the research integrates theoretical, contextual, and practical perspectives, offering a holistic framework that not only clarifies inconclusive evidence but also provides a roadmap for region-specific reforms. Ultimately, this endeavour aims to guide policymakers toward evidence-based interventions that reconcile policy aspirations with on-the-ground realities and to direct future researchers toward more integrative, cross-contextual studies that bridge the divide between global best practices and local contingencies.

Theoretical Framework

The theoretical framework of this study is anchored in the Human Capital Theory and the Governance and Leadership Models of Education, which together elucidate the pivotal role of education as both an economic driver and a societal equaliser (Ferreira et al., 2017). Human Capital Theory posits that investment in education enhances the skills, competencies, and productivity of individuals, thereby directly contributing to economic growth. Governance and leadership theories, on the other hand, underscore the importance of strategic policy formulation, institutional management, and cross-sectoral collaboration in maximising these returns. Within this comparative analysis of the EU and SAARC regions, the framework operationalises education not merely as a pedagogical process but as a systemic mechanism influenced by socio-political, cultural, and economic determinants that shape labour market outcomes, innovation capacity, and sustainable development. The EU's centralised and innovation-driven leadership model exemplifies how cohesive policy integration, collaborative governance, and resource-rich systems foster alignment between educational outputs and economic objectives. In contrast, the SAARC region's fragmented, under-resourced, and unevenly governed systems highlight the constraints of weak institutional leadership, inadequate collaboration, and inconsistent investment in human capital. Thus, the framework conceptualises educational leadership and management as mediating variables that bridge the relationship between education and economic growth, while socio-political stability, funding, and regional cooperation act as moderating factors, collectively explaining the disparities and opportunities in translating education into economic transformation across regional contexts (Ratzinger et al., 2018).

The following are related theories to the present research.

Human Capital Theory forms the foundational premise, originating from the works of Adam Smith (1776) and later formalised by Theodore Schultz (1961) and Gary Becker (1964), which conceptualises education as an investment that enhances the productive capacities, skills, and knowledge of individuals, thereby yielding returns in the form of higher wages, productivity, and aggregate economic growth. In the context of this study, Human Capital Theory directly relates to the role of educational systems in creating labour forces that drive economic progress, highlighting why disparities in quality, leadership, and access across the EU and SAARC result in differentiated developmental outcomes.

Educational Leadership Theory, emerging from early management theories and later adapted within education through the works of scholars like Leithwood and Hallinger, focuses on how leadership styles (transformational, instructional, or distributed) influence institutional performance, teacher effectiveness, and student achievement. Within this study, the theory elucidates how leadership paradigms in the EU (collaborative, multi-stakeholder, policy-integrated) contrast with SAARC's fragmented and often authoritarian approaches, shaping the capacity of education to contribute meaningfully to economic growth.

Systems Theory, derived from the work of Ludwig von Bertalanffy in the 1940s, views organisations as open systems that interact dynamically with their environment, emphasising interdependence, feedback loops, and systemic coherence. In applying this to education, the study situates schools, universities, and governance bodies as subsystems within broader socio-political and economic structures, where alignment (as in the EU's Bologna Process) yields coherence and efficiency. In contrast, misalignment (as in SAARC's fragmented governance) perpetuates inefficiency and weak outcomes.

Institutional Theory, tracing its origins to Selznick (1948) and later elaborated upon through neo-institutionalism (DiMaggio & Powell, 1983), explains how rules, norms, and legitimacy pressures within institutional environments shape organisational behaviour. This theory is particularly relevant to understanding how the EU's education systems have converged under supranational norms and policies (e.g., Erasmus+, Horizon Europe). In contrast, SAARC nations, driven by disparate political agendas and weak regional integration, have failed to institutionalise cohesive educational reforms.

Endogenous Growth Theory, advanced by Paul Romer and Robert Lucas in the 1980s, emphasises that long-term economic growth is primarily driven by knowledge, innovation, and human capital accumulation rather than external technological shocks. This theory complements the study by underscoring how regions with strong educational governance and leadership (such as the EU) succeed in fostering innovation-led growth. In contrast, areas with weaker educational infrastructures (such as SAARC) lag in leveraging knowledge economies.

Among these, Human Capital Theory serves as the central theoretical lens for this study, as it directly operationalises the nexus between education and economic growth. The other theories function as supporting frameworks, providing governance, systemic, institutional, and innovation-oriented dimensions to the analysis. Together, these theoretical perspectives enable the study to examine how leadership and governance influence the translation of educational inputs into economic outcomes, why disparities exist between the EU and SAARC, and what policy interventions are necessary to bridge the gap.

THEORETICAL PERSPECTIVES

The intricate relationship between educational leadership, management, and economic growth has been a focal point of scholarly inquiry for decades. The global discourse on this subject frequently explores the multifaceted mechanisms by which educational frameworks impact national and regional economies, particularly in the context of human capital development (Kivimäki, 2016). The role of education in driving economic transformation is unequivocally recognised, but the pathways through which this influence manifests remain a complex and evolving subject of study. The literature on educational leadership and management, particularly within regional contexts such as the European Union (EU) and the South Asian Association for Regional Cooperation (SAARC), reveals divergent models of governance, policy implementation, and socio-economic outcomes, with profound implications for regional development (Zahid et al., 2021).

One of the central tenets of the literature on educational leadership and management is the critical role of human capital in economic growth. Human capital theory posits that the skills, knowledge, and competencies acquired through education form the bedrock of economic productivity. It is widely acknowledged that an individual's capacity to participate effectively in the labour market is directly tied to the quality and accessibility of education (Z. S. Ahmed, 2018). Thus, educational systems that fail to equip students with the necessary tools for intellectual, technical, and vocational engagement are viewed as a hindrance to economic development (Sáez, 2014). In this respect, the leadership and management of educational systems are paramount, as these structures determine the distribution of resources, the design of curricula, and the methods of instructional delivery that ultimately shape the skills of the workforce.

Within the EU, educational leadership is often characterised by a highly centralised model, where policies and frameworks are coordinated across member states to promote integration and standardisation. This model is premised on the belief that a unified educational system, underpinned by common standards, will facilitate mobility and economic cohesion within the region. Research indicates that the EU's emphasis on cross-border cooperation in education—through initiatives such as the Bologna Process and Erasmus+—has led to the creation of a more harmonised educational landscape (Shaw et al., 2016). These initiatives seek to establish standard benchmarks for academic qualifications, enhance student mobility, and encourage inter-institutional collaboration, all of which have been linked to positive economic outcomes such as increased innovation, labour market integration, and overall productivity (Dixit & Bhatnagar, 2025; Miglani et al., 2025; Sharma et al., 2025).

The EU's educational framework is underpinned by a strategic vision that emphasises the cultivation of knowledge economies. Scholars have argued that the EU's commitment to research and development, innovation, and lifelong learning reflects a sophisticated understanding of how education can be leveraged to drive economic growth. The EU's leadership model promotes a collaborative, multi-stakeholder approach to policy formulation, where governments, academic institutions, and industry stakeholders engage in dialogue to ensure that education is aligned with the demands of the labour market (Gaurav et al., 2015). This approach, while highly effective in the context of well-resourced economies, has been critiqued for its tendency to overlook the nuances of local contexts and the diverse needs of its member states (Khanna et al., 2025).

In contrast, the educational leadership and management models within SAARC countries are often more fragmented, shaped by the complex socio-political landscapes of South Asia. The region's history of colonialism, combined with contemporary challenges such as political instability, economic inequality, and resource constraints, has resulted in educational systems that are often poorly coordinated and underfunded (Bhatta, 2019). Literature on education in South Asia suggests that, while there has been significant progress in expanding access to primary education, the quality of teaching and the leadership capabilities within the system remain highly inconsistent. Scholars argue that the lack of coherent leadership structures, combined with a history of political interference in educational policy, has led to systems that are ill-equipped to drive economic development.

The decentralisation of education in SAARC countries has been both a blessing and a curse. On the one hand, it allows for a degree of contextual flexibility, enabling educational policies to be tailored to the specific needs of local communities. On the other hand, the absence of a unified framework has led to a lack of standardisation, which has compounded issues of inequality and inefficiency. Research indicates that educational leadership in SAARC countries is often characterised by a top-down, authoritarian approach, where decision-making is concentrated in the hands of a few central authorities (Mohammad, 2011). This lack of inclusivity in policy development has led to education systems that are disconnected from the realities of local economies and labour markets. Furthermore, the failure to prioritise the development of educational leadership capacity has resulted in a shortage of skilled leaders capable of managing the complexities of modern educational systems.

While SAARC countries face significant challenges in terms of educational leadership and management, a growing body of literature also highlights the region's potential for educational reform. Some scholars have highlighted the region's youthful population as a key asset, suggesting that with the right investments in education and leadership development, South Asia could unlock significant economic growth. However, this potential remains largely untapped due to systemic inefficiencies and the lack of a coherent regional strategy for educational development (S. Y. S. Kumar, 2021). The literature on South Asian education emphasises the importance of establishing robust leadership structures that can effectively steer educational reform, responding to the needs of both the economy and society.

The comparative literature between the EU and SAARC regions reveals stark contrasts in their educational approaches and outcomes. While the EU's emphasis on standardisation, research-driven policy, and inter-regional cooperation has fostered a robust educational system that supports economic growth, the SAARC region's challenges in governance and policy implementation have hindered its ability to leverage education for economic advancement. Scholars have suggested that the EU's success can be attributed to its ability to align educational leadership with broader financial goals, thereby creating an ecosystem where education is directly tied to productivity, innovation, and competitiveness (Prasad, 2013). In contrast, SAARC countries have struggled to develop such linkages, with education often seen as a sector separate from economic development.

In recent years, however, there has been a growing recognition of the need for more integrated approaches to educational leadership and economic growth in South Asia (Pal et al., 2007). The literature suggests that SAARC countries must prioritise the development of human capital through strategic educational reforms, including the decentralisation of authority, enhancing leadership capacity, and integrating education with industry needs. Moreover, the importance of cross-regional collaboration and knowledge sharing has been emphasised as a means of overcoming the challenges posed by fragmented educational systems.

Ultimately, the existing body of literature underscores the critical role of educational leadership and management in shaping economic outcomes. While the EU provides a model of coordinated educational governance aligned with financial goals, the SAARC region offers valuable lessons in the challenges of educational reform in a diverse, resource-constrained context. The ongoing evolution of both regions provides a fertile ground for further research, particularly in the area of comparative education and its impact on regional economic growth. The literature affirms that, regardless of the regional context, the development of effective educational leadership and management is a crucial determinant of long-term economic prosperity.

METHODOLOGY

The research methodology for this comparative study of educational leadership and its impact on economic growth in the EU and SAARC regions adopts a qualitative, cross-regional approach. The study involves an in-depth analysis of secondary data sourced from a range of academic literature, policy documents, and regional reports on education and economic development. Comparative analysis is utilised to assess the differences and similarities in the educational frameworks, leadership structures, and financial outcomes between the two regions. Data are systematically gathered to explore key metrics, including literacy rates, PISA rankings, graduation rates, innovation capacity, and labour market conditions. Additionally, the research examines socio-economic factors that influence education, including economic and political stability, educational attainment, and social inequality. To gain insights into the effectiveness of educational policies, the study also examines regional integration, cross-country collaboration, and the alignment of educational leadership with labour market needs. The methodology incorporates case studies from both regions, supplemented by expert interviews, to gain a deeper understanding of the challenges and opportunities in educational reform.

DISCUSSION

The study's analytical framework is designed to provide a nuanced understanding of how educational leadership influences economic growth and to propose actionable recommendations for both the EU and SAARC regions to enhance their educational systems and financial outcomes.

Figure 1. Conceptual Framework

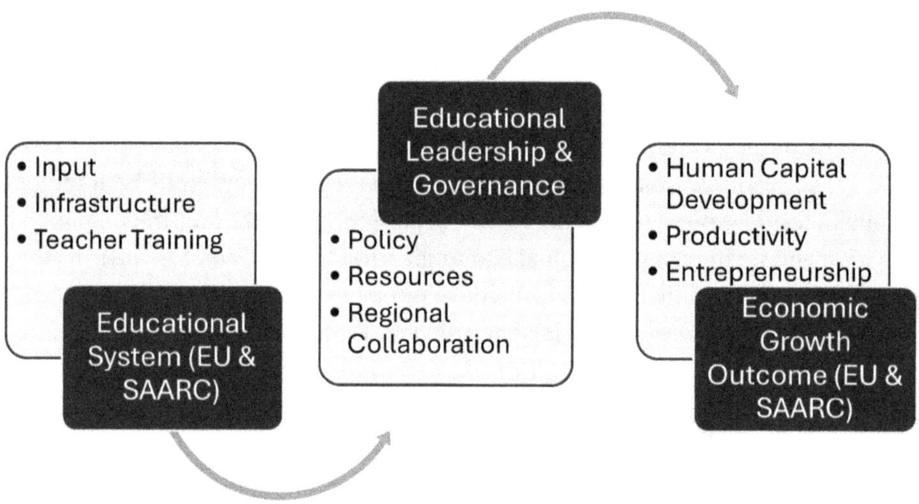

Figure 1 illustrates how educational systems, when mediated by effective leadership and governance and moderated by socio-political, financial, technological, and regional factors, translate into differentiated economic growth outcomes across the EU and SAARC contexts.

Analysis

Table 1. Comparative Overview of Educational Leadership Models in the EU and the SAARC Regions

Aspect	EU Region	SAARC Region
Leadership Structure	Centralised, multi-stakeholder involvement	Fragmented, predominantly top-down approach
Policy Development	Collaborative, with EU-wide agreements	Decentralised, influenced by national priorities
Governance Mechanisms	Standardised frameworks, EU-level policies (Bologna Process, Erasmus+)	Nationally driven policies, lack of regional integration
Focus on Innovation	Strong focus on research and innovation (Horizon Europe)	Limited focus on research and development
Decision-Making Process	Multi-tiered, inclusive decision-making	Authoritarian, often centralised at the top

Table 1 provides a comparative analysis of the educational leadership models in the European Union (EU) and the South Asian Association for Regional Cooperation (SAARC) regions. The comparison highlights significant differences in the structure, policy development, governance, innovation focus, and decision-making processes in the two areas, each of which has profound implications for both educational outcomes and economic growth.

The EU follows a centralised leadership structure, wherein educational governance is shaped by multi-stakeholder involvement, including EU institutions, national governments, and academic bodies. This collaborative framework enables the development of cohesive, region-wide policies, such as the Bologna Process and Erasmus+, which promote educational standardisation, mobility, and research collaboration across member states. This integrated approach not only ensures a high degree of cooperation but also allows for the alignment of educational systems with broader economic objectives. In contrast, the leadership in the SAARC region is much more fragmented (Khan, 2021). Academic governance is mainly national, with decisions being made at the country level without significant cross-border coordination. This top-down, hierarchical approach often yields policies that are inconsistent across the region, resulting in disparities in the quality of education. The lack of a unified leadership structure within SAARC impedes the region's ability to implement coordinated educational reforms that can foster economic integration and development.

In terms of policy development, the EU's approach is highly collaborative. The EU region benefits from a policy framework that includes agreements such as the

Bologna Process, which seeks to harmonise educational standards across member states, and Erasmus+, which facilitates student mobility and academic exchange. This collaborative approach to policy-making ensures that education is aligned with the region's economic and social needs, fostering a highly skilled, mobile workforce that is integral to the EU's competitive edge (Waqif, 1999). Conversely, policy development in SAARC is largely decentralised. While each country in the SAARC region sets its own educational priorities, the absence of a cohesive regional strategy means that these policies are often misaligned with the region's economic needs. The lack of coordination among the countries prevents the creation of a shared educational vision, making it difficult to implement reforms that could enhance regional economic growth.

Governance mechanisms in the EU are well-established and standardised, with frameworks such as the Bologna Process ensuring consistency in educational systems across member states. These governance structures are designed to facilitate integration, ensuring that education systems across Europe work in concert to support the region's economic ambitions. In contrast, the governance mechanisms within the SAARC region are primarily nationally driven, resulting in a lack of integration and standardisation across countries. The national-driven approach creates fragmented educational systems that vary significantly in terms of quality, resources, and outcomes, thus preventing the region from benefiting from a unified approach to academic leadership and development.

The EU places a significant emphasis on innovation, particularly through research funding and technological advancement. Initiatives like Horizon Europe have led to substantial investment in research and development, which has directly contributed to the region's economic growth and prosperity. By fostering innovation, the EU has positioned itself as a global leader in fields such as technology, healthcare, and sustainable development. However, the SAARC region has a relatively limited focus on research and innovation. While countries like India have made strides in areas such as technology and space exploration, the region as a whole lacks the cohesive policies and financial backing necessary to drive widespread innovation. The limited emphasis on research hampers the region's ability to create new economic opportunities and remain competitive in the global economy.

Ultimately, the decision-making processes in the EU and SAARC regions differ significantly. The EU's decision-making process is characterised by inclusivity and multi-tiered governance, where various stakeholders, including governments, academic institutions, and industry leaders, have a role in shaping policies. This inclusive approach enables the development of more flexible and adaptive educational strategies that can respond to the changing needs of the economy. In contrast, decision-making in the SAARC region is predominantly authoritarian and centralised, with education policies often being dictated by the central government. This lack of stakeholder involvement results in rigid educational policies that are not always responsive to the needs of the labour market or the demands of a dynamic, globalised economy.

In conclusion, the comparative analysis of educational leadership in the EU and SAARC regions, as illustrated in Table 1, underscores the vast differences between the two areas in terms of governance, policy development, and innovation. The EU's centralised, collaborative, and innovation-driven model has led to high-quality educational outcomes that align with economic growth. In contrast, the fragmented, top-down approach in the SAARC region has led to inconsistent educational standards, which hinder economic development. These disparities underscore the need for more cohesive and innovative educational leadership frameworks in the SAARC region to foster sustainable economic growth and regional integration.

Table 2. Educational Resources and Infrastructure in the EU and SAARC Regions

Resource/ Infrastructure	EU Region	SAARC Region
Funding for Education	High, consistent funding across member states	Varies greatly, often insufficient in low-income countries
School Infrastructure	Modern, well-maintained infrastructure in most countries	Inadequate, especially in rural and remote areas
Access to Technology	High access to technology, digital tools integrated	Limited access to technology, especially in rural areas
Teacher Training	Robust teacher training programs, continuous professional development	Inconsistent, often underfunded teacher training
Educational Institutions	Highly developed tertiary education systems, world-class universities	Inconsistent quality, with significant disparities in access and quality

Table 2 offers a comprehensive comparison of educational resources and infrastructure between the European Union (EU) and the South Asian Association for Regional Cooperation (SAARC) regions. This table highlights key areas, including funding, school infrastructure, access to technology, teacher training, and the development of educational institutions. The stark differences between the two regions in these critical areas reflect broader disparities in academic quality and, consequently, the ability of education systems to contribute to economic growth and social development.

Funding for Education is one of the most significant differentiators between the EU and SAARC regions. The EU benefits from high and consistent funding for education across its member states. This funding is not only robust but is also strategically allocated to ensure that all educational sectors—primary, secondary, and tertiary—are well-resourced to meet the evolving needs of students. This consistent investment in education has resulted in a highly developed educational system that serves as a model for other regions. In contrast, funding for education in the SAARC region varies widely across countries, and in many cases, it is insufficient, particularly in low-income nations. The lack of stable and equitable funding results in resource constraints that affect the quality of education, leading to disparities in learning outcomes and hindering the region's ability to foster economic growth through education.

School Infrastructure further illustrates the differences in educational resources between the EU and SAARC regions. In the EU, schools generally benefit from modern, well-maintained infrastructure that provides conducive learning environments. The infrastructure is equipped with the necessary facilities, such as libraries, sports complexes, and laboratories, which support a holistic approach to education. The SAARC region, however, faces significant challenges in this regard. Many schools, particularly in rural and remote areas, suffer from inadequate infrastructure. Poorly constructed classrooms, lack of sanitation facilities, and limited access to educational resources make it difficult for students in these areas to receive a quality education. This disparity in school infrastructure is a critical factor in perpetuating the academic divide between urban and rural areas within SAARC countries.

Access to Technology is another area where the EU region significantly outperforms the SAARC region. The EU has high access to technology, with digital tools integrated across the educational system. Schools in the EU are well-equipped with computers, smartboards, and high-speed internet access, enabling both teachers and students to leverage technology to enhance the learning experience. In contrast, access to technology in the SAARC region is often limited, especially in rural areas. While urban centres in countries like India and Pakistan may have better access to digital tools, the majority of rural schools lack the necessary infrastructure to incorporate technology into their teaching and learning processes. The digital divide exacerbates educational inequalities and limits students in less developed areas from accessing the resources needed to succeed in an increasingly digital world.

Teacher Training is a crucial aspect of educational quality, and here too, the EU region holds a distinct advantage over SAARC. The EU provides robust teacher training programs that are both comprehensive and continuous. Teachers are offered professional development opportunities, ensuring that they stay up-to-date with the latest pedagogical approaches and educational technologies. These programs aim to equip educators with the necessary skills and knowledge to engage students and foster learning in diverse settings effectively. In the SAARC region, teacher training is often inconsistent and underfunded. While there are efforts to improve the quality of teacher education, many countries still face challenges, including a lack of formal teacher certification, insufficient training resources, and inadequate professional development opportunities. This lack of quality teacher training is a significant barrier to improving educational outcomes in the region.

Educational Institutions in the EU are highly developed, with world-class universities and a well-established tertiary education system. The EU is home to some of the world's leading academic institutions, which attract students from all over the globe. These institutions are well-funded, internationally recognised, and offer a wide range of programs that cater to various academic and professional fields. In contrast, the quality of educational institutions in the SAARC region is inconsistent. While countries like India and Sri Lanka have numerous respected universities and academic institutions, the overall quality of higher education varies significantly across the region. Many institutions in SAARC countries suffer from outdated curricula, inadequate infrastructure, and insufficient funding, resulting in limited access to high-quality education for large segments of the population. The disparity in the quality and accessibility of educational institutions between urban and rural areas further exacerbates educational inequalities.

In conclusion, Table 2 reveals the significant disparities in educational resources and infrastructure between the EU and SAARC regions. The EU's strong and consistent funding for education, coupled with modern infrastructure, widespread access to technology, comprehensive teacher training, and world-class educational institutions, provides a strong foundation for its economic success. In contrast, the SAARC region faces considerable challenges in these areas, with inconsistent funding, inadequate infrastructure, limited access to technology, underfunded teacher training, and disparities in the quality of educational institutions. These differences underscore the need for substantial reforms in the SAARC region to enhance educational resources and infrastructure, which is crucial for promoting sustainable economic growth and reducing educational disparities.

Table 3. Student Performance and Learning Outcomes in the EU and SAARC Regions

Performance Indicator	**EU Region**	**SAARC Region**
Literacy Rates	High literacy rates across all member states	Literacy rates vary significantly, with lower rates in rural areas
PISA Rankings	Top rankings in global education assessments (OECD)	Low rankings, with significant regional disparities
Graduation Rates	High graduation rates, especially at tertiary levels	Graduation rates are lower, particularly at the tertiary level
Skills Development	Emphasis on both soft skills and technical expertise	Limited focus on vocational and technical education
Post-Education Employment	High rates of employment for graduates	Higher unemployment rates, particularly for educated youth

Table 3 provides a comparative analysis of student performance and learning outcomes between the European Union (EU) and South Asian Association for Regional Cooperation (SAARC) regions. This table examines key performance indicators, including literacy rates, rankings in global assessments (PISA), graduation rates, skills development, and post-education employment, shedding light on the disparities between the two regions and their implications for educational and economic outcomes.

Literacy Rates in the EU region are notably high across all member states, with most countries achieving near-universal literacy. This widespread literacy is a result of well-funded and accessible education systems that cater to diverse populations. The focus on early childhood education, primary and secondary schooling, and adult education programs ensures that literacy remains a priority in EU nations. Conversely, in the SAARC region, literacy rates exhibit significant variation across countries, with rural areas facing particular challenges. While urban centres may have relatively high literacy rates, rural and remote areas often lag due to inadequate educational infrastructure, limited access to quality teaching resources, and socio-economic barriers. The disparity in literacy rates within the SAARC region reflects broader educational inequalities and the ongoing challenges of ensuring equitable education across all demographics.

PISA Rankings further illustrate the differences in educational outcomes between the two regions. The EU consistently ranks highly in global education assessments, particularly in the areas of reading, mathematics, and science, as measured by the Programme for International Student Assessment (PISA) conducted by the OECD. These top rankings are indicative of strong educational systems that emphasise both academic excellence and the development of critical thinking skills. The EU's emphasis on research, innovation, and high educational standards has led to consistently strong performance on these global scales. In contrast, the SAARC region performs poorly in PISA rankings, with many countries scoring below the worldwide average. These low rankings are compounded by significant regional disparities, with some countries, such as India and Sri Lanka, performing better than others, including Afghanistan and Nepal. The lack of uniformity in educational quality, inadequate resources, and limited teacher training contribute to these poor outcomes in the SAARC region, hindering its ability to compete on a global scale.

Graduation Rates in the EU are relatively high, especially at tertiary levels. The EU benefits from a well-developed higher education system with numerous world-class universities and research institutions. These institutions offer a wide range of programs and are supported by substantial government funding, making education accessible to a larger portion of the population. High graduation rates at both secondary and tertiary levels reflect the EU's success in providing educational opportunities to a broad spectrum of students. In contrast, graduation rates in the SAARC region are lower, particularly at the tertiary level. Although access to primary and secondary education has improved in recent years, tertiary education remains out of reach for many students due to financial constraints, inadequate infrastructure, and limited availability of quality higher education institutions. As a result, many students in SAARC countries are unable to complete their education beyond high school, limiting their opportunities for upward social mobility and economic participation.

Skills Development is another key area where the two regions differ significantly. In the EU, there is a strong emphasis on both soft skills and technical expertise, with educational programs designed to equip students with the skills needed to thrive in the global workforce. This focus on holistic development ensures that students are not only academically proficient but also capable of navigating complex, ever-changing work environments. EU education systems integrate soft skills, such as communication, teamwork, and problem-solving, with technical skills, preparing students for diverse professional roles. On the other hand, in the SAARC region, there is a limited focus on vocational and technical education. While countries like India have made strides in technical education through initiatives such as the National Skill Development Corporation (NSDC), many other SAARC nations still lack a comprehensive approach to vocational training. The limited focus on skills development in the region contributes to a mismatch between the skills that students acquire and the demands of the labour market, resulting in high levels of underemployment and unemployment, particularly among young graduates.

Post-Education Employment - Outcomes reflect the impact of education on the broader economy. In the EU, graduates typically enjoy high employment rates, particularly in established industries such as technology, finance, healthcare, and engineering. The strong connection between educational institutions and industry, coupled with high-quality internships and apprenticeship programs, ensures that students are well-prepared to enter the workforce. Additionally, the EU's strong economic integration offers numerous opportunities for graduates to work across borders, thereby further enhancing their employability. In contrast, the SAARC region faces higher unemployment rates, particularly among educated youth. Despite improvements in educational access, many graduates struggle to find jobs due to factors such as a lack of job opportunities, skills mismatches, and economic instability. The relatively low rate of employment for educated youth in the SAARC region underscores the gap between education and the labour market, where many graduates are either underemployed or remain unemployed for extended periods after completing their studies.

In conclusion, Table 3 highlights the significant differences in student performance and learning outcomes between the EU and SAARC regions. While the EU excels in literacy rates, PISA rankings, graduation rates, skills development, and post-education employment, the SAARC region faces considerable challenges in these areas. These disparities reflect broader socio-economic differences, resource allocation, and the varying effectiveness of educational systems in both regions. The EU's robust and well-coordinated educational infrastructure has helped create a skilled and competitive workforce. At the same time, the SAARC region must overcome several obstacles to improve academic outcomes and better align education with labour market demands. Addressing these challenges will be crucial for the SAARC region to unlock the potential of its young population and foster sustainable economic growth.

Table 4. Socio-Economic Factors Influencing Education and Economic Growth

Factor	EU Region	SAARC Region
Economic Stability	Relatively high, stable economies	Varies, with some countries experiencing economic instability
Political Stability	Strong governance, relatively stable political systems	Political instability in several member countries
Educational Attainment	High levels of educational attainment, especially in higher education	Varied, with significant gaps in educational access and quality
Labour Market Conditions	Strong labour market, high demand for skilled workers	High youth unemployment and underemployment of skilled labour
Social Inequality	Lower levels of inequality, but challenges remain in certain areas	High levels of inequality, with disparities between urban and rural areas

Table 4 offers a detailed comparison of the socio-economic factors that influence education and economic growth in the European Union (EU) and South Asian Association for Regional Cooperation (SAARC) regions. The table examines key elements, including financial stability, political stability, educational attainment, labour market conditions, and social inequality. These factors are instrumental in shaping both the quality of education and the overall economic outcomes of a region, and the disparities between the EU and SAARC regions have profound implications for sustainable development.

Economic Stability plays a crucial role in both education and economic growth. The EU region benefits from relatively high and stable economies across its member states. The stability of EU economies enables consistent investment in education and infrastructure, thereby contributing to the region's overall prosperity. A robust economic environment provides governments with the financial resources to support and expand educational programs, creating a feedback loop where a skilled workforce drives further economic growth. In contrast, the SAARC region is marked by significant variation in economic stability. While countries such as India and Bangladesh have demonstrated impressive economic growth in recent years, others, like

Afghanistan and Nepal, have struggled with economic instability. This disparity in economic stability has a direct impact on the quality and accessibility of education in the region. In economically unstable countries, education systems often suffer from underfunding, inadequate resources, and limited access to quality learning opportunities, which in turn stifles the region's economic development.

Political Stability is another factor that has a profound effect on both education and economic outcomes. The EU region generally enjoys strong governance and relatively stable political systems, which are key drivers of policy continuity and social cohesion. Stable political environments in the EU enable long-term planning and the successful implementation of education and economic policies. These policies can focus on fostering innovation, improving infrastructure, and enhancing labour market participation. Conversely, political instability is a significant challenge in several SAARC countries, where fluctuating governments, political unrest, and corruption often disrupt educational reforms and economic policies. In countries experiencing political instability, the lack of continuity in governance can lead to fragmented education systems, inadequate policy execution, and a lack of investment in the education sector, thus hindering long-term economic growth.

Educational Attainment is a critical indicator of a region's ability to foster a skilled and productive workforce. In the EU, there are high levels of educational attainment, particularly in higher education. Most EU countries have well-established tertiary education systems that are accessible to a large portion of the population, with a significant emphasis on research, innovation, and skill development. The EU's focus on education at all levels has enabled its member states to develop a highly educated workforce, which is a key factor driving the region's economic growth and competitiveness on the global stage. In the SAARC region, however, educational attainment varies widely. While countries like Sri Lanka and India have made strides in improving access to education, significant gaps remain in terms of educational access and quality, particularly in rural areas. The disparities in educational attainment across the region result in an unevenly skilled workforce, which in turn hampers overall economic development and competitiveness. Many students in SAARC countries lack access to the resources and opportunities necessary to complete their education, particularly at higher levels, which limits their participation in the formal labour market.

Labour market conditions are closely tied to both educational outcomes and economic growth. The EU has a strong labour market characterised by high demand for skilled workers, particularly in sectors such as technology, healthcare, and engineering. This high demand for skilled workers is a direct result of the EU's emphasis on higher education, vocational training, and lifelong learning programs, which ensure that the workforce remains adaptable to the changing needs of the global economy. In contrast, labour market conditions in the SAARC region are characterised by high youth unemployment and underemployment of skilled labour. Despite an increasing number of young people obtaining higher education, the lack of job opportunities, particularly in the formal sector, leads to high levels of underemployment. This mismatch between the skills that graduates acquire and the demands of the labour market is one of the key barriers to economic growth in the SAARC region. Many educated youth in SAARC countries struggle to find meaningful employment, which limits their ability to contribute to economic growth and perpetuates cycles of poverty and inequality.

Social Inequality is a crucial socio-economic factor that affects both education and economic growth. In the EU, social inequality is relatively low, though challenges remain in certain areas. Many EU countries have implemented policies aimed at reducing social inequality, such as progressive taxation, social welfare programs, and initiatives to promote social mobility. These measures have contributed to relatively equitable access to education and economic opportunities, although disparities persist in certain areas, particularly in some Eastern European countries. On the other hand, the SAARC region experiences high levels of social inequality, with significant disparities between urban and rural areas, and among different socio-economic and ethnic groups. These inequalities limit access to education and economic opportunities for a large portion of the population, particularly in rural areas. The lack of access to quality education in underprivileged areas perpetuates cycles of poverty and restricts upward social mobility. Social inequality also manifests in labour market outcomes, where particular groups, particularly women and ethnic minorities, face discrimination and limited access to high-paying jobs, exacerbating the region's economic challenges.

In conclusion, Table 4 highlights the substantial differences in socio-economic factors between the EU and SAARC regions, as well as their impact on education and economic growth. The EU benefits from economic and political stability, high educational attainment, strong labour market conditions, and relatively low social inequality, all of which contribute to the region's financial success. In contrast, the SAARC region faces considerable challenges, including economic instability, political volatility, disparities in educational attainment, high youth unemployment, and significant social inequality. These socio-economic disparities must be addressed through targeted policies that aim to improve governance, invest in education, and reduce inequalities, to unlock the full economic potential of the SAARC region.

Table 5. Regional Integration and Cross-Country Collaboration in Education

Aspect	EU Region	SAARC Region
Regional Integration	Strong integration across member states	Limited integration, with minimal cooperation in educational policies
Educational Collaboration	Extensive collaboration (Erasmus+, research projects, student exchanges)	Few collaborative initiatives lack cross-border educational projects
Knowledge Sharing	Regular academic conferences, workshops, and forums	Limited exchange of knowledge, mainly at bilateral levels
Policy Harmonization	High degree of policy alignment across the EU	Minimal policy harmonisation, individual countries act independently
Research and Innovation Networks	Extensive research funding (Horizon Europe)	Minimal regional research funding and collaboration

Table 5 offers a comparative analysis of regional integration and cross-country collaboration in education between the European Union (EU) and the South Asian Association for Regional Cooperation (SAARC) regions. This table highlights critical aspects, including regional integration, educational collaboration, knowledge sharing, policy harmonisation, and research and innovation networks, illustrating the differences in how these regions approach educational development and regional cooperation.

Regional Integration in the EU is a cornerstone of its success in education and economic growth. The EU has established strong integration across its member states, with various frameworks that ensure that educational systems are interconnected and aligned. This integration is primarily driven by the EU's commitment to creating a unified European Education Area, where students, educators, and institutions can move freely across borders with recognised qualifications. The integration within the EU facilitates the free exchange of ideas, students, and research, leading to a more cohesive and competitive region. On the other hand, the SAARC region experiences limited integration, with minimal cooperation in educational policies. While SAARC has provided a platform for regional collaboration on various issues, educational integration has not been a priority. The lack of unified educational policies and frameworks across SAARC countries results in fragmented educational systems, which reduces the overall impact of education on regional economic development. The absence of robust integration in schooling also limits the potential for collaborative learning and the sharing of best practices among member states.

Educational Collaboration is another area where the EU excels compared to the SAARC region. The EU fosters extensive collaboration through initiatives such as Erasmus+, which supports student exchanges, academic cooperation, and inter-institutional research projects. These collaborative initiatives help promote a shared European identity in education, facilitate mobility for students and teachers, and encourage cross-border academic research, all of which have contributed to the

EU's educational and economic success. In addition to Erasmus+, numerous EU-funded research projects promote cooperation among universities, research centres, and industries. In contrast, the SAARC region has few collaborative initiatives in education, and cross-border educational projects are limited in scope. There is no regional program comparable to Erasmus+ that facilitates the free exchange of students and academic knowledge across the SAARC countries. The lack of significant collaboration results in missed opportunities for educational growth and regional development, especially in terms of pooling resources, sharing research, and developing joint curricula.

Knowledge sharing in the EU is a continuous and institutionalised process. Regular academic conferences, workshops, and forums are held across member states, encouraging the exchange of ideas, research findings, and best practices. These platforms facilitate collaboration among educators, researchers, policymakers, and students, thereby enhancing the quality of education across Europe. The EU's commitment to knowledge sharing is further exemplified by the establishment of various academic networks and initiatives that support lifelong learning and the professional development of educators. On the other hand, in the SAARC region, knowledge sharing is limited, with exchanges mostly occurring at the bilateral level rather than through regional platforms. Although some countries have begun to cooperate on educational initiatives, the lack of a formalised system for sharing knowledge and resources across the region hinders broader collaboration. The absence of regional academic forums or conferences reduces the opportunity for cross-border learning and the integration of diverse educational practices.

Policy Harmonisation is a key feature of the EU’s educational integration. The EU has achieved a high degree of policy alignment across member states, ensuring that educational standards, qualifications, and curricula are consistent throughout the region. This alignment enables greater mobility for students and workers, as qualifications earned in one member state are recognised throughout the entire EU. The harmonisation of policies also supports the creation of a unified educational framework that aligns with the region's economic goals. Conversely, the SAARC region exhibits minimal policy harmonisation, with each country pursuing its own educational policies largely independently of regional efforts. There are a few efforts to align educational standards across member states, leading to disparities in the quality of education and the recognition of qualifications. The lack of policy coordination in SAARC hinders the collective addressing of regional educational challenges and limits the potential for a cohesive regional strategy for economic development.

Finally, Research and Innovation Networks in the EU are robust and well-funded. The EU has extensive research funding programs, such as Horizon Europe, which support cross-border academic and industrial collaboration in research and innovation.

These research networks contribute to the development of cutting-edge technologies, address global challenges, and promote economic growth by commercialising research outcomes. The strong research infrastructure in the EU enables member states to compete on the worldwide stage in fields such as science, technology, and engineering. In stark contrast, the SAARC region has minimal funding for regional research and collaboration. Although some countries in the area have made progress in research and development, there is no coordinated effort to pool resources or fund joint research initiatives across the region. This lack of collaboration in research and innovation stifles the region's ability to develop competitive industries, particularly in high-tech and knowledge-driven sectors.

In conclusion, Table 5 highlights the significant contrasts between the EU and SAARC regions in terms of regional integration and cross-country collaboration in education. The EU's strong integration, collaborative initiatives, knowledge-sharing platforms, policy harmonisation, and well-funded research networks provide a solid foundation for educational and economic growth. In contrast, the SAARC region's limited integration, fragmented policies, and minimal collaboration hinder its ability to capitalise on education as a driver of regional development. For the SAARC region to achieve similar educational and economic success, greater emphasis must be placed on fostering regional cooperation, aligning educational policies, and enhancing research collaboration. These efforts would help unlock the region's full potential and contribute to its long-term socio-economic prosperity.

Table 6. Impact of Educational Leadership on Economic Growth

Impact Metric	EU Region	SAARC Region
Economic Growth Rate	Consistently high, driven by a skilled workforce and innovation	Moderate, constrained by low levels of educational quality and leadership
Human Capital Development	Strong alignment of education with labour market needs	Disconnected, with education often misaligned with market demands
Innovation Capacity	High innovation output, global leadership in R&D	Limited innovation, primarily in a few sectors such as agriculture
Productivity Growth	Driven by an educated workforce, high-skilled jobs	Low productivity growth due to skills mismatch and underemployment
Entrepreneurship Rates	High levels of entrepreneurship, especially in tech sectors	Lower levels of entrepreneurship are constrained by regulatory and educational barriers

Table 6 highlights the profound impact of educational leadership on economic growth in the European Union (EU) and South Asian Association for Regional Cooperation (SAARC) regions. By examining key metrics such as economic growth rates, human capital development, innovation capacity, productivity growth, and entrepreneurship rates, the table highlights how educational leadership in each region influences its financial trajectory. The differences in these factors reflect the varying degrees of success in aligning educational systems with the economy's needs and fostering environments conducive to innovation and economic productivity.

The economic growth rate in the EU has been consistently high, primarily driven by a skilled workforce and a strong focus on innovation. The EU's educational leadership emphasises the development of human capital through a robust system that aligns education with the needs of the labour market. The region's emphasis on research, development, and education in high-demand fields has cultivated a workforce that is not only highly skilled but also adaptable to changing economic conditions. This skilled workforce has been a primary driver of the EU's sustained economic growth. In contrast, the SAARC region experiences moderate economic growth, primarily constrained by low levels of educational quality and leadership. Many SAARC countries continue to struggle with fragmented educational systems and underdeveloped leadership structures that fail to align education with labour market demands effectively. As a result, while some countries in the region have made notable progress, overall economic growth is hindered by a workforce that lacks the advanced skills and knowledge required to drive large-scale, sustainable economic development.

A strong alignment between education and labour market needs characterises human capital development in the EU. The EU's education systems focus on both academic and vocational training, ensuring that graduates are well-prepared for the job market. Moreover, lifelong learning programs and continuous professional development initiatives enable workers to adapt to evolving economic demands. This alignment enables the EU to develop a highly skilled and competitive workforce, which is essential for sustaining economic growth. Conversely, in the SAARC region, human capital development is often disconnected from labour market needs. Educational systems in many SAARC countries produce large numbers of graduates; however, the lack of coordination between education curricula and labour market demands leads to a mismatch between the skills acquired by students and the skills needed by employers. As a result, many educated individuals in the SAARC region struggle to find relevant job opportunities, which hampers overall economic growth and increases unemployment rates, particularly among educated young people.

Innovation Capacity in the EU is one of the region's key strengths, with high levels of innovation output and global leadership in research and development (R&D). The EU invests heavily in R&D through programs like Horizon Europe, which fund collaborative research across member states and industries. These investments have enabled the EU to maintain its leadership in technological innovation, thereby contributing to economic growth in key sectors such as pharmaceuticals, information technology, and renewable energy. In contrast, the innovation capacity of the SAARC region is limited, with innovation primarily concentrated in a few sectors, such as agriculture. While countries like India have made significant strides in technology and space exploration, many other SAARC countries face challenges in fostering broad-based innovation. The region suffers from underinvestment in R&D, a lack of coordination among educational institutions and industries, and limited government support for innovation, which restricts the region's ability to develop and commercialise new technologies.

Productivity Growth in the EU is driven by a highly educated workforce, with a strong emphasis on high-skilled jobs in sectors such as engineering, finance, and technology. This focus on education ensures that workers are equipped with the skills needed to excel in high-productivity sectors, resulting in sustained growth in output per worker. The EU's emphasis on education and skill development supports economic efficiency, competitiveness, and long-term productivity growth. In contrast, the productivity growth in the SAARC region is low, primarily due to a mismatch between the skills workers possess and those required by the labour market. Many workers in the area are employed in low-productivity sectors, such as agriculture and informal labour, where educational attainment and skills are less relevant. Additionally, high levels of underemployment, particularly among educated youth, exacerbate the region's productivity challenges. Without significant improvements in education and skills training, SAARC countries face difficulties in increasing productivity and achieving economic growth.

Entrepreneurship Rates in the EU are notably high, especially in the technology sector, where a well-developed ecosystem supports innovative startups and businesses. The EU promotes entrepreneurship through various programs that offer funding, mentorship, and networking opportunities for emerging companies. The region's focus on education and research drives a culture of innovation and risk-taking, with many young entrepreneurs leading the charge in fields such as tech, biotechnology, and green energy. On the other hand, entrepreneurship rates in the SAARC region are lower, constrained by a combination of regulatory barriers and insufficient educational support for aspiring entrepreneurs. While entrepreneurship is growing in specific sectors, such as technology in India, many SAARC countries face bureaucratic obstacles, limited access to finance, and inadequate entrepreneurial training. These barriers prevent many individuals from pursuing entrepreneurial ventures, reducing the region's overall capacity for innovation-driven economic growth.

In conclusion, Table 6 reveals that the impact of educational leadership on economic growth in the EU and SAARC regions is profound and multifaceted. The EU benefits from high economic growth, strong human capital development, a robust innovation capacity, high productivity, and high rates of entrepreneurship, all of which are primarily driven by a well-developed educational system that aligns with labour market needs. In contrast, the SAARC region is experiencing moderate economic growth. Still, human capital development remains disconnected from the labour market, innovation is limited, productivity is low, and barriers to entrepreneurship persist. These disparities underscore the crucial role of educational leadership in promoting economic growth. The SAARC region must prioritise educational reforms, aligning them with labour market needs, investing in research and development, and removing regulatory barriers to entrepreneurship, to unlock its economic potential and drive sustainable growth.

Table 7. Recommendations for Enhancing Educational Leadership and Economic Growth

Recommendation	EU Region	SAARC Region
Strengthen Regional Collaboration	Continue to expand cross-border educational initiatives	Increase regional collaboration and knowledge sharing among SAARC nations
Improve Teacher Training	Maintain high standards and expand continuous professional development	Invest in comprehensive teacher training programs, especially in rural areas
Expand Vocational Education	Focus on technical skills alongside academic education	Increase investment in vocational education to align skills with labour market demands
Promote Inclusive Education	Ensure access for marginalised communities	Ensure equitable access to education for rural, poor, and minority populations.
Develop Regional Research Initiatives	Expand EU-wide research funding and partnerships	Establish regional research initiatives to foster innovation and economic growth.
Focus on Leadership Development	Enhance educational leadership through collaborative decision-making	Prioritise leadership development to drive systemic change and policy alignment in education

Table 7 presents a set of recommendations for enhancing educational leadership and promoting economic growth in both the European Union (EU) and the South Asian Association for Regional Cooperation (SAARC) regions. These recommendations aim to address specific challenges in each area by improving collaboration, teacher training, vocational education, inclusive education, research initiatives, and leadership development. While the EU is already relatively advanced in these areas, the SAARC region requires substantial investment and policy shifts to improve educational outcomes and support sustainable economic development.

Strengthening Regional Collaboration is a key recommendation for both regions. The EU is already highly integrated in terms of cross-border educational initiatives, such as Erasmus+ and Horizon Europe, which promote student exchanges, academic collaboration, and shared research projects across member states. The EU should continue to expand and refine these initiatives to further enhance the mobility of students and researchers, thereby strengthening regional cohesion and fostering economic growth. For the SAARC region, regional collaboration and knowledge sharing are limited. To improve, the SAARC nations should intensify their efforts to collaborate on educational initiatives, share best practices, and establish common platforms for dialogue. This could involve establishing a SAARC-wide educational network or collaborative research programs to promote inter-regional learning and solve everyday challenges in education.

Improving Teacher Training is essential for both regions, but requires different approaches. In the EU, teacher training is already of high quality, with continuous professional development programs in place to ensure educators remain up to date with the latest pedagogical techniques and technological advancements. Maintaining these high standards and expanding training opportunities for educators will be key to addressing future challenges. In the SAARC region, teacher training remains inconsistent, particularly in rural areas. A significant investment in comprehensive teacher training programs, especially in underserved rural areas, is necessary to improve the quality of education. Ensuring that teachers are well-equipped with both subject knowledge and teaching methodologies will lead to better educational outcomes and contribute to narrowing educational disparities within the region.

Expanding Vocational Education is a priority for both regions, but requires a different focus. The EU has made significant strides in integrating vocational education alongside academic education, ensuring that students gain both technical skills and academic knowledge, which are essential for the evolving labour market. The EU should continue to emphasise and expand technical skills training, particularly in emerging fields such as information technology, green energy, and biotechnology, to keep pace with the evolving economy. In the SAARC region, vocational education is often underfunded and lacks alignment with labour market demands. Increasing investment in vocational education to better align the skills provided by educational institutions with those needed in local and global labour markets will help reduce unemployment and underemployment in the region. Practical and job-ready skills should be prioritised, particularly in sectors such as manufacturing, construction, and healthcare.

Promoting Inclusive Education is crucial for both regions to ensure equitable access to education. The EU has made significant strides in providing access for marginalised communities. Still, challenges persist, particularly in some Eastern European countries, where access to higher education and vocational training remains limited for particular social groups. Ensuring that all individuals, regardless of their background, have access to high-quality education is key to social mobility and economic inclusion. In the SAARC region, equitable access to education is a significant issue, particularly for rural, poor, and minority populations. The region must prioritise policies that ensure children from these groups have access to quality education, thereby reducing educational disparities between urban and rural areas.

Efforts could include scholarship programs, infrastructural development in rural areas, and community engagement to increase awareness of the importance of education.

Developing Regional Research Initiatives is an area where the EU excels and can continue to lead. The EU's extensive research funding programs, such as Horizon Europe, have fostered collaboration and innovation across member states. The EU should continue expanding these initiatives to encourage more cross-border research in cutting-edge fields, such as artificial intelligence, climate change, and digital transformation, which can significantly contribute to economic growth. The SAARC region, however, suffers from a lack of coordinated research initiatives and under-investment in research and development. Establishing regional research initiatives that pool resources and expertise across member countries can foster innovation, particularly in sectors like agriculture, health, and renewable energy. By establishing research hubs and collaborative projects, SAARC countries can address common challenges and foster economic growth through innovation.

Focusing on Leadership Development is essential for driving systemic change in both regions. In the EU, educational leadership is well-established, with collaborative decision-making processes in place to guide policy development and implementation. However, there is always room for enhancing leadership skills to address emerging challenges such as digital transformation and climate change. In the SAARC region, leadership development is crucial for improving the quality of education and aligning it with broader economic objectives. Prioritising the development of strong educational leaders who can drive systemic reforms, enhance governance, and align educational policies with labour market needs is crucial. SAARC countries must invest in leadership training for academic administrators, teachers, and policymakers to establish a solid foundation for educational reform and enhanced outcomes.

In conclusion, Table 7 presents a set of tailored recommendations for both the EU and SAARC regions to enhance educational leadership and foster economic growth. While the EU has established a strong foundation in many areas, continuing to strengthen regional collaboration, expand vocational education, and focus on inclusive education will ensure its continued leadership in education and economic innovation. For the SAARC region, there is a pressing need to invest in teacher training, improve vocational education, promote inclusive education, develop regional research initiatives, and focus on leadership development to unlock the potential of its young population and drive economic growth. By addressing these areas, SAARC nations can establish a more robust educational framework that supports long-term economic development and reduces regional inequalities.

Managerial Implications

The managerial implications of enhancing educational leadership and its impact on economic growth are profound, particularly in the context of regional disparities, such as those between the European Union (EU) and the South Asian Association for Regional Cooperation (SAARC). These implications span policy formulation, resource allocation, and institutional restructuring, requiring astute strategic management to ensure that educational systems evolve in ways that bolster human capital development, innovation, and sustainable economic prosperity.

In the EU, the alignment between educational leadership and economic growth provides a model for effective governance. From a managerial perspective, the integration of education policies across member states has facilitated the development of a highly skilled workforce, thereby enabling the region to remain competitive in a globalised economy. The EU's focus on innovation-driven growth necessitates continuous investment in research and development, which, in turn, requires robust management strategies that foster collaboration between governments, educational institutions, and private industries. Managers in this context must prioritise the optimisation of resources to foster an ecosystem of academic excellence that not only meets current economic demands but is also agile enough to adapt to future challenges. Furthermore, the multi-stakeholder decision-making process prevalent in the EU provides a framework for inclusive governance, wherein managers must balance the diverse interests of national governments, educational institutions, and the private sector while ensuring that the region's academic outcomes are aligned with its economic goals.

On the other hand, for the SAARC region, the managerial implications are more complex due to the fragmented nature of its educational systems and the lack of coordinated leadership. Managers in SAARC countries face the challenge of transforming disparate educational systems into cohesive frameworks that contribute to regional economic integration. The fragmentation of educational policies across the region implies that national governments must play a pivotal role in creating and implementing policies that promote uniformity and coherence in education. This requires managers to facilitate cross-border collaboration among SAARC countries, which has historically been limited. By managing collaborative platforms, such as regional research initiatives or student exchange programs, managers can foster the sharing of best practices and research findings, thereby contributing to the development of human capital that is better equipped to meet labour market demands. Moreover, managers must oversee the allocation of resources to rural and underserved areas, ensuring that education infrastructure and training programs are equitable and accessible to all populations.

The focus on teacher training is another crucial area where managerial decision-making must be strategically focused. In the EU, where teacher training is already robust, managers are tasked with maintaining and enhancing these programs, ensuring that educators are continually exposed to the latest pedagogical practices and technological tools. However, the SAARC region faces significant challenges in this domain. Managers in SAARC countries must prioritise the professional development of educators, especially in rural and remote areas, by creating and sustaining comprehensive training programs. This would not only improve teaching standards but also enhance student outcomes and, ultimately, workforce readiness. The management of educational leadership in SAARC must be visionary, investing in long-term reforms that will create a sustainable and skilled workforce, which is essential for driving economic growth.

Lastly, the expansion of vocational education in both regions presents significant managerial implications. In the EU, the integration of technical and vocational education with academic curricula demands efficient management practices that align educational content with labour market needs. Managers must ensure that vocational programs are adaptable and responsive to the changing economic landscape, particularly in emerging sectors such as digital technologies and green energy. In the SAARC region, however, the underdevelopment of vocational education requires immediate managerial attention. Managers must advocate for increased investment in vocational training, ensuring that it aligns with market demands, thus reducing the skills gap and enhancing employability. This requires not only the creation of relevant curricula but also the establishment of partnerships between educational institutions, industries, and government agencies to ensure that the skills developed through vocational education are in high demand.

In conclusion, the managerial implications of educational leadership in both the EU and SAARC regions emphasise the need for strategic planning, resource management, and cross-border collaboration. Managers must be capable of balancing diverse interests, facilitating inclusive policy development, and fostering innovation in education to align with broader economic goals. In the SAARC region, addressing disparities in educational access and quality, coupled with investments in teacher training and vocational education, will be crucial to unlocking the region's full economic potential.

FUTURE DIRECTIONS AND RECOMMENDATIONS

The recommendations emanating from this comparative inquiry necessitate a paradigmatic reorientation wherein educational governance in both EU and SAARC regions is reconceptualised as a catalytic fulcrum of economic metamorphosis, demanding intensified investment in leadership capacity-building, harmonised policy architectures, and cross-border epistemic collaboration that transcend parochial national imperatives; concomitantly, future trajectories must interrogate the dialectics of innovation-driven curricula, equitable vocational inclusivity, and digitally mediated pedagogical ecosystems so as to engender a resilient, future-ready human capital reservoir, while simultaneously embedding region-specific contingencies of socio-political volatility, fiscal asymmetries, and cultural heterogeneities into adaptive governance models that not only align educational outputs with labor market exigencies but also galvanise sustainable economic integration, thereby establishing a research agenda that rigorously explores the multi-layered mediations between educational leadership, structural inequities, and long-term developmental competitiveness across divergent geopolitical contexts.

Practical Implications

The practical implications of this study underscore that effective educational leadership and governance must be operationalised as strategic levers for economic transformation, requiring policymakers and institutional managers in both EU and SAARC contexts to transcend rhetorical commitments and instead embed structural reforms that ensure curricular alignment with labor market exigencies, equitable allocation of resources to marginalised regions, systematic investment in teacher training and digital infrastructure, and the fostering of cross-border collaborations that facilitate knowledge exchange and innovation; by illuminating the divergent trajectories of the EU's cohesive, innovation-driven governance model and SAARC's fragmented, under-resourced systems, the study provides actionable insights for decision-makers to reconfigure educational ecosystems into engines of sustainable growth, thereby guiding future interventions that reconcile policy ambition with contextual realities while offering a roadmap for scholars and practitioners to develop adaptive, region-specific strategies that optimise human capital formation and economic competitiveness.

Theoretical Implications

The theoretical implications of this study lie in advancing an integrative lens that positions educational leadership and governance as mediating constructs within Human Capital Theory, thereby extending its explanatory power to account for institutional, systemic, and contextual contingencies shaping the education–economic growth nexus.

CONCLUSION

In conclusion, the comparative analysis of educational leadership and its impact on economic growth across the EU and SAARC regions underscores the critical role that education plays in shaping a region's financial trajectory. The EU's success in creating a cohesive, innovation-driven educational framework has significantly contributed to its sustained economic growth, competitiveness, and global leadership in key sectors, including technology, research, and development. The EU's emphasis on human capital development, vocational education, and regional collaboration provides a robust model for how education systems can be strategically aligned with labour market needs to foster long-term economic prosperity.

In contrast, the SAARC region faces several challenges that hinder its ability to leverage education for economic growth. The fragmentation of educational systems, disparities in access to quality education, and a lack of effective leadership in aligning educational policies with economic goals are key barriers to progress. In contrast, some countries within SAARC have made strides; the region as a whole struggles with underinvestment in education, insufficient teacher training, and limited regional cooperation. These challenges contribute to a workforce that is often disconnected from labour market demands, resulting in high levels of unemployment, underemployment, and low productivity growth.

To unlock the potential of the SAARC region, significant reforms are necessary. By investing in comprehensive teacher training, expanding vocational education, promoting inclusive access to education, and fostering regional collaboration, SAARC nations can create a more equitable and productive educational system. Additionally, aligning educational policies with labour market demands and increasing investment in research and innovation will help bridge the skills gap, promote entrepreneurship, and stimulate economic growth.

Ultimately, the findings of this study underscore the crucial role of educational leadership in fostering sustainable economic growth. By learning from the successes of the EU and addressing the systemic challenges within the SAARC region, it is possible to develop a more integrated, innovative, and resilient educational framework that can empower nations to build a future-driven economy. Education, when effectively managed and aligned with economic needs, becomes a powerful tool for fostering growth, innovation, and prosperity in both developed and developing regions.

REFERENCES

Ahmed, I. (2010). SAARC: Social charter and human security. In *The Emerging Dimensions of SAARC*. Foundation Books. DOI: 10.1017/UPO9788175968615.007

Ahmed, Z. S. (2018). The Role of SAARC and EU in Managing Refugees in South Asia and Beyond: Potential for North-South Cooperation. *Global Policy*, *9*(1), 76–84. DOI: 10.1111/1758-5899.12526

Bhatta, M. (2019). Challenges and opportunities in South Asia. In *New Futures for South Asia: Commerce and Connectivity*. Taylor and Francis., DOI: 10.4324/9780367816827-3

Dinda, S. (2014). Climate Change: An Emerging Trade Opportunity in South Asia. *South Asian Journal of Macroeconomics and Public Finance*, *3*(2), 221–239. DOI: 10.1177/2277978714548636

Dixit, P., & Bhatnagar, M. (2025). Advancing green economies through sustainable investment strategies for climate change mitigation and development: Adaptive strategies for green crypto investment. In *Adaptive Strategies for Green Economy and Sustainability Policies*. DOI: 10.4018/979-8-3693-7570-9.ch033

Ferreira, M., Kunn-Nelen, A., & De Grip, A. (2017). Work-related learning and skill development in Europe: Does initial skill mismatch matter? *Research in Labor Economics*, *45*, 345–407. DOI: 10.1108/S0147-912120170000045010

Gaurav, K., Bharti, N., & Sinha, P. (2015). ISFTA: Lessons for Bangladesh. In C. S., S. N.P., G. D.P., & G. N. (Eds.), *Springer Proceedings in Business and Economics: Vol. Part 111* (pp. 351 – 367). Springer Science and Business Media B.V. DOI: 10.1007/978-81-322-1979-8_28

Khan, O. H. (2021). Strengthening Regional Trade Integration in South Asia: A SAARC Perspective. In *Strengthening Regional Trade Integration in South Asia: A SAARC Perspective*. Springer Singapore. DOI: 10.1007/978-981-33-6777-7

Khanna, R., Bhatnagar, M., Sharma, P., Upreti, H., & Kanojia, P. (2025). Advancing circular-economy in food processing: Integrating waste management, policy support, and supply chain circularity. *Environment Conservation Journal*, *26*(3), 856–867. https://doi.org/https://doi.org/10.36953/ECJ.32323056. DOI: 10.36953/ECJ.32323056

Kivimäki, T. (2016). The EU-India-China Strategic Partnership and the Impact of Regional Constructs. In *The Role of the European Union in Asia: China and India as Strategic Partners*. Taylor and Francis., DOI: 10.4324/9781315553283-2

Kumar, S. (2024). Regional Organizations and States in International Relations: A Study of India's Approach Towards Regional Organizations. *Millennial Asia*, *15*(2), 259–277. DOI: 10.1177/09763996221105148

Kumar, S. Y. S. (2021). India Looking Beyond Saarc: Is it benefiting? In *Bilateral and Multilateral Cooperation in South Asia*. Taylor and Francis., DOI: 10.4324/9781003145271-10

Mehanna, R.-A. (2008). Strategic patterns in international business: Product differentiation or complementarity? *Journal of Transnational Management*, *13*(2), 112–131. DOI: 10.1080/15475770802255028

Miglani, M., Taneja, S., Bhatnagar, M., & Johri, A. (2025). Transforming Financial Services: Ethical Pathways of Workforce Automation towards Achieving SDG 9. *International Research Journal of Multidisciplinary Scope*, *6*(2), 1298–1308. DOI: 10.47857/irjms.2025.v06i02.03963

Mohammad, N. (2011). The role of global governance mechanisms to protect the environment for sustainability: A study on Bangladesh perspective. *Australian Journal of Basic and Applied Sciences*, *5*(10), 1175–1186. https://www.scopus.com/inward/record.uri?eid=2-s2.0-84864483785&partnerID=40&md5=55e74e63e8fef6f0e92899eb4a132775

Pal, D. P., Dietzenbacher, E., & Basu, D. (2007). Economic integration: Systemic measures in an input - Output framework. *Economic Systems Research*, *19*(4), 397–408. DOI: 10.1080/09535310701698464

Prasad, K. (2013). Building Bridges in South Asia: Regional Cooperation, Information Technologies and Opportunities for Integration. *Innovation. Technology and Knowledge Management*, *28*, 99–112. DOI: 10.1007/978-1-4614-5254-6_7

Ratzinger, D., Amess, K., Greenman, A., & Mosey, S. P. (2018). The impact of digital start-up founders' higher education on reaching equity investment milestones. *The Journal of Technology Transfer*, *43*(3), 760–778. DOI: 10.1007/s10961-017-9627-3 PMID: 31258242

Sáez, L. (2014). SAARC, the road-map for economic co-operation from a European perspective. In *The Merits of Regional Cooperation: The Case of South Asia*. Springer International Publishing., DOI: 10.1007/978-3-319-02234-5_8

Sharma, R., Bhatnagar, M., & Ozen, E. (2025). The role of intellectual capital in combatting deepfake threats to corporate reputation and trust. In *Mastering Deepfake Technology: Strategies for Ethical Management and Security*. River Publishers. https://www.scopus.com/inward/record.uri?eid=2-s2.0-105007657679&partnerID=40&md5=f313a80a3279f91fbedf7fd10c6a4f7a

Shaw, T. M., Grant, J. A., & Cornelissen, S. (2016). The Ashgate research companion to regionalisms. In *The Ashgate Research Companion to Regionalisms*. Taylor and Francis., DOI: 10.4324/9781315613499

Soni, V. K., & Sahoo, S. (2021). The Development Narratives in South Asia: A Case Study of Print Media. In *Development, Governance and Gender in South Asia: Perspectives, Issues and Challenges*. Springer Nature. DOI: 10.1007/978-981-16-5109-0_12

Sridharan, K., & Srinivasa-Raghavan, T. C. A. (2007). Regional cooperation in South Asia and Southeast Asia. In *Regional Cooperation in South Asia and Southeast Asia*. Institute of Southeast Asian Studies. https://www.scopus.com/inward/record.uri?eid=2-s2.0-84895082186&partnerID=40&md5=6a02e8b2020710393013f2e6e13e71fd

Srinivasan, V., Thomas, L., Peter, K. V., Remashree, A. B., & Cheriyan, H. (2024). Spices: Area, production, and export scenario. In *Handbook of Spices in India: 75 Years of Research and Development*. Springer Nature. DOI: 10.1007/978-981-19-3728-6_2

Waqif, A. A. (1999). Civil service capacity for regional cooperation: Some comparative aspects in the EU and SAARC regions. *South Asian Survey*, *6*(1), 75–88. DOI: 10.1177/097152319900600109

Zahid, M., Khalid, F., Ramzan, M., Haq, M. Z. U., Lee, W., Hwang, J., & Shim, J. (2021). The significance of monetary policy transmission mechanism in the sustainable development of the SAARC economic community. *Sustainability (Basel)*, *13*(23), 13171. Advance online publication. DOI: 10.3390/su132313171

KEY TERMS AND DEFINITIONS

Economic Growth: The sustained augmentation of a polity's productive frontier, measured not merely through quantitative indices of output but also through qualitative transformations in technological advancement, labour force adaptability, and institutional resilience, undergirded by the dynamic interplay of capital accumulation and knowledge creation.

Educational Leadership: The orchestrated exercise of authority, vision, and strategic acumen within scholastic ecosystems, wherein administrators and policy-makers mobilise resources, construct normative architectures, and inculcate epistemic cultures that transcend mere instructional oversight to become instruments of systemic transformation.

Governance: A multi-scalar constellation of regulatory mechanisms, institutional frameworks, and decision-making modalities through which educational systems are directed, coordinated, and legitimated, encompassing both formalised statutory structures and informal socio-political dynamics that determine policy coherence and implementation efficacy.

Human Capital: The aggregated reservoir of cognitive competencies, technical proficiencies, and socio-behavioural capacities embodied within individuals, conceived as an intangible economic asset whose augmentation through education, training, and innovation constitutes a principal determinant of productivity and growth.

Innovation Capacity: The systemic aptitude of a region to generate, diffuse, and commercialise novel knowledge and technologies, contingent upon the robustness of its educational institutions, research infrastructures, and entrepreneurial ecosystems, thereby serving as a fulcrum of endogenous growth.

Institutional Theory: An analytical paradigm postulating that organisational behaviour and structural configurations are not merely functional adaptations but also responses to external legitimacy imperatives, normative isomorphism, and cultural-cognitive pressures within their socio-political milieus.

Policy Harmonisation: The deliberate alignment of legislative, curricular, and governance structures across national or regional boundaries, designed to diminish regulatory divergence, standardise qualifications, and facilitate cross-border academic and economic mobility.

Regional Integration: The institutionalised interweaving of policies, educational standards, and economic frameworks across multiple sovereign entities, designed to harmonise objectives, reduce structural asymmetries, and create synergistic developmental trajectories that transcend national insularity.

Systems Theory: A holistic theoretical construct positing that educational and economic institutions operate as interdependent subsystems within broader socio-ecological orders, where feedback loops, equilibria, and systemic coherence determine functional efficiency and developmental outcomes.

Vocational Education: A pedagogical subdomain oriented toward praxis-based skill acquisition, wherein curricula are explicitly synchronised with labour market exigencies, thereby engendering occupational readiness, technical specialisation, and employability within volatile economic landscapes.

Chapter 4
Educational Leadership and Management for Economic Growth:
A Comparative Study of BRICS Nations

Sonia Munjal
Noida Institute of Engineering and Technology, India

Mukul Bhatnagar
https://orcid.org/0000-0002-7773-5641
Graphic Era University, India

ABSTRACT

This chapter explores the relationship between educational leadership, management, and economic growth in the BRICS nations (Brazil, Russia, India, China, and South Africa). By analysing educational policies, labour market demands, and educational outputs, the research investigates how educational disparities impact economic development. The study highlights the challenges faced by countries such as Brazil, India, and South Africa, where inequalities in access, quality, and skills mismatches hinder economic growth. In contrast, China and Russia have effectively aligned their education systems with industrial and technological goals, fostering economic competitiveness. Using a mixed-methods approach, which combines quantitative data analysis with qualitative case studies, the research provides insights into how educational reforms can drive economic integration and sustainable growth. Findings emphasise the need for systemic educational reforms to address inequality and improve workforce readiness, contributing to SDG 4 (Quality Education) and SDG 8 (Decent Work and Economic Growth).

DOI: 10.4018/979-8-3373-3616-9.ch004

INTRODUCTION

The intricate relationship between educational leadership and management and economic growth is a subject of perennial interest and significance in contemporary global discourse. Educational systems, as the bedrock of societal progress, wield immense potential to influence economic trajectories by equipping individuals with the necessary competencies, skills, and values to thrive in an increasingly complex and globalised economy. (Mohammadi, 2024). However, the role of educational leadership and management in fostering economic growth is not merely functional; it is strategic, implicating a deep integration of educational policy, institutional governance, pedagogical methodologies, and societal values that catalyse economic dynamism. Within this framework, a comparative study of the BRICS (Brazil, Russia, India, China, and South Africa) nations offers an invaluable lens to examine the intersection of these two vital domains, given the distinct political, social, and economic contexts within which these nations operate. (Daniels & Niemczyk, 2023). The BRICS nations, which collectively represent a significant proportion of the world's population, GDP, and global economic influence, stand as exemplary case studies in understanding how educational leadership and management can serve as catalysts for economic growth. Each nation, with its unique historical trajectory, cultural milieu, and socio-economic challenges, provides a distinct perspective on how the nexus between education and economic advancement is conceptualised and executed. The BRICS bloc, having emerged as a significant global economic force, is strategically positioned to influence and redefine global economic development norms. (Zvereva et al., 2020). As such, an exploration of the educational leadership and management practices within these nations is both timely and critical, offering insights that apply not only within the BRICS countries themselves but also to other emerging economies striving to replicate their success.

Educational leadership and management are integral to the formulation and implementation of policies that directly impact the quality, accessibility, and efficacy of education systems. Education leadership, encompassing both administrative and pedagogical dimensions, shapes the broader educational landscape by influencing curriculum design, teacher training, resource allocation, and infrastructural development. Effective management of educational institutions ensures that these resources are utilised efficiently, fostering environments conducive to learning and intellectual development (Carnoy et al., 2014). The dynamic interaction between these elements shapes the broader socio-economic fabric, with profound implications for economic growth. At the heart of the discourse on educational leadership is the notion of governance. Governance within educational institutions and across national education systems entails not only the formulation of educational policies but also their execution, monitoring, and evaluation. The political and institutional context in which educational leadership operates significantly influences the nature and scope of these policies.

In the BRICS nations, governance structures in education are often characterised by a blend of centralised and decentralised elements, reflecting the political diversity within the group. In countries such as China, where a centralised system prevails, the role of educational leadership is closely tied to the directives set by the state. (Shuangshuang et al., 2023). In contrast, countries like India and Brazil exhibit more decentralised educational management systems, which offer greater autonomy to local authorities and educational institutions, albeit with varying levels of efficacy and success. Moreover, the economic landscape of the BRICS nations offers a diverse set of challenges and opportunities for educational leadership and management. In countries such as India and Brazil, where significant portions of the population still lack access to quality education, the emphasis on educational equity is crucial. (Menter, 2024).

Meanwhile, in China and Russia, the focus has been on enhancing the global competitiveness of their educational systems, ensuring that their workforce is equipped with the requisite skills to thrive in a globalised economy. South Africa, meanwhile, grapples with the enduring legacy of apartheid, where educational disparities are still deeply entrenched, and significant efforts are required to address the socio-economic divide. The degree to which educational systems in these countries can be managed and led to address these multifaceted challenges will determine their ability to sustain long-term economic growth. The economic implications of educational leadership are profound, particularly in the context of the BRICS nations, where education is seen as a key driver of human capital development. The creation of a skilled and educated workforce is crucial for fostering innovation, entrepreneurship, and productivity —the primary engines of economic growth. Educational institutions not only act as providers of knowledge but also as incubators for creativity and innovation. (Zhu et al., 2022). By fostering critical thinking, problem-solving abilities, and specialised skills, educational leadership can enhance the capacity of individuals to contribute meaningfully to economic progress.

Furthermore, the management of education systems in the BRICS nations is inherently tied to the broader economic policies and developmental strategies of these countries. Economic growth, in this regard, becomes a cyclical process wherein investments in education lead to a more skilled and productive workforce, which in turn generates economic growth, thereby creating a positive feedback loop that strengthens the educational system further. (Yi et al., 2024). Conversely, the lack of effective educational leadership and management can stifle economic progress by hindering the development of a capable workforce. In terms of global competitiveness, the ability of the BRICS nations to align their educational systems with the demands of the global economy is crucial. Nations such as China and India have made remarkable strides in aligning their educational systems with the needs of modern industries, with a focus on technical education, science, technology, engineering, and mathematics (STEM) fields. Brazil and Russia, on the other hand, are increasingly focusing on enhancing their research and development capabilities, while South Africa is striving to overcome socio-economic inequalities that limit access to quality education. (Altbach et al., 2013).

A Comparative Approach

This comparative study of the BRICS nations is essential in elucidating how distinct educational leadership and management strategies can be leveraged to achieve sustainable economic growth. The complexities inherent in the educational systems of these nations, ranging from institutional challenges, political factors, economic pressures, and societal needs, make them ideal subjects for a cross-national analysis. By examining the strategies employed by educational leaders in these countries, this study aims to uncover the varied approaches to educational governance, management, and policymaking, as well as their resultant impact on economic development (İmre-Bıyıklı & Kamil, 2024). The nexus between educational leadership, institutional management, and macroeconomic performance has long been a topic of scholarly discourse, rooted in the recognition that education is not merely a social good but a catalytic instrument of human capital formation and national competitiveness. Since the early expositions of human capital theory, the intellectual lineage has evolved to underscore education as both a private investment and a public externality, shaping the very architecture of growth trajectories across diverse polities. (Kangotra & Sehajpal, 2025; Singh et al., 2025).

In the contemporary global landscape, education has been recast as a strategic lever in the knowledge economy, where empirical evidence demonstrates that nations with robust governance and effective management in education consistently outperform their peers in productivity indices and innovation benchmarks. (Xing & Imran, 2025). Recent statistics reveal that countries allocating above 5% of their GDP to education exhibit a median labour productivity growth rate nearly double that of those below this threshold. Meanwhile, data highlight persistent disparities in enrolment-to-employment transitions across emerging economies, including the BRICS bloc. (Iqbal et al., 2025). Notwithstanding such empirical affirmation, practical challenges proliferate. Disparities in resource allocation, rural–urban asymmetries, misalignment between curricular outputs and labour market requisites, and systemic inefficiencies in governance architectures collectively attenuate the transformative potential of educational investments. (Manzoor et al., 2025). The persistence of skill mismatches, as documented in reports, afflicts nearly 35% of graduates in developing economies, exemplifying the structural disjuncture between educational systems and economic imperatives. The extant literature, while voluminous, exhibits lacunae in two critical dimensions: first, comparative cross-national analyses that interrogate how divergent governance logics (centralised vs. decentralised) mediate educational effectiveness; second, integrative frameworks that bridge educational quality metrics with longitudinal economic outcomes. Most extant studies privilege either micro-level institutional analyses or macro-level economic correlations, rarely synthesising these into a holistic model that situates education as a governance-embedded developmental apparatus (Alfehaid et al., 2025).

This chapter endeavours to address these epistemic and policy gaps by offering a comparative analysis of educational leadership and management practices within the BRICS economies, juxtaposing them against economic performance indicators. By situating education within the dual contexts of governance complexity and labour market exigency, this work aims to provide a nuanced understanding of how leadership structures either facilitate or hinder economic dynamism. (Chisholm & Chissale, 2025). The guiding question animating this inquiry is thus: *How do variations in educational leadership and management across the BRICS nations shape their capacity to convert educational investments into sustained economic growth, and what governance configurations most effectively align education with labour market and developmental imperatives?* By addressing this question, the chapter furnishes policymakers with evidence-based blueprints for designing resilient educational systems while simultaneously offering scholars fertile ground for extending comparative, multidisciplinary research.

In doing so, this chapter positions itself as both diagnostic and prescriptive, diagnostic in unveiling structural impediments that constrain the education–growth nexus, and prescriptive in charting directions for future research and policy frameworks that seek to harmonise educational governance with the imperatives of sustainable economic transformation.

BACKGROUND

The genealogy of educational leadership as a determinant of national development is deeply intertwined with the evolution of governance paradigms, where the efficacy of institutional stewardship dictates the trajectory of human capital formation and, by extension, macroeconomic ascendancy. However, despite its theoretical elegance, the practice of operationalising educational leadership in diverse geopolitical contexts has encountered formidable impediments, revealing the complex interplay of political economy, sociocultural stratification, and institutional inertia (Zhang & Xiao, 2025).

Brazil epitomises the paradox of decentralisation: while constitutional reforms devolved authority to municipalities to enhance contextual responsiveness, empirical audits by UNESCO (2022) reveal a disjuncture wherein affluent urban jurisdictions flourish while peripheral regions languish in systemic deprivation. (Sart et al., 2025). The Bolsa Família initiative, though lauded for alleviating poverty, has struggled to translate stipends into qualitative educational outcomes, thereby underscoring the structural disequilibrium between policy intent and pedagogical reality. In contrast, Russia's hyper-centralised apparatus demonstrates the conundrum of homogeneity: while the federal state ensures curricular uniformity and alignment with industrial policy, ethnographic inquiries by literature illuminate how rural oblasts remain ensnared in infrastructural obsolescence, with pedagogical stagnation undermining the very objectives of technocratic centralism. (Valeeva et al., 2024). The rigidity of hierarchical governance has thus yielded conformity at the expense of innovation, exposing the latent tension between systemic cohesion and adaptive dynamism. India provides a further illustration of systemic dualism, where the simultaneity of a demographic dividend and an educational deficit engenders a policy impasse. National initiatives, such as "Digital India" and "Skill India," although ambitious in scope, have been hindered by infrastructural asymmetries and entrenched inequities in resource allocation. Case evidence from Bihar and Uttar Pradesh shows that digital learning interventions often falter due to electricity shortages, inadequate teacher training, and linguistic mismatches, thereby exacerbating rather than ameliorating the rural–urban educational divide. (Mussaiyib & Pradhan, 2024).

China's trajectory presents a counterfactual narrative of success punctuated by emergent contradictions. Its centralised orchestration of STEM-driven education has yielded prodigious outputs in technological innovation and workforce productivity. However, field-level ethnographies reveal that hinterland provinces remain disadvantaged, with rural schools struggling against urban magnetism, thus replicating structural disparities even within a putatively harmonised system. (Dong et al., 2024). The ostensible triumph of centralisation therefore conceals subterranean inequities that may erode long-term inclusivity. South Africa, finally, exemplifies the enduring shadow of historical injustice, where apartheid-era legacies continue to haunt the architecture of educational access. Despite post-apartheid reforms aimed at redistributive justice, evidence from Gauteng and Eastern Cape provinces indicates that schools remain stratified along socio-economic and racial lines, with quality differentials directly translating into labour market exclusion. The persistent unemployment rate of 30% or higher, despite relatively high educational expenditures, reflects the systemic inability to convert educational investment into equitable economic opportunities. Collectively, these case studies illuminate the praxis-oriented dilemmas of translating educational leadership into economic dividends: decentralisation risks exacerbating inequities; centralisation curtails adaptive innovation; digitisation collides with infrastructural fragility; and historical legacies impose path dependencies resistant to reform. These empirical realities necessitate a more nuanced comparative lens, one that transcends abstract theorisation to interrogate the political, cultural, and economic specificities that mediate the education–growth nexus.

The problem that animates this inquiry emanates from the persistent disjuncture between the *idealised state* of education as a universally accessible, equitably governed, and economically catalytic institution, and the *empirical reality* wherein contradictory evidence abounds, with some nations demonstrating positive correlations between educational leadership and growth, while others languish in stagnation despite significant investments (Menter et al., 2024a). The extant corpus of scholarship, though extensive, remains marred by inconclusive results; macro-level econometric analyses often establish correlations without explicating causal mechanisms, while micro-level institutional ethnographies reveal localised insights devoid of generalizability. The*oretical lacunae* persist in the absence of integrative frameworks that reconcile human capital theory with governance theories, and the *knowledge gaps* are accentuated by insufficient cross-national comparisons that examine how divergent political regimes, cultural architectures, and administrative modalities influence the education–growth nexus. Equally, *contextual deficits* are apparent in the tendency of existing research to privilege Western or OECD exemplars, thereby neglecting the heterogeneous realities of emerging economies such as the BRICS bloc (Masalimova et al., 2024). On the plane of praxis, *practical challenges* proliferate in the form of skill mismatches, inequitable resource allocation, entrenched socio-historical legacies, and the recurrent failure of policy interventions to translate access into employability or productivity. This study aims to address these interlocking deficiencies by conducting a comparative, empirically grounded, and governance-sensitive analysis of BRICS educational systems, thereby providing a comprehensive account that elucidates how leadership structures and management practices directly influence economic outcomes. In so doing, it not only addresses theoretical, knowledge, and context gaps but also provides a prescriptive roadmap for policymakers seeking to align education with labour market exigencies, while simultaneously delineating trajectories for future scholarly inquiry into the adaptive configurations of educational governance in a rapidly evolving global economy.

THEORETICAL PERSPECTIVES

The intricate interplay between educational leadership, management, and economic growth has been a subject of extensive academic scrutiny, attracting scholarly attention from various disciplines, including economics, political science, sociology, and education studies. Scholars have long debated the extent to which educational leadership and management can act as agents of economic transformation, particularly within emerging economies. Education is widely regarded as a critical determinant of human capital development, which in turn is a driving force for economic growth. (Tsaurai, 2017). However, the mechanisms through which educational leadership and management facilitate or hinder economic progress remain a contested field of inquiry. This literature review seeks to synthesise the key theoretical perspectives and empirical findings related to the nexus between educational leadership, management, and economic development, with a particular focus on the BRICS nations.

A foundational premise in the literature is that educational leadership plays a pivotal role in shaping the direction and quality of educational systems, which, in turn, influence the skills and competencies of the workforce. Education leadership is not a mere administrative function but rather a dynamic process involving the formulation, implementation, and evaluation of policies that directly impact teaching and learning outcomes. The quality of leadership in education systems has been shown to correlate positively with the overall effectiveness of educational institutions, fostering environments that are conducive to innovation, creativity, and the development of critical skills. (Amaral, 2016). It is widely acknowledged that strong educational leadership, characterised by vision, strategy, and a commitment to excellence, is essential for creating a skilled workforce capable of driving economic growth. Education leaders are tasked with navigating complex social, political, and economic landscapes, requiring them to balance competing interests, manage resources effectively, and implement policies that reflect both local needs and global trends. In parallel, the concept of educational management is integral to the broader discourse on educational governance and its economic implications. Educational management refers to the organisational processes and administrative practices that ensure the efficient functioning of educational institutions. The literature underscores the importance of management in ensuring that resources, whether financial, human, or material, are utilised optimally to enhance educational outcomes. Management in education is inextricably linked to accountability, transparency, and efficiency, all of which are crucial for improving the quality of education and ensuring equitable access to educational opportunities. (Chaudhary et al., 2012). The governance structures within educational systems, which vary significantly across countries, are a crucial determinant of how educational policies are implemented. Effective educational management, therefore, is not only a function of administrative skills but also a reflection of the broader institutional culture and political context in which these institutions operate.

In the context of economic growth, the role of education is crucial. Human capital theory, which posits that investment in education leads to increased productivity and economic output, serves as a key theoretical underpinning for many studies on the link between education and economic development (Fan et al., 2022). According to this theory, an educated workforce is more capable of innovation, entrepreneurship, and adaptation to changing market demands, all of which are critical to economic progress. The economic contributions of education are multifaceted, encompassing both direct and indirect effects on economic growth. Directly, education enhances individual productivity, thereby increasing the output of goods and services. Indirectly, a well-educated population fosters a culture of innovation and entrepreneurship, which is essential for creating new industries and sustaining long-term economic growth. Furthermore, education contributes to social mobility, reducing inequalities and enhancing social cohesion, which in turn promotes political stability and economic resilience (Xing & Imran, 2025). However, the relationship between education and economic growth is not always linear, and scholars have pointed to several moderating factors that influence this dynamic. Among the most salient of these is the quality of education. While access to education is necessary, it is not sufficient for driving economic growth. High-quality education systems, which emphasise the development of critical thinking, problem-solving, and technical skills, are more likely to produce graduates who can contribute meaningfully to the economy. This has been particularly relevant in the context of the BRICS nations, where rapid economic growth has been accompanied by significant educational reforms. (Ponomarev et al., 2024). In countries such as China and India, the focus has shifted toward strengthening vocational and technical education to equip the workforce with the specific skills required by the rapidly growing industrial sectors. In contrast, other BRICS nations, such as Brazil and South Africa, have faced challenges related to educational quality and equity, with large segments of the population still lacking access to high-quality education. These disparities in educational quality have direct implications for economic growth, as they limit the potential of large portions of the population to contribute to economic development. Additionally, the literature highlights the importance of aligning educational systems with the needs of the economy. This alignment ensures that the skills developed through education are relevant to the demands of the labour market, thereby enhancing employability and productivity. In the BRICS countries, there has been an increasing recognition of the need for educational systems to be more responsive to economic changes. For instance, in China, the state has prioritised the development of science, technology, engineering, and mathematics (STEM) education to position the country as a global leader in technological innovation. (Menter et al., 2024a). Similarly, India has made significant investments in technical education and higher education to foster a knowledge economy. However, in countries such as Brazil and South Africa, where economic growth has been uneven, there is a growing acknowledgement that education alone cannot spur economic development unless accompanied by structural reforms aimed at addressing underlying socio-economic challenges, such as poverty, inequality, and unemployment.

The governance and management of education systems in the BRICS nations vary considerably, reflecting the unique political, economic, and cultural contexts of each country. In China, education is heavily influenced by central government policies, with the state playing a dominant role in shaping educational priorities and outcomes. This centralised approach has facilitated rapid advancements in key areas such as infrastructure development and technological education. In contrast, countries like India and Brazil exhibit more decentralised educational systems, where state and local governments have greater autonomy in decision-making. (Saito et al., 2018). While decentralisation can lead to more context-specific educational policies, it can also result in disparities in educational quality and access, particularly in rural and marginalised areas. South Africa, with its complex history of apartheid, faces additional challenges in addressing educational inequities, as historical disparities in education continue to hinder efforts to create an inclusive and equitable educational system. In conclusion, the literature on educational leadership, management, and economic growth highlights the crucial role of education in shaping economic trajectories, particularly in emerging economies such as the BRICS nations. While significant progress has been made in aligning educational systems with the demands of modern economies, challenges remain in terms of educational quality, equity, and access. Educational leadership and management are crucial in navigating these challenges, ensuring that educational policies are effectively implemented and that the educational system responds dynamically to the needs of the economy (Novgorodtseva & Belyaeva, 2020). As the BRICS nations continue to grow and evolve, the ongoing development of their educational systems will play a crucial role in determining the sustainability and inclusivity of their economic growth.

Theoretical Framework

The first theoretical edifice underpinning this inquiry is Human Capital Theory, canonically articulated by Ferreira et al. (2017) and subsequently elaborated by Ratzinger et al. (2018). Emerging from the Chicago School tradition, the theory posits that investments in education, health, and training enhance the productive capacities of individuals, thereby constituting a form of capital analogous to physical or financial assets. Within this schema, education is not merely an individual good but a national imperative, wherein leadership and management of educational systems function as mediating conduits that determine the efficiency with which human capital is cultivated and mobilised. The theory's enduring relevance lies in its capacity to explicate the direct relationship between educational attainment and aggregate economic growth. This premise resonates strongly within the developmental trajectories of the BRICS nations.

A complementary yet distinct framework is the Systems Theory of Educational Management, whose intellectual origins can be traced to Ludwig von Bertalanffy's General Systems Theory (1950s) and its subsequent transposition into organisational and educational contexts. Systems theory conceptualises educational institutions as open, dynamic entities interacting with external environments, with leadership and management functioning as integrative nodes that harmonise inputs (resources, policies), processes (curricula, pedagogy), and outputs (graduates, skills) (Ligęza et al., 2021). Within the BRICS context, the theory highlights the systemic interdependencies between governance modalities, resource allocation, and labour market outcomes, illuminating why breakdowns at any node —whether infrastructural inadequacies or bureaucratic inefficiencies —reverberate across the entire educational–economic continuum.

The third relevant theoretical prism is Institutional Theory, advanced by early sociologists such as Silvestre, which interrogates the role of formal rules, norms, and cultural-cognitive schemas in shaping organisational behaviour. (Silvestre, 2015). In educational domains, institutional theory foregrounds how legitimacy, conformity to global standards, and normative isomorphism influence national education systems. The theory is particularly salient in explaining the BRICS nations' attempts to align domestic educational policies with international benchmarks (e.g., PISA scores, UNESCO directives), while simultaneously grappling with path dependencies rooted in local political economies and cultural matrices. It further highlights the paradox whereby conformity to global norms may enhance legitimacy but does not necessarily guarantee substantive improvements in educational quality or economic productivity.

Finally, Governance and Leadership Theories in Education, particularly transformational leadership (Chowdhury et al., 2023; Jenna Degan, 2013), offer a micro-foundational lens to examine the agency of educational leaders in navigating complex institutional landscapes. Transformational leadership posits that visionary, inspirational leaders can transcend structural constraints to mobilise followers toward higher-order goals, fostering innovation, adaptability, and organisational cohesion. In the educational context, such leadership is seen as vital in aligning institutional missions with national developmental imperatives, cultivating a culture of excellence, and bridging the disjuncture between policy and practice. This theory thus situates leadership not as a bureaucratic function but as a catalyst for systemic reform and economic renewal.

Among these four frameworks, Human Capital Theory is adopted as the principal theoretical lens for this study, given its explanatory power in elucidating the causal linkages between education and economic growth. However, the study deploys an integrative perspective wherein systems, institutional, and leadership theories function as subsidiary lenses that contextualise and enrich the analysis. By anchoring the inquiry in human capital theory while simultaneously drawing on complementary paradigms, this research endeavours to furnish a multidimensional account of how educational leadership and management shape the capacity of BRICS nations to convert educational investments into sustained economic advancement.

METHODOLOGY

The research methodology for this study involves a comparative analysis of the educational systems and economic outcomes across the BRICS nations (Brazil, Russia, India, China, and South Africa). The approach combines both qualitative and quantitative data to assess the relationship between educational policies, labour market demands, educational outputs, and economic growth. Data will be gathered from secondary sources, including government reports, educational policy documents, labour market statistics, and economic indicators. A mixed-methods approach will be employed, with statistical analysis of economic and educational data complemented by qualitative case studies to understand the contextual factors influencing the role of education in economic development. This methodology will enable the identification of patterns, disparities, and correlations between education systems and economic performance within the BRICS nations.

Analysis

Table 1. Educational Leadership Characteristics in BRICS Nations

Country	Educational Leadership Approach	Key Features	Impact on Economic Growth
Brazil	Decentralised with local autonomy	Emphasis on inclusivity and equality in education policies	Limited access to quality education in rural areas hampers workforce skill development
Russia	Centralised with state control over major decisions	Strong influence of the government on educational reforms and curriculum structure	Centralised control fosters uniformity but limits innovation in education
India	Hybrid approach with both central and state influence	Focus on increasing educational access and promoting STEM education	Disparities in educational quality slow overall workforce readiness
China	Highly centralised, top-down approach	Nationalisation of education policy, emphasis on STEM education	Centralisation allows for rapid reforms but may stifle localised innovation
South Africa	Mixed governance with emphasis on post-apartheid reforms	Educational reforms aimed at addressing racial disparities and socio-economic gaps	Educational inequities remain an obstacle to sustainable economic growth

The dynamics of educational leadership in the BRICS nations are marked by distinct governance structures that reflect the political, economic, and social contexts of each country. A comparative analysis of the educational leadership characteristics in these countries reveals not only the diverse ways in which education is governed but also the profound implications of these governance models on economic growth. Table 1, "Educational Leadership Characteristics in BRICS Nations," provides a detailed exploration of how these nations approach educational leadership, the key features that define these approaches, and the subsequent impact on their economic growth.

Brazil, with its decentralised educational leadership structure, has placed significant emphasis on inclusivity and equality within its educational policies. The Brazilian approach promotes local autonomy, allowing regions and municipalities to have considerable control over educational decisions, which facilitates the accommodation of local needs and contexts. While this decentralisation theoretically empowers local leaders to tailor educational strategies to their unique demographics, it has inadvertently led to disparities in the quality of education between urban and rural areas. As indicated in Table 1, limited access to quality education in rural regions hampers the development of a skilled workforce, which, in turn, constrains the nation's overall economic potential. This is particularly detrimental in an era where global competitiveness is increasingly dependent on the calibre of human capital, which Brazil's decentralised educational system struggles to nurture uniformly across its territory. The uneven educational access and quality across regions create a bottleneck, hindering Brazil's ability to leverage its population's potential for economic growth fully.

In contrast, Russia follows a more centralised approach to educational leadership, with the state exerting considerable control over educational reforms and curriculum structures. This centralised governance model ensures uniformity in the educational system across the nation, which can be beneficial for maintaining national standards and aligning educational policies with the country's long-term developmental goals. As highlighted in Table 1, Russia's strong government influence in the educational system has enabled the country to introduce large-scale reforms that emphasise technical education and industry-relevant skills. However, while this centralisation has its merits, it also limits innovation within the educational landscape. The rigidity of the system, shaped by top-down decision-making, constrains the flexibility needed for localised and innovative educational practices. Consequently, while Russia has made significant strides in educational uniformity, the inability to encourage diversity in educational approaches limits the creative and adaptive capacities of its education system, which are essential for fostering an innovative economy. In this regard, the centralised nature of educational leadership in Russia becomes a double-edged sword, fostering national cohesion while stifling the diverse educational reforms needed to match the rapidly evolving global economy.

India, as depicted in Table 1, employs a hybrid educational leadership model that balances both central and state influences. This duality enables the Indian government to craft nationwide policies while allowing states a certain degree of autonomy in their implementation. The focus of India's educational leadership has been on increasing access to education, particularly in rural areas, and promoting science, technology, engineering, and mathematics (STEM) education as key drivers of economic development. Despite these efforts, disparities in educational quality between different states persist as a significant challenge. While urban areas and some states have made considerable progress in educational outcomes, others continue to lag due to varying levels of resource allocation, administrative capacity, and political will. This unevenness in educational quality is a critical impediment to preparing India's workforce for the demands of a knowledge-based economy. Table 1 underscores that these disparities slow the readiness of the workforce, preventing India from fully capitalising on its demographic dividend. Although India's hybrid model allows for some customisation of educational policies, it also brings about challenges in standardisation and uniformity, making it difficult to ensure a consistently high quality of education across the country.

China, in stark contrast to Brazil and India, adheres to a highly centralised, top-down approach to educational leadership. The central government in China not only dictates educational policies but also directly shapes the curriculum and sets national standards. As noted in Table 1, China's nationalisation of education policies has prioritised STEM education, which aligns with its broader economic goals of technological innovation and industrial modernisation. The centralised approach has enabled China to rapidly implement reforms that address the nation's educational needs in a synchronised manner, fostering a highly skilled workforce integral to its economic success. However, this level of centralisation, while facilitating rapid policy changes, may inadvertently stifle localised innovation. The rigid structure of the system does not allow for much flexibility in adapting to regional needs or experimenting with alternative educational methodologies that could bring about more creative solutions. This top-down governance model, although effective in promoting national cohesion and rapid reform implementation, limits the scope for decentralised experimentation that better caters to diverse regional economic demands and individual learning needs.

South Africa's educational leadership model, as detailed in Table 1, is characterised by a mixed governance approach, which is heavily influenced by post-apartheid reforms aimed at addressing historical racial disparities and socio-economic inequalities. South Africa has made strides in reforming its education system to ensure greater inclusivity. However, the country still grapples with significant challenges related to educational access and quality, particularly among marginalised communities. Table 1 highlights that despite the efforts to address educational inequities, substantial barriers remain in providing quality education to all citizens, which hinders the development of a skilled and competitive workforce. The persistent educational inequities in South Africa impede its ability to achieve sustainable economic growth. These challenges are compounded by the country's legacy of apartheid, which left deep socio-economic divisions that continue to influence educational outcomes today. While the governance system has been restructured to foster greater equality in education, the pace of change has been slow, and the system's inability to fully address the needs of disadvantaged communities continues to hold back South Africa's economic potential.

In summary, Table 1 offers a nuanced understanding of the educational leadership characteristics across the BRICS nations, highlighting the diverse approaches each country takes to governance and education management. The differences in leadership structures, from Brazil's decentralised model to China's centralised approach, underscore the complexity of aligning educational systems with the economic goals of these nations. While each governance model has its advantages, such as increased local autonomy in Brazil or national uniformity in Russia and China, they also present challenges that directly affect economic growth. Disparities in educational access and quality, particularly in rural or marginalised areas, limit the potential of these nations to leverage education as a catalyst for economic growth fully. The analysis presented in Table 1 suggests that educational leadership is not only a matter of policy formulation but also of execution, resource allocation, and alignment with broader socio-economic goals. For the BRICS nations to harness the full potential of their educational systems for economic growth, they must address the inherent challenges within their respective leadership and management structures, ensuring that education systems are both equitable and adaptable to the changing demands of the global economy.

Table 2. Educational Management Practices in BRICS Nations

Country	Management Structure	Resource Allocation	Key Challenges
Brazil	Local autonomy in decision-making	Discrepancy in resource distribution between regions	Inequitable access to resources hampers educational quality
Russia	Centralised, government-driven	Government funding focuses on primary and secondary education	Resource allocation biases towards urban areas, leading to inequality
India	Mixed, with decentralised schools and centralised policy decisions	Disparities in funding allocation between states and rural areas	Limited resources for rural schools affect overall national productivity
China	Highly regulated by the national government	Focus on urban schools, with limited resources for rural institutions	The concentration of resources in cities exacerbates educational inequalities
South Africa	Decentralised management with national oversight	Disproportionate funding allocation based on historical socio-economic factors	Educational inequities from the apartheid era continue to affect resource equity.

Table 2, "Educational Management Practices in BRICS Nations," provides a detailed comparative analysis of the management structures and resource allocation within the educational systems of the BRICS nations, while also highlighting the key challenges each country faces in their efforts to improve educational outcomes. The management structures across these nations vary significantly, influencing how resources are distributed and the challenges that arise in the educational process. This variability plays a critical role in determining the overall effectiveness of their educational systems, especially in the context of their economic growth aspirations.

Brazil's educational management structure is characterised by local autonomy in decision-making, allowing regional and municipal authorities considerable freedom in shaping educational practices. This decentralised approach provides flexibility, enabling local educational leaders to tailor strategies and policies that reflect the unique needs of their communities. However, as highlighted in Table 2, this autonomy comes with significant challenges, particularly in terms of resource distribution. The country faces a glaring discrepancy in resource allocation between regions, with wealthier urban areas enjoying better access to educational resources compared to rural and poorer regions. This inequity hampers the overall quality of education, particularly in rural areas, where schools often lack sufficient infrastructure, outdated materials, and a shortage of qualified teachers. Consequently, these disparities in resource allocation negatively impact the development of a skilled workforce, which is essential for driving economic growth. In this way, Brazil's management structure, despite its ability to cater to local needs, exacerbates existing inequalities that limit educational quality and, by extension, economic progress.

Russia, on the other hand, operates with a centralised, government-driven educational management structure. The state exercises significant control over educational policies and decisions, ensuring uniformity across the country. This centralised governance model facilitates the implementation of national educational reforms and the establishment of a coherent curriculum that can be applied nationwide. However, as shown in Table 2, Russia faces a critical challenge in its resource allocation. The government predominantly focuses its funding on primary and secondary education, with less emphasis on higher education and vocational training, which are vital for preparing a workforce capable of competing in a globalised economy. Additionally, there is a pronounced bias in resource allocation towards urban areas, where the majority of educational infrastructure and services are concentrated. This urban-centric allocation exacerbates inequality, leaving rural regions underserved and depriving them of the resources necessary to build a robust educational system. The result is an uneven educational landscape that hampers the country's ability to fully capitalise on its human capital, thus limiting the potential for sustainable economic growth.

India's educational management structure is a hybrid model, combining decentralised schools with centralised policy decisions. This model allows for some degree of flexibility at the local level, with states and individual schools having the autonomy to adjust policies and practices to meet regional needs. However, as reflected in Table 2, this decentralisation is tempered by a significant challenge in funding allocation. There are notable disparities in funding between states, particularly between urban and rural areas, which contribute to an uneven educational experience across the nation. Rural schools, in particular, are underfunded, with limited access to essential resources, including qualified teachers, adequate infrastructure, and educational technology. This imbalance in resource allocation not only affects the quality of education but also exacerbates socio-economic disparities, as rural students are less prepared for the demands of the modern workforce. The limited resources available to rural schools contribute to the nation's overall productivity deficit, as a significant portion of the population remains underserved by the educational system. Despite the hybrid management structure offering some level of adaptability, the lack of equitable resource distribution remains a significant barrier to India's educational and economic advancement.

China, with its highly regulated educational management structure, operates under the central government's strict oversight. This system ensures that the educational policies and strategies align with national goals, particularly in the realms of technological innovation and industrial competitiveness. The government's focus is primarily on urban schools, which are considered the epicentre of China's educational reforms and development. As noted in Table 2, the centralisation of resources results in limited support for rural educational institutions, where infrastructure is often inadequate, and access to qualified teachers is scarce. This concentration of resources in urban areas exacerbates educational inequalities, as rural schools continue to lag in terms of quality and access to educational opportunities. The disparity in resource allocation between urban and rural schools creates a stark divide in educational outcomes, which can limit the overall productivity of the workforce and impede China's long-term economic growth. While urban educational institutions benefit from state-of-the-art resources and high-quality teaching staff, rural areas remain disadvantaged, thereby undermining the potential for nationwide human capital development.

South Africa's educational management structure is characterised by decentralisation with national oversight, reflecting the country's ongoing efforts to address the inequities created by the apartheid regime. In the post-apartheid era, South Africa has worked to reform its education system, aiming to provide equal opportunities to all citizens, regardless of their race or socio-economic status. However, as shown in Table 2, this decentralisation is complicated by the disproportionate funding allocation that still reflects the historical socio-economic factors of apartheid. Many schools in disadvantaged areas, particularly those in rural and historically marginalised communities, continue to receive insufficient funding, which affects the quality of education they can offer. This historical legacy of inequality has led to significant educational inequities, which continue to hamper the country's efforts to foster a skilled and productive workforce. Despite efforts to promote equity, South Africa's educational system remains deeply divided, with the unequal distribution of resources hindering the creation of a robust human capital base necessary for sustained economic growth.

In conclusion, the educational management practices of the BRICS nations, as detailed in Table 2, reflect a range of governance structures and resource allocation models that have varying impacts on educational outcomes and economic growth. While some countries, like Brazil and South Africa, have decentralised systems that allow for localised decision-making, they struggle with the inequitable distribution of resources, particularly in rural areas. Others, like Russia and China, operate under highly centralised systems, which ensure uniformity but also exacerbate urban-rural disparities in resource allocation. India's hybrid system, while offering a degree of flexibility, still faces significant challenges in ensuring equitable distribution of resources across states and regions. In all cases, the uneven allocation of resources, whether due to historical factors, urban biases, or insufficient funding for rural areas, remains a critical challenge that undermines the quality of education and hampers the development of a skilled workforce. Addressing these disparities in resource allocation and improving the management structures of educational systems are essential steps for the BRICS nations to fully leverage education as a driver of economic growth and development.

Table 3. Economic Indicators and Educational Investment in BRICS Nations

Country	GDP (2025, USD)	Education Spending (% of GDP)	Enrollment Rate (Primary/Secondary)	Labour Force Participation Rate (%)	Unemployment Rate (%)
Brazil	2.3 Trillion	6.2%	98% (Primary), 85% (Secondary)	59.3%	9.4%
Russia	1.8 Trillion	4.3%	100% (Primary), 95% (Secondary)	61.2%	5.0%
India	3.7 Trillion	3.1%	95% (Primary), 72% (Secondary)	53.6%	7.7%
China	16.8 Trillion	4.5%	99% (Primary), 94% (Secondary)	72.9%	4.0%
South Africa	0.5 Trillion	6.5%	94% (Primary), 80% (Secondary)	58.8%	33.9%

Table 3, titled "Economic Indicators and Educational Investment in BRICS Nations," presents a detailed comparison of key economic indicators, including GDP, education spending, enrolment rates, labour force participation rates, and unemployment rates across the BRICS countries. These indicators provide valuable insights into the relationship between a nation's educational investment and its economic outcomes, offering a window into how education systems can impact broader economic performance.

The table reveals a stark contrast between the economic sizes of the BRICS nations. China stands out as the largest economy by a significant margin, with a projected GDP of $16.8 trillion by 2025. This economic might is complemented by a robust education system, with near-total enrolment in primary education (99%) and secondary education (94%). China's education spending, at 4.5% of GDP, reflects its commitment to human capital development, which is essential for sustaining its position as a global economic powerhouse. The country's high labour force participation rate (72.9%) and low unemployment rate (4.0%) further underscore the positive effects of its substantial educational investments on its labour market. These factors suggest that China's investment in education has played a significant role in fostering a highly skilled workforce capable of driving its economic growth.

In contrast, South Africa, with a much smaller economy, has a GDP of just \$0.5 trillion and is facing profound challenges despite spending 6.5% of its GDP on education, the highest percentage among the BRICS countries. South Africa's enrolment rates are relatively high (94% in primary and 80% in secondary education). However, its labour force participation rate (58.8%) is lower than that of the other BRICS nations, and its unemployment rate is alarmingly high at 33.9%. These figures reflect the country's deep structural inequalities, many of which stem from the apartheid era. Despite significant educational investment, South Africa's high unemployment rate indicates that the education system is struggling to equip graduates with the skills demanded by the labour market. The educational system's inability to bridge the socio-economic divide and prepare young people for gainful employment remains a significant hurdle to South Africa's economic development.

Brazil, with a projected GDP of \$2.3 trillion by 2025, allocates 6.2% of its GDP to education, which is among the highest in the BRICS bloc. This level of investment reflects Brazil's recognition of the importance of education for economic growth. The enrolment rates in Brazil are commendable, with 98% of children enrolled in primary education and 85% in secondary education. However, Brazil's labour force participation rate (59.3%) and its unemployment rate (9.4%) reveal challenges in translating educational investment into employment outcomes. Although Brazil's educational access is relatively high, the quality of education and the alignment of educational outputs with labour market demands remain areas of concern. These gaps suggest that while Brazil's education system succeeds in providing access, it struggles to prepare its young workforce for the evolving demands of the labour market, contributing to persistent unemployment. Russia, with a GDP of \$1.8 trillion, spends 4.3% of its GDP on education, which is slightly below the BRICS average but still substantial. Russia boasts a 100% enrolment rate in primary education and a 95% enrolment rate in secondary education, indicating strong access to and completion rates in education. With a labour force participation rate of 61.2% and an unemployment rate of 5.0%, Russia's educational system appears to be relatively well-aligned with labour market needs, resulting in more stable employment outcomes. The government's focus on technical education and vocational training has contributed to a well-prepared workforce capable of supporting Russia's industrial and technological sectors. However, the centralisation of educational management, as discussed earlier, may limit localised innovation, potentially affecting the long-term adaptability of the workforce to rapidly changing global economic conditions. India, with the second-largest GDP in the BRICS group at \$3.7 trillion, allocates just 3.1% of its GDP to education, the lowest proportion among the BRICS nations. This relatively low level of educational investment is reflected in India's enrolment rates, with 95% of children enrolled in primary education and only 72% in secondary education. The discrepancy in secondary education enrolment highlights significant gaps in educational access, particularly in rural areas where resources and infrastructure are limited. India's labour force participation rate is the lowest in the group at 53.6%, and its unemployment rate is moderate at 7.7%. These figures suggest that while India has a large and growing workforce, the country's educational system has not fully equipped its labour force with the skills required for higher-paying and more stable employment. Additionally, the disparity in educational quality between urban and rural regions exacerbates socio-economic inequalities, limiting the country's ability to maximise its economic potential.

The data presented in Table 3 reveal a clear correlation between education spending and economic outcomes, although various factors, including the overall size of the economy, the effectiveness of the education system, and the socio-political context, influence this relationship. Countries like China and Russia, with relatively high educational investments and robust labour force participation rates, demonstrate the positive effects of a well-aligned education system on economic outcomes. In contrast, Brazil, India, and South Africa, despite investing significant portions of their GDP into education, face challenges related to unemployment, labour force participation, and disparities in educational access. These challenges highlight the complexity of the relationship between educational investment and economic growth, suggesting that while access to education is a crucial factor, it must be complemented by investments in quality, relevance, and equity to ensure that education yields meaningful economic outcomes.

In conclusion, Table 3 offers important insights into the economic implications of educational investments in the BRICS nations. While all the countries have made significant investments in education, their varying economic performance and labour market outcomes illustrate the need for more targeted educational policies that not only expand access but also enhance the quality and alignment of education with labour market demands. Education alone, as demonstrated in the cases of South Africa and Brazil, may not be sufficient to address deep-seated socio-economic challenges unless accompanied by structural reforms aimed at enhancing the quality of education and its relevance to the modern economy. These insights are essential for policymakers seeking to optimise educational investments to foster sustainable economic growth.

Table 4. Educational Quality Indicators and Workforce Productivity

Country	PISA Score (Reading/ Math/Science)	Adult Literacy Rate (%)	Higher Education Graduates (%)	Workforce Productivity	Economic Growth (Avg. 5-Year GDP Growth)
Brazil	400/375/385	93%	17%	Moderate, slow innovation	2.5%
Russia	470/475/475	99%	40%	High, competitive industries	3.0%
India	380/370/370	74%	25%	Low, needs skill enhancement	5.6%
China	515/510/505	96%	45%	High, technology-driven economy	6.4%
South Africa	415/400/410	88%	15%	Low, constrained by inequality	2.0%

Table 4, titled "Educational Quality Indicators and Workforce Productivity," offers a comprehensive analysis of the educational outcomes and their correlation with workforce productivity and economic growth across the BRICS nations. The table presents key indicators, including PISA (Program for International Student Assessment) scores, adult literacy rates, higher education graduation rates, workforce productivity, and the average five-year GDP growth, for each country. These factors provide valuable insights into the effectiveness of each nation's education system and its capacity to contribute to economic development.

Starting with Brazil, the PISA scores in reading, math, and science (400/375/385) indicate relatively low educational performance compared to the other BRICS nations. While Brazil boasts an adult literacy rate of 93%, which is above average, its higher education graduation rate is only 17%. This suggests that although many Brazilians can access basic education, a significant portion of the population struggles to attain higher education qualifications, which are crucial for a competitive, knowledge-based economy. The country's workforce productivity is described as "moderate," characterised by slow innovation, which suggests an educational system that, while offering basic education, struggles to equip its labour force with the advanced skills required to drive technological or industrial advancement. This is reflected in Brazil's economic growth rate of 2.5% over the past five years. Despite significant educational investment, Brazil faces challenges in translating its human capital into high-value economic output, highlighting the need to enhance workforce readiness and foster innovation.

Russia, in contrast, demonstrates a higher level of educational achievement, with PISA scores of 470/475/475. The country also boasts a very high adult literacy rate of 99% and a relatively high percentage of higher education graduates (40%). These indicators suggest that Russia's education system is producing a highly skilled workforce capable of contributing to competitive industries. Consequently, Russia's workforce productivity is categorised as "high," driven by industries that emphasise technological development and innovation. This alignment between education and industrial needs has contributed to Russia's relatively stable economic performance, reflected in its average GDP growth of 3.0% over the past five years. The combination of strong educational outcomes and a productive workforce positions Russia well for sustained economic growth, particularly in sectors that demand high levels of technical expertise and innovation.

India's educational performance, as indicated by its PISA scores (380/370/370), is lower than that of Russia and China, with particular deficiencies in math and science. India's adult literacy rate of 74% is considerably lower than that of other BRICS nations, and its higher education graduation rate of 25% is relatively modest. This limited access to higher education and the lower literacy rate suggest that India's education system has significant gaps in providing quality education, particularly in terms of higher education and skill development. As a result, India's workforce productivity is described as "low," with a pressing need for skill enhancement to meet the demands of an evolving global economy. Despite this, India's average GDP growth rate of 5.6% is the highest among the BRICS nations, indicating that the country's large and growing workforce, combined with recent strides in technology and services, has propelled economic growth. However, the challenge lies in harnessing the potential of the workforce by improving educational quality and aligning it with labour market needs, particularly in higher education and vocational training.

China's educational system stands out with high PISA scores (515/510/505) and an adult literacy rate of 96%. The country also has a strong higher education graduation rate of 45%, one of the highest in the BRICS bloc. These indicators reflect the success of China's education system in preparing a highly skilled workforce capable of supporting its fast-paced economic development. China's workforce productivity is categorised as "high" and driven by a "technology-driven economy," underscoring the country's substantial investments in STEM education and its focus on technological innovation. As a result, China's economic growth over the past five years has averaged 6.4%, the highest in the BRICS group. China's ability to align educational outputs with its industrial needs, particularly in technology and manufacturing, has enabled the country to maintain rapid economic growth and become a global leader in various high-tech sectors.

South Africa, with PISA scores of 415/400/410, ranks among the lower performers in terms of educational quality. The country's adult literacy rate of 88% is relatively high; however, its higher education graduation rate of just 15% suggests that access to advanced education remains limited, particularly among historically disadvantaged populations. This educational disparity is compounded by the structural inequalities that persist in the South African economy, limiting the potential for educational outcomes to translate into higher workforce productivity. South Africa's workforce productivity is described as "low," constrained by inequality and insufficient educational resources. These educational shortcomings are reflected in the country's modest economic performance, with an average GDP growth rate of just 2.0% over the past five years. The combination of educational inequities and the country's high unemployment rate continues to stifle South Africa's economic potential, as a significant portion of the population remains undereducated and underserved by the labour market.

In summary, Table 4 provides a comprehensive overview of the educational quality indicators and workforce productivity across the BRICS nations, illustrating a clear link between educational outcomes and economic performance. Countries like China and Russia, with higher educational achievement and stronger workforce productivity, have been able to leverage their education systems to drive high levels of economic growth (Kukreti et al., 2024). Conversely, Brazil, India, and South Africa, despite investing in education, face challenges in improving the quality of education and aligning it with labour market demands, which impacts their overall economic productivity. For these nations to enhance their economic performance, improving educational quality, particularly in higher education and vocational training, is crucial. Educational reform, focusing on both access and quality, is key to fostering a skilled workforce that can drive innovation, productivity, and long-term economic growth.

Table 5. Government Policies for Education and Economic Integration in BRICS

Country	Educational Policies Focus	Economic Integration	Policy Success Rate	Policy Effectiveness
Brazil	Expansion of access to primary and secondary education	Low-cost education policies for poverty alleviation	Moderate, slow progress due to inequality	Needs systemic reform
Russia	STEM education, vocational training	Strong industrialisation strategy, focus on technical and higher education.	High, aligning educational policy with industrial goals	Effective, but uneven in rural areas
India	Digital education, rural education initiatives	Focus on skill development for economic growth	Low, challenges in scaling rural education	Needs improvement in access

continued on following page

Table 5. Continued

Country	Educational Policies Focus	Economic Integration	Policy Success Rate	Policy Effectiveness
China	Focus on global competitiveness, technological and STEM education	Industrial policy aligning with educational advancements	Very high, education closely aligned with industry	Highly effective, globally competitive
South Africa	Equity in education, addressing apartheid-era disparities	Policies focusing on improving access for marginalised communities	Low needs more inclusive educational reforms	Needs significant policy overhaul

Table 5, titled "Government Policies for Education and Economic Integration in BRICS," provides a detailed overview of the educational policy priorities in each BRICS nation and their alignment with broader economic integration strategies. This table explores how each country's education policies are designed to foster economic development, the success rates of these policies, and their effectiveness in driving meaningful change. The interplay between educational policies and economic integration is crucial, as the education system plays a pivotal role in shaping the labour force and supporting industrial growth.

In Brazil, the primary focus of educational policies has been on expanding access to primary and secondary education, with the aim of alleviating poverty through low-cost education initiatives. This expansion is critical for ensuring that children across the country, particularly in underserved areas, have access to education. However, as Table 5 indicates, Brazil's policy success rate is moderate, with slow progress primarily due to systemic inequality within the education system. Despite efforts to improve access, significant disparities in the quality of education persist, particularly in rural and impoverished urban areas. The policies, while providing some access to education, fail to address the deeper structural issues within the system, such as underfunded schools and insufficient teacher training. These challenges hinder the full integration of education with economic growth strategies. Brazil's educational policies require a more systemic reform to better align with the nation's broader economic goals and to address inequality in the distribution of educational resources.

Russia, in contrast, has focused on STEM (Science, Technology, Engineering, and Mathematics) education and vocational training as part of a broader industrialisation strategy. The country's educational policies emphasise the importance of technical education and higher education, with a particular focus on fields that are aligned with the country's industrial goals. As noted in Table 5, Russia's policy success rate is high, and its education system is effectively aligned with the country's industrial needs. This alignment has been crucial in fostering a workforce capable of supporting technological and industrial growth. However, the effectiveness of these policies remains uneven, particularly in rural areas, where access to quality education and vocational training remains limited. The government has made significant strides in urban areas, but rural regions continue to face challenges in accessing the full benefits of the nation's educational reforms. Despite this, Russia's focus on STEM education has contributed to substantial industrial and technological growth, positioning the country as a key player in global markets.

India's educational policies have been centred around digital education and rural education initiatives, reflecting the country's recognition of the need for technological literacy and skill development to drive economic growth. Policies have been geared toward expanding educational access in rural areas, where access to quality education has historically been limited. However, as highlighted in Table 5, India's policy success rate is low, primarily due to the challenges in scaling educational initiatives in rural areas. Despite significant efforts to increase digital literacy and bridge the rural-urban divide, India continues to struggle with issues such as inadequate infrastructure, teacher shortages, and regional disparities in educational quality. These challenges hinder the country's ability to capitalise on its educational reforms and drive economic development fully. India's education system requires improvement, particularly in expanding access to quality education in rural areas, to more effectively support its economic goals, including skill development and technological growth.

China's educational policies place a strong emphasis on global competitiveness, technological innovation, and STEM education. The country's educational strategies are closely aligned with its industrial policies, creating a synergistic relationship between education and economic growth. China has invested heavily in developing a workforce skilled in technology and innovation, ensuring that its educational system produces graduates who are well-equipped to support the country's industrial and technological ambitions. As shown in Table 5, China's policy success rate is very high, with education closely aligned with industry needs. The effectiveness of these policies has been widely recognised, as China has become a global leader in manufacturing, technology, and innovation. The country's educational advancements have directly contributed to its economic growth, with an emphasis on producing graduates who can drive technological and industrial development. China's education system, with its strong alignment to economic goals, serves as a model for how educational policies can support and accelerate economic integration.

South Africa, in its post-apartheid era, has focused on equity in education and addressing the disparities created by apartheid. The country's educational policies aim to improve access to education for marginalised communities and promote inclusivity. However, as Table 5 indicates, South Africa's policy success rate is low, and the country continues to struggle with deeply entrenched educational inequalities. Despite efforts to improve access to education, particularly for disadvantaged groups, significant gaps remain in the quality of education provided to different communities. The need for more inclusive educational reforms is urgent, as the existing disparities prevent South Africa from fully integrating its education system with its economic goals. The country's education system requires a significant overhaul to address the socio-economic challenges stemming from its history and support economic growth by developing a skilled and diverse workforce.

In summary, Table 5 highlights the varying degrees of success in implementing educational policies across the BRICS nations and their impact on economic integration. Countries like China and Russia have successfully aligned their educational policies with economic goals, particularly in STEM fields, resulting in strong industrial and technological growth. On the other hand, nations like Brazil, India, and South Africa face significant challenges in scaling educational reforms and addressing systemic inequalities, which limit their ability to integrate education with economic development effectively. These disparities underscore the importance of aligning educational policies with national economic strategies and the need for continued reform to ensure that education systems produce the skilled workforce necessary for sustained economic growth.

Table 6. Labour Market Demands vs. Educational Outputs in BRICS Nations

Country	Labour Market Demand (STEM, Tech, Service Sectors)	Education System Output (STEM Graduates, Vocational Training)	Mismatch between Skills and Employment	Impact on Economic Growth
Brazil	High demand for service sector workers, tech skills	Moderate output in STEM fields, high output in service sectors	Mismatch in tech skills for a growing economy	Limits innovation and industrial growth
Russia	High demand for engineering and IT professionals	High output in STEM fields, especially in engineering	Minimal mismatch, industry-ready graduates	Drives technological and industrial growth
India	High demand for IT professionals, engineers, and skilled labour	Moderate STEM output, limited vocational training programs	Severe mismatch in vocational skills	Limits competitiveness in global markets
China	High demand for STEM professionals, innovation-driven sectors	High output of STEM and tech graduates, focused vocational training	Low mismatch, aligned with market needs	Enhances competitiveness and innovation
South Africa	High demand for skilled labour in mining, agriculture, and services	Low output of vocational training and skilled labour graduates	High mismatch in skills, particularly in mining and services	Limits job creation and economic integration

Table 6, titled "Labour Market Demands vs. Educational Outputs in BRICS Nations," provides an insightful comparison of the alignment between labour market demands and educational outputs across the BRICS countries. By examining the demand for various professional skills, the output of education systems in terms of graduates and vocational training, and the resulting skills mismatch, this table illustrates how well these countries are preparing their workforces to meet the evolving needs of their economies. Additionally, the table examines the implications of these dynamics on economic growth, shedding light on how educational outcomes impact national economic performance.

In Brazil, the labour market demands are high for workers in the service sector and for those with tech skills, reflecting the country's growing need for skilled labour in both traditional services and technology-driven industries. However, as indicated in Table 6, Brazil's education system produces a moderate output of STEM (Science, Technology, Engineering, and Mathematics) graduates, while its output in service sector-related fields is high. The mismatch in tech skills, particularly in engineering and computer science, is a critical challenge, as the growing economy increasingly requires a workforce proficient in technology and innovation. This gap in educational output hinders Brazil's ability to foster innovation and expand its industrial base, ultimately limiting its potential for industrial growth and economic diversification. While Brazil's education system is successful in addressing the demand for service sector workers, it falls short in aligning educational outputs with the needs of a rapidly evolving global economy, particularly in high-tech industries.

Russia, on the other hand, demonstrates a more favourable alignment between labour market demands and educational outputs. With a high demand for engineering and IT professionals, Russia's education system produces a strong output of STEM graduates, especially in the engineering sector. Table 6 shows that there is minimal mismatch between the skills produced by Russia's educational system and the needs of its labour market. This alignment has enabled Russia to develop a workforce that is well-prepared for the demands of technological and industrial growth. Russia's education system has been a driving force behind the country's technological advancements and industrial expansion, generating industry-ready graduates in key fields such as engineering and IT. As a result, Russia benefits from relatively high levels of productivity in its core industries, and its economy continues to develop as a competitive player in global markets, particularly in areas requiring high technical expertise.

India faces a significant challenge in aligning its educational outputs with labour market demands, particularly in the fields of IT and engineering. Table 6 reveals that India has a high demand for IT professionals, engineers, and skilled labour across various sectors. However, the country's education system produces only a moderate output in STEM fields, with limited emphasis on vocational training programs. The severe mismatch in vocational skills is particularly troubling, as many workers graduate from the education system without the specific skills required for high-demand sectors such as IT, engineering, and manufacturing. This mismatch limits India's ability to compete effectively in global markets, especially in technology-driven industries, where advanced skills are critical for maintaining competitiveness. While India has made significant strides in areas like information technology, the limited availability of skilled labour in key sectors restricts its overall economic growth and its ability to capitalise on its demographic advantage fully.

China's education system, as detailed in Table 6, is highly aligned with labour market demands, particularly in the STEM and technology sectors. The country faces a high demand for STEM professionals, particularly in innovation-driven sectors, and its educational output matches these needs. China produces a high number of STEM graduates and has focused its vocational training efforts on providing the technical skills required by the modern labour market. The low mismatch between China's educational outputs and the demands of the labour market ensures that the workforce is well-equipped to meet the needs of the country's rapidly evolving economy. This alignment has been a key factor in China's success in becoming a global leader in manufacturing, technology, and innovation. The result is enhanced competitiveness and a workforce capable of driving the country's economic growth in cutting-edge industries like artificial intelligence, robotics, and biotechnology. China's ability to foster this synergy between education and labour market needs has played a central role in its impressive economic performance.

South Africa, facing a distinct set of challenges, struggles to align its education system with the demands of the labour market. The country's economy requires skilled labour in sectors such as mining, agriculture, and services, yet South Africa's education system produces a low output of vocational training and skilled labour graduates. Table 6 highlights a significant mismatch in skills, particularly in industries such as mining and services, where the demand for skilled workers far exceeds the supply of adequately trained professionals. This skills gap limits job creation and hinders the country's ability to fully integrate its economy, preventing the generation of sufficient employment opportunities. The shortage of skilled labour further exacerbates South Africa's structural economic challenges, including high unemployment and inequality. As a result, the country faces challenges in achieving sustainable economic development and increasing its economic competitiveness on the global stage.

In conclusion, Table 6 presents a detailed analysis of the relationship between labour market demands and educational outcomes in the BRICS countries. The table illustrates the varying levels of alignment between educational systems and labour market needs, with significant implications for economic growth. While countries like Russia and China have successfully aligned their education systems with the demands of their labour markets, resulting in high workforce productivity and economic growth, others, like Brazil, India, and South Africa, continue to face challenges in bridging the skills gap. These mismatches between the skills produced by the education system and the needs of the economy limit innovation, industrial growth, and competitiveness in global markets. For BRICS nations to sustain long-term economic growth, it is essential to address these skills mismatches by adapting education systems to meet the evolving demands of the labour market, particularly in high-tech and innovation-driven sectors.

Table 7. Social Inequality and Education's Impact on Economic Development

Country	Educational Inequality Index	Impact on Economic Development	Policy Interventions	Effectiveness of Interventions
Brazil	High, with significant regional disparities	Economic growth is hindered by educational access disparities	Bolsa Família, education reforms for rural areas	Low, still a significant gap in access
Russia	Low, but disparities between urban and rural areas	Economic development is driven by higher education access, but rural areas lag	Government-funded education reforms in rural areas	Moderate, rural areas still lag behind
India	Very high, rural vs. urban education disparity	Economic growth stunted by inequality in access to quality education	Initiatives for digital learning and rural access improvement	Limited effectiveness, needs systemic change
China	Low, though disparities in rural areas persist	Economic growth is strongly bolstered by near-universal access to education.	Government investments in rural education and universal schooling	High, rural education is improving steadily
South Africa	Very high, with a legacy of apartheid disparities	Economic growth is severely limited by unequal access to quality education	Post-apartheid education reforms focus on equity	Slow progress, needs focused effort on inclusivity

Table 7, "Social Inequality and Education's Impact on Economic Development," highlights the relationship between educational inequality and economic growth across the BRICS nations. Countries such as Brazil, India, and South Africa face significant disparities in access to quality education, particularly between urban and rural areas, which hinders economic growth. While policy interventions, such as Brazil's Bolsa Família and India's digital learning initiatives, have been implemented, their effectiveness remains limited. In contrast, China and Russia have made notable strides in reducing educational inequality, particularly in rural areas, which has fostered stronger economic growth. However, persistent disparities in certain regions continue to affect overall development, necessitating continued policy focus.

DISCUSSION

The comparative examination of educational leadership and management across the BRICS polities reveals a paradoxical terrain where governance architectures, pedagogical imperatives, and economic exigencies converge yet often collide, producing outcomes that are simultaneously transformative and deficient (Menter et al., 2024b). Centralised regimes demonstrate remarkable efficacy in orchestrating systemic coherence and aligning curricular trajectories with industrial priorities; yet, they frequently suffocate localised innovation and contextual adaptability, thereby engendering structural rigidity that is inimical to long-term dynamism. Conversely, decentralised and hybrid frameworks confer autonomy and responsiveness. Still, they often exacerbate regional inequities and institutional fragmentation, undermining the universalism of educational opportunity and attenuating the capacity of human capital formation to translate into aggregate productivity (İmre-Bıyıklı & Kamil, 2024). Layered upon these structural dilemmas are entrenched socio-historical asymmetries, resource maldistributions, and persistent skill mismatches that compromise the very telos of education as a developmental instrument. The analysis thus foregrounds the ineluctable complexity of reconciling equity with efficiency, central oversight with local adaptability, and policy aspiration with practical execution, while simultaneously demonstrating that the economic dividends of education are neither automatic nor uniform but profoundly mediated by the quality of governance, the vision of leadership, and the capacity of management to synchronise institutional performance with national developmental trajectories (Yi et al., 2024).

RECOMMENDATIONS FOR FUTURE RESEARCH

The imperatives emergent from this inquiry necessitate a recalibration of educational governance wherein policymakers institutionalise hybridised architectures that judiciously reconcile the centripetal forces of central oversight with the centrifugal imperatives of localised adaptability, ensuring both systemic coherence and contextual responsiveness, while simultaneously enacting redistributive frameworks that ameliorate rural–urban asymmetries in infrastructure, pedagogy, and resource endowments. Leadership capacity-building must be elevated from a peripheral concern to a central policy priority, cultivating transformational actors capable of translating policy blueprints into practical realities. Robust monitoring and evaluative mechanisms should be embedded within the institutional fabric to generate longitudinal feedback loops, linking educational interventions to labour market dynamics and macroeconomic performance. Future research trajectories ought to transcend the descriptive orthodoxy of correlation by deploying longitudinal, mixed-method, and comparative methodologies that illuminate causal pathways, interrogate micro-level leadership styles, and explore the mediating role of institutional culture in conditioning systemic outcomes, while simultaneously incorporating emergent vectors such as digitalisation, artificial intelligence, and e-learning governance as transformative forces recalibrating the education–growth nexus. Moreover, scholarship must embed an equity-sensitive lens attentive to the differential experiences of marginalised constituencies, women, rural populations, and socio-economically disadvantaged groups, thus ensuring that the discourse on educational leadership transcends its technocratic moorings and contributes to a more inclusive and sustainable developmental paradigm that can furnish policymakers with actionable blueprints while furnishing future scholars with fertile epistemic terrain for inquiry.

CONCLUSION

In conclusion, the comparative analysis of the BRICS nations' educational systems and their impact on economic growth reveals a complex relationship between education, labour market demands, and economic development. Each country's academic leadership, management practices, policies, and the alignment of educational outputs with economic goals vary significantly, shaping their respective economic trajectories. Brazil, despite significant investment in expanding educational access, struggles with regional disparities and a mismatch in technical skills, which limits its innovation and industrial growth. Russia, with a strong focus on STEM education and vocational training, has aligned its education system with industrial goals, thereby fostering a competitive workforce; however, rural areas lag. India faces significant challenges in bridging the rural-urban educational divide, which limits its ability to harness its demographic advantage and compete effectively in the global market, despite efforts to increase digital education and rural access. China stands out with its highly aligned educational system that has fuelled technological innovation and industrial competitiveness, contributing significantly to its economic growth. South Africa, with its deep-rooted educational inequalities stemming from apartheid, continues to grapple with the challenge of providing equitable education for all, hindering its economic development despite post-apartheid reforms.

The educational inequalities in these nations, whether in access, quality, or alignment with labour market needs, remain a significant factor influencing their economic performance. While countries like China and Russia have made substantial progress in aligning education with economic goals, others, such as Brazil, India, and South Africa, face ongoing challenges that require systemic reforms to improve access, quality, and relevance of education. Addressing these disparities through focused and inclusive educational reforms is crucial for fostering sustainable economic growth and enhancing global competitiveness.

In essence, for BRICS nations to fully leverage education as a tool for economic advancement, they must continue to invest in addressing inequalities, aligning education systems with labour market demands, and fostering a highly skilled workforce capable of driving innovation and industrial development.

REFERENCES

Alfehaid, M. M. A., Johri, A., Sehajpal, S., & Jain, A. (2025). Exploring the Synergies Between SDG 9 and SDG 3: The Role of Innovation and Infrastructure in Enhancing Public Health. *International Journal of Sustainable Development and Planning, 20*(6), 2293–2315. DOI: 10.18280/ijsdp.200604

Altbach, P. G., Androushchak, G., Kuzminov, Y., Yudkevich, M., & Reisberg, L. (2013). The global future of higher education and the academic profession: The BRICs and the United States. In *The Global Future of Higher Education and the Academic Profession: The BRICs and the United States*. Palgrave Macmillan., DOI: 10.1057/9780230369795

Amaral, N. C. (2016). Higher education in Brazil: Dilemmas, challenges and comparison with oecd and brics countries [A educação superior brasileira: Dilemas, desafios e comparações com os países da OCDE e do BRICS]. *Revista Brasileira de Educação, 21*(66), 717–736. DOI: 10.1590/S1413-24782016216637

Carnoy, M., Froumin, I., Loyalka, P. K., & Tilak, J. B. G. (2014). The concept of public goods, the state, and higher education finance: A view from the BRICs. *Higher Education, 68*(3), 359–378. DOI: 10.1007/s10734-014-9717-1

Chaudhary, L., Musacchio, A., Nafziger, S., & Yan, S. (2012). Big BRICs, weak foundations: The beginning of public elementary education in Brazil, Russia, India, and China. *Explorations in Economic History, 49*(2), 221–240. DOI: 10.1016/j.eeh.2012.02.001

Chisholm, L., & Chissale, A. (2025). BRICS, sub-imperialism and education in Mozambique [ ]. *Comparative Education, 61*(2), 225–243. DOI: 10.1080/03050068.2024.2372209

Chowdhury, S., Dey, P., Joel-Edgar, S., Bhattacharya, S., Rodriguez-Espindola, O., Abadie, A., & Truong, L. (2023). Unlocking the value of artificial intelligence in human resource management through AI capability framework. *Human Resource Management Review, 33*(1), 100899. DOI: 10.1016/j.hrmr.2022.100899

Daniels, C., & Niemczyk, E. K. (2023). Towards Higher Education for Sustainable Development in BRICS: Focus on Brazil and South Africa. *Space and Culture, India, 11*(1), 68–77. DOI: 10.20896/saci.v11i1.1354

Dong, R., Song, J., Jiang, T., & Baloch, M. A. (2024). Environmental Sustainability Across BRICS Economies: The Dynamics Among the Digital Economy, Education, and CO2 Emissions. *Journal of the Knowledge Economy, 16*(1), 4125–4145. Advance online publication. DOI: 10.1007/s13132-024-02154-x

Fan, X., Liu, H., Wang, Y., Wan, Y., & Zhang, D. (2022). Models of Internationalization of Higher Education in Developing Countries, A Perspective of International Research Collaboration in BRICS Countries. *Sustainability (Basel)*, *14*(20), 13659. Advance online publication. DOI: 10.3390/su142013659

Ferreira, M., Kunn-Nelen, A., & De Grip, A. (2017). Work-related learning and skill development in Europe: Does initial skill mismatch matter? *Research in Labor Economics*, *45*, 345–407. DOI: 10.1108/S0147-912120170000045010

İmre-Bıyıklı, S., & Kamil, A. A. (2024). Measurement of Education Effectiveness in the BRICS countries and Turkey [Medición de la Eficacia de la Educación en los Países BRICS y Turquía]. *Multidisciplinary Journal of Educational Research*, *14*(3), 361–376. DOI: 10.17583/remie.8990

Iqbal, M., Ul-Durar, S., Arshed, N., Shahzad, K., & Ayub, U. (2025). Connecting higher education and renewable energy to attain sustainability for BRICS countries: A climate Kuznets curve perspective. *International Journal of Emerging Markets*, *20*(5), 2042–2060. DOI: 10.1108/IJOEM-04-2023-0555

Jenna Degan. (2013). Stronger Together: Team Teaching as a Strategy to Curb Burnout, Boost Teacher Efficacy, and Increase Student Engagement. *Uniwersytet Śląski*, *7*(1), 343–354. https://doi.org/10.2/JQUERY.MIN.JS

Kangotra, R., & Sehajpal, S. (2025). Voices without faces: The impact of Deepfake technology on authentic communication. In *Deepfake Technology Dilemmas: Mastering Managerial Navigation*. Nova Science Publishers Inc. https://www.scopus.com/inward/record.uri?eid=2-s2.0-105008365079&partnerID=40&md5=9c100d69117b318e7f59445149fea920

Kukreti, M., Sehajpal, S., Tiwari, R., & Sood, K. (2024). Driving global health and sustainable development goals with smart technology. In *Driving Global Health and Sustainable Development Goals With Smart Technology*. IGI Global., DOI: 10.4018/979-8-3373-0240-9

Ligęza, A., Kluza, K., Jemioło, P., Sepioło, D., Wiśniewski, P., & Jobczyk, K. (2021). Evaluation of Selected Artificial Intelligence Technologies for Innovative Business Intelligence Applications. In A. J. (Ed.), *Springer Proceedings in Mathematics and Statistics* (Vol. 364, pp. 111 – 126). Springer. DOI: 10.1007/978-3-030-92604-5_11

Manzoor, S., Abbas, A., Chen, S., Zhang, G., & Khan, A. (2025). Response of energy transition and education in promoting the ecological balance in the BRICS countries. *Renewable Energy*, *247*, 122859. Advance online publication. DOI: 10.1016/j.renene.2025.122859

Masalimova, A. R., Orekhovskaya, N. A., Pivovarov, V. A., Borovikova, Y. V., Zhirkova, G. P., & Chauzova, V. A. (2024). Analysing trends in online learning in higher education in the BRICS countries through bibliometric data. *Frontiers in Education, 9*, 1409013. Advance online publication. DOI: 10.3389/feduc.2024.1409013

Menter, I. (2024). The BRICS alliance and the impact of globalisation on teacher education worldwide. In *Globalisation and Teacher Education in the BRICS Countries: The Positioning of Research and Practice in Comparative Perspective*. Taylor and Francis., DOI: 10.4324/9781003388173-2

Menter, I., Valeeva, R. A., & Prata-Linhares, M. (2024a). Globalisation and Teacher Education in the BRICS Countries: The Positioning of Research and Practice in Comparative Perspective. In *Globalisation and Teacher Education in the BRICS Countries: The Positioning of Research and Practice in Comparative Perspective*. Taylor and Francis., DOI: 10.4324/9781003388173-11

Menter, I., Valeeva, R. A., & Prata-Linhares, M. (2024b). The impact of globalisation on teacher education in the BRICS countries. In *Globalisation and Teacher Education in the BRICS Countries: The Positioning of Research and Practice in Comparative Perspective*. Taylor and Francis., DOI: 10.4324/9781003388173-11

Mohammadi, M. (2024). Advancing an Integrative AI-assisted Adaptive Learning Environment for Teacher Education: Case of the BRICS Countries. *Education and Self Development, 19*(4), 82–95. DOI: 10.26907/esd.19.4.07

Mussaiyib, A. M., & Pradhan, K. C. (2024). An empirical analysis of causal nexus between higher education and economic growth in BRICS countries. *Transnational Corporations Review, 16*(3), 200057. Advance online publication. DOI: 10.1016/j.tncr.2024.200057

Novgorodtseva, A. N., & Belyaeva, E. A. (2020). Internationalization of higher education in Russia: Sociocultural interaction of students from the BRICS countries (Russia, China) [Интернационализация высшего образования в России: социокультурное взаимодействие студентов из стран БРИКС (Россия, Китай)]. *Perspektivy Nauki i Obrazovania, 45*(3), 517–526. DOI: 10.32744/pse.2020.3.37

Ponomarev, S. V., Mirgorod, E. E., Beilina, A. F., Chudaeva, A. A., & Maksaev, A. A. (2024). Online Education in BRICS Countries: New Opportunities for Post-pandemic Development. *Advances in Science. Technology and Innovation*, (Part F2356), 373–378. DOI: 10.1007/978-3-031-49711-7_62

Ratzinger, D., Amess, K., Greenman, A., & Mosey, S. P. (2018). The impact of digital start-up founders' higher education on reaching equity investment milestones. *The Journal of Technology Transfer*, *43*(3), 760–778. DOI: 10.1007/s10961-017-9627-3 PMID: 31258242

Saito, A. T., Dias Fouto, N. M. M., & De Angelo, C. F. (2018). Consumption and bank credit at the BRICS countries: A new light on the financial education process. *International Journal of Education Economics and Development*, *9*(4), 366–393. DOI: 10.1504/IJEED.2018.096064

Sart, G., Bayar, Y., Sezgin, F. H., Danilina, M. V., & Karagöz, E. (2025). The effect of shadow economy, life expectancy, education, and income on CO2 emissions: An analysis of BRICS countries. *Frontiers in Environmental Science*, *13*, 1550389. Advance online publication. DOI: 10.3389/fenvs.2025.1550389

Shuangshuang, Y., Zhu, W., Mughal, N., Aparcana, S. I. V., & Muda, I. (2023). The impact of education and digitalisation on female labour force participation in BRICS: An advanced panel data analysis. *Humanities & Social Sciences Communications*, *10*(1), 598. Advance online publication. DOI: 10.1057/s41599-023-02020-2

Silvestre, B. S. (2015). Sustainable supply chain management in emerging economies: Environmental turbulence, institutional voids and sustainability trajectories. *International Journal of Production Economics*, *167*, 156–169. DOI: 10.1016/j.ijpe.2015.05.025

Singh, M., Sehajpal, S., & Khati, K. S. (2025). Global branding partnerships for financial growth and SDG 17: Building sustainable and inclusive economic strategies. In *Brand Creation and Management in the Phygital Era* (pp. 307–340). IGI Global., DOI: 10.4018/979-8-3373-0948-4.ch012

Tsaurai, K. (2017). Education-economic growth nexus in BRICS countries: Does financial development matter? *International Journal of Education Economics and Development*, *8*(4), 250–265. DOI: 10.1504/IJEED.2017.088817

Valeeva, R., Kalimullin, A., & Baklashova, T. (2024). Editorial: BRICS Countries on the Improvement of Teacher Education. *Education and Self Development*, *19*(3), 6–8. DOI: 10.26907/esd.19.3.01

Xing, W., & Imran, A. (2025). Financial and Technological Drivers of Sustainable Development: The Role of Communication Technology, Financial Efficiency and Education in BRICS. *Sustainability (Basel)*, *17*(5), 2326. Advance online publication. DOI: 10.3390/su17052326

Yi, H., Wang, G., & Feng, J. (2024). Gender inequality: Policy responses to employment and education in BRICS countries. *African Journal of Reproductive Health, 28*(12), 88–96. DOI: 10.29063/ajrh2024/v28i12.10 PMID: 39764841

Zhang, X., & Xiao, L. (2025). Eco-literate societies: The interplay of education, environmental policy stringency, and digital innovation in BRICS nations. *Frontiers in Environmental Science, 13*, 1607166. Advance online publication. DOI: 10.3389/fenvs.2025.1607166

Zhu, Y., Zafar, S. M., & Salahodjaev, R. (2022). Mitigations pathways towards sustainable development: Assessing the influence of higher education on environmental quality in BRICS economies. *Environmental Science and Pollution Research International, 29*(57), 86851–86858. DOI: 10.1007/s11356-022-21772-z PMID: 35802318

Zvereva, E. V, Belenkova, N. M., & Kruse, I. I. (2020). From the economic union to the harmonisation of higher education in the BRICS countries: The experience of RUDN University. *Space and Culture, India, 7*(5), 60 – 69.://DOI: 10.20896/saci.v7i5.671

KEY TERMS AND DEFINITIONS

BRICS Context: An acronym for Brazil, Russia, India, China, and South Africa, BRICS denotes a geopolitical bloc of emerging economies whose heterogeneous governance architectures and developmental trajectories provide fertile ground for comparative inquiry into the education–growth nexus.

Economic Growth: Rooted in classical and neoclassical economic theory, economic growth signifies the sustained increase in a nation's productive capacity, often measured via GDP expansion, but more expansively construed to incorporate productivity, innovation, and equitable human development catalysed by education.

Educational Leadership: Deriving from the etymological root *ducere* (to lead), educational leadership refers to the strategic orchestration of vision, governance, and pedagogical direction within academic institutions, transcending mere administration to encompass the mobilisation of human and material resources toward the enhancement of learning outcomes and systemic resilience.

Educational Management: Originating in organisational theory, educational management denotes the technical and procedural coordination of inputs, processes, and outputs in the educational enterprise, emphasising accountability, efficiency, and optimisation of resource utilisation in alignment with broader institutional and national objectives.

Human Capital: Human capital encapsulates the aggregate stock of skills, knowledge, and competencies embodied in individuals, which, when cultivated through education and training, function as productive assets contributing to innovation, productivity, and economic growth.

Chapter 5
Sustainable Education and Economic Development:
A Critique of the Kerala (India) Model

Jipson Joseph
https://orcid.org/0009-0005-1795-5051
Christ University, India

ABSTRACT

Education is essential for society's growth and economic development. From the UDHR, all international conventions, national constitutions, and enactments have prioritised education for transforming society. This became more explicit with the SDG4 (quality education). Based on the UDHR and SDG4 guidelines, India also prioritises augmenting the educational sector in its policies and programs. The national education policies provide a foundational framework for this effort. Although many researchers praise the 'Kerala model' of education, several others sharply criticise it as not aligning with the demands of quality and job market requirements. In 2023, almost 250000 students emigrated from Kerala for educational purposes. The student emigration constitutes nearly 11.3% of the state's total emigration, raising serious concerns about the quality of education. From this perspective, this chapter critically examines sustainable education and economic development aspirations, evaluating the educational landscape of the most literate state in India, Kerala.

DOI: 10.4018/979-8-3373-3616-9.ch005

INTRODUCTION

According to Article 26 of the Universal Declaration of Human Rights (UDHR), education is a fundamental human right. Many national Constitutions, like India, have recognised this basic right and affirmed the importance of free and compulsory education of children for their well-being and sustainable growth. Article 21-A of the Constitution of India recognises and affirms the scope of this right. The central and state governments have shown positive and progressive attitudes towards the educational rights of the people of India (NITI Aayog, 2025). With the international shift towards sustainable development, people's academic aspirations were situated in the context of sustainable education (Kulal et al., 2024). Sustainable education revolves around the three pillars of sustainability: social, economic, and environmental. It affirms that the education provided to children should enable them to live a meaningful life in society with adequate financial strength and respect for the environment (Mohanty, 2018). Sustainable education encourages children to become the optimum members of society who prioritise its values and welfare (Schank & Rieckmann, 2019). Countries like India, through their national education policies and timely updates, underline the importance of sustainable education in both public and private sectors (NITI Aayog, 2025).

Quality education is often considered a prerequisite for economic growth (Hanushek & Wö mann, 2007). Increasing the educational levels and quality gives more opportunities and possibilities for financial advancement and economic development (Kumari et al., 2023). Compared to the developing world, the academic options are higher in the developed world. It provides more opportunities for their people to advance in economic matters. Advancements in education improve the possibilities of research, scientific and technological growth, and infrastructure development, leading to the country's economic development (Weber, 2011). Education and economic development are complementary. As the number of academic options increases, so does economic growth.

Although India is the most populous country, its educational level is not equal to that of developed countries. There are significant changes in the academic level of the country. However, there are regions and remote areas where education is not emphasised (Ghosh, 2011). It is also applicable to gender discrimination and education. Women are denied education in many regions of India (Husain, 2011). However, the State of Kerala remains a rare exception, as the government claims 96.2% literacy (Sawgiary, 2024). It also prioritises the academic growth of its children through public and private educational institutions. Kerala affirms that sustainable economic development is possible mainly through education (Bairagya & Joy, 2022). Kerala's achievements in the last 25 years establish this progressive vision. However, many public sector schools lack proper orientation and commitment, affecting students' academic progress. The private schools demand high fees, making them unapproachable for average families. Until recently, college education was a public sector monopoly, and no private university was permitted in the state (NITI Aayog, 2025). University life is associated with political ideologies and interactions, affecting students' academic progress (Kumar & George, 2009). On the one side, there is an affirmation that the State of Kerala is highly literate and prioritises children's educational progress. On the other hand, many students migrate to neighbouring states or other countries due to the lack of quality educational institutions (Sarkar, 2024).

From this perspective, the chapter critically examines the prestigious Kerala education model through the lens of sustainable education and economic development. The chapter analyses the various strategies, initiatives, and policies of the government of Kerala and their impact on the educational sector. The chapter critically explains this model's benefits and drawbacks, affirming the need for a policy change.

CONCEPTUAL FRAMEWORK

The changes in the economic landscape of the society also influence its social and other dimensions. During the agrarian economy, most families preferred more children, as they could be incorporated into the labour force of their fields. They did not prioritise their children's education, as it would affect their labour strength (Bentley et al., 1993). Society's shift toward an industrial economy changed this approach, which became more explicit with the growth of the professional sectors in the second half of the 20th century. It was realised that the higher the number of skilled labourers, the greater the productivity and the technological advancements (Apostu et al., 2022). Education primarily contributes to augmenting workers' skills and promoting technological advancements. Including educated and skilled workers in a particular sector redefines its functioning method. Highly educated and trained workers are given higher wages, increasing their spending. Production of goods and services also increases along with an increase in spending.

When both productivity and technological advancements increase, it contributes to economic development (Hanushek & Wö mann, 2007). Almost all countries prioritised knowledge generation and skill training, imagining that these would address the concerns of the market. They were predominantly oriented towards market empowerment. However, from the last quarter of the same century, the globe revolved around the inspirational idea of sustainability, which was propagated by the Brundtland Report (WECD, 1987). It also influenced the field of education, broadening its scope in connection with sustainability. The interplay between sustainability and education brings out the inspirational idea of sustainable education that revolves around sustainable development's economic, social, and cultural perspectives (Mohanty, 2018). The new growth theory affirms that education influences economic development by accumulating human capital. The policy that temporarily and permanently enhances education increases economic development with short-term and long-term effects (Bah, 2023).

EDUCATION

Any nation has specific socioeconomic, cultural, and developmental needs. These requirements can be effectively met through a systematic education system (Weber, 2011). Education is the most potent weapon to change society, as it prioritises enlightening individuals and communities. Education helps individuals understand things efficiently, apply them to their daily activities, and influence others to change their lives (Thangeda et al., 2016). Education thus functions as a tool to transform oneself and society. Its purpose is to impart knowledge and skills to learners to make them capable of achieving a dignified living. The central objective of education is to promote the learning skills of people (European Commission, 2013). Primary education is the solid foundation of the whole educational system. Secondary and tertiary education energise students to be more productive and achieve better outcomes. It is said that receiving quality education at a younger age has more scope than the quantity of education. Highly educated individuals are supposed to have the skills and positive attitudes to influence the economy and society (Apostu et al., 2022).

Education is often concerned with quality. Many parents, students, researchers, and policymakers usually argue that the current education system has no required quality. They say that the education system fails to provide proper knowledge and skills, offer adequate employment opportunities, and transform the lives of individuals and society. Quality education thus involves all these essential concerns. To be precise, quality education should incorporate excellence, perfection, value for money, commitment, competence, sustainability, and service to society (Bruçaj, 2014). Accordingly, quality education is a multidimensional concept with many vital components that significantly influence individuals and society (Sallis, 2002). An educational system's quality depends on various factors, like the offered program, the system of teaching, the academic quality and efficiency of the teachers, and the learning environment (European Commission, 2013). The program should be diverse enough to make the student competent and efficient in various fields. The qualification of the teachers matters. However, the most essential concern is how the teachers impart knowledge and skills to the students. The teaching system should prioritise research and development. It should encourage the students to do original research. The learning environment has great potential to transform the students. It consists of the institution's focus on providing enhanced infrastructure for the sustainable education of the students. The appropriate functioning of various labs, a systematic and up-to-date library system, effective methods of plagiarism check, and a systematic method of student-teacher interaction. It also insists that the institution must promote a learning environment to ensure better results from the students. The learning environment denotes an institution's standards of reference for its students (Thangeda et al., 2016).

SUSTAINABLE EDUCATION

Sustainable education evolved in the context of sustainable development (Mohanty, 2018). Chapter 36 of Agenda 21 states that education is a vital component of sustainable development, which improves people's capacity to address and balance environmental and developmental concerns. It received momentum by including education as a specific goal in the Millennium Development Goals (MDGs). MDG2 underlines the UN's inspirational objective to achieve universal primary education. It wanted to ensure a full course of primary schooling to every boy and girl, regardless of regional differences, by 2015. It tried to achieve just six years of compulsory education to realise this goal. It affirms that the globe has gained 91% of literacy by the end of 2015. However, such an effort ensured basic literacy without empowering people with appropriate knowledge and skills in many countries. In this context, the Sustainable Development Goals (SDGs) broadened the scope of the UN's goal of education. SDG4 stands for the UN's inspirational objective to ensure inclusive and equitable education and promote lifelong learning opportunities for all. Compared to MDG2, SDG4 does not impose any limitations on its scope. It is neither restricted to developing countries nor to elementary education. It has unique objectives: ensuring inclusive and equitable education and promoting lifelong learning opportunities. Education is not exclusive to any group. It includes everyone regardless of differentiating parameters, like sex, colour, economic status, and religion. It also underlines that education is a lifelong opportunity, not restricted to any particular age group. Accordingly, the SDGs (particularly SDG4) broadened the scope of education and included sustainability aspirations as a vital component.

Globalisation has redefined the global approach towards growth and development. It limited the international developmental approach to economic growth and market politics. Although the globe has realised the drawbacks of this uncontrollable attention towards economic growth, it requires time and a mindset change to adapt to the sustainable developmental objectives. It should function as a leitmotif for shifting people's mindset and making judgments and choices in favour of sustainable development (Schank & Rieckmann, 2019). Sustainable education is the framework that enables students to become protagonists of social, economic, and environmental transformation. Although attempts to achieve meaningful, sustainable education should start with elementary education, they can be substantially achieved only during higher education, when students become more aware of their social commitments (Agasisti & Petrenko, 2024). It underlines the importance of higher education for economic growth and societal transformation. Sustainable education demands that its primary objectives be within the progressive dimensions of sustainable development (economic, social, and environmental) (Abad-Segura & González-Zamar, 2021). Education should orient towards economic growth, environmental protection, and societal transformation. Absence of one of these core elements affirms that education has lost its sustainability radar to guarantee the desired objective.

ECONOMIC DEVELOPMENT

Any society's economic growth revolves around two central concepts: production and income level. If an economy shows a sustained increase in output and income level, it indicates substantial economic growth (Panayotou, 2016). Economic development is a broader term that also includes improving people's quality of life. People's quality of life can be observed with the advancements in various fields, like education, healthcare, society, economy, and politics (Abad-Segura & González-Zamar, 2021). Economic development is the sum of economic growth and improvements in people's quality of life. After the 2008 global financial crisis, many countries have focused on steadying their economic development. This move has become more explicit in the aftermath of the COVID-19 pandemic. However, the issue with economic growth is that it is a quantitative indicator, measured through a country's productive capacity and employment generation. Since it revolves around the calculation of GDP, it does not provide vital information, nor is it concerned with the quality of life in a society or its relevant factors, such as education and healthcare (Schank & Riekmann, 2019).

On the other hand, economic development is concerned with all these vital elements in addition to economic growth. Besides, with the evolution of sustainability, economic development has also included it in its ambit, advancing the idea of sustainable economic development. Abad-Segura and González-Zamar (2021) argue that this uncontrollable concentration on economic growth harmed sustainable economic development aspirations, as it did not equitably promote the inhabitants' quality of life and protect the environment. Sustainability in economic development means generating equitable wealth without degrading the environment.

Economic growth is mainly understood and measured in terms of GDP per capita. It follows the income-based calculation approach. However, it is often criticised as inefficient, as "it fails to measure the quality and well-being of economic development" (Kumari et al., 2023, p.4353). In contrast, economic development is measured by calculating the percentage of people above the poverty line, unemployment level, availability of basic infrastructure facilities, food security, healthcare facilities, human development, environmental protective measures, and societal well-being. By increasing people's living standards, education also positively contributes to economic development (Apostu et al., 2022). Education is a significant factor for eradicating poverty and achieving the SDGs. Poverty is the opposite of individual well-being and societal welfare. It continues through generations if people lack opportunities to excel through quality education. The advancements in education provide them with facilities to improve their standard of living. Since education positively changes people's quality of life, it implies that education leads to economic development. The SDGs affirm that the globe should strive to achieve social, economic, and environmental aspects of sustainable development to realise a sustainable future. The global population should know the national and international policies toward achieving the SDGs. It would only be possible when they can experience and evaluate the system's potential (Abu Alfoul et al., 2024).

Education increases an individual's earnings and productivity. Human capital engagement was considered the key driver of economic growth until the last decade of the 19th century. Thereafter, it was understood that the interplay between human capital and education can increase productivity and economic benefits (Valero, 2021). Similarly, a lack of education in a society due to financial matters or policy failures, or people's early withdrawal from the field of education due to a lack of encouragement and interest, can harm the economy (Camilla, 2023). However, scholars argue that when educational institutions increase considerably, their capacity to promote economic growth becomes marginal (Li et al., 2024). Since the economy is one of the easiest parameters to examine society's well-being, many undermine the importance of overall development to ensure a meaningful quality of life. The society should be explored through the prism of economic growth, which becomes explicit by analysing people's quality of life, for its march toward a sustainable future.

INTERPLAY BETWEEN EDUCATION AND ECONOMIC DEVELOPMENT

Various researchers have studied the influence of education on economic development. Education is the foundational element of human capital. Education adds quality and efficiency to human capital, increasing productivity. Romer (1986) and Lucas (1988) were the primary researchers who significantly studied the interconnection between education, human capital, and economic growth. Although some scholars doubt the influence of education on economic development, most researchers agree that they are closely interlinked. However, scholars affirm that if the education field compromises quality, it does not positively influence education (Abu Alfoul et al., 2024). Some studies state that the positive correlation between education and economic development cannot always be established in all countries. It varies depending on the level of wealth. However, it is argued that a minimum of 1% annual economic growth could be achieved if the secondary education enrolment is increased from 50% to 100% (Barro, 1991). It shows that, compared to primary education, secondary education is more beneficial to economic development.

Higher education has a vital role in the growth of an individual, society, and economy. The higher the level of education is, the greater the possibility of getting well-paid employment opportunities and contributing to society's economic development and welfare. Studies reveal that those with higher educational qualifications have an increased chance of employment opportunities. If the desired jobs are unavailable, they will have the skills and capacity to initiate their start-ups and other ventures, which can contribute to the economy. Since their creativity and innovation are more vibrant, they can influence the dynamics of the economy significantly (Thangeda et al., 2016). Regardless of the nature of countries, universities and higher education institutions have the potential to produce highly skilled human capital that can influence economic growth and the sustainable development of that country (Agasisti & Petrenko, 2024).

Education is closely associated with economic development, as studies have revealed that the inequality in education has more negative effects on economic development than the inequality in income (Blanden & McNally, 2015). Developed countries focus more on research and development, as they are economically stable to enforce such activities. It empowers them to promote more innovations and technological advancements, benefiting economic development. In contrast, developing countries cannot concentrate adequately on research and innovation, as their public funds are limited. They are supposed to become satisfied with an average higher education level, without pushing them to more innovative methods and research. Accordingly, many students with creative ideas and research capacity migrate to developed countries to continue their studies and research. After the studies, they remain in those countries, contributing to their economy and society (Agasisti & Petrenko, 2024). It creates a situation where the human capital of the developing world is systematically promoting the economic development of the developed world. It also causes the existing societal and economic disparity to continue. The current economic drawbacks cause a hindrance for developing countries to pursue success and economic development in the future. Such is primarily due to the failure of policy in developing countries. They fail to ensure an adequate and systematic educational system for their people. Accordingly, their economic development also becomes a huge concern.

Economic development of a country can promote the establishment of quality education institutions. It can improve the educational environment of a country. However, it cannot be assured that, along with economic growth, more students will enrol in higher educational systems (Reisz & Stock, 2012). They argue that it depends on the governmental policies and perspectives. If these provide favourable circumstances, education can enrich the efforts for economic development. Studies also note that the impact of private higher education on economic growth is relatively larger in developing countries than in developed countries (Agasisti & Petrenko, 2024). The developed world focuses more on the public educational system, as it has increased its infrastructure and other essential requirements. Private higher education institutions concentrate on the investments of committed and competent individuals, but the public sector emphasises spending public funds. Besides, since public funds and resources are relatively limited in poor countries (e.g., Romania, Chile, Myanmar, Uganda, and Senegal), they cannot completely guarantee the full functioning of the education system. In such a scenario, the private entrepreneurs focus on education, providing educational facilities for people and increasing their profit (Reisz & Stock, 2012).

THEORETICAL PERSPECTIVES

Marquez-Ramos and Mourelle (2019) analyse the correlation between education and economic growth in Spain through an empirical analysis of nonlinearities. They state that in some instances, there is significant economic growth due to the influence of education, whereas in other cases, the economic growth is comparatively small. No country's economic growth will be the same throughout. There will be variations, and the same applies to the influence of education on economic growth. Valero (2021) summarises the articles related to education and economic growth to broaden the perspective of sustainable education. The article claims that quality education can make significant progress in economic growth. Apostu et al. (2022) examine economic growth through the lens of sustainability, entrepreneurship, and innovation. They specifically focus on the importance of tertiary education in enhancing economic growth. Bairagya and Joy (2022) analyse the quality of higher education in India based on the responses of 416 commerce students from Kerala. They explore the quality of higher education based on the parameters of curriculum, analytical thinking, and communication skills. They argue that although Kerala is famous for quality school education, it fails to ensure quality in higher education. Using an index of human capital of 89 countries based on the mean years of education and returns to education, Bah (2023) states that the effect of education on economic growth relies on the accumulation of human capital rather than its stock. The author also underlines the importance of FDI (Foreign Direct Investment) in improving the educational sector and increasing economic growth. This study claims that low and middle-income countries can achieve higher economic growth in the same manner as high-income countries if they allocate enough resources for education and human capital accumulation.

Kannan (2023) argues that the often acclaimed Kerala development model can be appreciated only for social and human development. It failed to ensure economic development. Accordingly, a good number of educated youth migrate for adequate employment opportunities. Kulal et al. (2024) systematically study the 2020 National Education Policy to show its impact on sustainable development and its various challenges. They provide a basic framework to examine the education system in the country. Analysing the data of 18 Sub-Saharan African countries, Abu Alfoul et al. (2024) state that education contributes to economic growth and sustainable development if there is also a strong institutional framework. The robust institutions have a significant role in enhancing the effectiveness of education, which drives productivity and economic growth. Analysing 150 articles published in reputed journals during 1985-2022, Agasisti and Petrenko (2024) examine how human capital is built through investments in higher education and how it contributes to economic growth in a particular society. This biliometric study points to how higher education contributes to economic growth. Examining the empirical evidence from 38 OECD countries, Li et al. (2024) investigate the impact of popularising higher education on economic growth and poverty alleviation. They argue that it has a significant positive effect on GDP growth. Popularisation of higher education plays a meaningful role in the initial stages of socioeconomic development and enhances the global efforts for sustainable development. They argue that national and local governments are responsible for improving innovative talents and technological outcomes by encouraging higher education possibilities. Such attempts will produce economic growth and alleviate poverty across the globe.

SIGNIFICANCE OF THE STUDY

Blessinger et al. (2019) argue that the increasingly interconnected globe requires improvements in social, political, environmental, economic, and technological fields of human interactions, which can only be achieved through a systematic and progressive education. The global education system has also become complex, along with the global socioeconomic and political order. The complexity of the time demands that the globe experiment with different kinds of educational systems. It can be seen in the academic policies of various countries. The world cannot subscribe to a one-size-fits-all approach to education, as it may not be suitable everywhere. The question here is not about institutional diversity but the policy perspective. The government's policy is the primary concern, as it can positively or negatively influence education. If the policy is inclusive, equitable, and rights-based, it can promote the welfare of all. It should function as a roadmap to achieve universal education for all, individual well-being, sustainable development, and economic growth. To restrict merely to the elementary education demands cannot guarantee all citizens' sustainable development.

Education is a key determinant of individual well-being, human capital development, and economic growth (Marquez-Ramos & Mourelle, 2019). This is particularly true with higher education. Realising the scope of higher education, many developing countries, like India, have started to allocate more resources for advancements in the education system. However, this is not equally applied throughout the country. Some states, such as Kerala, have prioritised education from the very beginning of their formation; others are slowly developing new policies and programs. Kerala is among the most literate states and ranks top in female literacy. Its educational system is consistently regarded as a model in the country. However, the latest trends show that many students migrate abroad or to neighbouring states for higher education due to the limited availability of seats, politicisation of higher education, and a lack of placement opportunities. Besides, the state's lack of high-quality educational institutions also challenges its acclaimed education model. It also fails to provide employment opportunities to the educated youth. From this perspective, this chapter critically evaluates the Kerala education model and its impact on economic growth and sustainable development.

METHODOLOGY

Most studies that have analysed the impact of education on economic growth have used the empirical methodology. Some studies used a theoretical framework for examining and evaluating the interplay between them (Bah, 2023). However, the chapter primarily uses the critical analytical method of doctrinal methodology to explore the Kerala Model of Education from the perspective of sustainable education and economic growth. The objective of this chapter is to critically examine the available data on the Kerala model of education to evaluate whether it aligns with the goals of sustainable education and economic growth. It also uses explorative and analytical tools to explore and analyse the concepts deeply associated with sustainable education.

EDUCATION AND THE DEVELOPING WORLD

First and foremost, education should be examined from the right to education perspective. The UDHR affirmed all people's fundamental right to education in Article 26. Followed by the UDHR, the UNESCO Convention against Discrimination in Education (1960) and the International Covenant on Economic, Social, and Cultural Rights (ICESCR, 1966) further expanded the provisions of the UDHR. Many international covenants and guidelines have followed the same line, strengthening and enhancing the right to education. Based on these affirmations, most countries have included the right to free elementary education in their Constitutions (UNESCO, 2023). It also applies to developing countries. It is shown that countries with faster economic growth allocate more resources to education. Besides, countries with a higher education percentage are more productive than those with a lower rate (Bah, 2023). This can be understood inversely: countries allocating more resources to education can advance economic growth significantly. Researchers argue that the knowledge economy is essential for economic development, especially in developing countries. Suppose they do not design systematic policies and programs to become part of the information/knowledge revolution. In that case, they will again be left aside concerning the industrial and technological growth, leading to economic development (Weber, 2011).

According to the international human rights law, states must respect, protect, and fulfil the human rights framework for its meaningful implementation. It also applies to the right to education. When the international human rights law underlines a particular right as universal, inalienable, and indivisible, the legal protection guaranteed to that specific right and its components applies to all people (UNESCO, 2023). Human rights violations can easily be addressed only when people are more aware of their rights. It would be effective only when people are educated about the positives of human rights. Since most people are unaware of the scope of human rights, they fail to address violations by state authorities or other actors. Accordingly, the right to education is a fundamental right that tries to ensure the realisation of other rights. It implies that states are responsible for respecting, protecting, and fulfilling people's fundamental right to education. The West African country Sierra Leone allocated more budgetary resources to education in 2018. Many countries followed this model. The government's attention on improving a country's educational standards is essential for guaranteeing significant economic and societal growth. Some developing countries have also initiated a mid-day meal program in schools to attract students from low-income families. Some countries also extend the possibility of free education to higher education levels to encourage more participation of students (Bah, 2023). The free or charge concession to support the students' transportation is primarily oriented towards helping students from low-income families, with the objective that their education should not become a burden for the family to meet other bare essentials. This shows that the state is responsible for educating the children for the broadened objective of its future technological advancements, innovative outcomes, and economic growth. Since most constitutions have underlined the right to education as an essential component of the fundamental rights, it becomes a constitutionally assigned responsibility of the states (NITI Aayog, 2025). Compared to developed countries, developing countries should prioritise education in their policies and programs to maintain their growth standards and guarantee a human rights-based approach to education and economic growth.

EDUCATIONAL AND ECONOMIC DEVELOPMENT: INDIAN SCENARIO

Considering the country's population increase and demographic changes, India requires significant economic growth to meet people's demands. This can be achieved only when the country allocates adequate resources and attention to education (Kulal et al., 2024). Developing countries like India have to focus significantly on increasing the quality of human capital with the support of lifelong learning mechanisms to advance economic development objectives (Weber, 2011). India's political and administrative system emphasises education to ensure individual well-being, societal welfare, and sustainable economic development. India has a long history of societal and economic disparity, rooted in the caste system (Bapuji & Chrispal, 2020). The regional inequalities concerning economic development are also evident in India (Kumari et al., 2023). It also faces an unprecedented economic inequality, forcing researchers to affirm that India has moved from a British Raj to a Billionaire Raj (Chancel & Piketty, 2019). Socioeconomic inequality can happen among people and regions during economic growth. It becomes a serious concern for the country when it becomes highly significant and widespread. The wide gap resulting from such a scenario complicates the functioning and progress of Indian society. The concentration of income and wealth in the hands of a few without adequate opportunities for the larger portion of the Indian population to survive is a serious concern. Since GDP is the prime parameter for examining the growth of a country, policymakers and the administrative system are not worried about the prevailing regional and economic inequalities. Although there have been many attempts to eradicate the caste system, poverty, economic inequality, and social disparity, they continue to exist significantly (Ghosh, 2007).

India believes that societal and economic inequalities can easily be addressed through education. The Indian Constitution had listed education as a special category of the state list, entrusting the state governments to make laws, considering the situation of each state. However, with the 42nd Amendment of the Constitution in 1976, it was moved to the concurrent list. Such a move underlines the policymakers' interest in prioritising education over many other concerns, as it provided them with an opportunity for both the central and state governments to play key roles in developing the country's education field (NITI Aayog, 2025). Since education and economic growth are mutually reinforcing fields, progress in education can produce better results in economics (Li et al., 2024). However, India faces inequalities in children's educational opportunities. Das (2016) states that economic and regional disparities determine children's academic future. For instance, children from an Adivasi (indigenous people/forest dwellers) family may not get adequate educational facilities and opportunities compared to the children from the urban areas. Besides, children from low-income families face difficulties pursuing the desired education due to financial barriers.

India accounts for the second-highest higher education enrollment in the world. Enrollment of students cannot be considered a guarantee of quality education. Various agencies have started to assess the quality of education to ensure public accountability. Along with many international agencies, like the Academic Ranking of World Universities (ARWU) and QS World University Rankings, India also has its ranking agencies that evaluate the quality of higher education, like the National Assessment and Accreditation Council (NAAC) and the National Institutional Ranking Framework (NIRF). These mechanisms continuously check and balance the quality of the higher education system in India. However, the desired results have not yet been achieved. According to the US News (USN) source ranking, India ranks 42nd, whereas the World Top 20 rankings place it at 101st. Since there is a close correlation between a country's educational system and economic growth, the low positions in educational rankings also point to low economic development (World Population Review, 2025). This shows India's poor performance in ensuring quality education and significant economic growth. Although India accounts for progress in education and economic development, the data show its poor performance. This necessitates a more concentrated approach and a progressive vision from the policymakers.

ARTICLE 21A OF THE CONSTITUTION OF INDIA

The 86th Amendment Act of the Constitution of India inserted Article 21A, which provides free and compulsory education for all children aged 6 to 14. This Amendment of 2002 designed education as a fundamental right within the provisions of the UDHR. The state had the constitutional obligation to ensure free and compulsory education for children in that age group, even before the 86th Amendment. However, it was not part of the fundamental rights. The Constitutional Fathers had included it as part of the Directive Principles of State Policy. Since it was not part of the fundamental rights, it could not have been questioned in the court if there were failures in providing adequate education to children. The Supreme Court of India, in its historic judgement of 1993 in *Unnikrishnan vs. State of Andhra Pradesh*, affirmed that the right to education evolves from the right to life under Article 21 of the Constitution of India. Besides emphasising the importance of considering the right to education as a fundamental right, this judgment underlined its close connection with other fundamental rights. Besides, the Supreme Court of India in *Ashoka Kumar Thakur vs. Union of India and Others* (2008) affirmed Article 21A as the most fundamental right. It should be strictly implemented in the larger interests of the country. It noted that "without Article 21A, the other fundamental rights are effectively rendered meaningless. Education stands above other rights, as one's ability to enforce one's fundamental rights flows from one's education." Thus, the Supreme Court broadened the scope of Article 21A and insisted that the government prioritise education in its policies and programs.

Realising the importance of situating the right to education within the framework of fundamental rights, and to respect the Supreme Court's judgment, the Parliament enacted the 86th Amendment Act and inserted Article 21A in the Constitution as part of the fundamental rights. Thereafter, the government of India passed the Right of Children to Free and Compulsory Education Act (RTE Act) in 2009 to give full effect to Article 21A. The Right to Education implies that every child has "a right to a full-time elementary education of satisfactory and equitable quality in a formal school which satisfies certain essential norms and standards." Free education means that no child is liable to pay any charge for elementary education. However, this does not apply to those children whose parents admit them to a school that appropriate governments do not support. Compulsory education refers to the obligation of the government and local authorities to ensure admission, attendance, and completion of elementary education for children aged 6-14. Accordingly, India has moved towards a rights-based approach to education (Department of School Education & Literacy, 2021). With the provisions of the RTE Act, the scope of Article 21A has explicitly been established throughout the country.

NATIONAL EDUCATION POLICIES

The education system cannot be static; it should evolve with the changes and requirements of time. The regulatory bodies of any country introduce, modify, and implement specific educational policies to improve the education system, ensuring that it meets the demands of society (Mistry, 2022). Realising the importance of modernising and upgrading the education system, the central government of India framed the National Education Policy (NEP) to guide the country's initiatives on education. The government introduces NEP or other policies primarily based on the recommendations and suggestions of various commissions (Kaurav et al., 2020). The first NEP was introduced in 1968, based on the recommendations of the Kothari Commission, mainly focusing on educating children up to the age of 14 (Kalyani, 2020). Changes in the educational policies are essential to upgrade the education system and to guarantee competency and better results (Kulal et al., 2024). The second NEP was thus introduced in 1986, emphasising the need to standardise the education system and address the disparities between different social groups. It was revised in 1992 (Verma et al., 2021). The central government introduced the third NEP in 2020, based on the recommendations of the Kasturirangan Commission, prioritising the need for a holistic education and transforming India's educational system to address the 21st-century demands. The latest NEP revolves around three core concepts: quality, accessibility, and sustainability (Kulal et al., 2024).

The latest NEP was introduced to align with the demands of SDG4. At the same time, it also highlights the importance of inculcating and practising the core values (compassion, empathy, courage, and resilience) of India's cultural capital. It also encourages scientific curiosity and creative thinking among students, making them more productive and innovative. These measures can guarantee a fair, inclusive, and diverse society (National Education Policy, 2020). It aims to provide quality education from early childhood care to research (Kaurav et al., 2021). The most important transformation in the 2020 NEP is the shift towards a liberal, flexible, and skill-oriented education (Saini et al., 2021). Compared to the previous model of the education system, which prescribed a 10+2+3+2 standard of education, the 2020 NEP suggested a 5+3+3+4+4+1 model (Arun et al., 2022). The undergraduate system has become more student-friendly, designed for 3 or 4 years, with flexible multiple entry and exit options. The NEP 2020 also affirms the importance of the government's increased spending on education, encouraging multidisciplinary education, and promoting a research culture and innovative spirit (Kulal et al., 2024). However, the NEP 2020 is not without criticisms. Researchers have pointed out many areas of confusion and complexity, including cooperation from the states, difficulties in securing adequate funding, a lack of human resources, a shortage of basic infrastructure, complexities concerning the medium of language of instruction, as there are diverse languages, predominance of regional languages, an overburdened syllabus, and urban-rural disparities concerning human resources and infrastructure availability (Varma et al., 2021; Arun et al., 2022; Kulal et al., 2024)

KERALA EDUCATION MODEL: AN EXPOSITION

Kerala is acclaimed for its high literacy rate. The official sources affirm that its literacy rate is 96.2% (Swargiary, 2024). The Department of Economics & Statistics of the Government of Kerala states that there are 12951 schools in Kerala, consisting of government-owned, aided, and unaided schools. The state has 23 universities, and many colleges under them, covering a broader area of disciplines. Kerala's school education system has been appreciated by many as successful (Niti Aayog, 2019). However, it could not show excellence in higher or college-level education. Although Kerala has been acclaimed for its 'Kerala model' of education, the real picture does not affirm any significant model (John & Kumar, 2023). It is often criticised for inaccessibility and poor quality of education (Bairagya & Joy, 2022). Compared to previous decades, Kerala faces a significant issue of student emigration. While the earlier decades accounted for job seekers' emigration from Kerala, the present decade witnesses an unimaginable student emigration. "From 129763 student emigrants in 2018, the number has doubled to about 250000 in 2023." Kerala's student emigration constitutes almost 11.3% of its total emigration (Rajan, 2024). It adversely affects the education system and the future of the state. The increased emigration of students from the state imbalances the strength of educational institutions. Besides, their increased emigration for educational purposes causes them to remain in those countries. It adversely affects the future of society's economic development options.

Kerala Education Model: A Critique

Since there are several stakeholders, the quality of higher education is a complex topic. The perception of quality varies from person to person. Some scholars define it based on how students are taught. Others argue that it is not about teaching but about how students learn. It should be evaluated based on how the learning process helps students fit into the job market. Students understand it from the perspective of the institution's environment, infrastructure facilities, and scholarships; employers understand it as fitness for a purpose; and fund providers perceive it from the point of its value for money. Since there is no universally acceptable definition of quality, the discussions on the quality of higher education affirm that it is multidimensional. Although all the above-mentioned characteristics are vital considerations to assess the quality of higher education, they can be evaluated based on the students' subject knowledge, critical/analytical thinking, and communication skills (Bairagya & Joy, 2022). If the students inculcate all these essentials through their higher education, they can easily satisfy the concerns of all stakeholders, pointing to a quality higher education. However, the massive migration of students from Kerala raises serious concerns about the quality of the higher education system's capacity to provide these essentials. A close observation shows that the education system has the potential to ensure such an adequate education. But it fails to ensure certain vital elements associated with higher education's productivity and effectiveness. Concentrating on producing degrees rather than creative thinkers and decisive influencers has deteriorated the state's progressive and sustainable education spirit. The advantage of the 'Kerala model' of education is that it has made higher education, or an undergraduate degree, accessible to all. However, it faces many drawbacks as detailed in the following points.

Politicisation of Higher Education

In 1996, the Kerala High Court banned political activities in the schools, affirming the importance of education and a peaceful school environment. However, it continued in the higher education system. In 2003, the Kerala High Court further declared that colleges have the right to restrict political activities within the campus and will not violate any fundamental rights (Sojan Francis vs. M.G. University; the Principal, S.N. College, Punalur vs. State of Kerala). The rights guaranteed under 19(1), including peaceful assembly, do not mean they are absolute rights. The state or other authorities can enforce reasonable restrictions on these rights. Based on the judgments, several private colleges banned political activities on campus or enforced specific limits. However, the public colleges continue to politicise the higher education system. The involvement of political leaders, continuous fights between student political parties, strikes, and the encroachment of politicians in the decision-making bodies of the higher educational institutions damage their quality and standards. The education system should be separated from the interference of politics to ensure meaningful growth and sustainability. Many students do not pursue their educational aspirations due to their political agendas. Realising its harm to the state's future, the Kerala Governor, Rajendra Arlekar, stated that academic institutions should not be politicised (PTI, 2025).

Lack of Government Colleges

The Ministry of Human Resources' All India Survey on Higher Education (2019) states that 80.6% of the colleges in Kerala are in the private sector, and among them, 64.6% are self-financed. When the number of government colleges is low, it adversely affects the economically weaker sections' ability to pursue higher education opportunities in the state. Students from a low social background also find it a barrier to pursuing higher education (Bairagya & Joy, 2022). Besides, the communist government in Kerala advances the increasing privatisation of education for the benefit of students. Although it increases the number of seats and the educational environment in the state, it also tends to become part of the "vulgar commercialisation" of education, negatively affecting the academic aspirations of students from low-income families (Tilak, 2020).

Lack of Inclusiveness

Many students migrate to other countries or states seeking a more inclusive approach from the host society. They believe that migration not only helps them to get a better education but also offers a better lifestyle. A Centre for Public Policy Research study claims that 78% of female students migrate as a journey towards a more liberal setting of equality and opportunity. They argue that it also provides them freedom from social stigmas and stereotypes. They find education outside Kerala as a source of escape from a closed society to an open society. Compared to 78% of female students, just 48% of male students prefer education outside as a means of freedom (Sebastian, 2024). It shows that women still face significant social barriers to expressing their quality and freedom. Besides, high unemployment and underutilisation of labour among educated women indicate that Kerala society has not yet shown its full potential to affirm inclusiveness (Kannan, 2023). The exclusionary trends have shown serious drawbacks to Kerala's education system and economic development, forcing students to search for an egalitarian society that provides them with education and a free and positive lifestyle (Kumar & George, 2009).

Imbalance between Education and Employment Opportunities

Although Kerala ranks at the top in literacy, it holds one of the top positions concerning the percentage of educated youth unemployment. Kerala's youth unemployment in the age group of 15-29 is at a staggering 29.9%. Females (47.1%) face more unemployment than males (19.3%). Its unemployment percentage is even higher than the national average (Sharma, 2024). Authors criticise that Kerala fails to ensure quality higher education, enabling students to face the job market requirements (Bairagya & Joy, 2022). There is a mismatch between the qualifications of the job seekers and the requirements of the employment providers. The job market fails to incorporate some job seekers, as they are overly qualified. The employment opportunities are fewer compared to the inflow of job seekers. The state's industrial sector is not expanding exponentially to accommodate the increasing number of job seekers. The lower availability of employment increases competition among job seekers. These are ongoing reasons for the increased youth unemployment in Kerala (Sharma, 2024). The higher education system and the employment sectors should have a balance to ensure a sustainable future. The demand and supply principle is equally valid here. Kerala's higher education system supplies educated youth to the employment sector without systematically understanding its requirements.

Lack of Desired Wages

Although Kerala has the highest average monthly wages for casual male workers, it does not balance with the job seekers' qualifications. They are more qualified and skilled, and they look for such kinds of employment that satisfy their skill and wage preferences. This forces them to overlook other job opportunities (Sharma, 2024). The Kerala Migration Survey 2023 states that almost 30% of the youth prefer to remain unemployed rather than having jobs that do not align with their qualifications (Rajan, 2024). Since the local job market fails to satisfy their aspirations, most of them migrate to other places for better job opportunities.

Policy Recommendations

The state of Kerala has made tremendous progress in education due to many contributing factors, like the involvement of the Catholic Church and other religious denominations. The government policies and programs also prioritised education and healthcare, providing facilities to make people literate. However, the educational environment was not beneficial in producing more creative thinkers and researchers. Although the Kerala High Court banned politicisation of education in schools and private higher educational institutions, government colleges continue encouraging it, harming students' future. The government should make laws and policies that distance the academic sector from the interference of politics. Society needs creative thinkers for a sustainable future. Realising this perspective, the government should prioritise qualified specialists as members of the decision-making bodies concerning higher education. Incorporating their political party members as teachers and administrative officers of higher educational institutions will not transform society. They will be interested only in their political interests rather than the future of students.

Government support for students from low-income families, scheduled caste and tribe, and other marginalised sectors should be enhanced in such a way as to empower them to pursue the desired courses. Privatising the educational industry is advantageous as it provides competition and quality. However, the government should ensure that it also caters to the demands of the students from low-income families. Scholarships and other financial support mechanisms effectively ensure students have appropriate facilities in the state. Besides, it should also prioritise the quality of the education system. Compromises on the quality force students to try other options in other places, which will cause increased emigration of students.

Appropriate policies should be formulated to broaden the state's job market. Most educated youth have only one main option in Kerala – the service sector. The industrial sector is considered problematic in terms of the industry's job guarantee and permanence. Many good industries like 'Kitex' prefer other states to Kerala due to a lack of support from the government, increased corruption, and an unfriendly attitude towards industrialists. Putting aside political ideologies, political leaders should prioritise encouraging industrialists to promote the sustainable economic development of the state. When the state faces a lack of employment-generating industries, the qualified youth will be forced to migrate elsewhere.

CONCLUSION

Quality education is an essential component of the SDGs. Even before the proclamation of the SDGs, the 86th Constitutional Amendment, several central and state enactments, national education policies, and many Supreme Court judgments insisted on the importance of quality education for the country's economic development. However, after the declaration of SDG4, India also envisaged education within the ambit of sustainability, arguing that it should function from social, financial, and environmental perspectives. Accordingly, it insisted that education should function as a wheel for societal transformation, economic development, and environmental protection. From this perspective, this chapter critically analysed the sustainable education system of the most literate state of India, Kerala. Although it has a highly acclaimed "Kerala Model" of education, it merely focuses on promoting literacy and producing degrees, without prioritising creative thinking, analytical capacity, and communication skills. The increased emigration of students and young graduates from Kerala underlines the state's lack of quality education and employment opportunities. Many criticise the 'Kerala Model' for not aligning with the job market requirements. This necessitates changes in the government's educational and employment policies. Kerala has the potential to transform society and increase economic development. However, the uncontrollable politicisation of the educational system and employment sector complicates its functioning. A people-centred policy perspective should evolve to prioritise the concerns of students and job seekers. Changes in Kerala's educational system can influence the country's educational landscape, as it has always been a forerunner concerning educational sustainability.

REFERENCES

Aayog, N. I. T. I. (2025). Expanding Quality Higher Education through States and State Public Universities. https://www.niti.gov.in/sites/default/files/2025-02/Expanding-Quality-Higher-Education-through-SPUs.pdf

Abad-Segura, E., & González-Zamar, M.-D. (2021). Sustainable Economic Development in Higher Education Institutions: A Global Analysis within the SDGs Framework. *Journal of Cleaner Production*, *294*, 126133. DOI: 10.1016/j.jclepro.2021.126133

Abu Alfoul, M. N., Bazhair, A. A., Khatatbeh, I. N., Arian, A. G., & Abu Al-Foul, M. N. (2024). The Effect of Education on Economic Growth in Sub-Saharan African Countries: Do Institutions Matter? *Economies*, 12(11), 300. https://www.mdpi.com/2227-7099/12/11/300

Agasisti, T., & Petrenko, O. (2024). Higher Education and Economic Development: A Bibliometric Analysis 1985-2022. *European Journal of Education*, *59*(3), e12653. https://onlinelibrary.wiley.com/doi/10.1111/ejed.12653. DOI: 10.1111/ejed.12653

Apostu, S. A., Mukli, L., Panait, M., Gigauri, I., & Hysa, E. (2022). Economic Growth through the Lenses of Education, Entrepreneurship, and Innovation. *Administrative Sciences*, *12*(3), 74. https://www.mdpi.com/2076-3387/12/3/74. DOI: 10.3390/admsci12030074

Arun, D. P., Malik, J. S., & Shelar, R. (2022). Perceived Challenges of National Education Policy, 2020 by the Students. *Indian Journal of Extension Education*, *58*(2), 73–76. https://journals.acspublisher.com/index.php/ijee/article/view/209. DOI: 10.48165/IJEE.2022.58214

Ashoka Kumar Thakur vs. Union of India and Others (2008) 6 SCC 1.

Bah, I. A. (2023). The Relationship between Education and Economic Growth: A Cross-Country Analysis. *Research. Social Development*, *12*(5), e19312540522. https://rsdjournal.org/index.php/rsd/article/view/40522

Bairagya, I., & Joy, B. (2022). What Determines the Quality of Higher Education? A Study of Commerce Graduates in Kerala (India). *Journal of the Asia Pacific Economy*, *27*(1), 1–25. https://www.tandfonline.com/doi/full/10.1080/13547860.2020.1870067. DOI: 10.1080/13547860.2020.1870067

Bapuji, H., & Chrispal, S. (2020). Understanding Economic Inequality through the Lens of Caste. *Journal of Business Ethics*, *162*(3), 533–551. https://link.springer.com/article/10.1007/s10551-018-3998-8. DOI: 10.1007/s10551-018-3998-8

Barro, R. J. (1991). Economic Growth in a Cross Section of Countries. *The Quarterly Journal of Economics, 104*(2), 184–198. http://piketty.pse.ens.fr/files/Barro91.pdf. DOI: 10.2307/2937943

Bentley, G., Goldberg, T., & Jasienska, G. (1993). The Fertility of Agricultural and Non-Agricultural Traditional Societies. *Population Studies, 47*(2), 269–281. https://goldberglab.wisc.edu/pdf/P003.pdf. DOI: 10.1080/0032472031000147006

Blanden, J., & McNally, S. (2015). Reducing Inequality in Education and Skills: Implications for Economic Growth. *EENEE Analytical Report No. 21*. http://www.education-economics.org/dms/EENEE/Analytical_Reports/EENEE_AR21.pdf

Blessinger, P., Sengupta, E., & Makhanya, M. (2019). New Higher Education Literacies for a Sustainable Future. *University World News*, 571. https://www.universityworldnews.com/post.php?story=20191017120317521

Bruçaj, S. (2014). Quality in Private Higher Education System: New Challenges Regarding Students' Satisfaction. *The Online Journal of Distance Education and e-Learning : TOJDEL, 2*(2), 21–26. https://tojdel.net/journals/tojdel/articles/v02i02/v02i02-04.pdf

Camilla, S. (2023). The Design of Upper Secondary Education Across OECD Countries: Managing Choice, Coherence, and Specialisation. *OECD Education Working Papers*. https://www.oecd.org/en/publications/the-design-of-upper-secondary-education-across-oecd-countries_158101f0-en.html

Chancel, L., & Piketty, T. (2019). Indian Income Inequality, 1922-2015: From British Raj to Billionaire Raj? *Review of Income and Wealth, 65*(S1), S33–S62. https://onlinelibrary.wiley.com/doi/full/10.1111/roiw.12439. DOI: 10.1111/roiw.12439

Das, S. (2016). Inequality in Educational Opportunity in India: Evidence and Consequences of Social Exclusion. *Child Indicators Research, 9*(1), 51–71. https://link.springer.com/article/10.1007/s12187-014-9296-9. DOI: 10.1007/s12187-014-9296-9

Department of School Education & Literacy. (2021). Right to Education. https://dsel.education.gov.in/rte

European Commission. (2013). *High Level Group on the Modernization of Higher Education — Report to the European Commission on Improving the Quality of Teaching and Learning in Europe's Higher Education Institutions*. EU Publication Office. https://op.europa.eu/en/publication-detail/-/publication/fbd4c2aa-aeb7-41ac-ab4c-a94feea9eb1f

Ghosh, M. (2011). Regional Disparities in Education, Health, and Human Development in India. Indian. *Journal of Human Development*, *5*(1), 5–28. https://journals.sagepub.com/doi/10.1177/097370302011010l

Hanushek, E.A., & Wö mann, L. (2007). The Role of Education Quality in Economic Growth. *World Bank Paper Series 412*. https://documents1.worldbank.org/curated/en/260461468324885735/pdf/wps4122.pdf

John, K. T., & Kumar, K. S. (2023). Developmental Challenges to Internationalising the Higher Education Sector: A Critical Inquiry of Business Schools in Kerala. *Rajagiri Management Journal*, 17(1), 52-83. https://www.emerald.com/insight/content/doi/10.1108/ramj-07-2021-0058/full/html

Kalyani, P. (2020). An Empirical Study on NEP 2020 [National Education Policy] with Special Reference to the Future of Indian Education System and Its Effects on the Stakeholders. *Journal of Management Engineering and Information Technology*, *7*(5). https://zenodo.org/records/4159546

Kannan, K. P. (2023). Revisiting the Kerala 'Model' of Development: A Sixty-Year Assessment of Successes and Failures. *The Indian Economic Journal*, *71*(1), 120–151. https://journals.sagepub.com/doi/abs/10.1177/00194662221145290. DOI: 10.1177/00194662221145290

Kaurav, R. P. S., Narula, S., Baber, R., & Tiwari, P. (2021). Theoretical Extension of the New Education Policy 2020 Using Twitter Mining. *Journal of Content Community and Communication*, *13*(7), 17–26. https://www.amity.edu/gwalior/jccc/pdf/jun_03.pdf. DOI: 10.31620/JCCC.06.21/03

Kaurav, R. P. S., Suresh, K. G., Narula, S., & Baber, R. (2020). New Education Policy, 2020: Qualitative (Contents) Analysis and Twitter Mining (Sentiment) Analysis. *Journal of Content Community and Communication*, *12*(6), 4–13. https://www.amity.edu/gwalior/jccc/pdf/dec_02.pdf. DOI: 10.31620/JCCC.12.20/02

Kulal, A., Abhishek, N., Dinesh, S., Bhat, D. C., & Girish, A. (2024). Evaluating the Promise and Pitfalls of India's National Education Policy 2020: Insights from the Perspectives of Students, Teachers, and Experts. *SAGE Open*, *14*(4), 21582440241279367. https://journals.sagepub.com/doi/10.1177/21582440241279367. DOI: 10.1177/21582440241279367

Kumar, N. A., & George, K. K. (2009). Kerala's Education System: From Inclusion to Exclusion? *CSES Working Paper No. 2*. https://csesindia.org/wp-content/uploads/2020/08/Kerala%E2%80%99s-Education-System-From-Inclusion-to-Exclusion-1.pdf

Kumari, R., Raman, R., & Patel, R. K. (2023). Regional Disparities in Social, Environmental, and Economic Indicators among the Indian States. *GeoJournal, 88*(4), 4351–4371. https://link.springer.com/article/10.1007/s10708-023-10868-9. DOI: 10.1007/s10708-023-10868-9

Li, J., Xue, E., Wei, Y., & He, Y. (2024). How Popularising Higher Education Affects Economic Growth and Poverty Alleviation: Empirical Evidence from 38 Countries. *Humanities & Social Sciences Communications, 11*(1), 520. https://www.nature.com/articles/s41599-024-03013-5. DOI: 10.1057/s41599-024-03013-5

Lucas, R. E.Jr. (1988). On the Mechanics of Economic Development. *Journal of Monetary Economics, 22*(1), 3–42. DOI: 10.1016/0304-3932(88)90168-7

Marquez-Ramos, L., & Mourelle, E. (2019). Education and Economic Growth: An Empirical Analysis of Nonlinearities. *Applied Economic Analysis*, 27(29), 21-45. https://www.emerald.com/insight/content/doi/10.1108/aea-06-2019-0005/full/html

Mistry, B. (2022). An Analytical Review of NEP 2020. *International Journal of Research in All Subjects in Multi Languages, 10*(2), 9–12. https://www.raijmr.com/ijrsml/wp-content/uploads/2022/02/IJRSML_2022_vol10_issue_02_Eng_03.pdf

Mohanty, A. (2018). Education for Sustainable Development: A Conceptual Model of Sustainable Education for India. *International Journal of Development and Sustainability, 7*(9), 2242–2255. https://isdsnet.com/ijds-v7n9-02.pdf

National Education Policy. (2020). https://www.education.gov.in/sites/upload_files/mhrd/files/NEP_Final_English_0.pdf

Panayotou, T. (2016). Economic Growth and the Environment. In Haenn, N., Wilk, R. R., & Harnish, A. (Eds.), *The Environment in Anthropology: A Reader in Ecology, Culture, and Sustainable Living* (2nd ed., pp. 140–148). New York University Press.

PTI. (2025). Politicization of Educational Institutions Should not be Tolerated: Kerala Governor. *Deccan Herald* (March 22, 2025). https://www.deccanherald.com/india/kerala/politicisation-of-educational-institutions-should-not-be-tolerated-kerala-governor-3458061

Rajan, S. I. (2024). Kerala Migration Survey 2023. *Kerala Economy,* 5(3), 1-13. https://www.gift.res.in/wp-content/uploads/2024/09/Kerala-Migration-Survey-Report-2023-Irudaya-Raj.pdf

Reisz, R. D., & Stock, M. (2012). Private Higher Education and Economic Development. *European Journal of Education, 47*(2), 198–212. https://onlinelibrary.wiley.com/doi/abs/10.1111/j.1465-3435.2012.01518.x. DOI: 10.1111/j.1465-3435.2012.01518.x

Romer, P. M. (1986). Increasing Returns and Long-Run Growth. *Journal of Political Economy*, *94*(5), 1002–1037. https://www.jstor.org/stable/1833190. DOI: 10.1086/261420

Saini, M., Singh, M., Kaur, M., & Kaur, M. (2021). Analysing the Tweets to Examine the Behavioral Response of Indian Citizens over the Approval of National Education Policy 2020. *International Journal of Educational Development*, *82*, 102356. DOI: 10.1016/j.ijedudev.2021.102356

Sallis, E. (2002). *Total Quality Management in Education*. Taylor & Francis.

Sarkar, P. (2024). An Overview of Migration Study in Kerala: Analysing In-Migration and Out-Migration Trends Using Census 2011. *Journal of Migration Affairs*, *6*(1-2), 1–8. https://migrationaffairs.com/wp-content/uploads/2024/03/1-pinak-sarkar-commentary-migration-affairs-march-2024.pdf. DOI: 10.36931/jma.2024.6.1-2.1-8

Schank, C., & Rieckmann, M. (2019). Socio-Economically Substantiated Education for Sustainable Development: Development of Competencies and Value Orientations between Individual Responsibility and Structural Transformation. *Journal of Education for Sustainable Development*, *13*(1), 67–91. https://journals.sagepub.com/doi/epub/10.1177/0973408219844849. DOI: 10.1177/0973408219844849

Sebastian, C. (2024). Not Just Studies and Jobs: Why Kerala's Youth Choose to Migrate. *Center for Public Policy Research*. https://www.cppr.in/articles/youth-migrate

Sharma, S. (2024). Kerala Among the Top in India's Youth Unemployment Chart Despite High Literacy Rate: What are the Real Culprits? *The Times of India*. https://timesofindia.indiatimes.com/education/news/kerala-among-the-top-in-indias-youth-unemployment-chart-despite-high-literacy-rate-what-are-the-real-culprits/articleshow/113673214.cms

Swargiary, K. (2024). State-Wise Literacy Rates in India: Analysing Regional Disparities, Gender Gaps, and Policy Impacts. *SSRN*. https://papers.ssrn.com/sol3/papers.cfm?abstract_id=4886091

Thangeda, A., Baratiseng, B., & Mompati, T. (2016). Education for Sustainability: Quality Education is a Necessity in Modern Day. How far do the Educational Institutions Facilitate Quality Education? *Journal of Education and Practice*, *7*(2), 9–17. https://files.eric.ed.gov/fulltext/EJ1089752.pdf

The Hindu Bureau. (2023). 32nd Anniversary of Total Literacy Announcement Observed. *The Hindu* (April 18, 2023). https://www.thehindu.com/news/national/kerala/32nd-anniversary-of-total-literacy-announcement-observed/article66752754.ece

Tilak, J. B. G. (2020). Dilemmas in Reforming Higher Education in India. *Higher Education for the Future*, 7(1), 54-66. https://journals.sagepub.com/doi/abs/10.1177/00194662221145290

UNESCO. (2023). Bringing into Focus the Future of the Right to Education. https://articles.unesco.org/sites/default/files/medias/fichiers/2023/12/Future-of-right-to-education-working-document-en.pdf

Unnikrishnan vs. State of Andhra Pradesh (1993) 1 SCC 645.

Valero, A. (2021). Education and Economic Growth. In McCall, B. P. (Ed.), *The Routledge Handbook of the Economics of Education* (pp. 555–582). Routledge. DOI: 10.4324/9780429202520-20

Varma, A., Patel, P., Prikshat, V., Hota, D., & Pereira, V. (2021). India's New Education Policy: A Case of Indigenous Ingenuity Contributing to the Global Knowledge Economy? *Journal of Knowledge Management, 25*(10), 2385–2395. https://www.emerald.com/insight/content/doi/10.1108/jkm-11-2020-0840/full/html. DOI: 10.1108/JKM-11-2020-0840

Weber, A. S. (2011). The Role of Education in Knowledge Economies in Developing Countries. *Procedia: Social and Behavioral Sciences, 15*, 2589–2594. DOI: 10.1016/j.sbspro.2011.04.151

World Population Review. (2025). Education Rankings by Country 2025. https://worldpopulationreview.com/country-rankings/education-rankings-by-country

KEY TERMS AND DEFINITIONS

Fundamental Rights: Fundamental rights are essential human rights; without them, human flourishing would become challenging.

Inclusive Education: Inclusive education refers to the progressive vision of incorporating all sections of society with the sustainable education policy framework.

Quality Education: Quality education refers to the educational practices that support students' positive growth, value-based training, and increased productivity, which can increase their contributions to society.

Right to Education: Right to Education is a fundamental human right that guarantees people's basic claim to receive free and compulsory education up to a specific age.

SDGs: SDGs are the UN-framed international policy objectives for ensuring a sustainable future for the world.

Sustainable Development: Sustainable development is a policy framework that balances the developmental and environmental needs of the present and future generations.

UDHR: UDHR affirms a set of human rights as universal, inalienable, indivisible, and interdependent for people's sustainable future.

Chapter 6
Leadership and Management in Developing Countries:
Challenges and Opportunities for Socioeconomic Growth

Mustafa Kayyali
https://orcid.org/0000-0003-3300-262X
Maaref University of Applied Sciences, Syria

ABSTRACT

Leadership and management in developing countries operate amid volatility, policy drift, and thin infrastructure. Inside those frictions sits a growth engine. Effective educational leadership is an economic capability: it compounds human capital, improves allocative efficiency in local labour markets, professionalises routines that firms later mimic, and thickens the trust investors watch before they commit. Read this as an economics of leadership. We trace context-sensitive models and inclusive management that translate into development signals: higher retention and completion, faster school-to-work transitions, rising female labour-force participation, microenterprise formation, and multiplier effects. The claim is not romantic; it is empirical. Growth here is not only capital and technology. It is mediated by place-literate leadership that reduces wastage, compresses delays, and aligns schools with value chains, while holding equity, sustainability, and fiscal prudence together.

DOI: 10.4018/979-8-3373-3616-9.ch006

INTRODUCTION

Leadership and management have long been regarded as the cornerstones of progress in any society, but their importance becomes even more pronounced in the context of developing countries (Thelma & Chitondo, 2024). These nations, often characterised by fluctuating political climates, fragile economies, and evolving educational systems, present a unique landscape where leadership is not just a position—but a daily negotiation with adversity, aspiration, and limited resources. In such contexts, educational leaders and managers are more than administrators. They are mediators between policy and practice, visionaries who must operate within constraint, and often, they are the last line of hope in communities hungry for change. However, despite the attention paid to educational reform globally, the challenges and possibilities faced by leaders in developing countries remain underexplored, or worse, misunderstood. Much of the prevailing literature on educational leadership draws from Western paradigms, emphasising formal training, managerial efficiency, and standardised outcomes—models that often fall short when superimposed on the lived realities of schools and institutions in the Global South (Tian & Huber, 2021). Here, schools may be under-resourced, teachers may be underpaid or underprepared, and leadership must often contend with cultural traditions, political interference, donor expectations, and socioeconomic inequalities, all at once.

This chapter begins by situating leadership and management within the broader sociopolitical and economic contexts of developing countries. It unpacks how history, colonial legacies, corruption, infrastructure gaps, and rapidly shifting demographics shape not only what leaders can do, but also what they must become. Significantly, it shifts the gaze away from a deficit narrative. While challenges abound—from systemic inequity and policy instability to technological lags and brain drain—there is also robust evidence of innovation, adaptability, and deeply contextualised leadership practices that defy conventional metrics of success (Bachir & Vogel, 2025). In fact, it is within the very constraints of underdevelopment that some of the most creative and impactful leadership models are forged. At the heart of this discussion is a call to rethink what leadership means in spaces where formality and flexibility must coexist. Leadership in developing countries is not always about having access to resources; it is often about mobilising people, navigating complex systems with integrity, and leveraging limited means toward long-term, community-rooted goals. For many educational leaders in these contexts, the role includes being a moral compass, a social advocate, a cultural bridge-builder, and a pragmatic strategist—all in a single day. Moreover, leadership and management in developing countries cannot be divorced from issues of equity, gender, social justice, and the urgent demand for inclusive development (Kezar et al, 2021). Female leaders, for instance, often rise through systems not designed with them in mind, facing structural and cultural barriers that require additional resilience and creativity. Likewise, rural leaders must usually manage institutions that are not only educational spaces but also vital social centres in communities plagued by poverty, migration, or conflict. This chapter draws upon a wide range of case studies, research insights, and experiential knowledge to unpack the realities of leadership in developing countries. It explores both the visible structures—like policy frameworks and institutional governance—and the invisible forces—like cultural expectations, informal networks, and deeply rooted power dynamics—that shape leadership behaviour. It highlights how context matters, and how universal leadership principles must be interpreted through the lens of local culture, history, and need. Ultimately, the purpose of this chapter is not just to identify what makes leadership difficult in developing countries, but to illuminate what makes it meaningful. In doing so, it offers educators, policymakers, scholars, and practitioners a more nuanced, empathetic, and empowering understanding of what educational leadership can look like when grounded in the resilience, creativity, and cultural wealth of the Global South.

Economic growth in developing countries is often narrated through the big three—capital, technology, and trade—while the quiet fourth driver, institutional leadership in education, gets a footnote when it really deserves the headline. Schools and universities are not simply knowledge depots; they are production systems for skills, habits, and trust. When leadership is competent and context-sensitive, those systems begin to operate like flywheels: attendance stabilises, learning time is protected, pedagogy improves, and students leave with capabilities that firms can actually use. The result is not only higher private returns to schooling, but social returns—productivity spillovers, lower search costs in local labour markets, and a thicker pipeline for SMEs that hire locally rather than import talent from afar.

There is a direct macro story here. Better-led institutions reduce wastage (dropouts, repetition, idle infrastructure), which frees fiscal space; they professionalise management, which firms then mimic; they normalise data use, which improves the quality of public decisions beyond education. Over time, this creates a habit of coordination—schools in conversation with employers, municipalities aligning transport to class schedules, NGOs filling targeted gaps rather than building parallel systems. That coordination reduces frictions that keep economies stuck in low-productivity equilibria.

Growth also tracks who gets to participate. Leadership that centres equity changes household calculus: when girls are safe at school and see women leading those schools, families keep daughters in class longer, fertility patterns shift, and years later the labour supply looks different—more skilled, more diverse, more resilient. Inclusive leadership likewise reduces the cost of informality. When schools teach with the languages, schedules, and constraints of the community in mind, students from informal settlements transition into formal work with fewer frictions, and micro-enterprises formalise because the talent they need can now read regulations, file taxes, and speak the language of buyers.

Crucially, growth in fragile settings is about confidence. Competent leadership signals reliability: that exams will run, that teachers will show up, that the rulebook matters. Investors may not read the footnotes of an education policy, but they do notice the predictability of public services. In this sense, leadership in education acts like a credibility anchor for the broader economy—small signals, repeated over time, that lower risk premiums and attract the kind of patient capital that builds factories instead of pop-up kiosks. When leaders get the everyday basics consistently right, they create the conditions under which innovation can actually stick: apprenticeships that lead to real jobs, school-enterprise studios that solve local problems, and civic partnerships that move a region from subsistence to specialisation.

BACKGROUND - THE LEADERSHIP LANDSCAPE IN DEVELOPING COUNTRIES

To speak of leadership in developing countries without grounding the conversation in lived realities is to craft a map without the terrain (Ahmad & Islam, 2024). Too often, leadership discourse—especially in education—is plucked from global templates that, while tidy on paper, fray at the edges the moment they are applied to contexts shaped by centuries of imbalance, cultural pluralism, and structural asymmetries. Leadership here is not just about vision or efficiency (Kayyali, 2025 A); it is about navigating the thickets of uncertainty while carrying a load that was never evenly distributed to begin with. In developing nations, the very idea of leadership is a shapeshifter—unfixed, improvisational, contingent upon forces as wide-ranging as colonial residue, tribal hierarchy, currency devaluation, or the sudden absence of chalk.

The first challenge? Terrain. Not metaphorical terrain—actual, physical terrain. Schools nestled between craggy hills with no paved roads, institutions flanked by flood-prone fields, remote villages where electricity flickers on like a rumour and disappears before certainty can settle in. In such places, leadership is not abstract; it is visceral. The school principal might be the only formally educated adult in a 40-kilometre radius, called upon not just to manage staff and students, but to mediate land disputes, write grant proposals in languages foreign to their community, and convince dropout-prone parents that education will yield more than hope.

Table 1. Challenge   Leadership Response Matrix

System Challenge	Leadership Responses (Illustrative)	Evidence / KPIs	Time Horizon
Infrastructure Gaps	Community micro-projects; phased facilities plan; low-tech learning kits	Project log, maintenance records, and classroom uptime	Short
Funding Volatility	Scenario budgeting, diversified donors, and fee-waiver policies	Budget variance trend, donor MoUs, bursary counts	Short Mid
Governance Complexity	Local advisory councils; transparent procurement; policy briefs	Meeting minutes, public dashboards, policy memos	Mid
Teacher Shortages	Grow-your-own pipelines; coaching; flexible timetables	Teacher retention, observation rubrics, and class coverage	Short Mid
Technology Access	Offline-first tools; device rotation; radio/ WhatsApp learning	Device logs, offline content usage, and lesson reach	Short
Security/ Conflict	Safety protocols; psychosocial support; catch-up curricula	Incident reports, counselling uptake, and re-enrollment	Short Mid
Equity & Inclusion	Universal design; language supports; girls' safety routes	IEP coverage, language access, and attendance by subgroup	Mid Long

Then there is the question of systems—or the lack thereof. Bureaucracies in many developing nations are labyrinthine at best, dysfunctional at worst (Berda, 2022). Policies shift like sand underfoot, not because of deliberate reform, but because of political turbulence, regime changes, or donor influence (Brown et al, 2024). A principal might be told in January that there is funding for a computer lab, only to discover by April that the funds were reallocated for road construction—or worse, disappeared into an opaque spiral of paperwork and excuses. Leadership in such circumstances becomes a test of endurance. How does one lead in a system that, at times, seems actively designed to corrode initiative? However, it is not just the absence of infrastructure or coherence that defines the landscape—it is the complexity of presence. Cultural capital, local hierarchies, linguistic multiplicities, and social memory—all converge in these environments. Leadership must be multilingual, not just in spoken tongues, but in cultural fluencies (Leu Bonanno, 2023). One has to speak the language of the Ministry while honouring the idioms of the village. It is a kind of code-switching that's not taught in management seminars. Moreover, it is exhausting. However, it is also illuminating. Because in doing so, leaders become translators of hope, interlocutors between the possible and the permissible.

There is also the inherited weight of colonialism, which, despite decades of independence, continues to echo through institutional structures and leadership norms. Many educational models in the Global South were imported wholesale from the colonisers—designed not to liberate minds but to standardise them (Ndlovu-Gatsheni, 2023). Leadership, in this mould, was about control, order, and hierarchy. However, what happens when that mould no longer fits the local clay? Leaders in developing countries often inherit these rigid structures and must break them, slowly and carefully, while still appearing compliant to centralised authority. It is a balancing act—rebellion cloaked in respectability.

Compounding all this is the omnipresence of poverty—not just economic, but systemic, ideological, and generational. The poverty of expectation, where students have never seen someone who looks like them succeed in formal leadership (Leithwood, 2021). The poverty of access, where a single broken-down school bus means fifty children miss class. The poverty of morale, where teachers go unpaid for months and still show up because they are part of the same village and cannot afford to be absent in spirit, even if lacking in pay. Leadership in this climate is not about delegation or vision statements—it is about showing up. Every day. Even when the system forgets you.

Concerning gender, in many developing countries, women leaders exist in spaces that were not built for them. Patriarchal traditions run deep, sometimes silently, sometimes brazenly (Brulé, 2023). A female school director may need to wield authority in a room that reflexively discounts her voice. She may need to be twice as competent to be seen as half as legitimate. However, so often, she is the change-maker—the one who turns policy into practice with grace, grit, and a kind of steely optimism that defies cynicism. Her leadership is not just about school improvement; it is a quiet, daily defiance against structures designed to exclude her.

Ethnicity, too, casts its long shadow. In multi-ethnic societies with histories of marginalisation or outright violence, leadership often carries the burden of representation. A school leader from a minority background may be seen as both a symbol of progress and a target of resentment. Trust must be earned, and even when it is, it may still be withheld. Here, leadership becomes emotional labour, the kind that does not show up in metrics but is felt in every conversation, every decision, every act of restraint. However, despite all of this—despite the crumbling walls, the empty supply cupboards, the inconsistent curricula—there is something profoundly hopeful in the leadership that emerges. It is not glossy or tidy. It is often improvisational, deeply relational, and rooted in empathy more than expertise. Leaders in these settings know that their work is not only about students' test scores or inspection reports (Leithwood, 2021). It is about the long arc—about whether a girl in a conflict-affected zone gets to complete primary school, about whether a teacher decides not to migrate because she believes the system might change.

Leadership here is not about systems, but about souls. About belief in progress when everything around you signals regression. About finding room to breathe inside institutions that feel like they are suffocating (Mandala, 2023). About holding onto the idea that education can be more than survival—it can be transformation. It can be freedom. However, there is also a danger in valorising this kind of sacrificial leadership. Romanticising resilience, as if it is a virtue to lead without resources, is a trap. Leaders should not have to be martyrs to be effective. However, in so many cases, they are. This raises urgent questions: Who supports the leaders? Who listens when they are exhausted, disillusioned, or burnt out? What happens when their courage is mistaken for capacity, and the system continues to neglect them?

International donors and policymakers, well-intentioned as they may be, often misunderstand these landscapes (Hanson-DeFusco et al, 2024). They parachute in with frameworks, templates, toolkits—convinced that what works in Finland will work in Freetown. However, leadership does not unfold in a vacuum. It is shaped by place, by people, by the grain of daily life. What is needed is not just a transfer of knowledge but a deep listening—an attentiveness to nuance, to contradiction, to the spaces in between.

The leadership landscape in developing countries is, in many ways, a mirror. It reflects the aspirations and fractures of society. It reveals the disconnect between policy and practice, between intent and impact. However, it also reveals possibilities—moments where leadership becomes an act of reclamation, where a headteacher refuses to exclude pregnant girls from school, where a district supervisor decentralises decision-making, where a youth leader builds a learning hub in a refugee camp using recycled materials and borrowed books.

Leadership here is not static. It is responsive. It evolves with crisis. It bends with culture (Fernandez, 2023). It adapts because it has to. Moreover, in that adaptation lies a kind of genius—not always visible, not always rewarded, but undeniably transformative. What becomes clear, the longer one examines this terrain, is that leadership in developing countries cannot be studied solely through documents or policies. It must be observed in action, in small decisions made daily, in the quiet heroism of persistence. Moreover, it must be studied with humility. Because the stories, the struggles, the strategies—they are not failures of leadership. They are, more often, failures of context. Failures of global inequity. Failures of imagination from those who craft leadership paradigms without ever stepping into the dust and disorder where leadership is actually lived.

In these countries, leadership is not about control. It is about coherence in chaos. Not about authority, but authenticity. It is less a performance than a practice—of listening, adjusting, and continuing, even when the path ahead is dimly lit and the ground uncertain. Such tends to be the discourse of leadership in developing countries, not from a pedestal, but asking what we can learn from those who lead anyway—who lead not because the system supports them, but because the future demands it. Moreover, in doing so, perhaps we begin to reshape not only how we define leadership, but how we measure its worth.

SYSTEMIC CHALLENGES: FROM RESOURCE CONSTRAINTS TO GOVERNANCE GAPS

Something is disquieting about silence in a school—when it is not a mark of focus, but of absence. No hum of electric fans. No scribble of chalk. No low buzz of conversation. Just the kind of stillness that signals something is broken—physically, systemically, spiritually. That silence, thick and telling, is what many educational leaders in developing countries wake up to each day. And not just in the metaphorical sense (Ng, 2024). Often, the literal infrastructure of schooling has been so threadbare for so long that it is hard to tell whether the dysfunction is temporary or baked into the architecture of expectation.

To talk about leadership and management in developing countries without confronting the chronic, structural shortages that underpin the entire system is to miss the point. Not because those shortages define the worth of the people within them—but because they shape the battle lines of leadership itself. Here, resource constraints are not just hurdles. They are the backdrop, the stage, and sometimes, the main antagonist. Consider the most basic currency of any educational system—money. Or rather, the consistent lack of it. Public education budgets in many developing nations are skeletal, stretched thin between competing priorities: national debt repayments, military spending, foreign-dictated austerity programs, or the ever-lurking bureaucratic leakages that swallow funds faster than they are allocated. School leaders are often given mandates without means—told to improve literacy scores without access to books, or to increase digital access when the nearest computer is more of an exhibit than a tool.

Even when budgets exist, they tend to flow downward slowly, if at all. There is often a Kafkaesque web of approvals, sign-offs, and forms passed from one ministry office to another, each step bleeding urgency into inertia. Moreover, by the time funds arrive—if they arrive—they are often obsolete, either dwarfed by inflation or disconnected from the actual, immediate needs on the ground. You might get fifty whiteboards when what you really needed were roof repairs—or twenty desktop computers for a village without electricity. The issue runs deeper than funding—it is about systemic brittleness. Governance structures in many developing countries are often a blend of colonial residue, post-independence bureaucracy, and externally imposed reforms that fit like ill-tailored suits (Wright et al, 2023). Policies are written with lofty language, glittering with ambition, but they tend to float above ground level, untouched by dust, untested by the friction of actual school corridors. Implementation, if it happens, feels more like a trickle than a tide.

Leaders find themselves stuck in this in-between—accountable for executing visions they had no part in crafting, judged by indicators they cannot control, while operating in systems that rarely provide feedback loops or space for dissent

(London, 2023). Everything is top-down, yet nothing seems grounded. It is a kind of managerial purgatory, where you are not just asked to do more with less, but to do it without questioning why "less" is a permanent state.

The concept of accountability itself becomes slippery. In theory, leaders should be held to account by governing bodies, boards, and communities. In practice, accountability is often distorted. Sometimes it is performative—reduced to endless paperwork and compliance rituals that mask deeper inefficiencies. Other times, it is punitive—a system of blame-shifting where leaders become the scapegoats for institutional rot. Moreover, every so often, it is absent—where corruption or patronage renders any notion of accountability hollow, even dangerous.

Figure 1. Prevalent System Constraints in Education

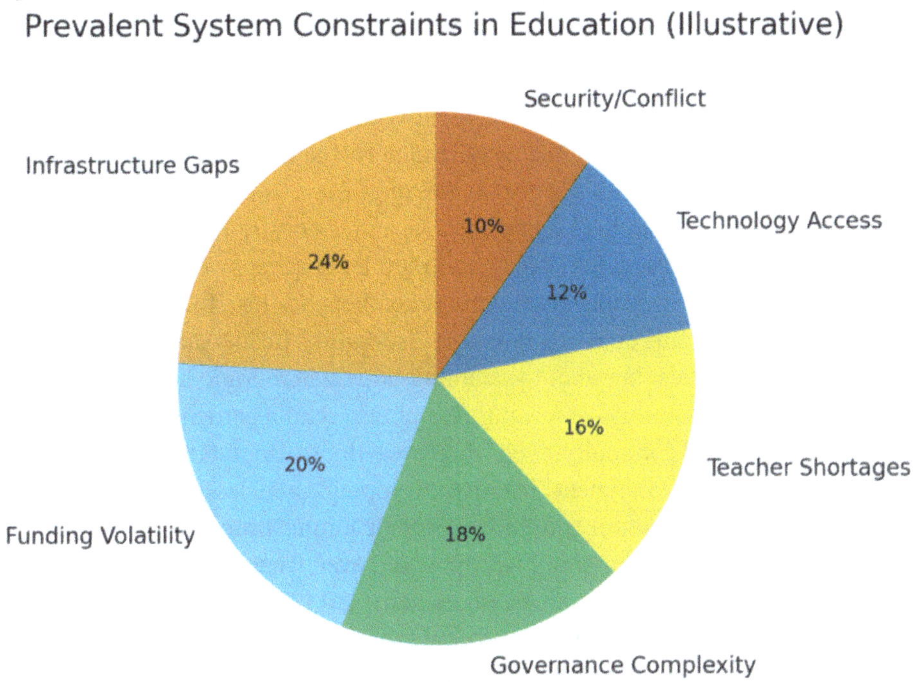

Corruption is one of those words that gets tossed around like a diagnosis, rarely with enough sensitivity to its symptoms. In some countries, the informal economy of favours, bribes, and under-the-table deals has become so normalised that it is almost invisible. Leaders are expected to navigate this terrain with tact—knowing when to resist, when to comply, when to look away (Lopez, 2024). Not because they condone it, but because surviving the system sometimes demands complicity. It is an impossible moral terrain. Moreover, for many, the most complex decisions are not pedagogical, but ethical: do you play the game to get resources for your school, or do you risk starving it for the sake of principle?

Even when corruption is not overt, there are governance gaps that are more insidious—forms of neglect that masquerade as neutrality. Ministries that have not updated teacher training curricula in two decades (Burns, 2023). Boards that rotate leadership every year due to political interference erode institutional memory before it can take root. Performance evaluations that value conformity over creativity. Policies that require internet access for reporting, despite schools functioning entirely offline. It is not always sabotage—sometimes it is disconnect, the slow erosion of alignment between decision-makers and reality. And then there is the issue of data—or, more precisely, the manipulation of it. In environments where reputation and funding depend on numeric targets, there is often a subtle pressure to cook the books. To inflate enrollment figures. To underreport dropout rates. To stage model classrooms for visiting officials that crumble the day after. Leadership, in this context, becomes a tightrope walk between honesty and survival (Swift, 2023). Speak the truth and risk censure. Play the game and perpetuate the farce. There is rarely a clear path forward that does not cost something.

One must also consider the human cost. Resource constraints are not just about a lack of supplies or money; they bleed into morale. Teachers working without pay for months lose faith. Students sitting on broken benches lose focus (Steiner et al, 2023). Principals begging donors for support lose dignity. Leadership, then, becomes not only about logistics, but about sustaining hope where logic has failed. About creating rituals of possibility—morning assemblies, school gardens, parent-teacher meetings—that signal continuity, even when everything else suggests collapse. And what of professional development? In most developing countries, leadership training is either perfunctory or entirely missing. A school administrator might rise through the ranks based on tenure, not training. Moreover, even when workshops exist, they are often generic, one-size-fits-all modules delivered by outside consultants with little sense of context. There is rarely a follow-up. No mentoring. No critical spaces to unpack the emotional toll of leadership or to exchange strategies with peers. Leaders are often left to learn on the job—an unpaid apprenticeship in managing chaos.

Technology, paradoxically, adds another layer of challenge. International bodies push digital innovation—smart classrooms, online reporting systems, e-learning platforms—as a panacea (Nair, 2024). However, technology without infrastructure is just decoration. What good is an app if there is no power? What is the point of a digital curriculum when teachers are not trained to use it? Leaders become intermediaries once again, trying to translate the techno-optimism of donors into something vaguely workable with the analogue realities of their schools.

Leadership in this context is emotionally taxing. There is a tiny margin for error, and yet, no real safety net. You are expected to inspire your staff, reassure parents, manage crises, interpret unclear policies, and somehow stay sane. Burnout is common, though rarely discussed. There is an unspoken expectation to be stoic, to shoulder everything quietly, because to admit exhaustion feels like weakness. Leaders often have no one to lead them.

It is tempting, in the face of all this, to succumb to cynicism. However, cynicism is a luxury many of these leaders cannot afford (Zaki, 2022). They persist. Not because they are blind to the failures of the system, but because they know the cost of giving up. They find workarounds. They crowdsource solutions. They tap into diasporas, build relationships with NGOs, lean on community elders, and organise school feeding programs through informal networks. They do what the system can not—or will not.

What is striking is not just the dysfunction, but the creativity it provokes. Leadership in developing countries is a masterclass in adaptive thinking. In one district, a headmaster turns old buses into mobile libraries. In another, a school leader partners with a local women's collective to fund uniforms through handmade crafts. These stories rarely make it into global reports, but they are the marrow of authentic leadership—the kind that builds bridges out of broken bricks.

However, the question remains: how sustainable is it to keep improvising when the system refuses to evolve? How long can one lead with heart when the body is exhausted? There is only so much that individual resilience can bear. Systemic challenges require systemic responses (Khaw, 2023). However, that will not happen until those in power recognise that reform cannot come solely from above. It must emerge from dialogue, from listening to those at the margins—not as recipients of wisdom, but as repositories of it.

In the end, leadership in developing countries is not just an administrative role—it is an existential one. It tests not only your competence, but your convictions. It is not about solving everything. Sometimes, it is about keeping things from falling apart. Other times, it is about planting something small—an idea, a ritual, a practice—that might bloom long after you have left. Moreover, perhaps, in these fractured systems, that is the quiet power of leadership: to hold space for what could be, even when what is seems relentlessly insufficient.

TRANSFORMATIVE OPPORTUNITIES: LOCAL AND GLOBAL LEVERAGE

Amid the exhaustion of persistent scarcity and the weight of systemic dysfunction, there lies—quiet but insistent—a current of possibility (Alifuoco, 2024). It does not roar; it murmurs. Sometimes it hides in the margins, in whispered solutions and sideways ideas. However, it is there, and it is growing. Because while developing countries may grapple with relentless constraints, they also sit on vast, untapped reservoirs of innovation, communal intelligence, and unspoken resilience. If leadership in these contexts is a test of survival, it is also—perhaps more radically—a doorway to reimagination (Kayyali, 2026).

It is tempting to assume that innovation is the privilege of those with access: to funding, technology, well-lit conference rooms, sleek think tanks, and pilot grants with international logos. However, that assumption fails to understand how innovation breathes. In many developing regions, innovation does not come prepackaged or backed by institutional logos—it emerges from necessity, shaped by improvisation, held together with thread and trust (Kayyali, 2025 B). It is messier, often invisible to outsiders, but no less profound. In fact, it might be more so. Because when the system offers no roadmap, those who persist must draw their own.

You can find it in the way a rural schoolteacher builds a makeshift projector using a smartphone, a bedsheet, and a borrowed power bank. Alternatively, the way a community leader orchestrates a rotational teaching scheme so that students in an isolated village can have access to subject experts who each walk ten kilometres to teach once a week. These are not footnotes in an innovation report—they are lifelines, drawn not from manuals, but from memory, intuition, and collective wisdom.

Innovation, in this sense, is not a product. It is a posture. A willingness to risk the unfamiliar. To test and tinker with the tools at hand, whether they are digital apps or age-old proverbs. In developing countries, innovation often dances with tradition—not in opposition, but in dialogue. There is a kind of elegance in how local wisdom intertwines with contemporary challenges, crafting solutions that feel both grounded and new. Take, for instance, conflict-resolution models in some African and South Asian schools that draw from indigenous customs—circle dialogue, storytelling, ritualised apology—to address bullying or classroom disputes (Mosima, 2022). No imported behavioural framework could do what these centuries-old practices achieve in minutes.

The problem is, such solutions are rarely spotlighted. They are too quiet, too localised, too hard to standardise. That may be the point. Fundamental transformation does not always scale. Sometimes it ripples. Sometimes it just takes root where it is planted. Moreover, if we insist on looking only at measurable outcomes, we risk missing the quiet revolutions already underway in courtyards, kitchens, and chalk-stained classrooms.

Leadership in this context, then, is about noticing—about paying attention to what is working not in theory, but in lived practice (Willocks, 2023). It is about asking, "What are we already doing that is worth naming, protecting, and nurturing?" That kind of leadership is deeply reflective, yes, but it is also deeply relational. It does not extract solutions—it listens to them into being. Leaders who recognise the value of local wisdom do not see themselves as saviours or technocrats; they see themselves as stewards of possibility, as midwives to emergent systems that may not yet have names. However, we would be naive not to acknowledge the growing pull of the global. Education, even in the most remote corners, is no longer an insulated endeavour. Curricula are benchmarked against international standards. Donor-funded programs carry the lexicon of metrics, outcomes, and impact assessments (Islam & Khan, 2022). There is pressure—subtle, and sometimes not so subtle—to modernise, digitise, and globalise. For many leaders, this creates a strange tension: how to embrace global tools without erasing local truths.

Figure 2. Leader-Led PD vs. Student Attendance Gains

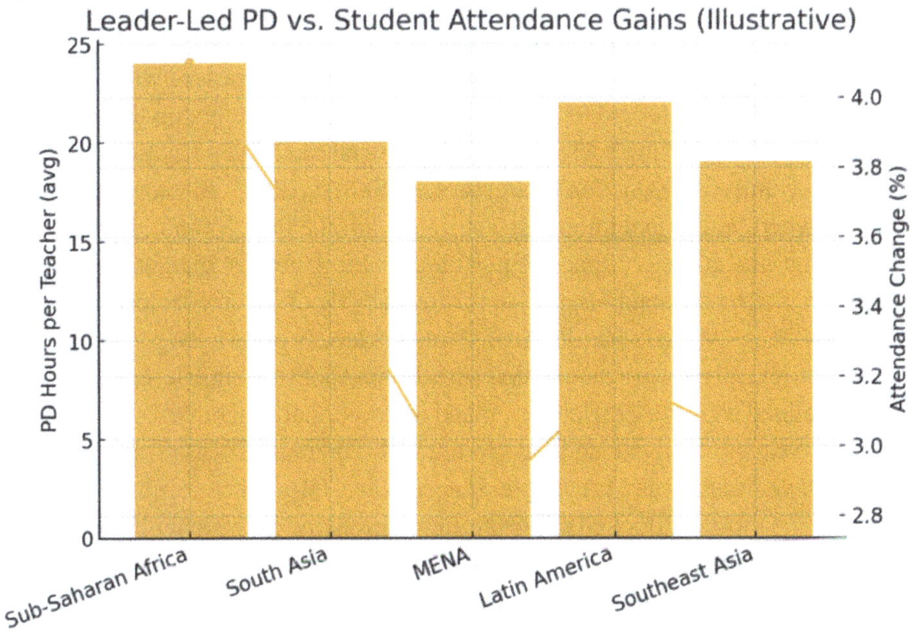

However, this tension may not be something to resolve. It could be something to lean into. The most transformative opportunities often arise not from choosing either the local or the global, but from daring to weave them together—imperfectly, messily, but meaningfully. Think of the young principal who teaches climate science using traditional agricultural calendars. Alternatively, the teacher uses WhatsApp voice notes to deliver inclusive lessons in multiple dialects because the school has no Wi-Fi, but every parent has a phone. These are not compromises—they are composites—hybrids born of necessity and imagination.

Technology, when wielded with care, becomes a tool not of dependency, but of empowerment. However, it has to be rooted in context. What good is an AI-based attendance tracker if a school has no electricity? However, what if the same technology could be reimagined to run offline and log attendance through biometric tokens? It is not impossible (Nithya et al, 2022). What is needed is not just technology transfer, but technology translation—tools reinterpreted by and for those who actually use them. Moreover, sometimes, global leverage does not come in the form of gadgets or grants. Sometimes it is about solidarity. About connecting leaders across borders who face similar struggles and can offer each other not solutions, but understanding (Nowak & Nowosielski, 2021). Leadership exchanges, virtual peer mentoring, collaborative research between schools in Nairobi and Dhaka—these kinds of networks allow leaders to step out of isolation, to realise they are not alone in the grind, and that their innovations, however local, are part of a wider, generative mosaic.

There is also something quietly radical in returning to the basics—not as a regression, but as a deliberate act of reclamation. In a world obsessed with speed and scale, leaders who focus on deep learning, on holistic well-being, on the rhythm of the school day, are pushing back against an industrial model of education that treats children like units of production (Hargreaves & Shirley, 2021). In many developing contexts, where traditional knowledge still hums in the background, there is room to reimagine education as a space of meaning-making, not just market preparation. Innovation is not a constant bloom—it is often a cycle of failures, adjustments, and small wins. Moreover, it is fragile. An inspired leader can build a program that transforms a district, only to see it dismantled with the next political shuffle. Local wisdom can be sidelined when new officials demand international benchmarks. Community trust takes years to cultivate and days to unravel (Kuzmuk, 2024). Transformation is possible, yes, but it is not inevitable. It needs care, infrastructure, and protection.

One of the most overlooked opportunities is investing in the inner life of leaders themselves. Too often, they are asked to innovate without rest, to inspire without support, to push boundaries without backup. However, creativity needs breathing space. Reflection. Dialogue. Leadership retreats, action-research residencies, time to write, to dream, to fail and try again—these are not luxuries (Hart, 2021). They are prerequisites. A leader cannot steward transformation if they are running on fumes. However, despite it all—the underfunding, the bureaucracy, the political meddling—transformation happens. Not everywhere. Not always. However, enough to suggest that the possibility is not just an idea—it is a practice. It is what happens when a group of teachers reimagines parent engagement as community storytelling (Markovich Morris & Cheng, 2025), when a school leader turns the annual exam day into a festival of learning and play, and when a region creates its own teacher accreditation system rooted in indigenous pedagogy and community feedback. These are not anomalies. They are signals. Moreover, they tell us something vital: that transformation in developing countries is not the exception—it is the undercurrent. All it needs is space, trust, and the audacity to believe that what grows slowly might one day shift everything.

So, perhaps the real opportunity is not to chase what others call innovation—but to recognise what we have already been doing under different names (Kayyali, 2023). Perhaps the work ahead is not just about scaling programs—but about deepening roots. About asking better questions, even if the answers take years to unfold. About honouring failure as part of the journey. About allowing leadership to be, at times, unruly, poetic, overly human for a spreadsheet. Moreover, if that sounds idealistic, maybe it is. However, in the face of systems that often feel like they are collapsing inward, maybe idealism is precisely the kind of defiance leadership needs.

EDUCATIONAL LEADERSHIP FOR GENDER EQUITY AND SOCIAL JUSTICE

Equity. A word that carries weight, and yet slips so easily into abstraction when stripped of context. In the polished vocabulary of global education conferences, it is tossed around like a moral compass—reassuring, noble, almost sterile. However, in the actual corridors of schools and the hearts of communities struggling to keep the doors of education open, equity is rarely a slogan (Kayyali, 2022). It is a fight. A layered, messy, ongoing reckoning with who gets to belong, who gets left out, and who holds the power to redraw the boundaries. In developing countries, where educational landscapes are textured by colonial scars, cultural codes, economic precarity, and the aftershocks of conflict or displacement, leadership for equity is not just an agenda item—it is a daily act of disruption. To lead equitably here is not about checking inclusion boxes; it is about questioning the very foundations upon which schools were built, who they were built for, and who continues to be marginalised by their structure and logic.

Concerning gender, "girls' education" unfolds, not only in the tokenistic way but into a footnote of policy, but as a full-bodied confrontation with the ways patriarchy runs its fingers through classrooms, curricula, leadership pipelines, and everyday school life. In many parts of the world, girls still walk miles to school only to sit at the back of the class, their voices swallowed by expectation and silence. Female teachers are often present in numbers but absent from leadership. Moreover, those who do make it into managerial positions usually carry double burdens—professional and domestic, visible and invisible, logistical and emotional.

A leadership that takes equity earnestly must contend with this imbalance, not merely by promoting women into roles, but by transforming the roles themselves (Alli et al, 2021). What good is promoting a woman to head a school if the leadership culture remains steeped in masculine norms—efficiency without empathy, command without care, competition over collaboration? What is needed is a fundamental shift, one that values emotional labour, communal leadership, and relational intelligence as core components of effective management. However, such values are often dismissed, precisely because they have been historically feminised. It is not that women cannot lead like men—it is that the entire architecture of leadership needs to be reimagined in a way that does not treat care as weakness or compassion as peripheral. Moreover, this reimagining cannot be surface-level. Take the curriculum. Gender equity is not only about who teaches or who learns—it is also about what is being taught, how, and whose stories are told. In far too many textbooks, the default human is still male (Kinchin et al, 2021). Women, if present, tend to be footnotes: the supportive wife, the nameless mother, the occasional exception who defied odds rather than shaped them. And then there is the silence—on gender-based violence, on reproductive health, on queerness, on consent, on the emotional complexity of being a young girl growing up in a world that does not always see her as fully human. Leadership for equity means curating a curriculum that does not erase, simplify, or sanitise reality, but leans into it—gently, bravely, and with cultural sensitivity that does not slide into cultural cowardice (McGee, 2024). However, gender is only one thread in the larger fabric of inclusion. The question of who belongs extends into disability, class, language, ethnicity, religion, and more (Müller, 2025). Consider students with disabilities—often euphemised as "special needs," as though their difference were something to be managed rather than respected. In many schools across developing regions, these students are either segregated, invisible, or painfully accommodated in ways that reinforce their marginality. Inclusion becomes a performance—an extra ramp here, a sympathetic teacher there—without the systemic shift in mindset that recognises difference as a resource, not a problem. Moreover, the problem is not just infrastructural. It is attitudinal. Leaders must move beyond compliance and into genuine transformation, asking hard questions about what assumptions underlie exclusion (Krieg, 2021). Why are some bodies deemed too inconvenient to teach? Why are some languages too burdensome to include? Why are some communities still waiting for a school to be built? Inclusion, when truly embraced, is not an act of charity; it is a radical assertion that the system must bend, not the learner.

This is especially urgent in contexts with deep ethnic or religious divides. Leadership in such places cannot afford to be neutral. Neutrality, in the face of structural injustice, is not objectivity—it is complicity (Vogler, 2024). Schools in these regions are not simply sites of learning; they are battlegrounds for identity, belonging, and memory. A leader tasked with managing such a school must possess not just pedagogical expertise, but political literacy, historical awareness, and emotional resilience. They must navigate community tensions without losing sight of the student's right to dignity and safety. They must ensure that the curriculum does not perpetuate erasure or hierarchy. They must be willing to interrupt traditions that exclude, while still honouring cultural integrity.

The challenge, of course, is that equity does not always come with applause. Often, it comes with resistance—from teachers who are uncomfortable with change, from parents who see inclusion as dilution, from systems that reward conformity over justice. Leaders who prioritise equity may be labelled as disruptive, idealistic, or impractical. However, leadership was never meant to be comfortable. At its core, leadership is about choosing discomfort when comfort comes at the cost of others' exclusion.

What complicates things further is that many educational leaders in developing countries were themselves products of unequal systems (Mitchell et al, 2025). They carry within them—consciously or not—biases shaped by years of gendered, racialised, and classed socialisation. To lead for equity, then, is to engage in self-interrogation. To ask: What prejudices have I inherited? Whose pain have I overlooked? Whose potential have I underestimated? This inner work is rarely part of formal training, but it is essential. Without it, policies remain hollow. Equity becomes just another word on a banner, detached from the everyday rhythms of school life. However, here is where it gets hopeful. In many communities, the most transformative shifts are not driven by external mandates or expensive interventions—they come from within. They come from leaders who dare to see differently. A principal who refuses to expel a pregnant girl. A teacher who fights for sign language interpreters in rural schools. A district officer who questions why all top-performing schools are located in wealthy urban zones (Lei & Yu, 2025). These small acts, often unnoticed, are what build equity from the inside out. Moreover, sometimes, equity work means slowing down. Not rushing to adopt every new inclusion framework, but taking time to understand what inclusion might mean in a specific context. It might mean consulting with community elders before introducing new sex education programs. It might mean adapting textbooks into local dialects. It might mean redesigning the school day so that children who help with farming chores in the morning can still attend classes in the afternoon. It is not always glamorous. It does not always fit neatly into global targets. However, it is deeply human.

Equity also demands coalition. No leader can do this work alone. They need allies—teachers, students, parents, policymakers, civil society actors (Theoharis, 2024). Building these alliances takes time. It takes trust. It requires letting go of control and embracing the messiness of shared power. However, when it works, it works beautifully. Because equity, at its heart, is not about leaders fixing things for others—it is about creating spaces where those who have been excluded can lead themselves.

Still, the road is long. Structural change is slow. Systems resist redistribution. Moreover, sometimes, in the thick of it, it is easy to feel like nothing is shifting.

However, the shift is there. In the girl who speaks up for the first time in class. In the parent who attends their first PTA meeting. In the teacher who chooses not to laugh at a homophobic joke in the staff room. These moments are the pulse of progress (Dunn, 2021). They may be small, but they are steady.

What equity asks of educational leaders is not perfection, but presence—a willingness to be awake. To notice who is not in the room. To ask why. And then to do something—however imperfect, however small—to change that. Not because it is strategic. Not because it looks good in a report. However, because leadership, in its most ethical form, is a practice of remembrance: remembering the humanity of every learner, and refusing to accept a system that forgets them.

Equity is not a destination. It is a direction. A compass that points toward justice, knowing the journey will be uneven, unfinished, sometimes disheartening (Manchala, 2023). However, leadership means anything in this century. In that case, it means learning to walk in that direction anyway—with humility, with courage, and with a heart big enough to hold the whole messy, beautiful, unfinished project of inclusion.

BUILDING RESILIENCE AND ADAPTIVE LEADERSHIP FRAMEWORKS

There comes a point in any reflection on leadership—especially within the labyrinth of developing contexts—where the question shifts from what is wrong to what might be possible. Not possible in a sweeping, romantic sense. However, in the gritty, granular, everyday way that systems begin to evolve—not through the thunder of revolutions, but through the steady pulse of quiet decisions. This is the terrain of the pathway forward. Not a clear highway with signs and exits, but a rough-cut trail through dense underbrush, where visibility is poor and faith often leads before certainty catches up.

Resilient leadership does not grow in laboratories. It is not the product of perfect conditions (Walsh et al, 2024). It grows in friction. It is shaped, not in ideal circumstances, but in the space between collapse and persistence. To build frameworks that truly support leaders in developing countries, one must begin by letting go of the idea that leadership can be standardised into neat competency lists or reduced to technical bullet points because it cannot. Not here. Not where crises are routine, policy is often a moving target, and the role of a school leader spills far beyond the office and into the lives of the communities they serve.

The first shift, then, is epistemological. We need to unlearn some of the dominant assumptions about what makes leadership effective (Özcan, 2021). Too often, frameworks are imported wholesale from Western models—models forged in vastly different socioeconomic and cultural conditions. They privilege efficiency, delegation, measurable outputs, and linear planning. All helpful in their own right, sure—but not always relevant, and sometimes, downright harmful when transplanted into ecosystems where relationships matter more than metrics, where flexibility is not a luxury but a survival tool, and where the informal is often more powerful than the formal.

Adaptive leadership, in the context of developing countries, must be rooted in responsiveness rather than rigidity (Mawaddah et al, 2025). A school leader in a drought-affected region, for instance, may need to pivot from academic priorities to emergency food distribution. Another, navigating a post-conflict zone, might find that the real leadership work lies in rebuilding trust before rebuilding syllabi. These are not outliers. They are archetypes. Moreover, any framework that does not account for this elasticity of role is simply out of step with reality.

So, what does a more grounded framework look like? Not a blueprint, but perhaps a constellation—guiding stars rather than fixed coordinates. First among them: relationality. In resilient systems, relationships are not just a "soft skill." They are infrastructure. Leaders must know how to build alliances across fractured communities, negotiate with local powerbrokers, mentor teachers with empathy, and navigate donor relationships without compromising dignity (Harris, 2024). None of this is taught in manuals. However, it should be. Because in times of instability, it is not policies that hold schools together—it is people.

Equally essential is reflective capacity. The kind that allows a leader to ask not just "What is going wrong?" but "What does this moment require of me?" Resilient leadership is not reactive; it is aware. It demands space—emotional, intellectual—to pause, to recalibrate, to make sense of complexity before acting. This is where most existing systems falter. Leaders are burdened with tasks, reports, audits, and inspections—little time is left for reflection. However, if we want adaptive leaders, we must create ecosystems where reflection is not indulgence, but investment.

Another star in this constellation: contextual literacy. Leadership training must be indigenised. It must speak the languages—literal and metaphorical—of the regions it aims to serve (Drouin-Gagné, 2021). This means rooting training in local histories, community dynamics, and socio-political realities. It means bringing in elders, activists, community healers alongside policymakers and academics. Because the knowledge needed to lead schools in fragile environments does not just sit in universities. It lives in lived experience. Moreover, any framework that ignores this is not just incomplete—it is arrogant. However, frameworks also need structures. Moreover, structures need resources. Resilience cannot be built on exhaustion. There must be investment—in professional development, yes, but also in the fundamental dignity of the leadership role itself. Salaries that do not demand side hustles. Workloads that do not swallow weekends. Support systems that go beyond "performance monitoring" and into the emotional terrain of burnout, grief, and moral injury.

There is also a case to be made for mentorship. Not the top-down, once-a-year, formal kind. However, embedded, horizontal mentorship—networks of practice where school leaders can share not just best practices, but doubts, failures, unfinished ideas. Imagine a peer-to-peer model where a headteacher in a refugee camp and a district supervisor in a flood-prone area swap strategies—not to "scale up" success, but to understand how improvisation works in different contexts. These networks already exist informally. A good framework would formalise them without formalising the life out of them.

Figure 3. Leadership Readiness Profile: Baseline vs 2025

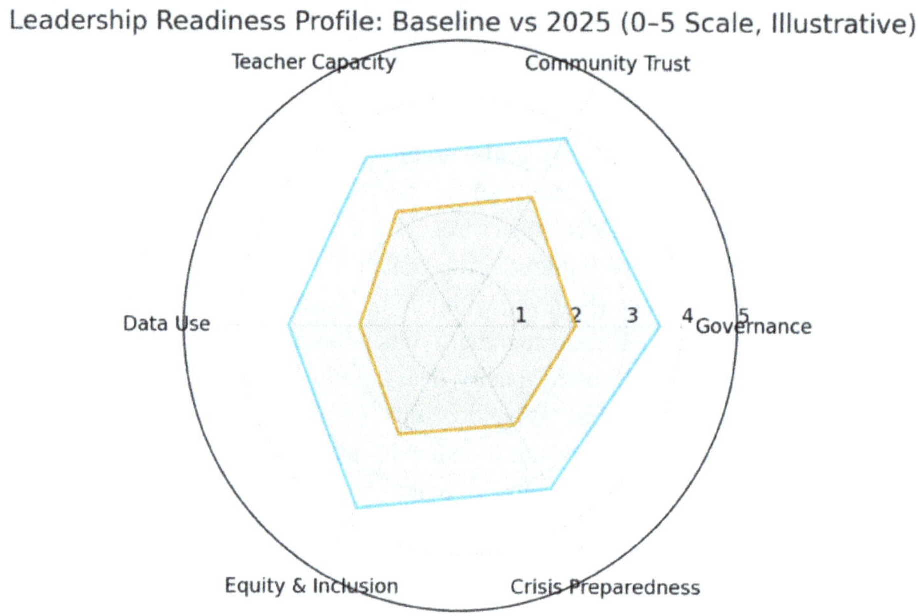

Technology, cautiously introduced, can support this too—but only when it is shaped by the needs of the user, not the fantasies of the funder (Matthijs Bal et al, 2025). Simple platforms for shared learning. Offline resources for remote areas. SMS-based updates for regions with poor connectivity. The question is not whether digital tools belong in leadership frameworks—the question is whether those tools are designed with humility and context in mind. And then there is the role of policy. No framework can flourish if it is constantly undermined by political volatility, corruption, or centralised micromanagement. Ministries must learn to listen—not in consultation sessions that tick boxes, but in ongoing, open-ended dialogue with those in the field. Policy must be porous—able to evolve in response to feedback, failure, and new realities. Leadership frameworks should not be laminated and locked away. They should be living documents—organic, iterative, shaped by practice as much as theory.

Courage, too, must be named. Not just as a character trait, but as a pillar of any fundamental leadership framework. Because in many contexts, to lead is to resist. To push back against inequity. To speak truth to bureaucracy. To protect the most vulnerable, even when it is politically risky. Courage cannot be taught in a module. However, it can be nurtured—in safe spaces, in stories, in solidarity. There is also room for imagination here. Resilient frameworks must not only respond to crisis—they must dare to envision (Tähtinen, 2022). What might it look like if leadership were not about control, but about co-creation? If school governance involved students, parents, teachers, and community members as equal stakeholders? If success were not measured only in test scores, but in student well-being, staff retention, and communal trust?

These are not utopian dreams. They are fragments of practice already unfolding—in pockets, in shadows, in places where leaders refuse to accept the script they have been handed. The role of a leadership framework, then, is not to dictate—but to notice. To gather these fragments, amplify them, legitimise them.

Of course, there will be resistance. Systems protect their shape. Change threatens comfort. However, if we are serious about building leadership frameworks that are not only resilient but just, we must be willing to disrupt the status quo. To ask uncomfortable questions. To let go of the idea that the Global North holds all the answers. Moreover, perhaps most radically, we must reframe failure (Selwyn, 2023), not as evidence of incompetence, but as an invitation to learn. Resilient leadership frameworks must normalise trial and error. Leaders must be allowed to experiment, to pivot, to revise. Without fear of punishment. Without shame. Because the truth is, leadership in developing contexts will always be a dance with uncertainty. The best we can do is to choreograph flexibility into the system.

So, what is the pathway forward? Not a single path, but many. Intersecting, diverging, winding. Some lit, some barely visible. What unites them is not uniformity, but intentionality. A commitment to lead with humility, to listen more than impose, to hold space for contradiction, and to build slowly, deeply, in relationship with those who live the consequences of leadership every day. In the end, resilient and adaptive leadership frameworks are less about control and more about cultivation. They are not fixed models to be replicated, but ecosystems to be tended. They require patience, courage, and a belief—against all odds—that change is possible. Not tomorrow. Not everywhere. But in this school, with these people, in this moment. Moreover, maybe, just maybe, that is enough to begin.

Treating educational leadership as an economic lever changes the conversation from "How do we run schools better?" to "Which constraints to growth can leadership loosen first?" Look at it through a growth-diagnostics lens. In many regions, the binding constraint is not only finance; it is coordination failure—skills that do not match vacancies, training that ignores local value chains, data that arrives too late to matter. Strong leadership narrows these gaps by institutionalising three simple but catalytic routines: (1) continuous evidence loops on attendance, learning, and transitions; (2) structured compacts with employers and municipalities; and (3) targeted, equity-first supports that keep the most vulnerable from dropping out at precisely the point where private and social returns begin to climb.

The mechanisms are mundane, which is why they work. A headteacher who co-designs timetables with nearby firms for staggered apprenticeships effectively lowers firms' training costs and students' search costs, speeding school-to-work transitions and raising local productivity. A district leader who ring-fences instructional time and ties procurement to local suppliers pushes cash into the community, creating a small but real multiplier. A university dean who rewires capstone projects toward local bottlenecks (cold-chain failures, water loss, micro-grid instability) seeds micro-innovations that firms can absorb without expensive consultants. None of this looks glamorous; all of it nudges GDP through better factor use.

Sequencing matters. Leadership can deliver quick wins—reliable timetables, safe transport corridors for girls, offline-first learning kits—that build legitimacy, then leverage that legitimacy to tackle slower, heavier lifts: teacher professionalism, data governance, regional skills compacts. Moreover, the political economy is never neutral. Good leaders translate reform into benefits that are legible to parents and councils—visible improvements that make it costly for politics to reverse course. That stickiness is growth-relevant: stability reduces investment risk, letting firms think in years rather than weeks.

There are risks to name. "Innovation" turns performative when it chases novelty rather than solves frictions; metrics can be gamed; partnerships drift if they are not renewed by shared problem-solving. The antidote is institutional humility: fewer grand launches, more iterative cycles; fewer dashboards, more decisions that actually move buses, books, and bodies on time. Moreover, equity is not a side plate. Systems that exclude large cohorts—rural learners, linguistic minorities, students with disabilities—leave human capital unused and depress demand. Inclusion, properly led, widens the market: more earners, more spenders, more entrepreneurs.

Growth must be future-proofed. Leadership that threads green skills into vocational tracks (repairing solar pumps, retrofitting buildings, waste valorisation) and treats digital public infrastructure as a utility (identity, payments, verifiable credentials) equips graduates for the opportunity frontier, not yesterday's labour market. Diaspora linkages can accelerate this shift: supervised internships, remote mentorships, and co-authored problem sets tied to local industries. These are small bridges; together, they form a corridor. If there is a single through-line, it is this: capable, place-literate leadership converts educational intent into economic momentum. Not by magic, but by steady choreography—aligning actors, compressing delays, reducing leakage, and insisting that the gains of schooling show up where households feel them: in jobs that exist, incomes that rise, and communities that finally have reason to plan beyond the next crisis.

CONCLUSION

Leadership and management in developing countries cannot be neatly summarised by frameworks imported from more developed contexts. The reality is far more layered, complex, and deeply human. As this chapter has explored, the everyday work of educational leaders in these settings often transcends the boundaries of their official roles. It requires constant improvisation, moral clarity, and an unwavering commitment to hope—despite conditions that would erode it.

Throughout the chapter, we have seen how the challenges facing educational leaders in developing nations are not simply logistical—they are structural, historical, and systemic. From the effects of colonial legacies and political instability to the burden of limited funding and inadequate training, leaders must operate within environments that often place them at a disadvantage from the outset. However, paradoxically, these very constraints can also become catalysts for ingenuity. When conventional tools are lacking, leaders in developing countries often build their own—rooted in local culture, community values, and a keen understanding of what is possible, not just ideal.

This context-sensitive form of leadership, while rarely celebrated in international policy circles, holds immense promise. It reframes success away from narrow performance indicators and instead focuses on sustained, community-oriented impact. It prioritises listening over dictating, collaboration over hierarchy, and long-term transformation over short-term results. In this sense, educational leadership in developing countries is not just about managing schools; it is about leading societal change from the ground up.

At the same time, we must be cautious not to romanticise resilience. The capacity of leaders to "make do" should not become an excuse to ignore the systemic injustices they endure. Instead, their daily innovation and perseverance should be seen as a powerful argument for greater investment, more equitable partnerships, and the urgent need for leadership development programs that honour context and complexity—not just standardisation.

What emerges from this exploration is a dual truth: leadership in developing countries is both extraordinarily challenging and profoundly hopeful. It operates at the intersection of resourcefulness and resistance, embodying a kind of leadership that is as much about heart and vision as it is about plans and protocols. Such leadership deserves not only recognition but also amplification—through policy support, international collaboration, and a reshaping of the global conversation about what it means to lead in education.

As we look toward the future, scholars, practitioners, and policymakers must approach leadership in developing countries not with a lens of deficiency, but with one of potential. By listening to the stories, strategies, and struggles of those who lead under pressure, we can begin to construct more inclusive, responsive, and human-centred paradigms of leadership. In the process, we also redefine leadership itself—not as a universal set of skills to be taught, but as a living practice to be understood, adapted, and co-created in every context where education dares to transform lives.

REFERENCES

Ahmad, I., & Islam, M. R. (2024). The Road Ahead in the 21st Century: Mapping Global Progress in Ethical Approaches to Inclusive Community Development. In Building Strong Communities: Ethical Approaches to Inclusive Development (pp. 91-131). Emerald Publishing Limited.

Alifuoco, A. (2024). Exhausting the (Human) Problem: A Performable Dys/Solution. *Performance Philosophy*, *9*(1), 183–204. DOI: 10.21476/PP.2024.91439

Alli, A., Lin, T., Thorndyke, L. E., Parekh, R., & Núñez, A. E. (2021). Advancing women to leadership positions through individual actions and institutional reform. Pediatrics, 148(Supplement 2).

Bachir, E., & Vogel, B. (2025). *Strategic Contextual Leadership: The Blueprint for CEOs and Executives to Master the Art of Leadership in Dynamic Contexts* (Vol. 8). Walter de Gruyter GmbH & Co KG. DOI: 10.1515/9783111382722

Berda, Y. (2022). *Colonial bureaucracy and contemporary citizenship*. Cambridge University Press. DOI: 10.1017/9781009053495

Brown, J. F., Fisher, S., Szilagyi, Z., Pehe, J., Woodward, S. L., Bugajski, J., & Ulrich, C. (2024). Issues In Foreign Policy. In The OMRI Annual Survey of Eastern Europe and the Former Soviet Union (pp. 369-407). Routledge. DOI: 10.4324/9781003580881-9

Brulé, R. E. (2023). Women and power in the developing world. *Annual Review of Political Science*, *26*(1), 33–54. DOI: 10.1146/annurev-polisci-062121-081831

Burns, M. (2023). *Distance Education for Teacher Training: Modes, Models, and Methods*. Education Development Center, Inc.

Drouin-Gagné, M. E. (2021). Beyond the "Indigenising the academy" trend: Learning from Indigenous higher education land-based and intercultural pedagogies to build trans-systemic education. *Engaged Scholar Journal*, *7*(1), 45–65.

Dunn, A. H. (2021). *Teaching on days after: Educating for equity in the wake of injustice*. Teachers College Press.

Fernandez, L. J. (2023). *The art of business Origami: folding your way to success*. Lloyd Jose Fernandez.

Hanson-DeFusco, J., Malik, S., Assamoi, R., Chiromba, A., Davis, D., Hounnouvi, F. M., Irfan, F. B., Faley, P., Matangwa, D. D., Muzenda, T., Nakiryowa, H., Obondoh, A., Parveen, S., Pinales, A. J., & Zimunya, R. (2024). Unethical issues in twenty-first century international development and global health policy. *International Studies Perspectives*, *25*(1), 60–85. DOI: 10.1093/isp/ekad016

Hargreaves, A., & Shirley, D. (2021). *Well-being in schools: Three forces that will uplift your students in a volatile world.* ASCD.

Harris, O. (2024). *Bridging the gap: strengthening school-community partnerships through cultural brokers*. Oscar Harris.

Hart, A. R. (2021). Increasing a Sense of Community in Campus Residences: An Action Research Study (Doctoral dissertation, Azusa Pacific University).

Islam, S., & Khan, M. N. I. (2022). Project impact assessment frameworks in non-profit development: A review of case studies from south asia. *American Journal of Scholarly Research and Innovation*, *1*(01), 270–294. DOI: 10.63125/eeja0t77

Kayyali, M. (2022). Equity, Equality, Diversity, and Inclusion as Key Performance Indicators in Higher Education. *Online Submission*, *3*(5), 1–3.

Kayyali, M. (2023). Promoting Entrepreneurship and Innovation in Higher Education. *Online Submission*, *2*(1), 1–26.

Kayyali, M. (2025a). Leadership's Role in Fostering a Resilient Organizational Culture. In *Enhancing Resilience in Business Continuity Management* (pp. 267–294). IGI Global Scientific Publishing. DOI: 10.4018/979-8-3693-8809-9.ch009

Kayyali, M. (2025b Introduction to Business Intelligence in Talent Management. In Harnessing Business Intelligence for Modern Talent Management (pp. 1-26). IGI Global Scientific Publishing.

Kayyali, M. (2026). Agile Leadership and Labor Dynamics: Navigating Organisational Change in the Digital Era. In Leading Inclusive Workplaces Through Digital Transformation and Organizational Change (pp. 1-36). IGI Global Scientific Publishing.

Kezar, A., Holcombe, E., Vigil, D., & Dizon, J. P. M. (2021). *Shared Equity Leadership: Making Equity Everyone's Work. On Shared Equity Leadership Series*. Pullias Center for Higher Education.

Khaw, K. W., Alnoor, A., Al-Abrrow, H., Tiberius, V., Ganesan, Y., & Atshan, N. A. (2023). Reactions towards organisational change: A systematic literature review. *Current Psychology (New Brunswick, N.J.)*, *42*(22), 19137–19160. DOI: 10.1007/s12144-022-03070-6

Kinchin, I. M., Derham, C., Foreman, C., McNamara, A., & Querstret, D. (2021). Exploring the Salutogenic University: Searching for the triple point for the becoming-caring-teacher through collaborative cartography. *Pedagogika, 141*(1), 94–112. DOI: 10.15823/p.2021.141.5

Krieg, T. R. (2021). Effective school leadership mentoring characteristics in the 21st century: Moving beyond compliance and conformity (Doctoral dissertation, Indiana State University).

Kuzmuk, O. M. (2024). Trust As A Catalyst For Community Development—Knowledge, Education, Law. *Management, 5*(65).

Lei, L., & Yu, W. H. (2025). Who Opts Out of Neighborhood Schools? Determinants and Consequences of School Choice Strategies in China. *Research in Social Stratification and Mobility, 98*, 101065. DOI: 10.1016/j.rssm.2025.101065

Leithwood, K. (2021). A review of evidence about equitable school leadership. *Education Sciences, 11*(8), 377. DOI: 10.3390/educsci11080377

Leu Bonanno, S. (2023). Examining the foundations of culturally and linguistically sustaining school leadership: Towards a democratic project of schooling in dual language bilingual education. *Educational Administration Quarterly, 59*(1), 72–111. DOI: 10.1177/0013161X221106972

London, M. (2023). Causes and consequences of adaptive leadership: A model of leaders' rapid responses to unexpected events. *Psychology of Leaders and Leadership, 26*(1), 22–43. DOI: 10.1037/mgr0000136

Lopez, I. (2024). *The EQ way: How emotionally intelligent school leaders navigate turbulent times*. ASCD.

Manchala, D. (2023). Dreaming a New Future: A Call from the Margins while on the Way to the Pilgrimage of Justice, Reconciliation, and Unity. International review of mission, 112(1), 24-36.

Mandala, C. R. (2023). Alternatively, Students Will Suffer: Feeling Rules in Identity Advocacy Centers at Institutions of Higher Education in the United States (Doctoral dissertation, University of Georgia).

Markovich Morris, E., & Cheng, Y. L. (2025). Parents as Allies: Innovative Strategies for (Re) imagining Family, School, and Community Partnerships. *Education Sciences, 15*(5), 533. DOI: 10.3390/educsci15050533

Matthijs Bal, P., Davids, J., Garcia, E., McKnight, C., Nichele, E., Orhan, M. A., & van Rossenberg, Y. (2025). The Psychology of Automation and Artificial Intelligence at Work: Exploring Four Fantasies and Their Leadership Implications. In *Power, Politics and Influence: Exercising Followership, Leadership, and Practicing Politics* (pp. 575–592). Springer Nature Switzerland.

Mawaddah, A. F., Hatta, A. H., Prasetya, A., & Saputra, A. A. (2025). Adaptive Leadership and Culturally Responsive Transformation in Contemporary Workplaces. *Oikos*, *17*(2), 1–18.

McGee, S. (2024). *Culturally Conscious Decision-Making for School Leaders: A Toolkit for Creating a More Equitable School Culture.* Taylor & Francis. DOI: 10.4324/9781003478928

Mitchell, R., Agbaire, J., Paulson, J., & Tikly, L. (2025). Endogenous systems leadership of education provision during crises in low-and middle-income countries: A conceptual framework: Endogenous systems leadership of education provision. *Prospects*, •••, 1–21. DOI: 10.1007/s11125-025-09732-0

Mosima, K. L. (2022). Exploring the Use of Culturally Responsive Leadership for Conflict Management in Secondary Schools to Enhance Teaching and Learning (Master's thesis, University of South Africa (South Africa)).

Müller, M. (2025). The Normativity of Diversity: Cultural Diversity and the Institutionalization of the Global Categories of People Race, Gender and Disability Cultural Diversity und die Institutionalisierung der globalen Personenkategorien Race, Gender und Disability. In *Ethnography and Diversity: Knowledge Production at the Boundaries and the Boundaries of Knowledge Production* (pp. 21–49). Springer Fachmedien Wiesbaden. DOI: 10.1007/978-3-658-47168-2_2

Nair, J. R. (2024). Educational Innovation and Digitalisation During Crises. In Global Higher Education Practices in Times of Crisis: Questions for Sustainability and Digitalization (pp. 59-76). Emerald Publishing Limited.

Ndlovu-Gatsheni, S. J. (2023). Beyond the coloniser's model of the world: Towards reworlding from the Global South. *Third World Quarterly*, *44*(10), 2246–2262. DOI: 10.1080/01436597.2023.2171389

Ng, S. T. Y. (2024). On Compromise: Neoliberalism, Postfeminism, and the Disappointed Promise of Personhood (Doctoral dissertation, UCL (University College London)).

Nithya, J., Vignesh, S. R., Devadarsan, A., & Venkatesh, S. (2022). AI based contactless attendance monitoring and management system. *International Journal of Health Sciences*, (III), 431063. DOI: 10.53730/ijhs.v6nS3.8365

Nowak, W., & Nowosielski, M. (2021). Leadership struggles and challenges for diaspora policies: A case study of the Polish institutional system. *Innovation (Abingdon)*, *34*(1), 93–110. DOI: 10.1080/13511610.2019.1594716

Özcan, M. (2021). The bottleneck metaphor of leadership culture: How shared understandings about leadership develop in groups and impede diversity and effectiveness of leaders—frontiers in Psychology, 12, 635751.

Selwyn, N. (2023). Lessons to be learnt? Education, techno-solutionism, and sustainable development. Technology and sustainable development, 71, 83.

Steiner, E. D., Woo, A., & Doan, S. (2023). *All work and no pay—Teachers' perceptions of their pay and hours worked.* Rand Corporation.

Swift, C. (2023). Lead Like No One Else.

Tähtinen, L. (2022). Exploring crisis resilience in the built environment: Institutional frameworks and crisis prioritisation in steering crisis management.

Thelma, C. C., & Chitondo, L. (2024). Leadership for sustainable development in Africa: A comprehensive perspective. *International Journal of Research Publications*, *5*(2), 2395–2410.

Theoharis, G. (2024). *The school leaders our children deserve: Seven keys to equity, social justice, and school reform*. Teachers College Press.

Tian, M., & Huber, S. G. (2021). Mapping the international knowledge base of educational leadership, administration and management: A topographical perspective. *Compare: A Journal of Comparative Education*, *51*(1), 4–23. DOI: 10.1080/03057925.2019.1585757

Vogler, G. (2024). *Judging Complicity: How to Respond to Injustice and Violence*. Edinburgh University Press. DOI: 10.1515/9781399522489

Walsh, S., Johnston, A., & Gabriel, C. L. (2024). Building resilient leadership: A study exploring leadership development during uncertainty. *Human Resource Management and Services*, *6*(2), 3474. DOI: 10.18282/hrms.v6i2.3474

Willocks, K. E. (2023). Making leadership as practice development visible: Learning from Activity Theory. *Management Learning*, *54*(5), 705–726. DOI: 10.1177/13505076221105870

Wright, C., Rolston, B., & Ní Aoláin, F. (2023). Navigating colonial debris: Structural challenges for Colombia's peace accord. *Peacebuilding, 11*(1), 62–77. DOI: 10.1080/21647259.2022.2027153

Zaki, J. (2022). Do not let cynicism undermine your workplace. *Harvard Business Review, 100*(5), 70–78.

KEY TERMS AND DEFINITIONS

Contextual Leadership: leadership that adapts actions to local political-economic realities, cultural norms, and resource constraints.

Governance Complexity: overlapping rules, agencies, and power centres that make decisions slow, opaque, or conflicting.

Adaptive Capacity: an institution's ability to pivot during shocks (conflict, disaster, funding cuts) while sustaining core learning.

Community Co-Production: services designed and delivered with parents, elders, NGOs, and learners rather than for them.

Offline-First EdTech: technology choices that work with scarce power/connectivity (SD-card libraries, SMS/WhatsApp routines).

Equity by Design: embedding inclusion (gender, disability, language) into policies, timetables, and budgets from the start.

Resilience Indicators: practical signals that a school/system is stabilising (attendance recovery, teacher retention, re-enrolment).

Chapter 7
Democratic Educational Leadership:
Effects on Organisational Citizenship Behaviours in Ethiopia's Socioeconomic Development

Wako Jio
https://orcid.org/0009-0003-6192-459X
Bule Hora University, Ethiopia

Zerihun Kinde Alemu
https://orcid.org/0000-0002-8546-2882
Ethiopian Civil Service University, Ethiopia

Shashi Kant
https://orcid.org/0000-0003-4722-5736
Lovely Professional University, India

Hirut Assegid
https://orcid.org/0009-0003-6192-459X
Bule Hora University, Ethiopia

ABSTRACT

This chapter asserts that educational institutions should embrace democratic leadership styles to enhance organisational commitment and a cooperative working culture. Evidence clearly demonstrates the importance of democratic educational reform in promoting economic development in Ethiopia. With the application of participatory approaches to leadership, schools can become both child and staff-centred, which

DOI: 10.4018/979-8-3373-3616-9.ch007

manifests in improved educational outcomes and economic growth. Study results suggest that democratic educational leadership creates the right environment that leads to enhanced OCB in teachers. KMO value was used to ensure that the analytical sample is suitable, whereas CFA was used to determine the reliability and validity of the measurement model. SEM analysis showed that democratic leadership may improve OCB indirectly and directly, through encouraging greater participation and engagement of teachers. This study proposes a policy change that is consistent with the democratic school practices to promote excellence in education as well as ensure socio-economic development.

INTRODUCTION

Democratic school leadership is an essential international approach to organisational change by incorporating collaboration and improving its performance (Sajuyigbe et al., 2024; Hermanto et al., 2024). This concept of governance is based on the shared decision-making power and responsibility of all stakeholders and developed on the principles of democracy in the field of government and the organisation (Daud et al., 2024). In a time where the standards and expectations of education are becoming more accountable for the performance of the students, democratic leadership becomes an essential element of encouraging positive Organisational Citizenship Behaviours (OCB) of the teachers (Debele, 2025). It has been shown that educators who contribute to decision-making tendencies are more prone to developing behaviour that leads to institutional success (Nassir & Benoliel, 2024). The practices of leadership in various contexts create a sense of belonging and commitment, which result in better educational performance (Edeh & Ikpor, 2025). However, in Ethiopia, the local governments face a critical obstacle to conducting their operational activities in the form of dealing with the democratic systems, which is mainly caused by the fact that the traditional hierarchical systems are still present in the developing regions (Yuliantini et al., 2024). The research has to be conducted further because the available sources lack adequate identification of the unique environmental aspects that determine the interaction between democratic leadership and the OCB practices in the educational systems (Bacha & Kosa, 2024). The chapter will fill these gaps by using the quantitative methodology and sampling 385 academic staff members, analysing KMO, CFA, and SEM with the help of AMOS software.

This study has more implications beyond the educational sector since improved OCB among educators can be of great help to the broader economic development. Teaching is enhanced by improved performance once teachers are empowered by democratic leadership, which also results in enhanced performance of both teachers and the students (Debele, 2025). This not only benefits the students but also produces a more skilled workforce, which is crucial in pushing forward the development of the economy. Educational institutions can contribute to developing the human capital required for sustainable growth in Ethiopia by establishing a culture of teamwork and collective responsibility (Bacha & Kosa, 2024). This study, thus, aims to shed light on the way democratic educational leadership can have an impact on OCB among Ethiopian teachers, which will eventually lead to a productive learning process and economic development in the area. To answer the main research question, i.e. ***how can organisational citizenship behaviours of Ethiopian educators be affected by democratic education leadership?*** This chapter sheds light on practical measures to be applied to address issues of teacher commitment and engagement in a way that brings about immense changes in the level of quality of education and the prosperity of the economy.

BACKGROUND

Contemporary leadership in democratic education has been developed as a result of the need to have transparency and inclusive governance in educational institutions (Debele, 2025). Nevertheless, the conventional authoritarian forms of leadership are still predominant in academic institutions, especially in Ethiopia, where such frameworks prevent cooperation between educators (Edeh & Ikpor, 2025). Democratic leadership, in turn, helps teachers to change their working environments by focusing on shared decision-making, which results in improved Organisational Citizenship Behaviours (OCB) (Yuliantini et al., 2024). However, it is complicated to maintain democratic leadership within established hierarchical structures that usually lead to the emergence of serious implementation issues (Bacha & Kosa, 2024). Indicatively, these issues were experienced in a secondary school in Addis Ababa when the principal tried to adopt democratic leadership styles. This program was to enrol teachers in making up school policies and curriculum, which was not welcomed by elderly staff who were used to the top-down methodology (Hermanto et al., 2024). A lot of the teachers were not sure if they could influence decisions and believed that leadership was not genuine about hearing their voices (De Clercq & Pereira, 2024). These cultural barriers are significant challenges to the process of introducing democratic practices to educational institutions (Chen et al., 2024).

Equally, a rural school district in Southern Ethiopia experienced a challenge in operating with regard to teachers participating in leadership (Jio et al., 2025). The development of a participatory culture was hindered by resource limitations, the lack of training in democratic leadership, and the inadequate support of the Ministry of Education (Lemi et al., 2025). Teachers claimed that they got overloaded with current roles, which did not leave them with time to contribute to decision-making procedures (Nassir & Benoliel, 2024). These instances depict how challenging it is to promote democratic settings in education where the organisation is not supportive (Dugo et al., 2025). The issues of democratic education leadership establishment in Ethiopia justify the need for a supportive framework that will help educators to adopt this leadership style, besides the need to overcome structural and cultural limitations (Tufa et al., 2025). Enhancement of OCB in teachers is not only vital in improving the outcomes of education but also in boosting economic development. A more involved and dedicated workforce to its educational mission may contribute to improved student performance, which makes the labour force more qualified. This further leads to the growth of the economy through innovation, productivity, and competitiveness in the economy at large. Therefore, this study will investigate these processes in greater detail, which will contribute to future efforts and policy formulation in the Ethiopian education system. The revelation on the effects of democratic leadership on OCB will help policymakers to establish the environment that will foster excellence in education and eventually associate enhanced educational practices with sustainable economic growth in Ethiopia.

The Democratic Education Challenge

Democratic education leadership implementation in the education system tends to encounter complex challenges because there remains a significant difference between perfect collaborative decision participation as well as everyday educational work conditions (Daud et al, 2024). Democratic leadership should establish teaching communities that facilitate decision participation, which then drives positive impacts on both OCB and educational outcomes (Debele, 2025). Data demonstrates that educational institutions primarily use traditional top-down management systems that run contrary to democratic practices (Yuliantini et al., 2024). Results from different research studies present a contradiction about democratic leadership's effect on OCB behaviour because scientists cannot establish its applicability in Ethiopian educational institutions (Bacha & Kosa, 2024). Present findings remain unclear about how socio-cultural and economic elements affect leadership practices in Ethiopian educational facilities, demanding targeted research in this setting (Tufa et al., 2025). Few systematic approaches exist to analyse how democratic leadership operates through OCB behaviour patterns inside developing countries (Edeh & Ikpor, 2025).

Insufficient research details the distinct obstacles which prevent educators from implementing democratic approaches in the educational setting (Sajuyigbe et al., 2024). Democratic leadership in schools faces obstacles from entrenched bureaucratic practices, as well as training deficiencies, and inadequate backing from the school system (Chen et al., 2024). Research reveals insufficient data about the way community customs influence perceptions of educational participation as well as leadership throughout different nations (Hermanto et al., 2024). Educational leaders experience multiple implementation difficulties because they face physical resource constraints alongside opposition from conservative current leadership figures (De Clercq & Pereira, 2024). The purpose of this research is to fill these gaps by thoroughly examining the connection between OCB and democratic leadership among Ethiopian educators (Nassir & Benoliel, 2024). A large sample size as well as sophisticated statistical methods will be used in the study to provide empirical data that accurately captures the distinctive setting of Ethiopian education (Jio et al., 2025). In addition to adding to the theoretical knowledge of democratic leadership in educational environments, the results will provide helpful information for educational leaders as well as policymakers (Maqbool et al., 2024). Finally, by shedding light on strategies to promote democratic behaviours that improve teacher cooperation as well as participation, this study hopes to direct future research as well as guide the creation of policies in Ethiopia's educational system.

THEORETICAL FOUNDATIONS

Transformational Leadership Theory: According to Transformational Leadership Theory, which James MacGregor Burns and Bernard Bass developed, effective leaders bring forth motivation in followers to perform duties above their individual interests for organisational success. According to this theory, leaders need to establish strong connections with followers while effectively communicating vision through open relationships. Transformational leaders in education create supportive settings in which teachers become more engaged, as well as work together as a group. Promoting shared vision enables these leaders to develop trust-based environments that allow educators to improve their OCB behaviours (Yuliantini et al., 2024).

Social Constructivism: The knowledge construction process depends heavily on social cooperation, according to Social Constructivism, which was developed by Lev Vygotsky alongside other theorists. Social constructivism demonstrates how people together generate knowledge by participating in conversations which help them learn. The application of social constructivism in educational institutions requires an acknowledgement that democratic leadership techniques will increase both group learning and student participation. Excellent OCB results from involving educators in team-based decision-making since such involvement fosters their feelings of value as well as respect. Schools develop their democratic culture through inclusive practices based on this critical theory (Daud et al, 2024).

Organisational Citizenship Behaviour (OCB) Theory: Belonging to the work of Dennis Organ, the OCB Theory examines unscripted actions from employees which enhance organisational success despite missing formal job requirements. The combination of altruism, conscientiousness, and civic virtue constitutes Organisational Citizenship Behaviour, which maintains the success of collaborative work settings. The implementation of Organisational Citizenship Behaviour practices among teachers in educational environments will produce better student development together through improved workplace cohesion. Democratic leadership theory demonstrates that it builds organisational citizenship behaviours when it fosters conditions which enable educators to perform tasks beyond their official responsibilities (Hermanto et al., 2024).

Situational Leadership Theory. Effective leadership under Situational Leadership Theory depends on both follower maturity levels as well as contextual factors established by Hersey and Blanchard. A leader needs to modify their approach according to their team members' readiness level as well as competence. The situational leadership approach helps the Ethiopian education system match democratic practices through different educational contexts by adjusting leadership styles to accommodate varying staff levels of experience as well as cultural elements in order to foster OCB (Debele, 2025).

The main theoretical framework used for this research is ***Transformational Leadership Theory***. The researchers selected this theory because it emphasises the inspiration as well as motivation of educators through democratic practices that support the study objective of analysing democratic education leadership as well as OCB relationships.

DEFINITION AND ORIGIN OF CONCEPT

Democratic Education Leadership: A leadership approach that centres on complete stakeholder involvement through decision-making, as well as shared duties in the educational environment, defines participatory leadership. The academic framework, which stems from democratic governance principles, enables teachers to actively join school leadership as well as become involved in policy development (Nassir & Benoliel, 2024).

Organisational Citizenship Behaviour (OCB): Employees demonstrate organisational citizenship behaviours when they voluntarily undertake work actions which receive no formal recognition yet support organisational operations. The three voluntary behaviours of altruism, as well as courtesy, through civic virtue serve as vital elements for building up a healthy workplace environment, as well as organisational success. During the 1980s, Dennis Organ established this concept to demonstrate formal as well as informal aspects necessary for organisational achievement (Daud et al, 2024).

Transformational Leadership: As a leadership approach, it helps leaders inspire their followers to deliver excellent results through building relationships based on mutual respect, trust, and shared organisational vision. James MacGregor Burns popularised transformational versus transactional leadership distinctions through his 1978 book "Leadership", which separated the two leadership approaches based on development as well as change inspiration among followers (Debele, 2025).

Social Constructivism: According to Social Constructivism, learning theory, knowledge forms through public relationship activities as well as wider cultural backgrounds. The learning process heavily depends on social interaction as well as dialogue according to the theory developed by Lev Vygotsky, as well as other theorists. Constructivism began its academic journey during the early 20th century as both an educational and psychological theory that promoted student participation throughout instructional activities (Edeh & Ikpor, 2025).

EMPIRICAL LITERATURE REVIEW

Democratic Education Leadership and Organisational Citizenship Behaviours
Research activity connecting democratic leadership in education to organisational citizenship behaviours (OCB) has expanded in recent years because of growing recognition of participatory leadership principles in educational environments (Edeh & Ikpor, 2025). Different research studies demonstrate that educators show better organisational citizenship behaviours under democratic leadership styles, which combine inclusiveness as well as shared decision-making through collaborative approaches (Daud et al, 2024). The research on Turkish schools showed that principals practising democratic leadership earned greater OCB results from their teaching staff (Bacha & Kosa, 2024). As teachers experience hearing as well as receiving value for their opinions in the workplace, they demonstrate enhanced altruistic behaviours that build support for their school environment (Maqbool et al., 2024). Iranian research confirmed the previous studies by establishing that democratic leadership practices cause teachers to demonstrate more substantial role commitment, which leads to increased OCB (Sajuyigbe et al., 2024). Educators experience higher job satisfaction after participating in decision-making activities, which leads them to deliver extra work beyond standard responsibilities (Demissie et al., 2024). The principles of Transformational Leadership theory show that motivation of followers through inspiration results in positive organisational outcomes (Debele, 2025).

The research investigated democratic leadership patterns inside Zimbabwean educational institutions from an African standpoint (Chen et al., 2024). The researchers demonstrated that through democratic practices, teachers both developed better leadership opinions and demonstrated increased commitment to help colleagues as well as develop the school environment (Sercu et al., 2025). The research underlined the importance of trust and respect because they serve as fundamental elements that build participative cultures necessary for increasing OCB (Hermanto et al., 2024). Research presents evidence about the problems that emerge when trying to establish democratic practices in educational environments (Ayane & Mihiretie, 2024). School leaders encounter two main obstacles while attempting to establish democratic environments, according to research, because staff members do not cooperate as well as institutions fail to provide appropriate backing (Yuliantini et al., 2024). Despite these challenges, their exploration indicated that schools that persisted in promoting democratic Headship saw gradual improvements in OCB, suggesting that sustained efforts can yield positive results over time (De Clercq & Pereira, 2024). Moreover, a meta-analysis synthesised various studies on OCB as well as identified key factors that influence these behaviours, including Headship style. Their findings underscored the significance of transformational as well as democratic Headship in promoting OCB, positioning these Headship styles as essential for enhancing organisational effectiveness (Nassir & Benoliel, 2024).

> H1: Democratic Education Leadership and Organisational Citizenship Behaviours have an empirical association

Democratic Education Leadership and Involvement

Numerous empirical studies have examined the connection between democratic education leadership and teacher participation, emphasising the vital role that participatory leadership plays in encouraging teachers to be actively involved (Yuliantini et al., 2024). Collaborative practices, shared governance, and inclusive decision-making are hallmarks of democratic education leadership and are crucial for promoting teacher participation in school operations (DeBele, 2025). Research continuously demonstrates that teachers' dedication to the school as well as excitement for teaching much rises when they feel empowered and included in decision-making (Edeh & Ikpor, 2025). One noteworthy research looked at how teacher participation in Canadian schools was affected by transformational as well as democratic leadership philosophies (Demissie et al., 2024). According to their results, teacher participation in curriculum creation as well as school improvement projects was greater in schools through principals who exercised democratic leadership (Hermanto et al., 2024). According to this research, democratic leaders foster an atmosphere in which teachers believe their input is appreciated, which boosts involvement as well as a sense of pride in their job (Bacha & Kosa, 2024). In a similar vein, research carried out in the United States found that teacher participation in collaborative planning as well as professional development was greater in schools through strong democratic leadership practices (Sajuyigbe et al., 2024). According to the study, teachers are more likely to participate in meaningful ways that advance their professional development as well as the school's overall efficacy when administrators actively seek out their opinions as well as establish discussion forums (Chen et al., 2024). Because involved instructors are more likely to use creative teaching techniques, this participation not only helps educators but also improves student results (Nassir & Benoliel, 2024).

Research conducted in Zimbabwe brought to light the difficulties as well as achievements of introducing democratic norms in schools within the framework of developing nations (Badada et al., 2025). They found that schools that promoted teacher engagement via democratic leadership reported more participation in school administration as well as projects, despite the presence of hierarchies as well as opposition to change (Daud et al, 2024). The significance of context in determining how much democratic leadership can promote educator participation was highlighted by this research (Jio et al., 2025). Additionally, studies conducted in China have shown that democratic leadership greatly increases teacher participation by creating a feeling of community as well as belonging in schools (Dugo et al., 2025). According to their results, teachers' job satisfaction as well as organisational commitment rise when they participate in decision-making processes, creating a more motivated and cohesive staff (Lemi et al., 2025). In demanding educational settings, this feeling of belonging is essential for encouraging teachers' engagement as well as retention (Badada et al., 2025). Even if the research has shown good connections, there are still obstacles in the way of entirely using democratic leadership's ability to increase teacher participation (De Clercq & Pereira, 2024). Implementing democratic principles may be hampered by obstacles, including deeply embedded hierarchical norms, a lack of institutional backing, and inadequate leadership training. However, research indicates that persistent initiatives to support democratic leadership may progressively foster an engaged culture, which will enhance academic results (Ayane & Mihiretie, 2024).

> H2: Democratic Education Leadership and Involvement has an empirical association

Involvement and Organizational Citizenship Behaviors

Organisational research has focused on the connection between engagement and organisational citizenship behaviours (OCB), especially in educational contexts (Daud et al, 2024). While OCB includes voluntary actions that enhance an organisation's overall efficacy, such as civic virtue, conscientiousness, and generosity, involvement refers to how much an employee participates in their job as well as decision-making processes (Nassir & Benoliel, 2024). Greater levels of participation among educators are continuously linked to greater OCB, according to empirical research, indicating that motivated educators are more inclined to go above and beyond the call of duty (Hermanto et al., 2024). The conceptual underpinning for OCB was developed from fundamental research that showed that workers are more likely to act in ways that benefit their coworkers as well as the company overall when they feel appreciated and invested in their job (Edeh & Ikpor, 2025). Building on this basis, other studies have shown the ways in which engagement affects OCB (Debele, 2025). For example, a research that meta-analysed a number of studies discovered a high positive correlation between OCB and employee participation in a variety of industries, including education (Demissie et al., 2024). According to their results, teachers are more inclined to act helpfully as well as support a pleasant school atmosphere when they believe they have a key role in decision-making (Bacha & Kosa, 2024).

Research in the educational setting emphasised the importance of perceived organisational support in raising OCB as well as participation (Badada et al., 2025). Their study showed that teachers' involvement in school activities rises when they perceive that their administrators value and encourage them, which in turn raises OCB levels (Yuliantini et al., 2024). This connection highlights how vital it is to create a welcoming atmosphere where instructors are encouraged to take an active role in school-related projects (Lemi et al., 2025). The relationship between teacher engagement and OCB was also studied in Iran, and the results showed that teachers who actively participate in decision-making are more likely to behave in ways that benefit their colleagues as well as the school community (Sajuyigbe et al., 2024). According to their research, participation not only improves work satisfaction but also helps educators feel more connected to one another, which further supports OCB (Ayane & Mihiretie, 2024). The findings imply that establishing opportunities for teacher involvement might result in a more cooperative and successful learning environment (Tufa et al., 2025). On the other hand, obstacles to participation may prevent OCB from manifesting. According to research, typical hierarchical school systems often restrict teachers' ability to participate in decision-making (Chen et al., 2024). According to their results, teachers are less likely to demonstrate OCB when they feel left out of crucial conversations (Kant et al., 2025). This emphasises how important it is for school administrators to adopt democratic procedures that promote participation in order to foster a supportive as well as cooperative atmosphere (De Clercq & Pereira, 2024).

H3: Involvement and Organisational Citizenship Behaviours have an empirical association.

Democratic Leadership, OCB and Involvement mediation

In educational research, the relationship among teacher participation, organisational citizenship behaviours (OCB), as well as democratic education leadership has received a lot of attention (Demissie et al., 2024). This highlights the significance of participatory leadership in creating a favourable school atmosphere (Sajuyigbe et al., 2024). According to empirical research, democratic leadership not only has a direct impact on OCB but also increases teacher participation, which acts as a mediator in this connection. Gaining an understanding of these interactions is essential to raising educational standards as well as encouraging teacher collaboration (Yuliantini et al., 2024). Research shows that democratic leadership techniques, such as inclusion as well as shared decision-making, boost teacher participation (Hermanto et al., 2024). According to their results, teachers feel more empowered to take an active role in school governance when school leaders embrace a democratic approach (Ayane & Mihiretie, 2024). In turn, this greater engagement cultivates a feeling of commitment as well as ownership, both of which are necessary for displaying OCB (Bacha & Kosa, 2024). According to the research, OCB as well as democratic leadership are critically mediated by teacher participation, indicating that leaders who place a high priority on democratic practices may foster a more engaged teaching staff (Edeh & Ikpor, 2025).

Research that indicated that teacher participation greatly improves OCB by giving educators the chance to make a meaningful contribution to their schools further supports this mediation effect (Chen et al., 2024). The researchers found that instructors are more inclined to act altruistically, such as helping colleagues as well as taking part in school activities, when they are engaged in decision-making processes (Debele, 2025). This research demonstrates how democratic leadership may result in greater levels of OCB via increased engagement among educators, hence confirming the mediation function of participation (Badada et al., 2025). Also, a meta-analysis supported the idea that engagement is a crucial connection among OCB as well as leadership behaviours (De Clercq & Pereira, 2024). According to their results, instructors are more inclined to act in ways that benefit their peers as well as the company when they are actively engaged in their job as well as decision-making (Ayane & Mihiretie, 2024). This connection emphasises how crucial it is to promote participation via democratic leadership to improve OCB in educational environments (Daud et al, 2024). On the other hand, studies also point out some obstacles to establishing this beneficial association (Jio et al., 2025). Spoke about how conventional hierarchical systems might restrict the possibilities for OCB by preventing teacher engagement (Abebe et al, 2024). According to their research, teachers may feel excluded in the absence of strong democratic leadership, which might lower their level of participation as well as discourage them from taking part in OCB (Dugo et al., 2025). This emphasises how important it is for school administrators to actively support inclusive policies in order to maximise the potential of their employees (Nassir & Benoliel, 2024).

> H4: Democratic Education Leadership, Organisational Citizenship Behaviours and Involvement mediation having an empirical association

Figure 1. Conceptual framework

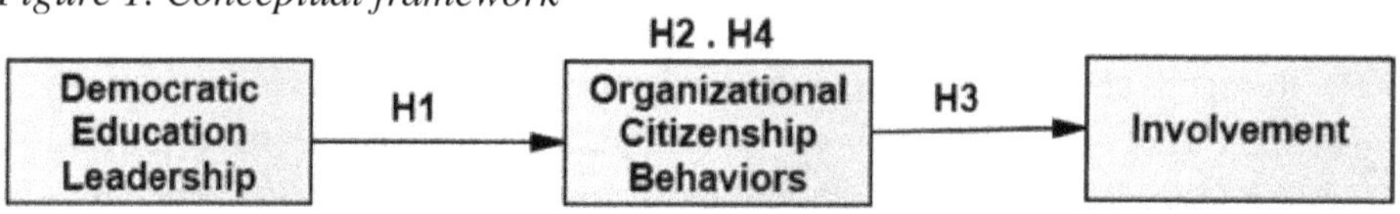

METHODOLOGY

A structured survey was used as part of the quantitative research technique in this study to gather information from a sample of 385 teachers in different Ethiopian schools. This method was used to make a statistical analysis of the connections among teacher participation, organisational citizenship behaviours (OCB), and democratic education leadership easier. The study instrument was created based on a thorough analysis of the relevant literature before data collection to make sure it appropriately captured the components of interest. In order to identify existing validated instruments relating to democratic leadership, OCB, as well as engagement, a thorough literature study was conducted before the scale-building process started. Based on their applicability as well as intelligibility, the items were modified and improved, producing a first scale through many dimensions. Items for democratic education leadership were taken from well-known frameworks that prioritise teacher empowerment as well as participatory decision-making. While the involvement scale focused on elements like involvement in school activities as well as decision-making, the OCB scale included questions that reflected conscientiousness, civic virtue, and altruism. The expert appraisals determined the content validity of each item to ensure that the scale measured what it was intended to measure.

After the completion of the instrument, data were collected and were also subjected to a range of statistical procedures. The adequacy of the sample in factor analysis was measured by the Kaiser-Meyer-Olkin (KMO) measure; a KMO measure of more than 0.70 implies sufficient sampling adequacy. The Exploratory Factor

Analysis (EFA) was then used to establish the underlying factor structures of the scales, and this confirmed that the items loaded onto the predicted constructs as expected. The proposed correlations between democratic education leadership, engagement and OCB were tested with both AMOS software and Structural Equation Modelling (SEM) after the factor structures had been determined. This method of analysis has enabled both the assessment of direct and indirect effects provided, and this provides an in-depth insight into the relationships between these concepts within the educational context. To ensure that the proposed model was a correct representation of the data, the model fit indices were evaluated to ensure that the proposed model was able to provide results on the correlations between the variables under study. Through this meticulous method, the research attempted to contribute to the literature, besides giving practical insights into the dynamics of democratic education leadership, engagement, and OCB. It also aimed at providing practical implications to both the Ethiopian educational policy and practice.

DATA ANALYSIS

Table 1. KMO and Bartlett's Test

Kaiser-Meyer-Olkin Measure of Sampling Adequacy.		**.974**
Bartlett's Test of Sphericity	Approx. Chi-Square	2516.73
	Df	163
	Sig.	.000

Source: Authors

Table 1 presents the results of the Test of Sphericity used by Bartlett and Kaiser-Meyer-Olkin (KMO) of sample adequacy, which are both critical in deciding whether or not the data is fit to be analysed using factor analysis. As the values near 1.0 mean that the data are appropriate to be subjected to factor analysis, it means that the KMO value of 0.974 represents a very high level of sampling adequacy. The current value is far above the acceptable value of KMO of 0.70, meaning that the relationships between the variables are strong enough to warrant further research. Moreover, a chi-square statistic of 2516.73 with 163 degrees of freedom and a level of significance (p-value) of 0.000 indicated the results of the Bartlett Test of Sphericity. This result rejects the null hypothesis that the correlation matrix is an identity matrix, suggesting that the degree of correlation among the variables is statistically significant. In other words, the large p-value supports the suitability of proceeding in the next stage of the analysis of the factors by demonstrating that the variables have significant relationships. Put together, these results are an excellent defence of the exploratory factor analysis that will be presented further, as it will prove that the data can reveal the underlying structure of the concepts being studied.

Table 2. Total Variance Explained

Component	Initial Eigenvalues			Extraction Sums of Squared Loadings			Rotation Sums of Squared Loadings		
	Total	% of Variance	Cumulative %	Total	% of Variance	Cumulative %	Total	% of Variance	Cumulative %
1	4.1	32.5	32.5	4.1	32.5	32.5	3.0	21.1	21.1
2	1.7	9.7	42.2	1.7	9.7	42.2	2.6	15.1	36.2
3	1.7	9.7	51.0	1.7	9.7	51.0	1.8	14.8	51.0
4	.99	6.2	57.2						
5	.81	6.3	64.5						
6	.73	5.9	69.4						

Extraction Method: PCA
Source: Authors

Table 2 presents the total variance of the components that have been acquired as a result of the Principal Component Analysis (PCA) of the exploratory factor analysis. The table contains the eigenvalues of each and every component, the percentage of its variance, and the cumulative percentage before and after rotation. The first component is explained by the first eigenvalue by 32.5 per cent of the total variance of the data, using an eigenvalue of 4.1. It means that the first component captures a substantial amount of the underlying structure of the dataset. They both explain 9.7% of the total variance each, through an eigenvalue of 1.7, when the second and third components are included in the model. The initial three elements still maintain the exact cumulative percentages in examining the extraction amounts of the squared loadings, indicating that the three components were retained during the extraction. Specifically, the three initial factors combined explain 51.0 per cent of the variance, and hence they capture a considerable amount of information on the initial data. The rotation sums of squared loadings are further used to explain the factor structure, where the first component has a total of 3.0 and explains 21.1% of the variance following rotation. After rotation, the second and third components explain 15.1% and 14.8% of the variation, respectively. This rotation leads to the possibility of reading the elements more clearly by simplifying the structure as well as enhancing the variation explained by each component.

Confirmatory Principal Component Examination

Table 3. Covariances

Covariance			**Estimate**	**SE.**	**CR.**	**P**	**Hy.**
Involvement	**<-->**	**Democratic Education Leadership**	**.242**	**.021**	**8.231**	**.00**	**H2**
Involvement	<-->	Organisational Citizenship Behaviours	.303	.032	7.692	.00	**H3**
Democratic Education Leadership	<-->	Organisational Citizenship Behaviours	.254	.24	7.831	.00	**H1**

Source: Authors

The covariance estimates among Organisational Citizenship Behaviours (OCB), teacher participation, and Democratic Education Leadership are shown in Table 3. The findings show that these constructs have meaningful connections with one another, underscoring their interdependence in the educational setting. Through a critical ratio (CR) of 8.231 as well as a standard error (SE) of 0.021, the estimated correlation between involvement and democratic education leadership is 0.242, resulting in a p-value of 0.00. This high statistical significance supports Hypothesis 2 (H2) by indicating that teacher participation rises in tandem with democratic leadership approaches. A p-value of 0.00 is also obtained from the covariance among involvement as well as organisational citizenship behaviours, which is 0.303 through an SE of 0.032 as well as a CR of 7.692. This result confirms Hypothesis 3 (H3), which states that engaged instructors are more likely to display behaviours that are advantageous to the organisation, as well as highlights the positive correlation between teacher participation and OCB. Last but not least, the estimated correlation among Democratic Education Leadership as well as Organisational Citizenship Behaviours is 0.254, through a p-value of 0.00, a SE of 0.24, as well as a CR of 7.831. This finding supports Hypothesis 1 (H1), which states that teachers who have strong democratic leadership have greater levels of OCB.

Table 4. Validity Concern

	CR	AVE	MSV	MaxR(H)		DEL	I	OCB
DEL	0.732	0.643	0.219	0.852		**0.654**		
I	0.758	0.657	0.132	0.763		0.171	**0.665**	
OCB	0.793	0.603	0.274	0.797		0.383	0.193	**0.684**

Note: DEL= Democratic Education Leadership; I= Involvement; OCB= Organizational Citizenship Behaviors

Source: Authors

Key validity indicators, through an emphasis on Composite Reliability (CR), Average Variance Extracted (AVE), Maximum Shared Variance (MSV), as well as Maximum Reliability (MaxR(H)), are shown in Table 4 for the constructs of Democratic Education Leadership (DEL), Involvement (I), as well as Organizational Citizenship Behaviors (OCB). These metrics are crucial for evaluating the validity as well as dependability of the study's measuring scales. Strong internal consistency is shown by the Composite Reliability (CR) ratings for all three components above the generally recognised cutoff of 0.70. In particular, OCB has the greatest CR of 0.793, followed by DEL through a CR of 0.732, as well as I through a CR of 0.758. These values imply that the items inside each construct are consistently measuring the desired ideas. The constructs' validity is further supported by the Average Variance Extracted (AVE) values, which show DEL at 0.643, I at 0.657, as well as OCB at 0.603. Convergent validity is demonstrated by the fact that all AVE values are higher than the suggested cutoff of 0.50, indicating that the latent constructs account for a substantial amount of the variation in the observable variables.

Additionally provided are the Maximum Shared Variance (MSV) values, which are OCB at 0.274, I at 0.132, as well as DEL at 0.219. Since the MSV should be less than the AVE for each construct, these numbers show that there is little overlap across the constructs, confirming the measures' discriminant validity. Finally, the scales' robustness is confirmed by the Maximum Reliability (MaxR(H)) values, which have DEL at 0.852, I at 0.763, as well as OCB at 0.797. These numbers show that the measurement scales are very reliable for all structures.

Mediating Role Examination

Figure 2. Structural Equation Model

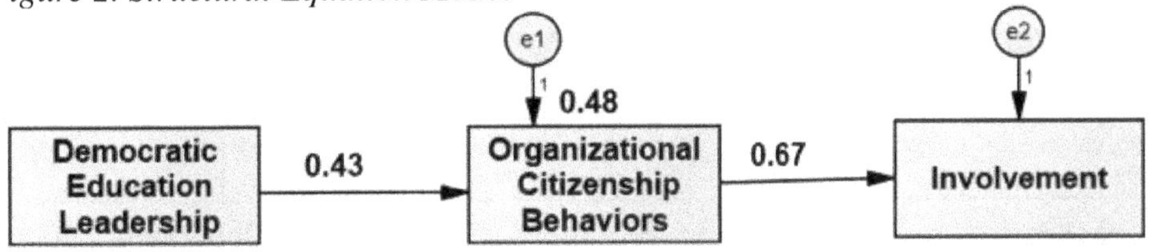

Model fit indices

Table 5. indices for Model Fit

Sig.	Chi-Sq	RMR	Fitness Goodness	Fitness Confirmatory	TLI	RMSEA
0.006	1.053	.032	0.924	0.904	0.903	.030

Source: Authors

The structural equation modelling (SEM) analysis's model fit indices are compiled in Table 5, which offers essential information about how well the suggested model represents the data. Through a stated significance value (Sig.) of 0.006, the model is statistically significant, implying that the proposed connections among the components are essential. The Chi-Square value shows excellent results at 1.053 owing to its low stature because more modest figures signify better correspondence between the model predictions and actual data observations. The predicted correlations sufficiently match observed values according to the Root Mean Square Residual figure, which reports 0.032 while showing minimal differences between actual and expected data points. The values for the Comparative Fit Index (CFI) reached 0.904, and the Goodness of Fit Index (GFI) attained 0.924. The data fit indicates a good model performance because these indices surpass the accepted cutoff threshold of 0.90. The high value of 0.903 for the Tucker-Lewis Index confirms a suitable model fit because it approaches the optimal benchmark of 1. The Researcher reported a Root Mean Square Error of Approximation (RMSEA) value of 0.030, which demonstrates a satisfactory match with standards. The model demonstrates a precise data match because its findings align very closely with the observed data.

Table 6. Regression Examination

Relative			**Approx.**	**SE.**	**CR.**	**P**	**Ass.**
Involvement	**<---**	**Democratic Education Leadership**	**.875**	**.152**	**7.693**	**.00**	**H2**
Organisational Citizenship Behaviours	<---	Involvement	.346	.142	2.961	.00	H3
Organisational Citizenship Behaviours	<---	Democratic Education Leadership	.968	.204	8.051	.00	H1

Source: Authors

The findings of the regression analysis performed to evaluate the connections among Democratic Education Leadership, Involvement, and Organisational Citizenship Behaviours (OCB) are shown in Table 6. Each path's coefficients, critical ratios (CR), standard errors (SE), as well as p-values, are given to show how strong and significant these associations are. The regression coefficient for the first path—from Democratic Education Leadership to Involvement—is 0.875, with a critical ratio of 7.693 as well as a standard error of 0.152. According to the indicated p-value of 0.00, there is a very significant association. This high coefficient supports the hypothesis (H2) that successful democratic leadership increases educator engagement, as well as indicates that democratic education leadership significantly improves teacher participation. The correlation among involvement as well as organisational citizenship behaviours is examined in the second route, which yields a critical ratio of 2.961, a regression coefficient of 0.346, as well as a standard error of 0.142. This path's p-value is also 0.00, indicating a statistically significant association. This result validates the hypothesis (H3) that teachers' participation in OCB is positively correlated with their level of involvement, suggesting that more active instructors are more likely to act in ways that benefit their peers as well as the school community. Lastly, a regression coefficient of 0.968, a standard error of 0.204, as well as a critical ratio of 8.051 are found for the direct association between Democratic Education Leadership and Organisational Citizenship Behaviours. Once again, a very significant impact is shown by the p-value of 0.00. The hypothesis (H1) that democratic education leadership has a direct effect on OCB is supported by this high coefficient, which implies that good leadership practices not only improve engagement but also raise citizenship behaviours among teachers.

Table 7. Mediating Role Effect

	Influence	Worth	Path Influence
Democratic Education Leadership → Organisational Citizenship Behaviours	Direct Influence	.43	Direct influence stated
Democratic Education Leadership → Involvement → Organisational Citizenship Behaviours	Indirect Influence	.74*.67=.48	Indirect Influence Ensued
	Whole influence	.91	Partial mediation

Source: Authors

The association between Democratic Education Leadership and Organisational Citizenship Behaviours (OCB) is mediated by involvement, as shown in Table 7. The table offers a thorough understanding of the interactions among these constructs by presenting both direct and indirect impacts. A considerable as well as favourable impact of leadership practices on teachers' civic behaviours is shown by the direct influence of Democratic Education Leadership on OCB, which is measured at 0.43. This direct consequence implies that OCB among educators is directly facilitated by competent democratic leadership. On the other hand, the chart also emphasises Democratic Education Leadership's indirect impact via involvement. The calculation of path influence yields an indirect impact of 0.48, which is equal to 0.74 (the effect of leadership on participation) times 0.67 (the impact of involvement on OCB). This result suggests that increased teacher participation accounts for a significant amount of the indirect effects of democratic leadership on OCB. The sum of the direct as well as indirect channels' combined effects, when taking into account the overall impact, is 0.91. This high overall impact shows that OCB, as well as Democratic Education Leadership, have a solid connection. Nonetheless, the fact that the direct influence is still substantial suggests that there is some mediation, which means that although involvement is essential in fostering the connection, Democratic Education Leadership also has a direct impact on OCB.

DISCUSSION

The results of this research emphasise the importance of Democratic Education Leadership in improving the engagement of teachers and the Organisational Citizenship Behaviours (OCB) in the classroom. Teachers are highly empowered, and this participation in decision-making processes has a significant effect on their engagement in their duties. These aspects have a substantial positive correlation with democratic leadership and teacher engagement practices. Studies have consistently shown that participatory leadership in schools provides desirable learning conditions that are critical in driving success in education. The close association between teacher participation and OCB indicates the basic relationship between these two variables. When teachers are active participants in school-related activities, they are more likely to perform behaviours that not only benefit those with whom they engage, but also the school society at large. This social attitude fosters a sense of solidarity and joint accountability, which is crucial in attaining improved learning results. The findings show that school leadership ought to focus on teacher engagement to foster a culture of cooperation among the teaching personnel, which eventually leads to improved education delivery to the students.

Further, the research finds a partial mediating role played by teacher involvement between Democratic Education Leadership and OCB, and confirms that strong leadership can directly relate to OCB without the need to have teacher involvement as a mediator. This autonomy implies that good leadership practices can trigger the change in OCB even in situations when the immediate teacher intervention is constrained. As a result, the educational leaders must be engaged in enacting direct democratic procedures that not only promote the creation of desirable school climates but also promote teacher involvement and encouragement. Connecting these results to the economic growth, one can see that it is not only an internal improvement of the educators to improve OCB; the result has systematic implications on the economy. Increased involvement of the teaching workforce will translate into better education results, vital to the production of a skilled workforce. The quality of education is also directly related to the economy of a country in an ever-competitive global economy. Through investment in democratic leadership practices, institutions of learning can establish a culture which facilitates innovation, performance increase and economic growth. The ripple effects could also create a more skilled and flexible labour force as the involvement of teachers and the level of OCB grow. This labour force will be critical towards satisfying the needs of such a vibrant economy, hence sustainable economic development in Ethiopia. The bottom line is that democratic education leadership implementation is a strategic investment in the future of the country's economy, as well as improving the education environment.

CONCLUSION

This research offers strong proof of the essential connections among Organisational Citizenship Behaviours (OCB), teacher participation, and Democratic Education Leadership. The results show that good democratic leadership techniques are critical for encouraging OCB among teachers in addition to increasing teacher participation. The significance of empowering teachers via collaborative practices as well as participatory decision-making is shown by the substantial direct effect of leadership on OCB. Furthermore, the mediating function of engagement emphasises how interrelated these concepts are, implying that active educators are more likely to demonstrate good citizenship practices that are advantageous to their institutions. The partial mediation effect further highlights how meaningful participation is, yet democratic leadership still has a significant direct influence. All things considered, this study adds to the body of knowledge by clarifying the dynamics of leadership as well as how they affect learning settings. The practical ramifications are evident: educational leaders need to give democratic leadership styles top priority, as well as make a concerted effort to include teachers in school administration. By doing this, they may create a cooperative as well as encouraging environment that raises teacher morale as well as fosters an organisational citizenship culture, both of which will eventually boost student learning results.

Managerial implications

The study's conclusions provide insightful information for administrators as well as educational leaders looking to improve their institutions' efficacy. First and foremost, the data demonstrating Democratic Education Leadership's beneficial effects on teacher participation emphasises how important it is for school administrators to embrace participatory decision-making techniques. The creation of inclusive environments by leaders serves as a strong approach to enhance staff engagement through conversations and decision-making opportunities with educators. The school administration should enact programs which promote engagement because teacher involvement clearly relates to Organisational Citizenship Behaviours (OCB). Educational forums for collaborative interaction should be established to allow teachers access to sharing ideas while pursuing joint assignments and developing professional competencies. Such programs enhance school-wide group unity and shared purpose, together with improved staff engagement. School administrators must receive ongoing training according to the report because it enables them to improve their democratic leadership performance. The mission of development programs should focus on teaching administrators effective ways to lead teachers while building positive work relationships throughout schools. Schools obtain better learning outcomes and teacher retention rates, and create a total positive environment through investments in leadership development programs.

Practical implications

The study's conclusions have significant real-world ramifications for academic institutions looking to improve their operational efficiency. First and foremost, school administrators need to aggressively adopt democratic leadership techniques that promote teacher involvement in decision-making. Regular meetings, cooperative committees, and feedback systems that let educators express their thoughts as well as participate in school governance help accomplish this. Establishing such inclusive systems encourages a feeling of responsibility as well as ownership among staff members, in addition to empowering instructors. Programs for professional development that emphasise abilities linked to democratic leadership as well as good communication should also be given top priority in schools. Training sessions may provide leaders with the skills they need to promote cooperation among teachers as well as conduct fruitful discussions. School administrators may foster an atmosphere that encourages participation as well as respect for one another by cultivating these qualities.

Additionally, the school's strategic planning should include activities to boost teacher participation. This includes setting up mentoring programs, collaborating across departments, and giving educators the chance to conduct training sessions or seminars. Since motivated teachers are more likely to encourage one another as well as foster a healthy school climate, such programs not only increase teacher participation but also have a favourable impact on OCB.

Theoretical implications

By emphasising the complex connections among Democratic Education Leadership, teacher participation, and Organisational Citizenship Behaviours (OCB), the study's results add to the body of research already available on educational leadership as well as organisational behaviour. This study supports theoretical frameworks that highlight how crucial participatory leadership approaches are to creating a cooperative learning environment in schools. Transformational as well as participatory leadership theories are supported as well as expanded by the research, which shows that democratic leadership not only increases teacher participation but also has a direct impact on OCB. Also, the discovery of engagement as a mediating element broadens our knowledge of how teacher actions in educational contexts are impacted by leadership approaches. This mediating function implies that democratic leadership functions via intricate as well as varied processes, which is consistent with more general theories of organisational behaviour that highlight the relationship among organisational performance, employee engagement, and leadership. By including the idea of OCB as a crucial consequence of successful leadership practices, the results also encourage a reassessment of current models of educational leadership. This integration stimulates further research into how different leadership philosophies may be used to advance both the effectiveness of the organisation as a whole and the performance of individual teachers.

RECOMMENDATIONS

Several suggestions may be made for educational leaders as well as legislators who want to improve the efficacy of their institutions in light of the study's results. First and foremost, school administrators must embrace and put into practice democratic leadership techniques that really give teachers more authority. Establishing advisory groups or holding frequent feedback sessions are two examples of organised ways to encourage teacher involvement in decision-making processes. Teachers may develop a feeling of ownership as well as dedication to the school's goal by actively participating in governance. Schools should also fund professional development initiatives that aim to improve leaders' abilities in collaborative as well as democratic leadership. Effective communication handling disagreement, as well as methods for really involving instructors, should be the main topics of training sessions. Giving school administrators these skills may contribute to the development of a more welcoming and encouraging school climate. Institutions of higher learning could also create programs primarily aimed at boosting teacher participation. This might include chances for instructors to conduct seminars for professional development, collaborative teaching techniques, and mentoring programs. Schools may improve teacher engagement as well as encourage excellent Organisational Citizenship Behaviours by supporting such efforts. Finally, to gauge the success of democratic practices as well as participatory programs, continuous assessment as well as feedback systems must be put in place. Gathering information on teacher engagement as well as satisfaction regularly might provide insightful information for ongoing development. Educational leaders may foster a more cooperative atmosphere that boosts teacher morale as well as advances the general efficacy and success of the school by implementing these suggestions.

FUTURE DIRECTIONS

The study's conclusions provide a number of directions for further investigation in the domains of organisational behaviour as well as educational leadership. Examining the precise processes by which Democratic Education Leadership affects teacher participation as well as Organisational Citizenship Behaviours (OCB) is one promising avenue. In order to better understand causal links, future research might use longitudinal designs to evaluate how changes in leadership practices affect teacher engagement as well as school culture over time. Researchers should also look at how contextual variables, such as neighbourhood demographics, school size, and cultural influences, can moderate the connections found in this study. Gaining insight into how these factors interact through democratic leadership approaches may highlight significant subtleties that might guide customised solutions in a range of educational contexts. Future research might also examine how OCB, as well as teacher participation, affect student results. A more thorough grasp of the advantages of democratic leadership methods would come from studying the effects of collaborative as well as engaged learning settings on student performance, motivation, and general well-being. Lastly, to get a deeper comprehension of the real-life experiences of educators as well as leaders in democratic contexts, qualitative research techniques like case studies or interviews should be used. This might reveal the difficulties as well as achievements of using such strategies in practical settings, providing insightful guidance for school administrators looking to improve their leadership styles.

REFERENCES

Abebe, Z. A., Admassu, K. A., & Belayneh, T. N. (2024). Interplay between civic engagement, political trust, and support for democracy: Insights from a study on youth students at Addis Ababa University, Ethiopia. *Social Sciences & Humanities Open*, *10*, 101152. DOI: 10.1016/j.ssaho.2024.101152

Ayane, Z. T., & Mihiretie, D. M. (2024). Developing good person and citizen through civic and ethical education in Ethiopia: A content analysis of secondary school textbooks. *Social Sciences & Humanities Open*, *10*, 100913. DOI: 10.1016/j.ssaho.2024.100913

Bacha, N. S., & Kosa, C. A. (2024). Nurturing a sense of institutional citizenship behaviour: Role of perceived transformational leadership style and organisationalorganisational support mediated by affective professional commitment. *Leadership and Policy in Schools*, *23*(2), 235–252. DOI: 10.1080/15700763.2022.2113799

Badada, B., Delina, G., Krishnaraj, R., & Thiruthuvanathan, M. M. (2025). Navigating Leadership and Technology Integration in the Digital Age: Success Factors and Determinants. *Insights Into Digital Business, Human Resource Management, and Competitiveness*, 349-376.

Chen, C., Duan, J., & Peng, Y. (2024). How does sense of power influence change-oriented organisational citizenship behavior? Evidence from China. *Public Performance & Management Review*, *47*(3), 732–760. DOI: 10.1080/15309576.2023.2298414

Daud, A., Dj, A. A., Adianita, H., & Mado, Y. J. (2024). The influence of participative leadership style on job satisfaction with organisational citizenship behavior as a moderating variable. *Reslaj: Religion Education Social Laa Roiba Journal*, *6*(4), 2192–2200. DOI: 10.47467/reslaj.v6i4.1918

De Clercq, D., & Pereira, R. (2024). How resilient employees can prevent family ostracism from escalating into diminished work engagement and change-oriented organisational citizenship behavior. *International Studies of Management & Organization*, *54*(1), 25–47. DOI: 10.1080/00208825.2023.2277968

Debele, E. T. (2025). Exploring Leadership's Impact on Working Culture, Organizational Culture, and Institutional Development at Samara University, Ethiopia: A Qualitative Study. *Social Sciences*, *14*(2), 94–108. DOI: 10.11648/j.ss.20251402.14

Demissie, A. D., Alemu, A. E., & Tensay, A. T. (2024). The nexus between servant leadership and organisational citizenship behavior through the mediating role of perceived organisational politics in Ethiopian federal public service organisations. *Cogent Business & Management*, *11*(1), 2336653. DOI: 10.1080/23311975.2024.2336653

Dugo, D., Kant, S., & Alemu, Z. K. (2025). Servant Leadership Influence on Organizational Citizenship Behavior With the Mediation Role of Emotional Intelligence: A Case of Public Universities in Ethiopia. In *Generation Alpha and Next Generation Leadership for Greener Futures* (pp. 269-292). IGI Global Scientific Publishing. DOI: DOI: 10.4018/979-8-3693-9281-2.ch014

Edeh, F. O., & Ikpor, I. M. (2025). Work-life balance in the service sector: Predicting organisational citizenship behaviour. *European Journal of International Management*, *25*(1), 122–137. DOI: 10.1504/EJIM.2025.143277

Hermanto, Y. B., Srimulyani, V. A., & Pitoyo, D. J. (2024). The mediating role of quality of work life and organisational commitment in the link between transformational leadership and organisational citizenship behavior. *Heliyon*, *10*(6), e27664. DOI: 10.1016/j.heliyon.2024.e27664 PMID: 38509945

Jio, W., Kant, S., & Lemi, K. (2025). Ethical Leadership: Effect on Future of Organizational Citizenship Behavior by Mediation of Organizational Culture in Ethiopia. In *Generation Alpha and Next Generaion Leadership for Greener Futures* (pp. 41-62). IGI Global Scientific Publishing. DOI: DOI: 10.4018/979-8-3693-9281-2.ch003

Jio, W., Kant, S., & Lemi, K. (2025). The Influence of Ethical Leadership on Organizational Citizenship Behavior by the Mediating Role of Organizational Commitment in Ethiopia. In *Humanising the Hyperconnected Workplace* (pp. 221–248). IGI Global Scientific Publishing., DOI: 10.4018/979-8-3693-8171-7.ch008

Kant, S., Adula, M., & Badi, S. (2025). Leading With Wisdom: The Role of Wise Leaders in Ethiopia. In *Harnessing Happiness and Wisdom for Organizational Well-Being* (pp. 361-390). IGI Global Scientific Publishing.

Lemi, K., Kant, S., & Jio, W. (2025). Greener Hospital Future in the Horn of Africa by Transactional Leadership: Outcome on Altruism Through Adaptability. In *Generation Alpha and Next Generation Leadership for Greener Futures* (pp. 1-22). IGI Global Scientific Publishing. DOI: DOI: 10.4018/979-8-3693-9281-2.ch001

Maqbool, S., Zafeer, H. M. I., Maqbool, S., Zeng, P., Draissi, Z., & Javed, S. (2024). Stance of numerous leadership styles and their effect on teaching to sustain academic performance at the high school level. *Heliyon*, *10*(16), e36438. DOI: 10.1016/j.heliyon.2024.e36438 PMID: 39253217

Nassir, M., & Benoliel, P. (2024). Teacher well-being and organisational citizenship behavior in Arab educational system in Israel: The implications of teacher collective involvement in decision making and organisational commitment. *School Psychology*, *39*(3), 256–268. DOI: 10.1037/spq0000610 PMID: 38166297

Sajuyigbe, A. S., Abiodun, A., Ayeni, A., & Ineba, H. L. (2024). Organisational Citizenship Behavior, Employee Voice and Academic Staff Retention in Nigerian Universities: Mediating Role of Conflict Resolution. *Revista Colombiana de Psicología, 33*(1), 87–106. DOI: 10.15446/rcp.v33n1.100117

Sercu, L., Ayana, D. K., & Mengistu, D. (2025). Intercultural Citizenship Education in Post-Conflict Contexts: The Case of Ethiopia. *African Journal of Education and Practice, 11*(2), 17–35. DOI: 10.47604/ajep.3287

Tufa, G., Kinde, Z., & Kant, S. (2025). Strategic Leadership: Effect on Employee Performance With Mediation of Dynamic Capabilities in Case of Ethiopian Public Organizations. In *Generation Alpha and Next Generation Leadership for Greener Futures* (pp. 115-138). IGI Global Scientific Publishing. DOI: DOI: 10.4018/979-8-3693-9281-2.ch006

Yuliantini, T., Ramli, Y., Kuswibowo, C., Zulfikar, R. R. O., & Soelton, M. (2024). Conceptualizing Work Engagement And Knowledge Sharing To Increase Organisational Citizenship Behavior. *Jurnal Riset Bisnis dan Manajemen, 17*(2), 105-116.

KEY TERMS AND DEFINITIONS

Collaborative Environment: The combination of workplace culture that emphasises teamwork among staff members leads to unified objectives as well as shared issue resolution approaches.

Democratic Education Leadership: The leadership method supports decision-making participation through staff involvement, which enables teachers to give input as well as collaborate for school governance processes.

Organisational Citizenship Behaviours (OCB): Workspace behaviours which employees perform beyond their required duties result in operational organisational success through social assistance to co-workers, as well as the creation of positive settings.

Participatory Leadership: A leadership methodology that brings stakeholders into decision-making together through appreciating their input while building a team-focused environment.

Professional Development: Educators benefit through specialised training programs, which enhance their capabilities, thus they teach better, leading to positive results for students.

Teacher Involvement: The committed involvement of educators in school events throughout decision-making tasks, as well as continued development, leads them to identify strongly with the institution.

Transformational Leadership: Please refer to this leadership style because it leads followers toward maximum potential while surpassing expectations by using genuine vision, motivational encouragement, and supportive strategies.

Chapter 8

Peace Education and National Security:
Implications for Educational Leadership and Economic Growth in Nigeria

Goodnews Osah
https://orcid.org/0000-0002-0276-0957
Babcock University, Nigeria

Chinedu Ekperechukwu Eti
https://orcid.org/0000-0001-8382-2488
Babcock University, Nigeria

Nnamdi Chijindu Azubuike
https://orcid.org/0009-0006-4667-5152
Babcock University, Nigeria

ABSTRACT

Nigeria faces persistent challenges to national security, arising from ethnic and religious conflicts, terrorism and widespread violence. This highlights the importance of both critical political and educational leadership and effective peace education. Peace education aims to equip individuals with the skills and knowledge to resolve conflicts peacefully, promote tolerance, political accountability and build inclusive societies. Leadership, particularly educational leadership that is focused on peace education, would prioritise adequate funding, educational quality and curricula reform, which will lead to innovation and human capital development that can foster environments where open dialogue and diverse viewpoints are valued, thus providing an opportunity for effective peacebuilding and meaningful economic

DOI: 10.4018/979-8-3373-3616-9.ch008

growth in various spheres. Through the nation's educational curriculum and willing educational leaders, there is great potential for ensuring national security through peacebuilding mechanisms, promoting a sense of civic responsibility and active citizenship, amidst diversity.

INTRODUCTION

Peace education is an intentional, transformative process designed to cultivate the knowledge, skills, values, and attitudes necessary for individuals to prevent and resolve conflict nonviolently, to create conditions conducive to peace, and to establish a global culture of peace. It is a holistic approach that moves beyond the mere absence of violence to advocate for the presence of justice, equity, and human dignity. Peace education addresses the conditions of injustice, intolerance, and inequality that contribute to internal conflict, a significant threat to modern national security. It produces citizens with the skills to manage disagreements and political differences through dialogue and democratic processes, reducing the likelihood of resorting to violence, insurgency, or civil disorder. By promoting respect for diversity, global citizenship, and human rights, peace education helps integrate disparate groups, leading to stronger social cohesion and a unified national identity. An educated citizenry equipped with critical thinking skills is better prepared to hold government institutions accountable, promoting good governance and the rule of law—key components of human security and national stability (Azadi & Das, 2024).

National security, on the other hand, is a contested concept that has evolved dramatically from its traditional, purely military focus to a multifaceted, comprehensive framework encompassing military, economic, societal, and environmental threats. It is fundamentally defined as the ability of a state to protect its vital interests, core values, and territory, while ensuring the safety and well-being of its citizens. Proper national security is not found in stronger walls, but in stronger communities. It is not just about defending the *state*; it is about safeguarding the people, their dignity, their rights, and their ability to thrive. By cultivating values such as empathy, nonviolence, and critical thinking, peace education transforms the conversation from one of military might to one of human resilience and compassion. It teaches individuals the skills to resolve conflicts peacefully, address the root causes of injustice, and build a society where 'freedom from fear' and 'freedom from want' are guaranteed for all.

Nigeria faces persistent threats to its national security. These threats are rooted in ethnic tensions, religious intolerance, political instability, youth unrest, terrorism, and a weak sense of national identity (Ojo, Oyewole & Aina, 2023). Efforts at resolving these concerns have often been reactive and militarised. Thus, creating new dimensions in the conflicts and leaving little or no progress in addressing the root causes (Mbagwu, 2016). In light of this, peace education has emerged as a viable and necessary strategy to foster long-term security through non-violent means.

Nigeria's sociological landscape is a complex blend of ethnic conflicts, political rivalries, and resource-based disputes that frequently disrupt social stability. Early exposure to these skills is crucial in helping learners and citizens manage and resolve these conflicts. In conflict-affected regions such as Kaduna, Benue, and Plateau states, as well as the Niger Delta region, community peacebuilding initiatives have demonstrated that when young people are equipped with these tools, they can play a vital role in breaking cycles of violence and mistrust (Bolanle, 2021). Therefore, peace education that prioritises conflict resolution and mediation skills not only improves individual social competence but also contributes to national efforts in building a more peaceful and cohesive society. For example, in the government secondary school in Chibok town, Borno State, north-east of Nigeria, 276 teenage girls were abducted overnight in 2014. This large-scale abduction was carried out by the Boko Haram terrorist group operating in northern Nigeria and some parts of West Africa. The abduction left many dead, and several others injured, displaced and separated in an attempt to secure their lives. In 2017, three years later, Peace Insight, through one of its programmes, "Counselling on Wheels", embarked on a psychological and trauma-support training programme to help victims and survivors build emotional resilience and break the cycle of repetitive violence. The training models included counselling, music, and dance therapy to heal and connect. Participants recounted how valuable the trainings were in helping to understand mental health and the effect of trauma (Kenneth, 2025).

Youths trained in mediation can serve as local peace ambassadors in areas plagued by communal violence, offering dialogue-based alternatives to retaliation. The preceding sections of this chapter explore how peace education can contribute to national security in Nigeria by examining key concepts, current challenges and pathways for meaningful integration into national life.

CONCEPTUAL BACKGROUND

Peace Education

Peace education is the process of acquiring the values, knowledge, and skills needed to promote peace, prevent conflict, and resolve disputes through dialogue and understanding (Kertyzia, 2021). It focuses on tolerance, empathy, cooperation, and respect for diversity. When embedded in the education system and social policies, peace education can contribute to building a culture of peace, strengthening civic responsibility, and reducing tendencies toward violence and extremism (Nelson, 2021).

One of the foundational pillars of peace education is equipping learners with the capacity to resolve conflicts peacefully. Conflict resolution involves identifying the underlying causes of a dispute, understanding the interests and needs of all parties involved, and working toward mutually satisfactory outcomes through dialogue, compromise, and collaboration (Hasan, 2023). In peace education, students are taught to recognise conflict not as something inherently negative, but as an opportunity for growth and relationship building. Through structured lessons, they learn how to de-escalate tensions, engage in active listening, and communicate assertively but respectfully. Mediation skills, in particular, enable them to act as neutral third parties who help others reach a mutually beneficial agreement (Terepyshchyi, 2021). These skills build emotional resilience, promote empathy and empower students to intervene constructively when conflicts arise. More importantly, these skills are transferable beyond the classroom, helping students navigate family disagreements, community tensions, and workplace or civic conflicts (Riyani, Brata, & Shintasiwi, 2021).

Escalating conflicts and societal fragmentations mark recent global dynamics. The concept of peace education in these circumstances illuminates a critical framework for addressing the root causes of fragmentation and violence, and fosters sustainable peace. Peace education provides the intellectual and practical tools necessary to understand conflict dynamics, identify underlying issues and develop effective strategies for conflict resolution. As Özel and Sümer (2025) observe, peace education has evolved over the past century into a multidimensional approach capable of addressing various forms of violence while creating pathways toward a more peaceful world.

Peace education is an intentional and systematic process that helps individuals, particularly students and young people, develop the knowledge, skills, values and attitudes necessary to prevent violence, resolve conflicts peacefully and contribute to a culture of peace. It is not just about teaching the absence of war, but also about fostering the presence of justice, tolerance, empathy, and mutual respect (UNESCO, 2023a). Thus, Emeodu and Famo (2023) describe peace education as an all-encompassing process that equips individuals with the knowledge, skills, values, and attitudes essential for resolving conflicts across diverse contexts—whether intrapersonal, interpersonal, intergroup, local, national, or international.

Cremin (2016) further emphasises that peace education extends beyond the mere transmission of knowledge. It incorporates dimensions of inner and outer peace, thus offering a more profound and holistic understanding of peace as both a personal and societal construct. Similarly, Cabezudo and Haavelsrud (2007) elaborate that peace education encompasses two interconnected approaches: its content and its communicative form. Together, these dimensions enable learners to engage meaningfully with the complexities of peace and violence.

Despite its significance, Danesh (2006) acknowledges the conceptual difficulties in defining peace education. Nevertheless, he argues that peace, as a foundational principle, provides a critical framework for addressing all forms of conflict. Also, Wilson (2009) contributes to this discourse by conceptualising peace education from two complementary perspectives: one focused on the absence of adverse conditions such as violence and hostility, and another centred on the presence of positive qualities such as harmony, empathy, respect for diversity, and an appreciation of human interconnectedness and interdependence.

UNESCO (2023) emphasises that peace education plays a crucial role in mitigating social prejudice and promoting intercultural competence. In educational settings, students who are exposed to diversity in a positive, structured way are more likely to develop empathy, engage in cooperative behaviour, and resist hate speech and group-based animosity. These attitudes contribute directly to social cohesion and national unity. Similarly, Wilson (2009) argues that peace education promotes a culture of peace rooted in nonviolence, compassion, fairness, cooperation, and reverence for all forms of life. Importantly, Oni and Ijove (2022) further note that peace education is not confined to formal education settings but can also be advanced through informal channels such as media, workshops, conferences, adult literacy programs, and family-based education.

The importance of peace education in breaking cycles of generational conflict has been highlighted by Emeodu and Famo (2023). They argue that without such interventions, unresolved tensions and fears perpetuate violence across generations, with younger cohorts often unaware of the original causes of the conflicts they inherit. This aligns with the perspective of the Global Partnership for Education (GPE) (2024), which identifies education as a crucial driver and pillar of a peaceful future. Education, they assert, fosters inclusivity and promotes tolerance and coexistence among diverse groups. As Wilson (2009) eloquently states, peace education is rooted in values such as love, compassion, fairness, cooperation, and respect for human dignity and life.

Recognising the global relevance of these principles, the United Nations Educational, Scientific, and Cultural Organisation (UNESCO) has positioned peace education as an integral part of peacebuilding, aimed at achieving inclusivity and fostering a culture of tolerance (Osah et al., 2021). They identify peace education as an essential element of nation-building, thus being a building block that cultivates the quality of leadership and governance necessary for sustainable peace and national security. Building on these perspectives, this chapter conceptualises peace education as a foundation for fostering quality leadership that strengthens governance and contributes to the realisation of sustainable peace and national security in Nigeria.

National Security

With the prevailing global insecurities and the rising incidences of violent conflicts, the concept of national security has come under increasing scrutiny. The frequent destruction of lives and property across various regions underscores the need to interrogate what constitutes national security, identify the missing elements in its implementation, and explore how it can promote sustainable peace alongside good governance. While the concept of national security has historical roots tracing back to the early 1940s, its prominence grew during World War II, an era characterised by the tension between interdependence and the assertion of national sovereignty (Grizold, 1994).

Grizold (1994) conceptualises national security as encompassing interdependence and cooperation among states while maintaining a focus on the sovereign functions of the nation-state. He broadly defines national security as a condition in which the state safeguards its territory, protects its citizens and their property, upholds sovereignty, and ensures the functioning of its economic, political, cultural, and ecological systems. Consequently, Wu (2025) averred that national security broadly refers to the defence of a sovereign state by its government, encompassing the protection of citizens, the economy, and institutions from military and non-military threats, including terrorism, crime, economic insecurity, energy and environmental challenges, food shortages, and cyber vulnerabilities.

Viter and Rudenko (2025) complement this view by advocating for a multi-domain approach to national security. They propose a comprehensive deterrence strategy that integrates diplomatic, informational, military, and economic instruments of power. Their framework emphasises the need for flexibility and resilience in responding to diverse adversaries and complex global threats. It also highlights the importance of striking a balance between security imperatives and sustainable societal development to ensure long-term strategic stability. Meanwhile, in striking a balance of sustainable societal development, Antai et al. (2025) introduce a critical dimension to the discourse by highlighting the interrelationship between national security, good governance, and human rights. They argue that human rights considerations are indispensable for building a democratic foundation that supports political and military stability. Integrating human rights into national security frameworks, they contend, enhances societal trust and strengthens the legitimacy of governance structures, laying the groundwork for a more secure and stable state. Incorporating these perspectives of national security and the promotion of sustainable peace, this chapter argues that a missing element is quality leadership, because how can a state achieve national security and sustainable peace without a leader providing good governance? Hence, it is important to understand the concept of leadership.

Leadership

Leadership is a multi-dimensional concept that has evolved, shaped by the intricacies of human societies and the demands of governance. Historically, leadership discourse has been grounded in a range of approaches reflecting different understandings of power and influence. Currie et al. (2012) highlight four classic approaches that have dominated leadership discourse over the past two centuries: the trait, situationist, contingency, and transactional approaches. These models underscore shifts in thinking from innate leader qualities (traits) to contextual and relational factors that determine effective leadership. Similarly, Weiskittel (1999) expands on this evolution by highlighting various leadership styles, including autocratic, democratic, situational, transformational, and free rein. These terminologies reflect different approaches to authority and decision-making, illustrating how leaders influence, guide, and inspire individuals, groups or even entire states towards achieving collective goals while addressing social, political, and economic challenges.

Miller and Sardais (2011) further broaden the conceptualisation of leadership, defining it as a process in which a leader influences and reshapes convictions of individuals, groups, or organisations. They emphasise that leadership is not restricted to formal hierarchies or superior-subordinate relationships; it may originate from subordinates and even extend across organisational boundaries to influence superiors. Fundamentally, leadership reflects both the capacity and process of motivating and guiding others toward shared objectives.

Adding to these perspectives, Burns (1978) conceptualises leadership as either transactional or transformational. Transactional leaders operate through social exchanges, such as politicians trading jobs for votes or business leaders offering financial rewards for productivity. In contrast, transformational leaders inspire and motivate followers to achieve extraordinary outcomes while fostering their personal growth and leadership capacity. They empower individuals, address their needs, and align personal aspirations with broader organisational goals, thereby creating a cohesive vision for collective success.

Despite extensive scholarly discourse, Haber (2012) argues that a general lack of understanding of leadership persists among the wider populace. To address this gap, she categorises leadership into thematic dimensions: the nature of leader-follower relationships, leadership characteristics and behaviours, and the outcomes of leadership. At the core of these themes, Haber emphasises the intentionality of the leader, suggesting that effective leadership is fundamentally driven by purposeful action and vision.

Adding a historical perspective, Sarachek (1968) links the essence of leadership to human nature itself, proposing that the direction of leadership is deeply influenced by qualities such as wisdom and craft. Drawing on Greek traditions,

Sarachek contrasts the ancient notion of leadership-centred on philosophical and moral excellence, with modern interpretations that often prioritise organisational efficiency and managerial capabilities.

These perspectives underscore leadership as a dynamic and relational process, deeply embedded in human interactions and responsive to the challenges of contemporary governance and societal transformation. Applying such conceptions of leadership is crucial in addressing national security lapses and fostering the sustainable peace required in today's volatile global environment. However, to achieve this, this chapter proposes the synergy of peace education, national security, and leadership.

Educational Leadership

There has been a growing interest in how educational leadership translates to outcomes in both the learning environment and the students. This interest is in seeing how school leaders and policymakers navigate their roles to make effective impacts and improvements in the educational system. Robinson et. al. (2008) have identified two leadership strategies – instructional and transformational – that are germane in measuring the impacts of educational leadership on students and society. The idea of the instructional leadership strategy is that the formulation of instructional leadership is the responsibility of the school administrators, where principals and university administrators play a critical role in establishing and maintaining the foundations of education (setting of goals, oversight of the teaching programmes and the development of a positive academic and learning culture (Hallinger & Murphy, 1985). This view, however, has been criticised for being too focused on the role of the principal or university administrator and ignoring the contributions of other staff in instructional leadership. Rahman et al. (2020) have argued that the instructional leadership strategy has become a challenge in educational leadership. This challenge involves a heavy workload, the inexperience of the principals, a lack of understanding of educational policy, and managing school finances. The point here is that the impact of instructional leadership on students' learning outcomes is insignificant because the principal does not have a direct impact on the students' outcomes. A more inclusive argument is that other staff should be included in the instructional leadership strategy in a school system.

The second leadership strategy is the transformational leadership strategy, which originated in the work of James McGregor Burns (1978). McGregor opines that transformational leadership strategy engages staff in ways that inspire them to make commitments to achieving a moral purpose, a common vision, and a shared goal (Robinson et al., 2008).

Transformational leadership in education, therefore, ensures that students acquire the knowledge, skills, attitudes, and values necessary for conflict resolution, tolerance, nonviolence, and an appreciation of diversity. Leaders are responsible for establishing school policies and a positive environment that models peace and security. This includes effective school-based conflict resolution mechanisms, promoting mutual respect among diverse student groups, and ensuring a safe and protective learning environment. They ensure that teachers and staff receive ongoing training in peace pedagogy, which promotes peace and effective crisis management. A well-trained teacher can effectively transmit peace values and serve as a conflict mediator. Transformational leaders act as liaisons between the school and the community. By involving parents, religious leaders, and community groups, they extend the reach of peace education, fostering unity and understanding that strengthen social cohesion —a key component of national security. As such, transformational strategic leadership allocates resources to support peace initiatives, such as funding for peace clubs, dialogue sessions, and materials that promote national unity and anti-violence campaigns.

Synergy between Peace Education, Leadership and National Security

Peace education, leadership, and national security are closely interconnected, with each reinforcing the others to foster sustainable peace and development. Peace education equips individuals with the skills and mindset to resolve conflicts nonviolently, which contributes to national security by reducing violence and promoting social cohesion. Effective leadership, in turn, is crucial for creating sustainable environments where peace education can thrive and where national strategies are developed and implemented with a focus on prevention and human security.

For instance, Bass and Riggio (2006) highlight transformational leadership, a form of leadership that prioritises collective good over self-interest and focuses on a transcendent goal in a complex, diverse environment; this form of leadership accounts for the aforementioned. However, transformative leadership cannot be achieved without the transformation of a mindset and intentionality, as highlighted by Haber (2012). Thus, this chapter questions how this transformation of mindset and intentionality can be achieved to promote sustainability and national security. Stephenson (2011) proposes a leadership educational framework that accommodates the wide range of leadership initiatives and concepts where one is trained on the deep structures, principles, skills and knowledge of leadership, accounting for organisational, family, and societal environments.

Ani (2025) elaborates on this, stating that peace education provides a system positioned as a crucial form of learning that safeguards human and material security, thereby supporting national resilience against crises, disasters and insecurity. Simply put, the synergy between peace education, national security, and leadership yields sustainable peace and development. Additionally, peace education leads to quality leadership, and through quality leadership and good governance, national security is enhanced, ultimately contributing to the nation's peaceful and sustainable development.

THE STATE OF NATIONAL SECURITY IN NIGERIA

Nigeria's national security landscape is marked by a complex web of threats, many of which are deeply rooted in historical grievances, socio-economic inequality, weak governance, and unresolved identity conflicts. These challenges are not only diverse in nature but also interconnected, creating a volatile environment that hinders development, displaces communities, and undermines national unity. Thus, Davis (2020) identifies Nigeria as a state engulfed in a high-intensity conflict webbed by multiple actors (internal and external), proxy forces, and transnational militant and criminal networks, making its insecurity protracted and multidimensional.

Boko Haram insurgency remains one of the most persistent and destabilising threats to national security in Nigeria. Since its violent escalation in 2009, the group, whose name loosely translates to "Western education is forbidden", has launched a campaign of terror primarily across Borno, Yobe, and Adamawa states in the North-East. Its ideological goal is the establishment of an Islamic caliphate governed by strict Sharia law, rejecting not only Western education but also the legitimacy of the Nigerian state. The insurgents have used extreme tactics to instil fear and assert control, including suicide bombings, mass executions, forced conversions, sexual slavery, and large-scale abductions. The 2014 abduction of over 270 Chibok school girls gained international attention and symbolised the group's strategic use of terror against educational institutions. In 2018, a similar mass abduction occurred in the Dapchi community, with some victims still missing years later. The emergence of the Islamic State West Africa Province (ISWAP), a splinter faction of Boko Haram, has added complexity to the conflict. Unlike Boko Haram's erratic attacks, ISWAP has adopted a more structured approach, targeting military outposts and civilians viewed as collaborators with the state, while attempting to win over local communities with limited social services.

The Global Terrorism Index (Institute for Economics and Peace, 2023) ranks Nigeria among the top countries globally affected by terrorism, despite a noticeable decline in attacks since 2021. Currently, the conflict-prone characteristics of Nigeria, further attributed by the clash between its military and non-state armed groups *Boko Haram* and *ISWAP,* have led the GPI [Institute for Economics & Peace] (2025) to rank Nigeria 148 out of 163 countries, as its peace level has worsened from the previous years. The long-term impact of the insurgency has been devastating, with over 2 million people displaced, thousands of schools destroyed or closed, widespread psychological trauma, and a weakened trust in government and security agencies. The humanitarian consequences are equally dire. Internally displaced persons (IDP) camps in Borno and surrounding states are overcrowded and under-resourced, making residents vulnerable to hunger, disease, and exploitation. In some areas, entire communities remain inaccessible due to security threats, limiting the delivery of aid and developmental support.

Despite military offensives, including the formation of the Multinational Joint Task Force (MNJTF) comprising forces from Nigeria, Chad, Niger, and Cameroon, Boko Haram and ISWAP continue to pose serious threats. The insurgency thrives on factors such as poverty, unemployment, poor governance, and local grievances, conditions that fuel recruitment and community tolerance or fear-induced silence. Addressing this crisis requires more than kinetic responses. Long-term solutions must include peace education, economic empowerment, regional cooperation, and robust reintegration programs for former militants and displaced populations. Without these, the cycle of violence is likely to continue, threatening not only the North-East but national stability as a whole.

Famer-Herder Violence

Another major threat to Nigeria's national security is the widespread violence driven by farmer-herder clashes and the rise of armed banditry, particularly in the North-Central and North-West regions. What began as localised disputes over land use and water access has escalated into deadly confrontations involving hundreds of communities, criminal networks, and heavily armed groups. Historically, nomadic Fulani herders have migrated across Nigeria in search of pasture for their livestock, especially during the dry season. However, increasing desertification, population growth, and agricultural expansion have led to more frequent contact and conflict with sedentary farming communities. These encounters often result in the destruction of crops by cattle or the killing of livestock by farmers, which then spiral into cycles of reprisal attacks. In states such as Benue, Plateau, and Nasarawa (North-Central), as well as Zamfara, Sokoto, and Katsina (North-West), this violence has taken on ethnic and religious dimensions. Armed groups, sometimes referred to as "bandits", have taken advantage of weak law enforcement and porous borders to carry out large-scale attacks. These include the raiding of villages, kidnapping for ransom, cattle rustling, sexual violence, and arson. Many of these groups operate with impunity in remote areas where state presence is minimal or nonexistent. According to the International Crisis Group (2021), over 8,000 people were killed and more than 300,000 displaced between 2011 and 2020 as a result of these conflicts. In many cases, violence is fueled not just by resource competition but by long-standing grievances, corruption, and failures in conflict resolution mechanisms. Traditional institutions that once helped mediate these disputes have been weakened or politicised, and the security forces are often under-resourced or accused of bias.

The Economy

The economic toll is equally severe. Agriculture, which is the mainstay of local economies in these regions, has been disrupted. Markets have shut down, rural-urban migration has increased, and food insecurity has worsened. Schools and health centres in conflict-prone areas often close, further entrenching poverty and inequality. In addition, the lucrative business of kidnapping for ransom, once rare, has become widespread, with students, commuters, and villagers regularly abducted. Banditry has grown into an organised criminal enterprise, sometimes involving former insurgents or ethnic militias. The Niger Delta region, rich in crude oil and natural gas, has long been a paradox of wealth and underdevelopment. Despite being the economic backbone of Nigeria, generating over 80% of the country's foreign exchange earnings, the region remains one of the most impoverished and environmentally degraded areas in the country. This reality has fueled resentment, activism, and eventually, violent militancy, posing a significant challenge to Nigeria's national security and economic stability. Militancy in the Niger Delta gained international attention in the early 2000s, especially with the rise of groups like the Movement for the Emancipation of the Niger Delta (MEND). These groups launched coordinated attacks on oil infrastructure, engaged in pipeline vandalism, and kidnapped oil workers, both local and expatriate, for ransom. Their demands typically centred on resource control, environmental justice, and increased inclusion in the nation's political and economic affairs.

The government responded with a mix of military crackdowns and political engagement. In 2009, the Amnesty Programme was introduced, offering militants monthly stipends, vocational training, and reintegration support in exchange for disarmament. This initiative resulted in a significant decrease in attacks and temporarily restored a measure of peace to the region. However, the underlying grievances that drove the militancy, such as environmental pollution from oil spills and gas flaring, poor infrastructure, unemployment, and political marginalisation, largely remain unresolved. In recent years, new militant groups and criminal networks have emerged, engaging in illegal oil bunkering, piracy, and artisanal refining, which continue to pose security threats. These activities result not only in massive economic losses, estimated to be in the billions of dollars annually, but also in further environmental damage and public health crises.

Politics and Militarisation

The rise of separatist agitation in Nigeria's South-East is one of the most politically sensitive and security-threatening issues confronting the country today. At the centre of this movement is the call for the restoration of the independent state of Biafra, an idea rooted in the painful legacy of the Nigerian Civil War (1967–1970), in which over a million people, mainly from the Igbo ethnic group, lost their lives. Although the war officially ended with a call for "no victor, no vanquished," many in the region continue to feel economically marginalised, politically excluded, and culturally alienated. The most prominent group spearheading the renewed Biafran secessionist movement is the Indigenous People of Biafra (IPOB), led by Nnamdi Kanu. IPOB has gained a broad following, especially among disaffected youth, through a combination of radio broadcasts, online activism, and street demonstrations. Its demands centre on the right to self-determination, which it claims is continually denied by the Nigerian state. To enforce its agenda, IPOB established the Eastern Security Network (ESN) in 2020, allegedly to protect communities from bandits and criminal herders. However, ESN operatives have been accused of clashing with security forces, destroying government infrastructure, and engaging in targeted violence. The Nigerian government declared IPOB a terrorist organisation in 2017, further deepening tensions between the group and the state. The situation has led to increasing militarisation of the region, and frequent raids, arrests, roadblocks, and military checkpoints have disrupted daily life. At the same time, "sit-at-home" orders issued by IPOB (particularly on Mondays) have crippled economic activity, closed schools and businesses, and fostered fear and instability across the South-East region. These directives are often violently enforced by splinter groups or criminal elements exploiting the movement's identity.

Ugwueze and Ojukwu (2023) argue that the separatist agitation is not solely about ethnic nationalism but a reflection of deep frustrations with governance, poverty, underdevelopment, and perceived injustice. Many young people in the region feel that peaceful avenues for political change have failed them. In the absence of inclusive dialogue, they turn to radical voices that promise dignity and control. The government's response has largely been security-driven, but this approach has proven insufficient and, at times, counterproductive. Reports of human rights abuses by security forces have further eroded public trust and given IPOB more legitimacy in the eyes of some citizens. Moreover, the absence of consistent efforts at national reconciliation and historical reckoning continues to fuel alienation. What is needed is a comprehensive peacebuilding strategy that includes genuine dialogue, political reform, economic revitalisation, and peace education that emphasises national unity, mutual respect, and civic engagement. Without addressing the root causes of the agitation, the cycle of unrest in the South-East is likely to persist and potentially intensify. Political violence and electoral unrest continue to pose significant threats to democratic consolidation and national security in Nigeria. From the local to the federal level, elections are often marred by violence, intimidation, vote-buying, and manipulation, undermining public trust in the democratic process and weakening state legitimacy. Historically, political contests in Nigeria are characterised by a zero-sum mentality, where the stakes of winning are so high that parties and candidates are willing to deploy violence to achieve their goals. This has led to the proliferation of political thuggery, the arming of youth, and the recruitment of cult groups and gangs to harass opponents, suppress votes, and disrupt election activities. Electoral periods often witness spikes in violence. During the 2011 post-election crisis, for instance, over 800 people were killed in Northern Nigeria. In more recent elections, such as the 2019 and 2023 general elections, numerous reports emerged of ballot box snatching, clashes between party supporters, arson attacks on electoral offices, and the killing of political actors and security personnel. Yagboyaju and Akinboye (2022) note that electoral violence is not just a symptom of political competition but a reflection of deeper structural problems, including poverty, youth unemployment, corruption, weak rule of law, and the politicisation of security agencies. Many citizens believe that elections do not offer genuine choices, which contributes to voter apathy, disenfranchisement, and frustration.

Social Media, Digitalisation and Cybersecurity

Social media has also added a new dimension to electoral unrest, with disinformation, hate speech, and incitement to violence spreading rapidly online. The lack of digital literacy and regulatory mechanisms has made these platforms both a tool for democratic engagement and a vector for chaos. Moreover, the Independent National Electoral Commission (INEC), though constitutionally independent, often faces credibility challenges due to logistical failures, accusations of bias, and inconsistent enforcement of electoral laws. When elections are perceived as unfair or predetermined, they can trigger widespread protests or violent resistance. The consequences of political violence are far-reaching. They delegitimise democratic institutions, discourage qualified candidates, especially women and youth, from running for office, and fuel public cynicism. In fragile states like Nigeria, where ethnic and regional loyalties often intersect with party politics, electoral violence can escalate into broader communal or sectarian conflict. Addressing electoral unrest requires more than security deployments on election day. It calls for systemic reform, including strengthening INEC's autonomy and capacity, enforcing campaign finance laws, ensuring accountability for electoral offenders, and expanding civic education. Importantly, peace education can equip young people with the tools to engage politically without resorting to violence, thereby fostering a culture of dialogue, tolerance, and democratic participation.

As Nigeria becomes more digitally connected, it also faces a growing wave of cyber-related security challenges. Cybercrime has evolved from isolated cases of email fraud to a complex web of internet-enabled crimes, now encompassing identity theft, ransomware attacks, financial scams, online blackmail, and coordinated misinformation campaigns. These digital threats have profound implications for national security, economic stability, and public trust in digital systems. Nigeria is one of the largest digital economies in Africa, with over 120 million internet users as of 2023. This expansion has enabled financial inclusion, e-commerce, and digital communication, but it has also exposed individuals, corporations, and government institutions to cyberattacks. The rise in online banking, mobile money transfers, and cloud-based data storage has made financial institutions and users vulnerable to exploitation.

One of the most prominent forms of cybercrime in Nigeria is advance-fee fraud, commonly known as "*Yahoo Yahoo.*" While initially dismissed as petty internet scams, the practice has grown into a sophisticated criminal enterprise involving networks of fraudsters, fake websites, identity impersonation, and, in some cases, ritual killings. The social glorification of cybercriminals among some youth populations reflects broader issues of unemployment, inequality, and the perception of state failure. Beyond fraud, ransomware attacks and phishing schemes have targeted government databases, hospitals, and private companies, often leading to significant financial losses and data breaches. The National Information Technology Development Agency (NITDA) and the Nigerian Communications Commission (NCC) have acknowledged that Nigeria lacks a robust cybersecurity infrastructure and skilled personnel to effectively track and prevent these attacks. Olayemi (2021) highlight that the absence of comprehensive cybersecurity laws, delayed prosecution of offenders, and poor inter-agency coordination have made Nigeria an attractive target for both domestic and international cybercriminals. Moreover, the country has also become a hub for digital disinformation, especially during elections, crises, and civil protests, fueled by fake news, doctored videos, and politically motivated propaganda. These threats are not merely technical; they can lead to social unrest, economic sabotage, and undermine public trust in digital governance. For instance, during the #EndSARS protests, online platforms were used to mobilise, but they were also used to spread misinformation and incite panic. The growing influence of online narratives makes digital literacy and regulation urgent national priorities.

Religious and ethnic intolerance remains one of the most enduring threats to peace and national security in Nigeria. With over 250 ethnic groups and significant religious diversity, primarily between Islam and Christianity, Nigeria's pluralism is both a strength and a source of friction. When poorly managed, this diversity often translates into deep social divisions, communal violence, and political instability. Conflicts framed along religious or ethnic lines have claimed thousands of lives and displaced entire communities. Incidents such as the Jos crises, Kafanchan religious riots, and Zaria Shia-military clashes, as well as retaliatory attacks in the South, underscore how rapidly tensions can escalate when identity is weaponised. Hate speech, inflammatory sermons, and the politicisation of ethnic and religious differences often contribute to these outbreaks of violence.

In some parts of Nigeria, people face discrimination in employment, housing, and education due to their ethnic or religious background. Inter-ethnic marriages are sometimes discouraged or stigmatised, and political appointments often reflect ethnic balancing rather than merit. These structural biases deepen mistrust and perpetuate cycles of grievance. Mustapha (2023) notes that intolerance in Nigeria is not merely about personal prejudice; it is systematically embedded in social institutions, political structures, and public discourse. When political elites invoke ethnic or religious loyalty to mobilise support or delegitimise opponents, it undermines national unity and promotes exclusion. Religious intolerance is especially pronounced in states where blasphemy laws are enforced.

Peace Education as a Strategic Investment

National security in Nigeria is often narrowly defined in terms of military strength, intelligence gathering, and policing. While these measures are important for managing immediate threats, they do little to address the root causes of conflict – such as inequality, mistrust, poor governance, youth disenfranchisement, and intergroup tensions. This is where peace education stands out, not as a short-term fix, but as a strategic, long-term investment in national stability. Peace education cultivates a generation of citizens equipped with the emotional, social, and civic competencies needed to prevent violence before it begins. It promotes values such as respect for human rights, empathy, tolerance, and critical thinking – all of which are essential for a peaceful society to flourish. By teaching young people how to manage differences constructively and resolve conflicts nonviolently, peace education reduces the likelihood that they will be drawn into extremism, political thuggery, or communal violence.

Countries that have embedded peace education in their national development plans have seen measurable socio-economic benefits. For example, Rwanda's post-genocide peace curriculum helped rebuild social trust, while Kenya's peace education programs reduced electoral violence. These examples demonstrate that education is not only about literacy and numeracy – it is also about shaping the attitudes and capacities that determine whether a society remains stable or fractures under pressure. In the Nigerian context, where violence is often rooted in political manipulation, ethnic competition, and historical grievances, peace education serves both a preventive and transformative function. It helps de-escalate tensions, rebuild intergroup relationships, and foster democratic engagement. It also encourages young people to become agents of peace in their homes, schools, and communities. Investing in peace education means allocating funding, training educators, integrating peace principles into curricula, and making it a policy priority. It is an investment in the kind of citizen who contributes to peace rather than undermines it – someone who can critically evaluate propaganda, resist hate speech, engage across differences, and participate meaningfully in society. In summary, peace education can be viewed as a form of national security policy. It may not carry the visibility of armed patrols or counterterrorism campaigns, but over time, it builds on a human infrastructure that makes a country resilient to conflict.

Educational Leadership and Economic Growth in Nigeria

Educational leadership involves the roles of principals, administrators, policymakers, and curriculum developers in guiding the education system. Effective leadership is needed for integrating peace education successfully, which in turn strengthens national security. Leaders are responsible for providing training and professional development for teachers to acquire the necessary knowledge, skills, and appropriate, interactive, and learner-centred methods, such as role-plays, negotiation, and consensus-building, to teach peace education effectively.

In Nigeria, socio-economic factors are often the root causes of conflict and insecurity in many conflict societies. High rates of poverty, mass unemployment, especially youth unemployment, and economic inequality are key causes of conflict and insecurity. These factors breed resentment and make disenfranchised youths susceptible to joining militant or insurgent groups to carry out violent activities relating to banditry, insurgency, and kidnapping. Educational leadership, well-structured and articulated, will directly influence economic growth and sustainability by developing human capital in equipping students with skills relevant to driving innovation and maintaining institutional stability (Obeten et al., 2024). The economic implications of this are far-reaching. For instance, where education is guided by effective leadership, it will translate to economic productivity. It then means that state managers must be able to understand economics and education and align educational policy with national development goals, by providing adequate funding in the educational sector to attain global benchmark, ensuring quality of education in all regions of the country, and undertaking comprehensive reform to update educational curricula to include skills that drive modern economies such as entrepreneurship and digital literacy (Okeke & Chukwudebelu, 2024).

In all ramifications, peace education deeply entrenched in educational leadership addresses the root causes of structural violence, such as poverty, injustice, and direct violence, by instilling values, attitudes, and skills to resolve problems nonviolently. A sound peace education guided by stable and efficient educational leadership will promote safety and security, reduce disruptions such as school attacks and other atrocities, and produce citizens with the values needed for social cohesion and national unity, as well as the knowledge and skills required for economic growth and development.

CHALLENGES

The potential of peace education in fostering national cohesion and security has been clearly articulated in this chapter. However, a range of obstacles that limit its effectiveness is palpable. These challenges are not merely logistical; they are also structural, political, and cultural. Addressing them is essential for transitioning from theory to practice and for making meaningful contributions to long-term national stability.

One of the biggest obstacles is that peace education has not been thoroughly or systematically integrated into Nigeria's formal education curriculum. While elements of civic education, moral instruction, or religious studies may touch on peace-related values, there is no nationwide framework that treats peace education as a distinct and essential subject. As a result, the teaching of conflict resolution, empathy, and tolerance tends to be fragmented or optional. According to the Nigerian Educational Research and Development Council (NERDC), curriculum reforms have not consistently prioritised peacebuilding or non-violent communication as core learning outcomes. Without a clear mandate, schools lack the necessary guidance to embed these values across subjects and grade levels effectively.

Even where peace education materials exist, there is often a gap in teacher preparedness. Many teachers lack training in delivering peace education content effectively and confidently. Some may be unfamiliar with participatory teaching methods, while others may struggle to facilitate discussions on sensitive issues, such as ethnic conflict or religious intolerance. Arowolo and Alani (2022) observe that without targeted pre-service and in-service training, teachers may resort to didactic instruction or avoid discussing peace-related topics altogether. Moreover, teachers themselves are products of the same divided society and may hold biases that go unexamined in the classroom.

Implementing peace education on a national scale requires political will, but this is often lacking. In some cases, leaders may view peace education as politically inconvenient, particularly when it challenges dominant narratives, exposes injustice, or promotes critical thinking about governance. There is also the issue of apathy: policymakers may see peace education as a soft or secondary concern compared to more visible infrastructure or security projects. However, as Udogu (2021) argues, ignoring peace education undermines long-term stability and leaves young people ill-equipped to participate in democratic life or resist radicalisation.

Peace education is rarely prioritised in education budgets. Most of the funding goes to infrastructure, teacher salaries, or examination bodies, while peacebuilding programs, when they exist, are often donor-driven and short-term. This leaves schools and NGOs scrambling for resources to sustain training, materials, or extracurricular peace clubs. The lack of a coherent national policy or strategy on peace education also means that implementation is uneven across states. In conflict-prone areas where peace education is most needed, schools may lack basic facilities, security, or qualified staff, making even foundational education a challenge.

Nigeria's diversity is both a strength and a source of tension. Any peace education program must navigate through deeply held cultural and religious beliefs. Some communities may resist content they perceive as conflicting with traditional authority, faith teachings, or historical grievances. For example, discussions around gender equality, pluralism, or interfaith dialogue may provoke discomfort or resistance, especially in conservative or rural contexts. Peace education must therefore be locally adapted and culturally sensitive; otherwise, it risks backlash or rejection. It is crucial to involve local leaders, religious scholars, and community elders in the design and delivery of peace education programs to ensure buy-in and relevance. As Shehu (2023) notes, inclusive peace education is most effective when it respects local values while still promoting universal principles of justice, respect, and nonviolence.

Pathways for Strengthening Peace Education in Nigeria

While peace education holds significant promise, its impact depends on how deliberately it is designed, funded, and implemented across Nigeria's diverse regions. For peace education to become a central force in promoting national security and cohesion, strategic pathways must be pursued at the institutional, community, and policy levels. To move peace education from the margins into the mainstream, it must be clearly embedded in Nigeria's national curriculum. This means not only creating standalone peace education courses but also integrating peace themes, such as conflict resolution, empathy, tolerance, and civic responsibility, into subjects like social studies, literature, history, and religious education. The curriculum should be age-appropriate, context-specific, and reflective of Nigeria's cultural diversity. The Nigerian Educational Research and Development Council (NERDC) can play a central role by developing a standardised framework that guides all public and private schools. As Okoh (2022) notes, peace education is most effective when it is systematically introduced from early childhood through secondary and tertiary education.

Teachers are the frontline facilitators of peace education. Without proper training, even the best-designed curriculum will fail to meet its objectives. Teacher education programs must include modules on peace pedagogy, facilitating classroom dialogue, bias awareness, and trauma-informed teaching. In-service training workshops can help practising teachers integrate peacebuilding activities into their daily lessons. Partnerships with teacher training colleges, NGOs, and international agencies can expand access to high-quality resources and methods for peace education. According to Osei and Eze (2023), empowering teachers to model peaceful behaviour also has a positive ripple effect on students' attitudes and interpersonal relationships.

Peace education should not stop at the school gate but involve citizen engagement. Community-based initiatives, such as youth peace clubs, interfaith dialogues, peer mediation teams, and local storytelling events, can help reinforce peacebuilding and citizenship values, creating safe spaces for dialogue in conflict-prone areas. These programs are critical in regions where formal schooling is disrupted by insecurity or underfunding. Local NGOs, faith-based organisations, and traditional leaders can play a critical role in tailoring peace initiatives to the unique needs and dynamics of their communities. When communities are engaged, peace education becomes a shared social project rather than a top-down intervention. In the digital age, media and technology provide powerful tools for promoting peace, particularly among young people. Educational radio and TV programs, social media campaigns, podcasts, and mobile apps can help spread messages of tolerance, empathy, and dialogue far beyond the classroom. Digital platforms can also host virtual peace clubs, connect learners from different parts of the country, and showcase positive examples of intercultural cooperation. However, to counter online hate speech and disinformation, digital peace education must also include media literacy and critical thinking skills. As UNESCO (2023c) emphasises, teaching youth how to navigate the digital world ethically and responsibly is a vital part of modern peace education.

Perhaps the most important pathway is the commitment of political leaders to institutionalise peace education through policy. Senior educational leaders at both federal and state levels must prioritise peace education in education sector plans, teacher training budgets, and youth development strategies. Legislative frameworks should support the implementation of peace curricula, protect inclusive educational spaces, and fund long-term peacebuilding programs. Cross-sector collaboration between ministries of education, youth, justice, and information can ensure that peace education is reinforced across different areas of governance. As Adesoji (2021) argues, peacebuilding cannot be effective without visible leadership and sustained policy attention.

Case Examples and Comparative Insights

Lessons from other countries show that peace education is not only feasible but effective in transforming societies affected by deep divisions and violence. These examples offer comparative insights that can guide Nigeria's efforts to institutionalise peace education, demonstrating both its practical potential and the importance of sustained political commitment.

Rwanda: Building Unity Through Peace Education

After the 1994 genocide in which over 800,000 people were killed, Rwanda undertook a national reconciliation project that placed peace education at the centre of its rebuilding efforts. The government integrated peace and values education into its formal school curriculum, emphasising citizenship, tolerance, genocide prevention, and national unity. According to Rutayisire and Kabwete (2022), Rwandan peace education includes classroom lessons, extracurricular clubs, and memorial activities that encourage reflection and empathy. Teachers were specifically trained to facilitate sensitive dialogue, and curricula were designed to confront hate ideology without reigniting tensions. Over time, this approach has helped to reduce ethnic polarisation, promote intergroup understanding, and rebuild a shared national identity. While Rwanda's experience is unique, it exemplifies how education can be leveraged to promote healing and cohesion following large-scale violence. For Nigeria, where ethno-religious conflicts and civil war memories remain part of the national consciousness, this model underscores the power of sustained, government-led peace education to reshape collective narratives.

Kenya: Peace Education to Curb Electoral Violence

Kenya provides another example where peace education has been utilised as a tool to mitigate politically motivated violence. Following the post-election crisis of 2007–2008, which resulted in over 1,000 deaths and massive displacement, the Kenyan Ministry of Education partnered with organisations like UNICEF and UNESCO to launch peace education programs in schools across the country. These programs focused on conflict resolution, civic responsibility, and ethnic tolerance. According to Ndethiu and Wamahiu (2021), peace education was integrated into teacher training colleges and included outreach to parents and the broader community. In subsequent elections, despite ongoing tensions, the scale and intensity of violence significantly declined, suggesting that peace education, combined with political reform, contributed to a more peaceful electoral environment. Kenya's approach highlights the importance of integrating peace education into both formal and informal education systems, particularly in politically volatile contexts. For Nigeria, where electoral violence remains a recurring threat, this example highlights how peace education can support democratic processes and reduce youth involvement in political thuggery.

Nigeria: Local Initiatives and the Need for Scale

In Nigeria, peace education initiatives have been mainly led by civil society organisations, international partners, and research institutions. The Institute for Peace and Conflict Resolution (IPCR), under the Ministry of Foreign Affairs, has developed peace education manuals and trained educators in conflict-sensitive teaching. NGOs such as the Global Peace Foundation Nigeria, the Peace Initiative Network, and WANEP-Nigeria have also conducted peace clubs, workshops, and community dialogues targeting youth and vulnerable groups. These initiatives demonstrate that peace education is not an abstract concept in Nigeria; it is already being practised in pockets across the country. However, the impact is limited by scale, funding, and lack of coordination. Many programs are pilot-based or donor-dependent, with minimal integration into state or national policy frameworks. Moreover, they often operate in isolation from the formal education system. As Adesina and Danjibo (2022) note, without sustained government commitment, peace education efforts in Nigeria risk remaining fragmented and unsustainable. To replicate the successes seen in Rwanda and Kenya, Nigeria requires a coordinated national strategy that integrates grassroots efforts with curriculum reform, teacher training, and policy implementation.

CONCLUSION

Peace education is not a quick fix, but it is a necessary, long-term investment in Nigeria's future. In a country marked by deep ethnic, religious, and political divisions, teaching young people how to engage differences peacefully is not optional; it is foundational. Peace education cultivates the skills and values that underpin a stable society, including empathy, dialogue, cooperation, tolerance, and critical thinking. While military and policy responses may address immediate security threats, they cannot replace the slow, deliberate work of building a culture of peace. By integrating peace education into schools, communities, and national policy, Nigeria can begin to address the root causes of conflict and nurture a generation capable of sustaining unity and democratic life. As the country continues to grapple with terrorism, political violence, cyber threats, and separatist tensions, peace education is both a strategic and moral imperative. It empowers citizens not only to reject violence but to actively participate in building the just and inclusive society they want to live in. With vision, commitment, and collaboration, peace education can help lay the foundation for a more secure and cohesive Nigeria.

To make peace education a powerful and lasting tool for national security in Nigeria, several targeted and strategic actions are necessary. These recommendations are informed by global best practices, local insights, and the challenges identified throughout this chapter.

Peace education should be formally embedded into Nigeria's education system, from early childhood to tertiary levels. This requires integrating peace concepts into existing subjects, as well as offering dedicated courses on conflict resolution, civic responsibility, and intercultural understanding. Pre-primary and primary schools should focus on developing empathy, cooperation, and emotional literacy. At the same time, secondary and tertiary institutions can address more complex issues, such as human rights, justice, and democratic engagement. The Nigerian Educational Research and Development Council (NERDC) and the Ministry of Education must champion this integration and ensure alignment with national goals for unity and security. Additionally, the implementation of peace education in these tiers of academic institutions will serve as a catalyst to foster high-quality leadership among future Nigerians.

A comprehensive national policy is needed to guide the rollout of peace education across states. This framework should define goals, curriculum standards, teacher competencies, assessment methods, and monitoring mechanisms. It should also outline how peace education will be adapted for different regions and conflict contexts. Such a framework would not only ensure consistency and accountability but also help mobilise funding and technical support. It would provide ministries, schools, and civil society groups with a common reference point and roadmap for action.

No single institution can advance peace education in isolation. The federal and state governments should foster partnerships with NGOs, religious bodies, media organisations, academic institutions, international donors, and the private sector. These collaborations can bring in resources, expertise, and grassroots reach. For example, NGOs can support school-based peace clubs and mediation programs; faith-based organisations can promote interfaith dialogue; and universities can offer peace education courses and training. A multi-stakeholder approach increases impact and sustainability.

Religious and traditional institutions continue to hold a profound influence in many Nigerian communities. Their involvement is crucial for ensuring community buy-in and cultural sensitivity. Leaders should be engaged not only as endorsers of peace education but as co-educators and peace ambassadors. Workshops, interfaith forums, and local peacebuilding initiatives should involve imams, pastors, chiefs, and emirs as facilitators of dialogue and reconciliation. Their voices can help counter hate speech, promote tolerance, and serve as a model for peaceful coexistence.

REFERENCES

Abdul-Rahman, A., Tahir, L. M., Anis, S. N. M., & Ali, M. F. (2020). Exploring challenges in practising instructional leadership: Insights from senior secondary principals. *Universal Journal of Educational Research*, *8*(11C), 83–96. DOI: 10.13189/ujer.2020.082310

Adesina, O. S., & Danjibo, N. D. (2022). *Mainstreaming peace education in Nigeria: Policy gaps and prospects*. Peace and Development Centre Press.

Adesoji, A. O. (2021). Governance and peacebuilding: A policy gap in Nigeria. *Journal of Development and Peace Studies*, *9*(2), 55–68.

Ani, K. J. (2025). Let peace reign: Introducing peace education for Nigerian national transformation. *Journal of Education and Learning Technology*, *6*(2), 60–68. DOI: 10.38159/jelt.2025624

Antai, G. O., Ekpenisi, C., Okonji, C. I., Kolo, E. A., & Okpong, D. E. (2025). Balancing national security and human Rights: A critical analysis of Nigeria's anti-terrorism laws. *NIU Journal of Social Sciences*, *11*(1), 287–299. DOI: 10.58709/niujss.v11i1.2148

Arowolo, D. O., & Alani, R. A. (2022). Peace education and the challenges of implementation in Nigerian schools. *Journal of Educational Sociology*, *14*(2), 33–47.

Azadi, N., & Das, P. P. P. (2024). A thematic analysis of the significance of peace education in managing aggression in adolescents. *Indian Journal of Psychological Medicine*, *XX*, 1–4. DOI: 10.1177/02537176241293635 PMID: 39588481

Bass, B. M., & Riggio, R. E. (2006). *Transformational leadership* (2nd ed.). Lawrence Erlbaum Associates Publishers. DOI: 10.4324/9781410617095

Bolanle, B. M. (2021). Integrating peace education into the curriculum of Nigerian teacher education programme to promote culture of peace. *Cumhuriyet Uluslararası Eğitim Dergisi*, *10*(4), 1356–1368.

Burns, J. M. (1978). *Leadership*. Harper & Row.

Cabezudo, A., & Haavelsrud, M. (2007). Rethinking peace education. In Webel, C., & Galtung, J. (Eds.), *Handbook of peace and conflict studies* (pp. 279–296). Routledge. DOI: 10.4324/9780203089163.ch18

Cremin, H. (2016). Peace education research in the twenty-first century: Three concepts facing crisis or opportunity? *Journal of Peace Education*, *13*(1), 1–17. DOI: 10.1080/17400201.2015.1069736

Currie, K., Conway, J., Johnson, S., Landry, B., & Lowther, A. (2012). Leadership concepts. In *Air Force Leadership Study: The Need for Deliberate Development* (pp. 11–20). Air University Press. https://www.jstor.org/stable/resrep13757.9

Danesh, H. B. (2006). Towards an integrative theory of peace education. *Journal of Peace Education, 3*(1), 55–78. DOI: 10.1080/17400200500532151

Davis, I. (2020). Armed conflict and peace processes in sub-Saharan Africa. In *SIPRI Yearbook 2020: Armaments, Disarmament, and International Security* (pp. 171–214). Oxford University Press. DOI: 10.1093/sipri/9780198869207.003.0007

Emeodu, E. N., & Famo, M. K. (2023). Peace education and national security: The need for its improvement in Nigerian schools. *Texas Journal of Multidisciplinary Studies, 25*, 1–12.

GPE. (2024, January 24). Education: A path to a peaceful future. *Global Partnership for Education.* https://www.globalpartnership.org

Grizold, A. (1994). The concept of national security in the contemporary world. *International Journal on World Peace, 11*(3), 37–53.

Haber, P. (2012). Perceptions of leadership: An examination of college students' understanding of the concept of leadership. *Journal of Leadership Education, 11*(2), 26–51. DOI: 10.12806/V11/I2/RF2

Hallinger, P., & Murphy, J. (1985). Assessing the instructional leadership behavior of principals. *The Elementary School Journal, 86*(2), 217–248. DOI: 10.1086/461445

Hasan, K. (2023). The four pillars of education By UNESCO and the Metaverse: Repositioning Islamic education. *Bidayah: Studi Ilmu-Ilmu Keislaman*, 85-105.

Institute for Economics & Peace. (2025). *Identifying and measuring the factors that drive peace: Global Peace Index briefing 2025.* https://www.visionofhumanity.org/wp-content/uploads/2025/06/Global-Peace-Index-2025-Briefing-Web.pdf

Institute for Economics and Peace. (2023). Global Terrorism Index 2023. https://www.visionofhumanity.org

International Crisis Group. (2021). Stopping Nigeria's spiraling farmer-herder violence. https://www.crisisgroup.org

Kenneth, C. (2025). "They moved from village to village with their *keke* to reach us": building positive peace through counselling in Borno, Nigeria. https://www.peaceinsight.org/en/article

Kertyzia, H. (2021). Peace education. In *The Palgrave handbook of positive peace* (pp. 1–29). Springer Singapore. DOI: 10.1007/978-981-15-3877-3_9-1

Lederach, J. P. (2003). *The little book of conflict transformation*. Good Books.

Miller, D., & Sardais, C. (2011). A concept of leadership for strategic organisation. *Strategic Organization*, *9*(2), 174–183. DOI: 10.1177/1476127011413757

Mustapha, A. R. (2023). *Ethnic and religious conflicts in Nigeria: Causes and solutions*. Spectrum Books.

Ndethiu, S., & Wamahiu, S. (2021). The Role of Peace Education in Kenya's Electoral Reforms. *East African Journal of Education and Development*, *3*(1), 41–58.

Nelson, L. L. (2021). Identifying determinants of individual peacefulness: A psychological foundation for peace education. *Peace and Conflict*, *27*(2), 109–119. DOI: 10.1037/pac0000517

Nigerian Educational Research and Development Council (NERDC). (2021). *Curriculum Reform Policy Brief*. NERDC.

Obeten, O. O., Okoringa, N., & Ossai, V. O. (2024). Leadership and economic development for nation building. *International Journal of Institutional Leadership. Policy and Management*, *6*(2), 169–179.

Ojo, J. S., Oyewole, S., & Aina, F. (2023). Forces of Terror: Armed Banditry and Insecurity in North-West Nigeria. *Democracy and Security*, *19*(4), 319–346. DOI: 10.1080/17419166.2023.2164924

Okeke, R. C., & Chukwudebelu, C. B. (2024). Educational policy and national development in Nigeria. *International Journal of Education and Evaluation*, *10*(4), 268–274.

Okoh, J. U. (2022). *Curriculum and peacebuilding in West Africa: Approaches and challenges*. Unity Press.

Olayemi, A. O. (2021). Cybercrime and National Security: Challenges for Nigeria. *Journal of African Cybersecurity*, *5*(2), 13–27.

Oni, M. B., & Ijov, T. M. (2022). Peace education as a catalyst for sustainable development in Nigeria. *International Journal of Peace. Education and Development*, *10*(2), 63–71. DOI: 10.30954/2454-9525.02.2022.5

Osah, G., Nwakanma, N. F., & Isikalu, A. A. (2021). Nomadic education and managing violent conflicts in Northern Nigeria. In Audu, B. J., & Hamza, M. (Eds.), *Conflicts and the vulnerable in Northern Nigeria: Festschrift in honour of Dr. Nafisat Dahiru Muhammad* (pp. 599–616). Pyla-Mak Press and Publishers.

Osei, K., & Eze, N. J. (2023). Teaching peace in fragile contexts: The role of teachers in Nigeria. *African Educational Review, 18*(1), 91–108.

Özel, D., & Sümer, Z. (2025). Adapting Peace Education Programs: A Sustainable Approach to Harmony. *Journal of Ethnic and Cultural Studies, 12*(2), 231–251. DOI: 10.29333/ejecs/2142

Riyani, M., Brata, N. T., & Shintasiwi, F. A. (2021). Making Peace with the Past: Peace Education in Post-Conflict Aceh Societies through the Application of Cognitive Behavioural Therapy. *Journal of Social Studies Education Research, 12*(2), 330–376.

Robinson, V. M. J., Lloyd, C. A., & Rowe, K. J. (2008). The impact of leadership on student outcomes: An analysis of the differential effects of leadership types. *Educational Administration Quarterly, 44*(5), 635–674. DOI: 10.1177/0013161X08321509

Rutayisire, T., & Kabwete, C. (2022). Post-genocide education and social healing in Rwanda. *International Journal of Peace Education, 19*(2), 115–134.

Sarachek, B. (1968). Greek concepts of leadership. *Academy of Management Journal, 11*(1), 39–48. DOI: 10.2307/255195

Shehu, A. B. (2023). *Culture, religion and peace education in Northern Nigeria.* Ahmadu Bello University Press.

Stephenson, L. (2011). Developing a Leadership Education Framework: A Transformative Leadership Perspective. *Counterpoints, 409*, 321–341. https://www.jstor.org/stable/42981314

Terepyshchyi, S. (2021). In search of peacebuilding strategies for the global civilisation: From "education for war" to "education for peace". *Philosophy and Cosmology, 27*(27), 153–162.

Udogu, E. I. (2021). Democratic governance and the neglect of peace education in Nigeria. *African Journal of Peace and Conflict Studies, 10*(1), 70–85.

Ugwueze, M. I., & Ojukwu, C. C. (2023). Secessionism and the crisis of federalism in Nigeria. *American Journal of Political Science, 27*(1), 55–70.

UNESCO. (2023a). *Education for peace and prevention of violence.* UNESCO Publishing.

UNESCO. (2023b). *Peace and global citizenship education: A guide for policy-makers*. UNESCO Publishing.

UNESCO. (2023c). *Transforming education for peace and sustainable futures*. UNESCO Publishing.

Viter, D., & Rudenko, O. (2025). National security in the multi-domain environment: Public administration issues. *Public Administration and Law Review*, *1*(21), 40–49. DOI: 10.36690/2674-5216-2025-1-40-49

Weiskittel, P. (1999). President's message: The concept of leadership. *ANNA Journal, 26*(5), 467, 536.

Wilson, R. (2009, May–June). The color green: A "go" for peace education. *Peace Education Exchange*, 40–43. https://www.exchangepress.com/library/5018740.pdf

Wu, C. (2025). Redefining concepts of nation and national security and establishing their models for the new era. *Journal of Safety and Sustainability*, *2*(1), 45–58. DOI: 10.1016/j.jsasus.2024.12.002

Yagboyaju, D. A., & Akinboye, S. O. (2022). *Elections and democratic consolidation in Nigeria*. University of Lagos Press.

Chapter 9
Bridging the Gap: Strengthening Community Involvement in Educational Leadership for Sustainable Growth

Md Mehedi Hasan Emon
https://orcid.org/0000-0002-6224-9552
American International University-Bangladesh, Bangladesh

Mohammad Kamrul Hasan
https://orcid.org/0000-0003-3866-0090
Tongling University, China

ABSTRACT

This chapter examines the pivotal role that community involvement plays in shaping educational leadership that promotes sustainable growth. It suggests that relying solely on top-down leadership is no longer enough to address the complex challenges facing education today. Instead, meaningful participation from communities is shown to improve accountability, relevance, and fairness within schools. Using a mix of theoretical insights and examples from different countries, the chapter explores various ways communities engage, the institutional structures that support this involvement, and approaches to building local capacity. Challenges such as decentralisation issues, power imbalances, and cultural barriers are also considered. The chapter concludes by emphasising that including community voices in educational decisions not only enhances learning but also supports broader social and economic progress, which is crucial for the future of education.

DOI: 10.4018/979-8-3373-3616-9.ch009

INTRODUCTION

In recent years, the nature of educational leadership has been undergoing a noticeable transformation. The traditional dependence on centralised, top-down governance is gradually being challenged by the rising demand for participatory structures based on community empowerment. This chapter argues that sustainable and equitable educational development is based on the concept of architecting the architecture of leadership, which is impossible unless community involvement is placed at the very Centre of the architecture of leadership. Rather than being regarded as an option or a fringe, community engagement serves as a centralising force with the capability of strengthening accountability, enhancing instructional practices and aligning educational efforts with the overall goals of social and economic development. The discussion begins by evaluating the limitations of traditional hierarchical structures, which often overlook the diverse social and cultural contexts in which schools are situated. With the predictability of these models, they are usually not flexible enough to solve the numerous challenges facing modern educational systems. In turn, participatory models based on mutual trust, place-based experience, and shared responsibility are being reviewed as more flexible and situational options. It discusses their operating mechanisms, the theoretical frameworks supporting them, and the policy changes that preceded their long-term adoption. It draws on various theoretical traditions, including transformational and distributed leadership theory, the theory of social capital, and the works of Paulo Freire, which are grounded in the concepts of dialogue and power. These perceptions collectively validate the need to involve not only educational leaders but also teachers, parents, and community stakeholders in influencing the course of conventional education. Although theoretical insights are a valuable source of conceptual clarity, the chapter also has a firm anchor point in the study of the practical manifestation of the ideas.

It moves forward by challenging the conventional understanding of leadership as something confined within school walls. As is contended here, effective leadership is no longer restricted to day-to-day management and is rooted more in the social crannies where education is practised. In cultures, especially those with cultural diversity or limited resource availability, strong community connections are highly beneficial to schools. Therefore, leadership is redefined as a collective initiative, one that thrives when local knowledge and engagement are centralised, as opposed to marginalised. An international experience comparative scan is added to this analysis. The chapter draws on examples from Sub-Saharan Africa, South Asia, and Latin America, focusing on village education committees and school management groups and how they have been adapted to local realities. These models demonstrate what has been successful, as well as the difficulties, trade-offs, and lessons that accompany community engagement. The ability to adjust to cultural and socio-economic situations is another recurring theme. The debate then questions the processes that promote long-term participation. The roles of Parent-Teacher Associations (PTAs), School Governing Bodies (SGBs), and partnerships with non-governmental organisations (NGOs) or faith-based organisations are discussed, including their strengths and weaknesses. The dynamics of token involvement, inadequate preparation, and power initiative balance are admitted. However, most of these institutions can be seen to be promising when properly resourced and managed. Capacity building proves to be another issue: community members should be well-prepared not only in terms of their knowledge of governance and planning, but also in communicating with school authorities. The amplification of the voices of marginalised people, in particular, women and the Indigenous peoples, is positioned at the forefront as a moral obligation and a condition of holistic development. The chapter concludes with a set of policy prescriptions to institutionalise participatory governance processes within national education systems, to motivate communities in underserved areas to assume the roles of community-based governance, and to improve school teacher education programs. These proposals are ambitious, but they are made both practical and necessary.

The discussion is further grounded through several case studies from countries such as Kenya, Nepal, Bangladesh, Brazil, and select indigenous communities in Canada or Australia. These examples demonstrate how local communities have assumed leadership roles in educational areas, often under significant constraints, and how such initiatives have yielded positive results for students, as well as practical benefits for local well-being. The scope is then broadened to explain how the nexus developed between community participation and the larger national development. Education in these discussions is not only thought of as a right but also a fundamental tool of economic empowerment and the development of human capital. In that regard, approaches to educational leadership have a community benefit that extends beyond the classroom into youth unemployment reduction, improved livelihoods of local communities, and the development of more resilient communities. Solid obstacles to reform, such as political opposition, established hierarchies and cultural obduracies, are stated to be endemic. However, the chapter also portrays the opportunities which open at the junction of strong leadership, favourable policy settings, and external relationships. The discussion is closed with a synthesis of key points of the debate and concludes that inclusive, community-based leadership is not only a good idea but offers potential solutions that require further exploration: longitudinal research into community involvement, the study of digital means of interaction and a more interdisciplinary approach to policymaking. By grounding its insights into both theory and lived experience, the chapter aims to offer a practical yet reflective contribution to the broader conversation on educational reform, one where schools are not isolated institutions, but active and responsive parts of the communities they serve.

EMPOWERMENT THROUGH PARTICIPATORY EDUCATION

A strict comprehension of community in the education leadership requires a holistic engagement of the theoretical underpinnings that inform educational leadership study as well as participatory practice. The paradigm of educational leadership has thereby undergone a significant transformation over the past, as the initially hierarchical forms of order gave way to more inclusive and collaborative versions, where the mutual interdependence between schools and their communities is recognised. The current discussion discusses some of the underlying theoretical frameworks, compares traditional forms of leadership with participatory models, clarifies how the theory of social capital can explain education partnerships, discusses how Freirean pedagogy can be used as a means of promoting communal empowerment, and questions the relationship between leadership agencies and collective efficacy in a school context.

Traditional versus Participatory Leadership Theories

Educational leadership has traditionally been studied from frameworks that rely upon formal authority and control. The traditional models tend to stick to the principles of transactional leadership, which puts strong emphasis on maintaining order, ensuring adherence, and completion of a given set of tasks (Wilkinson, 2021). However, top-down orientations have received criticism, especially when educational systems are required to adapt quickly and dynamically to the varied interests of the stakeholders (Azoury & Harvey, 2023). The ability to adapt to modern, rapidly changing social and educational settings is often limited in such styles and thus ineffective. In contrast, theories of participatory leadership have become well-known by redefining leadership as relational and collective in nature. Transformational leadership, say, focuses on the inspiration and motivation of stakeholders to go beyond personal interest and invest in the common good (Hong et al., 2021). This model focuses on the concept of developing the sense of vision and involvement but inspires other people to take responsibility for the processes of change. Distributed leadership goes further to decentralise authority and renders leadership as a shared practice, which is subject to various actors, and not a domain maintained by formal leaders (Nadeem, 2024). This strategy emphasises the partnership between a teacher, parents, and the community in the development of educational outcomes (Liu et al., 2021). The other important dimension that is provided by servant leadership is that leaders are meant to serve their communities. It lays more stress on the empathy, stewardship, and empowering of others instead of the control itself (Tsarkos, 2024). In education, servant leadership is closely related to participatory governance and is about the promotion of care and responsiveness to the needs of the community. The above participatory leadership models taken collectively imply that one has to rethink leadership as highly collaborative, context-specific, and social justice-oriented instead of hierarchical domination.

Social Capital Theory and Educational Partnerships

The theory of social capital explains why community engagement is an essential factor towards effective educational leadership. As resources integrated into social networks, i.e., trust, shared norms, and reciprocity, social capital enables mutual collaborative efforts among people (Brown et al., 2024). In education, such resources are manifested in relationships among teachers, families, and other community members, thus benefiting communication, collaboration, and joint problem-solving. The modern empirical research consistently shows that schools that are located within communities that have high levels of social capital have improved student achievements, greater accountability, and an increased innovative ability (Natung et al., 2025). As an example, when parents are engaged at a sufficient degree and with good contact, communication will be enhanced, and there will be a more integrated notion of shared responsibility for student achievement. These networks also help schools mobilise vital resources such as volunteers and local funding that can make a significant difference, particularly where financial resources are limited. That said, social capital is not equally available to all. Inequalities in social networks can deepen educational disparities if some groups are excluded or marginalised. This means educational leadership must be intentional in fostering inclusive social capital that brings together diverse groups and empowers marginalised voices (Aminudin & Jamal, 2024).

Freirean Pedagogy and the Role of Dialogue in Community Empowerment

The work of Paulo Freire offers a powerful lens through which community involvement in educational leadership can be understood. Critical pedagogy (especially as developed by Paulo Freire) emphasises the concepts of dialogue, critical consciousness (or conscientisation) and empowerment (Ferrada, 2020). Freire disagreed with the banking model of education to encompass a process of interaction whereby teacher and learner are both co-producers of knowledge through reflection and practice. In the context of leading, the Freire-based framework leads to the creation of democratic spaces where members of a given community are engaged participants in social functioning as opposed to passive receptors of policy in the educational process (Fernández-Aballí Altamirano, 2020). Dialogue in this context is a significant tool towards resolving power imbalances, along with establishing the importance of local knowledge and therefore empowering communities to speak out about their needs and determine those priorities they feel are essential to educational issues (Namoog & Agyekum, 2024). This dialogic orientation forms an integral component in the development of ownership and commitment, which requires that reforms must be both sustainable and convincing. The idea of the Praxis, which Freire discusses as the cycle of reflection and action, further facilitates constant learning and flexibility for the leaders and communities. By following this loop, schools may become centres of collective activism where marginalised voices can be heard and social change can be instigated (Elerian et al., 2025).

Figure 1. Freirean Pedagogy Cycle: Dialogue, Reflection, and Action

This figure illustrates Figure 1, a visual interpretation showing the cyclical model of praxis of Paulo Freire. The centre of the diagram is filled with Dialogue to emphasise its centrality of empowerment. Learners and educators enriched through dialogue progress to reflection and action, which are closely connected to each other and mutually supportive. The circular flow increases the dependence of these steps, explaining how they work in unison towards supporting critical pedagogy. The three thematic markers, Empowerment, Critical Consciousness, and Community Voice, surround the cycle and present the broad transformative goals of the Freirean philosophy of education.

Educational Leadership, Agency, and Collective Efficacy

Agency and collective efficacy are terms that are of significance to leadership and the engagement of the community. An agency can be defined based on the capacity of individuals or various groups to make decisions and take purposeful actions. Collective efficacy, in its turn, is the shared belief in the group's ability to achieve desired results (Hamann et al., 2024). In the classroom, the promotion of agency by educators, parents and community members helps to provoke active engagement and maintain collaborative work. The evidence supports the idea that in schools with leadership that fosters a high level of collective efficacy, there is a greater diversity of innovation, the quality of teaching, and the attainment of students. It is critical to mention that collective efficacy is no longer considered only an outcome but a dynamic, progressive journey, which is fostered by inclusive leadership practices based on the principles of sharing power, facilitating the engagement of stakeholders, and trusting them (Ahmad & Islam, 2024). The importance of community involvement is its contribution to the circle of responsibility related to education broadening and to the establishment of reciprocated relationships that build the level of motivation and commitment (Rodríguez-Zurita et al., 2025). In participatory governance, leaders who create situations for schools and communities to work independently strengthen one another to achieve educational objectives collectively.

EDUCATIONAL LEADERSHIP AS A COLLABORATIVE PROCESS AND BEYOND

The traditional interpretation of educational leadership locates authority as well as primary responsibility of decision-making in the confined space of the office of the principal and regular official administrative functions. However, this contested view does not reflect the complexity of schooling in the present-day world because social, cultural and economic forces beyond the school gates have far-reaching effects on the outcome of education. In the modern world, scholarship increasingly acknowledges that effective leadership should not be viewed as an individual in authority exercising, but as a shared activity that involves community members, families, local organisations, and other members of society to actively participate (Emon & Chowdhury, 2025; Mpuangnan & Ntombela, 2024). Schools are social institutions which are embedded, and their effectiveness depends on the nature of relations and partnerships linking them to the surrounding communities. The section talks about the need to extend educational leadership to encompass community actors, community values meeting school culture, the concept of shared accountability in strengthening mutual ownership of academic purposes and finally challenges and opportunities brought about by culturally diverse and resource-limited contexts.

Redefining School Leadership to Include Community Actors

The shift to distributed and participatory leadership has transformed the role of the school leader into a facilitator of an extended leadership framework instead of being a single decision-maker (Keding, 2021). Parents, local leaders, civil societies, and even students whose role as community actors are relevant in contributing to the educational process possess incomparable contextual knowledge and resources, which, in conjunction with that of teachers, make the teaching and learning experience unique. This widened model of leadership recognises the idea that educational issues, be it the student engagement issues, the mobilisation of resources or the social barriers, cannot be tackled by school staff necessarily. For example, local leaders and community organisations often serve as advocates for marginalised families and act as bridges between home and school environments, fostering trust and cooperation (Natung et al., 2025). In practice, this means that principals and administrators must cultivate meaningful partnerships, share leadership responsibilities, and create inclusive forums where diverse voices shape school policies and practices. Rather than diluting authority, this broader base of leadership enhances the school's adaptability and responsiveness to complex local realities. As Hargreaves and Candeias Fernandes & Franco (2022) argue, collaborative leadership builds resilience and fosters innovation by drawing on the collective strengths of a community.

The Interplay Between School Culture and Community Values

School culture, defined by shared norms, values, and behaviours, is deeply influenced by the social and cultural fabric of the community's school service (Fuad et al., 2022). Effective educational leaders recognise that aligning school culture with community values enhances student identity, belonging, and engagement, which are critical factors for academic success. When students see their languages, histories, and traditions reflected in the school environment, it validates their cultural identities and supports more meaningful learning experiences. However, leaders must carefully negotiate tensions between honouring community norms and promoting equity and inclusion, especially when some local values may perpetuate inequality or exclusion (Esquierdo-Leal & Houmanfar, 2021). For example, in some societies, accessibility to education might be limited to other gender roles or even caste issues. Culturally responsive leadership is associated with constant connection, cultural humility, and the capacity to reconcile conflicting values in such a way that they enhance reciprocity and other gradual improvements (Marujo & Wissing, 2024). When the culture of schools and community values engage in an active dialogue as opposed to conflicting with one another, a common ground of education can be cultivated, which both honours diversity and promotes social justice (Elias & Mansouri, 2020).

Figure 2. Interplay Between School Culture and Community Values

A Venn relationship between School Culture and Community Values is illustrated in Figure 2. The circle on the left side represents School Culture, which embodies things such as Beliefs, Norms, and Practices which influence the school ambience. The circle on the right is Community Values, including those of Traditions, Languages, and Norms that are significant to the local community. The intersection of these two circles depicts how culturally responsive leadership comes into place. This shared space focuses on some valuable things like Cultural Responsiveness,

Shared Identity and Equity. These factors are very important in enhancing school belonging, engagement, and inclusion among students.

Shared Accountability and Mutual Ownership of Educational Goals

The aspect of shared accountability removes the sole responsibility of educational outcomes from the school and transfers it to shared responsibility incorporated among families and stakeholders in the community (Dorji et al., 2023). This co-ownership grows trust and involvement, because community stakeholders are regarded as engaged stakeholders in tracking improvement, reform and allocation. The use of collaborative forms of governance, i.e., a school council or a PTA, serves to form significant platforms in which different stakeholders co-design learning priorities and co-design learning strategies (Asri et al., 2025). According to research, stronger schools exist regarding community partnerships and report greater amounts of trust and positive performance results among students (Mu et al., 2023). In addition, school and authority accountability before communities, which are part of the governance process, assist in the protection of transparency and fairness. Collective responsibility, hence, reinforces democratic practice in education and supports ongoing school improvement that is based on local situations.

Figure 3. Shared Accountability and Mutual Ownership Framework

A cyclical flowchart is used in Figure 3 to illustrate the flow of the process in a step-by-step manner, which encompasses the operation of the Shared Accountability and mutual ownership Framework. It begins with Transparent Communication, which will aid in the establishment of trust as well as unmistakable understanding between all the stakeholders involved. This is then shifted to Participatory Governance, such as through PTAs or School Councils, whereby decision-making is made more inclusive. Then the cycle will move to Mutual Goal Setting, whereby stakeholders will formulate shared goals, followed by Collective Monitoring and Support, which involves accountability by mutual monitoring and encouragement. The cycle continues generating continuous Improvement and Sustainability in educational or organisational contexts. This flow illustrates how the stages depend on and support each other to establish productive cooperation in the long term.

Leadership in Culturally Diverse and Resource-Constrained Settings

Leadership in educational matters in numerous regions across the globe occurs in an environment of cultural diversity and shortage. These circumstances require the kind of leadership that is radical, culturally competent, and inventive (Samaniego López et al., 2025). Leaders should find the linguistic and cultural diversity of their communities valuable and push to use curriculum and practices that embrace this diversity. In the case of indigenous communities, leadership sometimes presupposes the inclusion of local knowledge and pedagogies to make education relevant and empowering. The lack of resources will require such innovative mobilisation of community resources as the involvement of volunteers, local funding, and alliances with NGOs or companies (Altynbassov et al., 2024). At the school level, collaborative leadership helps in accessing social secondary capital and community networks, hence complementing limited governmental finances. This group work is instrumental in school sustainability and an intervention for needy students. Collaborative leadership can also be used in conflict or fragile contexts as a form of social cohesion: diverse communities are brought together around education and realise school as a dialogue space and a place of peacebuilding in needy environments (Emon & Khan, 2025; Murtadlo et al., 2025). Community-engaged leadership is thus valuable not only in terms of academic performance but also in terms of enhanced social stability and growth.

Furthermore, any redefinition of educational leadership outside the formal design of schools and the use of community actors with schools leads to more adaptive, culturally responsive, and equitable schools. This collaborative practice promotes cultures in schools that are based on localisation values, encourages collective responsibility, and leverages community assets and power in diverse and under-resourced settings. Sustainable educational development and community empowerment are based on such leadership practices.

COMPARATIVE INTERNATIONAL MODELS OF SCHOOL PARTNERSHIPS

Community involvement in education assumes various forms in various places. Developing nations have done this differently everywhere in the world, with each country trying to implement this concept, beguiled by their history and politics, as well as social life. Although this basic aim is often common, to achieve better results in education and to enhance the systems to be more responsive, the ways and facilities differ to a considerable extent. Here, the chapter considers models in Sub-Saharan Africa, South Asia, and Latin America to better understand how communities have been involved in schooling. It centres on what facilitates or inhibits the involvement, what sort of variation it imparts in educational availability as well as quality and what contribution it has to broader social improvement and integration.

Education Committees and Community-led School Construction (AFRICA)

In some regions in Sub-Saharan Africa, especially the rural and underserved communities, community involvement in schools is not only an exceptional measure but also often a necessity. There has been a consistently weak state infrastructure that has forced the local communities to act and fill in the gaps. The Village Education Committee (VEC) is one of the most widespread responses. These committees, consisting of parents, grassroots leaders and sometimes teachers, are also charged with a variety of responsibilities which may include monitoring attendance and enrolment of learners, purchase of materials, and the general running of day-to-day tasks. A good example is found in the Primary Education Development Programme (PEDP) in Tanzania: the communities did not just take the role of decision-making, but also contributed significant labour, arranged finance, and provided building materials, the literal building blocks of new facilities. This kind of intense participation is demonstrated to empower the perceived ownership and solidarity of households and school institutions. However, as Yu et al. (2024) warn, the developments come along with significant challenges. Not all communities had the skills or resources to manage these responsibilities. Technical shortcomings, gender inequalities within committees, and even political favouritism occasionally derailed the good intentions behind the VECs. In countries like Malawi and Uganda, the pattern holds but with variations. While school infrastructure and enrolment have seen some improvements thanks to community involvement, academic outcomes remain uneven. In wealthier or more organised communities, the model has worked relatively well, but in poorer areas, these committees have sometimes struggled, leading to inconsistent educational experiences across different regions. Despite these limitations, one cannot overlook the role such community-led models have played in expanding access to education in places where the government alone could not keep up.

School Management Committees and Mothers' Groups (SOUTH ASIA)

Turning to South Asia, one finds a more formalised structure of community engagement. School Management Committees (SMCs) in countries like India, Nepal, and Bangladesh are officially recognised governance bodies, often mandated by education policies. These are not informal groups; they come with legal backing and clear responsibilities, including budgeting, teacher hiring, planning school development, and monitoring student and teacher attendance among them (Guha, 2023). Nepal's case after the 1990 political reforms is particularly worth noting. With the decentralisation of school governance, SMCs became a tool for local empowerment. Interestingly, what made Nepal's experience stand out was the role played by mothers' groups. These were not just symbolic participants; they actively monitored attendance, advocated for girls' education, and even challenged gender-based norms in schooling. In remote or marginalised communities, these mothers became essential actors in pushing for inclusive education (Rafiki et al., 2025). However, the system is not without its flaws. Often, decision-making within SMCs is dominated by local elites or politically connected individuals, sidelining poorer or lower-caste parents. In some places, while the committee exists on paper, its actual influence is limited due to a lack of training or financial resources. This kind of "responsibility without capacity" has sometimes deepened inequalities rather than solving them (Kumar & Mishra, 2022). That said, where the system works as intended, it has contributed to making education more transparent, increasing teacher accountability, and creating stronger ties between schools and their communities.

Participatory Municipalities and Democratic School Governance (LATIN AMERICA)

Latin America presents a somewhat different picture, one driven more by political ideology and a vision of participatory democracy. Brazil, especially during the early 2000s under the Workers' Party, made bold moves in this space. In cities like Porto Alegre, school councils made up of teachers, parents, students, and other local stakeholders were given absolute power. They were not just advisory bodies; they influenced budgeting decisions, curricula, and evaluations (Ribeiro et al., 2025). What made these councils stand out was how they were tied into broader civic initiatives like participatory budgeting. Participatory education models have been at the centre stage in redefining schooling in terms of democratic participation. In some places of Colombia and Bolivia, the localities that were historically characterised by violence and marginalisation, such mechanisms offered agencies of social recuperation, where communities might rebuild vocal rights and agency (Bramwell, 2020). However, they are fragile with these enhancements. The changing nature of national political regimes and the instability which has accompanied these changes have encouraged some administrations to abandon decentralisation schemes in pursuance of a more centralised regime. Moreover, a contradiction has arisen between community involvement and professional independence among teachers. Participatory governance arrangements have occasionally been challenged by the teachers' unions, who feel that they have lost control of the curriculum and ways of teaching. Therefore, on the one hand, strong legal safeguards are necessary, but on the other hand, they are not a panacea. The continuity of the improvements depends on parallel cultural changes in the institutions of education and the community where they operate. It is only these changes that can enroot the participatory practices in the daily lives of schooling.

Cross-contextual Insights and Implications

A close evaluation of empirical literature reveals that educational models that are not always effective include vital insights. A particular example, Sub-Saharan Africa, highlights the possibility of grassroots mobilisation achieving quantifiable results even in situations of resource deficiency, but, at the same time, warns of over-emphasis on local involvement unless there is credible institutional support. On the contrary, the case of South Asia demonstrates that institution-based bureaucratic systems can yield significant gains provided that the decision-making process is not concentrated in the hands of a few people and is supported by a reasonable level of material resources. Latin America, in turn, contributes to the idea that education is not only to be viewed as service delivery, but as a democratic practice. These stories disclose the fact that the educational results tend to be more positive when such communal involvement is genuine instead of formal. This kind of participation facilitates local ownership, accountability and increases the ability of the schools to connect more closely with the cultural and social context within which they are operating.

Notwithstanding, these models all have their weaknesses, among which are captured by the elites and bureaucratic inefficiency and issues of mismatching between the allocated tasks and the resources at their disposal. The overall finding that is relevant to policymakers and practitioners is that Community School partnerships work best when schools are given actual powers and the appropriate means of exercising them. This means training, financing, and ongoing support, not just a seat at the table. Moreover, it requires time. Building trust and shared vision between schools and communities is not something that happens overnight. Suppose education is to fulfil its potential as a driver of both individual opportunity and collective well-being. In that case, it must be grounded in the lived experiences of the communities it serves. That means rethinking power structures, embracing inclusive participation, and recognising that schools do not just belong to states or teachers—but to the communities that sustain them.

INSTITUTIONAL MECHANISMS FOR ENGAGEMENT: PTAS, SGBS, AND LOCAL ORGANISATIONS

Engaging communities in educational leadership is not just a matter of sound policy; it often depends on the presence of effective institutional mechanisms. Across many education systems, bodies like PTAs, SGBs, and various local organisations (including religious and civil society groups) have been set up with the idea of giving the community a voice. These structures help bridge the gap between schools and the people they serve. Even though formal institutional participation mechanisms are articulated widely, applying them to substantial participation is often restricted. The adequacy with which such mechanisms operate depends on how they are designed, the presence of the necessary resources and norms and expectations on local systems of governance. The current section thus explores the actual functioning of these participatory forms and the demands to which they lead towards a conducive educational governance.

PTAs: Between Partnership and Symbolism

The most recognised mechanism of institutional engagement between families and schools is the parent-teacher association (PTA). In theory, they are meant to serve as more than a convening place; they should foster true partnerships, drive resource mobilisation, and foster accountability for the results related to students. The evidence provided by empirical analysis in both wealthier and poorer settings states that active PTAs can make a noticeable difference. According to some of the studies, the engagement of PTA is linked to improved parent-school communication, increased efficacy of conflict resolution, and a higher degree of transparency concerning resource disposition (Agyekum et al., 2025). This is not always the case, however. The role of PTAs in a good number of environments, many of which are characterised by constant underfunding or by a population of parents with little formal training, is essentially that of a perfunctory entity. In these situations, the legal jurisdiction necessary is often lacking, parent representatives are never subject to a system of organised training, and the school hierarchy may discourage normal parents from expressing themselves. Sometimes, there are even cultural or gender-based barriers that prevent mothers or certain minority groups from participating fully (Asri et al., 2025). In cases where PTAs do work well, it is usually because they are seen not as extras, but as essential to how the school operates. They help keep school leaders accountable and make sure that community voices shape school priorities.

SGBs: A Test of Decentralisation

SGBs are a more formalised type of engagement, often embedded directly into education policy. These bodies are tied to the broader push for decentralisation, that is, bringing decision-making closer to the local level. In theory, they include various stakeholders: parents, teachers, sometimes even students and community leaders. The idea is to make school management more inclusive and responsive (White et al., 2025). Countries like South Africa, India, and the UK have all embraced this model in different ways. In practice, though, how well SGBs function varies a lot. In places where communities are fairly educated and socially organised, these bodies can play a significant role in drafting development plans, overseeing finances, and even hiring staff (Peters et al., 2024). However, in many Global South contexts, these bodies struggle. Participation may be low, mandates may be vague, and there is often political interference. In Bangladesh, for example, SMCs (which are similar to SGBs) have at times been taken over by local politicians, who use them for personal gain rather than educational improvement (Bruder & Baar, 2024). Another issue is that school governance can be pretty technical. For members of the community without much formal education, understanding budgets or policies can be overwhelming. In such cases, school principals or administrators often retain absolute control, and community input becomes more symbolic than substantial. Still, there are signs of hope in training programs that specifically support women and disadvantaged groups have shown that it is possible to make these bodies more representative and effective (Nanda & Banerjee, 2021).

The Role of Faith-Based and Civil Society Organisations

Apart from the official structures, faith-based groups and civil society organisations (CSOs) also play a significant role, especially in areas where state capacity is weak or schools are underfunded. In countries across Sub-Saharan Africa and South Asia, religious institutions often run schools or support them by providing scholarships, meals, or teacher training (Ullah, 2022). These institutions are usually well-trusted and deeply embedded in their communities, which gives them a certain legitimacy that government actors sometimes lack. CSOs, particularly those focused on education and child rights, often act as a middleman between communities and the education system. They help raise awareness, support advocacy efforts, and sometimes train community members to better participate in school governance (Yu et al., 2024). In parts of Latin America, NGOs have even helped to design and implement participatory school models, especially in post-conflict or transitional political settings. However, it is not all positive. Sometimes, religious groups focus more on their own agendas than on inclusive, secular education. Moreover, many CSOs depend on donor funding, which can dry up quickly, leading to short-lived projects. Also, when multiple organisations are involved, there is the risk of confusion about who is responsible for what can become unclear, especially when different agendas are at play.

Barriers That Still Persist

Even with all these mechanisms in place, real engagement often falls short. One big problem is *tokenism*. Meetings might happen and minutes might be taken, but decisions are made in advance, and people's input does not really matter (Ahmad et al., 2021). Over time, this erodes trust and discourages community involvement. There is also a big *capacity gap*. Many community members do not have the background or confidence to participate meaningfully in school governance. When only the more educated or influential locals feel comfortable engaging, it ends up excluding the very people the process is meant to empower (Yu et al., 2024). Then there are *power dynamics* within the school and the community. School leaders may feel their authority is being questioned and resist change. On the other hand, some community leaders might distrust schools, especially if they are seen as tools of the state or not aligned with local interests. These dynamics make it challenging to establish truly collaborative relationships.

Reimagining Institutional Engagement

To make a real difference, there needs to be a shift from seeing participation as a box-ticking exercise to recognising it as something genuinely transformative. For starters, PTAs and SGBs need stronger legal backing so they have actual decision-making authority. Community members, especially women, young people, and marginalised groups, should receive targeted training that helps them engage more confidently. Educator preparation programs need to be redesigned so that they perceive the community involvement activity not as a possible disturbance, but as a vital source of resources. As a result, leadership studies programs should incorporate learning in participatory governance, cultural sensitivity, and inclusive leadership styles. Therefore, even though structures like parent-teacher associations (PTAs), school governing bodies (SGBs), and neighbourhood organisations provide the much-needed participatory avenues, their performance largely depends on how they are operationalised. Finally, it is essential to establish an inclusive, equal social atmosphere around such mechanisms; it is only then that they will be able to emerge as long-term solutions of education reform that will fully embrace the idea of community.

STRENGTHENING VOICES: CAPACITY-BUILDING AND EMPOWERMENT

The concept of meaningful community and educational leadership has emerged as a fundamental aspect of sustainable and inclusive development. Nonetheless, recognition of its importance is just halfway home; more meaningful is its realisation into action. The key concept in this undertaking is that of capacity. The most interested stakeholders will be unable to contribute meaningfully or over extended periods in the absence of essential skills, knowledge content and institutional support (Wahyuni et al., 2025). Too often, the engagement turns into a ritual of checking the boxes instead of a radical move. Engagement makes a difference when stakeholders can have the instruments needed to critique educational structures, engage in decisions, and form the future of their communities.

Building Competence in Educational Governance

To begin with, community members must first feel confident enough to engage and that confidence primarily comes from understanding. Governance structures, budgetary mechanisms, curriculum frameworks, and child rights issues often seem inaccessible to parents or community leaders, especially in under-resourced settings. Training programs focused on school management, financial literacy, and curriculum interpretation have shown positive outcomes in enhancing community participation (Gupta et al., 2024). When such stakeholders, particularly those in parent committees or school management boards, are equipped with foundational knowledge, their involvement often becomes more frequent, informed, and results-driven. One noteworthy example comes from Ghana's capitation grant initiative. Communities there were trained in budget tracking and basic financial management, which not only improved local oversight of school funds but also gave rise to broader advocacy efforts on behalf of students (Fontdevila et al., 2021). This case illustrates that capacity-building is not merely about competence; it is also about creating an agency. However, it should not stop there. One-off workshops or seasonal training programs often fade with time or turnover. Engagement as a constituent aspect of the school practice is maintained due to the systematic inclusion of modules of community-based training into the long-term continuous developmental regimen of school leaders and teachers. Many countries are currently introducing community-based pedagogies in their teacher-education programs, an important step which recognises the learning space as a co-learning context in classrooms where educators learn alongside students and the broader community, co-participants at the school.

Figure 4. Framework for Capacity-Building in Educational Governance

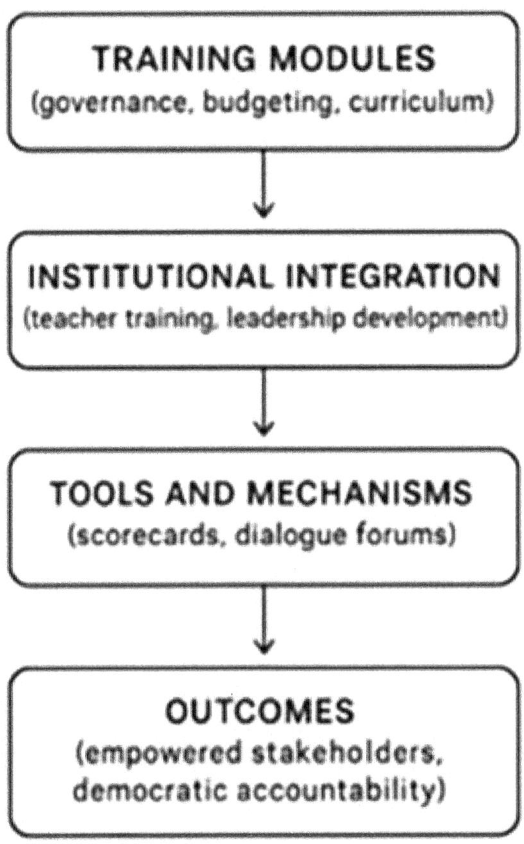

The current diagram outlines a stratified flow-type that is designed to provide the exposition of the community-related capacity-building operationalisation in education. It consists of four consecutive blocks, developed in a step-by-step order. The first block, Training Modules, deals with basic information including governance, budgeting and curriculum-related training. In the next block, "Institutional Integration", the preparation and development of leaders among teachers are discussed as the elements that are often left aside and of the most fundamental significance at the same time. The third block, called Tools and Mechanisms, presents the so-called concretely oriented tools, such as the community score cards and structured dialogue forums, which can be used to instigate transparency and inclusivity. The last block, "Outcomes" emphasises the expected outcome of all that, the increased community empowerment and the democratised accountability in the institutions of learning. Each block is also connected by arrows that illustrate the logical flow of the sequence in the stages and interdependence of its components on a larger goal of strengthening local educational governance.

Empowering the Marginalised: Inclusion as a Strategic Imperative

Exclusion of the marginalised groups, including women, Indigenous people, and low-income families, is institutionalised in numerous education systems. Even though systems like School Management Committees (SMCs) and Parent-Teacher Association (PTAs) claim to engage the community, they often contribute to the reassertion even more than breaking well-established hierarchies (Agyekum et al., 2025). Inclusion has thus to go beyond aspiration and be operationalised using systematic intervention. Good policies are the use of quota systems and sub-committees allocated explicitly to women and minority communities, to avoid mere tokenism. In Nepal, the active integration of mothers in SMCs has delivered a practical breakthrough in targeting Menstrual Hygiene Management and improving a gender-friendly schooling infrastructure (Asri et al., 2025). However, participation goes further than just being physically present: providing literacy support, programmes that build confidence, or cross mentoring of peers are equally important in terms of making such participation truly empowering instead of frightening. The digital innovations are also becoming channels through which inclusive engagement is realised. Community-based organisations in chosen rural spaces of Bangladesh use mobile learning and audio-visual aids to educate low-literate parents about children's rights and everything about their roles in governance, making abstract concepts tangible, and even out the playing field of historically marginalised communities.

Figure 5. Inclusive Representation Strategies in School Governance

Group	Strategy	Example
Women	Quotas	Nepal Mothers' Groups
Ethnic Minorities	Digital outreach	Bangladesh mobile training
Low-literacy Communities	Subcommittees	Village Council leadership mentoring

Figure 5 is a comparative matrix that juxtaposes different strategies that ensure the representation of marginalised groups in the school governance mechanisms in a systematic way. The table includes three columns: the column concerning the target constituency, the column containing the strategy that is to be followed, and the last column containing an illustrative example of the current practice. The focus is on groups that are often left out of decision-making, like women, ethnic minorities, and communities with lower literacy levels. Some of the approaches shown include things like quotas for female members, using mobile tech to reach people more effectively, and creating special subcommittees to make participation easier. Real-world cases like the Mothers' Groups in Nepal, mobile-based training efforts in Bangladesh, and local council mentoring programs are briefly mentioned to give practical context.

Trust-Building: The Invisible Currency of Collaboration

It is often overlooked, but trust is the quiet force that holds school-community collaboration together. Even when structural opportunities for engagement exist, distrust between educators and community members can derail them. Teachers might worry that parents will interfere in professional matters, while families may feel alienated by what they perceive as institutional arrogance or aloofness (Przytula, 2024). This mutual suspicion, left unaddressed, weakens the very fabric of shared educational responsibility. Creating trust takes time and intentionality. Spaces for genuine dialogue, whether through town hall-style meetings, informal cultural exchanges, or listening circles, are essential. These forums allow both sides to express concerns, share stories, and begin to see one another not as adversaries, but as collaborators. Importantly, school leaders and teachers must also build their own capacities, especially around cultural sensitivity and community engagement, so that they can approach families with empathy and openness rather than condescension. There is also value in legitimising local knowledge. When schools make room for indigenous ways of knowing, traditional ecological wisdom, or community-based approaches to discipline and mentorship, they send a powerful message: that knowledge does not just flow from textbooks or ministries, it also comes from lived experience (Druker-Ibáñez & Cáceres-Jensen, 2022). This form of epistemic respect is critical in communities where formal education has historically been used as a tool of exclusion. Accountability, too, must flow both ways. Communities deserve to know how decisions are made, how money is spent, and how well their children are learning. Schools that regularly share performance reports, financial summaries, or progress updates tend to cultivate more trust. Likewise, mechanisms such as community scorecards or parent feedback systems offer families a structured way to share concerns and recommendations.

Participatory Planning and Evaluation: Tools and Methodologies

Effective community engagement in education requires something that is more than face value consultation; what is needed is a stakeholder that has significant power in assessing the whole educational process, including determining the vision and evaluating the programs. The need to understand through participation by the stakeholder has led to the development of participatory planning and evaluation (PPE) as an essential framework. In co-developed school development plans (SDPs), the strategies are more representative of local realities because community members can integrate actions into a School Development Plan (SDP) that is based on unique regional conditions. Similarly, participatory rural appraisal (PRA) methods, including mapping activities, transect walks, and seasonal calendars, allow families to identify other local problems, which may otherwise be missed by conventional audits, such as dangerous walkways or toilets which are out of reach (Emon, 2025b; Ryan et al., 2024). These tools not only offer usable data but also build local authorship to instructional outcomes. Assessment is another critical platform without which community voice is non-negotiable. Qualitative techniques, such as Most Significant Change (MSC) or Outcome Harvesting, are effective in recording unmeasurable but essential changes in the school culture, such as improved parent-teacher relationships and an increased sense of agency among learners, especially in districts where more standard measures of student learning, such as test scores, may not be able to present a complete picture of improvement (Nnamani, 2024).

Figure 6. Tools for Participatory Planning and Evaluation (PPE)

The figure accompanying illustrates a circular, cyclic mechanism which connotes the action involved in practising participatory school governance. It includes five consecutive steps: Community Needs Assessment, Collaborative Planning (including the development of School Development Plans), Co-Implementation, Participatory Monitoring (through such tools as community scorecards or participatory rural appraisal), and Evaluation (which is well captured by Most Significant Change and Outcome Harvesting methodologies). The stages relate to arrows to reflect the fact that there is no stopping of the cycle, and it is everlasting; at every point, participants are educated by tools and processes to remain involved to ensure the translation of the fact that the engagement goes beyond the introduction phase to continue being present throughout the entire process.

From Participation to Transformation

The empowerment of communities cannot be regarded as a mere procedural measure; it is a long-term optimisation of educational governance. The success of capacity-building can lead to communities being more than watchdogs or voluntary actors; they can become co-partners in designing the vision and the execution of education. This implies that donor agencies, education ministries, and governments must invest the resources, not just financial capital, but also ideological capital in decentralised power, inclusive leadership styles and a sense of participation not only as a discrete, bounded event but as an ongoing process. In this age of digital advancement, a changing world economy, and increasing climate demands, strong education systems will be those that are based upon community power. Moreover, that strength must be cultivated through trust, inclusion, and shared learning.

POLICY RECOMMENDATIONS

Enhancing community involvement in educational leadership is not just a matter of policy rhetoric; it must be part and parcel of the structures that shape how schools operate and how decisions are made. As discussed earlier, community engagement cannot be viewed as a peripheral addition to education systems. Instead, it must be seen as a vital part of ensuring that education remains responsive, inclusive, and equitable. The following policy recommendations are proposed, rooted in both the challenges and possibilities presented in previous sections. To begin with, there is an urgent need to establish legal and regulatory frameworks that do not merely encourage but require community participation in school governance. In many countries, especially in parts of the Global South, involvement by community members in educational decision-making remains informal, and sometimes, unfortunately, symbolic (Carrasco & Perez Lopez, 2025). Without legal mandates, community bodies like PTAs and SGBs tend to operate on the margins. Laws should not only formalise their existence but also give these groups specific, actionable responsibilities in areas like budgeting, teacher recruitment, and curriculum oversight. South Africa's approach through the South African Schools Act is a frequently cited example, which grants substantial autonomy to SGBs. However, outcomes vary significantly depending on each school's socio-economic context (Nakidien et al., 2021). Still, having these provisions in law gives legitimacy to local involvement and provides communities with a point of leverage.

However, having a law on paper does not always translate into participation in practice. That is why incentive structures are just as important. In regions where people struggle with daily livelihoods, civic engagement may not be a priority.

Participation becomes less likely when it is perceived as time-consuming or fruitless. Here, modest incentives, whether monetary, symbolic, or social, can play a critical role. Community members who volunteer for school governance might be offered transportation reimbursements, recognition awards, or conditional grants for community-led school improvement projects. In fact, empirical evidence from Bangladesh and rural Ghana indicates that performance-linked block grants tied to community participation can boost both enrolment and learning outcomes (Emon, 2025a). Though not a silver bullet, these incentives send a powerful message: that communities are valued partners in educational transformation. Another key area of reform concerns the professional development of teachers and school leaders. Historically, teacher training has emphasised instructional techniques and classroom management, often ignoring the relational and social aspects of education. However, effective collaboration with communities requires a different skillset. Educators must be trained to listen, to mediate conflicts, and to co-plan with non-experts. Therefore, teacher education curricula, both pre-service and in-service, should include modules on community engagement, participatory governance, and cross-cultural communication. International programs like UNESCO's Teacher Task Force have already begun emphasising the importance of leadership that is participatory and contextually aware (Göregen et al., 2024). Teachers and headteachers who are equipped to lead inclusive dialogue with communities often become the bridge between policy and practice.

Moreover, if governments are serious about community engagement, they must also rethink how they monitor school performance. Most education systems rely heavily on quantitative metrics such as test scores or attendance without really capturing how communities perceive quality. Participatory Monitoring and Evaluation (PM&E) tools, such as citizen report cards or community scorecards, offer an alternative. These tools allow community members to express satisfaction, voice grievances, and co-define success criteria. They have been successfully implemented in places like India and Kenya, where they have contributed to higher levels of transparency and better teacher attendance (Mouta et al., 2024). While these methods may seem messy or "subjective," they bring to the forefront insights that conventional indicators often miss. That said, participatory structures can reproduce existing social hierarchies if safeguards are not in place. It is not uncommon for local elites' men, the affluent, or dominant ethnic groups to monopolise community forums. That is why policies need to be intentional about inclusivity. One of the ways a voice and agency can be redistributed in educational governance is by instituting quotas of women and marginal groups on school boards. The relevant example would be the education reform in Nepal of 2007, where the focus was on ensuring that mothers' groups were included in school management committees. These committees have been effective in making gender issues take Centre stage and protecting children in danger (Gupta et al., 2024). Additional complementary approaches like gender responsibilities, budgeting, and the integration of cultural concerns in the development of curriculum further ensure that cultures that have been marginalised are reflected.

The collaborative practice across sectors should also be emphasised in policies. Schools live in the scope of health, nutrition, social protection and community development of the population. Therefore, there should be the synchronisation of community-engagement activities across the pertinent ministries. A notable example of this process is the participatory budgeting model in Brazil: connecting the education plans of municipalities with the corresponding health and social services helps the community to anchor the need to educate children in their growth perspectives (Almazroa et al., 2024). Such a comprehensive policy helps in creating policy coherence and prevents duplication. However, policy rigidity must be discouraged to an extent. Though national frameworks are imperative, they still need to be flexible enough to include local contexts. Innovative funds or competitive grants which promote creative solutions on the community level, through peer learning networks that spread good practices, may thus be initiated by governments. The big picture would be to establish a culture whereby bottom-up experimentation is not only allowed but encouraged. Altogether, community engagement policy development does not focus only on the development of legislative tools and technical interventions, but also on redistribution of power, respecting local knowledge and building cultures of mutual trust relationships. They are expected to view policies as open invitations to participate in co-creation within which community members will engage as equals and will have a say in the future of their schools. Finally, authentic engagement is a big-time investment, a long-term process that demands patience and utmost faith in the possibility of people, regardless of their background, to make effective changes in education.

CASE STUDIES: LOCAL VOICES, GLOBAL LESSONS

Involvement of communities in educational leadership takes on what one may find to be a specific salience when judged based on situationally particular contexts. The following presented case studies comprise the cases of Kenya, Nepal, Bangladesh, Brazil, Indigenous people in Canada, and Indigenous people in Australia, which could be used to define the ability of local actors to overcome educational issues within their specific social and political contexts. Taken together, they could attest to the concrete improvements in learning achievements and provide transferable knowledge that can be used more broadly.

Kenya: VECs and Grassroots School Leadership

In Kenya, the push toward decentralised educational governance resulted in the establishment of Village Education Committees (VECs), particularly in rural areas where educational facilities are not readily available. These committees, which include community members, parents, community leaders, or teachers, have been operating since 2003, when the Free Primary Education program was introduced; their duties consist of taking administrative charge, mobilising resources, and managing accountability practices (Yu et al., 2024). The social and political context of Kenya, which consists of regional inequality and ethnic diversity, often affects the quality of education. VECs aim to increase ownership of schools at the community level, and in response to this aim, their duties have embraced fundraising activities to build/repair classrooms, recruiting volunteer teachers, and tracking the attendance of teachers. The distinguished enrollment and retained status in schools with proactive VECs, as reported by empirical studies, refers to the high levels of enrollment and retention compared to schools with no similar community outreach (Natarajarathinam et al., 2021). These committees also help in integration by introducing a cultural component and allowing elders in the community to make school decisions, thus increasing their presence in the communities. Combined, the experience in Kenya highlights the need to normalise these ways of community participation in the official governance structures to achieve sustainability. The trained governance capacity, however, is lacking in considerable parts of VEC members, and this limits its reach (Gupta et al., 2024). Therefore, the legal recognition should be complemented by long-term capacity-building processes.

Nepal: Mothers' Groups and SMCs Advancing Gender Equity

Nepal's school reforms have increasingly recognised how critical mothers' groups and SMCs are to governance, particularly given the country's patriarchal norms and historically low female literacy rates. Mothers' groups actively support girls' education by keeping an eye on school conditions and tackling issues like early marriage and menstrual hygiene (Fitzgerald et al., 2024). These groups run awareness campaigns and work closely with teachers to create safer, more supportive environments. A common approach has been monthly meetings facilitated by NGOs that provide training on leadership, budgeting, and education rights. The results have been encouraging, with schools with active mothers' groups reporting rises in girls' enrollment and retention, with some districts seeing attendance improve by 20% over three years (Omanyo & Ndiege, 2025). Beyond numbers, the presence of mothers in governance strengthens social bonds and trust in schools. Empowering women in these roles also challenges traditional gender norms, promoting broader social change. Nepal's experience shows how targeted efforts to include marginalised groups can make a meaningful difference.

Bangladesh: Community-Led School Building and Participatory Governance

Bangladesh has made remarkable progress in primary education access, but challenges remain in quality and governance, especially outside urban centres. Here, community involvement has been critical to sustaining improvements. In Khulna's coastal areas, local NGOs teamed up with communities to construct schools using volunteer labour and local fundraising, cutting back reliance on external donors. Alongside this, SMCs formed with parents, teachers, and local leaders to oversee school affairs. This study used a two-pronged intervention strategy that combined the ability to increase enrolment rates and the ability to improve the school infrastructure. The intervention was especially effective among the marginalised groups, especially the ethnic minorities, whose involvement in education rose significantly. Statistical data reveal that such schools where local populations took direct oversight responsibility showed 25% better retention percentage than comparative government-run schools, which were not under direct supervision of communities (Emon, 2025a). However, the administration system has experienced significant challenges that demonstrate the importance of open governance systems and constant administrative services. An early signal of trouble would be that certain community committees had been hijacked by elite interests, even though the governing government machinery was also uneven in its monitoring. Such results support the significance of institutional transparency, continuity and consistent collaborative support.

Brazil: Participatory Budgeting and Democratic Governance in Schools

In Brazil, the Municipal Participatory Budgeting (PB) process, where citizens have a direct say in the municipal fiscal decisions, has been used in the education system as well, so that the community gets to vote on where the money should go to counters that require repairing, hiring of teachers, and extracurricular programmes. This mechanism has created additional transparency by placing the fiscal power in the local hands and promoting the relevance of educational services to the priorities of the communities, especially in low-income urban neighbourhoods. The experience of some cities like Porto Alegre proves that there exists a connection between PB and decreased dropout percentage and higher rates of attendance (Touchton et al., 2019). The involvement of the local voices in financial decision-making also serves to spur participation and civic foundations, as well as strengthen the norms of democracy. Nevertheless, the involvement has its limitations and is based on the side of more prosperous residents; thus, such developed long-term outreach and capacity-building programs are required to provide the full and equal representation of all members of the community.

Indigenous Communities in Canada and Australia: Embracing Culturally Responsive Leadership

Educational leadership in the case of Indigenous people differs in the context of settler-colonial nations like Canada and Australia due to various issues associated with language maintenance, the upholding of traditions, and governance practices. In Canada, the First Nations Education Steering Committee supports communities to manage their schools to run under band-operated school systems (Friesen & Jacobsen, 2020). The committee believes in culturally responsive curriculum, increased participation of elders, and changes in administration patterns to be consistent with Indigenous forms of governance. In Australia, community-controlled schools are organised by Aboriginal people and locally applied in local languages and local practices, where community members take up leadership roles in school councils (Williams, 2020). These have been traced to be characterised by positive student participation, reinforced cultural awareness and gradual academic growth. However, these programs are inherent in the history of marginalisation and hence they necessitate continuous policy encouragement and reconciliation work. Collectively, these cases demonstrate that education is tied to the cultural existence and Indigenous self-determination.

Lessons Learned and Transferability

In various settings, some critical lessons should be considered when it comes to facilitating community involvement in educational governance. First, good participation must be integrated into institutionalised frameworks of governance that clearly indicate roles and duties. Second, to ensure that the engagement is worthwhile, continuous capacity building is essential, as meaningful work cannot be implied without the necessary support. Third, deliberate efforts should be made with respect to historically disadvantaged populations, such as women, ethnic minority groups, and Indigenous populations, as elements that are crucial to equity. Lastly, strict accountability systems that embrace societal consideration are essential towards building trust and transparency. These principles can be modified, though it is dependent on the specificities of the nation and community. Politicians and educationalists are thus urged to make them more specific to their environment and develop their leadership, which appreciates local knowledge and shared responsibility. The cross-world experience of community-school alliances has shown the true potential of participatory action in education at the ground level to make it more sustainable, equitable and relevant.

COMMUNITY PARTICIPATION AND ECONOMIC DEVELOPMENT

The connection between community participation in education and broader national economic development has increasingly drawn attention from both researchers and policymakers. Modern learning has now come to the realisation that when education is fueled and influenced through meaningful community involvement, it supersedes mere benefits in personal learning; it goes further ahead to participate in the process of creating human capital, which is a fundamental precursor of long-term economic development and societal development. Based on that, the broader effects of community involvement in education are discussed, which clarifies how it serves as a driver of local economic empowerment, addresses the existing skills shortages and social inequalities, and maintains cross-sector partnerships between education, health, and economic prosperity. At the centre of this relationship is the ability of education to empower the local economy. Communities that are directly involved in the governance of the school commonly report an increased sense of ownership and responsibility. This ownership increases the segmentation of education to the local geographical and labour-market contexts and necessities (Li, 2023). The involvement will facilitate the inclusion of relevant skills in curriculum and training programmes, which include both vocational and entrepreneurial aptitude, consequently resulting in increased employment and income-earning capabilities. In many rural settings across the globe, local communities have employed such schools where agricultural labour or crafts work has been part of the curriculum, thereby resembling the economic and livelihood systems of the local people. This practice shifts education again out of academic performance towards a more practical, economically more favourable direction. Human capital theory provides such an intellectual skeleton: within this framework, participatory governance of education enhances national development through increasing the productive capacity of individuals and, therefore, boosts economic growth (Lubis et al., 2024). However, the past potential of the top-down systems has been quite often squandered because of the lack of fit with the local needs and the insufficient responsiveness of the traditional systems. Conversely, participatory governance or participation with parents, local and civil society actors can help fill this gap by establishing and prioritising the competencies that are most essential to community development. The social capital is enhanced in the same direction, and the creation of knowledge is achieved in this way through the co-creation mechanism, thus solidifying the composition of human capital. (Ohnishi et al., 2024).

Community engagement is a critical tool in overcoming the current issues that are peculiar to numerous countries, the most notable ones being a lack of skills, unemployment among youth and inequality. The educational mismatch with the labour-market needs and abilities is regularly described as a formidable barrier to economic growth, particularly in rapidly changing environments brought about by technological changes and globalisation pressures. The participatory platforms enable the communities to express the competencies which they feel do not adequately meet their needs and to demand changes in the curriculum, access to apprenticeship programs or increased collaboration with local businesses. An example is in different parts of Sub-Saharan Africa, where community engagement has played a significant role in the institution of youth training centres, either affiliated to agricultural cooperatives or small businesses, thus allowing the youth to gain practical skills as well as to become more employable. Unemployment among the youth and its unequal effect on marginalised populations is a problem that usually creates social instability and reproduces impoverishment. The more open the schools are to community contributions, the more inclusive the school programmes aimed at the vulnerable groups, like young women or ethnic minorities, become, which reduces the levels of social ostracism. Moreover, learning through participation tends to ensure more profound learning experiences as well as mentorship, which instils the youth with highly desirable soft skills such as communication, leadership, and teamwork, vital in the modern fast-paced workplaces. This holistic view on the development of human capital in general is key to breaking the systemic barrier and enabling social mobility.

Education, health and economic productivity are bound together, and such meetings often lack proper attention. Local-level community engagement usually enables coordinated interventions that combine learning with learner wellbeing due to the understanding of the intense relationship between these areas (Forshaw & Woods, 2023). An example of school-feeding programs run by the community, such as the school, is that better nutrition shows direct cognitive results and improved school attendance. Similarly, the health-education campaigns that are co-designed by the schools and their surrounding communities will lead to healthier populations, which will minimise illness, cut down on absences and improve the general learning outcomes. These compounding benefits unearth how educational systems do not actually exist in a vacuum; they are isomorphic to a greater developmental ecosystem that also covers health, social protection and economic empowerment. The total capital in human resources produced as a result of these synergies then brings increased productivity, innovation and resilience on local and national levels (Kokkinopoulou et al., 2025). Despite the positive evidence base, there are also several adverse challenges. Without a particular ability to maintain participation in the community in a constant manner, with proper provision of resources and a stridently supported policy, the phenomenon is likely to lose appeal. Additionally, there should be genuine inclusiveness and representativeness of participation processes because, without them, there is a risk of an established group's algorithms ruling and such a vulnerable population being underrated. Lastly, the measurement of the effects of community-initiated education programs on the economy is still in its complicated stages, requiring monitoring systems that provide a balance between both the quantitative and qualitative evidence.

CHALLENGES, ENABLERS, AND THE PATH FORWARD

Educational leadership aimed at integrating the meaningful presence of a community is not a simple affair, and a variety of limitations tend to hinder the process. Although it is well documented that decentralisation and inclusive governance are highly beneficial, transforming these concepts into a practical reality is not always easy. In the section below, we analyse the significant constraints to community participation, which are political opposition, elite capture, cultural barriers to participation by women, and technical and infrastructural constraints. One of the major hindrances that has continued to reduce active community participation in the management of education remains political opposition to decentralisation. In many nations, control of education has retained the form of the Ministry or local bureau, which is unwilling to cede power. Their reluctance can be explained by concerns about a lack of control, accountability problems, and the feeling that decentralisation will worsen the current inequities (Sánchez Galera, 2020).

Decentralisation of the administration of education is made difficult by political insecurity and the activities of patronage systems. School committees can be seen as venues of partisan conflict and not as collaborative efforts in a milieu in which education is highly politicised and corrodes both trust and performance. Influences of sections of Sub-Saharan Africa point toward the reality that local political actors tend to take over school governance organisations to maintain their grip, hence leaving local community members without representation in the actual expression. These observations serve to remind us that decentralisation should not be viewed as an administrative reform only; it has deep roots in local politics of power. Another sharp issue that exists in participatory structures is the exclusion of the elite and the marginalised groups. Even though policies may be geared towards co-opting community participation, decision-making circles are often dominated by better-off and wealthier families, males, or more dominant ethnic groups and societies. As a result, pre-existing social disparities are maintained in which women, minorities, indigenous peoples, and disadvantaged groups are often marginalised or overlooked. Similar results are available in South Asia and Latin America in terms of empirical undertakings, which show how there are social hierarchies that reinstate participation. As an example, caste and gender bias in Nepalese SMCs undermine the role of lower-caste and female members despite the formal policies of inclusion. Related processes can be observed in Brazil's participatory budgeting forums, where members with high incomes tend to have much more weight in decision-making related to education. The solution to elite capture is conscious decision-making involving quotas, capacity-building efforts, and transparency, but these solutions are not always consistent in use.

The fact that cultural norms limit the role of women in the process of governance is a significant barrier to effective governance. Many societies still restrict the extent to which women can participate in society or exercise power, and this is highly experienced in rural or conservative settings. Despite the formal inclusion of women through their inclusion in the school governance processes, there is a general societal anticipation that negates the full participation of women. These variables include time poverty due to high domestic commitments, recurring lack of confidence, and even poor education levels, all of which impede women's participation in decision-making forums. These cultural obstacles undermine female equity in leadership roles in education and affect the overall quality of community participation. More importantly, female voices cannot be disregarded when it comes to addressing school-safety concerns, the good nutrition of children, and inclusive pedagogical approaches, yet they are often overlooked. Effective interventions have been known to incorporate the legally required representation of women with community-awareness campaigns and specifically an empowerment programme aimed at normalising female leadership. Technological and infrastructural deficiency helps to enhance social and political issues, especially in the impoverished and rural areas. The lack of adequate electricity, quality and access to the internet and quality transportation systems may hinder the flow of information, access to training opportunities and the complete inclusion in the digitised decision-making processes that define modern-day governance. The COVID-19 pandemic has increased these gaps by locking many marginalised groups out of participating in remote activities, thus expanding the gap.

Infrastructure is often the most referenced barrier to civic engagement, as there is a need to facilitate participation. A lack of enough meeting areas and the poor condition of schooling resources may also hinder the frequency with which community members gather and the inclusiveness of these gatherings. The inability to move or spend time in a convenient location makes it even more challenging to maintain long-term participation once the potential participants are exposed to some barriers. The solution to these problems does not only require specific capital investment in physical infrastructure but also wise solutions regarding digital literacy and access to affordable connectivity. Despite these barriers, a series of enabling factors has emerged that can result in everlasting community engagement. One, local and national supportive leadership is essential. Leaders support decentralisation, and their emphasis on the involvement of the community contributes to the development of participatory cultures. As an example, principals who have been trained to be inclusive leaders usually develop more coherent ties of trust and collaboration with parents and other stakeholders in the area. Similarly, institutional changes are facilitated by political elites who express their support for community-based governance publicly. A policy atmosphere is also essential. Formalised, such as the Schools Act (South Africa), and participatory budgeting policies (Brazil), allow the community a defined role within a law and provide said duties a clear role which protects and empowers its residents. When these mechanisms are combined with capacity-building actions, communities are in a better position and more prepared to interact effectively.

The contributions of donors and cooperation with the international organisations have involved essential resources in many scenarios to provide technical knowledge, financial funds, and knowledge-sharing platforms. Multilateral agencies and NGOs also often launch community-training programs, organise policy discussions and test new forms of engagement. Even though external support should never overshadow community ownership, such partnerships can trigger systematic changes and share the good practices. Future directions require a complex understanding of the complex nature of the various issues involved in community participation. The aspect of decentralisation is not an easy correction of administration, but is critically influenced by political and social forces. At the same time, it is possible to alleviate these challenges by creating coalitions between governments, civil society organisations, and the targeted populations. The significant investment in social inclusion, gender-sensitive programming, and the growth of digital infrastructure will become essential. It is also important to develop a culture of constant learning and adaptability. Feedback systems and transparent evaluation-based participatory governance mechanisms, in turn, should be incorporated into participatory governance processes to reveal weaknesses and come up with better solutions. The potential role of technology here is as a tool that can be used effectively, so that accessibility is increased, but the population at risk does not get further marginalised.

CONCLUSION

The current chapter aims at shedding light on the necessity of bridging the gap between the educational institutions and the communities they serve, emphasising that long-term progress in the sphere of education can only be secured in the case of effective involvement of the communities in leadership and governance. Modern evidence indicates that a dependence on the traditional, vertical leadership models is insufficient to solve the complex social, cultural, and economic forces defining the contemporary learning environment. A participatory paradigm, which places the members of the community first and as active stakeholders, is thus cited as more effective in terms of enhancing education quality and meeting greater goals like social cohesion and economic empowerment. The discussion shows that engagement with the community cannot be reduced to a marginal or token factor; it is one of the pillars of effective educational leadership. The chapter uses theoretical threads grounded in transformational leadership and distributed leadership, to social capital and Freirean pedagogy to show how participation in the community fosters collective efficacy, agency and mutual responsibility. In accordance with international case studies, the introduction of the community perspective tends to lead to even greater access, higher equity, and locally adaptive education, with local development agendas strengthened, even though the contextual frameworks involved have varied significantly. The move towards a participatory governance of educational processes has, however, been filled with pitfalls. The problem of political opposition, capture of the elite, cultural factors, and torments of infrastructure still appear to be formidable obstacles. The overview of the presented issues indicates that a monolith approach or an approach or strategy where universality is presumed is simply insufficient. A good intervention should thus take into consideration localised settings and weigh between bottom-up empowerment and inclusive mechanisms. The literature emphasises that enabling community engagement relies heavily on the supportive leadership style, well-consistent legal frameworks, capacity-building efforts, and collaborations with other stakeholders outside a community. Therefore, the chapter prescribes systematic changes that incorporate community involvement in the heart of educational leadership and management as opposed to peripheral and marginal supply. However, these reforms hold the potential to engage the lived experience, commitment, and resources of communities to create school settings that promote educational institutions and society in a synergistic relationship with one another. In the future, further consolidation in community engagement will call not only for long-term but also flexibility and resilience to work in political realities and social intricacies of educational governance. The future work and practice will be able to explore new forms of participation, utilise new technologies to be more inclusive, and understand that community-based educational leadership can enhance human capital development and sustainable economic growth.

REFERENCES

Agyekum, B., Salifu, I., Eshun, S. N., & Asamoah, M. K. (2025). Exploring the implications of using parent-teacher associations (PTAs) as a pathway for school-community development. *Journal of Professional Capital and Community*, *10*(4), 465–480. Advance online publication. DOI: 10.1108/JPCC-06-2024-0092

Ahmad, I., & Islam, M. R. (2024). Empowerment and Participation: Key Strategies for Inclusive Development. In *Building Strong Communities: Ethical Approaches to Inclusive Development* (pp. 47–68). Emerald Publishing Limited. DOI: 10.1108/978-1-83549-174-420241003

Ahmad, J., Khan, A. W., & Khan, H. U. (2021). Role of Critical Success Factors in Offshore Quality Requirement Change Management Using SLR. *IEEE Access : Practical Innovations, Open Solutions*, *9*, 99680–99698. DOI: 10.1109/ACCESS.2021.3096663

Almazroa, H., Alotaibi, W., & Alrwaythi, E. (2024). Sustainable Development Goals and Future-Oriented Teacher Education Programs. *IEEE Transactions on Engineering Management*, *71*, 13517–13530. DOI: 10.1109/TEM.2022.3165686

Altynbassov, B., Bayanbayeva, A., Tolegen, M., & Zhamankarin, M. (2024). A comprehensive bibliometric analysis of trends in higher education leadership in the Global South, 2013-2023: Contemporary perspectives and developments. *International Journal of Educational Research*, *127*, 102421. DOI: 10.1016/j.ijer.2024.102421

Aminudin, N., & Jamal, S. A. (2024). Social capital and economic mobility in tourism: A systematic literature review. *Cogent Social Sciences*, *10*(1), 2321665. Advance online publication. DOI: 10.1080/23311886.2024.2321665

Asri, F. H. M., Singh, D., Mansor, Z., Norman, H., Alshurideh, M. T., Alzoubi, M. R., Falaki, N., Mohammad, S. I., & Mohammad, A. A. S. (2025). *An Insight of the Importance of Stakeholders in Collaborative Online Learning*. COLAB., DOI: 10.1007/978-3-031-74220-0_10

Azoury, N., & Harvey, S. (2023). The Changing Role of Governance in Education. In *Governance in Higher Education* (pp. 211–231). Springer Nature Switzerland., DOI: 10.1007/978-3-031-40586-0_10

Bramwell, D. (2020). Systematic review of empirical studies on citizenship education in Latin America 2000 to 2017 and research agenda proposal. *Citizenship. Social and Economics Education*, *19*(2), 100–117. DOI: 10.1177/2047173420922506

Brown, C., Luzmore, R., O'Donovan, R., Ji, G., & Patnaik, S. (2024). How educational leaders can maximise the social capital benefits of inter-school networks: Findings from a systematic review. *International Journal of Educational Management*, *38*(1), 213–264. DOI: 10.1108/IJEM-09-2023-0447

Bruder, M., & Baar, T. (2024). Innovation in humanitarian assistance—A systematic literature review. *Journal of International Humanitarian Action*, *9*(1), 2. DOI: 10.1186/s41018-023-00144-3

Candeias Fernandes, A. J., & Franco, M. (2022). The role of entrepreneurial resilience in forms of collaboration: A systematic literature review with bibliometric analyses. *EuroMed Journal of Business*, *17*(4), 752–789. DOI: 10.1108/EMJB-05-2021-0075

Carrasco, S., & Perez Lopez, I. (2025). Linking education and practice gaps for inclusive architecture in the AEC industry. *Archnet-IJAR: International Journal of Architectural Research*, *19*(1), 128–148. DOI: 10.1108/ARCH-11-2023-0297

Dorji, T., Morrison-Saunders, A., & Blake, D. (2023). Understanding How Community Wellbeing is Affected by Climate Change: Evidence From a Systematic Literature Review. *Environmental Management*, *72*(3), 568–586. DOI: 10.1007/s00267-023-01833-w PMID: 37209142

Druker-Ibáñez, S., & Cáceres-Jensen, L. (2022). Integration of indigenous and local knowledge into sustainability education: A systematic literature review. *Environmental Education Research*, *28*(8), 1209–1236. DOI: 10.1080/13504622.2022.2083081

Elerian, M., Yemini, M., Khavenson, T., & Jasikowska, K. (2025). Systematic literature review of school-age youth activism in post-socialist countries. *Educational Review*, •••, 1–25. DOI: 10.1080/00131911.2025.2451091

Elias, A., & Mansouri, F. (2020). A Systematic Review of Studies on Interculturalism and Intercultural Dialogue. *Journal of Intercultural Studies (Melbourne, Vic.)*, *41*(4), 490–523. DOI: 10.1080/07256868.2020.1782861

Emon, M. M. H. (2025a). Leveraging AI on Social Media & Digital Platforms to Enhance English Language Teaching and Learning. In *AI-Powered English Teaching* (pp. 211–238). IGI Global Scientific Publishing., DOI: 10.4018/979-8-3373-1952-0.ch007

Emon, M. M. H. (2025b). Navigating the Digital Labyrinth: Personal Data Privacy and Security at Individual and Organizational Levels. In *User-Centric Cybersecurity Implications for Sustainable Digital Transformation* (pp. 257–288). IGI Global Scientific Publishing. DOI: 10.4018/979-8-3373-3171-3.ch008

Emon, M. M. H., & Chowdhury, M. S. A. (2025). Safeguarding Student Data: Privacy and Security Challenges in AI-Powered Education Tools. In *Enhancing Student Support and Learning Through Conversational AI* (pp. 191–228). IGI Global Scientific Publishing. DOI: 10.4018/979-8-3373-3316-8.ch008

Emon, M. M. H., & Khan, T. (2025). Corporate Social Responsibility for Sustainable Development: A Systematic Review of Business Contributions to Address Global Challenges. *Review of Business and Economics Studies*, *13*(2), 6–39. DOI: 10.26794/2308-944X-2025-13-2-6-39

Esquierdo-Leal, J. L., & Houmanfar, R. A. (2021). Creating Inclusive and Equitable Cultural Practices by Linking Leadership to Systemic Change. *Behavior Analysis in Practice*, *14*(2), 499–512. DOI: 10.1007/s40617-020-00519-7 PMID: 33613858

Fernández-Aballí Altamirano, A. (2020). The Importance of Paulo Freire to Communication for Development and Social Change. In *Handbook of Communication for Development and Social Change* (pp. 309–327). Springer Singapore., DOI: 10.1007/978-981-15-2014-3_76

Ferrada, D. (2020). Dialogic pedagogy linking worlds: Participatory community classrooms. *Pedagogy, Culture & Society*, *28*(1), 131–146. DOI: 10.1080/14681366.2019.1615534

Fitzgerald, A., Avirmed, T., & Battulga, N. (2024). Exploring the factors informing educational inequality in higher education: a systematic literature review. *Perspectives: Policy and Practice in Higher Education*, 1–11. DOI: 10.1080/13603108.2024.2381121

Fontdevila, C., Verger, A., & Avelar, M. (2021). The business of policy: A review of the corporate sector's emerging strategies in the promotion of education reform. *Critical Studies in Education*, *62*(2), 131–146. DOI: 10.1080/17508487.2019.1573749

Forshaw, E., & Woods, K. (2023). Student participation in the development of whole-school wellbeing strategies: A systematic review of the literature. *Pastoral Care in Education*, *41*(4), 430–448. DOI: 10.1080/02643944.2022.2148175

Friesen, S., & Jacobsen, M. (2020). *The Education System of Canada.*, DOI: 10.1007/978-3-319-93443-3_37-1

Fuad, D. R. S. M., Musa, K., & Hashim, Z. (2022). Innovation culture in education: A systematic review of the literature. *Management in Education*, *36*(3), 135–149. DOI: 10.1177/0892020620959760

Göregen, M. S., Tanghe, E., & Schelfhout, W. (2024). What Works to Retain Beginning Teachers in the Profession? A Mixed Methods Approach to Detect Determining Factors. *Education Sciences*, *14*(12), 1319. DOI: 10.3390/educsci14121319

Guha, P. (2023). School committee composition: Exploring the role of parental and female representation in India. *Development Policy Review*, *41*(3), e12677. Advance online publication. DOI: 10.1111/dpr.12677

Gupta, S. L., Mittal, A., Singh, S., & Dash, D. N. (2024). Demand-driven approach of vocational education and training (VET) and experiential learning: A thematic analysis through systematic literature review (SLR). *Asian Education and Development Studies*, *13*(1), 45–63. DOI: 10.1108/AEDS-07-2023-0083

Hamann, K. R. S., Wullenkord, M. C., Reese, G., & van Zomeren, M. (2024). Believing That We Can Change Our World for the Better: A Triple-A (Agent-Action-Aim) Framework of Self-Efficacy Beliefs in the Context of Collective Social and Ecological Aims. *Personality and Social Psychology Review*, *28*(1), 11–53. DOI: 10.1177/10888683231178056 PMID: 37386819

Hong, P. C., Chennattuserry, J. C., Deng, X., & Hopkins, M. M. (2021). Purpose-driven leadership and organizational success: A case of higher educational institutions. *Leadership and Organization Development Journal*, *42*(7), 1004–1017. DOI: 10.1108/LODJ-02-2021-0054

Keding, C. (2021). Understanding the interplay of artificial intelligence and strategic management: Four decades of research in review. *Management Review Quarterly*, *71*(1), 91–134. DOI: 10.1007/s11301-020-00181-x

Kokkinopoulou, E., Vrontis, D., & Thrassou, A. (2025). *The impact of education on productivity and externalities of economic development and social welfare: a systematic literature review*. Central European Management Journal., DOI: 10.1108/CEMJ-04-2024-0124

Kumar, A., & Mishra, S. (2022). Exploring Future Research Agenda for Rural Mother's Empowerment: A Study at the Intersection of Bibliometric and Systematic Literature Review. *South Asian Journal of Business and Management Cases*, *11*(3), 254–275. DOI: 10.1177/22779779221115804

Li, M. (2023). Adapting Legal Education for the Changing Landscape of Regional Emerging Economies: A Dynamic Framework for Law Majors. *Journal of the Knowledge Economy*, *15*(3), 10227–10256. DOI: 10.1007/s13132-023-01507-2

Liu, Y., Bellibaş, M. Ş., & Gümüş, S. (2021). The Effect of Instructional Leadership and Distributed Leadership on Teacher Self-efficacy and Job Satisfaction: Mediating Roles of Supportive School Culture and Teacher Collaboration. *Educational Management Administration & Leadership*, *49*(3), 430–453. DOI: 10.1177/1741143220910438

Lubis, S., Purnomo, E. P., Lado, J. A., & Hung, C.-F. (2024). Electronic governance in advancing sustainable development goals through systematic literature review. *Discover Global Society*, *2*(1), 77. DOI: 10.1007/s44282-024-00102-3

Marujo, H. A., & Wissing, M. P. (2024). *Community Peace and Character Strengths*., DOI: 10.1007/978-3-031-66928-6_6

Mouta, A., Pinto-Llorente, A. M., & Torrecilla-Sánchez, E. M. (2024). Uncovering Blind Spots in Education Ethics: Insights from a Systematic Literature Review on Artificial Intelligence in Education. *International Journal of Artificial Intelligence in Education*, *34*(3), 1166–1205. DOI: 10.1007/s40593-023-00384-9

Mpuangnan, K. N., & Ntombela, S. (2024). Community voices in curriculum development. *Curriculum Perspectives*, *44*(1), 49–60. DOI: 10.1007/s41297-023-00223-w

Mu, G. M., Gordon, D., Xu, J., Cayas, A., & Madesi, S. (2023). Benefits and limitations of partnerships amongst families, schools and universities: A systematic literature review. *International Journal of Educational Research*, *120*, 102205. DOI: 10.1016/j.ijer.2023.102205

Murtadlo, M., Albana, H., Nisa, Y. F., Izazy, N. Q., Sumiati, N. T., Dewi, M. S., Abdullah, H., & Henry, C. (2025). Inclusive education in Africa: Transforming higher education in low-income countries. *Scientific African*, *28*, e02708. DOI: 10.1016/j.sciaf.2025.e02708

Nadeem, M. (2024). Distributed leadership in educational contexts: A catalyst for school improvement. *Social Sciences & Humanities Open*, *9*, 100835. DOI: 10.1016/j.ssaho.2024.100835

Nakidien, T., Singh, M., & Sayed, Y. (2021). Teachers and Teacher Education: Limitations and Possibilities of Attaining SDG 4 in South Africa. *Education Sciences*, *11*(2), 66. DOI: 10.3390/educsci11020066

Namoog, M. Y., & Agyekum, B. (2024). Non-formal education and women's empowerment: An assessment of the contemporal relevance of Freire's concept of conscientisation in increasing district assemblywomen's participation in community development and governance in Northen Ghana. *Cogent Arts & Humanities*, *11*(1), 2313338. Advance online publication. DOI: 10.1080/23311983.2024.2313338

Nanda, A. P., & Banerjee, R. (2021). Consumer's subjective financial well-being: A systematic review and research agenda. *International Journal of Consumer Studies*, *45*(4), 750–776. DOI: 10.1111/ijcs.12668

Natarajarathinam, M., Qiu, S., & Lu, W. (2021). Community engagement in engineering education: A systematic literature review. *Journal of Engineering Education*, *110*(4), 1049–1077. DOI: 10.1002/jee.20424

Natung, B., Awuor, E., Mall, M., & Mishra, M. (2025). The role of self-help groups in social capital development: A systematic review. *Cogent Social Sciences*, *11*(1), 2527393. Advance online publication. DOI: 10.1080/23311886.2025.2527393

Nnamani, G. (2024). An ecosystemic perspective of the factors affecting the learning experiences of learners with dyslexia in mainstream schools in England. *Dyslexia (Chichester, England)*, *30*(3), e1768. Advance online publication. DOI: 10.1002/dys.1768 PMID: 38845553

Ohnishi, S., Osako, M., Nakamura, S., Togawa, T., Kawai, K., Suzuki, K., Yoshida, A., Gomi, K., & Tsuji, T. (2024). A Framework for Analyzing Co-Creation Value Chain Mechanisms in Community-Based Approaches: A Literature Review. *Sustainability (Basel)*, *16*(7), 2919. DOI: 10.3390/su16072919

Omanyo, J. O., & Ndiege, J. R. (2025). Knowledge management considerations in learning management systems in higher education institutions: A systematic review, synthesis and research agenda. *VINE Journal of Information and Knowledge Management Systems*, *55*(3), 586–603. DOI: 10.1108/VJIKMS-09-2022-0305

Peters, A.-K., Capilla, R., Coroamă, V. C., Heldal, R., Lago, P., Leifler, O., Moreira, A., Fernandes, J. P., Penzenstadler, B., Porras, J., & Venters, C. C. (2024). Sustainability in Computing Education: A Systematic Literature Review. *ACM Transactions on Computing Education*, *24*(1), 1–53. DOI: 10.1145/3639060

Przytula, S. (2024). Expatriate academics: What have we known for four decades? A systematic literature review. *Journal of Global Mobility*, *12*(1), 31–56. DOI: 10.1108/JGM-03-2023-0024

Rafiki, A., Mohd Subri, I., Mohiddin, M. N., Hidayat, S. E., & Mohd Salleh, M. M. (2025). Salient practices of halal management in Southeast Asia: A systematic literature review. *Journal of Islamic Marketing*, *16*(7), 1821–1843. Advance online publication. DOI: 10.1108/JIMA-02-2024-0059

Ribeiro, J. D., Falanga, R., & Moniz, J. (2025). Assessing the Role of Democratic Innovations in Environmental Sustainability: A Systematic Literature Review. *Sustainable Development (Bradford), 33*(5), 7775–7790. Advance online publication. DOI: 10.1002/sd.3545

Rodríguez-Zurita, D., Jaya-Montalvo, M., Moreira-Arboleda, J., Raya-Diez, E., & Carrión-Mero, P. (2025). Sustainable development through service learning and community engagement in higher education: A systematic literature review. *International Journal of Sustainability in Higher Education*, *26*(1), 158–201. DOI: 10.1108/IJSHE-10-2023-0461

Ryan, A. W., Kolås, L., Nilsen, A. G., & Almås, A. G. (2024). Systematic literature review as a digital collaborative research-like learning activity: A case study. *Education and Information Technologies*, *29*(5), 5243–5257. DOI: 10.1007/s10639-023-11997-x

Samaniego López, M. V., Orrego Riofrío, M. C., Barriga-Fray, S. F., & Paz Viteri, B. S. (2025). Technologies in Inclusive Education: Solution or Challenge? A Systematic Review. *Education Sciences*, *15*(6), 715. DOI: 10.3390/educsci15060715

Sánchez Galera, M. D. (2020). Facing Cultural and Education Challenges at the EU Level: Fragmentation and Multiple Solutions. In *Educational and Cultural Challenges of the European Sustainability Model* (pp. 179–266). Springer International Publishing. DOI: 10.1007/978-3-030-38716-7_5

Touchton, M., Wampler, B., & Spada, P. (2019). The digital revolution and governance in Brazil: Evidence from participatory budgeting. *Journal of Information Technology & Politics*, *16*(2), 154–168. DOI: 10.1080/19331681.2019.1613281

Tsarkos, A. (2024). *Servant Leadership and Transformative Change.*, DOI: 10.4018/979-8-3693-4119-3.ch007

Ullah, M. S. (2022). *Under the Wheel of Decolonization and Recolonization: The Crossroads of Journalism Education in South Asia* (pp. 139–163). DOI: 10.1007/978-3-031-13749-5_7

Wahyuni, A. S., Málovics, G., & Gébert, J. (2025). Critical factors influencing sustainable and impactful university–community engagement: A systematic review of top-down and bottom-up initiatives. *International Journal of Sustainability in Higher Education*. Advance online publication. DOI: 10.1108/IJSHE-02-2024-0089

White, R., Lowery, C., & Johnson, J. (2025). Enhancing high-quality education through systemic school leadership: A systematic review. *Quality Education for All*, *2*(1), 227–244. DOI: 10.1108/QEA-09-2024-0096

Wilkinson, J. (2021). *Educational Leadership through a Practice Lens*. Springer Singapore., DOI: 10.1007/978-981-16-7629-1

Williams, S. S. (2020). Culturally Sustaining Leadership: Supporting the Resilience of Indigenous Students in the United States and Australia. *Journal of School Leadership, 30*(6), 565–587. DOI: 10.1177/1052684620951725

Yu, Y., Appiah, D., Zulu, B., & Adu-Poku, K. A. (2024). Integrating Rural Development, Education, and Management: Challenges and Strategies. *Sustainability (Basel), 16*(15), 6474. DOI: 10.3390/su16156474

KEY TERMS AND DEFINITIONS

Capacity-Building: Capacity-building refers to the package of actions and procedures through which persons and groups are empowered with the necessary knowledge, skills and material resources, thus empowering them to engage in educational leadership and governance effectively.

Collective Efficacy: Collective efficacy is an expression that implies the level of communal trust among group members about their ability to coordinate and perform the necessary steps to achieve educational goals and promote student performance. Effectively, it refers to a group-based belief about its effectiveness.

Community Involvement: It refers to the direct involvement of the local stakeholders, such as parents, educators, and other members of the community, in the decision-making and management operations of the schools and the institutions of education. Their constant participation often defines the daily operations of these entities.

Decentralisation: Decentralisation is a movement of decision-making frequencies of the centralised education agencies, which transfer to school or community stakeholders. This power shift has a twofold rationale: first, it is meant to increase the flexibility of education systems, but second, it is intended to promote a local feeling of ownership over education provision.

Educational Leadership: Educational leadership is most often characterised as a continuous activity meant to guide and manage schools or the complete education system. The domain of this practice has included the development of a shared vision, the establishment of a positive school culture and the selection of policy decisions, which seek to improve educational outcomes.

Participatory Governance: The concept in question constitutes a model of governance in which power and task responsibility are simultaneously assigned to formally established authorities in the educational field, as well as to members of the wider community. The general goal of this arrangement is to offer transparency, accountability and inclusiveness in the running of schools.

Social Capital: Social capital is also how people relate and trust using networks and relations that define a community. Networking enables better collective work towards common goals, such as the improvement in the quality of education.

Sustainable Growth: Sustainable growth in education is a developmental path that persists, not only over time, but that protects, at the same time, ensures quality and equity, and responds to community demands. It aims at developing educational success as well as social and economic development.

Chapter 10
Innovative Management Strategies for Achieving Educational Quality

Mustafa Kayyali
https://orcid.org/0000-0003-3300-262X
Maaref University of Applied Sciences, Syria

ABSTRACT

In an era defined by complexity, uncertainty, and rapid change, traditional management approaches in education often fall short in delivering quality outcomes. This chapter explores innovative management strategies that reimagine how educational institutions can lead with vision, agility, and inclusivity. Drawing on global examples and evidence-informed practices, the chapter examines how educational leaders can foster a culture of continuous improvement, embed innovation into strategic planning, and leverage data to make context-sensitive decisions. It also emphasises the role of inclusive governance and stakeholder collaboration in sustaining quality across diverse educational landscapes. Rather than offering a one-size-fits-all solution, the chapter highlights the necessity of adapting strategies to local needs while maintaining a global awareness. In doing so, it argues for a reframing of leadership—one that is proactive, reflective, and deeply committed to the human dimensions of education as a lever for economic and societal growth.

INTRODUCTION

In recent decades, education systems around the world have faced unprecedented shifts—economic globalisation, technological acceleration, demographic diversification, and the ever-evolving demands of labour markets have all transformed the

DOI: 10.4018/979-8-3373-3616-9.ch010

landscape of education. These changes have placed immense pressure on educational institutions to not only provide access but also to ensure consistent, measurable quality. Amid such complexity, one pressing question arises: How can we manage education differently to achieve better and sustain quality?

Traditional paradigms of educational management, rooted in bureaucratic rigidity and top-down control, often prove inadequate in responding to the fluid and dynamic needs of learners and societies (Lunenburg & Ornstein, 2021). What is required now is not mere reform but transformation—a shift in mindset, systems, and strategies. At the heart of this transformation lies innovation: in leadership, in governance, in assessment, in stakeholder engagement, and in the very ways schools and universities define and pursue excellence.

This chapter is grounded in the belief that educational quality is not a fixed benchmark but a living, breathing pursuit—deeply influenced by cultural, economic, and social contexts. Quality must be dynamic, inclusive, and contextually grounded. It is not achieved through compliance alone, but through creativity, shared vision, reflective practice, and the courage to depart from convention when necessary. To explore this further, the chapter delves into innovative management strategies that disrupt outdated models and instead centre on adaptability, inclusivity, and evidence-based planning (Kayyali, 2026). These strategies recognise the increasing complexity of educational systems and the necessity of involving all stakeholders—leaders, teachers, students, parents, and policymakers—in crafting a collective path forward. They reject the notion that excellence can be engineered through rigid top-down systems or over-reliance on standardised metrics. Instead, they embrace educational quality as a multi-dimensional, evolving ideal that must be nurtured through holistic, strategic, and innovative means.

This chapter begins by unpacking how education leadership must be reimagined for the 21st century—how strategic foresight, ethical vision, and system-wide collaboration can serve as the foundation of educational reform. It then examines the pivotal role of innovation—not just in technology, but in management practices, organisational design, and pedagogical responsiveness. It proceeds to explore how data can be utilised not just for accountability, but for meaningful insight and continuous improvement. Furthermore, it highlights the need for inclusive governance, recognising that educational quality cannot be sustained without trust, ownership, and dialogue across all levels of the system (Kayyali, 2022).

Finally, the chapter presents international case studies of transformative practice—drawing from diverse regions, sectors, and leadership models to illustrate how innovative management can tangibly reshape the quality of educational delivery and outcomes. These case studies serve not as templates to be copied, but as mirrors through which educators can reflect on what might be possible in their own contexts.

Ultimately, this chapter does not aim to provide all the answers but to provoke critical thought and action. It is an invitation to educational leaders, policymakers, and practitioners to ask bold questions, challenge inherited assumptions, and reimagine what quality means—not only for today's learners but for the uncertain futures they will inherit. In doing so, it affirms that innovative management is not a luxury or a trend, but a necessity—central to building education systems that are not only excellent but equitable, resilient, and responsive to the world's ever-shifting demands.

REDEFINING EDUCATIONAL LEADERSHIP IN THE 21ST CENTURY

To speak of leadership in education today is to wade into turbulent waters. The word itself—*leadership*—once so firmly grounded in authority, vision, and institutional command, now trembles under the weight of contradiction (George, 2024). On the one hand, there is the inherited legacy of hierarchies, protocols, and systems meticulously designed to maintain order, compliance, and measurable outputs. On the other hand, there is the sobering realisation that many of those systems—despite their meticulous design—have failed to keep pace with the kaleidoscopic complexity of the modern world. The 21st century has not simply challenged educational leadership; it has cracked it open.

We are not just managing schools or directing policy anymore. We are confronting fractured social fabrics, existential climate threats, political volatility, and technological transformations unfolding at warp speed. Amid all this, schools have become microcosms of a world in flux—chaotic, beautiful, unjust, hopeful. Thus, the question is not simply, "What should leaders do?" but rather, "Who must they become?"

Leadership today is not about being the one who knows (Schiuma et al, 2022). It is about being the one who listens, who convenes, who holds ambiguity with grace. It is about navigating the silence between competing truths, the dissonance between equity and tradition, between innovation and tradition, between data and lived experience. To lead now is to engage in an unending conversation between the possible and the practical—and to do so without the comfort of a script.

The traditional image of the leader at the helm—singular, decisive, stoic—is increasingly anachronistic (Brown, 2023). That model, forged in the crucible of industrial efficiency and bureaucratic order, may have served an earlier era. However, education no longer unfolds on a factory floor. It is organic, relational, and often unruly. It grows at the pace of trust and dies in the absence of it. Students, teachers, parents, communities—each brings a story, a history, a set of wounds and hopes.

The leader who cannot or will not make space for those stories is leading no one at all. What, then, does it mean to lead in such times?

It begins with unlearning the idea that control is the same as leadership. Unlearning the myth that impact can always be measured in test scores or quarterly benchmarks (Cadet et al, 2024). Unlearning the belief that success is about preserving the past. The 21st-century leader is not merely an executor of plans but a curator of culture, a steward of meaning. They do not just ask how to raise achievement—they ask what achievement should mean in the first place. Moreover, the answers are not simple.

In one district, it may mean disrupting a curriculum that's been blind to indigenous knowledge. In another, it may mean confronting a deeply entrenched culture of exclusion masked as discipline. Elsewhere, it might require letting go of long-cherished traditions that no longer serve the learners they were meant to uplift. These are not cosmetic changes. They demand courage—the kind that upsets people, the kind that makes the room fall silent.

Leadership, in this evolving landscape, is not for the faint of heart. Nor is it for the overly confident (Garcia & Fisher, 2023). The best leaders I have encountered (and it bears noting, they rarely call themselves "leaders") possess a kind of quiet restlessness. The status quo unsettles them, but they are not undone by it. They question not for the sake of provocation but because they are haunted by the possibility that we can do better, that we *must* do better. Moreover, they do not just act—they reflect, deeply and often, not out of self-doubt, but out of responsibility.

Indeed, reflection is the heartbeat of modern leadership. Not reflection as a checkbox in a performance review, but the kind that comes late at night when the building is empty and the question lingers: *Did I listen well today? Did I make space for dissent? Did I mistake silence for agreement?* These are not questions of policy, but of conscience (Kayyali, 2025 A). Moreover, conscience, too, is back on the table. For far too long, educational leadership has been sanitised of emotion. There was always a spreadsheet, a report, a framework to lean on. However, frameworks do not carry the grief of a marginalised student (Thacker & Duran, 2022). They do not sit with a teacher whose creativity has been suffocated by standardisation. They do not hold the gaze of a community still waiting for justice. That work falls to people. Real people. Fallible, tired, hopeful people. It is no longer enough to be efficient. Leaders must also be human.

This humanity is expressed not in grand gestures, but in the small, often invisible decisions—choosing to pause a meeting to ask how someone's mother is doing; rethinking a policy when a single student falls through its cracks; admitting, out loud, "I got it wrong." These are not signs of weakness. They are, in fact, radical acts of strength. Because vulnerability, when wielded wisely, builds the kind of trust upon which all meaningful transformation rests.

That trust becomes especially critical in pluralistic societies where schools function as crucibles of cultural negotiation. In classrooms where students speak a dozen languages, carry ten different passports, or none at all, leadership becomes a delicate choreography of empathy and decisiveness (Egitim & Sandu, 2023). The best leaders do not erase differences in the name of cohesion. They hold the tension. They learn to speak across it. Moreover, let us not forget: to lead now is to face the machines.

Artificial intelligence, automation, surveillance technologies—these are no longer fringe concerns. They shape how we learn, how we teach, and how we are measured (Gilliard & Selwyn, 2023). Some herald these changes as liberating; others fear the dehumanisation they portend. The truth, as always, lies somewhere in the messy middle. The real question is not whether technology belongs in education, but how leaders can harness it without surrendering to it. How do we protect the sacred unpredictability of learning—the surprise insight, the accidental discovery—from being flattened into an algorithmic pattern?

This requires a different kind of intelligence. Emotional intelligence, indeed. But also moral intelligence. Cultural intelligence. Systems intelligence. The capacity to see the whole without losing sight of the parts. Moreover, to act in ways that honour both.

Let us be honest: the metrics do not always capture this kind of leadership. It is not always reflected in funding formulas or rankings. However, you feel it in a school's hallways—in the way teachers speak to students, in the energy of assemblies, in the quiet confidence of learners who know they are seen. You feel it in moments when a community turns to its school not just for education, but for healing. Moreover, healing may be the most radical form of leadership today because our institutions are wounded. Generations of students have internalised failure not as feedback but as identity. Teachers carry burnout like a second skin (Donop et al, 2023). Leaders, too, are not immune—they are exhausted, often lonely, sometimes afraid to admit they do not have the answers. In this context, the most powerful thing a leader can do might not be to innovate, but to *repair*—to restore dignity where it has been stripped, to reweave trust where it has frayed.

This, too, is a kind of innovation—one that does not rely on new gadgets but on renewed relationships. Still, we cannot be naïve. Leadership is not all heart (Kayyali & Christiansen, 2024). It also demands strategy, acuity, and the ability to navigate policy, budgets, and politics. However, what we often forget is that these skills are not ends in themselves. They are tools in service of something more profound: the flourishing of human potential. When strategy loses its soul, it becomes machinery. When the soul loses its structure, it becomes chaos. The leader's task is to hold both. Thus, we circle back: who must leaders become?

Not heroes. Not saviours. Not mere managers of broken systems. However, cultivators of conditions in which others can thrive. Builders of bridges where walls once stood. Interpreters of silences. Learners among learners. Not flawless. However, faithful to the idea that education, at its best, is an act of love (Yun, 2025). That kind of leadership is not always visible. It does not always win awards. However, it leaves a trace—in the lives it touches, the systems it bends toward justice, the possibilities it whispers into being.

In the end, redefining educational leadership in the 21st century is not about adding new layers (Kezar, 2023). It is about peeling back the noise to return to what matters most—the child in the back of the classroom who stopped raising their hand. The teacher is quietly innovating against the odds. The community is waiting to be heard. Moreover, the leader—somewhere in the middle—navigating the in-between, with eyes wide open, heart heavy, but feet still moving forward. That is the kind of leadership this century demands. That is the kind of leadership education that deserves.

STRATEGIC INNOVATION AND THE QUEST FOR QUALITY

Quality in education is often talked about like a destination on a map—as if it lies at the end of a well-marked trail paved with reforms, performance targets, and checklists (Stolz & Megerle, 2022). You follow the signs, check the boxes, align the curriculum, measure the outcomes, and voilà—excellence. However, that notion, neat as it may seem on paper, rarely holds up in practice. Real quality is far messier, more elusive. It is not a fixed endpoint but a moving horizon, shaped by shifting societal needs, evolving pedagogical understandings, and, perhaps most unpredictably, by the human beings at the centre of the educational experience—teachers and learners, each one a universe of complexity.

So, if quality cannot be engineered like a factory product, if it resists standardisation and refuses to settle into static definitions, then how do we pursue it without losing ourselves in the chase? That is where the concept of strategic innovation enters—not as a buzzword dragged from the latest management fad, but as a quiet recalibration of how we think about change, agency, and the architecture of possibility within educational systems (Whitney, 2024). Strategic innovation, when stripped of corporate jargon, is simply the art of *seeing differently*. It means stepping outside the gravitational pull of "the way we have always done it" and asking, sometimes uncomfortably, "What if we are wrong?" or even more provocatively, "What if we are right, but it is no longer working?" It is about creating space for reimagining rather than just tweaking. Moreover, more than anything, it is about aligning that reimagining with a deeper purpose: cultivating learning environments where quality does not just exist—it breathes, evolves, and includes (Kayyali, 2024).

Let us be real for a moment—schools and universities are not naturally fertile grounds for innovation (Nyka & Marczak, 2023). They are steeped in tradition, weighed down by bureaucracy, and constantly measured against frameworks that often prioritise order over imagination. Risk-taking is rarely rewarded. Failure is penalised. Novelty is eyed with suspicion, especially when budgets are tight and stakes are high. However, this makes innovation no less necessary, but more urgent. The question is not whether we innovate, but how—and with what kind of intent.

Intent matters. Because innovation for its own sake—innovation unmoored from values—can be just as dangerous as stagnation. One can disrupt a system into dysfunction as easily as one can bureaucratise it into paralysis. True strategic innovation in education starts not with technology, nor with policy, nor even with pedagogy (Fawns, 2022). It starts with purpose. What are we actually trying to do here? What kind of human beings are we hoping to nurture? What kind of society do we hope they will shape? These are not abstract questions. They are directional. They determine whether an innovation is merely clever or genuinely transformative.

When purpose leads, the tools follow. Moreover, the tools, in this era, are abundant—AI-driven learning analytics, adaptive content platforms, project-based models, flipped classrooms, blockchain credentialing, microlearning ecosystems, and more (Omona & O'dama, 2024). However, tools are not a strategy. Nor are they inherently innovative. A poorly conceived flipped classroom can replicate the worst aspects of traditional teaching, just upside-down. An AI-based grading system, without ethical guardrails, can reinforce systemic bias with a polished interface. Strategic innovation asks not just "What can we do?" but "What should we do, given the people we serve and the world they are entering?" It demands that every new design, every new practice, answer to that north star of relevance and responsibility.

However, there is a more profound, more slippery truth: quality does not emerge from systems alone. It emerges from *interactions*. From the spaces between teacher and student, between curriculum and context, between vision and reality. Strategic innovation must target these spaces—not by trying to control them, but by cultivating conditions in which they can thrive (Lamine et al, 2021). That is a subtle distinction, but a critical one. We cannot script every outcome, nor should we try. What we *can* do is design with intention—design for trust, for agency, for curiosity, for connection.

Figure 1. Illustrative Allocation of Innovation Investment for Educational Quality

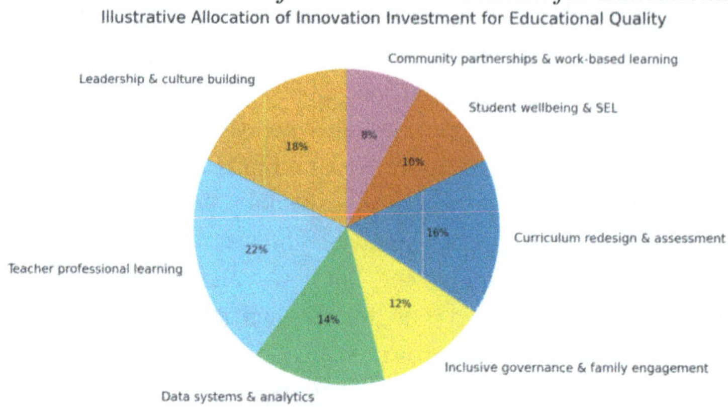

In schools that embody this spirit, innovation looks less like a glossy new device and more like a power shift (REHAN, 2025). A teacher reconfigures their classroom around inquiry, giving students ownership over their learning journey. A principal rethinks parent engagement, not as a once-a-semester conference, but as an ongoing dialogue that acknowledges families as co-educators. A university restructures its curriculum to dissolve the artificial barriers between disciplines, allowing learners to follow questions across fields instead of being locked into silos (Domanic, 2025). These moves are not flashy. They do not always make headlines. But they ripple. They signal to the ecosystem that thinking differently is allowed, that experimentation is welcome, that failure is not fatal. Moreover, failure, let us talk about that because any honest conversation about innovation must include it. The dirty little secret of every successful educational initiative is that it likely emerged from a graveyard of ideas that did not pan out. Strategic innovation is a process of iterative becoming—it is messy, nonlinear, sometimes heartbreaking. Not every new approach works. Not every pilot scales. However, in the wreckage of failed experiments lie the seeds of insight. The key is to build cultures where people *can* fail—safely, reflectively, generatively.

That requires leadership willing to absorb risk. Structures are flexible enough to adapt. Moreover, systems are brave enough to question their own assumptions. Too often, our education systems punish deviation, treat experimentation as indulgence, and equate stability with success. However, stagnation wears a mask—it often looks like order, but beneath the surface, it is a slow erosion of vitality. Innovation, even when uncomfortable, is a form of care. It is a commitment not to let the system go numb.

Still, innovation does not happen in a vacuum (Owens, 2021). Context is king. A strategy that revolutionises a private school in Finland might buckle under the weight of resource scarcity in rural Ghana. An initiative that empowers students in Singapore might trigger resistance in a region where authority structures are more rigid. Strategic innovation, then, must be contextual—attuned to history, culture, power dynamics, and the lived realities of the communities it aims to serve. Moreover, sometimes, innovation means slowing down. It means saying no to the relentless churn of "new" in favour of depth. It means resisting the market logic that equates speed with progress. Because not all change is progress, and not all progress is human-centred. Innovation that dehumanises—by over-quantifying, by automating judgment, by erasing voice—is not innovation. It is efficiency in disguise. So, what does *real* quality look like in a strategically innovative system?

It looks like a student who once felt invisible raising their hand without fear. It looks like a teacher designing a lesson that responds to the lived experiences of her students, not just the demands of a test. It looks like an institution willing to ask hard questions about whose knowledge counts, whose histories are told, and whose dreams are made possible.

Quality, in this light, is relational. It is ecological. It is slow-cooked. Moreover, it often defies the metrics we use to define it. That does not mean we abandon measurement—but we expand it. We measure what matters. We use data not as a whip, but as a mirror. We ask not just whether students are achieving, but whether they are thriving. There is something almost paradoxical about it: the more we pursue quality as a fixed outcome, the more it slips through our fingers. However, when we centre meaning, when we align our strategies with purpose, when we treat innovation not as a disruption but as a form of love—we find ourselves stumbling into quality almost accidentally, like discovering a quiet clearing after a long, disorienting hike. It is easy to romanticise this. However, the work is hard. It involves conflict. Pushback. Disappointment. Strategic innovation demands not only vision, but stamina. Not only creativity, but also political savvy. Not only hope, but the ability to endure when hope falters.

Still, the alternative—clinging to systems that no longer serve us—is not just untenable. It is unjust. Education has always carried the potential to transform lives (Akour & Alenezi, 2022). However, that potential cannot be fulfilled through replication alone. It requires regeneration. Reimagination. Renewal. Strategic innovation is the path—not because it guarantees perfection, but because it dares to ask the right questions. Moreover, in asking those questions, it honours the sacredness of education not as a product, but as a human act.

So, we return to the quest for quality. Not as a checklist, not as a final destination, but as a journey we take again and again—with each new cohort of learners, each shift in the world outside, each revelation that challenges our assumptions. It is a quest defined not by the pursuit of certainty, but by a commitment to keep asking: What does good education look like—*here, now, for these people, in this moment?* Moreover, how do we build it—not alone, but together?

DATA-DRIVEN DECISION-MAKING AND CONTINUOUS IMPROVEMENT

The phrase *data-driven decision-making* has become something of a sacred chant in modern educational discourse—a mantra recited in policy briefs, echoed in staff rooms, etched into the bones of school development plans (Munoz, 2025). On the surface, it sounds indisputably sensible. Who would argue with the idea of making choices informed by evidence? However, scratch beneath that polished surface, and complexities spill out—quiet contradictions, ethical quandaries, unintended consequences. Because data, for all its perceived objectivity, is never neutral. It comes shaped, filtered, and often warped by the instruments we use to collect it and the assumptions we make when interpreting it. In education, where the terrain is overwhelmingly human, messy, and fluid, treating data like divine truth can be both seductive and dangerous.

The trouble begins when data stops being a tool for insight and starts functioning as a weapon of control (OLASYA & Kiamba, 2025). The kind of data that gets prioritised—test scores, attendance rates, graduation percentages—tends to flatten the lived reality of learners into tidy digits that fit neatly into spreadsheets and dashboards. Moreover, while those figures have their place, they often tell a partial story, a curated fragment of something far more textured and dynamic.

Figure 2. Waterfall of Interventions Increasing Educational Quality (Illustrative)

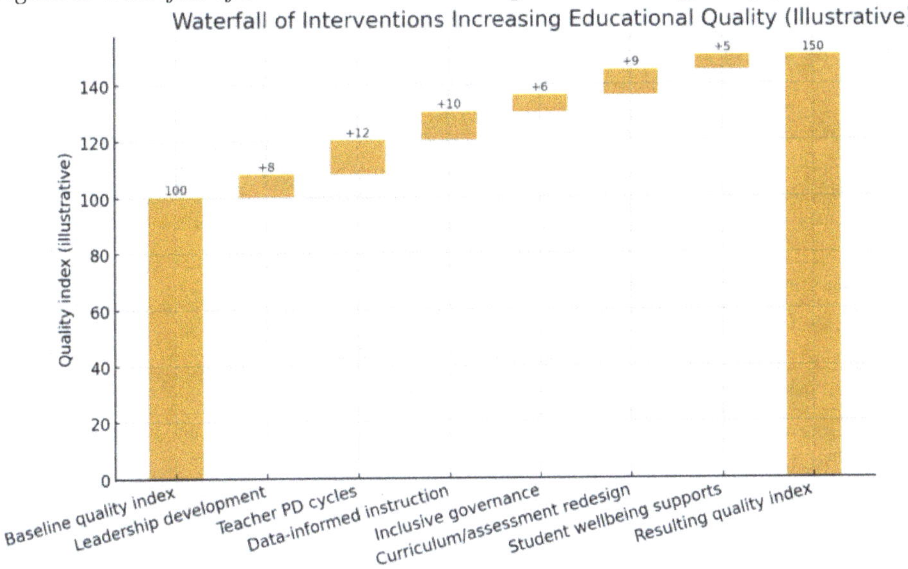

Imagine a student whose test scores are low, who skips class often, whose record paints a picture of disengagement. Now imagine that same student composing poetry late at night, translating for their parents, resisting systems that have never quite seen them. None of that richness shows up in the metrics. None of it counts in school improvement plans. So the question becomes: what are we missing when we reduce students to numbers? What gets erased when decision-making is guided exclusively by what can be measured? However, the answer is not to abandon data. That would be equally misguided. The answer is to rehumanise it. To ask better questions. To expand what counts as data, and more importantly, to interrogate who decides what counts. Because metrics do not just reflect reality—they construct it. They shape which stories get told, whose experiences are validated, which problems are deemed urgent, and which are quietly ignored.

This is where continuous improvement comes in—not as a mechanistic cycle of measure-fix-repeat, but as an ethos of humility. It is the recognition that education is a living system, and living systems require constant listening—feedback loops matter. However, not all loops are created equal. Some capture noise. Others surface the truth. Actual continuous improvement does not begin with data points. It begins with curiosity (Friederich et al, 2022). What is really happening here? Why is this pattern emerging? Who is benefiting—and who is being left out? These are questions that cannot be answered by dashboards alone. They demand dialogue, triangulation, and contextual wisdom. They demand that we sit with complexity instead of rushing to simplify it.

Table 1. Quality and Equity KPI Dashboard

KPI	Definition	Baseline (2024)	Target (2027)	Owner
Foundational literacy (%)	Grade-level reading by the end of the cycle	62	82	Curriculum & T&L
Differential growth (pp)	Gap closure for priority groups	0	12	Equity team
Authentic assessment coverage (%)	Courses using projects/ portfolios	22	50	Program leads
Teacher PD (hrs/term)	Avg hours in targeted PD	8	20	Faculty dev.
Family engagement (% events multilingual)	Events with translation/ interpretation	35	80	Community office
Student wellbeing (1"5)	Composite of belonging/ mental-health items	3.2	4.2	Student services
Graduate pathway match (%)	Graduates in the desired next-step pathway	58	75	Careers & partners

Unfortunately, the pressure to perform—fueled by league tables, funding formulas, and political cycles—often incentivises the opposite. Educators are nudged, sometimes shoved, toward metrics that are visible, quantifiable, and easy to report (Beach, 2021). It is understandable. Policy systems crave clarity. However, learning is rarely linear. Growth is uneven, recursive. Students leap, stall, backtrack, surge. Moreover, the most significant changes often happen just beyond the reach of the data we know how to collect.

Take, for instance, the development of critical thinking. Or empathy. Or resilience. Multiple-choice exams or rubric grids do not easily capture these. However, they are arguably the most important outcomes of any educational experience. When decision-making ignores them, it narrows the horizon of what education is *for*. Moreover, still, data has its role—when wielded with care, when coupled with stories, when treated as a flashlight rather than a blueprint (Jones, 2022). When school leaders use data to start conversations instead of ending them, to question assumptions rather than confirm them, it becomes a powerful tool for reflection and responsiveness.

Some of the most compelling examples of data-informed transformation are not grand reforms but small shifts—a teacher analysing patterns in student work to adapt their instruction mid-course; a principal tracking disciplinary referrals and realising they are disproportionately targeting a particular group; a policymaker reading drop-out rates alongside community interviews to understand where the system is failing and why. In these cases, data is not abstract. It is personal. Moreover, it becomes a lever for equity when used to amplify the voices of those often unheard. However, to get there, we have to dismantle the illusion that more data automatically means better decisions. We are drowning in data, and still, many schools feel starved for clarity. Because what matters is not just *having* data, but knowing what to *do* with it—and having the time, training, and trust to do it well.

This brings us to an uncomfortable truth: most educators are not data analysts (Raffe & Loughland, 2021). Nor should they have to be. However, they are often expected to sift through complex dashboards with minimal support, draw conclusions in high-pressure environments, and act on them quickly. It is a recipe for superficial compliance, not profound change. The answer is not to technocratize the profession but to build cultures of inquiry—places where asking questions is valued more than finding the "right" answer, where data is a prompt for exploration rather than a justification for punishment. That kind of culture cannot be mandated from above. It must be nurtured, slowly and relationally, over time. And what about students? Too often, they are the objects of data collection, not participants in the meaning-making process. What would it look like to share data with students—not as a score to fear, but as a mirror to reflect on? What if learners were co-interpreters of the data that shapes their lives? That shift alone could change everything. It would transform data from something done *to* students into something done *with* them.

Continuous improvement, when truly practised, has a rhythm to it. Not the frenzied tempo of reform cycles, but the steady pulse of reflection-action-adjustment (Venegas, 2024). It is a posture of learning embedded in the fabric of the organisation. It says: *We are not finished. We are not perfect. However, we are paying attention.* It is slow work, often invisible, occasionally frustrating. However, over time, it builds resilience. Not the brittle kind that resists change, but the adaptive kind that grows from it.

Still, improvement must not be improvement for its own sake. Just because we *can* tweak does not mean we *should*. The question is not just "How do we improve?" but "Toward what end?" Because systems can become more efficient at perpetuating inequity. They can become better at sorting, faster at excluding, and more sophisticated in their failure. If the destination is misguided, then the journey—no matter how refined—is still heading in the wrong direction.

This is why data and continuous improvement must be anchored in values. In justice. In care. In the messy, radical belief that every child deserves not just a place in the classroom, but a voice in shaping it. When improvement is detached from purpose, it becomes performance. When it is connected to human dignity, it becomes a transformation. There is a word that rarely appears in data conversations: *love*. However, love—deep, sustaining, inconvenient love—is often what fuels the best educators. Love for the child who will not look you in the eye. Love for the subject that still gives you goosebumps. Love for the belief that something better is possible, even when the evidence says otherwise.

That kind of love does not show up on spreadsheets. However, you can feel it in the decisions people make—the extra hour spent revising a lesson, the awkward conversation initiated because a pattern in the data did not sit right, the risk taken to challenge a practice that everyone else had accepted as usual. Those decisions, driven by both information and emotion, are what make data-driven decision-making *human*.

It is not a binary—data *or* intuition, metrics *or* meaning. It is a dance. A negotiation. A willingness to let evidence inform, not dictate. To let numbers start the story, but never finish it. Education is not an exact science. It is an ecosystem. Moreover, ecosystems thrive not because they are engineered to perfection, but because they adapt, regenerate, and respond to feedback in real time (Yakubovna, 2024). That is the essence of continuous improvement—not a race toward flawless efficiency, but a commitment to becoming more alive, more responsive, more just. It will not always feel clean. It will not always feel certain. However, if we can make peace with the messiness—if we can approach data not with reverence but with responsibility—then we might begin to build systems worthy of the complexity of the lives they aim to shape.

INCLUSIVE GOVERNANCE AND STAKEHOLDER ENGAGEMENT

Governance in education has long been misunderstood—often mistaken for a series of tidy flowcharts, policy documents, and committee chairs (Anderson, 2023). However, real governance, the kind that pulses through classrooms and corridors, does not live in procedural manuals. It lives in relationships. It lives in the quiet tensions of a parent-teacher meeting. It lives in the pause before a principal speaks. It lives in the invisible hierarchies that shape who gets to speak and who does not.

For years, the dominant model of governance in educational institutions has leaned toward centralisation—decision-making parked at the top, information trickling down, voices filtered through layers of formality. It is clean. It is efficient. It is comforting to those who fear chaos. However, the cost of this comfort has been steep: alienated communities, tokenised voices, and systems so brittle they break the moment fundamental disagreement enters the room.

Inclusive governance does not aim for control. It aims for coherence (Wilkes, 2022). Not sameness, but shared direction. Moreover, it starts from a premise both radical and simple: that those most affected by educational decisions should have a meaningful role in shaping them. Not just consultation, not just symbolic inclusion, but real, reciprocal engagement. That sounds good on paper. Who would not want a more inclusive system? However, in practice, it is slow, it is messy, and it is uncomfortable. Because inclusion requires listening. Moreover, listening—truly listening—means being open to change. It means that the principal might have to let go of their perfect plan. It means the policymaker might hear something that disrupts their metrics. It means that teachers, who are already exhausted, might have to make room for student agency that does not fit their timeline. It means letting go of the illusion of control, and leaning instead into the unpredictability of collaboration.

Stakeholder engagement, in this context, becomes less of a task and more of a stance (Mitchell et al, 2022). It is about approaching others not as data points or political chess pieces, but as co-owners of a shared vision. Moreover, that is hard—because it means giving up power. Not all of it. Not irresponsibly. However, enough to make the engagement real. Enough to make it matter.

Figure 3. Institutional Maturity for Innovative Quality Management

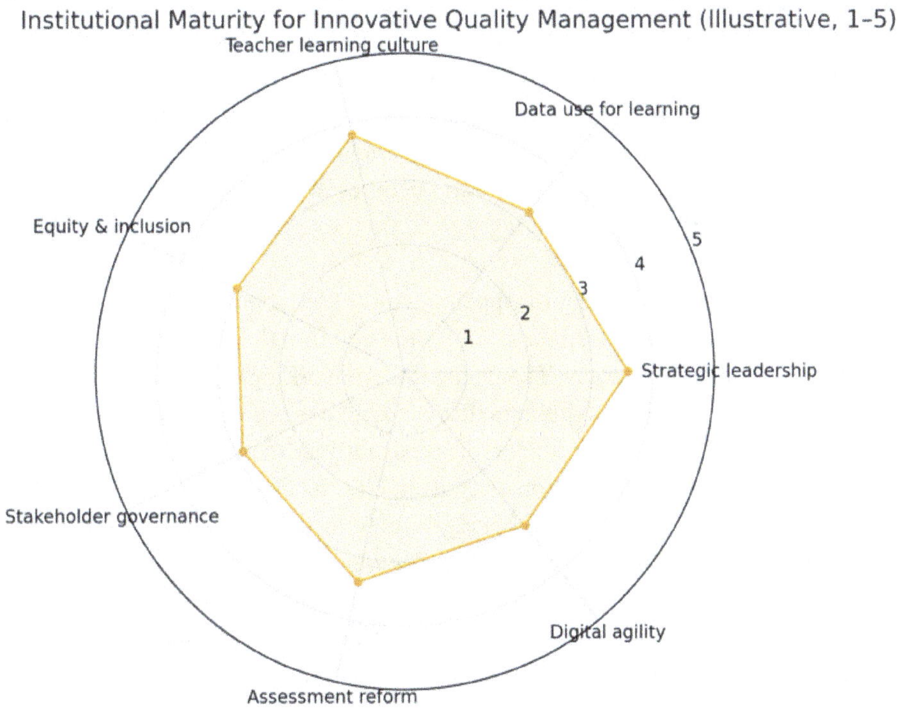

There is something deeply human in the need to be heard. Moreover, in education, where so much is done *to* people in the name of outcomes, giving stakeholders a genuine seat at the table becomes a small act of restoration (Palmer et al, 2022). When a student is asked not just to answer, but to question the curriculum. When a parent is invited not just to bake for the fundraiser, but to help shape school policy. When a teacher is asked not just to implement reforms, but to co-design them, these moments matter.

Still, the word "stakeholder" itself is problematic. It flattens people into roles. It makes the student, the parent, the janitor, the policymaker—all sound interchangeable. However, they are not. Each brings a different history, a different stake, a different story. Inclusive governance must resist the urge to homogenise and instead ask: who is not in the room? Whose silence is being mistaken for consent?

In some places, engaging with the community means knocking on doors. In others, it means hosting meetings in five languages. In others still, it means creating anonymous channels for feedback because trust has been broken too many times before. There is no single blueprint. Moreover, anyone promising one is selling convenience, not inclusion.

Trust, that elusive thread, is the currency of any inclusive system. Moreover, trust is built not in grand gestures, but in consistent, small acts. Showing up. Following through. Saying "we heard you" and meaning it. Saying "we got it wrong" and meaning that too. Without trust, engagement becomes performance (Carter, 2022). A photo op. A ticked box. And people know. They can smell disingenuousness from a mile away. However, when trust is present, something powerful happens. Governance stops being about enforcement and becomes about alignment. Stakeholders stop resisting change and start driving it because they see themselves in it. Not just as beneficiaries, but as architects.

This does not mean conflict disappears—quite the opposite. Real engagement brings disagreement to the surface. It forces tension into the open. However, that is not a failure. That is democracy. That is the system working. The challenge is not to avoid conflict, but to create containers that can hold it—processes rooted in respect, spaces designed for listening, leaders trained not just to decide but to facilitate. Moreover, leadership, again, becomes central. Not the charismatic figurehead, but the leader who knows how to build bridges, how to step back, how to hold space without dominating it. The leader who understands that governance is not about having the answers, but about convening the right questions.

There is a story from a school in a post-conflict region—a place where trauma hung in the air like dust. The principal, newly appointed, did not start with reforms or metrics. He started with chairs. Dozens of them, placed in a circle in the school courtyard. Moreover, every evening, he sat there. Anyone could join. Teachers. Parents. Students. Elders. There was no agenda—just space. Slowly, people came. Stories were shared. Trust was rebuilt. Policy came later. The chairs came first. That image—the circle of chairs—has stuck because it captures something that no strategic plan can: the power of presence. The act of making space. The willingness not to rush.

In high-functioning inclusive systems, engagement is not reactive. It is not a fire drill after a scandal or a community meeting after a policy misstep. It is built into the fabric. Into the rhythms of the institution. Into the lunch breaks, the board meetings, the design labs, and the staff training. Engagement is not a project. It is a posture. Moreover, let us not ignore power. Inclusion does not dissolve it. It redistributes it. Moreover, that can feel threatening to those who have held it for a long time. The fear is often unspoken: *If they get more voice, do I lose mine?* However, power is not a finite pie. When shared well, it multiplies. When hoarded, it rots.

The trick is to design structures that both empower and protect. Because not all engagement is safe. Marginalised voices, when brought into systems unprepared to hear them, often get tokenised—or worse, punished (Olson et al, 2023). So, inclusion must come with safeguards. With listening protocols. With trauma-informed practices. With facilitators trained to notice who is being interrupted, who is shrinking in their chair, and who has not spoken at all.

Technology, while no panacea, can support this process. Digital platforms can widen access, archive voices, and allow asynchronous participation (Co et al, 2023). However, they can also replicate exclusion if not carefully designed. The digital divide is real. Algorithms carry bias. Online spaces, without moderation, can become hostile. So even here, intentionality matters. The tool is only as inclusive as the mindset behind it.

There is also a temptation to focus only on the loudest voices—the activist parent, the eloquent student leader, the veteran teacher. Moreover, while these voices are valuable, the quieter ones often hold the most profound insights. The janitor who sees every corner of the school. The shy student whose drawings speak volumes. The refugee parent is still learning the language, but is fluent in wisdom. Inclusive governance must make space for these voices too—not just by inviting them in, but by meeting them where they are.

Ultimately, the goal is not to create harmony but to create *authenticity*. Not everyone will agree. Not every decision will please all. However, if the process is dignified, if the engagement is real, people will walk away feeling respected—even if they walk away disappointed.

That is the paradox of inclusive governance: it takes more time but often leads to stronger, more durable outcomes. It requires slowing down to move forward. It demands that we hold both complexity and clarity, both structure and fluidity, both courage and humility. Moreover, what emerges, slowly, unpredictably, is a community—not just of learners, but of co-leaders. A place where governance is not done *to* people, but *with* them. A place where engagement is not extracted, but invited. A place where everyone—regardless of title or background—feels the subtle shift of being not just included, but essential. In a world where many feel voiceless, that shift can be revolutionary.

GLOBAL LESSONS: CASE STUDIES OF TRANSFORMATIONAL EDUCATIONAL MANAGEMENT

Transformation in education rarely announces itself with fanfare (Rosenberg, 2023). More often, it creeps in sideways—quiet, persistent, and almost always inconvenient. Not because it is flawed, but because it resists the comfort of convention. What makes it "transformational" is not the scale or budget, but the audacity to break from what is familiar and the courage to build what has never been tried before. Moreover, perhaps what is most remarkable is how often such stories—often dismissed as outliers—emerge from unexpected corners of the world.

Look long enough, and you will notice a pattern: the most compelling case studies of educational renewal tend to be local in heartbeat but global in resonance. They are specific, deeply rooted in context, yet they somehow echo across borders, offering lessons to anyone paying close enough attention, not as templates to mimic, but as provocations—questions in motion.

Take, for instance, the small municipality of Sobral in northeastern Brazil. Once plagued by illiteracy and plagued even more by bureaucratic inertia, it is now frequently cited as a miracle in educational reform. However, the story is not really about miracles. It is about consistency. The local leadership, instead of launching grandiose reform packages, started with a deceptively simple question: Are our children learning to read? The answer, at the time, was a disheartening no.

So, they recalibrated—not everything, but the right things. Literacy became the north star. Curriculum materials were revised. Teacher training was aligned with clear, specific goals. Monitoring was tight, but not punitive (MacPhail et al, 2023). Results were not weaponised; they were treated as feedback. Moreover, year after year, gains came—not spectacularly at first, but steadily, to the point where Sobral now outperforms most of the country. The lesson here is not that centralisation or decentralisation is better. It is that clarity of purpose, coupled with local autonomy and dignified accountability, that can move mountains. And then there is the story of Finland. Yes, Finland—the oft-romanticised example in international education circles, sometimes held up with such reverence that it risks becoming folklore. However, beneath the myth lies something very real: a deeply intentional design. Finnish education is not successful because it is laissez-faire, nor because it is rigorously managed. It is successful because it is values-driven. Equity is not a policy add-on; it is baked into the system's DNA. Teachers are not treated as instruments of policy delivery—they are architects of learning. Trust flows not from metrics but from the integrity of relationships built over time (Schilke et al, 2021). Homework is light, standardisation is minimal, yet learning thrives.

However, the Finnish story also cautions against easy replication. Try to cut and paste it into a different context, ext, and it will wilt. Because what is often missing from surface-level analyses is the cultural infrastructure underneath—respect for public institutions, social cohesion, and low levels of income inequality. These are not policy levers; they are societal conditions. Still, the Finnish case urges us to ask: what does it mean to design a system around trust instead of surveillance? What kind of outcomes might emerge if we measure less and listen more?

Meanwhile, in Kenya, the story looks different, and no less vital. In the semi-arid county of Turkana, the challenge is not curriculum reform—it is access, relevance, survival. Here, learning must compete with livestock herding, climate displacement, and generational trauma. However, community schools—often supported by hybrid coalitions of NGOs, tribal elders, and teachers—have begun to reimagine what education *means* in such a place. Instead of importing textbook models, they have embedded indigenous knowledge, oral histories, and land-based learning into the curriculum. Governance is communal. Decision-making is participatory. Children are taught not only how to write in English, but how to navigate their land, how to preserve water, and how to tell the stories that carry their identity.

This is not modernisation in the usual sense. It is reclamation. It is education bending to fit the people, not the other way around. Moreover, it raises uncomfortable questions: who decides what counts as knowledge? Who benefits from standardised curricula? What does "quality" mean in a place where survival itself is an educational achievement (Kayyali, 2023)?

In Tokyo, the challenge shifts yet again. Here, in the world's largest metropolis, some schools have begun experimenting with "lesson study" models, where teachers collaboratively design, observe, and revise lessons over time. It is not a flashy innovation. There are no apps involved: just deeply professionalised dialogue, slow observation, rigorous peer feedback. The premise is simple: teaching is a craft, and crafts improve through shared inquiry. It is a model rooted in humility—a collective acknowledgement that no one has it all figured out, but together we can get closer. There is a kind of quiet genius in this. In a world obsessed with speed and disruption, Tokyo's lesson study reminds us that transformation can be slow, even meditative. That maybe the next frontier in educational leadership is not in scaling innovations, but in deepening them.

Of course, no conversation about transformation would be complete without acknowledging the work happening under constraint—sometimes invisible, often heroic. In Syria, for instance, amidst the ruins of conflict, teachers have held classes in tents, in half-destroyed buildings, in underground shelters, not out of obligation, but out of conviction. Moreover, in doing so, they have kept the flame of learning alive for thousands of children. Here, "transformational" does not mean new models. It means fierce continuity. It means defiance against erasure. These are not case studies you will often find in glossy reports. However, they should be. And then there are the digital stories—those scattered across virtual platforms, where learning communities have bloomed in places previously disconnected from global discourse (Abrahamsen, 2023). In India's Bihar state, for instance, a group of female school leaders formed an online network during the pandemic. Many had never used Zoom before. However, over time, they began exchanging ideas, troubleshooting local challenges, and co-developing professional development resources. No one told them to do it. No ministry approved it. However, in this grassroots network, something began to shift: isolation turned into solidarity, passive implementation turned into active co-creation. The medium was digital, but the impact was deeply human.

What these stories show—across continents, income brackets, and political systems—is that transformation does not follow a script. It thrives in paradox. It grows in tension. It blooms in the in-between spaces where rigid systems falter and human ingenuity takes root.

Still, there are common threads worth naming.

- First, transformation is almost always led by insiders—not consultants or donors or distant policymakers, but people within the system who see both its promise and its pain. Teachers who decide they have had enough of teaching to the test. Principals who refuse to suspend students for being hungry. District leaders who are willing to say, "We do not know yet, but we are listening."
- Second, transformation rarely begins with scale. It begins with seeds. A single pilot class. A redesigned timetable. A partnership with local elders. The goal is not to go big fast. It is to go deep first—and only then, when the roots are strong, to think about replication.
- Third, context matters. What works in Bogotá might collapse in Bangkok. What liberates students in Johannesburg might backfire in Jakarta. That is not an argument against learning from others. It is a reminder to translate, not transplant. To ask not "How can we copy this?" but "What spirit of this might nourish our own soil?"
- Fourth, every example of transformation holds tension—between tradition and change, between local control and systemic alignment, between urgency and sustainability. Navigating those tensions requires more than technical skill. It requires moral clarity, emotional intelligence, and political acumen. It requires leaders who can hold ambiguity without rushing to resolution.

Finally—and maybe most profoundly—transformational systems are characterised not just by what they do, but by *how they make people feel*. Do students feel seen? Do teachers feel respected? Do parents feel invited in rather than pushed out? Do communities feel that education belongs to them—not as a service, but as a shared inheritance? Because at the end of the day, management is not just about logistics. It is about love (Matthews et al, 2022). It is about the care with which systems are designed, the attentiveness with which voices are heard, and the dignity with which change is pursued. Moreover, that is the unspoken thread that binds these case studies together. Not perfection. Not uniformity. But love, in practice.

If there is one final lesson from these global stories, this: transformation does not arrive on schedule. It does not always follow logic. However, it does follow courage. The courage to disrupt without discarding. The courage to centre those who have long been pushed to the margins. The courage to begin again, even when the odds say do not bother.

These stories are not a roadmap. However, they are a compass. Moreover, if we listen carefully—really listen—they might help us find our own way forward, not toward someone else's idea of success, but toward an educational future that feels just a little more human.

CONCLUSION

As we reflect on the global pursuit of educational quality, it becomes clear that the path forward demands more than incremental reform—it requires a fundamental rethinking of how we lead, manage, and sustain learning. Innovation in educational management is not a singular solution, but a broad and evolving mindset, one that places curiosity above compliance, adaptability above rigidity, and inclusiveness above hierarchy.

Throughout this chapter, we have explored the critical components of innovative management—strategic leadership grounded in purpose, data-informed planning anchored in empathy, and systems of governance that recognise education as a shared societal endeavour. We have seen how bold leadership can cultivate a culture of experimentation and reflection, how purposeful innovation can reorient institutions toward learners' real-world needs, and how inclusive governance practices can empower communities to take ownership of educational outcomes.

Perhaps most importantly, this chapter has highlighted that educational quality is not an end state but a continuous process. It cannot be legislated into existence or measured solely through test scores. It lives in the day-to-day practices of educators, in the evolving aspirations of students, and in the systems that support or hinder meaningful learning. Quality arises when institutions dare to question the status quo, to listen deeply to the voices of the marginalised, and to adapt proactively in response to global and local shifts.

The international case studies referenced throughout this chapter show that there is no universal formula for educational excellence. What works in one setting may falter in another. However, what connects successful examples across diverse contexts is a shared commitment to relevance, responsiveness, and reinvention. Whether in rural classrooms or urban universities, in high-income countries or resource-constrained regions, the principles of innovation remain constant: empathy, collaboration, evidence, and courage.

To move forward, educational systems must embrace complexity rather than fear it. They must design management structures that are not only efficient but also human-centred. Leaders must be equipped not merely with technical skills, but with moral imagination—the ability to see beyond metrics and navigate the ethical terrain of what education should do and whom it should serve.

Moreover, education must be reclaimed as a public good—a collective investment in human potential and societal well-being. Innovative management strategies, when designed thoughtfully, can help redistribute power, reframe accountability, and reignite the purpose of education in ways that foster both excellence and equity.

As the world becomes increasingly interconnected and interdependent, the role of education in shaping sustainable, just, and resilient societies has never been more vital. Educational leaders and managers are not merely administrators of systems; they are architects of futures. Moreover, in this pivotal role, they must constantly ask: What kind of world are we preparing students for? What kind of citizens are we shaping? Moreover, what kind of institutions do we need to support both? These are not easy questions. However, they are necessary ones. Moreover, it is through the lens of innovation—courageous, inclusive, and ethically grounded—that we may begin to find answers worthy of the learners we serve.

REFERENCES

Abrahamsen, J. (2023). Tools to create interactive digital communities as our world embraces virtual learning—the annual, 1.

Akour, M., & Alenezi, M. (2022). Higher education future in the era of digital transformation. *Education Sciences*, *12*(11), 784. DOI: 10.3390/educsci12110784

Anderson, J. D. (2023). Exploring the misalignment between state and federal policies: Trials and tribulations in a west texas school district (Doctoral dissertation, The University of Texas at El Paso).

Beach, J. M. (2021). *Can we measure what matters most?: Why educational accountability metrics lower student learning and demoralise teachers.* Rowman & Littlefield.

Brown, A. C. (2023). *Redefining Stoicism: How Crisis and Disaster Leaders Demonstrate Positive Behaviours Found in the Ancient Philosophy*. University of Florida.

Cadet, X. F., Borovykh, A., Malekzadeh, M., Ahmadi-Abhari, S., & Haddadi, H. (2024). Deep unlearn: Benchmarking machine unlearning. arXiv preprint arXiv:2410.01276.

Carter, J. A. (2022). Trust as performance. *Philosophical Issues*, *32*(1), 120–147. DOI: 10.1111/phis.12214

Co, E., Dirig, R., Halstead, J., Hendrie, M., & Masilko, T. (2023). Reimagining access: Improving access to digital archives through participatory design. *Journal of Digital Media Management*, *11*(4), 324–333. DOI: 10.69554/IAGK5522

Domanic, M. (2025). Breaking Down the Silos. A hypothesis for Redesigning the Academic Spatial Environment to Encourage Interdisciplinary collaborations (Doctoral dissertation, Politecnico di Torino).

Donop, J., Walderon, T., & Etchells, M. J. (2023). Identity flux: Educator narratives in the face of Burnout. In Drawn to the Flame: Teachers' Stories of Burnout (pp. 181-198). Emerald Publishing Limited.

Egitim, S., & Sandu, R. (2023). Intercultural Language Education Through Leaderful Pedagogy: A Collaborative Autoethnographic Approach. In *Leaderful classroom pedagogy through an interdisciplinary lens: Merging theory with practice* (pp. 159–174). Springer Nature Singapore. DOI: 10.1007/978-981-99-6655-4_10

Fawns, T. (2022). An entangled pedagogy: Looking beyond the pedagogy—technology dichotomy. *Postdigital Science and Education*, *4*(3), 711–728. DOI: 10.1007/s42438-022-00302-7 PMID: 40477872

Friederich, J., Francis, D. P., Lazarova-Molnar, S., & Mohamed, N. (2022). A framework for data-driven digital twins of intelligent manufacturing systems. *Computers in Industry*, *136*, 103586. DOI: 10.1016/j.compind.2021.103586

Garcia, S., & Fisher, D. (2023). *The end of leadership as we know it: what it takes to lead in today's volatile and complex world*. John Wiley & Sons.

George, A. S. (2024). The symbiotic relationship between visionary and pragmatic leadership in propelling organisational success. *Partners Universal International Innovation Journal*, *2*(3), 57–79.

Gilliard, C., & Selwyn, N. (2023). Automated surveillance in education. *Postdigital Science and Education*, *5*(1), 195–205. DOI: 10.1007/s42438-022-00295-3

Jones, M. (2022). *More Judgment Than Data: Data Literacy and Decision-making*. Palgrave Macmillan. DOI: 10.1007/978-3-030-99472-3

Kayyali, M. (2022). Equity, Equality, Diversity, and Inclusion as Key Performance Indicators in Higher Education. *Online Submission*, *3*(5), 1–3.

Kayyali, M. (2023). The Evolution of Quality Assurance Systems in Higher Education. *Online Submission*, *2*(1), 1–9.

Kayyali, M. (2024). Quality enhancement frameworks in higher education. In *Quality Assurance and Accreditation in Higher Education: Issues, Models, and Best Practices* (pp. 61–141). Springer Nature Switzerland. DOI: 10.1007/978-3-031-66623-0_2

Kayyali, M. (2025). Leadership's Role in Fostering a Resilient Organizational Culture. In *Enhancing Resilience in Business Continuity Management* (pp. 267–294). IGI Global Scientific Publishing. DOI: 10.4018/979-8-3693-8809-9.ch009

Kayyali, M. (2026). Innovative Sustainability Models in the MENA Region: A Corporate Perspective. In Sustainable Innovation in the Middle East and North Africa (MENA) Region (pp. 243-270). IGI Global Scientific Publishing.

Kayyali, M., & Christiansen, B. (Eds.). (2024). *Insights Into International Higher Education Leadership and the Skills Gap*. IGI Global. DOI: 10.4018/979-8-3693-3443-0

Kezar, A. J. (Ed.). (2023). *Rethinking leadership in a complex, multicultural, and global environment: New concepts and models for higher education*. Taylor & Francis. DOI: 10.4324/9781003446842

Lamine, W., Anderson, A., Jack, S. L., & Fayolle, A. (2021). Entrepreneurial space and the freedom for entrepreneurship: Institutional settings, policy, and action in the space industry. *Strategic Entrepreneurship Journal, 15*(2), 309–340. DOI: 10.1002/sej.1392

Lunenburg, F. C., & Ornstein, A. (2021). *Educational administration: Concepts and practices*. Sage Publications.

MacPhail, A., Tannehill, D., Leirhaug, P. E., & Borghouts, L. (2023). Promoting instructional alignment in physical education teacher education. *Physical Education and Sport Pedagogy, 28*(2), 153–164. DOI: 10.1080/17408989.2021.1958177

Matthews, J., Love, P. E., Porter, S. R., & Fang, W. (2022). Smart data and business analytics: A theoretical framework for managing rework risks in mega-projects. *International Journal of Information Management, 65*, 102495. DOI: 10.1016/j.ijinfomgt.2022.102495

Mitchell, J. R., Mitchell, R. K., Hunt, R. A., Townsend, D. M., & Lee, J. H. (2022). Stakeholder engagement, knowledge problems and ethical challenges. *Journal of Business Ethics, 175*(1), 75–94. DOI: 10.1007/s10551-020-04550-0

Munoz, G. M. A. (2025). Navigating in the Shadows: Undocumented Latina Experiences in Early Care and Education and Workforce Equity (Doctoral dissertation, San Francisco State University).

Nyka, L., & Marczak, E. (2023). Frontier education for a sustainable future-speculative design in architecture as a transdisciplinary experiment. *Global Journal of Engineering Education, 25*, 6–11.

OLASYA, D. P., & Kiamba, A. (2025). Weaponisation of data: the role of data in modern warfare. BULLETIN OF" CAROL I" NATIONAL DEFENCE UNIVERSITY, 14(1), 90-107.

Olson, L., Guzmán, E., & Kunneman, F. (2023, May). Along the margins: Marginalised communities' ethical concerns about social platforms. In 2023 IEEE/ACM 45th International Conference on Software Engineering: Software Engineering in Society (ICSE-SEIS) (pp. 71-82). IEEE.

Omona, K., & O'dama, M. K. (Eds.). (2024). *Global perspectives on micro-learning and micro-credentials in higher education*. IGI Global. DOI: 10.4018/979-8-3693-0343-6

Owens, T. (2021). The innovation delusion: How our obsession with the new has disrupted the work that matters most. *The American Archivist, 84*(2), 545–548. DOI: 10.17723/0360-9081-84.2.545

Palmer, C. G., Fry, A., Libala, N., Ralekhetla, M., Mtati, N., Weaver, M., Mtintsilana, Z., & Scherman, P. A. (2022). Engaging society and building participatory governance in a rural landscape restoration context. *Anthropocene*, *37*, 100320. DOI: 10.1016/j.ancene.2022.100320

Raffe, C. P., & Loughland, T. (2021). "We are not data analysts": Teachers' perspectives on factors impacting their use of student assessment data. *Issues in Educational Research*, *31*(1), 224–240.

REHAN, S. (2025). A paradigm shift in storytelling and narrative styles: a study of anime effect.

Rosenberg, B. (2023). *"Whatever it is, I am against it": Resistance to change in higher education*. Harvard Education Press.

Schilke, O., Reimann, M., & Cook, K. S. (2021). Trust in social relations. *Annual Review of Sociology*, *47*(1), 239–259. DOI: 10.1146/annurev-soc-082120-082850

Schiuma, G., Schettini, E., Santarsiero, F., & Carlucci, D. (2022). The transformative leadership compass: Six competencies for digital transformation entrepreneurship. *International Journal of Entrepreneurial Behaviour & Research*, *28*(5), 1273–1291. DOI: 10.1108/IJEBR-01-2021-0087

Stolz, J., & Megerle, H. E. (2022). Geotrails as a medium for education and geotourism: Recommendations for quality improvement based on the results of a research project in the Swabian Alb UNESCO Global Geopark. *Land (Basel)*, *11*(9), 1422. DOI: 10.3390/land11091422

Thacker, N. E., & Duran, A. (2022). Operationalising intersectionality as a framework in qualitative grief research. *Death Studies*, *46*(5), 1128–1138. DOI: 10.1080/07481187.2020.1795749 PMID: 32692617

Venegas, C. (2024). *Flow in the office: implementing and sustaining lean improvements*. CRC Press. DOI: 10.4324/9781003576440

Whitney, D. E. (2024). Manufacturing by design. In *Revitalizing Manufacturing* (pp. 282–292). CRC Press. DOI: 10.4324/9781003571872-24

Wilkes, J. (2022). Reconnecting with nature through good governance: Inclusive policy across scales. *Agriculture*, *12*(3), 382. DOI: 10.3390/agriculture12030382

Yakubovna, Y. B. (2024). CONDUCT OF EXACT SCIENCES IN AN INTERACTIVE WAY IN THE SYSTEM OF PROFESSIONAL EDUCATION. *PEDAGOGICAL SCIENCES AND TEACHING METHODS*, *3*(32), 118–121.

Yun, J. S. (2025). To Reflect & to be Reflective: Student Experiences of Critique in Art & Design Higher Education.

KEY TERMS AND DEFINITIONS

Innovative management: a values-driven approach that redesigns leadership, processes, and culture to make quality dynamic, contextual, and inclusive.

Strategic innovation: change anchored to purpose (not gadgets) that iterates toward learner-relevant, equity-centred outcomes.

Data-informed improvement: using multiple forms of evidence as a flashlight (not a weapon) to refine teaching and support, continuously.

Inclusive governance: decision-making shared with students, families, staff, and communities to build trust and durable reforms.

Teacher learning culture: PLCs, peer observation, and reflective practice that translate strategy into day-to-day classroom change.

Authentic assessment: portfolios and projects that evidence transfer of learning beyond standardised tests.

Equity by design: proactively closing opportunity gaps through targeted supports, multilingual access, and shared accountability.

Chapter 11
Fostering Sustainable Education Through AI and Social Media Integration:
A New Frontier for Educational Leadership

Md Mehedi Hasan Emon
https://orcid.org/0000-0002-6224-9552
American International University-Bangladesh, Bangladesh

Most. Sharmin Ara Chowdhury
https://orcid.org/0009-0005-1050-8283
Uttara University, Bangladesh

ABSTRACT

This chapter takes a closer look at the powerful role that artificial intelligence (AI) and social media can play in shaping sustainable and inclusive education systems. It focuses on how educational leaders are essential in managing the tricky balance between embracing new technologies and addressing ethical concerns, especially around fairness and human values. Through several cross-cultural examples, the chapter shows how different regions approach AI integration, highlighting common challenges like digital gaps and biases in algorithms. It also explores how these technologies impact human capital growth, economic sustainability, and policy-making. By offering practical advice for policymakers and education leaders, the

DOI: 10.4018/979-8-3373-3616-9.ch011

chapter encourages leadership that is flexible, collaborative, and ethically aware, aiming to use AI and social media as tools to promote fair and meaningful change in education today.

INTRODUCTION

The rapid development of digital technologies has brought about significant changes across many areas of society, and education is no exception. In the current paradigm, the presence of Artificial Intelligence (AI) and social media in educational systems has become a political issue not only within the confines of prospects but also because of the intensities of future necessities in terms of sustainability and equal human progress. This chapter explores the possible role of educational leadership to take a transformative horizon, in which these technologies can be used to promote sustainable education. By doing that, it not only supports progress toward the Sustainable Development Goals (SDGs), especially SDG 4 on Quality Education, but also more general socioeconomic development. It is assumed that the functional area of educational leadership is not limited merely by the traditional administrative roles traditionally assigned to it. It is also increasingly recognised as the combination of strategic visioning, inclusive governance and ethical responsibility in understanding the complex interrelationship between technology and pedagogy in its management. The discussion starts with a focus on placing educational leadership within a sustainability perspective, showing how increasing demands are leading to a need for transformational, distributed, and digital models of educational leadership. Utilising the established tools, including the UNESCO guidelines on Education for Sustainable Development, one can realise that leaders who can define what needs to be changed and lead through cooperation of various stakeholders, collaboration, and adjustment of the management to the new conditions will achieve the most success. Artificial Intelligence, considered the next major frontier in technology, offers promising opportunities for personalising education and broadening inclusion. The chapter is a critical discussion of how artificial intelligence (AI) may be used to personalise instruction, diagnose individual learner needs, and provide marginalised populations with greater access to education through adaptive learning systems and predictive analytics. The discussion is based on empirical evidence in both developed and developing countries to show that there are still existing disparities in access and practical implementations. These results highlight why educational leaders are faced with the vital task of reducing these disparities. Moreover, added ethical issues related to data privacy and algorithmic bias are in focus, and one should address the integration of AI carefully and with a strict dedication to equality. At the same time, social media sites have become dynamic environments which mediate participatory and collaborative learning. The chapter discusses the role of YouTube, Facebook, LinkedIn, and the emerging technologies, such as TikTok platforms, as interactive platforms where the learners are co-constructing knowledge, offering peer feedback, and participating in peer schools. Even though these digital ecosystems expand opportunities and empower learners, it is associated with the development of some challenges concerning misinformation, distraction, and cognitive load. Therefore, it becomes clear that educational leadership must also focus on developing digital literacy and critical engagement skills among both learners and educators to maximise benefits and minimise potential harms.

The shift brought about by AI and social media is closely tied to changes in digital pedagogy and educational management. The current chapter argues that phenomena such as blended learning, flipped classrooms, gamification, and Massive Open Online Courses (MOOCs) are only some of the evidence to postulate that educational practice heavily depends on new technologies. Such innovations challenge the traditional curricular framework, the design of instruction and faculty readiness, hence the need for leaders who can guide the capacity-building initiatives as well as institutional change. These pedagogical shifts demand nimble and proactive leadership that would find a balance between innovation on the one hand and conservation of academic standards on the other, and foster inclusivity. Sustainable technology integration becomes one of the key concerns at the organisational level. Through an appeal to accepted constructs, namely the technology acceptance models, change management theories, and stakeholder involvement concepts, this chapter provides the audience with helpful information on how to plan, implement, and maintain the usage of artificial intelligence (AI) and social-media tools. The criticality of continuous professional learning, participatory decision making, and policies that draw on the goals of the institution and social values of the community is emphasised. The topic of digital transformation cannot be complete without mentioning the constant digital divide and ethical issues related to AI utilisation in learning. Disparities based on geography, socioeconomic factors and gender are looked at and how AI may strengthen or address the gap. These ethical issues, like potential bias in the algorithms, monitoring the data and student choice, are addressed within the framework of global regulations like the General Data Protection Regulation (GDPR) and Staff Working Paper: Recommendations on the Ethics of Artificial Intelligence by UNESCO. Exploration is a reminder that educational leaders have a pressing need to espouse ethical models and policies that protect the rights and dignity of learners. To bridge theory and practice, a series of cross-cultural case studies from regions such as Finland, Bangladesh, Rwanda, and Brazil is presented. The deployment of artificial intelligence (AI) and social media within the education system depends on various factors such as leadership approach, institutional situation, and policymaking. The examples of case studies provided below indicate that variances in leadership paradigms, institutional frameworks, and regulatory frameworks influence the implementation of such innovations and influence the pursuit of sustainable education goals. Through these illustrations, the chapter explores the challenges that tend to be faced, including poor infrastructure, poor cultural predispositions, and restrictive resource endowment, as well as strategies that can be transferred in overcoming these challenges. In the concluding part, the case-related findings are synthesised and generalised on the potential of technology-promoted eco-education to support the development of human capital and ensure economic sustainability. It offers a strong case in support of the long-term partnership between government, schools, and business as a precondition to long-term social and economic progress. The discussion is concluded by evidence-based prescriptions to managers and policymakers in terms of investments in digital infrastructure, data privacy governance, capacity building, inclusive policy making, as well as effective monitoring and evaluation. Through this, the chapter highlights the impact of AI and social media in reshaping sustainable education implementation. Still, it warns that before it is realised, it must not be implemented blindly or unjustly. It advocates for visionary, ethical, and context-sensitive educational leadership capable of leveraging technology to create learning environments that are inclusive, adaptive, and sustainable, thereby shaping the educational landscape for the future.

EDUCATIONAL LEADERSHIP IN THE AGE OF SUSTAINABILITY

In today's world, marked by swift social, environmental, and technological transformations, the role of educational leadership has grown increasingly important and complex. The modern education leadership can no longer be reduced to the managerial functions of overseeing the processes of daily institutional functions; instead, it has become one of the drivers of systemic change, with a task to incorporate the principles of sustainability into the educational systems. The basis of this shift in the conception is proposed by global plans like the Sustainable Development Goals (SDGs) of the United Nations, and on the understanding of education as one of the pillars of resilience and overall well-being in a society (Saxena et al., 2021). In this context, educational leadership is theoretically framed as a strategic necessity, which organises institutional visioning, brokers participatory action across the various stakeholders, and mobilises flexible forms of governance to foster sustainable educational processes. The key concept in this transformation is the change in leadership paradigms, transcending the obsolete hierarchical paradigm. Transformational leadership has been a subject of great academic interest due to its focus on motivating a common picture, innovation and empowering stakeholders. This kind of leadership is generally believed to be capable of promoting sustainability in education settings (Owusu-Agyeman, 2021). Leaders assuming this orientation typically inspire educators, learners and communities to look beyond. A sense of purpose in the form of a clear mission that resonates with social justice, environmental responsibility and inclusion is required. This form of vision-driven leadership does not simply motivate change; it also fosters a culture of ongoing learning and ethical accountability, which are crucial for navigating the complexities of sustainability challenges (Zhang & Huang, 2024).

Alongside transformational leadership, distributed leadership has increasingly been recognised as vital for achieving sustainability goals. As opposed to having a centralised authority empowered by one person, distributed leadership encourages shared stewardship of teachers, school administrators, students, and outside stakeholders (Khilji, 2022). This position of collective action, which is also consistent with the participatory nature of the practice of sustainability, allows an abundance of viewpoints to influence policy, the teaching practice and the community interest. The empirical evidence suggests that distributed leadership may support organisational resilience and innovation, the qualities that are considered key to surviving the changes in the current imperative of sustainability education (Nadeem, 2024). In addition, the model tends to strengthen democratic systems of governance, hence the sustainability of inclusiveness and equity as core aspects of sustainable education systems (Hariram et al., 2023). At the same time, digital leadership has become more relevant, mainly due to the extent to which educational facilities are applying technology with an eye toward sustainable development. Digital leadership also refers to the abilities that are necessary to imagine, implement, and support digital interventions which redefine teaching, learning, and administrative procedures (Karakose et al., 2024). In the area of sustainability, this type of leadership allows educational institutions to utilise the possibilities provided by such tools as Artificial Intelligence (AI), social media, and data analytics to personalise education, broaden access, and bring a greater understanding of the environment.

Nevertheless, to perform this leadership role, both technical-related skills are required as well as underlying issues of ethical considerations, such as digital equity and data privacy, which highlight the heightened challenges that digital eras impose on their leaders (Grande et al., 2022). The two leadership paradigms fit well in the UNESCO Education for Sustainable Development (ESD) framework that further advances leadership as a catalyst of system transformation toward sustainability. According to Miao & Nduneseokwu (2024), leaders in the education field should act like visionaries who foster what was coined as transformative competencies, i.e., critical thinking, collaborating, and problem-solving, which are essential in ensuring sustainable futures. Leaders are also expected to engage stakeholders meaningfully by bridging formal and informal educational settings and fostering partnerships across sectors and communities. Importantly, such stakeholder engagement is not an add-on but a central element of adaptive governance, which acknowledges the complex and dynamic nature of educational systems (Linzalone et al., 2024). This underlying reality of sustainability problems, that of uncertainties, has led to the development of adaptive governance as a leadership paradigm that helped to make educational institutions more adaptable to the challenges of education. This method allows removing the strict policy prescriptions and encourages consistent reflection, feedback loop and iterative decision-making (Burns et al., 2022). As a result, leaders can guide through the dynamic landscapes of policy, technological shocks, and varied community needs with a focus on sustainability goals. The strategy can also build resiliency through the building of learning organisations that become resilient under crises and emerging opportunities, a characteristic that was tested through recent shocks of the global system, i.e., the COVID-19 situation (Khan et al., 2024a; Shaya et al., 2023). Education leaders whose goals include sustainability should also consider issues of equity and inclusiveness, as new and green interventions should not only favour some students. In this regard, leadership requires a strong ethical position harbouring affiliative social justice, environmental responsibility, and cultural responsiveness (Mahmoud & Mousa, 2025). These commitments guide resource employment, construction of curriculum content, and community involvement and provoke changes in the way leaders address the systematised obstacles and introduce democratised access to quality educational activities.

Figure 1. Adaptive Governance Cycle in Educational Sustainability Leadership

Educational sustainability leadership is a knowledge-based, learning loop of adaptive governance. This recursive dynamic is summarised in the spiral diagram shown herein, which identifies six interrelated phases, namely Environmental Scanning, Vision Alignment, Policy Formulation, Implementation, Monitoring & Evaluation and adaptive Feedback. A perimeter exegesis makes out the essential skills and abilities necessary at every turn, which are cooperation, moral thinking, and tactical forecasting. Even the very construction of the building as a spiral can serve as an emphasis on the understanding of the fact that every process of leadership, such as this, is always iterative and transformative. All these elements define the character of leadership as a part and parcel of achieving the objectives of sustainability. Modern educational leaders are supposed to integrate features of transformational, distributed and digital leadership within unified models which prioritise emphasis on vision, engagement and flexibility. By so doing, they mentor institutions through complex processes of change and together with the other processes make significant contributions to the international agenda of sustainable development material-wise. The challenges are significant, but leadership as a strategic necessity in the present age of sustainability is ensured by the possibility of pushing forward toward equity, resiliency, and innovative education systems.

ARTIFICIAL INTELLIGENCE IN EDUCATION: PATHWAYS TO INCLUSION

Artificial Intelligence (AI) has increasingly been recognised as a transformative force in education, with the potential to fundamentally change how learning is delivered, assessed, and accessed. It is expected that the implementation of artificial intelligence (AI) in education in every corner of the world will contribute to improvements in the customisation of educational experiences, the specificity of identifying the needs of learners, and increased access to historically underserved and disadvantaged populations. However, the adoption and consequences of AI vary significantly with geographical location, and it is dependent on the infrastructural potential, regulatory standards, and socioeconomic inequities. This discussion critically reflects the existing practices in fostering personalisation and inclusion in the education sector, involving reference to empirical research to outline possible directions and existing gaps and differences. One of the main benefits of the application of AI in education is the possibility of individual learning paths. The traditional classroom, with its limited curriculum and large ratio of students to sales desks, is often unable to meet the individual needs of the students, in terms of rates of progress and interests. In contrast, adaptive learning systems run on AI deliver algorithms that adapt to teaching content in real time according to data on constantly computed performance (Sayed et al., 2023). These platforms change the difficulty, sequence, and presentation mode of lessons to fit the individual profile of each learner, thus maintaining interaction and understanding. As an illustration, when using AI systems, repetitive problem areas can be spotted and resources or exercises can be recommended, thus reducing the risk of student regression. Although there are significant benefits associated with the adoption of AI, its adoption is uneven across the regions.

Differences among regions vary, primarily dependent on infrastructure, policy environments and socioeconomics. Empirical research findings on the Global North and the Global South reveal that despite the high potential of AI, regionalised challenges in terms of implementing capabilities, governance, and socioeconomic stratification continue to influence adoption and performance. Such tailored approaches are particularly valuable for students with learning disabilities or those requiring differentiated instruction, as they enable educators to provide more precise and timely support. The application of intelligent tutoring systems (ITS) is one of the most advanced applications of artificial intelligence in recent literature, the conditions of which can be determined as imitating one-to-one tutoring, by providing feedback and instruction to learners in real-time and adapting to their individualised needs as they progress through curricular materials (Lin et al., 2023). ITS AI interprets student responses, identifies misconceptions and responds to them with a similar scaffolding behaviour of human tutors; however, with the scalability where services are provided to much larger groups of students. Empirical evidence suggests that, in mathematics, languages, and science, ITS improve the quality of learning due to prolonged, individualised communication with the students (Darling-Hammond et al., 2020). Furthermore, the paradigm has gained greater significance in Internet and blended learning environments where the ability to monitor remotely and adapt in real-time became essential in times of disturbances, the likes of which occurred during the COVID-19 pandemic (González et al., 2023).

Figure 2. Intelligent Tutoring Systems (ITS) Workflow

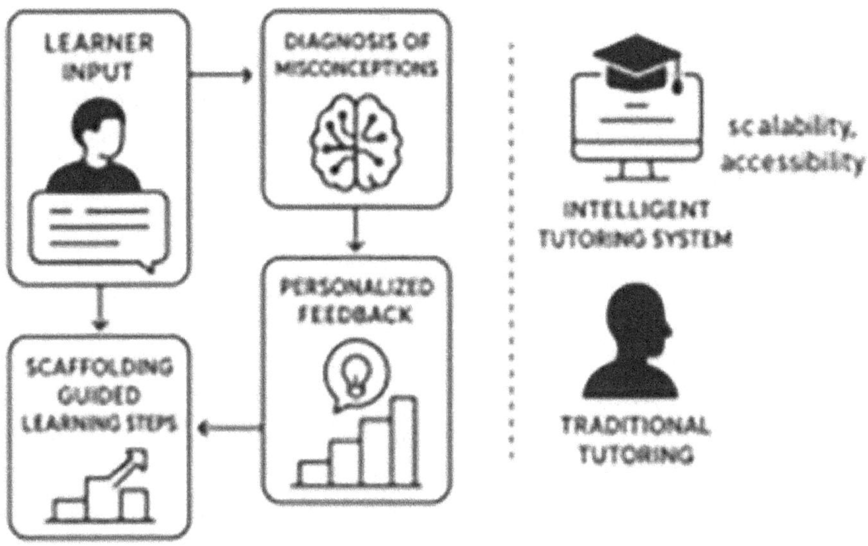

The diagram shows the major elements of an Intelligent Tutoring System (ITS), which are learner input, automated AI diagnosis, individual feedback, and stepping through learning tasks, as well as a comparison with typical tutoring. The difference between ITS and other similar systems is that under ITS, you will have features like a high level of scalability and enhanced accessibility. The existence of a continuous feedback loop implies that the system produces repeated feedback, shifting the instructional process forward to adjust to personal requirements. This is due to the cyclic manner of presenting each element, which shows the dynamic nature of ITS to the progress of the learner. Predictive analytics based on AI also plays an important role: through processing large amounts of data, which include attendance indicators, interaction engagement, test results, and even socio-demographic characteristics, these models can reveal those students who are at risk of poor performance or school dropout. With this kind of prediction, educators and administrators will manage to channel resources and interventions better, contributing to better retention and academic achievement. Structural inequalities can also be identified through predictions on the existence of patterns based on socioeconomic background, ethnicity, or place of residence (Schaper et al., 2025).

Nevertheless, the application of such technologies poses ethical issues, especially in matters of data privacy, algorithmic bias, and the risk of entrenching the current disparities in the case of their limited application due to a lack of oversight and transparency (Hakimi et al., 2021). In terms of inclusion, the marginalised learners, either poverty-affected, disability affected, language-barrier-affected, remote-location-affected, etc., would get the most out of individual AI interventions. Artificial intelligence-based systems may surmount both the distance and the barriers to distance barriers and allow knowledge of high quality to reach students who may otherwise not have had access to traditional schools. As an example, AI-driven language translation and speech recognition technologies have presented new avenues and opportunities to the learners, who are in a multilingual environment and can engage with material in their first languages but still access it despite the language barriers (Lee et al., 2023). Similarly, AI applications designed for students with disabilities, such as screen readers, predictive text input, and adaptable interfaces, can foster more inclusive and accessible learning environments (Chopra et al., 2024).

Nevertheless, despite these promising developments, significant challenges remain in the Global South, where the full potential of AI for inclusion is often hindered. A combination of unresolved infrastructure underdevelopment, low levels of digital fluency, and variation in policy support to AI adaptation are active barriers to mass adoption of AI and therefore continue to contribute to the digital divide and, potentially, the educational disparity (Polozhentseva et al., 2025). Although countries in the Global North have already made significant progress in developing AI as an integrated part of the comprehensively financed education system, many developing nations continue to struggle to deliver even the basic possibilities of digital penetration. In areas where there is low internet connectivity or a lack of adequate technological infrastructure, AI tools are out of reach for most learners and teachers. In addition, the cost of both implementing and sustaining sophisticated AI solutions is often unaffordable for schools looking to make substantial limitations to their budgets (Emon, 2025a). There is also suspicion that the cultural applicability of AI models can be under threat since most of them are trained and tested on data sets compiled in Western or developed environments. This practice may lead to unfair or inaccurate performance of the systems in various learning settings, and it may negatively affect marginalised students (Yared et al., 2023). As a result, increasing recognition of the significance of transferring the development of AI instruments to local educators and society to guarantee contextual sensitivity and sensitivity to culture (Balzer, 2020). These participatory design processes have a positive effect on building trust and the probability of sustainability adoption. Policy-wise, there is a crucial need to teach the governments and educational institutions not only to attain the AI technologies but also to shape the faculty of their educators to use AI tools effectively and proficiently. The focus on increasing digital literacy and ethical awareness among professionals should form a significant part of AI-integration efforts to ensure that teachers become proactive rather than passive adapters of a new technology (Nedungadi et al., 2024). Moreover, large governance structures are required to disclose data privacy, transparency across AI decision-making, as well as equitable access, thus reducing the harm and maximising possible advantages (Qasmi & Fatima, 2024). Altogether, AI has a significant potential for personalising learning and increasing inclusion, with the tools having the potential to appeal to the exceptional needs of individual learners and those who have been systematically marginalised. However, the actualisation of such advantages is not well distributed in different global scenes, continuing to depend on infrastructure, economic capacity, and social-political status. For AI to truly become a catalyst for equitable and sustainable education systems, educational leaders and policymakers must approach its integration with a balanced mindset embracing innovation while remaining critically aware of ethical, cultural, and contextual considerations.

SOCIAL MEDIA AND PARTICIPATORY DEMOCRATIC LEARNING SPACES

In recent years, social media platforms have increasingly been recognised as influential spaces for learning and knowledge exchange, fundamentally changing the educational landscape beyond the traditional classroom. Digital applications and forums like YouTube, Facebook, LinkedIn, and TikTok have evolved both in terms of being spaces of social interaction, but have also become essential spaces where learners are involved in making content, peer-to-peer connections, and with educators across geographical and institutional boundaries. The current discussion questions the degree to which social media enables participatory learning by prioritising the agency of the learners, constructive peer input, and community-based knowledge-sharing practices. Meanwhile, it would address potential danger brought by misinformation and online distractions. The principal value of social media to education is that it democratises access to information and fosters agency of the learners, that is, their capability to control their own educational processes. Unlike the more traditional models of education that are one-sided and based on passive information intake, the given platforms encourage active learning and autonomous pursuit. As an example, the YouTube video platform can be mentioned as it operates as a broad and publicly accessible library anywhere in the world of educational material, which can be as narrow as tutorials or as broad as scholarly lectures (Ziguras, 2023). Learners can gain control of what they study, go back to studying failed concepts at their own pace, and produce and remix their own instructional material, moving beyond being a consumer towards being a co-producer of knowledge. Such a paradigm transformation brings about learners who are characterised by more autonomy and intrinsic dedication to educational endeavours.

In addition to supporting individual learning, social media also fosters collaborative learning by enabling peer-to-peer interactions and feedback, which are critical elements in the co-creation of knowledge. Facebook groups and LinkedIn communities are a subtype of digital space in which learners and professionals come together to share common thoughts, share relevant material, and support each other in any educational projects (Staziaki et al., 2021). Digital learning platforms trigger discussions that regularly go beyond the scope of official courses and include various viewpoints and experiences of reality that enhance the study process. TikTok, even though it is mainly viewed as an entertainment app, has also turned out to be an informal means of learning, especially among younger generations. Its short and entertaining videos allow content creators to make complicated topics simple and more accessible to most users, and comments and duets between the viewers create an interactive learning environment (Abdullah, 2022). This feedback loop is iterative, whereby it motivates the learners to critically reflect and be involved in the co-construction of knowledge, which conforms to the constructivist theory of education. Social media is also community-based, and this orientation causes learning to be a socially situated activity. The education process is a collaborative production of knowledge in the virtual community of practices that breaks the walls of formal classrooms (Hilli, 2020). These communities offer social capital, social and resource networks that assist in skill acquisition, career enhancement and lifelong learning to the learners (Dlamini et al., 2024).

Most importantly, the spaces have the potential of enhancing the voices which are often underrepresented in formal education, thus creating more inclusive and diversified knowledge environments (Timmis & Muñoz-Chereau, 2022). As a result, social media acts as a new sphere of democracy where learners not only interact with the content but with each other, which shatters old hierarchies of knowledge construction. Even though social media has much potential in terms of educational practice, the implementation of the tool is fraught with a set of complexities and risks. The most notable of them is the prevalence of misinformation and disinformation that can undermine the plausibility and general vitality of educational content (Jiménez-Aleixandre & Puig, 2022). This is because social media websites are not controlled, and information appears as suspicious or inaccurate data is shared, often causing confusion and informing poor learner choices. Therefore, teachers and heads of education should respond to the necessity to promote digital literacy skills that would enable students to analyse the trustworthiness of sources and filter valuable data in the digital ocean (George & Wooden, 2023).

One more noticeable issue is that of digital distraction. At the same time, those specific features that make social media so captivating, notifications, infinite scrolling, and opportunities to observe the feed produced by the algorithms may impair concentration on long-term, reflective thinking. This contradiction puts social media simultaneously as an excellent teaching instrument as well as a possible bottleneck to focus on. Thus, educators also embrace an approach to teaching and learning that reflects mindful and intentional interactions to employ social media in instructional practice, instead of viewing it as an automatic remedy (Mandinach & Gummer, 2025). Inequalities in digital equity also need a close look. Although social media can expand access to learning, internet connectivity, access to devices, and digital skills leaves a big gap both across borders and within respective societies (Czerniewicz & Carvalho, 2022). Such inequalities mean that not all learners will receive social media opportunities on an equal basis, so the possible closing of the pre-existing educational gaps will be compromised. To resolve these inequalities, specific policy efforts and institutional facilitation are needed, as without those resources, social media can merely be a tool of participatory learning that would have no chance of inclusivity. Finally, the pedagogical mission of social media is rather convoluted and dynamic. It has outstanding benefits related to the advancement of learner agency, creation of collaborative learning processes and community-based knowledge creation in a kind of decentralised and democratised manner. At the same time, it also presents other issues, including misinformation, distraction, and inequity that require strict handling. Social media should not be seen as a technological tool in future education law, but as a social revolutionary discovery that is changing both the boundaries of learning; the former will require the creation of new literacies, a deeper awareness of critical consciousness, as well as inclusive planning. Equally weighing these opportunities and limitations, teachers may utilise social media as a truly disruptive power of participatory and sustainable learning.

DIGITAL PEDAGOGIES AND THE TRANSFORMATION OF EDUCATIONAL MANAGEMENT

Over the last ten years or so, educational practices have undergone significant shifts, much of it pushed forward by rapid technological progress, changing expectations from learners, and the growing complexity of the global education landscape. The spread of digital pedagogies, and most prominently the flipped classroom, blended learning, gamification and MOOC (Massive Open Online Courses) has been a key theme in the sphere of contemporary higher education. It is not true that these innovations have been short-lived trends but are rather now pillars of teaching and learning in all institutions and around the world. Artificial intelligence-powered and influenced by social media, these practices have developed both at the micro-adaptation level, as well as at the macro-level of substantial changes to the institutional structure and its management. The reconsideration of the fundamentals of instruction is the basic postulate of digital pedagogy. The example of the flipped classroom represents this concern. Instead of opening a lecture to start a course, students are pre-exposed to curricular materials, such as videos or readings, before they meet as a group during the course, during which the group work or a discussion can be facilitated (Chen et al., 2023).

Nevertheless, this model requires a high level of expertise in instructional design practitioners need to create compelling online content, learn how to make proper use of learning-management systems, and create new methods to keep the learners online and involved. Blended learning, which unites synchronous and asynchronous learning environments, provides more flexibility to the students but also forces institutions to redesign both delivery modalities as well as assessment schemes (Valtonen et al., 2021). Under these circumstances, technology is no longer an accessory tool but the fundamental medium of teaching. The other important aspect of digital pedagogy is gamification. By using some form of badges, points, or leaderboards, this method aims to increase the engagement of the learners by introducing game-like motivators into educational activities. Although opponents argue that gamification can be used to diminish a learning process into shallow competition, it could strengthen motivation and increase academic results when the learning activity can be undertaken seriously with clear objectives and prompts, as stated in research (Balzer, 2020). To these mechanisms, adaptive learning systems, exemplified by Carnegie Learning and Squirrel AI, participate in AI algorithms to track students' progress and suggest individualised materials in real-time (Khan & Hasan Emon, 2024; Srinivasa et al., 2022). However powerful, these systems need ample instructor training to be put successfully into practice. One more thing that deserves attention is MOOCs. Initially proposed as a possible democratiser of higher education, today they are used more tactically as a part of institutional portfolios, whether as an add-on to degree programs or, even more substantially, as supporting ongoing-education programs, micro-credentialing and other provision of lifelong learning. This change in motion is forcing universities to renegotiate their international status and team up with provider giants, like edX and Coursera. Digital pedagogies have progressed past the minor tweaks in the delivery of instructions to a point where there are fundamental changes in organisational and managerial practices within the higher-education sector.

These changes in how teaching happens also affect how institutions are managed. Educational administrators now face questions about whether their infrastructure can handle new tech demands, whether faculty are ready for the digital shift, and how to make sure students from all backgrounds can access these tools equally. A key issue is curriculum reform. Older, more rigid curricula are often not well-suited to digital learning environments, which tend to be modular, interdisciplinary, and focused on competencies rather than just content (Redecker, 2022). Another issue is faculty readiness. While some educators take digital tools with ease, others find it overwhelming or lack confidence with tech. This has made faculty development programs essential, though they do not always work as well as hoped. Research suggests that whether instructors engage in digital transformation depends not just on training, but also on support from leadership and whether they see real value in changing their methods (Khan et al., 2025). The quick move to online teaching during the COVID-19 pandemic made this even more apparent. Many faculty were overworked and stressed, and some even burned out, which raises questions about the long-term sustainability of digital teaching models if institutions do not provide enough support (Morze & Trybulska, 2021). Beyond the classroom, digital tools are changing how education is managed. More institutions are using data analytics to track student progress, evaluate teaching, and guide strategic planning. Tools like learning analytics dashboards can highlight which students are struggling, allowing for more targeted interventions (Paulsen & Lindsay, 2024).

However, here, too, ethical issues arise: how much data is too much? Are students being surveilled? What about algorithmic bias? These are not easy questions, and administrators need to tread carefully to make sure technology serves the students, not the other way around. Equity is another big concern. Yes, digital tools can open doors, but they can also widen existing gaps. Students in rural areas or low-income communities might not have reliable internet, updated devices, or even quiet places to study (Emon, 2025b; Mousumi, 2023). These are real barriers. If institutions do not address them head-on through things like subsidies, offline access options, or community support, then digital learning will continue to benefit some more than others. Even with all the challenges, there is no denying the potential of digital pedagogies. They allow institutions to reimagine their role not just as places that deliver knowledge, but as platforms for continuous learning, creativity, and inclusion.

For this to happen, educational management must evolve, becoming more flexible, open to experimentation, and centred around student needs. This is not just about upgrading technology; it is about changing culture.

Figure 3. Evolution of Digital Pedagogical Models

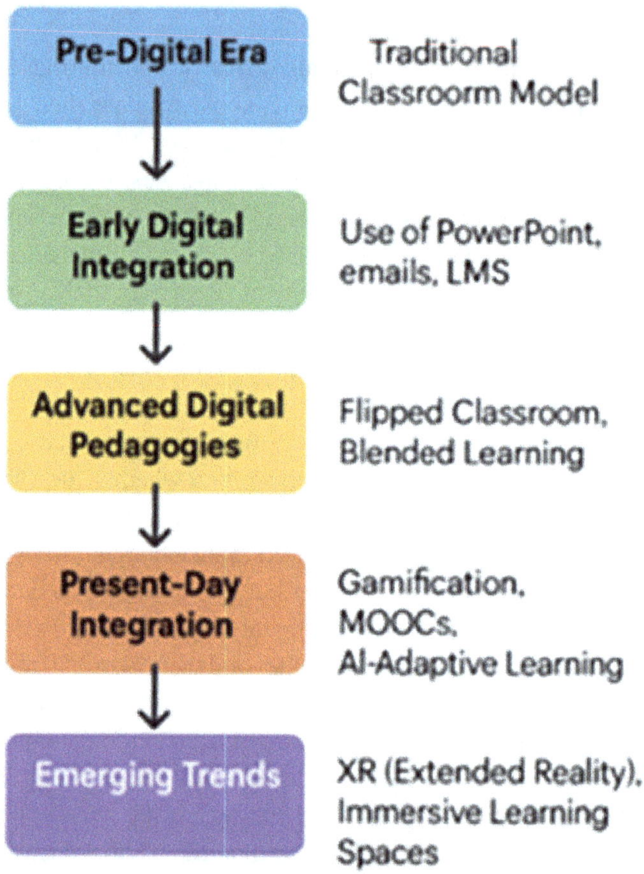

This flowchart presents a timeline showing how teaching methods have changed over time, starting from the Pre-Digital Era and moving towards current and emerging trends. The education process has changed between the Traditional Classroom Model and Early Digital Integration, a period which saw the integration of educational tools like PowerPoint presentations, email, and Learning Management Systems. The other stages involve Advanced Digital Pedagogies, which include the Flipped Classrooms and the Blended Learning strategies. The current Integration now has Gamification, Massive Open Online Courses, and Adaptive learning powered by AI, and the Emerging Trends are portrayed, which are extended reality and Immersive learning space options. All these developments prove the fact that digital pedagogies, enabled with the aid of AI and social media, are transforming the whole educational ecosystem. Thoughtful instructional design, wide-ranging support of faculty, and procedures installed in advance of forthcoming trajectories are all-important to institutions that need to stay on course. Finally, it is essential to ensure that the digital transformation is not divided, but needs to be reduced, rather than increasing the gaps in education.

LEADERSHIP STRATEGIES FOR RESPONSIBLE TECHNOLOGY INTEGRATION

The modern education context is in a state of fast-track digitalisation, which makes the integration of artificial intelligence (AI) and social media into the classrooms, campus-wide, and back-office infrastructure not hypothetical or experimental, but a real process happening and gaining momentum. However, what tends to get overlooked amidst the rush for innovation is the critical role that leadership plays in ensuring such technology does not just get implemented, but that it genuinely adds value. Technology on its own is never truly neutral. It reflects and reinforces the values, assumptions, and intentions of those who design and deploy it. This is where responsible leadership steps in, not just to facilitate access to tools, but to navigate the messiness that often accompanies systemic change. Leading technology integration is not merely about procurement decisions or signing off on the latest edtech vendor's proposal. It is about steering complex institutions, filled with diverse stakeholders and competing priorities, toward meaningful change. One-size-fits-all solutions rarely work. Instead, the process often involves compromise, creativity, and a whole lot of listening. Frameworks like the Technology Acceptance Model (TAM) or the Unified Theory of Acceptance and Use of Technology (UTAUT) are helpful starting points in understanding how teachers, staff, and students react to new systems (Ursavaş, 2022). However, real-world leadership goes beyond these models, because people's responses to technology are often emotional, cultural, and unpredictable.

A core part of effective leadership in this space involves gauging an institution's readiness for change. This includes both the hardware, whether the school or university has reliable internet, functioning devices, and interoperable platforms and the human elements: skill levels, trust in leadership, and openness to trying new things. It is not unusual to see significant investments in AI-driven platforms that end up underused or even abandoned because teachers were not adequately trained or consulted (Bernasconi et al., 2025). That is not a failure of the technology; it is a failure of leadership to ask the right questions early on. Moreover, this brings us to professional development. Frankly, the traditional model of a one-off "training day" does not cut it anymore. Digital transformation is not a static goal; it is a moving target. So, educators and staff need continuous, meaningful, and context-sensitive learning opportunities. These do not always need to be expensive or externally delivered. Peer mentoring, communities of practice, and reflective spaces where teachers can experiment and share what works (and what does not) can go a long way. Of course, leaders must lead by example. If those at the top are unwilling to engage with digital tools themselves, it sends a message, intentionally or not, that this transformation is someone else's job (Banerjee-Batist et al., 2022). Equally important is stakeholder consultation. It is hard to overstate how often tech implementation becomes a top-down affair, orchestrated by leadership teams or IT units who may be several steps removed from the day-to-day classroom realities. However, technology used in education affects everyone: students, parents, instructors, and even surrounding communities. Participatory approaches, such as surveys, student-led panels, co-design sessions, or pilots, can make a significant difference. This not only improves decision-making but fosters a sense of ownership and inclusion. When students see themselves as co-creators of their learning environment, they are more likely to engage meaningfully with the tools provided.

One practical tool that can help leaders navigate this complexity is a Leadership Decision Matrix for Technology Adoption. While it might sound bureaucratic at first glance, it is a helpful way to ensure that key factors are not overlooked in the excitement of adopting something "new." The matrix prompts leadership teams to evaluate proposed tools across dimensions like pedagogical fit, equity, data ethics, scalability, user readiness, and system compatibility. Ideally, this scoring exercise should not happen in a closed boardroom, but through a process that involves varied voices. It is not foolproof, of course, but it encourages slower, more deliberate choices (Zhang et al., 2025), a necessary counterbalance to the often-breathless pace of edtech marketing. In terms of overall direction, successful leadership for digital transformation leans more on building a culture of experimentation than on enforcing compliance. A school or university that tolerates a degree of failure, that celebrates small wins, and that creates room for innovative uses of AI and social media, even if they do not always stick, is more likely to thrive in the long term. It is about creating safe spaces for trying things out and learning together. Importantly, leaders need to recognise variation across departments or regions. What works brilliantly in one faculty may flop in another. That is okay as long as the institution remains adaptable and aligned to its broader mission, whether that is equity, excellence, or something else altogether.

Communication, too, plays a vital role. Not just in the usual newsletters and press releases, but in how consistently leaders explain *why* specific digital changes are being made. Transparency, especially around decision-making and progress updates, builds trust. Moreover, in the absence of clear information, people will usually fill in the gaps with assumptions, which can quickly derail even the best-planned initiatives. Communication should also extend outside the campus to include parents, policymakers, alums, and industry partners, all of whom shape the broader educational ecosystem. Lastly, in a time when algorithms are increasingly influencing how learners are evaluated, what content they see, and how they interact with institutions, ethical leadership becomes non-negotiable. It is not just about "what works", it is about what is *right*. Predictive analytics, for example, might help flag students at risk of dropping out, but it could also lead to stereotyping if not handled sensitively. Similarly, using social media platforms for learning requires an understanding of how data is collected and used. Leaders must remain vigilant, asking not only what AI *can* do, but what it *should* do (Demeke, 2024).

Figure 4. Leadership Decision Matrix for Technology Adoption

Leadership Decision Matrix for Technology Adoption

PEDAGOGICAL ALIGNMENT	EQUITY & ACCESS	DATA PRIVACY & ETHICS	SCALABILITY & SUSTAINABILITY	FACULTY & STUDENT READINESS
Does the tool support or hinder learning outcomes?	Can all learners benefit regardless of background or ability?	Does it comply with GDPR / local data laws Any ethical concerns?	Is long-term use cost-effective and realistic?	Are users trained and confident to use this tool?
Does the tool support or hinder learning outcomes?	Can all learners benefits regardless of background or ability?		Are users trained and confident to use this tool?	Can it integrate with existing platforms (e.g., LMS, SIS)?

This figure, labelled as Figure 3, depicts Paulo Freire's cyclical model of praxis. It shows dialogue at the centre, acting as the base for empowerment, which is then followed by reflection and action in an ongoing cycle. The circular design is meant to emphasise how these parts depend on each other to support critical pedagogy. Around the cycle, important ideas like Empowerment, Critical Consciousness, and Community Voice are displayed to highlight the transformative aims of Freire's educational approach. The figure, therefore, visually represents how these interconnected stages work together to promote learning that empowers learners and their communities. To wrap it up, the integration of AI and social media into education is not a purely technical shift; it is a deep cultural and organisational one. Moreover, at the centre of it all are leaders who must balance vision with caution, innovation with equity, and speed with sustainability. Those who get it right will not just digitise education, they will humanise it in the process.

BRIDGING DIGITAL DIVIDES AND ENSURING ETHICAL USE OF AI IN EDUCATION

Over the last few years, artificial intelligence (AI) has quietly become a transformative force within educational systems. It is changing how students learn, how teachers instruct, and how institutions manage resources. However, while these innovations offer great promise, like making learning more personalised or automating routine tasks, they also bring with them a host of complicated ethical and equity-related questions. If care is not taken, AI could end up widening the very gaps it is supposed to bridge. The dream of educational equity might remain just that dream if the digital transformation does not consider the deeper social and ethical issues surrounding its use (Czerniewicz & Carvalho, 2022). One ongoing problem is the digital divide, which, unfortunately, is not a new issue. It has been discussed for decades, yet in many parts of the world, the situation has barely improved. Some students live in environments where reliable internet is a luxury, if it exists at all. This is especially true in rural areas or low-income urban neighbourhoods where both infrastructure and support systems are fragile. In places like Bangladesh or rural Nigeria, for instance, even when schools do have digital equipment, students might not be able to access it at home. Power outages, lack of devices, and shared living spaces can make digital learning feel like an uphill battle (Fayed & Cummings, 2021).

Gender gaps in technology use are also a significant concern. While there has been global momentum around getting more girls and women online, progress remains uneven. According to Gupta & Kiran (2025) women globally are still significantly less likely than men to use the internet, with the gap being vast in low-income regions. This phenomenon under analysis is not only a technological limitation, but a reflection of general societal and cultural limitations that define the extent to which women can participate on the internet. Those asymmetries are more acute in the framework of educational experiences supported by artificial intelligence (AI). Due to access differences, as well as to social instructions that canonically locate women on the periphery of technology-based practices, girls are often subjected to limited access to interactions with AI tools. Native, on the other hand, AI-facilitated learning has the potential to suffer from some structural obstacles. The pedagogical systems supplemented with the technologies can facilitate individual pace, provide immediate feedback, and provide signals at an early stage in case learners are losing their way. These tools could help struggling learners or those with special needs. However, reality is often more complicated. High-quality AI systems are usually expensive and are more accessible in well-funded schools or wealthier countries. Students from less privileged backgrounds might end up using lower-quality tools that do not adapt well to their learning needs. So ironically, what is designed to level the playing field may end up reinforcing existing inequalities. Beyond questions of access, there are also significant concerns about how ethical these technologies are. One of the major issues is bias in algorithms.

AI systems are built on data, and if that data contains biases, as most real-world datasets do, then the AI will replicate those biases in its decisions. A well-documented example involves facial recognition software that performs poorly on darker-skinned individuals (Khan et al., 2024). In schools, this could mean misidentifying students or unfairly grading assignments. Automated essay graders, for instance, have shown a tendency to favour specific sentence structures or vocabulary that reflect a narrow standard of "good writing." Data privacy is another ethical minefield. Many of these AI systems collect vast amounts of data, sometimes without users being fully aware. From keystrokes and login patterns to facial expressions and emotional responses, everything becomes a data point. While this can help teachers understand student behaviour, it also raises serious concerns about surveillance. Are students being watched too closely? Who owns this data? Moreover, what happens if it gets into the wrong hands? These are not hypothetical questions. In several cases, third-party edtech providers have accessed student data without explicit consent, creating a legal and moral grey area (Khan et al., 2024).

Global frameworks like the General Data Protection Regulation (GDPR) in Europe have tried to tackle this. GDPR emphasises things like informed consent, transparency, and the right to opt out, important protections in an age of algorithmic decision-making. UNESCO has also stepped in with its 2021 Recommendation on the Ethics of AI, laying out guiding principles such as inclusiveness, explainability, and human oversight. These frameworks are certainly a step in the right direction, but in practice, many countries, especially those with limited resources, struggle to enforce them. Laws are only helpful if there are systems in place to monitor and uphold them. Another subtle but important issue is the risk to student autonomy. AI systems can become too good at predicting outcomes. They may recommend specific courses, highlight career paths, or even nudge students toward certain behaviours. While that sounds helpful on the surface, it also reduces room for exploration and critical thinking. If an algorithm tells a student they are likely to succeed in one field but not another, does that become a self-fulfilling prophecy? There is a real danger that students may begin to rely too much on machines and stop questioning or challenging the system. Education, after all, should empower individuals to think independently, not simply to follow instructions (Boyadjieva & Ilieva-Trichkova, 2021; Emon & Mazid-Ul-Haque, 2025). Given these complexities, what can be done?

First and foremost, infrastructure investment is crucial. Governments need to ensure that all students, regardless of background, can access the internet and digital tools. However, access alone is not enough. Schools must also design culturally relevant content, offer materials in multiple languages, and make sure students with disabilities are included. Teachers, too, need support not just in using AI tools, but in understanding how they work, what their limitations are, and how to push back when necessary.

Figure 5. The Layers of the Digital Divide in Education

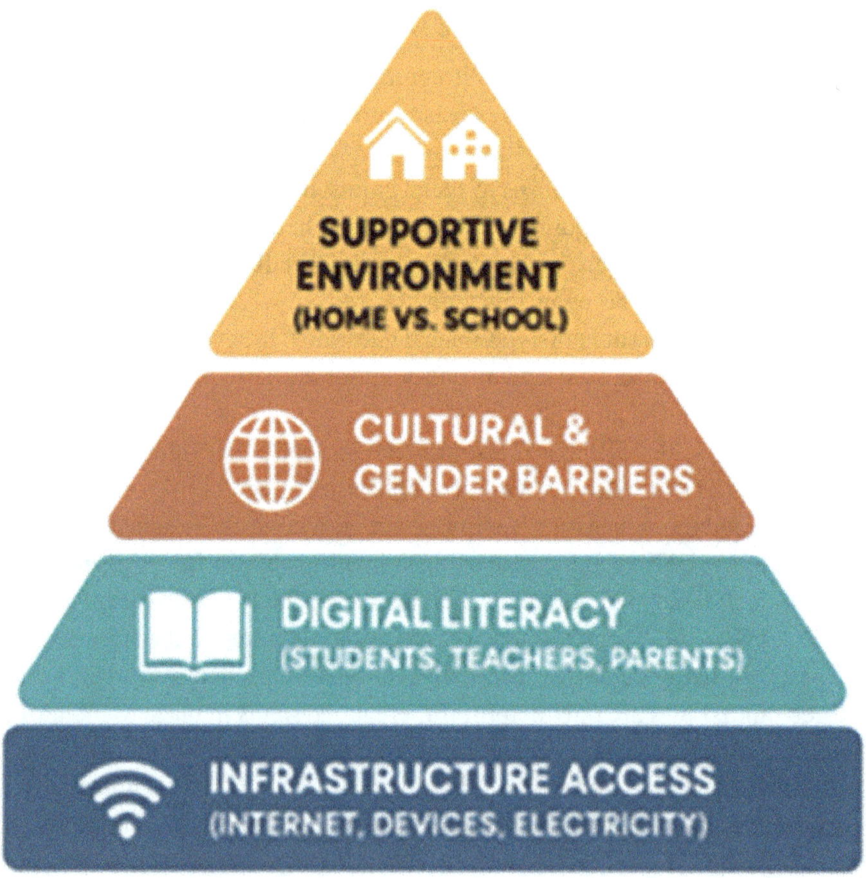

The figure represents a multi-level model of a pyramid that would be used to demonstrate the aspect of the digital divide in the education sector. At the very bottom of the pyramid lies the level of Infrastructure Access that may include critical areas, including internet access points, availability of devices, and the emergence of electricity. On ascending, the second layer is the issue of Digital Literacy, a term used to signify the different skills and abilities of students, teachers and even parents to use digital tools. On top of the layer, we have Cultural and Gender Barriers, which are social norms and preferences that may restrict equitable access to technologies. At the apex of the pyramid is the Supportive Environment, which alerts to the variability in the home and school environments of facilitating or inhibiting digital learning. All these layers are supported by ordinary icons to explain the ideas.

CASE STUDIES IN GLOBAL EDUCATIONAL LEADERSHIP AND TECHNOLOGY INTEGRATION

Teaching administrators across the globe are facing educational issues as well as a prospective challenge in brainstorming in a bid to integrate artificial intelligence (AI) and social media in their learning institutions. Such efforts are flavoured by the social, political, and economic environment within which they shape schools and universities, but also by the basic ability of these technologies on their own scales. The examples of cross-cultural case studies below, covering Finland, Bangladesh, Rwanda, and Brazil, represent the implementation of different education systems and their leaders in dealing with the complexity of technology integration, and in many cases, a sense of sustainability and equity. Altogether, the cases clarify important questions of leadership, flexibility, and the continuous dilemma of promoting innovation and maintaining inclusiveness.

Finland, a leading country in terms of progressive education, tends to apply the technology-infusion more carefully with pedagogical consideration. At both primary school and university, there are high levels of teacher autonomy and cooperation in Finnish classrooms, attributes that are important in the successful introduction of AI tools (Koski et al., 2024). Instead of following the rush to implement, only because new technologies are available, the Finnish leaders have concentrated on making sure that AI applications are consistent with the long-standing promises of equity and all-around student growth that have defined the nation. Consequently, the use of AI-powered systems is primarily to aid in individualised learning programs and to be able to identify potential learning difficulties as early as possible, without exception, along with the instructor's discretion and sensitivity to student needs. Another example of successful integration is that of Bangladesh, which uses a model of public-private partnerships. The partnership between the governmental agencies, nongovernmental organisations, and information-communication-technology sector has led to the creation and mass deployment of digital curricula that focus specifically on digital literacy and civic engagement-related competencies (Riaz et al., 2020). Though the overall structure of the nation in terms of public education can be regarded as on the modest end, the program has not only been thriving, but mainly in the cases of underserved and rural communities.

Another integration model of focused integration is in Rwanda. The educational leadership of the country has put much emphasis on aligning AI-enabled tools with the future of education more generally, such as social inclusion and the furtherance of national development (Mwansa et al., 2025). All these are aimed at achieving these outcomes by setting up community-based digital learning centres, increasing the scope of teacher preparation and using AI-assisted open educational resources. An example of the integration of the systems on a large scale can be seen in Brazil. The Digital Access Program was the initiative introduced on the state level in 2019 to provide digital resources and access to over 100,000 schools in the nation (Pozzer & dos Reis Neuhold, 2025). The program has used social media, inexpensive devices, and selected open educational material to increase access to education materials in an equitable manner.

Collectively, they indicate how complex technological integration can be, and how numerous factors arose in it, structural, social, cultural, and economic, impacting educational practice. They demonstrate that successful leadership does not depend only on technological know-how but also on resilience and a highly sensitive orientation to the context-dependent needs of the population of learners. Social media is also used cautiously, typically to foster professional communities and support for educators rather than directly engaging students, which helps avoid some of the common issues like distraction or misinformation. This case illustrates how leadership based on trust and shared goals can promote sustainable use of technology that enhances rather than replaces human involvement. On the other hand, Bangladesh offers a very different picture, characterised by fast changes but also significant infrastructural limitations. Education leaders there operate within a context of scarce resources and significant gaps between urban and rural areas. Despite these challenges, innovative leadership has been able to make some important progress through government initiatives such as “Digital Bangladesh.” At the secondary and higher education levels, AI-powered learning management systems have increasingly been introduced to complement in-person teaching, especially following the disruptions caused by the COVID-19 pandemic. In modern informal learning experiences, social networking sites like Facebook and YouTube have become a crucial online tool for marginalised groups to have opportunities to access learning materials and those who share common interests. However, these benefits are not without their burdens: the facilitation and preservation of equal access; the protection of privacy on data; and addressing faculty resistance to using new digital opportunities. Bangladesh's experience shows that sound leadership requires bold objectives, simultaneously without being insensitive to pragmatic limitations and the exploitation of local people. Rwanda presents a valuable case study of the way in which a coherent national development strategy can be built on technological integration. Educational technology holds a pivotal role in economic growth and transforming societal trends developed by Vision 2050 (Sooryamoorthy, 2023). At a tertiary level, the University of Rwanda uses analytics based on AI to track student progress and to provide customised support services. Simultaneously, there is a push to introduce young students to social media literacy in a bid to develop a digitally literate citizenry that can serve the enlarging knowledge economy. Although Rwandan teachers operate under an impoverished infrastructure, they incorporate technological advancements in interdisciplinary and international collaborations, which highlights the significance of partnerships with the private sector and international donors. This example shows how visionary leadership can adopt technology as a tool of inclusive growth and achievement of sustainable development goals.

The context of Brazil, with its strong socioeconomic divisions, makes the strength of the grassroots movement in the development of technology deployment even more prominent. Due to the unbalanced nature of digital penetration, unequal access to digital resources is common in public schools in favelas. In contrast, more affluent private schools are more likely to implement advanced technologies (Pinto, 2021). Political leaders are forced to operate in a complicated sociopolitical context where distrust of all-powerful hierarchies and fears of social stratification and hyper-technology are prevalent. Despite this, community groups use social media, including Instagram and TikTok, to promote participatory learning and civic participation by the marginalised youth. Digital storytelling projects help young people learn to connect and tell their stories through digital literacy beyond the academic walls. Brazilian teachers emphasise co-creation and empowerment policies, and support technology policies focused on local demands as opposed to fixed policies handed down by a centralised authority. The case of Rwanda proves that integration of leadership, inclusive and context-sensitive, is essential to fair technology adoption. In total, these case studies give us several lessons on educational leadership. First, the implementation of AI and social media is not only determined by the complexity of technology, but rather by human aspects, specifically dynamic leadership, stakeholder involvement, cultural awareness, and continuous moral questioning. In both the middle-resourced setting, like in Finland and in the developing country setting, like in Rwanda, collaborative and fair methods produce more sustainable results. Second, there is no exaggeration when it comes to the salience of contextual particularities. The approaches shown to be successful in one system or grade level are invalid in another unless approached with sensitivity. Digital divides can only be minimised by understanding the local existence thoroughly, including infrastructure, social disparities, and cultural demands and expectations. Third, equity remains a constant concern. Educational leaders must actively work to close gaps in access, skills, and representation to make sure technology acts as a bridge rather than a barrier. However, challenges persist. Across all these examples, tensions remain between the hopeful potential of AI-driven personalisation and concerns about surveillance, data privacy violations, and algorithmic bias. Leaders in these diverse settings are often tasked with balancing innovation with caution, promoting critical digital literacy and ethical awareness among both educators and students. The governance of technology integration often involves working through fragmented policies, budget constraints, and competing interests. Successful leaders are often described as being strategic planners who are skilled at adapting to problems and have high-quality, inclusive communication skills.

IMPLICATIONS FOR HUMAN CAPITAL DEVELOPMENT AND ECONOMIC SUSTAINABILITY

In today's fast-changing global economy, the importance of education as a key driver of human capital development has never been more apparent. The modern spread of artificial intelligence (AI) and the epidemic of social media settings have caused significant changes in educational systems that are not limited to the traditional learning activities but affect economic sustainability and social progress on a large scale. Sustainable education, which is based on the affordances of digital technologies, is conceptualised by scholarly discourse as one of the critical mechanisms in terms of increasing employability level, hastening digital entrepreneurship and reinforcing cognitive competencies as well as educational outcomes that are better aligned to the needs of the labour market. The discussion below questions the associations, upon which these developments thrive, and explains how they are helpful towards long-term national economic stability and national-building at large. The first of the direct impacts of education with the assistance of AI is its ability to expand employability. The modern labour market is marked by a high rate of change, and routine jobs continue to be automated and new professions requiring the combination of high-level digital skills and non-technical skills like creativity, flexibility, and analytical thinking to appear (Cox, 2021). Individualised learning steps and flexible education programmes are implemented with the help of AI-powered platforms to address these changes and provide personalised content, instantaneous feedback, and a constant skill-evaluation system tailored to the strong and weak points of the learners (Trajkovski & Hayes, 2025). In exemplary fashion, adaptive learning technologies can empower students and working professionals to eliminate digital-literacy gaps and lock in technical expertise, thus preparing them to enter the field of emerging data-science expertise, cybersecurity, and AI ethics. At the same time, social media is a supportive facilitator, providing places of professional networking and keeping communities of practice alive, which are independent of traditional classrooms and support career development.

Furthermore, the education powered by AI and mediated by social processes is becoming positively entwined with the development of digital entrepreneurship, which proves to be an even greater trigger of economic growth in various environments, both developed and developing. Digital spaces can bypass most of the historical obstacles to becoming an entrepreneur, allowing new business owners to reach markets, funding, mentorship, and customers with little difficulty. Learners develop entrepreneurial skills, develop feasible business models, and engage in a peer-learning network via the available online courses, interactive webinars, and social-networking groups that strengthen their businesses (Palmquist et al., 2025). The latter mechanisms are especially relevant when there are no or few formal employment opportunities, and digital entrepreneurship presents a plausible alternative pathway to the economy and youth empowerment (Baxter et al., 2022). Therefore, education policy leaders are forced to prioritise not only imparting learners with domain-specific vocational skills but with an entrepreneurial mindset and the ability to operate within a digitalised environment that is changing very rapidly, aspects without which innovation and adaptation in a continuously changing global context are impossible.

The development of cognitive skills, in particular higher-order skills including those of critical reasoning, creativity and metacognition, too, has received significant assistance via AI-assisted learning platforms. In contrast to memorisation-based pedagogies, most AI systems frequently facilitate active participant interaction by requiring the analysis of encrypted data, solving complex problems, and automating critical thinking about the learning process (Chasokela & Hlongwane, 2025). The effects are further enhanced by social media, which enables collaborative knowledge building, provides peer feedback, and introduces learners to a wide variety of opinions, which are the necessary conditions to develop critical thinking in the current world of digitalisation (Meirbekov et al., 2022). The combination of these platforms nurtures students ready to face complex, not-so-much-black-or-white problems, a positive trait in the modern knowledge economy. Also important is the enhancement of the congruence between education programmes and labour-market needs, which is easier to achieve with the help of the data-driven analytical power of AI. Learning analytics and labour-market-information systems are being exploited by governments, education institutions and employers to identify current skill deficiencies, future labour demands and to design the curricula that cater to current labour conditions with flexibilities to adapt to changing labour dynamics (Kopackova et al., 2024). The resulting inter-sectoral collaboration will keep educational innovations within the development of economies that develop a resilient, future-ready workforce. Lifelong partnerships, e.g., help to co-create content based on issues that workers are facing daily at their jobs, and the policies of lifelong learning help support lifelong upskilling and reskilling during the work life of individuals (Field, 2020). The consequences of these combined strategies on economic sustainability and nation-building are tremendous. The success of an economy is benchmarked by human capital, which has traditionally been interpreted as its fundamental pillar of development, stability, and innovation. The development of agile, responsive education systems able to use the power of AI and social media to provide an inclusive, high-quality approach to learning produces a more successful, flexible and interested population. This kind of stability strengthens national capabilities available to resolve intricate challenges, such as demographic transitions, changes in weather, and an accelerating rate of technological change. (Wang et al., 2024). Moreover, through the emphasis on fair access and inclusive approaches, sustainable education will also contribute to the mitigation of social inequalities and subsequent social cohesion; it is the key to stable governance and democratic government.

However, these potential advantages are conditional and linked to a solid governance structure, extensive infrastructure, and clear policy structures. Without an adequate investment into digital infrastructures, teacher professional learning and effective data-governance processes, the transformative power of AI and social media may be uselessly distributed and can even worsen the existing disparities. The issue of ethical privacy of data security, algorithmic bias, and online surveillance are topics that also require constant supervision to protect the rights and dignity of learners. Finally, AI and social media-driven education have significant potential to evolve human capital and support the sustainability of the economy. These technologies have the potential to make significant contributions to the process of nations building and economic resilience by enhancing employability, enhancing digital entrepreneurship, deepening critical cognitive skills and developing greater alignment with labour-market demands. However, realisation of this potential would need multisectoral cooperation, inclusive policymaking, and imperturbable ethical custodianship. As the educational landscape continues to evolve, it is vital that stakeholders work together to create learning ecosystems that are innovative, equitable, sustainable, and attuned to the complexities of the 21st-century economy.

POLICY AND MANAGERIAL RECOMMENDATIONS

In modern educational frameworks, the current proliferation of artificial intelligence (AI), social media, and other associated technologies of the digital world has highlighted the need to consider policy development in a strategic context. The digital transformation follows an increase in pace, which equally offers educators, policymakers, and administrators both essential opportunities and challenges. This gives rise to the imminence of real-world advice, magnified by empirical bases and practice of advice that can guide investment decisions, development of laws and regulations, and development of infrastructures among capacity-building programs. In the following overview, pertinent suggestions that can be made based on the recent scholarship are synthesised with the focus on the ideas of coherence, inclusivity, and robust monitoring and evaluation systems, which could have dealt with making digital education reforms sustainable and fair. In the first place, policymakers must focus on strategic investment in digital infrastructure. The lack of good-quality internet access, modern and well-maintained equipment, and effective data management solutions highlights any attempt to automate education with the usage of AI or social media and causes such an initiative to be fragmented or unavailable to significant proportions of students. Second, the policy interventions need to be adjusted to the peculiarities of various institutional settings. A generic strategy is not likely to cover the non-homogeneous technological, societal, and cultural realities of various education systems (Sonetti et al., 2020).

Third, policies are necessary to ensure that context-specific uses accompany generic competences of digital skills. The opportunities presented by integrating AI and social media in education do not generate only competencies related to traditional digital tools, e.g., word processing, web searching, and data analysis, but promote an extended range of domain-specific competencies that have their origins in social, cultural, and pedagogical space (H. Zhang & Tian, 2025). Fourth, the policy mechanisms should refer to addressing the digital divide. Since the affordances of digital technologies are heterogeneous, policymakers should explicitly acknowledge and work on inequities of access, affordability, and digital literacy, especially among disadvantaged groups within and between contexts (Memon & Memon, 2024). Fifth, fair access to digital devices and internet connectivity must be established not just throughout the regular hours of learning but also thereafter. Learning experiences are also increasingly transferred to non-formal contexts, including family life, extra-curricular activities, and leisure activities, which all require similar digital infrastructures (Allaste et al., 2022).

Sixth, institutional preparedness is essential before the implementation of large-scale initiatives. Educational institutions' readiness goes beyond the technical abilities but also includes the leadership, professional growth, pedagogical shift, and cultural adjustments necessary to institute and successfully incorporate technology into the curriculum (Grimus, 2020). Seventh, implementation ought to use an iterative, staged roll-up as opposed to one big rollout as a pathway to implementation. Incrementalism encourages flexibility, teaching innovation, and social learning, and thus reduces the chances of a system breakdown (Tan, 2023). Eighth, stakeholder engagement should be whole-hearted and iterative. The collaborative construction of digital education solutions cannot be possible and practical without meaningful input by teachers, students, parents, community members, and other stakeholders (Ari et al., 2022). Ninth, the evaluation frameworks need to be designed before the evaluation and should include both the quantitative and qualitative aspects. Efficient assessment helps to improve the digital education programs constantly and ensures the relevance of policy solutions to the changing situations (Alenezi, 2023).

The overall implications of these guidelines are massive. A strategic orientation concentrated on coherence, inclusivity, and vigorous monitoring and evaluation empowers policymakers, school leaders, and administrators to make the most of AI and social media capacities, yet also meet the challenges of digital transformation to a full extent. This coherence, inclusiveness and evaluation are preconditions to reforms that are sustainable and equitable in type. Governments and educational bodies need to focus on expanding broadband access, especially in rural and underserved areas, where digital divides are often the widest. Investment should also cover more than just hardware, software platforms, learning management systems, and data analytics tools that enable personalised learning. However, these investments must be planned with a long-term view in mind, considering ongoing maintenance, scalability, and the risk of technologies becoming obsolete too quickly, which could otherwise lead to wasted resources. Alongside investment, robust regulatory safeguards are equally necessary. Growing concerns about data privacy, algorithmic biases, and the ethical implications of AI mean that clear policies need to be put in place regarding the collection, storage, and usage of educational data. Policymakers would do well to align these regulations with international frameworks such as the GDPR and UNESCO's AI Ethics Recommendations, while adapting them thoughtfully to local contexts.

Furthermore, responsibilities must be clearly defined among educational institutions, technology providers, and third-party vendors, with mechanisms for accountability and recourse in cases of misuse or breaches. Without such legal clarity, trust in digital learning innovations may falter, hindering their adoption. Developing digital infrastructure is closely tied to the need for comprehensive capacity-building programs. Experience shows that simply investing in technology does not guarantee success unless educators, administrators, and students themselves are equipped with the necessary digital skills and pedagogical know-how. Professional development programs need to move beyond one-off workshops to continuous, embedded learning experiences that build both technical competence and a critical understanding of AI's educational and ethical implications. Leadership training for school administrators is also essential to help them guide digital transformations effectively, manage resistance to change, and nurture inclusive, innovation-friendly learning environments (Buchanan et al., 2022). Capacity-building efforts should also focus on students, fostering digital citizenship skills so that learners can navigate online spaces responsibly and critically.

For maximum effectiveness, policy coherence is a must. Digital education policies cannot operate in isolation but need to be harmonised with broader national development plans, labour market strategies, and social inclusion policies. Without such coordination, fragmented or contradictory policies risk creating implementation gaps and duplicated efforts. For example, digital education initiatives will likely falter if they are not supported by complementary health, infrastructure, and social welfare policies addressing barriers faced by disadvantaged learners. Inter-ministerial collaboration and inclusive consultation with educators, students, parents, civil society, and the private sector can foster policy designs that are integrated, context-sensitive, and widely accepted. This approach also builds stronger legitimacy and ownership of policies. Inclusivity must be placed at the centre of all policy and managerial decisions around technology integration. Marginalised groups, including girls, learners with disabilities, ethnic minorities, and low-income families, often suffer disproportionately from digital divides. Therefore, targeted policies are needed to prevent these learners from being left behind. Digital education reform requires, among others, the creation of accessibility regulation of the content and platforms, device subsidisation or distribution schemes, and the encouragement of universal pedagogical practices that take advantage of technology to meet the diverse learning needs. The idea of equity needs to be integrated with monitoring systems, and data collection should be done not just in showing access in general, but in showing the response and the participation of specific demographic groups.

The monitoring and evaluation (M&E) mechanisms cannot be avoided to ensure that the digital education reforms are still objective-oriented. Constant data collection and analysis allow stakeholders to evaluate technology integration, define obstacles, and perform the necessary adjustments promptly. M&E frameworks entail indicators as per policy priorities such as infrastructure deployment, capacity development, innovations in teaching, equity, and performance of learners. Educators and students' qualitative insights enhance the evaluation process since they can capture the situational aspects and experiences that might not be represented in numerical measures. Accountability can be improved by open reporting and the publication of the results of the research, which makes it easier to learn collectively. National-level recommendations are not the only action that has to take place in educational institutions: they too need to play an active part in developing digital leadership. It implies expressing a consistent strategy on technology application that aligns with institutional mission and values, the promotion of experiments and innovations, and the maintenance of constant dialogue on ethical and pedagogical issues arising due to AI and social media. Technological decisions should be made cross-functionally and well-balanced by the establishment of IT specialists, curriculum designers and the teaching staff of the institutional managers. Additionally, the leadership must ensure enough resources and win favourable partnerships with its technology accelerators and ensure that the digital projects are faithfully carried out to shun fragmentation.

The managerial policies and strategies must be made flexible and adaptable. The world of digital technologies tends to change quickly, and the strategies that are working today can be outdated in a short period of time. Consequently, horizon scanning, reiterated piloting, and third-party feedback mechanisms are necessary to pilot projects to predict change and reset projects. This forward-looking posture must be supplemented by risk management strategies that will govern the potential of digital exhaustion, data overuse, or increasing disparities. A comprehensive policy and managerial approach requiring investment, control, capacity building, inclusivity, and non-exempt investigation would be needed to integrate AI and social media into the education sector successfully. The education systems can leverage the power of digital transformation to facilitate sustainable and quality learning by encouraging the promotion of cross-sector coherence, the prioritisation of equitable access, and the development of leadership competencies. It requires long-term dedication, teamwork, and moral diligence so that technology can be used not as a system of disempowerment but one of empowerment.

CONCLUSION

Artificial intelligence (AI) and social media integration into the educational systems are a unique chance to create sustainable, inclusive, and transforming learning settings. Although integration holds some notable potential, it is itself more complex and requires an appropriate understanding of the capabilities of the technology and constant awareness of the issues and ethical dilemmas it entails. Artificial intelligence and social media can no longer be seen as merely objects of application, but instead as drivers of redefining the process of teaching, learning, and experiencing education, which is necessary to address the new demands of the twenty-first-century learners, societies, and economies. One of the main insights is that sustainable education supported by AI and social media cannot be disconnected from leadership that involves critical thinking, flexibility, and firm adherence to equity. Digital transformation of education is not a simple technological update, but it is essentially a big change process in an organisation. The leaders will have to balance innovation, inclusiveness, agility, stability, and technological possibilities with a base of human values. Therefore, leadership needs to wisely weigh the potential of AI, i.e., personalised learning, data-driven decision-making, and improved connectivity, in boosting equity, and should avoid building or deepening the already-present disparities. This bilateral mandate makes educational leadership the centre of digital adoption, ethical stewardship and social justice practice.

The case studies that were given throughout the chapter demonstrate how far the integration of AI and social media in education can be conditioned by contextual factors. The reflective, pedagogy-focused approach of Finland is set in contrast against the adventurous antics of Bangladesh amid limited infrastructure, a futurist approach towards the national development goals in Rwanda, and the bottom-top empowering practices of Brazil. Nonetheless, successful leadership always responds to local conditions of doing business, such as cultural norms, resource access, and governance, as well as a broad range of stakeholders, including teachers, students and parents, policymakers, and private partners. Technology, when properly done, does not become the mechanism of exclusion; instead, it becomes the real facilitating means of learning and empowerment. This chapter also explains the greater aspects of AI and social media in terms of human capital and the sustainability of an economy. The inventions which make use of these technologies enhance the possibilities of employability and entrepreneurship and help develop the higher-order cognitive skills that are necessary to succeed in a world of uncertainties and increased complexity. Moreover, better matching processes of education with labour-market needs may improve economic stability and societal development. However, this potential will be hindered by the need for cross-sector cooperation, uniform policy frameworks, and governance systems which connect education with labour, infrastructure, and social welfare sectors. Education leadership should therefore not simply be individual leadership within a single institution, but more of systems and strategic thinking, leadership and partnerships. The managerial and policy directions presented in the chapter highlight the need for a holistic and interrelated response to digital education transformation. The key to the responsible use of technology is establishing decent digital infrastructure and providing transparent rules that protect data privacy and guarantee that algorithms are fair. Simultaneously, capacity-building activities relating to ongoing professional growth enable educators and leaders to utilise AI and social media productively in terms of intellectual principles and ethical accountability. The essence of these suggestions is the focus on inclusivity: sustainable education can become a reality only when there is specific attention to marginalised communities and bridging the digital divide. Accountability, learning, and continuous improvement also rely on the strenuous monitoring and evaluation systems. Moreover, AI and social media leadership should be more fluid as opposed to stubborn. The fast-changing nature of technology demands horizon scanning, piloting activities, and active involvement of the membership of stakeholders over a long period of foresight, adjusting strategies as needs arise. The moral issues that will guide decision-making should be upstream rather than downstream: data management, risks of surveillance, bias in the algorithm, and respect for student autonomy. At the same time, it is crucial to promote critical digital literacy among teachers and students not only as a skill of becoming technically proficient but also as the skill of developing reflective, responsible forms of digital citizenship. Despite the potential power of AI and social media being so significant, the chapter warns against invocations that are unachievable. Technology is not a silver bullet, but it depends on the purpose, values, and leaders accompanying the implementation of technology. Without inclusive policies, equal access, and long-lasting capacity-building work, digital education programs can promote social inequality and reduce the quality of education. A blind eye towards moral demands is also capable of removing trust and violating the dignity and rights of learners. Ethical and responsible leadership is consequently imperative to guarantee that AI and social media become entities of empowerment as opposed to isolation.

Moving in the future, the integration of AI and social media into the field of education will become even more intricate and comprehensive. New opportunities and challenges will be brought by novel innovations like AI-based assessments, immersive learning technologies and worldwide digital citizenship education. These developments must be explored in future research and practice; however, it is important to consider them through the prism of participatory governance, intercultural sensitivity, and sustainability. Finding a balance between high-aspiring innovation and the defence of central values of education equality, inclusion, human dignity, and democratic life will continue to be necessary. The current chapter invites educational leaders, policymakers, and practitioners to think of AI and social media as transgressive agents who are naturally ingrained within a broader social construct rather than construed as independent agents. The process of nurturing sustainable education by harmonising them requires a strategic, inclusive, ethical and dynamic leadership. Through this undertaking, educational leaders will be able to contribute to making the learning ecosystem sustainable, fair, active, and responsive to preparing learners towards the future labour market as well as contributing well to a rapidly shifting world.

REFERENCES

Abdullah, M. A. (2022). Using the educational tablet: An evaluation study of teachers' and pupils' views in Egyptian primary schools. *Education and Information Technologies*, *27*(6), 8771–8792. DOI: 10.1007/s10639-022-10958-0

Alenezi, M. (2023). Digital Learning and Digital Institution in Higher Education. *Education Sciences*, *13*(1), 88. DOI: 10.3390/educsci13010088

Allaste, A.-A., Beilmann, M., & Pirk, R. (2022). Non-formal and Informal Learning as Citizenship Education: The Views of Young People and Youth Policymakers. *Journal of Applied Youth Studies*, *5*(1), 19–35. DOI: 10.1007/s43151-021-00059-z

Ari, R., Altinay, Z., Altinay, F., Dagli, G., & Ari, E. (2022). Sustainable Management and Policies: The Roles of Stakeholders in the Practice of Inclusive Education in Digital Transformation. *Electronics (Basel)*, *11*(4), 585. DOI: 10.3390/electronics11040585

Balzer, W. K. (2020). *Lean Higher Education*. Productivity Press., DOI: 10.4324/9781351216944

Banerjee-Batist, R., Gajjar, K., Saxena, P., Smetana, J. B., & Muduli, A. (2022). Leadership response to COVID-19: A comparative analysis of the education sector in USA and India. *Human Resource Development International*, *25*(3), 321–341. DOI: 10.1080/13678868.2022.2073119

Baxter, M., Novy-Marx, M., & D'Angelo, S. (2022). Improving pathways for girls and disadvantaged youth through secondary education and into work: Evidence and reflections from practice. *Development Policy Review*, *40*(S2), e12651. Advance online publication. DOI: 10.1111/dpr.12651

Bernasconi, E., Redavid, D., & Ferilli, S. (2025). Enhancing Personalised Learning with a Context-Aware Intelligent Question-Answering System and Automated Frequently Asked Question Generation. *Electronics (Basel)*, *14*(7), 1481. DOI: 10.3390/electronics14071481

Boyadjieva, P., & Ilieva-Trichkova, P. (2021). *Adult Education as an Agency and Empowerment Process.*, DOI: 10.1007/978-3-030-67136-5_4

Burns, L., Le Roux, N., Kalesnik-Orszulak, R., Christian, J., Hukkelhoven, M., Rockhold, F., & O'Donnell, J. (2022). Real-World Evidence for Regulatory Decision-Making: Guidance From Around the World. *Clinical Therapeutics*, *44*(3), 420–437. DOI: 10.1016/j.clinthera.2022.01.012 PMID: 35181179

Chasokela, D., & Hlongwane, J. (2025). *Assessing Higher-Order and Critical Skills in the Era of Artificial Intelligence.*, DOI: 10.4018/979-8-3693-6351-5.ch010

Chen, A. M. H., Brown, S., Mark, K., & McBane, S. (2023). An overview of Instructional approaches and decision-making strategies to curtail curricular overload. *American Journal of Pharmaceutical Education, 87*(8), 100013. DOI: 10.1016/j.ajpe.2022.12.001 PMID: 37597910

Chopra, A., Patel, H., Rajput, D. S., & Bansal, N. (2024). *Empowering Inclusive Education: Leveraging AI-ML and Innovative Tech Stacks to Support Students with Learning Disabilities in Higher Education* (pp. 255–275). DOI: 10.1007/978-981-97-0914-4_15

Cox, A. M. (2021). Exploring the impact of Artificial Intelligence and robots on higher education through literature-based design fictions. *International Journal of Educational Technology in Higher Education, 18*(1), 3. DOI: 10.1186/s41239-020-00237-8

Czerniewicz, L., & Carvalho, L. (2022). Open, Distance, and Digital Education (ODDE) – An Equity View. In *Handbook of Open, Distance and Digital Education* (pp. 1–20). Springer Nature Singapore. DOI: 10.1007/978-981-19-0351-9_93-1

Darling-Hammond, L., Flook, L., Cook-Harvey, C., Barron, B., & Osher, D. (2020). Implications for educational practice of the science of learning and development. *Applied Developmental Science, 24*(2), 97–140. DOI: 10.1080/10888691.2018.1537791

Demeke, W. (2024). *Selective Integration.*, DOI: 10.4018/979-8-3693-8130-4.ch005

Dlamini, R., Ramatsetse, B., Zenda, R., Gorimbo, J., & Mpungose, C. B. (2024). *Establishing Professional Communities of Practice to Enhance Teacher Development in Technical Schools.*, DOI: 10.1007/978-3-031-58206-6_11

Emon, M. M. H. (2025a). Leveraging AI on Social Media & Digital Platforms to Enhance English Language Teaching and Learning. In *AI-Powered English Teaching* (pp. 211–238). IGI Global Scientific Publishing., DOI: 10.4018/979-8-3373-1952-0.ch007

Emon, M. M. H. (2025b). Circularity Meets AI: Revolutionizing Consumer Engagement Through Green Marketing. In *Transforming Business Practices With AI-Powered Green Marketing* (pp. 169–208). IGI Global Scientific Publishing. DOI: 10.4018/979-8-3373-3017-4.ch007

Emon, M. M. H., & Mazid-Ul-Haque, M. (2025). Balancing Usability and Security: Enhancing User Experience Without Compromising Privacy. In *User-Centric Cybersecurity Implications for Sustainable Digital Transformation* (pp. 309–342). IGI Global Scientific Publishing. DOI: 10.4018/979-8-3373-3171-3.ch010

Fayed, I., & Cummings, J. (Eds.). (2021). *Teaching in the Post COVID-19 Era*. Springer International Publishing., DOI: 10.1007/978-3-030-74088-7

Field, J. (2020). Lifelong Learning for Working People. In *Encyclopedia of Education and Information Technologies* (pp. 1093–1104). Springer International Publishing., DOI: 10.1007/978-3-030-10576-1_61

George, B., & Wooden, O. (2023). Managing the Strategic Transformation of Higher Education through Artificial Intelligence. *Administrative Sciences*, *13*(9), 196. DOI: 10.3390/admsci13090196

González, C., Ponce, D., & Fernández, V. (2023). Teachers' experiences of teaching online during COVID-19: Implications for postpandemic professional development. *Educational Technology Research and Development*, *71*(1), 55–78. DOI: 10.1007/s11423-023-10200-9 PMID: 36785811

Grande, V., Kinnunen, P., Peters, A.-K., Barr, M., Cajander, Å., Daniels, M., Lewis, A. N., Sabin, M., Sánchez-Peña, M., & Thota, N. (2022). Role Modeling as a Computing Educator in Higher Education. *Proceedings of the 2022 Working Group Reports on Innovation and Technology in Computer Science Education*, 37–63. DOI: 10.1145/3571785.3574122

Grimus, M. (2020). *Emerging Technologies: Impacting Learning*. Pedagogy and Curriculum Development., DOI: 10.1007/978-981-15-0618-5_8

Gupta, M., & Kiran, R. (2025). Digital exclusion of women: A systematic review. *Global Knowledge, Memory and Communication*, *74*(3/4), 938–957. DOI: 10.1108/GKMC-12-2022-0301

Hakimi, L., Eynon, R., & Murphy, V. A. (2021). The Ethics of Using Digital Trace Data in Education: A Thematic Review of the Research Landscape. *Review of Educational Research*, *91*(5), 671–717. DOI: 10.3102/00346543211020116

Hariram, N. P., Mekha, K. B., Suganthan, V., & Sudhakar, K. (2023). Sustainalism: An Integrated Socio-Economic-Environmental Model to Address Sustainable Development and Sustainability. *Sustainability (Basel)*, *15*(13), 10682. DOI: 10.3390/su151310682

Hilli, C. (2020). Extending classrooms through teacher collaboration in Virtual Learning Environments. *Educational Action Research*, *28*(4), 700–715. DOI: 10.1080/09650792.2019.1654901

Jiménez-Aleixandre, M. P., & Puig, B. (2022). *Educating Critical Citizens to Face Post-truth: The Time Is Now* (pp. 3–19). DOI: 10.1007/978-3-030-92006-7_1

Karakose, T., Polat, H., Tülübaş, T., & Demirkol, M. (2024). A Review of the Conceptual Structure and Evolution of Digital Leadership Research in Education. *Education Sciences*, *14*(11), 1166. DOI: 10.3390/educsci14111166

Khan, T., Emon, M. M. H., & Nath, A. (2024). Quantifying the Effects of AI-Driven Inventory Management on Operational Efficiency in Online Retail. *2024 27th International Conference on Computer and Information Technology (ICCIT)*, 2092–2097. DOI: 10.1109/ICCIT64611.2024.11021996

Khan, T., Emon, M. M. H., Rahman, K. M., Nipa, M. N., & Fuad, M. N. (2025). The Role of AI in Driving Customer Engagement Through Technological, Organizational and Environmental Enablers in E-Commerce. *2025 International Conference on Quantum Photonics, Artificial Intelligence, and Networking (QPAIN)*, 1–6. DOI: 10.1109/QPAIN66474.2025.11171949

Khan, T., Emon, M. M. H., & Rahman, M. A. (2024a). A systematic review on exploring the influence of Industry 4.0 technologies to enhance supply chain visibility and operational efficiency. *Review of Business and Economics Studies*, *12*(3), 6–27. DOI: 10.26794/2308-944X-2024-12-3-6-27

Khan, T., & Hasan Emon, M. M. (2024). Determinants of AI Image Generator Adoption Among Marketing Agencies: The Mediating Effects of Perceived Usefulness. *2024 IEEE 3rd International Conference on Robotics, Automation, Artificial-Intelligence and Internet-of-Things (RAAICON)*, 177–182. DOI: 10.1109/RAAICON64172.2024.10928548

Khilji, S. E. (2022). An Approach for Humanizing Leadership Education: Building Learning Community & Stakeholder Engagement. *Journal of Management Education*, *46*(3), 439–471. DOI: 10.1177/10525629211041355

Kopackova, H., Simonova, S., & Reimannova, I. (2024). Digital transformation leaders wanted: How to prepare students for the ever-changing demands of the labor market. *International Journal of Management Education*, *22*(1), 100943. DOI: 10.1016/j.ijme.2024.100943

Koski, J., Metsäpelto, R.-L., Kyllönen, M., & Poikkeus, A.-M. (2024). Finnish student teachers as a focus of teacher education research: A 10-Year scoping review of empirical research. *Educational Review*, •••, 1–24. DOI: 10.1080/00131911.2024.2432256

Lee, H. Y., Hamid, M. O., & Hardy, I. (2023). Language and education policies in Southeast Asia: Reorienting towards multilingualism-as-resource. *International Journal of Multilingualism, 20*(3), 1106–1124. DOI: 10.1080/14790718.2021.2002333

Lin, C.-C., Huang, A. Y. Q., & Lu, O. H. T. (2023). Artificial intelligence in intelligent tutoring systems toward sustainable education: A systematic review. *Smart Learning Environments, 10*(1), 41. DOI: 10.1186/s40561-023-00260-y

Linzalone, R., Ammirato, S., Felicetti, A. M., Corvello, V., & Santarsiero, F. (2024). Exploring stakeholder engagement network behavior: Strategic and managerial implications for corporate social responsibility. *Business Ethics, the Environment & Responsibility*. Advance online publication. DOI: 10.1111/beer.12692

Mahmoud, S. E., & Mousa, M. E.-S. (2025). Does benevolent leadership affect the organizational identification of nursing staff? The mediating role of forgiveness climate and the moderating role of positive emotions. *Future Business Journal, 11*(1), 35. DOI: 10.1186/s43093-025-00442-9

Mandinach, E. B., & Gummer, E. S. (2025). Shining Light on Ethical Uses of Data in Education: Emerging Importance. *Teachers College Record, 127*(2), 141–162. DOI: 10.1177/01614681251334784

Meirbekov, A., Maslova, I., & Gallyamova, Z. (2022). Digital education tools for critical thinking development. *Thinking Skills and Creativity, 44*, 101023. DOI: 10.1016/j.tsc.2022.101023

Memon, F. N., & Memon, S. N. (2024). *Digital Divide and Equity in Education.*, DOI: 10.4018/979-8-3693-1854-6.ch004

Miao, Q., & Nduneseokwu, C. (2024). Advancing Environmental Leadership: Education, Development, and Training. In *Environmental Leadership in a VUCA Era* (pp. 467–538). Springer Nature Singapore. DOI: 10.1007/978-981-96-0324-4_10

Morze, N., & Trybulska, E. S. (2021). Web-based community-supported online education during the COVID-19 pandemic. *International Journal of Web Based Communities, 17*(1), 9. DOI: 10.1504/IJWBC.2021.112858

Mousumi, M. A. (2023). Access and equity: What do we know about government primary school students' remote learning experience during school closures in Bangladesh? *Kokusai Kyoiku Kyoryoku Ronshu, 25*(1), 80–95. DOI: 10.1108/JICE-07-2022-0018

Mwansa, G., Ngandu, M. R., & Mkwambi, Z. (2025). Bridging the digital divide: Exploring the challenges and solutions for digital exclusion in rural South Africa. *Discover Global Society*, *3*(1), 54. DOI: 10.1007/s44282-025-00189-2

Nadeem, M. (2024). Distributed leadership in educational contexts: A catalyst for school improvement. *Social Sciences & Humanities Open*, *9*, 100835. DOI: 10.1016/j.ssaho.2024.100835

Nedungadi, P., Tang, K.-Y., & Raman, R. (2024). The Transformative Power of Generative Artificial Intelligence for Achieving the Sustainable Development Goal of Quality Education. *Sustainability (Basel)*, *16*(22), 9779. DOI: 10.3390/su16229779

Owusu-Agyeman, Y. (2021). Transformational leadership and innovation in higher education: A participative process approach. *International Journal of Leadership in Education*, *24*(5), 694–716. DOI: 10.1080/13603124.2019.1623919

Palmquist, A., Alves, J., Baranyi, R., Munkvold, R., Carvalho, V., & Oliveira, E. (2025). Blended Realities - Higher Education Student Reflections on Acquiring Skills for Game Creation in a Project-Based- and Blended Learning Environment. *Games: Research and Practice*, *3*(1), 2–26. DOI: 10.1145/3704414

Paulsen, L., & Lindsay, E. (2024). Learning analytics dashboards are increasingly becoming about learning and not just analytics - A systematic review. *Education and Information Technologies*, *29*(11), 14279–14308. DOI: 10.1007/s10639-023-12401-4

Pinto, J. M. de R. (2021). *The Education System of Brazil: Financing of Education in Brazil* (pp. 265–289). DOI: 10.1007/978-3-030-41651-5_21

Polozhentseva, I., Zhilkibaeva, R., Luzina, T., & Vijaya Kumar, K. (2025). *AI Digital Learning Adaptation Challenges and Issues in Current Higher Education Field.*, DOI: 10.1007/978-981-96-1981-8_12

Pozzer, M. R. O., & dos Reis Neuhold, R. (2025). Vocational education and training and regional development in Brazil. *Journal of Vocational Education and Training*, *77*(1), 207–228. DOI: 10.1080/13636820.2025.2449657

Qasmi, F., & Fatima, S. K. (2024). *Enhancing Education and Well-Being Through Artificial Intelligence: Opportunities and Challenges* (pp. 154–164). DOI: 10.1007/978-3-031-65996-6_13

Riaz, B. K., Ali, L., Ahmad, S. A., Islam, M. Z., Ahmed, K. R., & Hossain, S. (2020). Community clinics in Bangladesh: A unique example of public-private partnership. *Heliyon*, *6*(5), e03950. DOI: 10.1016/j.heliyon.2020.e03950 PMID: 32420500

Saxena, A., Ramaswamy, M., Beale, J., Marciniuk, D., & Smith, P. (2021). Striving for the United Nations (UN) Sustainable Development Goals (SDGs): What will it take? *Discover Sustainability*, *2*(1), 20. DOI: 10.1007/s43621-021-00029-8

Sayed, W. S., Noeman, A. M., Abdellatif, A., Abdelrazek, M., Badawy, M. G., Hamed, A., & El-Tantawy, S. (2023). AI-based adaptive personalized content presentation and exercises navigation for an effective and engaging E-learning platform. *Multimedia Tools and Applications*, *82*(3), 3303–3333. DOI: 10.1007/s11042-022-13076-8 PMID: 35789938

Schaper, M.-M., Tamashiro, M. A., Smith, R. C., & Iversen, O. S. (2025). *Diversity in AI Education: Tailoring students' learning paths for inclusive learning about facial recognition*. ACM Transactions on Computing Education., DOI: 10.1145/3727985

Shaya, N., Abukhait, R., Madani, R., & Khattak, M. N. (2023). Organizational Resilience of Higher Education Institutions: An Empirical Study during Covid-19 Pandemic. *Higher Education Policy*, *36*(3), 529–555. DOI: 10.1057/s41307-022-00272-2 PMID: 35529423

Sonetti, G., Barioglio, C., & Campobenedetto, D. (2020). Education for Sustainability in Practice: A Review of Current Strategies within Italian Universities. *Sustainability (Basel)*, *12*(13), 5246. DOI: 10.3390/su12135246

Sooryamoorthy, R. (2023). *Barriers to Self-Reliance*., DOI: 10.1007/978-981-99-5577-0_6

Srinivasa, K. G., Kurni, M., & Saritha, K. (2022). *Harnessing the Power of AI to Education*., DOI: 10.1007/978-981-19-6734-4_13

Staziaki, P. V., Santo, I. D. de O., Skobodzinski, A. A., Park, L. K., & Bcdi, H. S. (2021). How to Use YouTube for Radiology Education. *Current Problems in Diagnostic Radiology*, *50*(4), 461–468. DOI: 10.1067/j.cpradiol.2020.11.007 PMID: 33261926

Tan, S. (2023). Exploiting Disruptive Innovation in Learning and Teaching. In *Learning Intelligence: Innovative and Digital Transformative Learning Strategies* (pp. 149–176). Springer Nature Singapore. DOI: 10.1007/978-981-19-9201-8_4

Timmis, S., & Muñoz-Chereau, B. (2022). Under-represented students' university trajectories: Building alternative identities and forms of capital through digital improvisations. *Teaching in Higher Education*, *27*(1), 1–17. DOI: 10.1080/13562517.2019.1696295 PMID: 34584277

Trajkovski, G., & Hayes, H. (2025). *Foundations of AI in Educational Assessment*., DOI: 10.1007/978-3-031-88252-4

Ursavaş, Ö. F. (2022). *Conducting Technology Acceptance Research in Education.* Springer International Publishing., DOI: 10.1007/978-3-031-10846-4

Valtonen, T., Leppänen, U., Hyypiä, M., Kokko, A., Manninen, J., Vartiainen, H., Sointu, E., & Hirsto, L. (2021). Learning environments preferred by university students: A shift toward informal and flexible learning environments. *Learning Environments Research*, *24*(3), 371–388. DOI: 10.1007/s10984-020-09339-6

Wang, R., Qamruzzaman, M., & Karim, S. (2024). Unveiling the power of education, political stability and ICT in shaping technological innovation in BRI nations. *Heliyon*, *10*(9), e30142. DOI: 10.1016/j.heliyon.2024.e30142 PMID: 38707328

Yared, H., Grové, C., & Chapman, D. (2023). *Who Belongs in Schools?* How the Education System Fails Racially Marginalised Students., DOI: 10.1007/978-981-16-5908-9_13

Zhang, H., & Huang, H. (2024). Low-Carbon Transformational Leadership: Conceptualization, Measurement, and Its Impact on Innovation Outcomes. *Sustainability (Basel)*, *16*(24), 10844. DOI: 10.3390/su162410844

Zhang, H., & Tian, M. (2025). Unpacking the multi-dimensional nature of teacher competencies: A systematic review. *Scandinavian Journal of Educational Research*, *69*(5), 1004–1025. DOI: 10.1080/00313831.2024.2369867

Zhang, Y., Chen, D., & Xu, J. (2025). The relationship between faculty members' perceptions of technology leadership and their technology integration into higher education—Evidence from China. *British Educational Research Journal*, berj.4204. Advance online publication. DOI: 10.1002/berj.4204

Ziguras, C. (2023). *The Global Market for Digital Educational Content and its Impact on Institutional Strategy*. Program Design and Teaching Practice., DOI: 10.1007/978-3-031-16065-3_9

KEY TERMS AND DEFINITIONS

Algorithmic Bias: In numerous instances, discriminatory approaches that are built as a bias in AI software or data design are often systemic and unfair.

Artificial Intelligence (AI): The field of computer science focuses on developing systems that can perform tasks such as learning, reasoning, and problem-solving that require human intelligence.

Digital Divide: The digital divides are inequalities in access to electronic technologies and the internet among people or residential groups, often based on socio-economic, geographic and demographic factors.

Educational Leadership: Educational governance can be referred to as the process by which educational institutions and systems are guided and managed in a way that maximises the learning results and drives innovation, whereby ethical standards and consideration to sociocultural issues.

Human Capital Development: It is the process of systematic improvement of skills, knowledge, and potential of people, and thus their productivity, and ability to contribute to economic growth.

Policy Coherence: The alignment and consistency among various policies across sectors and levels of governance to ensure effective and integrated implementation

Social media: Digital platforms and tools that aid the user in generating, distributing and interactive consumption of content, and aid communication and collaboration.

Sustainable Education: Inclusive, adaptive learning is the new practice that education to improve social equity, environmental responsibility, and economic viability should embrace.

Chapter 12
Harnessing Disciplinary Networks:
A Global Educational Leadership Perspective on Positive Behavioural Management

Tahsina Khan
https://orcid.org/0000-0001-8032-3376
Bangladesh University of Professionals, Bangladesh

Md Mehedi Hasan Emon
https://orcid.org/0000-0002-6224-9552
American International University-Bangladesh, Bangladesh

ABSTRACT

This chapter explores the vital role of disciplinary networks in fostering positive behavioural management through a global leadership lens. It examines how distributed and transformational leadership theories, combined with social learning and systems thinking, provide a robust framework for understanding and improving behaviour governance in schools. Drawing on diverse international case studies from Finland's collaborative culture to Bangladesh's community engagement, the chapter highlights culturally responsive strategies that empower educators, students, and stakeholders. It underscores the impact of inclusive leadership on school climate, equity, and academic outcomes, while offering policy recommendations to align disciplinary practices with broader social and economic goals. Finally, the chapter argues that strategic leadership, rooted in collaborative networks, is essential for creating sustainable, equitable, and effective behavioural management systems across varied educational contexts worldwide.

DOI: 10.4018/979-8-3373-3616-9.ch012

INTRODUCTION

This chapter explores the ways in which relationships between educators, students, administrators and stakeholders can play a significant role in behaviour management in schools. It seeks to shift viewpoints, making behaviour regulation a planned action by leaders, where it is firmly embedded in school culture and its effects last beyond the walls of the school. Approaching this topic from a worldwide leadership standpoint, the inquiry believes that making sure behaviour is governed wisely depends on network structures that are culturally aware and guided by diverse guidance, rather than strictly by organisation leaders. The beginning of the chapter explains how connected academic networks bring about a sense of responsibility and cohesive behaviour among staff members in educational institutions. After that, it strengthens its theoretical structure by bringing together themes from distributed leadership, transformational leadership, social learning theory and systems thinking. All these approaches help us understand the ways leadership can form behavioural standards, affect the climate in institutions and encourage participation. In order to put theory into practice, the chapter looks at four international case studies: Finland's teamwork in schools, Bangladesh's actions led by the community, South Africa's difficulties after colonialism and Canada's approaches involving restorative justice. The cases highlight how discipline practices are structured and influenced by the cultures, politics and economies around them, stressing that managing students is tied to their broader environments. The following sections provide practical guidelines for leaders on constructing and continuing inclusive disciplinary groups. In practice, the goal is to help stakeholders use the strengths of the community and choose leadership methods that are flexible and not reliant on discipline. There is a special focus on establishing ecosystems that support fair treatment and work against differences between students.

Then, the chapter looks at the broader effects of disciplinary leadership. It points out how behavioural culture relates to student performance and discusses how proper behaviour management helps build the human capital of students for the future. Building students' confidence in their actions, responsibility and social unity through disciplinary networks helps to make education an essential factor in boosting both the economy and society. At the end, the chapter outlines a set of recommendations aimed at educators, training institutes and development agencies. It encourages rethinking how policies are made in leadership, to ensure they focus on equity, inclusion and relevance to people in schools. The chapter's main points are brought together in the final section and set priorities for additional study, urging researchers to work on empirical studies, multi-year research and more examples of leadership styles that encourage national growth. It is concluded that if educators apply inclusive, adaptable and culture-based leadership to network groups, behaviour in schools improves, and students gain the skills and morals vital for a prosperous and equal society.

DISCIPLINARY NETWORKS AS STRATEGIC LEADERSHIP IN EDUCATION

Educational institutions are always centres where social issues are being negotiated in every community. In most cases, behaviour management is seen as a separate duty handled by a chosen teacher or by disciplinary committees. Now, most social scientists are challenging the previous view by referring to behaviour management as a joint goal for all leaders in a school that is closely connected to the school's community values and culture (Chatzipanagiotou & Katsarou, 2023). A key idea in this shift is disciplinary networks, which are the patterns of interactions, both set and spontaneous, among educators, students, administrators, parents and various community actors that help shape the moral and behavioural culture in a school. Disciplinary networks should not be treated as hierarchical bosses or written codes for good behaviour. Instead, customs are flexible and moulded by each environment, where behaviours are discussed, shared and adopted by individuals. These networks cover many areas, including school policies made by leaders, meetings between students and teachers and parent and community involvement (Kelty & Wakabayashi, 2020). Embedding behavioural regulations in a network of people enables disciplinary networks to provide effective and inclusive standards, lessen the need for punishment and encourage good behaviours to flourish. Therefore, behavioural management becomes seen as an essential tool for learning, as well as a key role in leading people. A leadership approach to behaviour management needs us to see influence and power in education differently. Leadership happens everywhere in a school, not just in the offices of the principal or in official policies made by the Ministry of Education. It includes all groups in the school, for example, teacher leadership, student voice, parental engagement and peer influence. In educational research, distributed leadership frameworks are being valued more for stressing the need for people to share their duties and build each other's strengths to meet institutional goals (Nadeem, 2024). The paradigm supports the creation of disciplinary methods in schools that are friendly to all students and flexible to the needs of each student group. In addition, transformational leadership underlines that being motivating involves having a vision, gaining trust from employees and maintaining strong relationships (Akdere & Egan, 2020).

In contrast to authoritarian methods, which mainly use coercion, a transformational approach helps bring out good feelings of identity, belonging and self-motivation in students. Using this approach, behavioural management is used to promote both personal growth and good relationships in society, not only to obey rules in the institution. Transformational leadership does this by guiding kids' actions, resorting to shared values and building trust, resulting in better student behaviour over time.

School behavioural culture influences many aspects of life, not only what happens in the classroom. There is increasing knowledge that a favourable school climate and consistent behavioural norms influence student learning, well-being and future pathway (White et al., 2023). Establishing a school's culture of inclusivity, respect, and collaboration helps students stay interested in school and reduce the rate of dropping out, while also teaching them the social skills that employers need today. Therefore, behavioural management naturally aligns with primary educational and economic growth objectives. According to UNESCO (2023), the best strategy for achieving Sustainable Development Goal 4 (SDG 4) is focusing on social and emotional learning environments. How schools are run is now connected to global economic factors, mainly because of ongoing education reform. In developing countries, where there are more young people and employment patterns are changing, improving human capital through education is considered very important (Emon & Khan, 2025; Lauder & Mayhew, 2020). But if there is also no attention to skills like self-control, teamwork, empathy and being responsible, knowledge gained from school is not always sufficient for today's jobs and social situations. If used well, disciplinary networks can help develop these skills by encouraging them through interactions, peer rules and what is expected from the institution. Having a global leadership perspective in this case is more about action than only about theory. Educational institutions globally are dealing with common concerns: students not being engaged, students' behaviour varying widely by their social and economic backgrounds, the rise of mental health concerns and less respect for group norms due to online influences (Ainscow, 2020; Emon, 2025b). The way these challenges develop, and the best solutions are influenced strongly by where, when and how culture, history and institutions play a role. Educational leaders with a global mindset can discover different tactics, choose the best ones and avoid making errors when applying policies from other cultures.

Furthermore, having a global perspective on disciplinary networks points out that leaders should be culturally responsive. In countries like Canada and New Zealand, the idea of restorative practices has become popular because it fits with the indigenous belief in togetherness and healing (Asamoah et al., 2023). In South Asia, Bangladesh and India, among them, people often use behavioural governance in a way that depends on family and community involvement, influenced by cultural values (Hamilton et al., 2022). This diversity highlights the ways disciplinary networks can work best locally, but continue to follow the basic principles of equity, respect and inclusion. In the end, this chapter describes disciplinary networks as both a way to understand the field and a helpful structure for leaders promoting positive, just and effective schools. The chapter strives to advance the conversation by incorporating a global leadership approach and considering behaviour management as the foundation of innovation and social change (Khan et al., 2024). The approach claims that by carefully forming discipline-focused networks, schools can change from a responsive approach to one that proactively encourages improvements in both learning and citizenship.

INTEGRATING LEADERSHIP AND BEHAVIOURAL PERSPECTIVES

A strong theoretical basis covering leadership, behaviour and the relationship in the system is needed to see how disciplinary networks work in schools. The following chapter uses Distributed Leadership Theory, Transformational Leadership, Social Learning and Behavioural Theories and Systems Thinking in Educational Management to analyse behavioural governance in schools. All of these frameworks, together, help us understand how leadership shapes behaviour, how behaviour is picked up and encouraged and how the right policies and culture influence good results.

Distributed Leadership Theory: Collective Responsibility and Shared Authority

In recent years, distributed leadership has become more critical than the traditional model where authority rests with only one person, usually the principal (Mifsud, 2024). Leadership in schools is spread among numerous actors, including teachers, administrators, support staff, students and parents, all helping to work towards the school's goals and making things function smoothly. Distributed leadership stresses in behavioural management that the responsibility for positive behaviour should be shared among various leaders in the system, not just given to the designated disciplinary staff. Therefore, all stakeholders should take part in shaping the expected behaviours, demonstrate good behaviours themselves and act when things go wrong (Roszkowska & Melé, 2021). Adopting this method encourages everyone to help regulate behaviour, instead of automatically responding with punishment whenever needed. According to studies, having distributed leadership in behavioural governance leads to better qualities in the school environment and a reduction in unacceptable behaviours (Abdulmuhsin et al., 2021; Emon & Chowdhury, 2025). Nowadays, when people look for more inclusive approaches, the distributed system encourages teamwork and fair answers to different types of behaviour. It further pays attention to the role peers and student leaders have in influencing conduct, so social elements are also part of formal leadership.

Transformational leadership: Inspiring Behavioural Change

Complementing distributed leadership, transformational leadership theory highlights the motivational and relational dimensions of effective behavioural management. Leithwood and Azah (2022) articulate transformational leadership as a process whereby leaders inspire and mobilise followers through a compelling vision, intellectual stimulation, individualised consideration, and the fostering of trust and respect. Applied to behavioural governance, transformational leadership reframes discipline from mere rule enforcement to a developmental process aimed at nurturing internal motivation and ethical commitment among students (Emon, 2025c; Memon et al., 2024). Leaders who embody transformational qualities seek to create school environments where behavioural expectations are shared values rather than externally imposed restrictions. Through positive role modelling and meaningful relationships, transformational leaders cultivate a culture of mutual respect and accountability. Studies indicate that transformational leadership in schools contributes to heightened student engagement, reductions in disruptive behaviour, and enhanced teacher morale (Emon, 2025a; Ogwumike et al., 2024). This approach also recognises the diversity of student backgrounds and experiences, promoting culturally responsive leadership that attends to individual and collective needs. By inspiring behavioural change from within, transformational leadership supports sustainable behavioural improvements and aligns with broader educational goals of fostering responsible citizenship.

Figure 1. Transformational Leadership Model in Behavioural Change

Figure 1 shows how transformational leadership helps change the behaviour of students. It shows how each of the four traits (Vision, Intellectual Stimulation, Individualised Consideration and Trust & Respect) encourages important mediating factors such as Internal Motivation, Ethical Reasoning, Behavioural Responsiveness and School Climate. All these mediators help contribute to better behaviour by students. It visually demonstrates that transformational leadership encourages motivation, makes people aware of ethics, helps them respond well and creates a positive environment at the school, which supports behavioural transformation.

Social Learning and Behavioural Theories: Behaviour as Learned

Behavioural management depends on how psychological and social factors shape behaviours. According to Granziera & Perera (2019), working in educational psychology, people observe and imitate others, and they are reinforced for their actions in order to learn how to behave in society. Modern studies suggest that students learn how to behave by working with peers, teachers and the rest of their school community (Darling-Hammond et al., 2020). Social learning happens in these networks through both official systems (rules and consequences) and less formal actions by peers. For example, students watching other students get praised for good actions tend to act the same way. Negative behaviours might grow more common if they are ignored or are sometimes honoured with good results (van der Oord & Tripp, 2020). Therefore, for behavioural management to work correctly, the same behavioural standards should be applied consistently throughout the organisation. Adding social learning to leadership insights points out that a group's culture and bond are vital for shaping each person's behaviour. Encouraging students to take part in pccr mentoring, restorative justice, and collaboratively shaping rules leads them to take responsibility for their actions and for the entire community (Emon & Mazid-Ul-Haque, 2025; Moran et al., 2025). This way of thinking matters most in settings where students from many cultures interact, since it means expectations must be agreed upon instead of being forced.

Systems Thinking in Educational Management: Interconnectedness of Roles, Policies, and Culture

Finally, system thinking provides a holistic framework for understanding the multifaceted Systems thinking adds a whole-picture approach to understanding the different aspects of behavioural management in schools. Systems theory focuses on the way other parts of a system interact and depend on one another, pointing out how outcomes can be established by how policies, school leadership, culture and behaviours work together (Norqvist & Ärlestig, 2020). It becomes clear through systems thinking that behavioural management does not stand alone but is connected to many aspects of the institution. Leadership actions about funding, employees' growth and involvement in the community create an environment where behaviour is controlled. Initiatives that integrate disciplinary actions with values and equity guidelines make the disciplinary process cohesive and acceptable to people. School behaviours are also influenced by the cultural background found within the school, such as attitudes concerning authority, diversity and conflict. A systems approach helps leaders believe that behaviour problems are usually signs of underlying issues in the organisation, not just due to individual mistakes. A more effective solution means applying integrated actions to fix fundamental problems like social-emotional difficulties or unfair practices, in addition to just using disciplinary actions. When stakeholders' goals are in line and policies are unified, systems thinking encourages lasting improvements in behaviour and helps organisations stay resilient. In reality, schools that use systems thinking build feedback loops so they can always review and adapt their behavioural strategies. Around the world, governments are supporting this method because it promotes inclusive, flexible and student-centred institutions (Islam et al., 2022; Khan et al., 2025). This approach supports both distributed and transformational leadership because it stresses patients, families and health professionals working together. All four of these perspectives provide a complete and well-structured way to look at how networks impact positive behaviour management. The basic framework and relationships come from distributed leadership, transformational leadership sparks motivation for change, social learning theory explains how behaviour is taught, and systems thinking makes sure behaviour fits within the overall institution. The analysis of global case studies and leadership shows that such governance relies on effective leadership, connections among individuals and having clear goals across all parts of the organisation.

GLOBAL PERSPECTIVES ON DISCIPLINARY NETWORKS IN EDUCATION

Behavioural management in schools can't be fully grasped without understanding how it varies from one country, culture and economy to another. A set of collaborative experts and ways of doing things addressing positive student behaviour are influenced strongly by the past, current leaders, society and policy directions where each network works. Learning about how leadership looks in various parts of the world helps us realise how much leaders have in common while still being unique in their management approaches. The chapter includes international comparisons of behaviour management practices, points out how discipline is handled differently across cultures and provides example cases from Finland, Bangladesh, South Africa and Canada to show how disciplinary leadership operates in practice.

Cross-National Comparisons: Behavioural Management in Developed and Developing Contexts

The presence of strong institutions, fixed policies and a significant focus on helping students shape their learning in developed places helps disciplinary networks thrive. In Finland, Canada and the Netherlands, behaviour management puts emphasis on restoring relationships, involving everyone and preventing issues. In such schools, students are involved, learning social-emotional skills becomes part of the culture and making decisions together is encouraged by the staff (Morgan et al., 2022). In addition, these nations report better inclusion, greater student happiness and better results in school, thus proving that having humane and supportive policies supports education in the long run.

In another way, Bangladesh, Kenya or Pakistan are countries where schools are not sufficiently funded, class sizes are enormous, and access to social or psychological support is hard for many. Management of student behaviour is often done reactively and harshly, showing strong control from teachers, which may be related to colonial tradition and inequality. Still, we must refrain from setting things up into overly simple "good vs. bad" categories. In many emerging countries, people are coming up with new approaches, including support from the community, active parent involvement and leadership models aligned with culture, which add to the world's discussions on behavioural governance. Cross-country studies indicate that the details of discipline networks depend significantly on their local context; even so, principles like delegating authority, involving stakeholders, and cultural sensitivity usually help achieve positive behaviour in students, no matter a country's development status (UNESCO, 2022).

Socio-Cultural Variations in Disciplinary Approaches and Leadership Responses

Cultural norms play a crucial role in shaping how behaviour is understood, managed, and negotiated within schools. In collectivist societies, for instance, behaviour is often perceived as a reflection of family honour and community values, thereby placing significant emphasis on external accountability and social cohesion. In more individualistic cultures, on the other hand, behavioural expectations may focus on personal responsibility, autonomy, and intrinsic motivation (Urhahne & Wijnia, 2023).

Figure 2. Socio-Cultural Dimensions Shaping Disciplinary Leadership

The figure shows an informed example of how various cultural factors affect leadership styles and how different groups are involved in education. It mainly includes four areas: Collectivism vs Individualism, Norms of Religious Behaviour, Language and Contemporary Condition and Ways Leadership Organises Society (Hierarchical, Participatory or Restorative). Disciplinary Leadership Style is indicated by arrows from each of these two elements, and this then leads into Stakeholder Engagement. Figure 2 shows how leaders address behaviour changes a lot depending on the local culture, suggesting that behaviour management is not standard worldwide.

Leaders handle behaviour problems differently based on the cultural context. In certain Asian situations, the influence of Confucianism supports a leadership system where things are given from the top, yet there are more and more attempts to challenge and change this practice. There are also Indigenous laws in countries such as Canada and New Zealand, which base their approaches on talking, respecting differences and finding ways to heal; such practices can show how to become a culturally respectful leader in discipline (Asamoah et al., 2023; Emon et al., 2025).

In addition, religious, historical and language values shape how different disciplines work. In several African scenarios, issues related to who is in charge, rules and how leadership is viewed still have a significant impact on school discipline. The fact that these factors interact clearly shows why it is important to study disciplinary networks in the context of their social and cultural environment. The approach is no more correct than others; what matters is whether leaders and the community share similar values.

Case Study 1: Finland-Collaborative School Culture and Low Exclusion Rates

Finland is regularly seen as a role model for fairness in education and a healthy culture of positive behaviour. In Finland, schools are based on trust; they test students infrequently, allow teachers to guide their own lessons and make sure all students grow holistically. Disciplinary action in Finland is based on cooperation between teachers, school psychologists, social workers and parents in creating positive behaviour plans (Paju et al., 2022). Finnish schools choose to focus on early intervention, encourage inclusiveness in learning and make sure students feel good about themselves. Exclusion, expulsion and detention are uncommon, and teachers are taught to view poor behaviour as caused by development or special situations instead of thinking it is bad behaviour. The leadership culture encourages equality in leadership and makes sure principals assist staff rather than control them. The model explains that having mutual trust and teamwork among professional groups can keep learning environments calm and lively.

Case Study 2: Bangladesh-Parental Involvement and Community Leadership

The availability of resources, large class sizes and inequality faced by many in Bangladesh make behavioural management more difficult in this country. However, one of the important benefits is that parents, along with communities, play a bigger part in managing children's behaviour. In rural schools, committees known as SMCs are made up of parents, religious leaders and leaders from the local community, and they help create rules for behaviour and manage conflicts (Al Marjuk, 2023). They usually rely more on the strength of social relationships and influence, rather than formal regulations. In many cases, teachers and headteachers team up with guardians to address continuous behavioural challenges, using the customs and culture of the community. The leadership role is not usually official and depends on cultural respect and influence among people in the community. Though corporal punishment and unfair treatment of children based on gender continue, teachers and parents are increasingly concerned about how children are treated at school and are calling for training, rights-based systems and for children to have a say in their education. The case of Bangladesh explains how the involvement of the community can help disciplinary networks work well in challenging situations.

Case Study 3: South Africa-Addressing Post-Colonial Disciplinary Inequalities through Networks

In South Africa, behaviour managers deal with inequalities left over from apartheid, changes in institutions and a mix of various cultures. Before, school discipline in South Africa was directed by both authoritarian and racially biased regulations. In the years since 1994, people in South Africa have focused on creating inclusive communities, using restorative efforts and overcoming past punitive approaches (Ricart-Huguet, 2021). Nowadays, school governing bodies (SGBs), youth forums and civil society organisations are commonly part of disciplinary networks. Programmes like Whole School Development and Safe Schools work towards making schools more welcoming and supportive, where teachers and students have positive interactions and focus on the effects of trauma. Nevertheless, making these changes happen is not smooth for certain township schools that are still affected by old challenges. South Africa shows that successful change in education happens when politicians support it, history is acknowledged, and agencies cooperate.

Case Study 4: Canada – Inclusive and Restorative Disciplinary Systems

Behavioural management in Canada is guided by including all people, encouraging reconciliation and focusing on respecting human rights. Recently, Canadian schools have used restorative justice to help make things right, restore relationships and help people feel accountable, without shutting anyone out (Weaver & Swank, 2020). The leadership role is shared by teachers, counsellors, Indigenous elders and peer mediators in such systems. Canada stands out for making sure Indigenous ways of knowing are considered in how governmental decisions are made. Educational policies in British Columbia and Ontario officially support safety for cultural identity, anti-racist actions and taking care of trauma (Cénat et al., 2025). The Truth and Reconciliation Commission encouraged changes to help decolonise classrooms and give Indigenous students meaningful support. Disciplinary networks in Canada show that including policymakers, teachers and the community helps reduce behavioural differences and makes schools more democratic. In Canada, restorative leadership has helped produce schools that are both more resilient and more empathetic.

Figure 3. Conceptual Model (Elements of Effective Global Disciplinary Networks)

As shown in Figure 3, global disciplinary networks work well when they concentrate on Contextual Responsiveness, Distributed Leadership, Student-Centred Practices, Cultural Legitimacy and Collaboration with Stakeholders. All of these elements are connected as nodes in a flowing loop to stress how they support and rely on each other. The directional arrows highlight the ongoing communication between various systems, which makes the model a functional theory guiding future research, policy making and education globally.

LEADERSHIP STRATEGIES FOR BEHAVIOURAL MANAGEMENT

In recent years, managing behaviour in schools has grown from a minor task for administration to a primary responsibility for leaders. As the approach changes, behavioural management is now considered a strategic leadership role that needs long-term vision, teamwork and readiness to change. A good approach to leadership should build on values of equity, empowerment and interdependence, which lead to a long-lasting, positive corporate culture. The following section presents important leadership strategies required to form and uphold effective networks for disciplinary affairs, empower teachers and students, unite stakeholders, embrace cultural respect and develop proactive and restorative school systems.

Designing and Sustaining Effective Disciplinary Networks

It is difficult to shape disciplinary networks because they must have a clear vision, an organised structure and flexible leaders. A good network consists of educators, counsellors, parents, administrative staff, students and community agents. They exist to promote good behaviour and provide an atmosphere where students can grow and learn in many ways. It is through leadership that important networks are formed and kept together over time. These structures are started by visionary school leaders who include behavioural expectations as part of the school's mission and values. However, these visions should be turned into reality by setting up institutional rules, protocols and everyday work habits. Investing in behaviour support teams and ongoing training, as well as using data, helps schools better deal with behaviour disruptions.

Figure 4. Structure of an Effective Disciplinary Network

The model in Figure 4 shows the way an effective disciplinary network should be put together. In the diagram, Educators, Counsellors, Parents, Administrative Staff,

Students and Community Agents are linked because they depend on each other. The directional arrows between these entities show how workers and departments work together and provide constant feedback to each other. The circular shape demonstrates that every stakeholder should cooperate, and that authentic, effective behavioural leadership comes from shared efforts rather than one person acting alone. However, a significant condition for stability is when these groups are accepted and operated under strong government policies, continuous support from experts and routine interaction with stakeholders. A sustainable disciplinary network changes when required to deal with changing student behaviour, shifts in the population and new situations in society. A lack of strong leadership that promotes agility and steadiness could turn networks into bureaucratic or ineffective systems.

Empowering Educators, Students, and Support Staff through Distributed Authority

An effective discipline policy depends on the principal moving beyond authoritarianism and passing responsibility to other administrators and staff. Decision-making power shared among teachers, support staff, and students makes everyone responsible and involved in the school community. When teachers participate in creating and carrying out behaviour policies, their dedication and steadiness in applying them is shown to be much greater.

Figure 5. Distributed Leadership Model in Behavioural Management

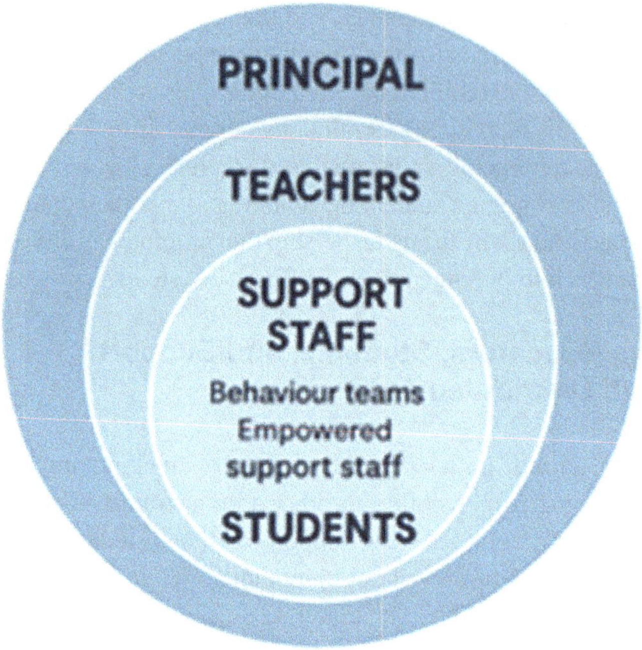

The figure illustrates that four different groups within the school community are involved in behaviour management with their own roles. The principal is found at the outermost circle because they provide general leadership. Coming from the next circle, Teachers and then Support Staff, who are highly encouraged and given authority to assist in making important decisions as part of the behaviour team. At the centre are Students, who are made clear they play the central role in taking charge and being held accountable. Figure 5 demonstrates that all stakeholders have leadership and authority roles to ensure everyone collaborates and is involved. Students must be empowered in the same way. When schools include students in peer mediation, student councils or restorative justice, they teach them to take responsibility and lead in managing how people behave. The effectiveness of restorative circles relies mainly on how involved students are and how much trust there is between them. Students who feel empowered help shape the expectations and understand them better, which discourages arguments and disobedience. Often, support staff are less discussed in behavioural management studies, even though they should be empowered. It is common for cleaners, cafeteria workers and security people to be the first to observe any troubling changes in behaviour. Making them part of the training and decisions increases the effectiveness of behavioural monitoring and intervention. Everyone in the school being involved as stakeholders in behavioural leadership helps to make the culture stronger and more unified (Nadeem, 2024).

Stakeholder Collaboration: Integrating Parents, Community Leaders, and Policymakers

The positive effects of good behavioural leadership reach further than the boundaries of the classroom. The involvement of people like parents, community leaders and policymakers is essential for a disciplinary network. When families are involved in behavioural support plans, it helps to keep the same rules at home and school and increases mutual trust and respect (Ihmeideh et al., 2020). Community leaders such as religious figures, NGO specialists, and people involved in cultural life can transmit behavioural guidelines in ways that match students' identities and values. Their presence makes these behavioural models sound and can address issues of resistance because of any perceived cultural or moral gaps. Many times, in developing countries, community members help with problems left by institutions by solving disagreements, guiding youngsters or supporting activities that reward good behaviour in schools (Khlaif et al., 2021).

Meanwhile, policymakers need to be viewed as partners who help support behavioural leadership, not only as people who set rules. Educational leaders must step forward to champion policies that back active, inclusive and resource-based behavioural approaches. It requires supporting mental health care services, funding programs for teachers, and law changes that stop punishment and instead work on restoring those involved.

Figure 6. Stakeholder Collaboration Framework

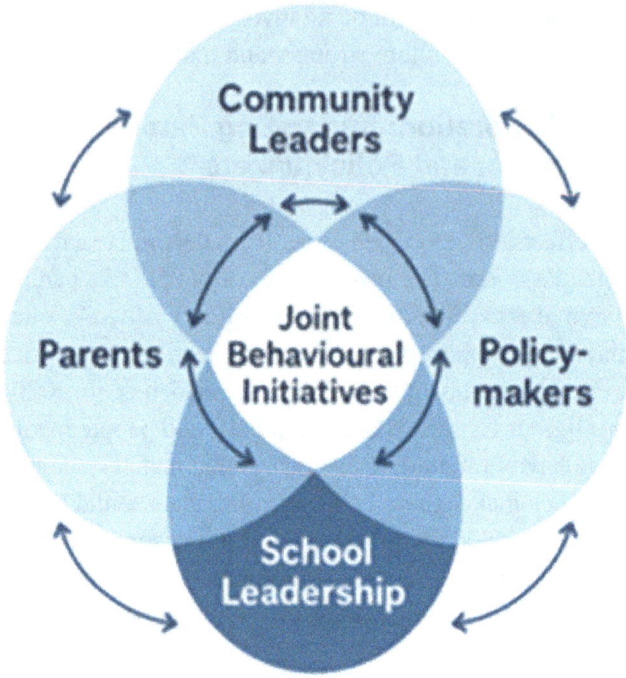

A Venn diagram that overlaps complements intersections is used to show a stakeholder collaboration framework in Figure 6. It explains how student behaviour is managed by parents, community leaders, policymakers and school leadership working together. The core point where Joint Behavioural Initiatives appear highlights the work done when companies team up. Arrows show two-way communication and coordination among all groups. The framework explains that connecting with external organisations increases the accepted nature, spread and consistency of school strategies outside of classrooms. Collaborative efforts work best when there is open talking, the group has common aims, and all members respect each other's unique impact on behaviour.

Culturally Responsive Leadership: Adapting Behavioural Strategies to Local Realities

There are always culture-specific rules for how we behave, and these rules vary from place to place. Social standards for respect, how to communicate, who holds authority and dealing with conflict differ widely among different cultures. Therefore, school leaders should use culturally responsive leadership, changing their behaviour according to the community's values and habits. A school leader should understand the community and be open to making changes to imported models that might not suit them. Inclusive leadership, use of local language and images and awareness of traditional ways to resolve conflict are all elements of culturally responsive behavioural leadership. In Indigenous communities in Canada, leaders build restorative justice programs on their traditions of circle sharing and communal responsibility (Asadullah & Morrison, 2021). Similarly, a lot of African and South Asian schools depend on intergenerational talk and community mediation to help students behave.

Figure 7. Principles of Culturally Responsive Behavioural Leadership

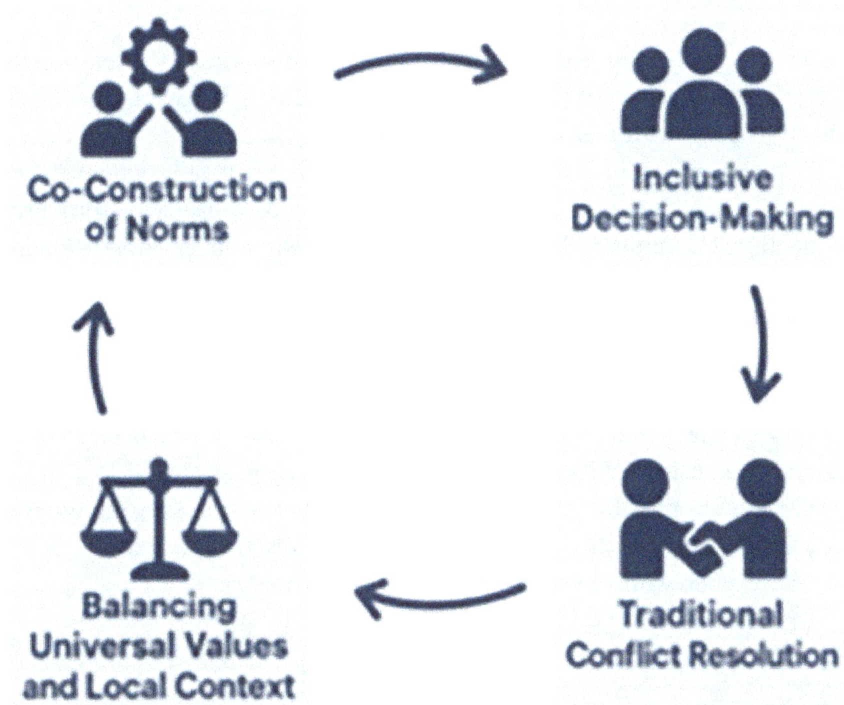

Figure 7 represents a cycle including four main ideas needed for behaving effectively as a culturally responsive leader. The process commences with individuals determining Norms by coming together under the gear, which signifies they are sharing in developing the behavioural guidelines. Inclusive Decision-Making is shown by a gathering of three figures who suggest that all should be part of the decision-making process. Then, Traditional Conflict Resolution, two individuals shaking hands, represents the acceptance of different approaches to settling arguments. The process follows Balancing Universal Values and Local Context, which is shown by a balanced scale that integrates universal and local concepts. Once more, the leadership approach moves to Co-Construction of Norms, demonstrating that it is ongoing.

A good school leader practices universal ideas such as dignity, empathy and fairness with respect to how these values look in their setting. They do not set rules but join students and families to develop them together. As a result, behavioural strategies are chosen that are just and can last over time and the legal system is widely accepted and less opposed.

Building Restorative and Proactive Disciplinary Ecosystems

Modern school leaders are changing from reactive solutions to create environments that aid and encourage restoration. In these practices, behaviour management goes hand in hand with teaching, learning and daily activities at school. Restorative ecosystems put value on strong relationships, empathy and accountability, so incidents of misconduct rarely arise. For example, some proactive efforts involve social-emotional learning (SEL), trauma-informed teaching and positive behavioural interventions and support (PBIS). These programs teach students to control their emotions and handle social situations, which also helps reduce behavioural incidents and improve how engaged students are in learning (Riggs & Landrum, 2023). The approaches of making supportive statements, using conflict conferences and setting reparation agreements allow students to address and resolve conflicts, improving the relationship. Instead of harsh disciplinary actions, these strategies look at issues of misbehaviour as possibilities for learning, discussion and healing. In ecosystem schools, leaders set up a climate where people treat mistakes as learning opportunities and everyone works to support and respect each other.

Figure 8. Restorative and Proactive Disciplinary Ecosystem Model

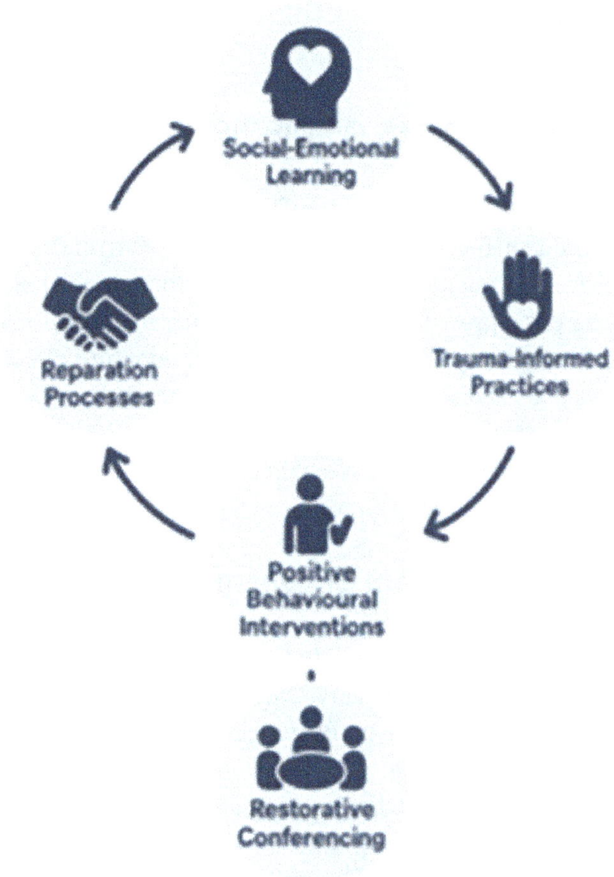

Figure 8 describes a model where restorative and proactive disciplinary techniques are applied to foster emotional growth, make individuals accountable and bring about community healing. The process starts by teaching Social-Emotional Learning to help people become more in touch with their emotions, empathy and relationship skills. It supports Trauma-Informed Practices, which require that reactions to behaviour address the feelings and thoughts caused by trauma in a person. Furthermore, the model takes advantage of Positive Behavioural Interventions, which use kindness and motivate students instead of depending on disciplinary approaches. Afterwards, Restorative Conferencing helps people involved in conflict or harm to meet and have a dialogue, aiming for everyone to understand, be accountable and agree on what to do next. In addition, the model covers Reparation Processes, which involve actual steps people take to fix issues and rebuild relationships. The five aspects are always linked in a cycle that shows how one element helps reinforce the others to form a solid and persistent system.

IMPACTS AND OUTCOMES OF DISCIPLINARY LEADERSHIP

A disciplinary leader is expected to influence more than only the immediate management of student behaviour. It plays a significant role in shaping school life, which impacts how engaged students are, how they perform and their lasting development. There is a growing focus on how proper behaviour management can affect education and society, which highlights why adopting effective leadership techniques to create good disciplinary practices is crucial. This part focuses on the different effects and outcomes tied to being a disciplinary leader, including school climate, student achievements, their social and moral values, managing behaviour with fairness and managing the institution properly.

School Climate and Student Engagement

Educational success and how well students are involved in their learning are greatly affected by how students perceive safety, their relationships and the learning environment in school. A climate of respect, fairness and inclusiveness in an organisation is driven by disciplinary leaders, who set clear rules and follow cultural customs. Leaders who use methods like restorative discipline and inclusion help students feel appreciated, so they do not feel controlled by punishments. When relational approaches are used instead of punitive measures, students feel safer, which helps them participate more in their learning and interact better with their peers (Lodi et al., 2021). A supportive atmosphere in schools comes about intentionally by leaders investing time in healthy relationships and including students in running the school. In addition, how a school is disciplined affects both teachers' morale and their effectiveness. Empowering teachers to deal with behaviour and give them appropriate resources and training, while making leaders available for help, increases both their job satisfaction and the manner in which they instruct their students, making their classes more meaningful. The strong relationships in the group lead to more joining, which results in fewer behavioural problems.

Positive Behavioural Culture and Academic Performance

It has been proven again and again by research that schools with good behavioural climates perform better academically. Different behavioural habits can make disruptions happen often and have an impact on the school atmosphere, helping or hindering students' abilities to focus, collaborate and risk technological challenges (Chatzipanagiotou & Katsarou, 2023). Multiple studies now show that PBIS, managed by strong administrative authority, increases student performance while cutting down on the number of students sent to the office for discipline (Khan et al., 2024; McLaughlin et al., 2025). It is clear from these findings that behavioural culture plays a significant and at times neglected role in improving education. There are many ways behavioural culture affects achievement. A regular and well-explained way of handling student behaviour makes them feel more secure, so they use their mental energy on academics. In addition, when leaders ensure inclusivity and equality, it lessens the effects of marginalisation and leads to increased involvement and success for people from disadvantaged groups. Therefore, leadership-shaped culture influences learning in the context of a larger educational system that helps students do well academically.

Preparing Socially Responsible, Economically Productive Citizens

Disciplinary leadership is essential for shaping students' social and economic futures in addition to influencing their education. In schools, young people gain knowledge as well as the social behaviours, morals and beliefs that will play a role in how they act in society and at work. Leaders in schools help guide students to act responsibly and connect with others, which supports their ability to have a positive role in democratic societies. According to research studies that have followed students over time, those who study in schools with supportive discipline systems are less likely to become involved in antisocial actions, delinquency or crime (Khan & Hasan Emon, 2024; Mowen et al., 2020). In terms of economy, schools focused on positive behaviour help their students by preparing them for work by developing skills such as cooperation, speaking and controlling their actions. These soft skills are now being highlighted as essential skills by many employers alongside technical skills. Disciplinary leadership that focuses on the overall development of students helps students succeed in the workplace and workforce, which improves both the economy and social status.

Reducing Disparities in Exclusion, Punishment, and Opportunity

A key effect of successful disciplinary leadership is to encourage fairness in people's behaviour. Over the years, educational systems globally have faced problems with unequal use of discipline that affects groups identified by race, ethnicity, socioeconomic background or disability (Kikabhai, 2022). This situation holds back individual students and helps maintain bigger problems of systemic inequality in education.

Behavioural policies with an equity focus on school leadership work to fix exclusionary and strict guidelines that mostly harm vulnerable students. For instance, if restorative justice initiatives are applied carefully, suspensions for minority students are cut, and these students gain better educational chances. Good discipline leaders use data and analysis to find where problems exist and to make intentional changes. Leaders need to encourage a thoughtful environment, respect different cultures and always strive to improve in handling behaviour inequality. This leadership style makes us understand behavioural management differently, as working for the formulation of justice and support for all members of the community.

Contributions to Institutional Efficiency and Human Capital Development

A well-structured system can increase institutional efficiency, also supporting the development of human resources in the future. When disciplinary procedures are properly organised, schools have fewer disruptions and more time for teaching activities. Because of this efficiency, human resources and materials are used more effectively, and the organisation runs better. In addition, encouraging positive school experiences and fair treatment of everyone improves the chances of both students and staff sticking with the school. A decrease in staff turnover ensures that organisations are more stable and knowledge keeps getting transferred, which supports their success over a long period (Akdere & Egan, 2020).

Figure 9. Impact of Effective Disciplinary Leadership on Institutional Efficiency

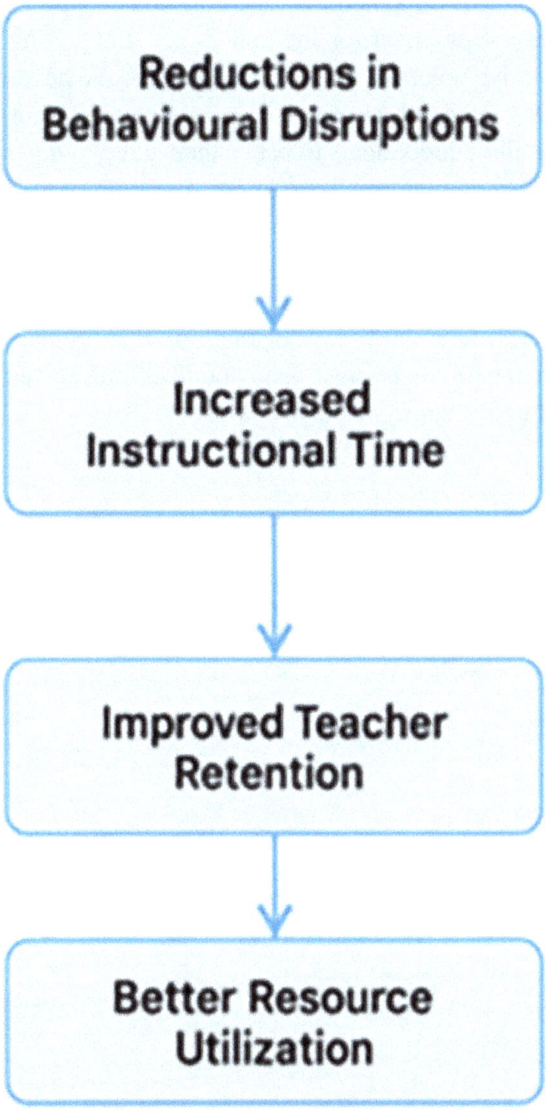

As shown in Figure 9, effective leadership in a discipline reduces the effort needed for the institution to operate smoothly. At the start, the diagram points to Reductions in Behavioural Disruptions, which helps to increase the student's learning time. As a result, teachers tend to stay in their positions for a longer period, which advances Better Use of Available Resources. The figure shows how strong leadership in behaviour can spread in an organisation, making it both more successful and efficient. Through human capital development, schools contribute to the growth of social and learning skills that are practical for life and career. Integrating social-emotional learning and restorative practices into leadership helps the developmental mission by teaching students to be self-aware, feel empathy and solve conflicts (Huguley et al., 2022). They allow individuals to better themselves, which also boosts community health and economic growth. In short, disciplinary leadership influences more aspects than just controlling student behaviour. The way school leaders affect school climate, student achievement, social values, equity and how the school is significantly run affects the future of individuals and the community. Therefore, it is essential for leaders to employ ways of thinking that are purposeful, including all staff and look to the future, because behavioural culture and educational success are closely related in our quickly changing world.

Figure 10. Integration of Social-Emotional Learning (SEL) and Restorative Practices in Human Capital Development

A conceptual model is shown in Figure 10, bringing together Social-Emotional Learning (SEL) and Restorative Practices in the context of disciplinary leadership. The central role is held by SEL, which is supported by "Disciplinary Leadership" and helps develop abilities like empathy and solving conflicts through it. The combination of these skills and improved "Community and Economic Health" helps create "Human Capital." The arrows indicate that there are active connections between all these factors, again highlighting how people skills help the community develop beyond today and support ongoing economic growth.

POLICY IMPLICATIONS AND STRATEGIC RECOMMENDATIONS

As leadership in schools is now recognised as crucial for good school climates and fair behaviour, this should lead to significant new policies. It is essential that this shift in emphasis moves away from simply enforcing rules and uses leadership and team networks to help support long-term, inclusive and easily adaptable behaviour cultures.

This section discusses what recent research and practice imply for policies and advises that strategies should put emphasis on leadership development, fairness, effective use of policies and cooperation with international partners to support disciplinary governance worldwide.

Reframing Behaviour Policies Through Leadership and Network Lenses

In various educational areas, behaviour policies are mainly based on punishments, are spread out and rarely pay attention to stopping future problems or fixing relationships. Nevertheless, recent studies promote treating behaviour policies as active leadership tools that form part of the disciplinary networks where teachers, students, parents and communities share responsibilities, cooperate and provide support (Lodi et al., 2021).

A shift in viewing behaviour policies in this manner guides policymakers to improve collaborative leadership and support restorative and preventive approaches to discipline. A better approach for policies is to support leadership that creates trust, involves everyone and uses cultural strategies fitted to each community. The network approach is consistent with systems thinking in education, as it sees that the behaviour of individuals is shaped by the system of relationships, roles and cultures within an organisation (Iacovidou et al., 2021).

Recommendations for School Leadership Development Programs

As leadership is key to changing disciplinary cultures, special attention should be given to developing leadership. It is essential that these programs educate school leaders on how to put into practice inclusive governance correctly and shared behavioural governance. Training in restorative justice, the use of data to resolve behaviour issues and pedagogy that relates to every culture are essential for leadership development. It is also necessary for leaders to learn facilitation skills and how to engage teachers, students, parents and community members in developing suitable behaviour policies and techniques (Yulianti et al., 2022). In addition, continuous professional development at all levels is essential, with coaching and peer groups, allowing people to exchange difficulties and solutions. These programs should be able to change with the context, address local issues and rely on research and evidence from different education systems (Rich et al., 2021).

Aligning Disciplinary Practices with Equity and Inclusion Goals

A major policy issue is behavioural equity, since unfair exclusion or punishment of groups often leads to greater educational inequalities (Lodi et al., 2021). The use of equity as a central principle in disciplinary practices should mean that schools must break down and review students' behaviour by race, ethnicity, gender, disability and socioeconomic status. Social and emotional contexts affecting behaviour must be recognised by equity-aligned policies that encourage the application of restorative and trauma-informed practices in schools. Ensuring that zero-tolerance rules do not funnel children into issues with the law should be a primary goal of these policies, which should instead look for ways to address individuals' needs (Green et al., 2021). Additionally, making sure marginalised voices are part of creating policies allows schools to address behaviour and ensure it fits the needs and culture of all students (Fuentes et al., 2021). This inclusive strategy is essential for earning trust and legitimacy for disciplinary authorities.

Strategies for Policy Transfer and Contextual Adaptation

The exchange of policies and best practices among nations has been sped up, though it is still tricky to adapt them to different cultures and societies. When creating leadership policies, it is essential to adapt them to the individual context to prevent incomplete or unintended results.

Co-making the processes for behaviours with several levels of stakeholders means the policies fit with the culture, norms and limited resources in the area. Pilot programs and step-by-step introduction of reforms should be encouraged by policymakers since they provide opportunities to fix issues based on actual experiences and information (Sotiriou et al., 2020). It is essential to build capacity among national ministries, teachers and other community leaders to help reform last. International collaboration and partnerships help transfer knowledge, address common issues and design leadership strategies that fit the needs of each organisation (George et al., 2024).

Guidelines for International Agencies Supporting Education Reform

International organisations such as UNESCO, UNICEF and the World Bank contribute significantly to advising countries to include effective leadership strategies and encourage fairness in managing students' behaviour. These agencies should plan their work according to the principles of distributed leadership, equity and cultural responsiveness mentioned in current research.

Leadership at every level need support; so, education should focus on increasing capacity by organising networks that include schools, families and communities (Óskarsdóttir et al., 2020). Flexibility in programs helps them fit different needs, and including mechanisms for local changes prepares them for feedback. In addition, such agencies should promote openness with data and strict checking to point out successful and problematic approaches. Partnerships in research and the spread of knowledge can close the differences between global guidelines and the actual work being done in different areas (Farrell et al., 2022). All policies related to behaviour in schools should be fair, address unequal access and lead to the development of communities where all feel included. By promoting these values, international agencies support actions toward justice in education and help students do better.

CONCLUSION

This chapter highlights the vital interaction between leadership, different fields within education and behaviour management, showing the importance of a strategic and global outlook. It is clear from looking at several approaches that behavioural management rests more on encouraging teamwork, trust among staff and responsiveness to different cultures than on just making rules and enforcing them. The theories discussed highlight the value of distributing leadership to allow educators, students and others involved to share authority and responsibility, which makes the behavioural governance system more robust. In addition, transformational leadership helps through its ability to inspire change based on a vision and improve relationships, which leads people to change their behaviours. At the same time, social learning and behavioural theories show us that behaviour develops in communities and is supported by connections among them, which highlights the importance of having interconnected and friendly academic cultures. It shows that policies, roles and institutional culture are not separate but work together, so behavioural management should be looked at as a whole instead of focusing only on single elements. Comparing different countries like Finland, Bangladesh, South Africa, and Canada demonstrates that disciplinary approaches are affected by social, economic and historical differences. These cases prove that strong leadership needs to support community involvement, favour restorative actions and promote equity. In Finland, Bangladesh, South Africa or Canada, strengthening teamwork shows that distributed leadership is key to improving student behaviour. The leadership ideas mentioned here, in addition, point out that discipline plans thrive when everyone in the school, from students to support staff, feels responsible for their actions and for interventions.

Managing students' behaviour is most successful when parents, community leaders and policymakers are true allies in creating disciplinary actions that fit local culture. It is necessary to value culturally responsive leaders and utilise restorative systems so behavioural challenges are handled proactively, and all students can feel included. As the impacts and outcomes explain, effective leadership and a good behavioural culture help create a positive atmosphere, involve students more and increase learning results. In addition to assisting students to become more disciplined right now, this kind of leadership gets them ready to be responsible and successful citizens in the long run. Also, having equal discipline systems lowers the unfair differences in punishing and excluding students, bringing more justice and equality to schools. Moreover, such cultures assist institutions in being more efficient and help create a stronger workforce, which benefits society and the economy. Instead of the traditional approach, this chapter suggests developing behaviour policies by looking at leadership and how people are connected in networks. Instead of remaining punitive, policies should focus on building programs that help create effective, inclusive and distributed rules by leaders. Ensuring that schools align equity and inclusion with all subjects is necessary to address unfairness and allow all students to do well.

Furthermore, finding good ways to take and change policies among various educational systems helps promote global education while still caring for local differences. Leadership, equity and flexibility are essential qualities in education programs, and international agencies stress these qualities in their support for schools. Moving forward, researchers should pay special attention to studies that follow people over time to see how distributed and transformational leadership affects their actions. Assessing leadership training for managing behaviour will supply information needed for improving professional development. Also, investigating how disciplinary networks function differently in various cultural and economic settings can improve the ways leaders are trained.

REFERENCES

Abdulmuhsin, A. A., Zaker, R. A., & Asad, M. M. (2021). How exploitative leadership influences on knowledge management processes: The moderating role of organisational citizenship behaviour. *The International Journal of Organizational Analysis, 29*(3), 529–561. DOI: 10.1108/IJOA-09-2020-2424

Ainscow, M. (2020). Inclusion and equity in education: Making sense of global challenges. *Prospects, 49*(3–4), 123–134. DOI: 10.1007/s11125-020-09506-w

Akdere, M., & Egan, T. (2020). Transformational leadership and human resource development: Linking employee learning, job satisfaction, and organizational performance. *Human Resource Development Quarterly, 31*(4), 393–421. DOI: 10.1002/hrdq.21404

Al Marjuk, O. (2023). Comparing Secular and Religious Primary Education: Bangladesh's Marriage of Convenience? In *Multifaceted Development* (pp. 23–52). Springer Nature Singapore. DOI: 10.1007/978-981-99-1798-3_2

Asadullah, M., & Morrison, B. (2021). 'Communities are not at the periphery, rather they are at the centre of Restorative Justice in BC': An inquiry into the praxis of Restorative Justice in British Columbia, Canada. *Contemporary Justice Review, 24*(2), 172–196. DOI: 10.1080/10282580.2021.1881893

Asamoah, G. D., Khakpour, M., Carr, T., & Groot, G. (2023). Exploring Indigenous Traditional Healing programs in Canada, Australia, and New Zealand: A scoping review. *Explore (New York, N.Y.), 19*(1), 14–25. DOI: 10.1016/j.explore.2022.06.004 PMID: 35768321

Cénat, J. M., Manoni-Millar, S., David, A., Moshirian Farahi, S. M. M., Jacob, G., Darius, W. P., Beogo, I., & Dalexis, R. D. (2025). Racism in Education among Black Youth in Canada and its Association with Depression, Anxiety, Stress, and Post-Traumatic Stress Disorder. *Research on Child and Adolescent Psychopathology, 53*(7), 999–1015. Advance online publication. DOI: 10.1007/s10802-025-01316-y PMID: 40186816

Chatzipanagiotou, P., & Katsarou, E. (2023). Crisis Management, School Leadership in Disruptive Times and the Recovery of Schools in the Post COVID-19 Era: A Systematic Literature Review. *Education Sciences, 13*(2), 118. DOI: 10.3390/educsci13020118

Darling-Hammond, L., Flook, L., Cook-Harvey, C., Barron, B., & Osher, D. (2020). Implications for educational practice of the science of learning and development. *Applied Developmental Science, 24*(2), 97–140. DOI: 10.1080/10888691.2018.1537791

Emon, M. M. H. (2025a). Leveraging AI on Social Media & Digital Platforms to Enhance English Language Teaching and Learning. In *AI-Powered English Teaching* (pp. 211–238). IGI Global Scientific Publishing., DOI: 10.4018/979-8-3373-1952-0.ch007

Emon, M. M. H. (2025b). Purpose-Driven Intelligence in Green Marketing: Leveraging AI for CSR-Centric and Sustainable Brand Positioning. In *Transforming Business Practices With AI-Powered Green Marketing* (pp. 89–122). IGI Global Scientific Publishing. DOI: 10.4018/979-8-3373-3017-4.ch004

Emon, M. M. H. (2025c). Navigating the Digital Labyrinth: Personal Data Privacy and Security at Individual and Organizational Levels. In *User-Centric Cybersecurity Implications for Sustainable Digital Transformation* (pp. 257–288). IGI Global Scientific Publishing. DOI: 10.4018/979-8-3373-3171-3.ch008

Emon, M. M. H., & Chowdhury, M. S. A. (2025). Safeguarding Student Data: Privacy and Security Challenges in AI-Powered Education Tools. In *Enhancing Student Support and Learning Through Conversational AI* (pp. 191–228). IGI Global Scientific Publishing. DOI: 10.4018/979-8-3373-3316-8.ch008

Emon, M. M. H., & Khan, T. (2025). Corporate Social Responsibility for Sustainable Development: A Systematic Review of Business Contributions to Address Global Challenges. *Review of Business and Economics Studies*, *13*(2), 6–39. DOI: 10.26794/2308-944X-2025-13-2-6-39

Emon, M. M. H., & Mazid-Ul-Haque, M. (2025). Balancing Usability and Security: Enhancing User Experience Without Compromising Privacy. In *User-Centric Cybersecurity Implications for Sustainable Digital Transformation* (pp. 309–342). IGI Global Scientific Publishing. DOI: 10.4018/979-8-3373-3171-3.ch010

Emon, M. M. H., Nath, A., & Nipa, M. N. (2025). *AI for a Greener Tomorrow: Harnessing Artificial Intelligence for Environmental Sustainability*. IGI Global Scientific Publishing., DOI: 10.4018/979-8-3373-2387-9.ch010

Farrell, C. C., Penuel, W. R., Allen, A., Anderson, E. R., Bohannon, A. X., Coburn, C. E., & Brown, S. L. (2022). Learning at the Boundaries of Research and Practice: A Framework for Understanding Research–Practice Partnerships. *Educational Researcher*, *51*(3), 197–208. DOI: 10.3102/0013189X211069073

Fuentes, M. A., Zelaya, D. G., & Madsen, J. W. (2021). Rethinking the Course Syllabus: Considerations for Promoting Equity, Diversity, and Inclusion. *Teaching of Psychology*, *48*(1), 69–79. DOI: 10.1177/0098628320959979

George, G., Fewer, T. J., Lazzarini, S., McGahan, A. M., & Puranam, P. (2024). Partnering for Grand Challenges: A Review of Organizational Design Considerations in Public–Private Collaborations. *Journal of Management*, *50*(1), 10–40. DOI: 10.1177/01492063221148992

Granziera, H., & Perera, H. N. (2019). Relations among teachers' self-efficacy beliefs, engagement, and work satisfaction: A social cognitive view. *Contemporary Educational Psychology*, *58*, 75–84. DOI: 10.1016/j.cedpsych.2019.02.003

Green, A. L., Hatton, H., Stegenga, S. M., Eliason, B., & Nese, R. N. T. (2021). Examining Commitment to Prevention, Equity, and Meaningful Engagement: A Review of School District Discipline Policies. *Journal of Positive Behavior Interventions*, *23*(3), 137–148. DOI: 10.1177/1098300720951940

Hamilton, S. H., Merritt, W. S., Carter, L., Chakraborty, A., Cosijn, M., Lim-Camacho, L., Mishra, R., Syme, G., Das, M., & Ray, D. (2022). Affecting behavioural change through empowerment: Conceptual insights from theory and agricultural case studies in South Asia. *Regional Environmental Change*, *22*(3), 85. DOI: 10.1007/s10113-022-01939-7 PMID: 35761800

Huguley, J. P., Fussell-Ware, D. J., McQueen, S. S., Wang, M.-T., & DeBellis, B. R. (2022). Completing the Circle: Linkages Between Restorative Practices, Socio-Emotional Well-Being, and Racial Justice in Schools. *Journal of Emotional and Behavioral Disorders*, *30*(2), 138–153. DOI: 10.1177/10634266221088989

Iacovidou, E., Hahladakis, J. N., & Purnell, P. (2021). A systems thinking approach to understanding the challenges of achieving the circular economy. *Environmental Science and Pollution Research International*, *28*(19), 24785–24806. DOI: 10.1007/s11356-020-11725-9 PMID: 33289042

Ihmeideh, F., AlFlasi, M., Al-Maadadi, F., Coughlin, C., & Al-Thani, T. (2020). Perspectives of family–school relationships in Qatar based on Epstein's model of six types of parent involvement. *Early Years Journal of International Research and Development*, *40*(2), 188–204. DOI: 10.1080/09575146.2018.1438374

Islam, M. K., Sarker, M. F. H., & Islam, M. S. (2022). Promoting student-centred blended learning in higher education: A model. *E-Learning and Digital Media*, *19*(1), 36–54. DOI: 10.1177/20427530211027721

Kelty, N. E., & Wakabayashi, T. (2020). Family Engagement in Schools: Parent, Educator, and Community Perspectives. *SAGE Open*, *10*(4), 2158244020973024. Advance online publication. DOI: 10.1177/2158244020973024

Khan, T., Emon, M. M. H., & Nath, A. (2024). Quantifying the Effects of AI-Driven Inventory Management on Operational Efficiency in Online Retail. *2024 27th International Conference on Computer and Information Technology (ICCIT)*, 2092–2097. DOI: 10.1109/ICCIT64611.2024.11021996

Khan, T., Emon, M. M. H., Rahman, K. M., Nipa, M. N., & Fuad, M. N. (2025). The Role of AI in Driving Customer Engagement Through Technological, Organizational and Environmental Enablers in E-Commerce. *2025 International Conference on Quantum Photonics, Artificial Intelligence, and Networking (QPAIN)*, 1–6. DOI: 10.1109/QPAIN66474.2025.11171949

Khan, T., Emon, M. M. H., & Rahman, S. (2024). Marketing Strategy Innovation via AI Adoption: A Study on Bangladeshi SMEs in the Context of Industry 5.0. *2024 6th International Conference on Sustainable Technologies for Industry 5.0 (STI)*, 1–6. DOI: 10.1109/STI64222.2024.10951050

Khan, T., & Hasan Emon, M. M. (2024). Determinants of AI Image Generator Adoption Among Marketing Agencies: The Mediating Effects of Perceived Usefulness. *2024 IEEE 3rd International Conference on Robotics, Automation, Artificial-Intelligence and Internet-of-Things (RAAICON)*, 177–182. DOI: 10.1109/RAAICON64172.2024.10928548

Khlaif, Z. N., Salha, S., Affouneh, S., Rashed, H., & ElKimishy, L. A. (2021). The Covid-19 epidemic: Teachers' responses to school closure in developing countries. *Technology, Pedagogy and Education*, *30*(1), 95–109. DOI: 10.1080/1475939X.2020.1851752

Kikabhai, N. (2022). How educational systems respond to diversity, inclusion and social justice: Disability, power, discipline, territoriality and deterritorialization. *The British Journal of Sociology*, *73*(4), 685–698. DOI: 10.1111/1468-4446.12969 PMID: 35842905

Lauder, H., & Mayhew, K. (2020). Higher education and the labour market: An introduction. *Oxford Review of Education*, *46*(1), 1–9. DOI: 10.1080/03054985.2019.1699714

Lodi, E., Perrella, L., Lepri, G. L., Scarpa, M. L., & Patrizi, P. (2021). Use of Restorative Justice and Restorative Practices at School: A Systematic Literature Review. *International Journal of Environmental Research and Public Health*, *19*(1), 96. DOI: 10.3390/ijerph19010096 PMID: 35010355

McLaughlin, A., Walls, J. H., & Kruse, S. (2025). Principal discipline decision-making: Choices and challenges. *Educational Management Administration & Leadership*, 17411432251330958. Advance online publication. DOI: 10.1177/17411432251330958

Memon, N. A., Abdalla, M., & Chown, D. (2024). Laying Foundations for Islamic Teacher Education. *Education Sciences, 14*(10), 1046. DOI: 10.3390/educsci14101046

Mifsud, D. (2024). A systematic review of school distributed leadership: Exploring research purposes, concepts and approaches in the field between 2010 and 2022. *Journal of Educational Administration and History, 56*(2), 154–179. DOI: 10.1080/00220620.2022.2158181

Moran, E., Walsh, E., & Sloan, S. (2025). Promoting a restorative culture in schools: Insights from school leaders. *International Journal of Educational Research Open, 8*, 100397. DOI: 10.1016/j.ijedro.2024.100397

Morgan, L., Close, S., Siller, M., Kushner, E., & Brasher, S. (2022). Teachers' experiences: Social emotional engagement – knowledge and skills. *Educational Research, 64*(1), 41–59. DOI: 10.1080/00131881.2021.1988865

Mowen, T. J., Brent, J. J., & Boman, J. H.IV. (2020). The Effect of School Discipline on Offending across Time. *Justice Quarterly, 37*(4), 739–760. DOI: 10.1080/07418825.2019.1625428 PMID: 34262239

Nadeem, M. (2024). Distributed leadership in educational contexts: A catalyst for school improvement. *Social Sciences & Humanities Open, 9*, 100835. DOI: 10.1016/j.ssaho.2024.100835

Norqvist, L., & Ärlestig, H. (2020). Systems thinking in school organizations – perspectives from various leadership levels. *Journal of Educational Administration, 59*(1), 77–93. DOI: 10.1108/JEA-02-2020-0031

Ogwumike, I., Rangel, V. S., & Johnson, D. D. (2024). The Promise and Pitfalls of Transformational Leadership for Decreasing the Use of Out-of-School Suspensions and Reduce the Racial Discipline Gap. *Education and Urban Society, 56*(2), 230–259. DOI: 10.1177/00131245221106710

Óskarsdóttir, E., Donnelly, V., Turner-Cmuchal, M., & Florian, L. (2020). Inclusive school leaders – their role in raising the achievement of all learners. *Journal of Educational Administration, 58*(5), 521–537. DOI: 10.1108/JEA-10-2019-0190

Paju, B., Kajamaa, A., Pirttimaa, R., & Kontu, E. (2022). Collaboration for Inclusive Practices: Teaching Staff Perspectives from Finland. *Scandinavian Journal of Educational Research, 66*(3), 427–440. DOI: 10.1080/00313831.2020.1869087

Ricart-Huguet, J. (2021). Colonial Education, Political Elites, and Regional Political Inequality in Africa. *Comparative Political Studies, 54*(14), 2546–2580. DOI: 10.1177/0010414021997176

Rich, P. J., Mason, S. L., & O'Leary, J. (2021). Measuring the effect of continuous professional development on elementary teachers' self-efficacy to teach coding and computational thinking. *Computers & Education, 168*, 104196. DOI: 10.1016/j.compedu.2021.104196

Riggs, L., & Landrum, T. (2023). Trauma-Informed PBIS: How Educators Can Combine Evidence-Based Practices for Behavior Management With Trauma-Informed Care. *Beyond Behavior, 32*(3), 152–161. DOI: 10.1177/10742956231201351

Roszkowska, P., & Melé, D. (2021). Organizational Factors in the Individual Ethical Behaviour. The Notion of the "Organizational Moral Structure.". *Humanistic Management Journal, 6*(2), 187–209. DOI: 10.1007/s41463-020-00080-z

Sotiriou, S. A., Lazoudis, A., & Bogner, F. X. (2020). Inquiry-based learning and E-learning: How to serve high and low achievers. *Smart Learning Environments, 7*(1), 29. DOI: 10.1186/s40561-020-00130-x

Urhahne, D., & Wijnia, L. (2023). Theories of Motivation in Education: An Integrative Framework. *Educational Psychology Review, 35*(2), 45. DOI: 10.1007/s10648-023-09767-9

van der Oord, S., & Tripp, G. (2020). How to Improve Behavioral Parent and Teacher Training for Children with ADHD: Integrating Empirical Research on Learning and Motivation into Treatment. *Clinical Child and Family Psychology Review, 23*(4), 577–604. DOI: 10.1007/s10567-020-00327-z PMID: 32968886

Weaver, J. L., & Swank, J. M. (2020). A Case Study of the Implementation of Restorative Justice in a Middle School. *RMLE Online: Research in Middle Level Education, 43*(4), 1–9. DOI: 10.1080/19404476.2020.1733912

White, J. L., Chávez, A. F., & Longerbeam, S. D. (2023). *Teaching Across Cultural Strengths*. Routledge., DOI: 10.4324/9781003447344

Yulianti, K., Denessen, E., Droop, M., & Veerman, G.-J. (2022). School efforts to promote parental involvement: The contributions of school leaders and teachers. *Educational Studies, 48*(1), 98–113. DOI: 10.1080/03055698.2020.1740978

KEY TERMS AND DEFINITIONS

Disciplinary Networks: Involving the roles of educators, administrators, students and stakeholders in formal and informal structures to support the regulation and assistance of students' behavior.

Behavioural Management: The systems and approaches schools use to guide students toward good behaviour and solve disciplinary problems.

Distributed Leadership: A way of leadership where several people work together and share control in managing schools and their operations.

Transformational Leadership: A leadership way that inspires individuals to behave differently by relying on a vision, helping them and fostering positive relationships.

Social Learning Theory: A theory presented by psychologists that mentions behaviour can be picked up by watching, copying and practicing it in society.

Systems Thinking: A thinking process that believes schools work as part of a larger system, where the way rules, jobs and culture interact shapes the outcomes.

Culturally Responsive Leadership: Leadership that values and responds to cultural aspects and needs of the school community to ensure good behaviour is managed efficiently.

Restorative Practices: Strategies that help repair the problem and rebuild relationships instead of simply punishing offenders show more inclusivity and accountability.

Chapter 13
Leading With Purpose: The Role of Academic Heads of Departments in South African Universities

Emmanuel Kojo Oseifuah
https://orcid.org/0000-0002-5362-3514
University of Venda, South Africa

ABSTRACT

This chapter examines the role of academic heads in accounting departments, as endorsed by the South African Institute of Chartered Accountants, with a focus on Historically Disadvantaged Institutions. Drawing on the author's ten years of experience as Academic Head of the Accounting Department, combined with document analysis and an integrated theoretical framework, the chapter offers a holistic lens for understanding lived academic leadership in accounting education in South Africa. The chapter outlines the academic head's role, responsibilities, and expectations, as well as the challenges, opportunities, and core competencies required to fulfil their roles. Additionally, the chapter outlines the key outcomes of the SAICA endorsement journey, including the formal endorsement of the BCom programme, staff capacity development, and improvements in students' performance. It concludes by emphasising the need for a more strategic and integrated approach to leadership development for academic heads of accounting departments.

INTRODUCTION

The role of the Academic Head of Department (HoD) has undergone a significant transformation over the past century, shaped by the changing landscape of higher

DOI: 10.4018/979-8-3373-3616-9.ch013

education, institutional governance, and academic professionalism. This chapter examines the role of the Academic Head of Department within a Historically Disadvantaged Institution (HDI) accredited/endorsed by the South African Institute of Chartered Accountants (SAICA) to offer its professional accounting programmes. Positioned at the intersection of higher education and the accounting profession, the HoD plays a strategic leadership role in shaping curriculum delivery, fostering academic excellence, and ensuring alignment with SAICA's rigorous professional accounting standards. Given the unique challenges and transformative potential within HDIs, this chapter explores how academic heads navigate institutional constraints, drive innovation, and contribute to the broader goals of equity, professional relevance, and educational quality in accounting education.

To fully appreciate the complexities of academic leadership, one must first consider how the role of the HoD has historically evolved within university systems. According to Western (2008), the concept of academic leadership has undergone significant transformation over the past century, shaped by institutional reforms, socio-political dynamics, and evolving educational paradigms. The emergence of departmental leadership in universities is closely tied to the formalisation of academic departments in the early 20th century, particularly within Western institutions, where disciplinary specialisation became the norm. University leadership initially centred around scholar-leaders who embodied academic excellence and intellectual stewardship. However, as higher education systems expanded and became more complex, leadership roles evolved to include managerial responsibilities. Duderstadt (2007) highlights this transition, noting the rise of shared governance models and the increasing administrative demands placed on academic leaders. These changes marked a shift from purely academic oversight to hybrid roles that required balancing scholarship with institutional management. Historical contexts have also played a critical role in shaping leadership philosophies. Townsend (2024) traces the evolution of educational leadership from ancient systems to the transformational models of the 1970s, emphasising how broader societal changes, such as industrialisation and bureaucratisation, influenced leadership structures and expectations. At the departmental level, leadership is often characterised by paradoxes and tensions. Kruse (2022) and Caron (2019) explore the challenges faced by department chairs, who must navigate the delicate balance between academic autonomy and administrative accountability. These roles demand adaptive leadership strategies, as chairs are responsible for faculty development, curriculum oversight, and aligning departmental goals with institutional priorities. Caron (2019) further notes that many departmental leaders operate within a dual academic-administrative framework, often without formal leadership training, which can lead to role ambiguity and stress. This highlights the importance of leadership development programmes tailored to the unique demands of academic departments.

Recent scholarship has identified ideological shifts in academic leadership, driven by neoliberal reforms and market-oriented policies. Macfarlane, Bolden, and Watermeyer (2024) categorise leadership discourses into three dominant perspectives: traditionalist, reformist, and pragmatist. Their review of over 250 sources reveals how performance metrics, accountability, and strategic planning have become central to leadership expectations in contemporary higher education. Global trends in academic leadership research further illustrate the increasing complexity of leadership roles. Mohamud, Farah, & Osman et al. (2025), through a bibliometric analysis of over 4,000 publications, identify emerging themes such as distributed leadership, inclusive governance, and digital transformation. In the African context, including South Africa, the HoD position has been influenced by post-colonial restructuring, resource constraints, and the imperative for transformational leadership in historically disadvantaged institutions (HDIs). The role often entails navigating systemic inequalities, fostering inclusive academic cultures, and driving curriculum reform to meet national development goals. Moreover, the career trajectory of HoDs reflects broader challenges in academic identity. Floyd (2009) highlights that many academics enter departmental leadership with limited preparation, which can lead to role ambiguity and identity conflict. The balancing act between being a scholar, manager, and leader often results in professional dilemmas, particularly in environments where leadership development is under-resourced.

The body of literature collectively reveals that academic leadership, particularly at the departmental level, has evolved from informal scholarly stewardship to multifaceted roles embedded within institutional governance structures. This evolution reflects broader ideological, structural, and pedagogical shifts in higher education. Understanding this trajectory is essential for developing leadership models that are both contextually relevant and strategically effective. In the South African higher education landscape, HoDs in accounting departments play a critical role in shaping academic quality, fostering transformation, and ensuring compliance with professional standards set by SAICA. This leadership position is particularly complex within Historically Disadvantaged Institutions (HDIs), where HoDs must navigate systemic challenges such as resource constraints, institutional politics, high administrative workload, legacies of inequality, and the pressure to meet rigorous SAICA endorsement standards while promoting inclusive and contextually relevant education (Woldegiorgis & Chiramba, 2025; Letshwene & Du Plessis, 2021; HRSC, 2025). Despite the centrality of the HoD in driving academic excellence and institutional reform, there is a conspicuous lack of scholarly inquiry into their lived experiences, leadership practices, challenges, and opportunities they encounter in SAICA-endorsed accounting programmes (Kativhu, 2025). Existing literature tends to focus broadly on leadership in higher education or on curriculum transformation, without adequately capturing the unique realities of departmental leadership in professional accounting education within historically marginalised contexts (CHE, 2025; Govender & McDonald, 2022). This gap in the literature limits the development of leadership models and support mechanisms that are responsive to the unique demands of HDIs and the professional expectations of SAICA. Without a deeper understanding of what constitutes effective leadership in this context, efforts to strengthen accounting education and improve student outcomes may remain misaligned with institutional realities.

BACKGROUND

According to the commemorative volume *Celebrating 30 Years of Education at the University of Venda (Molapo,* Nyamukondiwa, & Chingombe, 2012), which chronicles the institution's development from its founding in 1982 to 2012, the University of Venda (Univen) was initially established as a branch of the University of the North (now the University of Limpopo) on February 18, 1981. Initially, Univen had a student population of 177 individuals who had completed their first year at the University of the North. The establishment of the university was influenced by the South African Black Students' Constitution Act of 1971, which specifically excluded black students from university education. To address this educational gap, the Parliament of the Venda homeland enacted the University of Venda Act, 1981 (Act No. 19 of 1981) on November 6 1981. Univen officially opened its doors in 1982, using the facilities at Dimani Agricultural High School. Like other historically black universities in South Africa, the university's mission was to serve the black communities, particularly those speaking Venda. Its primary objective was to function as a higher education institution within the Venda homeland, aiming to train and upgrade teachers' academic qualifications. Additionally, it sought to cultivate an educated elite with the managerial skills necessary to foster entrepreneurship and meet the workforce needs of the Venda homeland, specifically in the fields of agriculture and business. Since the dawn of democracy in 1994, the University of Venda has operated under the Higher Education Act (Act 101 of 1997) as amended. By the vision[1] and mission,[2] Moreover, the Statute of the University of Venda, the Council, and senior management (at the initiation of the SAICA-endorsed project) committed themselves to growing Univen into a quality-driven, financially sustainable, comprehensive university, to be among the top five South African universities by 2030.

The University of Venda for Science and Technology, as it was known since its establishment, underwent a name change to its current name, the University of Venda (Univen), in the late 2000s. Until 2013, the university only offered the Bachelor of Commerce in Accounting (general) programmes. This has disadvantaged the local community from benefiting from the training of Chartered Accountants through the offering of the prestigious SAICA-endorsed professional Bachelor of Commerce in Accounting Sciences qualification, which forms the basis for the training of Chartered Accountants in South Africa. The situation, however, changed positively when a tripartite partnership agreement involving the University of Venda, Bankseta, and the South African Institute of Chartered Accountants (SAICA) was reached on September 3 2013. The purpose of the partnership was to enhance the Department of Accountancy at the University of Venda's capacity to offer a four-year Bachelor of Commerce degree in Accounting Sciences. The actual implementation of the project commenced in January 2014 with the recruitment of the first cohort of 50 students on a full Bankseta bursary. The intake has increased from 100 annually in the 2015 academic year to the current number. Furthermore, the university has partnered with the University of Johannesburg to implement the project, serving as an SAICA endorsement partner/mentor.

The objectives of this collaboration are as follows: 1. To support and guide the development of strong academic capacity and resources at UNIVEN that meet the SAICA accreditation requirements and competency framework, ensuring the sustainable delivery of the Chartered Accountant (CA) program. 2. To assist in building sufficient operational, management, and physical capacity at UNIVEN for the sustainable delivery of the CA program. 3. To guide UNIVEN through the SAICA accreditation process. 4. To support pilot groups of learners in obtaining a qualification that will grant them access to Part 1 of the SAICA Qualifying Examination (QE Part 1) during the timeframe of the project. 5. To collaboratively foster support among academic, student, and community stakeholders for the reaccreditation process.

It is important to emphasise that the groundwork for the SAICA endorsement initiative began in the early 2000s. At that time, the University of Venda was the last public university in South Africa to offer DHET-approved and CHE-accredited Bachelor of Commerce in Accounting programmes that were not endorsed by SAICA. This situation caused dissatisfaction among BCom graduates, prospective students, and, importantly, the public, resulting in negative publicity surrounding the credibility of the university's BCom (Accounting) programmes (City Press, 2007; Sowetan, 2007). This discontent is not surprising. Long before the unfavourable publicity, the Department of Accounting and Auditing (as it was known at the time) had repeatedly sought permission from SAICA to initiate the endorsement process but was unsuccessful. The primary obstacles included inadequate infrastructure—such as ICT labs, lecture and tutorial venues, library facilities, student accommodation, and staff offices—and an insufficient academic staff complement needed to support a prestigious SAICA-endorsed programme.

THEORETICAL PERSPECTIVES

This study is grounded in a multi-theoretical framework that draws on four interrelated yet distinct theoretical perspectives: Critical Pedagogy, Transformational Leadership Theory, Institutional Theory, and Stakeholder Theory. These frameworks collectively provide a robust analytical lens for examining the complex dynamics influencing the role of academic heads of accounting departments in HDIs in South Africa.

Critical Pedagogy, as articulated by Freire (2017), emphasises the transformative potential of education in challenging oppressive structures and fostering critical consciousness. It positions learners and educators as co-creators of knowledge through dialogical engagement, thereby aligning with the emancipatory goals of inclusive and socially responsive accounting education. Within the context of HDIs, this perspective is particularly relevant for interrogating how pedagogical practices can empower students from marginalised backgrounds and promote epistemic justice.

Transformational Leadership Theory, conceptualised initially by Burns (1978) and later expanded by Bass (2008), provides a framework for understanding leadership as a process of inspiring and motivating followers to achieve higher levels of performance and moral development. Stewart (2006) examined the evolution of transformational leadership in educational settings, noting its adaptability in response to systemic change and accountability pressures. Salanova, Lorente, & Martínez (2011) elaborated on the psychological mechanisms underpinning transformational leadership, highlighting its role in fostering trust, self-efficacy, and high-quality leader-member relationships. Collectively, these studies emphasise the enduring relevance of transformational leadership theory in guiding leadership development, organisational transformation, and follower empowerment. The theory's integration into diverse domains, from corporate management to education, demonstrates its robustness and adaptability in addressing contemporary leadership challenges.

Institutional Theory provides a robust structural lens for examining how institutional norms, formal rules, and isomorphic pressures shape organisational behaviour and strategic decision-making (DiMaggio & Powell, 1983). Recent scholarship has extended Institutional Theory to higher education leadership, particularly in settings marked by historical inequities and reform pressures (Moikanyane, 2023). These studies demonstrate how institutional pressures (coercive, mimetic, and normative) affect leadership decisions related to curriculum transformation, accreditation compliance, and responsiveness to socio-political imperatives. For instance, Muchiri and Muathe (2024) highlight how HDIs must align with national accreditation standards while simultaneously adapting to global reforms in accounting education. Drawing on Institutional Theory, this chapter aims to illuminate the structural and normative forces that shape educational reform efforts in HDIs, particularly in the integration of emerging technologies and global standards into accounting education.

Stakeholder Theory (Freeman, 2010) complements the aforementioned perspectives by outlining the ethical and relational dimensions of organisational governance. It emphasises the importance of engaging a diverse array of stakeholders (students, faculty, professional bodies, government agencies, and local communities) in decision-making processes that shape institutional direction and curriculum development. Recent scholarship has expanded this view, highlighting stakeholder engagement as a critical mechanism for enhancing educational quality, inclusivity, and responsiveness (Bridoux & Stoelhorst, 2022; Yang, Qiu, & Yu, 2024). In the context of historically disadvantaged institutions (HDIs), stakeholder expectations are deeply influenced by historical inequities and contemporary imperatives for transformation, decolonisation, and accountability (Ajani, 2024; Mahabeer, 2025; Bidandi, Byaruhanga, & Malinga, 2022).

This chapter integrates these theoretical perspectives to establish a comprehensive framework for analysing the multifaceted role of academic heads in shaping accounting education within marginalised contexts. By synthesising stakeholder theory with leadership and curriculum transformation literature, the framework enables an understanding of the interplay between pedagogy, institutional structures, leadership practices, and stakeholder engagement. Such an integrative approach contributes to both theoretical advancement and practical insight into curriculum transformation in HDIs, offering pathways for inclusive, contextually relevant, and socially just educational reform (Gerwel, Reddy, & Govender, 2025; Moikanyane, 2023).

Integrated Framework

The integrated framework positions the academic head as a transformative agent operating at the intersection of four interrelated domains: 1) Pedagogical Transformation (Critical Pedagogy), 2) Visionary Leadership (Transformational Leadership), 3) Institutional Legitimacy (Institutional Theory), and 4) Stakeholder Engagement (Stakeholder Theory). These domains are mutually reinforcing. For example, a commitment to critical pedagogy may drive curriculum reform, which in turn requires transformational leadership to implement, institutional navigation to legitimise, and stakeholder engagement to sustain. The framework can be visualised as a four-quadrant model with the academic head at the centre, symbolising their role as a nexus of influence and coordination.

Figure 1. Multi-theoretical framework for analysing the role of academic heads

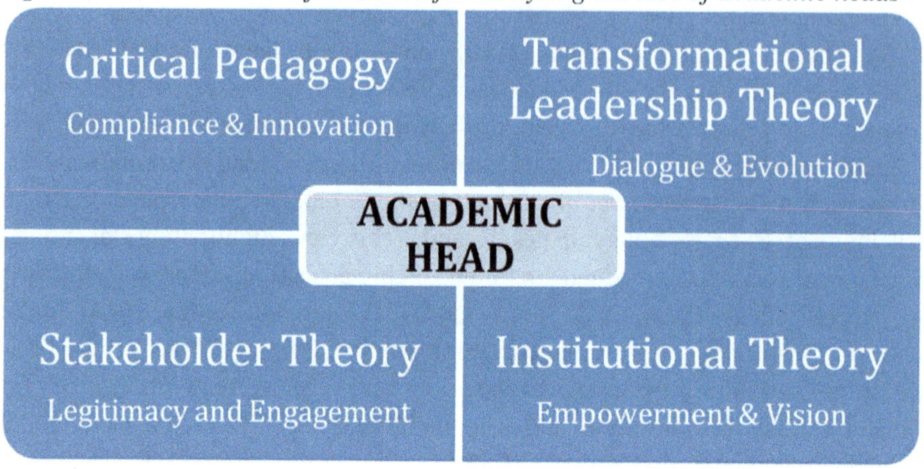

Source: Author's Construction

Empirical literature

As stated in the introduction section, a growing body of empirical research has explored the multifaceted role of academic department heads in universities, highlighting the complexity of their leadership responsibilities and the contextual factors that shape their effectiveness. The multifaceted nature of the academic head's responsibilities encompasses student affairs, staff wellbeing, departmental governance, financial oversight, and external representation within institutional leadership structures (Gmelch, 2019; Geschwind et al., 2019; Walker, 2022). These studies provide valuable insights into how these leaders navigate their roles as academic leaders and administrative managers.

Ngare (2024) emphasises the importance of transformational and collaborative leadership styles in promoting academic success, while also noting the significant accountability pressures academic heads face. This aligns with findings by Fung and Gordon (2016), who examine academic heads in research-intensive universities and reveal the tensions between academic identity and managerial responsibilities. Their study highlights the need for distributed leadership models and more explicit role definitions to support mid-level managers. Building on Ngare's work, Kariyana (2024) examines how academic heads navigate institutional politics and resource constraints while upholding academic standards. This study reinforces the need for strategic leadership training and institutional support mechanisms.

The influence of professional background is explored by Rybnicek, Leitner, and Plakolm (2019), who find that academic department heads with prior industry or leadership experience often bring innovative and adaptive approaches to departmental management. This suggests that leadership development programmes should consider diverse career trajectories when preparing future academic leaders. Other studies explore how leadership in higher education must evolve to meet the demands of crisis and transformation, albeit from different geographical and contextual perspectives. For example, Lalani, Crawford, & Butler-Henderson (2021) identify a range of leadership styles, authentic, servant, situational, distributed, leader-member exchange, and ineffective, that emerged during the early COVID-19 pandemic. The authors noted that these styles interacted with environmental factors such as social networks and financial management, emphasising the need for adaptive and innovative leadership. The study highlights the importance of developing specific leadership behaviours that can enhance institutional preparedness for future crises, especially in leveraging educational technology.

Anthony and Antony (2017) argue that while academic leadership shares principles with conventional leadership theory, it is uniquely shaped by the cultural and political dynamics of academic institutions. They question whether effective leadership requires traits developed through academic career progression or if exceptional external leaders can successfully lead within academia. Expanding on this, Kazi (2025) explores leadership dynamics in UK universities, focusing on the interactions between heads of academic units and senior leaders. Using a five-part model, the study highlights how personal, social, structural, and contextual factors influence leadership relationships, revealing the need for adaptive and responsive leadership practices.

Seale (2019) examines the role of middle-level academic leaders in African universities, arguing that leadership development must be reimagined to respond to both local and global disruptions effectively. These include student-led movements such as *#RhodesMustFall* and *#FeesMustFall*, which emerged in South Africa as calls for decolonisation, equity, and systemic reform in higher education. Recent scholarship has emphasised the need for contextually grounded leadership development in higher education. Zulfqar, Valcke, et al (2021) present a compelling case for a holistic and integrated leadership intervention, designed to address the complex socio-political and cultural realities of academic institutions in developing contexts. Their study, although situated in Pakistan, offers valuable parallels to South African HDIs, where structural inequalities, historical legacies, and calls for transformation demand leadership that is both responsive and reflective. Incorporating this perspective into the current study enriches the theoretical framework by aligning leadership development with curriculum transformation efforts in HDIs. It supports the argument that academic leadership must be reimagined not only in terms of administrative competence but also in terms of ethical responsiveness, stakeholder engagement, and pedagogical innovation.

In South Africa, academic leadership is further complicated by post-apartheid imperatives of transformation, equity, and redress (Badat, 2010). Heads of Departments (HoDs), particularly in HDIs, must balance academic quality with socio-political goals, often under resource constraints and governance tensions (Jansen, 2004). Mouton et al. (2015) advocate for distributed leadership to address these challenges. Nevertheless, tensions between vocational training and academic research, especially in commerce faculties, are highlighted by Coetzee and Schmulian (2013) and Tewari and Ilesanmi (2022). Ngwenya and Maseko (2022) emphasise the importance of resilience and adaptability in navigating systemic challenges such as funding limitations and digital transformation. Relational leadership also emerges as a key theme. Nkomo, Horne, and du Plessis (2015) demonstrate that high-quality leader-member exchange (LMX) relationships significantly influence academic staff perceptions of institutional support, underscoring the importance of interpersonal dynamics in talent development. Finally, Crawford (2021) explores the emotional and personal dimensions of leadership, advocating for self-awareness and emotional intelligence as essential tools for navigating institutional politics and fostering collaboration. Together, these studies present a multidimensional view of academic leadership—one that integrates strategic competence, relational engagement, emotional insight, and contextual responsiveness to meet the evolving demands of higher education.

METHODOLOGY

Research design

A qualitative approach, employing a single-case study design, was used to explore the role of the academic head of the accounting department in a historically disadvantaged Institution (HDI) in the Limpopo Province, South Africa. This approach enabled a holistic understanding of the phenomenon (Creswell & Creswell, 2018). By focusing on HDIs, the chapter aims to provide insight into leadership practices, institutional dynamics, and the influence of professional bodies' endorsement standards in these under-resourced universities.

Data Collection and Analysis

Secondary data were collected mainly through document analyses (e.g., departmental reports, personal experiences, institutional policies, SAICA site visit reports, among others). These data sources provided a comprehensive picture of the role of HoDs, including their responsibilities, leadership styles, challenges, opportunities, and impact on the university. The findings are systematically presented and discussed in alignment with each of the stated research objectives.

> Objective 1: To examine the strategic roles of the academic head of accounting departments within SAICA-endorsed universities in South Africa.

This objective explores the key strategic roles and leadership functions performed by the HoD. The roles include: 1) Academic leadership, 2) Strategic planning, 3) Academic quality assurance, 4) Staff development and transformation, and 4) Stakeholder engagement.

Academic leadership

Academic leadership in SAICA-endorsed accounting departments encompasses strategic, pedagogical, and operational responsibilities that align with both institutional goals and the professional standards set by SAICA. A primary focus of this role is ensuring that programmes meet the requirements of the CA2025 Competency Framework, which emphasises ethical leadership, integrated thinking, and sustainable value creation (SAICA, 2021). Key components of academic leadership include:

- Strategic and Academic Oversight
- Quality Assurance and Compliance
- Faculty Development and Mentorship
- Student Success and Transformation
- External Engagement and Professional Collaboration
- Administrative and Institutional Leadership

Strategic and Academic Oversight involves aligning academic content with SAICA's technical and enabling competencies while integrating pervasive skills such as ethical reasoning, communication, and decision-making. In terms of Quality Assurance and Compliance, Heads of Departments (HoDs) must ensure that programs are endorsed by SAICA, which follows accreditation by the Council on Higher Education (CHE) and registration on the National Qualifications Framework (NQF). Conducting regular curriculum reviews is crucial for maintaining relevance in a dynamic professional environment. Faculty Development and Mentorship are critical for success. HoDs should recruit and support qualified staff, preferably Chartered Accountants (CA(SA)), and promote excellence in teaching, research, and postgraduate supervision. Implementing quality assurance processes, including moderation, peer review, and continuous improvement, is necessary to uphold academic standards and meet SAICA's endorsement criteria. Student Success and

Transformation are also top priorities. Academic leaders should create inclusive learning environments, support historically disadvantaged students, and promote initiatives such as Thuthuka. Enhancing relational and decision-making skills is vital for graduate employability and professional readiness. External Engagement and Professional Collaboration are essential for maintaining relevance and fostering partnerships. HoDs are expected to facilitate internships, guest lectures, and joint research initiatives to strengthen links between academia and industry. Research leadership includes promoting scholarly work in accounting education, ethics, and emerging technologies. Encouraging faculty participation in publications and conferences enhances the department's academic profile and contributes to thought leadership. Operational responsibilities include managing budgets, staffing, timetabling, and ensuring compliance with institutional policies. Strategic planning and departmental reviews are crucial for maintaining continuous improvement and ensuring alignment with evolving academic and professional standards. In summary, academic leadership in SAICA-accredited departments demands a balanced focus on strategic vision, academic integrity, professional relevance, and transformative impact.

Strategic planning

Regarding strategic planning, the HoD is responsible for guiding the department in creating and implementing strategies that align with the institution's overarching goals and national priorities. This involves encouraging innovation in teaching and learning, promoting excellence in research, and ensuring that the department plays a significant role in advancing the university's transformation agenda. Through visionary guidance and collaborative engagement, the HoD facilitates the development and implementation of strategies that position the department as a key driver of academic and societal impact.

Academic quality assurance

Within this framework, the HoD is entrusted with overseeing the standards of teaching, learning, and assessment across the department. This responsibility includes monitoring the effective delivery of the curriculum, upholding academic integrity, and ensuring the quality of student outcomes meets the rigorous endorsement criteria set by SAICA. Through continuous quality assurance and academic leadership, the HoD plays a critical role in maintaining the department's credibility and alignment with professional accreditation standards.

Staff development and transformation

The HoD also plays a critical role in staff development and institutional transformation. This includes advancing equity and diversity within the department, fostering the professional growth of academic staff, and cultivating an inclusive academic environment that supports and empowers emerging scholars—particularly those from historically underrepresented groups. Through strategic mentorship and capacity-building initiatives, the HoD contributes to the creation of a vibrant, diverse, and socially responsive academic community.

Stakeholder engagement

Stakeholder engagement constitutes a vital dimension of the HoD's leadership role. This involves actively liaising with key external and internal stakeholders (including SAICA, industry partners, funding entities, alumni, and relevant university structures) to ensure the department remains professionally relevant and responsive to the evolving needs of students and employers. Through strategic partnerships and continuous dialogue, the HoD fosters a dynamic interface between academia and the professional world, thereby enhancing curriculum relevance, graduate employability, and institutional impact.

CHALLENGES

Curriculum Compliance and Alignment

Onc of the primary challenges is ensuring that the curriculum complies with SAICA's evolving competency frameworks, such as CA2025, which emphasise ethical leadership, integrated thinking, and digital acumen (SAICA, 2021). This necessitates ongoing curriculum review and alignment, often with limited institutional resources.

Resource Constraints

Resource constraints are particularly severe in historically disadvantaged institutions (HDIs), where funding shortages, inadequate infrastructure, and high student-to-staff ratios impede the delivery of quality education (Frans, 2022; Clerkiq, 2025).

Staff Recruitment and Retention

These limitations also impact the recruitment and retention of qualified academic staff, especially those with CA(SA) credentials, who are often attracted to more lucrative opportunities in the private sector (Thryv, 2024).

Transformation and Equity Pressures

Transformation imperatives add a layer of complexity. Academic leaders must spearhead efforts to increase access for Black students and staff, decolonise curricula, and promote gender equity, all while ensuring the academic and professional integrity of their programs (Badat, 2010).

Student Preparedness and Throughput

Moreover, many students enter university underprepared due to systemic inequalities in basic education, which necessitates the implementation of academic support systems to improve throughput rates (Du Plessis & Gerber, 2012)

Ethical and Professional Conduct

The ethical dimension of accounting education has gained prominence in light of corporate scandals. Academic leaders are expected to ensure that ethics is not only taught but also meaningfully integrated into the curriculum, in accordance with SAICA's emphasis on responsible leadership (SAICA, 2021).

Transformation and Equity Pressures

Transformation imperatives add another layer of complexity. Academic heads must lead efforts to increase access for black students and staff, decolonise curricula, and promote gender equity, all while maintaining the academic and professional integrity of their programmes (Badat, 2010).

Ethical and Professional Conduct

The ethical dimension of accounting education has also gained prominence in the wake of corporate scandals. Academic heads are expected to ensure that ethics is not only taught but meaningfully integrated into the curriculum, in line with SAICA's emphasis on responsible leadership (SAICA, 2021).

OPPORTUNITIES

Curriculum Innovation and Digital Transformation

The CA2025 framework encourages the integration of digital competencies and value creation, offering opportunities to modernise curricula and adopt blended learning models (SAICA, 2021).

Leadership in Transformation

Leadership in transformation is another key opportunity. Institutions such as the University of Johannesburg have shown that strategic leadership can lead to significant progress in equity and inclusion.

Partnerships and Funding

Partnerships and funding initiatives, such as the Thuthuka Bursary Fund, provide critical support for disadvantaged students, enabling academic heads to improve access and success rates (SAICA, 2023).

Research and Thought Leadership

Moreover, academic heads can position their departments as thought leaders by promoting research in emerging areas such as ESG accounting, ethics, and African accounting practices (Universities South Africa, 2024).

Graduate Employability and Impact

Finally, SAICA-endorsed programmes are highly respected, and graduates enjoy strong employment prospects. Academic heads thus play a pivotal role in shaping future business leaders and contributing to national development.

CORE COMPETENCIES AND LEADERSHIP PRACTICES

This objective is analysed and discussed under the following domains: Academic leadership, Strategic and operational management skills, Interpersonal and team leadership, Communication and stakeholder engagement, and ethical and professional integrity. Academic leadership remains a foundational competency for HoDs. Subject matter expertise enables leaders to guide curriculum development, uphold academic standards, and mentor faculty members (Black, 2015). In addition to disciplinary depth, HoDs must foster a research-oriented culture that promotes scholarly productivity and interdisciplinary collaboration (Garcia et al., 2023). The ability to lead curriculum innovation, particularly in response to technological advancements and evolving pedagogical practices, is also critical (Adams, 2023).

Strategic and operational management skills are vital for aligning departmental goals with institutional priorities. Strategic planning allows HoDs to anticipate and respond to internal and external changes, ensuring that departmental initiatives remain relevant and impactful (Schoemaker, Krupp and Howland, 2013). Effective resource management, encompassing budgeting, staffing, and infrastructure oversight, is crucial for maintaining departmental performance (City & Curtis, 2025). Furthermore, a sound understanding of academic governance and policy implementation is essential for ensuring compliance with quality assurance frameworks and accreditation standards (Black, 2015).

Interpersonal and team leadership competencies are equally important. The ability to support staff development through mentoring and performance management contributes to faculty growth and departmental cohesion. Conflict resolution skills enable HoDs to mediate disputes and foster a collegial work environment (Deming, 2017). Inclusive leadership, which promotes diversity, equity, and inclusion, is increasingly viewed as a strategic imperative in higher education (City and Curtis, 2025).

Communication and stakeholder engagement are critical dimensions of effective leadership. Clear and empathetic communication with faculty, students, and administrative units enhances transparency and trust (Deming, 2017). Advocacy and representation of departmental interests in institutional forums and external partnerships are necessary for securing resources and recognition (City & Curtis, 2025). Responsiveness to student needs and the ability to foster a supportive learning environment further contribute to departmental success (Black, 2015).

In the context of rapid institutional change, HoDs must demonstrate adaptability and innovation. Leading through digital transformation, curriculum reform, and evolving pedagogical models requires flexibility and vision (Bazerman, 2020). Encouraging innovative teaching and research practices not only enhances academic quality but also positions the department as a leader in its field (Gampala, 2023). Finally, ethical and professional integrity underpins all aspects of effective leadership. Transparency and accountability in decision-making are essential for maintaining credibility and trust within the department (Ko et al., 2018). Fairness and confidentiality in handling staff and student matters are essential for reinforcing the ethical standards expected of academic leaders (Bazerman, 2020). These core competencies collectively define the profile of an effective Head of Department in universities. As higher education continues to evolve, the ability of HoDs to integrate these competencies will remain critical to institutional resilience, academic excellence, and stakeholder satisfaction.

THE IMPACT OF SAICA ENDORSEMENT

The South African Institute of Chartered Accountants' endorsement of the Bachelor of Commerce in Accounting Sciences programme at the University of Venda marks a significant milestone in the university's academic development and its strategic commitment to transformation and excellence. This accreditation has had a far-reaching impact on both the Accounting Department and the university as a whole, affirming its capacity to deliver a programme that meets the rigorous standards required for the training of Chartered Accountants in South Africa.

As part of the BCom Accounting Sciences endorsement process, SAICA carried out a 3-day site visit (11-13 March 2019) at Univen (four and a half years after the pilot project was launched). Before the visit, the department prepared and submitted a 134-page Self-Evaluation Report (SER) to SAICA. The SER is a critical document that demonstrates how the university's accounting programme aligns with SAICA's standards for academic quality, governance, and professional readiness. The SER was organised into the following sections: Executive Summary, Institutional Overview, Programme Overview, Academic Quality and Standards, Faculty and Staff, Student Profile and Support, Infrastructure and Resources, Stakeholder Engagement, Quality Assurance and Continuous Improvement, Compliance with SAICA Requirements, and Appendices.

The executive summary provides a concise overview of the university, the purpose of the report, and key highlights regarding the accounting programme's alignment with SAICA's endorsement criteria. This section sets the tone for the report and outlines the university's commitment to academic excellence and professional readiness. Following the summary, the report provides a detailed institutional overview, describing the university's history, mission, and strategic direction. It outlines the governance structures, leadership roles, and how the university's values and goals align with SAICA's vision for developing future chartered accountants.

The programme overview section introduces the accounting qualification under review, detailing its objectives, structure, and intended learning outcomes. It explains how the curriculum is designed to meet SAICA's competency framework and prepares students for the professional pathway. Academic quality and standards are then discussed, focusing on teaching and learning strategies, assessment practices, moderation processes, and the integration of ethics, sustainability, and emerging technologies. This section highlights how the institution ensures that graduates possess the necessary technical and professional competencies. The report continues with a profile of the faculty and staff, including their qualifications, professional experience, and scholarly contributions. It includes information on staff development initiatives, workload management, and the university's commitment to maintaining high teaching standards.

Student profile and support services are addressed next, providing data on student demographics, admission criteria, progression rates, and academic support mechanisms. This section emphasises how the institution fosters student success and prepares learners for the accounting profession. Infrastructure and resources are then described, including physical facilities, ICT systems, library access, and availability of accounting software and databases. The report demonstrates how these resources support effective teaching, learning, and research.

Stakeholder engagement is explored through the institution's partnerships with industry, alum networks, and advisory boards. It outlines how feedback from employers and graduates informs curriculum development, enhancing the relevance of the programme. The report then discusses quality assurance and continuous improvement processes. This section reflects the university's commitment to continually enhancing academic standards. Finally, the report presents a comprehensive mapping of the programme's outcomes to SAICA's competency framework, demonstrating compliance with SAICA's endorsement requirements. It includes evidence of alignment with SAICA's standards for learning, teaching, and professional development. Supporting documents, including subject files, curriculum maps, faculty CVs, assessment rubrics, and institutional policies, are included in the appendices to substantiate the claims made throughout the report.

The BCom in Accounting Sciences programme at the University of Venda (UNIVEN) was officially endorsed by SAICA, following a successful review of the Self-Evaluation Report and related supporting evidence. This endorsement marks a historic milestone, as it is the first time that SAICA has allowed UNIVEN to offer a professional BCom Accounting programme. This enviable achievement signifies the university's full integration into the national framework for chartered accountancy education. The endorsement was met with widespread celebration, recognising the collaborative efforts of UNIVEN, SAICA, the University of Johannesburg (UJ), BANKSETA, and Thuthuka. More importantly, by endorsing the BCom Accounting programme, SAICA certifies that UNIVEN has put the appropriate resources in place that, if utilised effectively, should enable it to deliver the programme at the required standards and levels of quality; and also that the BCom Accounting Sciences programme meets SAICA's requirements in terms of the standards of learning and teaching.

The endorsement reflects the culmination of sustained institutional efforts to enhance academic quality, reform curriculum structures, and build capacity within the Accounting Department. It also signifies the university's successful alignment with national imperatives aimed at redressing historical inequities in higher education, particularly among Historically Disadvantaged Institutions (HDIs). The collaborative engagements with the University of Johannesburg, BANKSETA, and SAICA's Thuthuka programme were instrumental in facilitating this transformation, providing critical support in areas such as staff development, curriculum design, and quality assurance.

The Accounting Department has undergone a comprehensive academic review and restructuring process to meet the standards of SAICA's accreditation. This has resulted in the implementation of a curriculum that is both professionally relevant and pedagogically sound, equipping students with the competencies required to enter the Chartered Accountancy profession. The department's enhanced academic standing has enabled it to attract a more diverse and academically capable student body, while also laying the groundwork for the introduction of a SAICA-endorsed Postgraduate Diploma in Accounting (PGDA) Sciences programme.

Students have benefited significantly from the endorsement, gaining access to professional networks, mentorship opportunities, and financial support mechanisms such as the Thuthuka Education Upliftment Fund. These resources have improved student retention, academic performance, and graduate employability, particularly among those from disadvantaged backgrounds. The endorsement has thus contributed meaningfully to the diversification of the accounting profession and the empowerment of students from rural and underserved communities.

At the institutional level, the SAICA endorsement aligns with the University of Venda's two-decade Strategic Plans, which prioritise academic excellence, transformation, and societal impact. The university's recognition as a SAICA-endorsed institution enhances its national profile and affirms its role as a key contributor to the development of a skilled and inclusive workforce.

Beyond the university, the accreditation is expected to yield positive socioeconomic outcomes for the Limpopo province and the broader South African context. By producing highly skilled accounting professionals, the University of Venda is contributing to job creation, poverty alleviation, and economic development in regions historically excluded from mainstream economic participation.

To consolidate the gains achieved through SAICA endorsement and to ensure sustained impact, the following strategic actions are recommended. First, the university should expedite the development and accreditation of a Postgraduate Diploma in Accounting, thereby providing a seamless academic pathway for students aspiring to qualify as Chartered Accountants. Second, continued investment in staff development is crucial to maintaining academic standards and supporting the delivery of a dynamic and responsive curriculum. This includes encouraging faculty participation in professional development programmes and academic research aligned with SAICA competencies. Third, strengthening student support services, including academic advising, career counselling, and mentorship programmes, will be critical in enhancing student success and professional readiness. Fourth, the university should deepen its engagement with industry stakeholders to ensure that the curriculum remains relevant and that students are exposed to practical experiences through internships, work-integrated learning, and guest lectures. Fifth, ongoing monitoring and evaluation of programme outcomes should be institutionalised to assess the effectiveness of the curriculum, identify areas for improvement, and ensure alignment with evolving professional standards. Finally, the university should leverage its SAICA accreditation to foster regional partnerships and community outreach initiatives that promote financial literacy, entrepreneurship, and economic empowerment in Limpopo and surrounding areas. In conclusion, the SAICA endorsement has positioned the University of Venda as a transformative force in the field of accounting education. By implementing the above recommendations, the university can further strengthen its academic offerings, enhance student outcomes, and make a meaningful contribution to national development objectives.

DISCUSSION

This chapter examines the role of the HoD within an HDI endorsed by SAICA to offer the professional BCom Accounting Sciences programme. The findings reveal that leadership in this context extends beyond administrative duties, requiring a purpose-driven approach that aligns with broader educational and societal objectives. A central theme is dual accountability to both internal university governance and external bodies, such as government regulatory bodies (e.g., DHET, CHE, SAQA), professional bodies (e.g., SAICA), and funding bodies (e.g., Bankseta, FASSET, ISFAP, and Thuthuka). This duality necessitates a leadership style that is collaborative, visionary, and adaptive, capable of harmonising departmental objectives with evolving national and global standards in accounting education.

The chapter further emphasises the need for transformational leadership. That is, leaders who inspire innovation in curriculum development, foster research excellence, and promote graduate employability. Academic heads of accounting departments are increasingly expected to act as change agents, particularly in response to SAICA's evolving competency frameworks (e.g. CA2025 project, now known as the CA of the Future), technological advancements, and the imperative for transformation and inclusivity in higher education. Equally important is the role of relational leadership. Effective heads of department cultivate trust-based relationships with faculty, students, professional bodies, and university executives. They must balance academic freedom with performance accountability, and collegiality with strategic oversight. This relational dynamic is especially critical in the South African context, where historical inequities and institutional transformation remain pressing concerns. Ultimately, the chapter argues that purpose-driven leadership (grounded in ethical stewardship, social responsiveness, and a commitment to excellence) is essential for navigating the multifaceted responsibilities of leading an accounting department in a SAICA-endorsed institution.

FUTURE RESEARCH DIRECTIONS

This chapter examines the complex role of academic leaders in SAICA-endorsed accounting departments within South African universities, with a focus on a case study in a historically disadvantaged institution (HDI). The findings reveal that leadership in this context goes beyond administrative responsibilities; it requires a purpose-driven approach that aligns with broader educational and societal goals. Based on these insights, several directions for future research are suggested: 1. Future studies could investigate the differences in leadership styles and departmental governance across HDIs, as well as how these differences impact curriculum innovation and student outcomes. 2. Empirical research is necessary to assess the relationship between academic leadership practices and the success of departments in maintaining SAICA accreditation, particularly in resource-constrained environments. 3. Further exploration is needed into how academic leaders manage the tension between SAICA's global standards and the local needs for curriculum transformation and decolonisation in post-apartheid South Africa. 4. There is an opportunity to explore how universities prepare future academic leaders in accounting, including aspects such as mentorship, leadership training, and succession planning strategies. 5. As accounting education increasingly integrates emerging technologies (e.g., AI, data analytics, blockchain), future research could investigate how academic leaders drive digital transformation initiatives and manage related change processes. 6. Research could also focus on the representation and experiences of women and other underrepresented groups in academic leadership roles within accounting departments. 7. Additionally, studies might explore how academic leaders collaborate with external stakeholders, such as SAICA, industry partners, and alumni, to co-create relevant and future-ready accounting curricula.

CONCLUSION

The chapter suggests that the Head of the Accounting Department within a SAICA-endorsed South African university is a strategic and multifaceted leadership position. This role is instrumental in shaping the direction of the accounting profession by ensuring that graduates are not only technically competent but also ethically grounded. Leading effectively in this context necessitates a capacity to navigate complexity, drive transformation, and foster a shared vision that harmonises academic objectives with professional standards and societal imperatives. As the higher education landscape and the accounting profession continue to evolve, the significance of academic leadership will intensify, requiring inclusive, adaptive, and visionary approaches. Accordingly, future research and policy initiatives should prioritise the professional development and institutional support of these leaders, acknowledging their pivotal role at the intersection of academia and professional practice. Such investment will enable South African universities to sustain accounting departments that are globally competitive, locally responsive, and purposefully governed.

REFERENCES

Adams, J. (2023). *Curriculum innovation in higher education.* Routledge.

Ajani, O. (2024). Stakeholder expectations and governance challenges in historically disadvantaged institutions. *Journal of Educational Policy and Transformation, 18*(2), 145–162.

Anthony, S. G., & Antony, J. (2017). Academic leadership – special or simple. *International Journal of Productivity and Performance Management, 66*(5), 630–637. DOI: 10.1108/IJPPM-08-2016-0162

Badat, S. (2010). *The challenges of transformation in higher education and training institutions in South Africa.* Development Bank of Southern Africa.

Bass, B. M. (2008). *The Bass handbook of leadership: Theory, research, and application* (4th ed.). Free Press.

Bazerman, M. H. (2020). A new model for ethical leadership. *Harvard Business Review, 98*(5), 90–97.

Bidandi, F., Byaruhanga, J., & Malinga, T. (2022). Governance and accountability in historically disadvantaged higher education institutions in South Africa. *African Journal of Public Affairs, 14*(3), 78–95.

Black, S. A. (2015). Qualities of effective leadership in higher education. *Open Journal of Leadership, 4*(2), 54–66. DOI: 10.4236/ojl.2015.42006

Bridoux, F., & Stoelhorst, J. W. (2022). Stakeholder governance: Solving the collective action problems in joint value creation. *Academy of Management Review, 47*(2), 214–236. DOI: 10.5465/amr.2019.0441

Burns, J. M. (1978). *Leadership.* Harper & Row.

Caron, R. M. (2019). Departmental leadership: Navigating productive tension while in a paradoxical role. *Frontiers in Education, 4*, 97. DOI: 10.3389/feduc.2019.00097

City, E. L., & Curtis, R. (2025). *Leading strategically: Achieving ambitious goals in education.* Harvard Education Press.

City Press. (2007). *BCom degrees shocker: Lowly qualifications mean graduates are unemployable by Chuenyame.* Gershwin.

Clerkiq. (2025) *Navigating accounting resource constraints and the talent shortage in South Africa.* Available at: https://clerkiq.io/blog/navigating_accounting_resource_constraints (Accessed: September 20 2025).

Coetzee, S. A., & Schmulian, A. (2013). Relevance of a competency framework for accounting education: Perspectives from South Africa. *Accounting Education, 22*(4), 345–368.

Council on Higher Education (CHE). (2025). *Reflecting, renewing, and realigning: A baseline study of conceptions of curriculum transformation in South African universities.*

Crawford, M. (2021). Being a head of department in an English university. *Educational Review, 75*(6), 1168–1180. DOI: 10.1080/00131911.2021.2000368

Creswell, J. W., & Creswell, J. D. (2018). *Research design: Qualitative, quantitative, and mixed methods approach* (5th ed.). SAGE Publications.

Deming, D. J. (2017). The Growing Importance of Social Skills in the Labour Market. *The Quarterly Journal of Economics, 132*(4), 1593–1640. DOI: 10.1093/qje/qjx022

DiMaggio, P. J., & Powell, W. W. (1983). The iron cage revisited: Institutional isomorphism and collective rationality in organisational fields. *American Sociological Review, 48*(2), 147–160. DOI: 10.2307/2095101

Du Plessis, L., & Gerber, D. (2012). Academic preparedness of students – an exploratory study. *The Journal for Transdisciplinary Research in Southern Africa, 8*(1), 81–94. DOI: 10.4102/td.v8i1.7

Duderstadt, J. J. (2007). Academic leadership. In *The View from the Helm: Leading the American University during an Era of Change* (pp. 111–132). University of Michigan Press. DOI: 10.3998/mpub.168531

Floyd, A. (2009). *Focusing the kaleidoscope: Investigating the newly formed role of 'academic lead' at a research-led university.* Leadership Foundation for Higher Education.

Freeman, R. E. (2010). *Strategic management: A stakeholder approach.* Cambridge University Press., DOI: 10.1017/CBO9781139192675

Freire, P. (2017). *Pedagogy of the Oppressed.* Penguin Classics.

Fung, D., & Gordon, C. (2016). *Rewarding educators and education leaders in research-intensive universities.* Higher Education Academy.

Gampala, M. (2023). Innovative Approaches to Teaching and Learning. *Shanlax International Journal of English, 12*(S1-Dec, S1), 138–145. DOI: 10.34293/rtdh.v12iS1-Dec.86

Garcia, D., Clemente Fuentes, R. W., Hyer, S., & Broszko, C. M. (2023). Cultural Influences Catalysing Resident Scholarly Productivity. *Family Medicine*, *55*(10), 653–659. DOI: 10.22454/FamMed.2023.239179 PMID: 37540530

Geschwind, L., Aarrevaara, T., Berg, L. N., & Lind, J. K. (2019). The changing roles of academic leaders: Decision-making, power, and performance. In Pinheiro, R., Geschwind, L., Foss Hansen, H., & Pulkkinen, K. (Eds.), *Reforms, organisational change and performance in higher education*. Palgrave Macmillan. DOI: 10.1007/978-3-030-11738-2_6

Gmelch, W. H. (2019). The call for department chair leadership: Why chairs serve, what they do, how they develop, how long they serve, and is there life after chairing? *International Journal of Leadership and Change*, *7*(1), 1.

Govender, L., & McDonald, Z. (2022). *Understanding epistemic access and success for historically disadvantaged students in South African public universities*. CHE.

Human Sciences Research Council (HSRC). (2025). *Policy brief: Historically disadvantaged institutions and research funding*. HSRC.

Jansen, J. D. (2004). Autonomy and accountability in the regulation of the teaching profession: The case of South Africa. *Research Papers in Education*, *19*(1), 51–66. DOI: 10.1080/0267152032000176972

Kariyana, I. (2024). Aspirations and constraints of middle managers in higher education institutions: A systematic literature review. *Journal of Public Administration and Development Alternatives*, *9*(3), 128–145. DOI: 10.55190/JPADA.2024.347

Kativhu, S. (2025). *Historically disadvantaged institutions and the SARChI initiative: Addressing research deficits*. HSRC Policy Brief.

Kazi, D. D. (2025). Leading up: Perspectives of the heads of departments and schools on their interactions with hierarchy in UK universities. *Journal of Educational Administration and History*, •••, 1–17. DOI: 10.1080/00220620.2024.2446884

Ko, M., Reich, M. R., Takemi, T., & Howland, S. (2018). The Core Roles of Transparency and Accountability in the Governance of Global Health Public–Private Partnerships. *Health Systems and Reform*, *4*(3), 239–248. DOI: 10.1080/23288604.2018.1465880 PMID: 30207904

Kruse, S. D. (2022). Department chair leadership: Exploring the role's demands and tensions. Portland State University. https://www.pdx.edu/academic-affairs/sites/academicaffairs

Lalani, K., Crawford, J., & Butler-Henderson, K. (2021). Academic leadership during COVID-19 in higher education: Technology adoption and adaptation for online learning during a pandemic. *International Journal of Leadership in Education, 28*(1), 1–17. DOI: 10.1080/13603124.2021.1988716

Letshwene, M. J., & Du Plessis, E. C. (2021). The challenges of implementing the Curriculum and Assessment Policy Statement in accounting. *South African Journal of Education, 41*(Suppl. 2), 1–10. DOI: 10.15700/saje.v41ns2a1978

Macfarlane, B., Bolden, R., & Watermeyer, R. (2024). Three perspectives on leadership in higher education: Traditionalist, reformist, pragmatist. *Higher Education, 88*(4), 1381–1402. DOI: 10.1007/s10734-023-01174-x

Mahabeer, P. (2025). Curriculum transformation in South African HDIs: Navigating equity and epistemic justice. *South African Journal of Higher Education, 39*(1), 1–20.

Mohamud, Z. A., Farah, M. A., Osman, L. A., Mohamed, M. A., & Mohamud, I. H. (2025). Mapping the evolution of leadership in higher education: A bibliometric analysis. *Cogent Education, 12*(1), 2554957. DOI: 10.1080/2331186X.2025.2554957

Moikanyane, M. (2023). Reimagining curriculum reform in historically disadvantaged institutions: A participatory approach. *Journal of Curriculum Studies in Africa, 11*(4), 56–74.

Molapo, S., Nyamukondiwa, P., & Chingombe, K. (2012). Celebrating 30 years of education at the University of Venda: From inkpot to iPad – Towards an educational centre of excellence. In B. Rootman (Ed.), *University of Venda*. Thohoyandou: University of Venda.

Mouton, J., Louw, H., & Strydom, A. (2015). A typology of research capacity development initiatives. *South African Journal of Higher Education, 29*(1), 1–22.

Muchiri, C. W., & Muathe, S. M. (2024). Strategic orientation and organisational performance: Evidence from Rotary Clubs in Kenya. *Journal of Business and Management Sciences, 12*(2), 99–110. DOI: 10.12691/jbms-12-2-3

Ngare, R. (2024). The role of heads of departments (HODs) in university management: Leadership and accountability in academic success. *Greener Journal of Social Sciences, 14*(2), 203–211. DOI: 10.15580/gjss.2024.2.102024140

Ngwenya, T., & Maseko, P. (2022). Leadership in historically disadvantaged universities: Challenges and opportunities. *Journal of Higher Education Policy, 34*(3), 210–225.

Nkomo, S., Horne, A. L., & Du Plessis, Y. (2015). Role of department heads in academic development: A leader-member exchange and organisational resource perspective. *Educational Management Administration & Leadership*, •••, 44.

Rybnicek, R., Leitner, K. H., Baumgartner, L., & Plakolm, J. (2019). Industry and leadership experiences of the heads of departments and their impact on the performance of public universities. *Management Decision*, *57*(12), 3321–3345. DOI: 10.1108/MD-10-2018-1173

Salanova, M., Lorente, L., Chambel, M. J., & Martínez, I. M. (2011). Linking transformational leadership to nurses' extra-role performance: The mediating role of self-efficacy and work engagement. *Journal of Advanced Nursing*, *67*(10), 2256–2266. DOI: 10.1111/j.1365-2648.2011.05652.x PMID: 21535088

Schoemaker, P. J. H., Krupp, S., & Howland, S. (2013). *Strategic Leadership: The Essential Skills*. Harvard Business Review, January–February Issue.

Seale, O. (2019). Re-imagining leadership development for middle-level academic leaders in Africa. *Journal of Higher Education in Africa / Revue de l'enseignement supérieur en Afrique, 17*(1), 1–26.

South African Institute of Chartered Accountants (SAICA). (2021). *CA2025 Competency Framework: Pathways to relevance*. Johannesburg.

South African Institute of Chartered Accountants (SAICA). (2023). *SAICA-accredited academic programmes: CA (SA) and AGA (SA).*

Sowetan. (2007). "Concerns About the Graduate Quality of the University of Venda's BCom Accounting Programme".

Stewart, J. (2006). Transformational Leadership: An Evolving Concept Examined through the Works of Burns, Bass, Avolio, and Leithwood. *Canadian Journal of Educational Administration and Policy*, (54), 1–29.

Tewari, D. D., & Ilesanmi, O. A. (2022). Conflicting Goals of SAICA and South African Universities: Implications for Accounting Research. *South African Journal of Accounting Research, 36*(1), 1–15.

Thryv, 2024. Small Business Index Report, available at: https://www.thryv.com/2024-smb-index/ (accessed September 20 2025).

Townsend, T. (2024). Transforming educational leadership: A historical context. *Education Sciences*, *14*(8), 890. DOI: 10.3390/educsci14080890

Universities South Africa. (2024) *Thought Leadership Series*. Available at: https://usaf.ac.za/thought-leadership-series/ (Accessed: September 27 2025).

Walker, J. G. (2022). How to develop and nurture academic leaders at our universities. https://usaf.ac.za/how-to-develop-and-nurture-academic-leaders-at-our-universities

Western, S. (2008). An overview of the leadership discourses. In Preedy, M., Bennett, N., & Wise, C. (Eds.), *Leadership and Management in Education: Cultures, Change and Context* (pp. 11–16). SAGE Publications.

Woldegiorgis, E. T., & Chiramba, O. (2025). Access and success in higher education: Fostering resilience in historically disadvantaged students in South Africa. *Journal of Applied Research in Higher Education, 17*(2), 759–776. DOI: 10.1108/JARHE-05-2023-0217

Yang, J., Qiu, H., & Yu, W. (2024). Surging currents: A systematic review of the literature on dynamic stakeholder engagements in higher education in the generative artificial intelligence era. *Journal of Asian Public Policy*. Advance online publication. DOI: 10.1080/17516234.2024.2429046

Zulfqar, A., Valcke, M., Devos, G., & Tuytens, M. (2021). Developing academic leaders: Evaluation of a leadership development intervention in higher education. *SAGE Open, 11*(3), 1–13. DOI: 10.1177/2158244021991815

KEY TERMS AND DEFINITIONS

Accounting Education: The teaching and learning processes, curricula, and activities designed to develop knowledge, skills, and competencies in accounting.

Academic Head of Department: A senior academic and administrative leader of a specific department, responsible for providing strategic direction, academic leadership, and operational management in alignment with the institution's mission and national higher education policies.

Critical Pedagogy: An educational philosophy and approach that emphasises the role of education in challenging social injustices and empowering learners to question and transform oppressive structures in society.

Higher Education: Post-secondary level of education offered by universities, universities of technology, and other accredited institutions, leading to qualifications such as diplomas, degrees, and postgraduate certifications.

Historically Disadvantaged Institution (HDI): A university or higher education institution in South Africa that was systematically underfunded, marginalised, and deprived of resources under apartheid policies. These institutions primarily served Black African, Coloured, and Indian populations and were excluded from equitable access to infrastructure, academic development, and research funding.

Institutional Theory: A sociological framework that explains how institutions (such as universities) develop, operate, and change in response to external pressures, cultural norms, and regulatory environments. It emphasises the role of established rules, routines, and shared beliefs in shaping organisational behaviour and decision-making.

Leading with Purpose: The practice of guiding individuals or organisations by articulating and embodying a clear, inspiring mission or set of values that motivates others, aligns efforts, and drives meaningful outcomes.

SAICA endorsement: The formal recognition by the South African Institute of Chartered Accountants of specific academic programmes offered by higher education institutions that meet the professional and educational standards required for entry into SAICA's Chartered Accountant [CA(SA)] and Associate General Accountant [AGA(SA)] designations.

Stakeholder Theory: A framework in business ethics and organisational management that posits that an organisation should create value not only for its shareholders but for all its stakeholders – individuals or groups who are affected by or can affect the organisation's operations. This includes employees, customers, suppliers, communities, regulators, and investors.

Transformational Leadership: A leadership style in which leaders inspire and motivate followers to exceed expectations by transforming their attitudes, beliefs, and values to align with a shared vision and purpose. It emphasises personal development, innovation, and positive change within individuals and organisations.

1 A university leading in engaged scholarship.

2 The University of Venda produces graduates who are locally relevant and globally competitive.

Compilation of References

Aayog, N. I. T. I. (2025). Expanding Quality Higher Education through States and State Public Universities. https://www.niti.gov.in/sites/default/files/2025-02/Expanding-Quality-Higher-Education-through-SPUs.pdf

Abad-Segura, E., & González-Zamar, M.-D. (2021). Sustainable Economic Development in Higher Education Institutions: A Global Analysis within the SDGs Framework. *Journal of Cleaner Production*, *294*, 126133. DOI: 10.1016/j.jclepro.2021.126133

Abdullah, M. A. (2022). Using the educational tablet: An evaluation study of teachers' and pupils' views in Egyptian primary schools. *Education and Information Technologies*, *27*(6), 8771–8792. DOI: 10.1007/s10639-022-10958-0

Abdulmuhsin, A. A., Zaker, R. A., & Asad, M. M. (2021). How exploitative leadership influences on knowledge management processes: The moderating role of organisational citizenship behaviour. *The International Journal of Organizational Analysis*, *29*(3), 529–561. DOI: 10.1108/IJOA-09-2020-2424

Abdul-Rahman, A., Tahir, L. M., Anis, S. N. M., & Ali, M. F. (2020). Exploring challenges in practising instructional leadership: Insights from senior secondary principals. *Universal Journal of Educational Research*, *8*(11C), 83–96. DOI: 10.13189/ujer.2020.082310

Abebe, Z. A., Admassu, K. A., & Belayneh, T. N. (2024). Interplay between civic engagement, political trust, and support for democracy: Insights from a study on youth students at Addis Ababa University, Ethiopia. *Social Sciences & Humanities Open*, *10*, 101152. DOI: 10.1016/j.ssaho.2024.101152

Abouzeid, M., Muthanna, A., Nuwayhid, I., El-Jardali, F., Connors, P., Habib, R. R., Akbarzadeh, S., & Jabbour, S. (2022). Barriers to sustainable health research leadership in the Global South: Time for a Grand Bargain on localisation of research leadership? *Health Research Policy and Systems*, *20*(1), 136. DOI: 10.1186/s12961-022-00910-6

Abrahamsen, J. (2023). Tools to create interactive digital communities as our world embraces virtual learning—the annual, 1.

Abu Alfoul, M. N., Bazhair, A. A., Khatatbeh, I. N., Arian, A. G., & Abu Al-Foul, M. N. (2024). The Effect of Education on Economic Growth in Sub-Saharan African Countries: Do Institutions Matter? *Economies*, 12(11), 300. https://www.mdpi.com/2227-7099/12/11/300

Acton, K. S. (2021). School leaders as change agents: Do principals have the tools they need? *Management in Education*, *35*(1), 43–51. DOI: 10.1177/0892020620927415

Adams, J. (2023). *Curriculum innovation in higher education*. Routledge.

Adesina, O. S., & Danjibo, N. D. (2022). *Mainstreaming peace education in Nigeria: Policy gaps and prospects*. Peace and Development Centre Press.

Adesoji, A. O. (2021). Governance and peacebuilding: A policy gap in Nigeria. *Journal of Development and Peace Studies*, *9*(2), 55–68.

Agasisti, T., & Petrenko, O. (2024). Higher Education and Economic Development: A Bibliometric Analysis 1985-2022. *European Journal of Education*, *59*(3), e12653. https://onlinelibrary.wiley.com/doi/10.1111/ejed.12653. DOI: 10.1111/ejed.12653

Agyekum, B., Salifu, I., Eshun, S. N., & Asamoah, M. K. (2025). Exploring the implications of using parent-teacher associations (PTAs) as a pathway for school-community development. *Journal of Professional Capital and Community*, *10*(4), 465–480. Advance online publication. DOI: 10.1108/JPCC-06-2024-0092

Ahmad, I., & Islam, M. R. (2024). Empowerment and Participation: Key Strategies for Inclusive Development. In *Building Strong Communities: Ethical Approaches to Inclusive Development* (pp. 47–68). Emerald Publishing Limited. DOI: 10.1108/978-1-83549-174-420241003

Ahmad, I., & Islam, M. R. (2024). The Road Ahead in the 21st Century: Mapping Global Progress in Ethical Approaches to Inclusive Community Development. In Building Strong Communities: Ethical Approaches to Inclusive Development (pp. 91-131). Emerald Publishing Limited.

Ahmad, J., Khan, A. W., & Khan, H. U. (2021). Role of Critical Success Factors in Offshore Quality Requirement Change Management Using SLR. *IEEE Access : Practical Innovations, Open Solutions*, *9*, 99680–99698. DOI: 10.1109/ACCESS.2021.3096663

Ahmed, I. (2010). SAARC: Social charter and human security. In *The Emerging Dimensions of SAARC*. Foundation Books. DOI: 10.1017/UPO9788175968615.007

Ahmed, Z. S. (2018). The Role of SAARC and EU in Managing Refugees in South Asia and Beyond: Potential for North-South Cooperation. *Global Policy*, *9*(1), 76–84. DOI: 10.1111/1758-5899.12526

Ainscow, M. (2020). Inclusion and equity in education: Making sense of global challenges. *Prospects*, *49*(3–4), 123–134. DOI: 10.1007/s11125-020-09506-w

Ajani, O. (2024). Stakeholder expectations and governance challenges in historically disadvantaged institutions. *Journal of Educational Policy and Transformation*, *18*(2), 145–162.

Akdere, M., & Egan, T. (2020). Transformational leadership and human resource development: Linking employee learning, job satisfaction, and organizational performance. *Human Resource Development Quarterly*, *31*(4), 393–421. DOI: 10.1002/hrdq.21404

Akour, M., & Alenezi, M. (2022). Higher education future in the era of digital transformation. *Education Sciences*, *12*(11), 784. DOI: 10.3390/educsci12110784

Al Marjuk, O. (2023). Comparing Secular and Religious Primary Education: Bangladesh's Marriage of Convenience? In *Multifaceted Development* (pp. 23–52). Springer Nature Singapore. DOI: 10.1007/978-981-99-1798-3_2

Alenezi, M. (2023). Digital Learning and Digital Institution in Higher Education. *Education Sciences*, *13*(1), 88. DOI: 10.3390/educsci13010088

Alfehaid, M. M. A., Johri, A., Sehajpal, S., & Jain, A. (2025). Exploring the Synergies Between SDG 9 and SDG 3: The Role of Innovation and Infrastructure in Enhancing Public Health. *International Journal of Sustainable Development and Planning*, *20*(6), 2293–2315. DOI: 10.18280/ijsdp.200604

Alifuoco, A. (2024). Exhausting the (Human) Problem: A Performable Dys/Solution. *Performance Philosophy*, *9*(1), 183–204. DOI: 10.21476/PP.2024.91439

Allaste, A.-A., Beilmann, M., & Pirk, R. (2022). Non-formal and Informal Learning as Citizenship Education: The Views of Young People and Youth Policymakers. *Journal of Applied Youth Studies*, *5*(1), 19–35. DOI: 10.1007/s43151-021-00059-z

Alli, A., Lin, T., Thorndyke, L. E., Parekh, R., & Núñez, A. E. (2021). Advancing women to leadership positions through individual actions and institutional reform. Pediatrics, 148(Supplement 2).

Allison, S. T., & Goethals, G. R. (2024). *Heroic leadership: An influence taxonomy of 100 exceptional individuals*. Routledge. DOI: 10.4324/9781003328681

Almazroa, H., Alotaibi, W., & Alrwaythi, E. (2024). Sustainable Development Goals and Future-Oriented Teacher Education Programs. *IEEE Transactions on Engineering Management, 71*, 13517–13530. DOI: 10.1109/TEM.2022.3165686

Altbach, P. G., Androushchak, G., Kuzminov, Y., Yudkevich, M., & Reisberg, L. (2013). The global future of higher education and the academic profession: The BRICs and the United States. In *The Global Future of Higher Education and the Academic Profession: The BRICs and the United States*. Palgrave Macmillan., DOI: 10.1057/9780230369795

Altynbassov, B., Bayanbayeva, A., Tolegen, M., & Zhamankarin, M. (2024). A comprehensive bibliometric analysis of trends in higher education leadership in the Global South, 2013-2023: Contemporary perspectives and developments. *International Journal of Educational Research, 127*, 102421. DOI: 10.1016/j.ijer.2024.102421

Amaral, N. C. (2016). Higher education in Brazil: Dilemmas, challenges and comparison with oecd and brics countries [A educação superior brasileira: Dilemas, desafios e comparações com os países da OCDE e do BRICS]. *Revista Brasileira de Educação, 21*(66), 717–736. DOI: 10.1590/S1413-24782016216637

Aminudin, N., & Jamal, S. A. (2024). Social capital and economic mobility in tourism: A systematic literature review. *Cogent Social Sciences, 10*(1), 2321665. Advance online publication. DOI: 10.1080/23311886.2024.2321665

Anderson, J. D. (2023). Exploring the misalignment between state and federal policies: Trials and tribulations in a west texas school district (Doctoral dissertation, The University of Texas at El Paso).

Ani, K. J. (2025). Let peace reign: Introducing peace education for Nigerian national transformation. *Journal of Education and Learning Technology, 6*(2), 60–68. DOI: 10.38159/jelt.2025624

Ansell, C., Sørensen, E., & Torfing, J. (2022). *Co-creation for sustainability: the UN SDGs and the power of local partnerships*. Emerald Publishing. DOI: 10.1108/9781800437982

Antai, G. O., Ekpenisi, C., Okonji, C. I., Kolo, E. A., & Okpong, D. E. (2025). Balancing national security and human Rights: A critical analysis of Nigeria's anti-terrorism laws. *NIU Journal of Social Sciences, 11*(1), 287–299. DOI: 10.58709/niujss.v11i1.2148

Anthony, S. G., & Antony, J. (2017). Academic leadership – special or simple. *International Journal of Productivity and Performance Management, 66*(5), 630–637. DOI: 10.1108/IJPPM-08-2016-0162

Apostu, S. A., Mukli, L., Panait, M., Gigauri, I., & Hysa, E. (2022). Economic Growth through the Lenses of Education, Entrepreneurship, and Innovation. *Administrative Sciences, 12*(3), 74. https://www.mdpi.com/2076-3387/12/3/74. DOI: 10.3390/admsci12030074

Ari, R., Altinay, Z., Altinay, F., Dagli, G., & Ari, E. (2022). Sustainable Management and Policies: The Roles of Stakeholders in the Practice of Inclusive Education in Digital Transformation. *Electronics (Basel), 11*(4), 585. DOI: 10.3390/electronics11040585

Arora, P. (2024). *From pessimism to promise: Lessons from the Global South on designing inclusive tech.* MIT Press.

Arowolo, D. O., & Alani, R. A. (2022). Peace education and the challenges of implementation in Nigerian schools. *Journal of Educational Sociology, 14*(2), 33–47.

Arun, D. P., Malik, J. S., & Shelar, R. (2022). Perceived Challenges of National Education Policy, 2020 by the Students. *Indian Journal of Extension Education, 58*(2), 73–76. https://journals.acspublisher.com/index.php/ijee/article/view/209. DOI: 10.48165/IJEE.2022.58214

Asadullah, M., & Morrison, B. (2021). 'Communities are not at the periphery, rather they are at the centre of Restorative Justice in BC': An inquiry into the praxis of Restorative Justice in British Columbia, Canada. *Contemporary Justice Review, 24*(2), 172–196. DOI: 10.1080/10282580.2021.1881893

Asamoah, G. D., Khakpour, M., Carr, T., & Groot, G. (2023). Exploring Indigenous Traditional Healing programs in Canada, Australia, and New Zealand: A scoping review. *Explore (New York, N.Y.), 19*(1), 14–25. DOI: 10.1016/j.explore.2022.06.004 PMID: 35768321

Ashoka Kumar Thakur vs. Union of India and Others (2008) 6 SCC 1.

Asri, F. H. M., Singh, D., Mansor, Z., Norman, H., Alshurideh, M. T., Alzoubi, M. R., Falaki, N., Mohammad, S. I., & Mohammad, A. A. S. (2025). *An Insight of the Importance of Stakeholders in Collaborative Online Learning*. COLAB., DOI: 10.1007/978-3-031-74220-0_10

Avolio, B. J., Bass, B. M., & Jung, D. I. (1999). Reexamining the components of transformational and transactional leadership using the multifactor leadership questionnaire. *Journal of Occupational and Organizational Psychology, 72*(4), 441–462. DOI: 10.1348/096317999166789

Ayane, Z. T., & Mihiretie, D. M. (2024). Developing good person and citizen through civic and ethical education in Ethiopia: A content analysis of secondary school textbooks. *Social Sciences & Humanities Open, 10*, 100913. DOI: 10.1016/j.ssaho.2024.100913

Azadi, N., & Das, P. P. P. (2024). A thematic analysis of the significance of peace education in managing aggression in adolescents. *Indian Journal of Psychological Medicine, XX*, 1–4. DOI: 10.1177/02537176241293635 PMID: 39588481

Azoury, N., & Harvey, S. (2023). The Changing Role of Governance in Education. In *Governance in Higher Education* (pp. 211–231). Springer Nature Switzerland., DOI: 10.1007/978-3-031-40586-0_10

Bacha, N. S., & Kosa, C. A. (2024). Nurturing a sense of institutional citizenship behaviour: Role of perceived transformational leadership style and organisationalorganisational support mediated by affective professional commitment. *Leadership and Policy in Schools, 23*(2), 235–252. DOI: 10.1080/15700763.2022.2113799

Bachir, E., & Vogel, B. (2025). *Strategic Contextual Leadership: The Blueprint for CEOs and Executives to Master the Art of Leadership in Dynamic Contexts* (Vol. 8). Walter de Gruyter GmbH & Co KG. DOI: 10.1515/9783111382722

Badada, B., Delina, G., Krishnaraj, R., & Thiruthuvanathan, M. M. (2025). Navigating Leadership and Technology Integration in the Digital Age: Success Factors and Determinants. *Insights Into Digital Business, Human Resource Management, and Competitiveness*, 349-376.

Badat, S. (2010). *The challenges of transformation in higher education and training institutions in South Africa*. Development Bank of Southern Africa.

Bah, I. A. (2023). The Relationship between Education and Economic Growth: A Cross-Country Analysis. *Research. Social Development, 12*(5), e19312540522. https://rsdjournal.org/index.php/rsd/article/view/40522

Bairagya, I., & Joy, B. (2022). What Determines the Quality of Higher Education? A Study of Commerce Graduates in Kerala (India). *Journal of the Asia Pacific Economy, 27*(1), 1–25. https://www.tandfonline.com/doi/full/10.1080/13547860.2020.1870067. DOI: 10.1080/13547860.2020.1870067

Balzer, W. K. (2020). *Lean Higher Education*. Productivity Press., DOI: 10.4324/9781351216944

Banerjee-Batist, R., Gajjar, K., Saxena, P., Smetana, J. B., & Muduli, A. (2022). Leadership response to COVID-19: A comparative analysis of the education sector in USA and India. *Human Resource Development International, 25*(3), 321–341. DOI: 10.1080/13678868.2022.2073119

Banwo, B. O., Khalifa, M., & Seashore Louis, K. (2022). Exploring trust: Culturally responsive and positive school leadership. *Journal of Educational Administration, 60*(3), 323–339. DOI: 10.1108/JEA-03-2021-0065

Bapuji, H., & Chrispal, S. (2020). Understanding Economic Inequality through the Lens of Caste. *Journal of Business Ethics, 162*(3), 533–551. https://link.springer.com/article/10.1007/s10551-018-3998-8. DOI: 10.1007/s10551-018-3998-8

Barro, R. J. (1991). Economic Growth in a Cross Section of Countries. *The Quarterly Journal of Economics, 104*(2), 184–198. http://piketty.pse.ens.fr/files/Barro91.pdf. DOI: 10.2307/2937943

Bass, B. M. (1985). *Leadership and performance beyond expectations*. Free Press.

Bass, B. M. (2008). *The Bass handbook of leadership: Theory, research, and application* (4th ed.). Free Press.

Bass, B. M., & Riggio, R. E. (2006). *Transformational leadership* (2nd ed.). Lawrence Erlbaum Associates Publishers. DOI: 10.4324/9781410617095

Baxter, M., Novy-Marx, M., & D'Angelo, S. (2022). Improving pathways for girls and disadvantaged youth through secondary education and into work: Evidence and reflections from practice. *Development Policy Review, 40*(S2), e12651. Advance online publication. DOI: 10.1111/dpr.12651

Bazerman, M. H. (2020). A new model for ethical leadership. *Harvard Business Review, 98*(5), 90–97.

Beach, J. M. (2021). *Can we measure what matters most?: Why educational accountability metrics lower student learning and demoralise teachers*. Rowman & Littlefield.

Bentley, G., Goldberg, T., & Jasienska, G. (1993). The Fertility of Agricultural and Non-Agricultural Traditional Societies. *Population Studies, 47*(2), 269–281. https://goldberglab.wisc.edu/pdf/P003.pdf. DOI: 10.1080/0032472031000147006

Berda, Y. (2022). *Colonial bureaucracy and contemporary citizenship*. Cambridge University Press. DOI: 10.1017/9781009053495

Bernasconi, E., Redavid, D., & Ferilli, S. (2025). Enhancing Personalised Learning with a Context-Aware Intelligent Question-Answering System and Automated Frequently Asked Question Generation. *Electronics (Basel), 14*(7), 1481. DOI: 10.3390/electronics14071481

Bhatta, M. (2019). Challenges and opportunities in South Asia. In *New Futures for South Asia: Commerce and Connectivity*. Taylor and Francis., DOI: 10.4324/9780367816827-3

Bidandi, F., Byaruhanga, J., & Malinga, T. (2022). Governance and accountability in historically disadvantaged higher education institutions in South Africa. *African Journal of Public Affairs, 14*(3), 78–95.

Black, S. A. (2015). Qualities of effective leadership in higher education. *Open Journal of Leadership, 4*(2), 54–66. DOI: 10.4236/ojl.2015.42006

Blain, J. (2024). *Unleash the Inner CEO: Make Distributed Leadership a Reality*. Jaico Publishing House.

Blanden, J., & McNally, S. (2015). Reducing Inequality in Education and Skills: Implications for Economic Growth. *EENEE Analytical Report No. 21*. http://www.education-economics.org/dms/EENEE/Analytical_Reports/EENEE_AR21.pdf

Blessinger, P., Sengupta, E., & Makhanya, M. (2019). New Higher Education Literacies for a Sustainable Future. *University World News*, 571. https://www.universityworldnews.com/post.php?story=20191017120317521

Bolanle, B. M. (2021). Integrating peace education into the curriculum of Nigerian teacher education programme to promote culture of peace. *Cumhuriyet Uluslararası Eğitim Dergisi, 10*(4), 1356–1368.

Boyadjieva, P., & Ilieva-Trichkova, P. (2021). *Adult Education as an Agency and Empowerment Process*., DOI: 10.1007/978-3-030-67136-5_4

Bramwell, D. (2020). Systematic review of empirical studies on citizenship education in Latin America 2000 to 2017 and research agenda proposal. *Citizenship. Social and Economics Education, 19*(2), 100–117. DOI: 10.1177/2047173420922506

Bridoux, F., & Stoelhorst, J. W. (2022). Stakeholder governance: Solving the collective action problems in joint value creation. *Academy of Management Review, 47*(2), 214–236. DOI: 10.5465/amr.2019.0441

Brown, J. F., Fisher, S., Szilagyi, Z., Pehe, J., Woodward, S. L., Bugajski, J., & Ulrich, C. (2024). Issues In Foreign Policy. In The OMRI Annual Survey of Eastern Europe and the Former Soviet Union (pp. 369-407). Routledge. DOI: 10.4324/9781003580881-9

Brown, A. C. (2023). *Redefining Stoicism: How Crisis and Disaster Leaders Demonstrate Positive Behaviours Found in the Ancient Philosophy*. University of Florida.

Brown, C., Luzmore, R., O'Donovan, R., Ji, G., & Patnaik, S. (2024). How educational leaders can maximise the social capital benefits of inter-school networks: Findings from a systematic review. *International Journal of Educational Management*, *38*(1), 213–264. DOI: 10.1108/IJEM-09-2023-0447

Bruçaj, S. (2014). Quality in Private Higher Education System: New Challenges Regarding Students' Satisfaction. *The Online Journal of Distance Education and e-Learning : TOJDEL*, *2*(2), 21–26. https://tojdel.net/journals/tojdel/articles/v02i02/v02i02-04.pdf

Bruder, M., & Baar, T. (2024). Innovation in humanitarian assistance—A systematic literature review. *Journal of International Humanitarian Action*, *9*(1), 2. DOI: 10.1186/s41018-023-00144-3

Brulé, R. E. (2023). Women and power in the developing world. *Annual Review of Political Science*, *26*(1), 33–54. DOI: 10.1146/annurev-polisci-062121-081831

Bryant, W., & Bryant, C. (2023). *Leadership Practices: A Global and Biblical Perspective*. Christian Faith Publishing, Inc.

Burns, J. M. (1978). *Leadership*. Harper & Row.

Burns, L., Le Roux, N., Kalesnik-Orszulak, R., Christian, J., Hukkelhoven, M., Rockhold, F., & O'Donnell, J. (2022). Real-World Evidence for Regulatory Decision-Making: Guidance From Around the World. *Clinical Therapeutics*, *44*(3), 420–437. DOI: 10.1016/j.clinthera.2022.01.012 PMID: 35181179

Burns, M. (2023). *Distance Education for Teacher Training: Modes, Models, and Methods*. Education Development Center, Inc.

Cabezudo, A., & Haavelsrud, M. (2007). Rethinking peace education. In Webel, C., & Galtung, J. (Eds.), *Handbook of peace and conflict studies* (pp. 279–296). Routledge. DOI: 10.4324/9780203089163.ch18

Cadet, X. F., Borovykh, A., Malekzadeh, M., Ahmadi-Abhari, S., & Haddadi, H. (2024). Deep unlearn: Benchmarking machine unlearning. arXiv preprint arXiv:2410.01276.

Cairney, P., & Toomey, C. (2025). Systems Leadership: A qualitative systematic review of advice for policymakers. *Open Research Europe*, *5*, 6. DOI: 10.12688/openreseurope.18982.1

Camilla, S. (2023). The Design of Upper Secondary Education Across OECD Countries: Managing Choice, Coherence, and Specialisation. *OECD Education Working Papers*. https://www.oecd.org/en/publications/the-design-of-upper-secondary-education-across-oecd-countries_158101f0-en.html

Candeias Fernandes, A. J., & Franco, M. (2022). The role of entrepreneurial resilience in forms of collaboration: A systematic literature review with bibliometric analyses. *EuroMed Journal of Business*, *17*(4), 752–789. DOI: 10.1108/EMJB-05-2021-0075

Carnoy, M., Froumin, I., Loyalka, P. K., & Tilak, J. B. G. (2014). The concept of public goods, the state, and higher education finance: A view from the BRICs. *Higher Education*, *68*(3), 359–378. DOI: 10.1007/s10734-014-9717-1

Caron, R. M. (2019). Departmental leadership: Navigating productive tension while in a paradoxical role. *Frontiers in Education*, *4*, 97. DOI: 10.3389/feduc.2019.00097

Carrasco, S., & Perez Lopez, I. (2025). Linking education and practice gaps for inclusive architecture in the AEC industry. *Archnet-IJAR: International Journal of Architectural Research*, *19*(1), 128–148. DOI: 10.1108/ARCH-11-2023-0297

Carter, J. A. (2022). Trust as performance. *Philosophical Issues*, *32*(1), 120–147. DOI: 10.1111/phis.12214

Cénat, J. M., Manoni-Millar, S., David, A., Moshirian Farahi, S. M. M., Jacob, G., Darius, W. P., Beogo, I., & Dalexis, R. D. (2025). Racism in Education among Black Youth in Canada and its Association with Depression, Anxiety, Stress, and Post-Traumatic Stress Disorder. *Research on Child and Adolescent Psychopathology*, *53*(7), 999–1015. Advance online publication. DOI: 10.1007/s10802-025-01316-y PMID: 40186816

Chairez, C. C. (2022). Principal perspectives on the dual roles of manager and instructional leader (Doctoral dissertation, Walden University).

Chancel, L., & Piketty, T. (2019). Indian Income Inequality, 1922-2015: From British Raj to Billionaire Raj? *Review of Income and Wealth*, *65*(S1), S33–S62. https://onlinelibrary.wiley.com/doi/full/10.1111/roiw.12439. DOI: 10.1111/roiw.12439

Chasokela, D., & Hlongwane, J. (2025). *Assessing Higher-Order and Critical Skills in the Era of Artificial Intelligence.*, DOI: 10.4018/979-8-3693-6351-5.ch010

Chatzipanagiotou, P., & Katsarou, E. (2023). Crisis Management, School Leadership in Disruptive Times and the Recovery of Schools in the Post COVID-19 Era: A Systematic Literature Review. *Education Sciences*, *13*(2), 118. DOI: 10.3390/educsci13020118

Chaudhary, L., Musacchio, A., Nafziger, S., & Yan, S. (2012). Big BRICs, weak foundations: The beginning of public elementary education in Brazil, Russia, India, and China. *Explorations in Economic History*, *49*(2), 221–240. DOI: 10.1016/j.eeh.2012.02.001

Chen, A. M. H., Brown, S., Mark, K., & McBane, S. (2023). An overview of Instructional approaches and decision-making strategies to curtail curricular overload. *American Journal of Pharmaceutical Education*, *87*(8), 100013. DOI: 10.1016/j.ajpe.2022.12.001 PMID: 37597910

Chen, C., Duan, J., & Peng, Y. (2024). How does sense of power influence change-oriented organisational citizenship behavior? Evidence from China. *Public Performance & Management Review*, *47*(3), 732–760. DOI: 10.1080/15309576.2023.2298414

Chen, J., Ghardallou, W., Comite, U., Ahmad, N., Ryu, H. B., Ariza-Montes, A., & Han, H. (2022). Managing hospital employees' burnout through transformational leadership: The role of resilience, role clarity, and intrinsic motivation. *International Journal of Environmental Research and Public Health*, *19*(17), 10941. DOI: 10.3390/ijerph191710941 PMID: 36078657

Chisholm, L., & Chissale, A. (2025). BRICS, sub-imperialism and education in Mozambique [ ]. *Comparative Education*, *61*(2), 225–243. DOI: 10.1080/03050068.2024.2372209

Chopra, A., Patel, H., Rajput, D. S., & Bansal, N. (2024). *Empowering Inclusive Education: Leveraging AI-ML and Innovative Tech Stacks to Support Students with Learning Disabilities in Higher Education* (pp. 255–275). DOI: 10.1007/978-981-97-0914-4_15

Chowdhury, S., Dey, P., Joel-Edgar, S., Bhattacharya, S., Rodriguez-Espindola, O., Abadie, A., & Truong, L. (2023). Unlocking the value of artificial intelligence in human resource management through AI capability framework. *Human Resource Management Review*, *33*(1), 100899. DOI: 10.1016/j.hrmr.2022.100899

City Press. (2007). *BCom degrees shocker: Lowly qualifications mean graduates are unemployable by Chuenyame*. Gershwin.

City, E. L., & Curtis, R. (2025). *Leading strategically: Achieving ambitious goals in education*. Harvard Education Press.

Clerkiq. (2025) *Navigating accounting resource constraints and the talent shortage in South Africa*. Available at: https://clerkiq.io/blog/navigating_accounting_resource_constraints (Accessed: September 20 2025).

Co, E., Dirig, R., Halstead, J., Hendrie, M., & Masilko, T. (2023). Reimagining access: Improving access to digital archives through participatory design. *Journal of Digital Media Management, 11*(4), 324–333. DOI: 10.69554/IAGK5522

Coetzee, S. A., & Schmulian, A. (2013). Relevance of a competency framework for accounting education: Perspectives from South Africa. *Accounting Education, 22*(4), 345–368.

Copp, S., Olorunsola, V. O., & Alola, U. V. (2021). Achieving environmental sustainability through green transformational leadership policy: Can green team resilience help? *Business Strategy and the Environment, 30*(1), 671–682. DOI: 10.1002/bse.2646

Council on Higher Education (CHE). (2025). *Reflecting, renewing, and realigning: A baseline study of conceptions of curriculum transformation in South African universities.*

Cox, A. M. (2021). Exploring the impact of Artificial Intelligence and robots on higher education through literature-based design fictions. *International Journal of Educational Technology in Higher Education, 18*(1), 3. DOI: 10.1186/s41239-020-00237-8

Crawford, M. (2021). Being a head of department in an English university. *Educational Review, 75*(6), 1168–1180. DOI: 10.1080/00131911.2021.2000368

Cremin, H. (2016). Peace education research in the twenty-first century: Three concepts facing crisis or opportunity? *Journal of Peace Education, 13*(1), 1–17. DOI: 10.1080/17400201.2015.1069736

Creswell, J. W., & Creswell, J. D. (2018). *Research design: Qualitative, quantitative, and mixed methods approach* (5th ed.). SAGE Publications.

Currie, K., Conway, J., Johnson, S., Landry, B., & Lowther, A. (2012). Leadership concepts. In *Air Force Leadership Study: The Need for Deliberate Development* (pp. 11–20). Air University Press. https://www.jstor.org/stable/resrep13757.9

Czerniewicz, L., & Carvalho, L. (2022). Open, Distance, and Digital Education (ODDE) – An Equity View. In *Handbook of Open, Distance and Digital Education* (pp. 1–20). Springer Nature Singapore. DOI: 10.1007/978-981-19-0351-9_93-1

Danesh, H. B. (2006). Towards an integrative theory of peace education. *Journal of Peace Education, 3*(1), 55–78. DOI: 10.1080/17400200500532151

Daniels, C., & Niemczyk, E. K. (2023). Towards Higher Education for Sustainable Development in BRICS: Focus on Brazil and South Africa. *Space and Culture, India, 11*(1), 68–77. DOI: 10.20896/saci.v11i1.1354

Darling-Hammond, L., Flook, L., Cook-Harvey, C., Barron, B., & Osher, D. (2020). Implications for educational practice of the science of learning and development. *Applied Developmental Science, 24*(2), 97–140. DOI: 10.1080/10888691.2018.1537791

Das, S. (2016). Inequality in Educational Opportunity in India: Evidence and Consequences of Social Exclusion. *Child Indicators Research, 9*(1), 51–71. https://link.springer.com/article/10.1007/s12187-014-9296-9. DOI: 10.1007/s12187-014-9296-9

Daud, A., Dj, A. A., Adianita, H., & Mado, Y. J. (2024). The influence of participative leadership style on job satisfaction with organisational citizenship behavior as a moderating variable. *Reslaj: Religion Education Social Laa Roiba Journal, 6*(4), 2192–2200. DOI: 10.47467/reslaj.v6i4.1918

Davis, I. (2020). Armed conflict and peace processes in sub-Saharan Africa. In *SIPRI Yearbook 2020: Armaments, Disarmament, and International Security* (pp. 171–214). Oxford University Press. DOI: 10.1093/sipri/9780198869207.003.0007

De Clercq, D., & Pereira, R. (2024). How resilient employees can prevent family ostracism from escalating into diminished work engagement and change-oriented organisational citizenship behavior. *International Studies of Management & Organization, 54*(1), 25–47. DOI: 10.1080/00208825.2023.2277968

Debele, E. T. (2025). Exploring Leadership's Impact on Working Culture, Organizational Culture, and Institutional Development at Samara University, Ethiopia: A Qualitative Study. *Social Sciences, 14*(2), 94–108. DOI: 10.11648/j.ss.20251402.14

Demeke, W. (2024). *Selective Integration.*, DOI: 10.4018/979-8-3693-8130-4.ch005

Deming, D. J. (2017). The Growing Importance of Social Skills in the Labour Market. *The Quarterly Journal of Economics, 132*(4), 1593–1640. DOI: 10.1093/qje/qjx022

Demissie, A. D., Alemu, A. E., & Tensay, A. T. (2024). The nexus between servant leadership and organisational citizenship behavior through the mediating role of perceived organisational politics in Ethiopian federal public service organisations. *Cogent Business & Management, 11*(1), 2336653. DOI: 10.1080/23311975.2024.2336653

Deng, W. (2021). Impact of the Western Developed Leadership Theories on the Promotion of Confucian Asian into Administrative Position (Doctoral dissertation, South University).

Department of School Education & Literacy. (2021). Right to Education. https://dsel.education.gov.in/rte

DiMaggio, P. J., & Powell, W. W. (1983). The iron cage revisited: Institutional isomorphism and collective rationality in organisational fields. *American Sociological Review*, *48*(2), 147–160. DOI: 10.2307/2095101

Dinda, S. (2014). Climate Change: An Emerging Trade Opportunity in South Asia. *South Asian Journal of Macroeconomics and Public Finance*, *3*(2), 221–239. DOI: 10.1177/2277978714548636

Dixit, P., & Bhatnagar, M. (2025). Advancing green economies through sustainable investment strategies for climate change mitigation and development: Adaptive strategies for green crypto investment. In *Adaptive Strategies for Green Economy and Sustainability Policies*. DOI: 10.4018/979-8-3693-7570-9.ch033

Dlamini, R., Ramatsetse, B., Zenda, R., Gorimbo, J., & Mpungose, C. B. (2024). *Establishing Professional Communities of Practice to Enhance Teacher Development in Technical Schools.*, DOI: 10.1007/978-3-031-58206-6_11

Domanic, M. (2025). Breaking Down the Silos. A hypothesis for Redesigning the Academic Spatial Environment to Encourage Interdisciplinary collaborations (Doctoral dissertation, Politecnico di Torino).

Dong, R., Song, J., Jiang, T., & Baloch, M. A. (2024). Environmental Sustainability Across BRICS Economies: The Dynamics Among the Digital Economy, Education, and CO2 Emissions. *Journal of the Knowledge Economy*, *16*(1), 4125–4145. Advance online publication. DOI: 10.1007/s13132-024-02154-x

Donop, J., Walderon, T., & Etchells, M. J. (2023). Identity flux: Educator narratives in the face of Burnout. In Drawn to the Flame: Teachers' Stories of Burnout (pp. 181-198). Emerald Publishing Limited.

Dorji, T., Morrison-Saunders, A., & Blake, D. (2023). Understanding How Community Wellbeing is Affected by Climate Change: Evidence From a Systematic Literature Review. *Environmental Management*, *72*(3), 568–586. DOI: 10.1007/s00267-023-01833-w PMID: 37209142

Drouin-Gagné, M. E. (2021). Beyond the "Indigenising the academy" trend: Learning from Indigenous higher education land-based and intercultural pedagogies to build trans-systemic education. *Engaged Scholar Journal*, *7*(1), 45–65.

Druker-Ibáñez, S., & Cáceres-Jensen, L. (2022). Integration of indigenous and local knowledge into sustainability education: A systematic literature review. *Environmental Education Research*, *28*(8), 1209–1236. DOI: 10.1080/13504622.2022.2083081

Du Plessis, L., & Gerber, D. (2012). Academic preparedness of students – an exploratory study. *The Journal for Transdisciplinary Research in Southern Africa*, *8*(1), 81–94. DOI: 10.4102/td.v8i1.7

Duderstadt, J. J. (2007). Academic leadership. In *The View from the Helm: Leading the American University during an Era of Change* (pp. 111–132). University of Michigan Press. DOI: 10.3998/mpub.168531

Dugan, J. P. (2024). *Leadership theory: Cultivating critical perspectives*. John Wiley & Sons.

Dugo, D., Kant, S., & Alemu, Z. K. (2025). Servant Leadership Influence on Organizational Citizenship Behavior With the Mediation Role of Emotional Intelligence: A Case of Public Universities in Ethiopia. In *Generation Alpha and Next Generation Leadership for Greener Futures* (pp. 269-292). IGI Global Scientific Publishing. DOI: DOI: 10.4018/979-8-3693-9281-2.ch014

Dunn, A. H. (2021). *Teaching on days after: Educating for equity in the wake of injustice*. Teachers College Press.

Eaton, L., Bridgman, T., & Cummings, S. (2024). Advancing the democratisation of work: A new intellectual history of transformational leadership theory. *Leadership*, *20*(3), 125–143. DOI: 10.1177/17427150241232705

Edeh, F. O., & Ikpor, I. M. (2025). Work-life balance in the service sector: Predicting organisational citizenship behaviour. *European Journal of International Management*, *25*(1), 122–137. DOI: 10.1504/EJIM.2025.143277

Egitim, S., & Sandu, R. (2023). Intercultural Language Education Through Leaderful Pedagogy: A Collaborative Autoethnographic Approach. In *Leaderful classroom pedagogy through an interdisciplinary lens: Merging theory with practice* (pp. 159–174). Springer Nature Singapore. DOI: 10.1007/978-981-99-6655-4_10

El Hawi, R. (2021). Transformational leadership and rhetoric competencies for organisational success: Analysis of Jack's rhetoric. *International Journal of Recent Technology and Engineering*, *8*, 892–896.

Elerian, M., Yemini, M., Khavenson, T., & Jasikowska, K. (2025). Systematic literature review of school-age youth activism in post-socialist countries. *Educational Review*, •••, 1–25. DOI: 10.1080/00131911.2025.2451091

Elias, A., & Mansouri, F. (2020). A Systematic Review of Studies on Interculturalism and Intercultural Dialogue. *Journal of Intercultural Studies (Melbourne, Vic.)*, *41*(4), 490–523. DOI: 10.1080/07256868.2020.1782861

Emeodu, E. N., & Famo, M. K. (2023). Peace education and national security: The need for its improvement in Nigerian schools. *Texas Journal of Multidisciplinary Studies*, *25*, 1–12.

Emon, M. M. H. (2025b). Circularity Meets AI: Revolutionizing Consumer Engagement Through Green Marketing. In *Transforming Business Practices With AI-Powered Green Marketing* (pp. 169–208). IGI Global Scientific Publishing. DOI: 10.4018/979-8-3373-3017-4.ch007

Emon, M. M. H. (2025b). Navigating the Digital Labyrinth: Personal Data Privacy and Security at Individual and Organizational Levels. In *User-Centric Cybersecurity Implications for Sustainable Digital Transformation* (pp. 257–288). IGI Global Scientific Publishing. DOI: 10.4018/979-8-3373-3171-3.ch008

Emon, M. M. H. (2025b). Purpose-Driven Intelligence in Green Marketing: Leveraging AI for CSR-Centric and Sustainable Brand Positioning. In *Transforming Business Practices With AI-Powered Green Marketing* (pp. 89–122). IGI Global Scientific Publishing. DOI: 10.4018/979-8-3373-3017-4.ch004

Emon, M. M. H., & Chowdhury, M. S. A. (2025). Safeguarding Student Data: Privacy and Security Challenges in AI-Powered Education Tools. In *Enhancing Student Support and Learning Through Conversational AI* (pp. 191–228). IGI Global Scientific Publishing. DOI: 10.4018/979-8-3373-3316-8.ch008

Emon, M. M. H., & Mazid-Ul-Haque, M. (2025). Balancing Usability and Security: Enhancing User Experience Without Compromising Privacy. In *User-Centric Cybersecurity Implications for Sustainable Digital Transformation* (pp. 309–342). IGI Global Scientific Publishing. DOI: 10.4018/979-8-3373-3171-3.ch010

Emon, M. M. H. (2025a). Leveraging AI on Social Media & Digital Platforms to Enhance English Language Teaching and Learning. In *AI-Powered English Teaching* (pp. 211–238). IGI Global Scientific Publishing., DOI: 10.4018/979-8-3373-1952-0.ch007

Emon, M. M. H., & Khan, T. (2025). Corporate Social Responsibility for Sustainable Development: A Systematic Review of Business Contributions to Address Global Challenges. *Review of Business and Economics Studies*, *13*(2), 6–39. DOI: 10.26794/2308-944X-2025-13-2-6-39

Emon, M. M. H., Nath, A., & Nipa, M. N. (2025). *AI for a Greener Tomorrow: Harnessing Artificial Intelligence for Environmental Sustainability*. IGI Global Scientific Publishing., DOI: 10.4018/979-8-3373-2387-9.ch010

Esquierdo-Leal, J. L., & Houmanfar, R. A. (2021). Creating Inclusive and Equitable Cultural Practices by Linking Leadership to Systemic Change. *Behavior Analysis in Practice, 14*(2), 499–512. DOI: 10.1007/s40617-020-00519-7 PMID: 33613858

European Commission. (2013). *High Level Group on the Modernization of Higher Education — Report to the European Commission on Improving the Quality of Teaching and Learning in Europe's Higher Education Institutions*. EU Publication Office. https://op.europa.eu/en/publication-detail/-/publication/fbd4c2aa-aeb7-41ac-ab4c-a94feea9eb1f

Facer, K., & Selwyn, N. (2021). *Digital technology and the futures of education: Towards 'Non-Stupid'optimism. Futures of Education initiative*. UNESCO.

Fan, X., Liu, H., Wang, Y., Wan, Y., & Zhang, D. (2022). Models of Internationalization of Higher Education in Developing Countries, A Perspective of International Research Collaboration in BRICS Countries. *Sustainability (Basel), 14*(20), 13659. Advance online publication. DOI: 10.3390/su142013659

Farrell, C. C., Penuel, W. R., Allen, A., Anderson, E. R., Bohannon, A. X., Coburn, C. E., & Brown, S. L. (2022). Learning at the Boundaries of Research and Practice: A Framework for Understanding Research–Practice Partnerships. *Educational Researcher, 51*(3), 197–208. DOI: 10.3102/0013189X211069073

Fawns, T. (2022). An entangled pedagogy: Looking beyond the pedagogy—technology dichotomy. *Postdigital Science and Education, 4*(3), 711–728. DOI: 10.1007/s42438-022-00302-7 PMID: 40477872

Fayed, I., & Cummings, J. (Eds.). (2021). *Teaching in the Post COVID-19 Era*. Springer International Publishing., DOI: 10.1007/978-3-030-74088-7

Fernández-Aballí Altamirano, A. (2020). The Importance of Paulo Freire to Communication for Development and Social Change. In *Handbook of Communication for Development and Social Change* (pp. 309–327). Springer Singapore., DOI: 10.1007/978-981-15-2014-3_76

Fernandez, L. J. (2023). *The art of business Origami: folding your way to success*. Lloyd Jose Fernandez.

Ferrada, D. (2020). Dialogic pedagogy linking worlds: Participatory community classrooms. *Pedagogy, Culture & Society, 28*(1), 131–146. DOI: 10.1080/14681366.2019.1615534

Ferreira, M., Kunn-Nelen, A., & De Grip, A. (2017). Work-related learning and skill development in Europe: Does initial skill mismatch matter? *Research in Labor Economics, 45*, 345–407. DOI: 10.1108/S0147-912120170000045010

Field, J. (2020). Lifelong Learning for Working People. In *Encyclopedia of Education and Information Technologies* (pp. 1093–1104). Springer International Publishing., DOI: 10.1007/978-3-030-10576-1_61

Fitzgerald, A., Avirmed, T., & Battulga, N. (2024). Exploring the factors informing educational inequality in higher education: a systematic literature review. *Perspectives: Policy and Practice in Higher Education*, 1–11. DOI: 10.1080/13603108.2024.2381121

Floyd, A. (2009). *Focusing the kaleidoscope: Investigating the newly formed role of 'academic lead' at a research-led university*. Leadership Foundation for Higher Education.

Fontdevila, C., Verger, A., & Avelar, M. (2021). The business of policy: A review of the corporate sector's emerging strategies in the promotion of education reform. *Critical Studies in Education, 62*(2), 131–146. DOI: 10.1080/17508487.2019.1573749

Forshaw, E., & Woods, K. (2023). Student participation in the development of whole-school wellbeing strategies: A systematic review of the literature. *Pastoral Care in Education, 41*(4), 430–448. DOI: 10.1080/02643944.2022.2148175

Freeman, R. E. (2010). *Strategic management: A stakeholder approach*. Cambridge University Press., DOI: 10.1017/CBO9781139192675

Freire, P. (2017). *Pedagogy of the Oppressed*. Penguin Classics.

Friederich, J., Francis, D. P., Lazarova-Molnar, S., & Mohamed, N. (2022). A framework for data-driven digital twins of intelligent manufacturing systems. *Computers in Industry, 136*, 103586. DOI: 10.1016/j.compind.2021.103586

Friesen, S., & Jacobsen, M. (2020). *The Education System of Canada*., DOI: 10.1007/978-3-319-93443-3_37-1

Fry, L. W., & Vu, M. C. (2024). Leading without a self: Implications of buddhist practices for pseudo-spiritual leadership. *Journal of Business Ethics, 190*(1), 41–57. DOI: 10.1007/s10551-023-05416-x

Fuad, D. R. S. M., Musa, K., & Hashim, Z. (2022). Innovation culture in education: A systematic review of the literature. *Management in Education, 36*(3), 135–149. DOI: 10.1177/0892020620959760

Fuentes, M. A., Zelaya, D. G., & Madsen, J. W. (2021). Rethinking the Course Syllabus: Considerations for Promoting Equity, Diversity, and Inclusion. *Teaching of Psychology, 48*(1), 69–79. DOI: 10.1177/0098628320959979

Fullan, M. (2001). *Leading in a culture of change*. Jossey-Bass.

Fullan, M. (2011). *The moral imperative realised.* Corwin Press.

Fung, D., & Gordon, C. (2016). *Rewarding educators and education leaders in research-intensive universities*. Higher Education Academy.

Gampala, M. (2023). Innovative Approaches to Teaching and Learning. *Shanlax International Journal of English, 12*(S1-Dec, S1), 138–145. DOI: 10.34293/rtdh.v12iS1-Dec.86

Garcia, D., Clemente Fuentes, R. W., Hyer, S., & Broszko, C. M. (2023). Cultural Influences Catalysing Resident Scholarly Productivity. *Family Medicine*, *55*(10), 653–659. DOI: 10.22454/FamMed.2023.239179 PMID: 37540530

García-Morales, V. J., Lloréns-Montes, F. J., & Verdú-Jover, A. J. (2008). The effects of transformational leadership on organisational performance through knowledge and innovation. *British Journal of Management, 19*(4), 299–317. DOI: 10.1111/j.1467-8551.2007.00547.x

Garcia, S., & Fisher, D. (2023). *The end of leadership as we know it: what it takes to lead in today's volatile and complex world.* John Wiley & Sons.

Gaurav, K., Bharti, N., & Sinha, P. (2015). ISFTA: Lessons for Bangladesh. In C. S., S. N.P., G. D.P., & G. N. (Eds.), *Springer Proceedings in Business and Economics: Vol. Part 111* (pp. 351 – 367). Springer Science and Business Media B.V. DOI: 10.1007/978-81-322-1979-8_28

George, A. S. (2024). The symbiotic relationship between visionary and pragmatic leadership in propelling organisational success. *Partners Universal International Innovation Journal*, *2*(3), 57–79.

George, B., & Wooden, O. (2023). Managing the Strategic Transformation of Higher Education through Artificial Intelligence. *Administrative Sciences, 13*(9), 196. DOI: 10.3390/admsci13090196

George, G., Fewer, T. J., Lazzarini, S., McGahan, A. M., & Puranam, P. (2024). Partnering for Grand Challenges: A Review of Organizational Design Considerations in Public–Private Collaborations. *Journal of Management, 50*(1), 10–40. DOI: 10.1177/01492063221148992

Geschwind, L., Aarrevaara, T., Berg, L. N., & Lind, J. K. (2019). The changing roles of academic leaders: Decision-making, power, and performance. In Pinheiro, R., Geschwind, L., Foss Hansen, H., & Pulkkinen, K. (Eds.), *Reforms, organisational change and performance in higher education.* Palgrave Macmillan. DOI: 10.1007/978-3-030-11738-2_6

Ghaleb, B. (2024). The concept of alienation and alienation in organisations. *Pancasila International Journal of Applied Social Science*, *2*(2), 206–223. DOI: 10.59653/pancasila.v2i02.714

Ghosh, M. (2011). Regional Disparities in Education, Health, and Human Development in India. Indian. *Journal of Human Development*, *5*(1), 5–28. https://journals.sagepub.com/doi/10.1177/0973703020110101

Gilliard, C., & Selwyn, N. (2023). Automated surveillance in education. *Postdigital Science and Education*, *5*(1), 195–205. DOI: 10.1007/s42438-022-00295-3

Gmelch, W. H. (2019). The call for department chair leadership: Why chairs serve, what they do, how they develop, how long they serve, and is there life after chairing? *International Journal of Leadership and Change*, *7*(1), 1.

González, C., Ponce, D., & Fernández, V. (2023). Teachers' experiences of teaching online during COVID-19: Implications for postpandemic professional development. *Educational Technology Research and Development*, *71*(1), 55–78. DOI: 10.1007/s11423-023-10200-9 PMID: 36785811

Gordon, C. (2023). Reading literature in/against the digital age: Shallow assumptions, deep problems, expectant pedagogies. *Convergence (London)*, *29*(1), 28–46. DOI: 10.1177/13548565221148105

Göregen, M. S., Tanghe, E., & Schelfhout, W. (2024). What Works to Retain Beginning Teachers in the Profession? A Mixed Methods Approach to Detect Determining Factors. *Education Sciences*, *14*(12), 1319. DOI: 10.3390/educsci14121319

Govender, L., & McDonald, Z. (2022). *Understanding epistemic access and success for historically disadvantaged students in South African public universities*. CHE.

GPE. (2024, January 24). Education: A path to a peaceful future. *Global Partnership for Education*. https://www.globalpartnership.org

Grande, V., Kinnunen, P., Peters, A.-K., Barr, M., Cajander, Å., Daniels, M., Lewis, A. N., Sabin, M., Sánchez-Peña, M., & Thota, N. (2022). Role Modeling as a Computing Educator in Higher Education. *Proceedings of the 2022 Working Group Reports on Innovation and Technology in Computer Science Education*, 37–63. DOI: 10.1145/3571785.3574122

Granziera, H., & Perera, H. N. (2019). Relations among teachers' self-efficacy beliefs, engagement, and work satisfaction: A social cognitive view. *Contemporary Educational Psychology*, *58*, 75–84. DOI: 10.1016/j.cedpsych.2019.02.003

Green, A. L., Hatton, H., Stegenga, S. M., Eliason, B., & Nese, R. N. T. (2021). Examining Commitment to Prevention, Equity, and Meaningful Engagement: A Review of School District Discipline Policies. *Journal of Positive Behavior Interventions, 23*(3), 137–148. DOI: 10.1177/1098300720951940

Grimus, M. (2020). *Emerging Technologies: Impacting Learning*. Pedagogy and Curriculum Development., DOI: 10.1007/978-981-15-0618-5_8

Grizold, A. (1994). The concept of national security in the contemporary world. *International Journal on World Peace, 11*(3), 37–53.

Güçlü, H. (2024). Transformational educational leadership for shaping Education 4.0 in higher education. *Journal of Innovation in Practice and Development, 4*(1), 4900. Advance online publication. DOI: 10.57237/jipd.2024.4900

Guha, P. (2023). School committee composition: Exploring the role of parental and female representation in India. *Development Policy Review, 41*(3), e12677. Advance online publication. DOI: 10.1111/dpr.12677

Gupta, M., & Kiran, R. (2025). Digital exclusion of women: A systematic review. *Global Knowledge, Memory and Communication, 74*(3/4), 938–957. DOI: 10.1108/GKMC-12-2022-0301

Gupta, S. L., Mittal, A., Singh, S., & Dash, D. N. (2024). Demand-driven approach of vocational education and training (VET) and experiential learning: A thematic analysis through systematic literature review (SLR). *Asian Education and Development Studies, 13*(1), 45–63. DOI: 10.1108/AEDS-07-2023-0083

Haber, P. (2012). Perceptions of leadership: An examination of college students' understanding of the concept of leadership. *Journal of Leadership Education, 11*(2), 26–51. DOI: 10.12806/V11/I2/RF2

Hakimi, L., Eynon, R., & Murphy, V. A. (2021). The Ethics of Using Digital Trace Data in Education: A Thematic Review of the Research Landscape. *Review of Educational Research, 91*(5), 671–717. DOI: 10.3102/00346543211020116

Hallinger, P., & Murphy, J. (1985). Assessing the instructional leadership behavior of principals. *The Elementary School Journal, 86*(2), 217–248. DOI: 10.1086/461445

Hamann, K. R. S., Wullenkord, M. C., Reese, G., & van Zomeren, M. (2024). Believing That We Can Change Our World for the Better: A Triple-A (Agent-Action-Aim) Framework of Self-Efficacy Beliefs in the Context of Collective Social and Ecological Aims. *Personality and Social Psychology Review, 28*(1), 11–53. DOI: 10.1177/10888683231178056 PMID: 37386819

Hamilton, S. H., Merritt, W. S., Carter, L., Chakraborty, A., Cosijn, M., Lim-Camacho, L., Mishra, R., Syme, G., Das, M., & Ray, D. (2022). Affecting behavioural change through empowerment: Conceptual insights from theory and agricultural case studies in South Asia. *Regional Environmental Change*, *22*(3), 85. DOI: 10.1007/s10113-022-01939-7 PMID: 35761800

Hanson-DeFusco, J., Malik, S., Assamoi, R., Chiromba, A., Davis, D., Hounnouvi, F. M., Irfan, F. B., Faley, P., Matangwa, D. D., Muzenda, T., Nakiryowa, H., Obondoh, A., Parveen, S., Pinales, A. J., & Zimunya, R. (2024). Unethical issues in twenty-first century international development and global health policy. *International Studies Perspectives*, *25*(1), 60–85. DOI: 10.1093/isp/ekad016

Hanushek, E.A., & Wö mann, L. (2007). The Role of Education Quality in Economic Growth. *World Bank Paper Series 412*. https://documents1.worldbank.org/curated/en/260461468324885735/pdf/wps4122.pdf

Hargreaves, A., & Shirley, D. (2021). *Well-being in schools: Three forces that will uplift your students in a volatile world.* ASCD.

Hariram, N. P., Mekha, K. B., Suganthan, V., & Sudhakar, K. (2023). Sustainalism: An Integrated Socio-Economic-Environmental Model to Address Sustainable Development and Sustainability. *Sustainability (Basel)*, *15*(13), 10682. DOI: 10.3390/su151310682

Harris, O. (2024). *Bridging the gap: strengthening school-community partnerships through cultural brokers*. Oscar Harris.

Hart, A. R. (2021). Increasing a Sense of Community in Campus Residences: An Action Research Study (Doctoral dissertation, Azusa Pacific University).

Hasan, K. (2023). The four pillars of education By UNESCO and the Metaverse: Repositioning Islamic education. *Bidayah: Studi Ilmu-Ilmu Keislaman*, 85-105.

Heikkilä, M. (2021). Finnish teachers' participation in local curriculum development: A study of processes in five school contexts. *Policy Futures in Education*, *19*(7), 752–769. DOI: 10.1177/1478210320967816

Hermanto, Y. B., Srimulyani, V. A., & Pitoyo, D. J. (2024). The mediating role of quality of work life and organisational commitment in the link between transformational leadership and organisational citizenship behavior. *Heliyon*, *10*(6), e27664. DOI: 10.1016/j.heliyon.2024.e27664 PMID: 38509945

Hernandez, J. O. S. É. (2022). *Servant-leadership as a cornerstone for restoration of human dignity. Servant-Leadership, Feminism, and Gender Well-Being: How Leaders Transcend Global Inequities through Hope*. Unity, and Love.

Hilli, C. (2020). Extending classrooms through teacher collaboration in Virtual Learning Environments. *Educational Action Research, 28*(4), 700–715. DOI: 10.1080/09650792.2019.1654901

Hong, P. C., Chennattuserry, J. C., Deng, X., & Hopkins, M. M. (2021). Purpose-driven leadership and organizational success: A case of higher educational institutions. *Leadership and Organization Development Journal, 42*(7), 1004–1017. DOI: 10.1108/LODJ-02-2021-0054

Hood, M. K. (2024). *Improvisation and Creativity in Educational Leadership.* Gwynedd Mercy University.

Huguley, J. P., Fussell-Ware, D. J., McQueen, S. S., Wang, M.-T., & DeBellis, B. R. (2022). Completing the Circle: Linkages Between Restorative Practices, Socio-Emotional Well-Being, and Racial Justice in Schools. *Journal of Emotional and Behavioral Disorders, 30*(2), 138–153. DOI: 10.1177/10634266221088989

Human Sciences Research Council (HSRC). (2025). *Policy brief: Historically disadvantaged institutions and research funding*. HSRC.

Iacovidou, E., Hahladakis, J. N., & Purnell, P. (2021). A systems thinking approach to understanding the challenges of achieving the circular economy. *Environmental Science and Pollution Research International, 28*(19), 24785–24806. DOI: 10.1007/s11356-020-11725-9 PMID: 33289042

Ide, Y., & Beddoe, L. (2022). Attitude or skills?: Cultural competence development within an Aotearoa New Zealand bicultural framework. *Aotearoa New Zealand Social Work, 34*(4), 47–60. DOI: 10.11157/anzswj-vol34iss4id954

Ihmeideh, F., AlFlasi, M., Al-Maadadi, F., Coughlin, C., & Al-Thani, T. (2020). Perspectives of family–school relationships in Qatar based on Epstein's model of six types of parent involvement. *Early Years Journal of International Research and Development, 40*(2), 188–204. DOI: 10.1080/09575146.2018.1438374

İmre-Bıyıklı, S., & Kamil, A. A. (2024). Measurement of Education Effectiveness in the BRICS countries and Turkey [Medición de la Eficacia de la Educación en los Países BRICS y Turquía]. *Multidisciplinary Journal of Educational Research, 14*(3), 361–376. DOI: 10.17583/remie.8990

Institute for Economics & Peace. (2025). *Identifying and measuring the factors that drive peace: Global Peace Index briefing 2025.* https://www.visionofhumanity.org/wp-content/uploads/2025/06/Global-Peace-Index-2025-Briefing-Web.pdf

Institute for Economics and Peace. (2023). Global Terrorism Index 2023. https://www.visionofhumanity.org

International Crisis Group. (2021). Stopping Nigeria's spiraling farmer-herder violence. https://www.crisisgroup.org

Ionela, S. (2021). Leadership: from classic theories to the 21th century's challenges. In SHS Web of Conferences (Vol. 120, p. 02023). EDP Sciences.

Iqbal, M., Ul-Durar, S., Arshed, N., Shahzad, K., & Ayub, U. (2025). Connecting higher education and renewable energy to attain sustainability for BRICS countries: A climate Kuznets curve perspective. *International Journal of Emerging Markets, 20*(5), 2042–2060. DOI: 10.1108/IJOEM-04-2023-0555

Islam, M. K., Sarker, M. F. H., & Islam, M. S. (2022). Promoting student-centred blended learning in higher education: A model. *E-Learning and Digital Media, 19*(1), 36–54. DOI: 10.1177/20427530211027721

Islam, S., & Khan, M. N. I. (2022). Project impact assessment frameworks in non-profit development: A review of case studies from south asia. *American Journal of Scholarly Research and Innovation, 1*(01), 270–294. DOI: 10.63125/eeja0t77

Jain, V., Gupta, S. S., Shankar, K. T., & Bagaria, K. R. (2022). A study on leadership management, principles, theories, and educational management. *World Journal of English Language, 12*(3), 203–211. DOI: 10.5430/wjel.v12n3p203

Jansen, J. D. (2004). Autonomy and accountability in the regulation of the teaching profession: The case of South Africa. *Research Papers in Education, 19*(1), 51–66. DOI: 10.1080/0267152032000176972

Jenna Degan. (2013). Stronger Together: Team Teaching as a Strategy to Curb Burnout, Boost Teacher Efficacy, and Increase Student Engagement. *Uniwersytet Śląski, 7*(1), 343–354. https://doi.org/10.2/JQUERY.MIN.JS

Jian, G. (2022). From empathic leader to empathic leadership practice: An extension to relational leadership theory. *Human Relations, 75*(5), 931–955. DOI: 10.1177/0018726721998450

Jiménez-Aleixandre, M. P., & Puig, B. (2022). *Educating Critical Citizens to Face Post-truth: The Time Is Now* (pp. 3–19). DOI: 10.1007/978-3-030-92006-7_1

Jimerson, J. B., & Myers, R. D. (2024). Scaffolding Criticality: Iterations of Theory in Principal Preparation. *Education Sciences, 14*(12), 1298. DOI: 10.3390/educsci14121298

Jio, W., Kant, S., & Lemi, K. (2025). Ethical Leadership: Effect on Future of Organizational Citizenship Behavior by Mediation of Organizational Culture in Ethiopia. In *Generation Alpha and Next Generaion Leadership for Greener Futures* (pp. 41-62). IGI Global Scientific Publishing. DOI: DOI: 10.4018/979-8-3693-9281-2.ch003

Jio, W., Kant, S., & Lemi, K. (2025). The Influence of Ethical Leadership on Organizational Citizenship Behavior by the Mediating Role of Organizational Commitment in Ethiopia. In *Humanising the Hyperconnected Workplace* (pp. 221–248). IGI Global Scientific Publishing., DOI: 10.4018/979-8-3693-8171-7.ch008

Johannesson, P. (2022). Development of professional learning communities through action research: Understanding professional learning in practice. *Educational Action Research, 30*(3), 411–426. DOI: 10.1080/09650792.2020.1854100

John, K. T., & Kumar, K. S. (2023). Developmental Challenges to Internationalising the Higher Education Sector: A Critical Inquiry of Business Schools in Kerala. *Rajagiri Management Journal*, 17(1), 52-83. https://www.emerald.com/insight/content/doi/10.1108/ramj-07-2021-0058/full/html

Jones, M. (2022). *More Judgment Than Data: Data Literacy and Decision-making*. Palgrave Macmillan. DOI: 10.1007/978-3-030-99472-3

Kalyani, P. (2020). An Empirical Study on NEP 2020 [National Education Policy] with Special Reference to the Future of Indian Education System and Its Effects on the Stakeholders. *Journal of Management Engineering and Information Technology*, 7(5). https://zenodo.org/records/4159546

Kangotra, R., & Sehajpal, S. (2025). Voices without faces: The impact of Deepfake technology on authentic communication. In *Deepfake Technology Dilemmas: Mastering Managerial Navigation*. Nova Science Publishers Inc. https://www.scopus.com/inward/record.uri?eid=2-s2.0-105008365079&partnerID=40&md5=9c100d69117b318e7f59445149fea920

Kannan, K. P. (2023). Revisiting the Kerala 'Model' of Development: A Sixty-Year Assessment of Successes and Failures. *The Indian Economic Journal, 71*(1), 120–151. https://journals.sagepub.com/doi/abs/10.1177/00194662221145290. DOI: 10.1177/00194662221145290

Kant, S., Adula, M., & Badi, S. (2025). Leading With Wisdom: The Role of Wise Leaders in Ethiopia. In *Harnessing Happiness and Wisdom for Organizational Well-Being* (pp. 361-390). IGI Global Scientific Publishing.

Karakose, T., Polat, H., Tülübaş, T., & Demirkol, M. (2024). A Review of the Conceptual Structure and Evolution of Digital Leadership Research in Education. *Education Sciences*, *14*(11), 1166. DOI: 10.3390/educsci14111166

Kariyana, I. (2024). Aspirations and constraints of middle managers in higher education institutions: A systematic literature review. *Journal of Public Administration and Development Alternatives*, *9*(3), 128–145. DOI: 10.55190/JPADA.2024.347

Kativhu, S. (2025). *Historically disadvantaged institutions and the SARChI initiative: Addressing research deficits*. HSRC Policy Brief.

Kaurav, R. P. S., Narula, S., Baber, R., & Tiwari, P. (2021). Theoretical Extension of the New Education Policy 2020 Using Twitter Mining. *Journal of Content Community and Communication*, *13*(7), 17–26. https://www.amity.edu/gwalior/jccc/pdf/jun_03.pdf. DOI: 10.31620/JCCC.06.21/03

Kaurav, R. P. S., Suresh, K. G., Narula, S., & Baber, R. (2020). New Education Policy, 2020: Qualitative (Contents) Analysis and Twitter Mining (Sentiment) Analysis. *Journal of Content Community and Communication*, *12*(6), 4–13. https://www.amity.edu/gwalior/jccc/pdf/dec_02.pdf. DOI: 10.31620/JCCC.12.20/02

Kayyali, M. (2025 B). Understanding Innovation in Higher Education: Challenges and Future Directions. In Cultivating Creativity and Navigating Talent Management in Academia (pp. 117-138). IGI Global Scientific Publishing.

Kayyali, M. (2025b Introduction to Business Intelligence in Talent Management. In Harnessing Business Intelligence for Modern Talent Management (pp. 1-26). IGI Global Scientific Publishing.

Kayyali, M. (2026). Agile Leadership and Labor Dynamics: Navigating Organisational Change in the Digital Era. In Leading Inclusive Workplaces Through Digital Transformation and Organizational Change (pp. 1-36). IGI Global Scientific Publishing.

Kayyali, M. (2026). Innovative Sustainability Models in the MENA Region: A Corporate Perspective. In Sustainable Innovation in the Middle East and North Africa (MENA) Region (pp. 243-270). IGI Global Scientific Publishing.

Kayyali, M. (2022). Equity, Equality, Diversity, and Inclusion as Key Performance Indicators in Higher Education. *Online Submission*, *3*(5), 1–3.

Kayyali, M. (2023). Promoting Entrepreneurship and Innovation in Higher Education. *Online Submission*, *2*(1), 1–26.

Kayyali, M. (2023). The Evolution of Quality Assurance Systems in Higher Education. *Online Submission*, *2*(1), 1–9.

Kayyali, M. (2024). Quality enhancement frameworks in higher education. In *Quality Assurance and Accreditation in Higher Education: Issues, Models, and Best Practices* (pp. 61–141). Springer Nature Switzerland. DOI: 10.1007/978-3-031-66623-0_2

Kayyali, M. (2025). A). Leadership's Role in Fostering a Resilient Organizational Culture. In *Enhancing Resilience in Business Continuity Management* (pp. 267–294). IGI Global Scientific Publishing. DOI: 10.4018/979-8-3693-8809-9.ch009

Kayyali, M., & Christiansen, B. (Eds.). (2024). *Insights Into International Higher Education Leadership and the Skills Gap*. IGI Global. DOI: 10.4018/979-8-3693-3443-0

Kazi, D. D. (2025). Leading up: Perspectives of the heads of departments and schools on their interactions with hierarchy in UK universities. *Journal of Educational Administration and History*, •••, 1–17. DOI: 10.1080/00220620.2024.2446884

Keding, C. (2021). Understanding the interplay of artificial intelligence and strategic management: Four decades of research in review. *Management Review Quarterly*, *71*(1), 91–134. DOI: 10.1007/s11301-020-00181-x

Kelty, N. E., & Wakabayashi, T. (2020). Family Engagement in Schools: Parent, Educator, and Community Perspectives. *SAGE Open*, *10*(4), 2158244020973024. Advance online publication. DOI: 10.1177/2158244020973024

Kenneth, C. (2025). "They moved from village to village with their *keke* to reach us": building positive peace through counselling in Borno, Nigeria. https://www.peaceinsight.org/en/article

Kertyzia, H. (2021). Peace education. In *The Palgrave handbook of positive peace* (pp. 1–29). Springer Singapore. DOI: 10.1007/978-981-15-3877-3_9-1

Kezar, A. J. (Ed.). (2023). *Rethinking leadership in a complex, multicultural, and global environment: New concepts and models for higher education*. Taylor & Francis. DOI: 10.4324/9781003446842

Kezar, A., Holcombe, E., Vigil, D., & Dizon, J. P. M. (2021). *Shared Equity Leadership: Making Equity Everyone's Work. On Shared Equity Leadership Series*. Pullias Center for Higher Education.

Khan, O. H. (2021). Strengthening Regional Trade Integration in South Asia: A SAARC Perspective. In *Strengthening Regional Trade Integration in South Asia: A SAARC Perspective*. Springer Singapore. DOI: 10.1007/978-981-33-6777-7

Khan, T., & Hasan Emon, M. M. (2024). Determinants of AI Image Generator Adoption Among Marketing Agencies: The Mediating Effects of Perceived Usefulness. *2024 IEEE 3rd International Conference on Robotics, Automation, Artificial-Intelligence and Internet-of-Things (RAAICON)*, 177–182. DOI: 10.1109/RAAICON64172.2024.10928548

Khan, T., Emon, M. M. H., & Nath, A. (2024). Quantifying the Effects of AI-Driven Inventory Management on Operational Efficiency in Online Retail. *2024 27th International Conference on Computer and Information Technology (ICCIT)*, 2092–2097. DOI: 10.1109/ICCIT64611.2024.11021996

Khan, T., Emon, M. M. H., & Rahman, S. (2024). Marketing Strategy Innovation via AI Adoption: A Study on Bangladeshi SMEs in the Context of Industry 5.0. *2024 6th International Conference on Sustainable Technologies for Industry 5.0 (STI)*, 1–6. DOI: 10.1109/STI64222.2024.10951050

Khanna, R., Bhatnagar, M., Sharma, P., Upreti, H., & Kanojia, P. (2025). Advancing circular-economy in food processing: Integrating waste management, policy support, and supply chain circularity. *Environment Conservation Journal*, *26*(3), 856–867. https://doi.org/https://doi.org/10.36953/ECJ.32323056. DOI: 10.36953/ECJ.32323056

Khan, T., Emon, M. M. H., Rahman, K. M., Nipa, M. N., & Fuad, M. N. (2025). The Role of AI in Driving Customer Engagement Through Technological, Organizational and Environmental Enablers in E-Commerce. *2025 International Conference on Quantum Photonics, Artificial Intelligence, and Networking (QPAIN)*, 1–6. DOI: 10.1109/QPAIN66474.2025.11171949

Khan, T., Emon, M. M. H., & Rahman, M. A. (2024a). A systematic review on exploring the influence of Industry 4.0 technologies to enhance supply chain visibility and operational efficiency. *Review of Business and Economics Studies*, *12*(3), 6–27. DOI: 10.26794/2308-944X-2024-12-3-6-27

Khaw, K. W., Alnoor, A., Al-Abrrow, H., Tiberius, V., Ganesan, Y., & Atshan, N. A. (2023). Reactions towards organisational change: A systematic literature review. *Current Psychology (New Brunswick, N.J.)*, *42*(22), 19137–19160. DOI: 10.1007/s12144-022-03070-6

Khilji, S. E. (2022). An Approach for Humanizing Leadership Education: Building Learning Community & Stakeholder Engagement. *Journal of Management Education*, *46*(3), 439–471. DOI: 10.1177/10525629211041355

Khlaif, Z. N., Salha, S., Affouneh, S., Rashed, H., & ElKimishy, L. A. (2021). The Covid-19 epidemic: Teachers' responses to school closure in developing countries. *Technology, Pedagogy and Education, 30*(1), 95–109. DOI: 10.1080/1475939X.2020.1851752

Kikabhai, N. (2022). How educational systems respond to diversity, inclusion and social justice: Disability, power, discipline, territoriality and deterritorialization. *The British Journal of Sociology, 73*(4), 685–698. DOI: 10.1111/1468-4446.12969 PMID: 35842905

Kinchin, I. M., Derham, C., Foreman, C., McNamara, A., & Querstret, D. (2021). Exploring the Salutogenic University: Searching for the triple point for the becoming-caring-teacher through collaborative cartography. *Pedagogika, 141*(1), 94–112. DOI: 10.15823/p.2021.141.5

Kivimäki, T. (2016). The EU-India-China Strategic Partnership and the Impact of Regional Constructs. In *The Role of the European Union in Asia: China and India as Strategic Partners*. Taylor and Francis., DOI: 10.4324/9781315553283-2

Kokkinopoulou, E., Vrontis, D., & Thrassou, A. (2025). *The impact of education on productivity and externalities of economic development and social welfare: a systematic literature review*. Central European Management Journal., DOI: 10.1108/CEMJ-04-2024-0124

Ko, M., Reich, M. R., Takemi, T., & Howland, S. (2018). The Core Roles of Transparency and Accountability in the Governance of Global Health Public–Private Partnerships. *Health Systems and Reform, 4*(3), 239–248. DOI: 10.1080/23288604.2018.1465880 PMID: 30207904

Kopackova, H., Simonova, S., & Reimannova, I. (2024). Digital transformation leaders wanted: How to prepare students for the ever-changing demands of the labor market. *International Journal of Management Education, 22*(1), 100943. DOI: 10.1016/j.ijme.2024.100943

Koski, J., Metsäpelto, R.-L., Kyllönen, M., & Poikkeus, A.-M. (2024). Finnish student teachers as a focus of teacher education research: A 10-Year scoping review of empirical research. *Educational Review*, •••, 1–24. DOI: 10.1080/00131911.2024.2432256

Krieg, T. R. (2021). Effective school leadership mentoring characteristics in the 21st century: Moving beyond compliance and conformity (Doctoral dissertation, Indiana State University).

Kruse, S. D. (2022). Department chair leadership: Exploring the role's demands and tensions. Portland State University. https://www.pdx.edu/academic-affairs/sites/academicaffairs

Kukreti, M., Sehajpal, S., Tiwari, R., & Sood, K. (2024). Driving global health and sustainable development goals with smart technology. In *Driving Global Health and Sustainable Development Goals With Smart Technology*. IGI Global., DOI: 10.4018/979-8-3373-0240-9

Kulal, A., Abhishek, N., Dinesh, S., Bhat, D. C., & Girish, A. (2024). Evaluating the Promise and Pitfalls of India's National Education Policy 2020: Insights from the Perspectives of Students, Teachers, and Experts. *SAGE Open*, *14*(4), 21582440241279367. https://journals.sagepub.com/doi/10.1177/21582440241279367. DOI: 10.1177/21582440241279367

Kumar, N. A., & George, K. K. (2009). Kerala's Education System: From Inclusion to Exclusion? *CSES Working Paper No. 2*. https://csesindia.org/wp-content/uploads/2020/08/Kerala%E2%80%99s-Education-System-From-Inclusion-to-Exclusion-1.pdf

Kumar, A., & Mishra, S. (2022). Exploring Future Research Agenda for Rural Mother's Empowerment: A Study at the Intersection of Bibliometric and Systematic Literature Review. *South Asian Journal of Business and Management Cases*, *11*(3), 254–275. DOI: 10.1177/22779779221115804

Kumari, R., Raman, R., & Patel, R. K. (2023). Regional Disparities in Social, Environmental, and Economic Indicators among the Indian States. *GeoJournal*, *88*(4), 4351–4371. https://link.springer.com/article/10.1007/s10708-023-10868-9. DOI: 10.1007/s10708-023-10868-9

Kumar, S. (2024). Regional Organizations and States in International Relations: A Study of India's Approach Towards Regional Organizations. *Millennial Asia*, *15*(2), 259–277. DOI: 10.1177/09763996221105148

Kumar, S. Y. S. (2021). India Looking Beyond Saarc: Is it benefiting? In *Bilateral and Multilateral Cooperation in South Asia*. Taylor and Francis., DOI: 10.4324/9781003145271-10

Kuzmuk, O. M. (2024). Trust As A Catalyst For Community Development—Knowledge, Education, Law. *Management*, *5*(65).

Lalani, K., Crawford, J., & Butler-Henderson, K. (2021). Academic leadership during COVID-19 in higher education: Technology adoption and adaptation for online learning during a pandemic. *International Journal of Leadership in Education, 28*(1), 1–17. DOI: 10.1080/13603124.2021.1988716

Lamine, W., Anderson, A., Jack, S. L., & Fayolle, A. (2021). Entrepreneurial space and the freedom for entrepreneurship: Institutional settings, policy, and action in the space industry. *Strategic Entrepreneurship Journal, 15*(2), 309–340. DOI: 10.1002/sej.1392

Lauder, H., & Mayhew, K. (2020). Higher education and the labour market: An introduction. *Oxford Review of Education, 46*(1), 1–9. DOI: 10.1080/03054985.2019.1699714

Lederach, J. P. (2003). *The little book of conflict transformation.* Good Books.

Lee, H. Y., Hamid, M. O., & Hardy, I. (2023). Language and education policies in Southeast Asia: Reorienting towards multilingualism-as-resource. *International Journal of Multilingualism, 20*(3), 1106–1124. DOI: 10.1080/14790718.2021.2002333

Lei, L., & Yu, W. H. (2025). Who Opts Out of Neighborhood Schools? Determinants and Consequences of School Choice Strategies in China. *Research in Social Stratification and Mobility, 98*, 101065. DOI: 10.1016/j.rssm.2025.101065

Leithwood, K. (2021). A review of evidence about equitable school leadership. *Education Sciences, 11*(8), 377. DOI: 10.3390/educsci11080377

Lemi, K., Kant, S., & Jio, W. (2025). Greener Hospital Future in the Horn of Africa by Transactional Leadership: Outcome on Altruism Through Adaptability. In *Generation Alpha and Next Generation Leadership for Greener Futures* (pp. 1-22). IGI Global Scientific Publishing. DOI: DOI: 10.4018/979-8-3693-9281-2.ch001

Letshwene, M. J., & Du Plessis, E. C. (2021). The challenges of implementing the Curriculum and Assessment Policy Statement in accounting. *South African Journal of Education, 41*(Suppl. 2), 1–10. DOI: 10.15700/saje.v41ns2a1978

Leu Bonanno, S. (2023). Examining the foundations of culturally and linguistically sustaining school leadership: Towards a democratic project of schooling in dual language bilingual education. *Educational Administration Quarterly, 59*(1), 72–111. DOI: 10.1177/0013161X221106972

Ligęza, A., Kluza, K., Jemioło, P., Sepioło, D., Wiśniewski, P., & Jobczyk, K. (2021). Evaluation of Selected Artificial Intelligence Technologies for Innovative Business Intelligence Applications. In A. J. (Ed.), *Springer Proceedings in Mathematics and Statistics* (Vol. 364, pp. 111 – 126). Springer. DOI: 10.1007/978-3-030-92604-5_11

Li, J., Xue, E., Wei, Y., & He, Y. (2024). How Popularising Higher Education Affects Economic Growth and Poverty Alleviation: Empirical Evidence from 38 Countries. *Humanities & Social Sciences Communications, 11*(1), 520. https://www.nature.com/articles/s41599-024-03013-5. DOI: 10.1057/s41599-024-03013-5

Li, M. (2023). Adapting Legal Education for the Changing Landscape of Regional Emerging Economies: A Dynamic Framework for Law Majors. *Journal of the Knowledge Economy, 15*(3), 10227–10256. DOI: 10.1007/s13132-023-01507-2

Lin, P. (2024). Investigating leadership in formal school clusters: The case of Education Collectives in China (Doctoral dissertation, Institute of Education).

Lin, C.-C., Huang, A. Y. Q., & Lu, O. H. T. (2023). Artificial intelligence in intelligent tutoring systems toward sustainable education: A systematic review. *Smart Learning Environments, 10*(1), 41. DOI: 10.1186/s40561-023-00260-y

Linzalone, R., Ammirato, S., Felicetti, A. M., Corvello, V., & Santarsiero, F. (2024). Exploring stakeholder engagement network behavior: Strategic and managerial implications for corporate social responsibility. *Business Ethics, the Environment & Responsibility*. Advance online publication. DOI: 10.1111/beer.12692

Liu, Y., Bellibaş, M. Ş., & Gümüş, S. (2021). The Effect of Instructional Leadership and Distributed Leadership on Teacher Self-efficacy and Job Satisfaction: Mediating Roles of Supportive School Culture and Teacher Collaboration. *Educational Management Administration & Leadership, 49*(3), 430–453. DOI: 10.1177/1741143220910438

Lodi, E., Perrella, L., Lepri, G. L., Scarpa, M. L., & Patrizi, P. (2021). Use of Restorative Justice and Restorative Practices at School: A Systematic Literature Review. *International Journal of Environmental Research and Public Health, 19*(1), 96. DOI: 10.3390/ijerph19010096 PMID: 35010355

London, M. (2023). Causes and consequences of adaptive leadership: A model of leaders' rapid responses to unexpected events. *Psychology of Leaders and Leadership, 26*(1), 22–43. DOI: 10.1037/mgr0000136

Lopez, L. (2025). Culturally Responsive Leadership: Shaping Inclusive Classrooms For Diverse Learners.

Lopez, I. (2024). *The EQ way: How emotionally intelligent school leaders navigate turbulent times*. ASCD.

Lubis, S., Purnomo, E. P., Lado, J. A., & Hung, C.-F. (2024). Electronic governance in advancing sustainable development goals through systematic literature review. *Discover Global Society, 2*(1), 77. DOI: 10.1007/s44282-024-00102-3

Lucas, R. E.Jr. (1988). On the Mechanics of Economic Development. *Journal of Monetary Economics*, *22*(1), 3–42. DOI: 10.1016/0304-3932(88)90168-7

Lunenburg, F. C., & Ornstein, A. (2021). *Educational administration: Concepts and practices*. Sage Publications.

Macfarlane, B., Bolden, R., & Watermeyer, R. (2024). Three perspectives on leadership in higher education: Traditionalist, reformist, pragmatist. *Higher Education*, *88*(4), 1381–1402. DOI: 10.1007/s10734-023-01174-x

MacPhail, A., Tannehill, D., Leirhaug, P. E., & Borghouts, L. (2023). Promoting instructional alignment in physical education teacher education. *Physical Education and Sport Pedagogy*, *28*(2), 153–164. DOI: 10.1080/17408989.2021.1958177

Mahabeer, P. (2025). Curriculum transformation in South African HDIs: Navigating equity and epistemic justice. *South African Journal of Higher Education*, *39*(1), 1–20.

Mahmoud, S. E., & Mousa, M. E.-S. (2025). Does benevolent leadership affect the organizational identification of nursing staff? The mediating role of forgiveness climate and the moderating role of positive emotions. *Future Business Journal*, *11*(1), 35. DOI: 10.1186/s43093-025-00442-9

Makoe, M. (2023). Resilient leadership in time of crisis in distance education institutions in Sub-Saharan Africa. In *Handbook of Open, Distance and Digital Education* (pp. 547–561). Springer Nature Singapore. DOI: 10.1007/978-981-19-2080-6_30

Manchala, D. (2023). Dreaming a New Future: A Call from the Margins while on the Way to the Pilgrimage of Justice, Reconciliation, and Unity. International review of mission, 112(1), 24-36.

Mandala, C. R. (2023). Alternatively, Students Will Suffer: Feeling Rules in Identity Advocacy Centers at Institutions of Higher Education in the United States (Doctoral dissertation, University of Georgia).

Mandinach, E. B., & Gummer, E. S. (2025). Shining Light on Ethical Uses of Data in Education: Emerging Importance. *Teachers College Record*, *127*(2), 141–162. DOI: 10.1177/01614681251334784

Manzoor, S., Abbas, A., Chen, S., Zhang, G., & Khan, A. (2025). Response of energy transition and education in promoting the ecological balance in the BRICS countries. *Renewable Energy*, *247*, 122859. Advance online publication. DOI: 10.1016/j.renene.2025.122859

Maqbool, S., Zafeer, H. M. I., Maqbool, S., Zeng, P., Draissi, Z., & Javed, S. (2024). Stance of numerous leadership styles and their effect on teaching to sustain academic performance at the high school level. *Heliyon, 10*(16), e36438. DOI: 10.1016/j.heliyon.2024.e36438 PMID: 39253217

Marginson, S. (2024). The new geo-politics of higher education 2: Between nationalism and globalism.

Markovich Morris, E., & Cheng, Y. L. (2025). Parents as Allies: Innovative Strategies for (Re) imagining Family, School, and Community Partnerships. *Education Sciences, 15*(5), 533. DOI: 10.3390/educsci15050533

Marquez-Ramos, L., & Mourelle, E. (2019). Education and Economic Growth: An Empirical Analysis of Nonlinearities. *Applied Economic Analysis*, 27(29), 21-45. https://www.emerald.com/insight/content/doi/10.1108/aea-06-2019-0005/full/html

Marujo, H. A., & Wissing, M. P. (2024). *Community Peace and Character Strengths.*, DOI: 10.1007/978-3-031-66928-6_6

Masalimova, A. R., Orekhovskaya, N. A., Pivovarov, V. A., Borovikova, Y. V., Zhirkova, G. P., & Chauzova, V. A. (2024). Analysing trends in online learning in higher education in the BRICS countries through bibliometric data. *Frontiers in Education, 9*, 1409013. Advance online publication. DOI: 10.3389/feduc.2024.1409013

Matthews, J., Love, P. E., Porter, S. R., & Fang, W. (2022). Smart data and business analytics: A theoretical framework for managing rework risks in mega-projects. *International Journal of Information Management, 65*, 102495. DOI: 10.1016/j.ijinfomgt.2022.102495

Matthijs Bal, P., Davids, J., Garcia, E., McKnight, C., Nichele, E., Orhan, M. A., & van Rossenberg, Y. (2025). The Psychology of Automation and Artificial Intelligence at Work: Exploring Four Fantasies and Their Leadership Implications. In *Power, Politics and Influence: Exercising Followership, Leadership, and Practicing Politics* (pp. 575–592). Springer Nature Switzerland.

Mawaddah, A. F., Hatta, A. H., Prasetya, A., & Saputra, A. A. (2025). Adaptive Leadership and Culturally Responsive Transformation in Contemporary Workplaces. *Oikos, 17*(2), 1–18.

Mazurkiewicz, G. (2021). Educational leadership in times of crisis. *Risks, 9*(5), 90. DOI: 10.3390/risks9050090

McGee, S. (2024). *Culturally Conscious Decision-Making for School Leaders: A Toolkit for Creating a More Equitable School Culture*. Taylor & Francis. DOI: 10.4324/9781003478928

McLaughlin, A., Walls, J. H., & Kruse, S. (2025). Principal discipline decision-making: Choices and challenges. *Educational Management Administration & Leadership*, 17411432251330958. Advance online publication. DOI: 10.1177/17411432251330958

Mehanna, R.-A. (2008). Strategic patterns in international business: Product differentiation or complementarity? *Journal of Transnational Management*, *13*(2), 112–131. DOI: 10.1080/15475770802255028

Meirbekov, A., Maslova, I., & Gallyamova, Z. (2022). Digital education tools for critical thinking development. *Thinking Skills and Creativity*, *44*, 101023. DOI: 10.1016/j.tsc.2022.101023

Memon, F. N., & Memon, S. N. (2024). *Digital Divide and Equity in Education.*, DOI: 10.4018/979-8-3693-1854-6.ch004

Memon, N. A., Abdalla, M., & Chown, D. (2024). Laying Foundations for Islamic Teacher Education. *Education Sciences*, *14*(10), 1046. DOI: 10.3390/educsci14101046

Menter, I. (2024). The BRICS alliance and the impact of globalisation on teacher education worldwide. In *Globalisation and Teacher Education in the BRICS Countries: The Positioning of Research and Practice in Comparative Perspective*. Taylor and Francis., DOI: 10.4324/9781003388173-2

Miao, Q., & Nduneseokwu, C. (2024). Advancing Environmental Leadership: Education, Development, and Training. In *Environmental Leadership in a VUCA Era* (pp. 467–538). Springer Nature Singapore. DOI: 10.1007/978-981-96-0324-4_10

Mifsud, D. (2024). A systematic review of school distributed leadership: Exploring research purposes, concepts and approaches in the field between 2010 and 2022. *Journal of Educational Administration and History*, *56*(2), 154–179. DOI: 10.1080/00220620.2022.2158181

Miglani, M., Taneja, S., Bhatnagar, M., & Johri, A. (2025). Transforming Financial Services: Ethical Pathways of Workforce Automation towards Achieving SDG 9. *International Research Journal of Multidisciplinary Scope*, *6*(2), 1298–1308. DOI: 10.47857/irjms.2025.v06i02.03963

Miller, D., & Sardais, C. (2011). A concept of leadership for strategic organisation. *Strategic Organization*, *9*(2), 174–183. DOI: 10.1177/1476127011413757

Mistry, B. (2022). An Analytical Review of NEP 2020. *International Journal of Research in All Subjects in Multi Languages*, *10*(2), 9–12. https://www.raijmr.com/ijrsml/wp-content/uploads/2022/02/IJRSML_2022_vol10_issue_02_Eng_03.pdf

Mitchell, J. R., Mitchell, R. K., Hunt, R. A., Townsend, D. M., & Lee, J. H. (2022). Stakeholder engagement, knowledge problems and ethical challenges. *Journal of Business Ethics, 175*(1), 75–94. DOI: 10.1007/s10551-020-04550-0

Mitchell, R., Agbaire, J., Paulson, J., & Tikly, L. (2025). Endogenous systems leadership of education provision during crises in low-and middle-income countries: A conceptual framework: Endogenous systems leadership of education provision. *Prospects*, •••, 1–21. DOI: 10.1007/s11125-025-09732-0

Mohammadi, M. (2024). Advancing an Integrative AI-assisted Adaptive Learning Environment for Teacher Education: Case of the BRICS Countries. *Education and Self Development, 19*(4), 82–95. DOI: 10.26907/esd.19.4.07

Mohammad, N. (2011). The role of global governance mechanisms to protect the environment for sustainability: A study on Bangladesh perspective. *Australian Journal of Basic and Applied Sciences, 5*(10), 1175–1186. https://www.scopus.com/inward/record.uri?eid=2-s2.0-84864483785&partnerID=40&md5=55e74e63e8fef6f0e92899eb4a132775

Mohamud, Z. A., Farah, M. A., Osman, L. A., Mohamed, M. A., & Mohamud, I. H. (2025). Mapping the evolution of leadership in higher education: A bibliometric analysis. *Cogent Education, 12*(1), 2554957. DOI: 10.1080/2331186X.2025.2554957

Mohanty, A. (2018). Education for Sustainable Development: A Conceptual Model of Sustainable Education for India. *International Journal of Development and Sustainability, 7*(9), 2242–2255. https://isdsnet.com/ijds-v7n9-02.pdf

Moikanyane, M. (2023). Reimagining curriculum reform in historically disadvantaged institutions: A participatory approach. *Journal of Curriculum Studies in Africa, 11*(4), 56–74.

Molapo, S., Nyamukondiwa, P., & Chingombe, K. (2012). Celebrating 30 years of education at the University of Venda: From inkpot to iPad – Towards an educational centre of excellence. In B. Rootman (Ed.), *University of Venda*. Thohoyandou: University of Venda.

Moran, E., Walsh, E., & Sloan, S. (2025). Promoting a restorative culture in schools: Insights from school leaders. *International Journal of Educational Research Open, 8*, 100397. DOI: 10.1016/j.ijedro.2024.100397

Morgan, L., Close, S., Siller, M., Kushner, E., & Brasher, S. (2022). Teachers' experiences: Social emotional engagement – knowledge and skills. *Educational Research, 64*(1), 41–59. DOI: 10.1080/00131881.2021.1988865

Morze, N., & Trybulska, E. S. (2021). Web-based community-supported online education during the COVID-19 pandemic. *International Journal of Web Based Communities, 17*(1), 9. DOI: 10.1504/IJWBC.2021.112858

Mosima, K. L. (2022). Exploring the Use of Culturally Responsive Leadership for Conflict Management in Secondary Schools to Enhance Teaching and Learning (Master's thesis, University of South Africa (South Africa)).

Mousumi, M. A. (2023). Access and equity: What do we know about government primary school students' remote learning experience during school closures in Bangladesh? *Kokusai Kyoiku Kyoryoku Ronshu, 25*(1), 80–95. DOI: 10.1108/JICE-07-2022-0018

Mouta, A., Pinto-Llorente, A. M., & Torrecilla-Sánchez, E. M. (2024). Uncovering Blind Spots in Education Ethics: Insights from a Systematic Literature Review on Artificial Intelligence in Education. *International Journal of Artificial Intelligence in Education, 34*(3), 1166–1205. DOI: 10.1007/s40593-023-00384-9

Mouton, J., Louw, H., & Strydom, A. (2015). A typology of research capacity development initiatives. *South African Journal of Higher Education, 29*(1), 1–22.

Mowen, T. J., Brent, J. J., & Boman, J. H.IV. (2020). The Effect of School Discipline on Offending across Time. *Justice Quarterly, 37*(4), 739–760. DOI: 10.1080/07418825.2019.1625428 PMID: 34262239

Mpuangnan, K. N., & Ntombela, S. (2024). Community voices in curriculum development. *Curriculum Perspectives, 44*(1), 49–60. DOI: 10.1007/s41297-023-00223-w

Muchiri, C. W., & Muathe, S. M. (2024). Strategic orientation and organisational performance: Evidence from Rotary Clubs in Kenya. *Journal of Business and Management Sciences, 12*(2), 99–110. DOI: 10.12691/jbms-12-2-3

Mudd-Fegett, K., & Mudd, H. K. (2024). Transformational Leadership. In Transformational Learning in Social Work and Human Services Education (pp. 63-83). IGI Global. DOI: 10.4018/979-8-3693-2407-3.ch004

Mu, G. M., Gordon, D., Xu, J., Cayas, A., & Madesi, S. (2023). Benefits and limitations of partnerships amongst families, schools and universities: A systematic literature review. *International Journal of Educational Research, 120*, 102205. DOI: 10.1016/j.ijer.2023.102205

Müller, M. (2025). The Normativity of Diversity: Cultural Diversity and the Institutionalization of the Global Categories of People Race, Gender and Disability Cultural Diversity und die Institutionalisierung der globalen Personenkategorien Race, Gender und Disability. In *Ethnography and Diversity: Knowledge Production at the Boundaries and the Boundaries of Knowledge Production* (pp. 21–49). Springer Fachmedien Wiesbaden. DOI: 10.1007/978-3-658-47168-2_2

Munoz, G. M. A. (2025). Navigating in the Shadows: Undocumented Latina Experiences in Early Care and Education and Workforce Equity (Doctoral dissertation, San Francisco State University).

Murtadlo, M., Albana, H., Nisa, Y. F., Izazy, N. Q., Sumiati, N. T., Dewi, M. S., Abdullah, H., & Henry, C. (2025). Inclusive education in Africa: Transforming higher education in low-income countries. *Scientific African, 28*, e02708. DOI: 10.1016/j.sciaf.2025.e02708

Mussaiyib, A. M., & Pradhan, K. C. (2024). An empirical analysis of causal nexus between higher education and economic growth in BRICS countries. *Transnational Corporations Review, 16*(3), 200057. Advance online publication. DOI: 10.1016/j.tncr.2024.200057

Mustapha, A. R. (2023). *Ethnic and religious conflicts in Nigeria: Causes and solutions.* Spectrum Books.

Mwansa, G., Ngandu, M. R., & Mkwambi, Z. (2025). Bridging the digital divide: Exploring the challenges and solutions for digital exclusion in rural South Africa. *Discover Global Society, 3*(1), 54. DOI: 10.1007/s44282-025-00189-2

Nadeem, M. (2024). Distributed leadership in educational contexts: A catalyst for school improvement. *Social Sciences & Humanities Open, 9*, 100835. DOI: 10.1016/j.ssaho.2024.100835

Nair, J. R. (2024). Educational Innovation and Digitalisation During Crises. In Global Higher Education Practices in Times of Crisis: Questions for Sustainability and Digitalization (pp. 59-76). Emerald Publishing Limited.

Nakidien, T., Singh, M., & Sayed, Y. (2021). Teachers and Teacher Education: Limitations and Possibilities of Attaining SDG 4 in South Africa. *Education Sciences, 11*(2), 66. DOI: 10.3390/educsci11020066

Namoog, M. Y., & Agyekum, B. (2024). Non-formal education and women's empowerment: An assessment of the contemporal relevance of Freire's concept of conscientisation in increasing district assemblywomen's participation in community development and governance in Northen Ghana. *Cogent Arts & Humanities*, *11*(1), 2313338. Advance online publication. DOI: 10.1080/23311983.2024.2313338

Nanda, A. P., & Banerjee, R. (2021). Consumer's subjective financial well-being: A systematic review and research agenda. *International Journal of Consumer Studies*, *45*(4), 750–776. DOI: 10.1111/ijcs.12668

Nassir, M., & Benoliel, P. (2024). Teacher well-being and organisational citizenship behavior in Arab educational system in Israel: The implications of teacher collective involvement in decision making and organisational commitment. *School Psychology*, *39*(3), 256–268. DOI: 10.1037/spq0000610 PMID: 38166297

Natarajarathinam, M., Qiu, S., & Lu, W. (2021). Community engagement in engineering education: A systematic literature review. *Journal of Engineering Education*, *110*(4), 1049–1077. DOI: 10.1002/jee.20424

National Education Policy. (2020). https://www.education.gov.in/sites/upload_files/mhrd/files/NEP_Final_English_0.pdf

Natung, B., Awuor, E., Mall, M., & Mishra, M. (2025). The role of self-help groups in social capital development: A systematic review. *Cogent Social Sciences*, *11*(1), 2527393. Advance online publication. DOI: 10.1080/23311886.2025.2527393

Ndethiu, S., & Wamahiu, S. (2021). The Role of Peace Education in Kenya's Electoral Reforms. *East African Journal of Education and Development*, *3*(1), 41–58.

Ndlovu-Gatsheni, S. J. (2023). Beyond the coloniser's model of the world: Towards reworlding from the Global South. *Third World Quarterly*, *44*(10), 2246–2262. DOI: 10.1080/01436597.2023.2171389

Nedungadi, P., Tang, K.-Y., & Raman, R. (2024). The Transformative Power of Generative Artificial Intelligence for Achieving the Sustainable Development Goal of Quality Education. *Sustainability (Basel)*, *16*(22), 9779. DOI: 10.3390/su16229779

Nelson, L. L. (2021). Identifying determinants of individual peacefulness: A psychological foundation for peace education. *Peace and Conflict*, *27*(2), 109–119. DOI: 10.1037/pac0000517

Ng, S. T. Y. (2024). On Compromise: Neoliberalism, Postfeminism, and the Disappointed Promise of Personhood (Doctoral dissertation, UCL (University College London)).

Ngare, R. (2024). The role of heads of departments (HODs) in university management: Leadership and accountability in academic success. *Greener Journal of Social Sciences*, *14*(2), 203–211. DOI: 10.15580/gjss.2024.2.102024140

Ngwenya, T., & Maseko, P. (2022). Leadership in historically disadvantaged universities: Challenges and opportunities. *Journal of Higher Education Policy*, *34*(3), 210–225.

Nigerian Educational Research and Development Council (NERDC). (2021). *Curriculum Reform Policy Brief*. NERDC.

Nithya, J., Vignesh, S. R., Devadarsan, A., & Venkatesh, S. (2022). AI based contactless attendance monitoring and management system. *International Journal of Health Sciences*, (III), 431063. DOI: 10.53730/ijhs.v6nS3.8365

Nkomo, S., Horne, A. L., & Du Plessis, Y. (2015). Role of department heads in academic development: A leader-member exchange and organisational resource perspective. *Educational Management Administration & Leadership*, •••, 44.

Nnamani, G. (2024). An ecosystemic perspective of the factors affecting the learning experiences of learners with dyslexia in mainstream schools in England. *Dyslexia (Chichester, England)*, *30*(3), e1768. Advance online publication. DOI: 10.1002/dys.1768 PMID: 38845553

Norqvist, L., & Ärlestig, H. (2020). Systems thinking in school organizations – perspectives from various leadership levels. *Journal of Educational Administration*, *59*(1), 77–93. DOI: 10.1108/JEA-02-2020-0031

Novgorodtseva, A. N., & Belyaeva, E. A. (2020). Internationalization of higher education in Russia: Sociocultural interaction of students from the BRICS countries (Russia, China) [Интернационализация высшего образования в России: социокультурное взаимодействие студентов из стран БРИКС (Россия, Китай)]. *Perspektivy Nauki i Obrazovania*, *45*(3), 517–526. DOI: 10.32744/pse.2020.3.37

Nowak, W., & Nowosielski, M. (2021). Leadership struggles and challenges for diaspora policies: A case study of the Polish institutional system. *Innovation (Abingdon)*, *34*(1), 93–110. DOI: 10.1080/13511610.2019.1594716

Nurohman, D. A. (2025). *SILENT INFLUENCE: How Great Leaders Lead Without Shouting Preface*. PT Indonesia Delapan Kreasi Nusa.

Nyka, L., & Marczak, E. (2023). Frontier education for a sustainable future-speculative design in architecture as a transdisciplinary experiment. *Global Journal of Engineering Education*, *25*, 6–11.

Obeten, O. O., Okoringa, N., & Ossai, V. O. (2024). Leadership and economic development for nation building. *International Journal of Institutional Leadership. Policy and Management, 6*(2), 169–179.

Odeh, M. R. B. S., Obeidat, B. Y., Jaradat, M. O., Masa'deh, R., & Alshurideh, M. T. (2023). The transformational leadership role in achieving organisational resilience through adaptive cultures: The case of Dubai service sector. *International Journal of Productivity and Performance Management, 72*(2), 440–468. DOI: 10.1108/IJPPM-02-2021-0093

OECD. (2019). *OECD future of education and skills 2030: OECD learning compass 2030*. OECD Publishing. https://www.oecd.org/education/2030-project/

Ogwumike, I., Rangel, V. S., & Johnson, D. D. (2024). The Promise and Pitfalls of Transformational Leadership for Decreasing the Use of Out-of-School Suspensions and Reduce the Racial Discipline Gap. *Education and Urban Society, 56*(2), 230–259. DOI: 10.1177/00131245221106710

Ohnishi, S., Osako, M., Nakamura, S., Togawa, T., Kawai, K., Suzuki, K., Yoshida, A., Gomi, K., & Tsuji, T. (2024). A Framework for Analyzing Co-Creation Value Chain Mechanisms in Community-Based Approaches: A Literature Review. *Sustainability (Basel), 16*(7), 2919. DOI: 10.3390/su16072919

Ojo, J. S., Oyewole, S., & Aina, F. (2023). Forces of Terror: Armed Banditry and Insecurity in North-West Nigeria. *Democracy and Security, 19*(4), 319–346. DOI: 10.1080/17419166.2023.2164924

Okeke, R. C., & Chukwudebelu, C. B. (2024). Educational policy and national development in Nigeria. *International Journal of Education and Evaluation, 10*(4), 268–274.

Okoh, J. U. (2022). *Curriculum and peacebuilding in West Africa: Approaches and challenges*. Unity Press.

OLASYA, D. P., & Kiamba, A. (2025). Weaponisation of data: the role of data in modern warfare. BULLETIN OF" CAROL I" NATIONAL DEFENCE UNIVERSITY, 14(1), 90-107.

Olayemi, A. O. (2021). Cybercrime and National Security: Challenges for Nigeria. *Journal of African Cybersecurity, 5*(2), 13–27.

Olson, L., Guzmán, E., & Kunneman, F. (2023, May). Along the margins: Marginalised communities' ethical concerns about social platforms. In 2023 IEEE/ACM 45th International Conference on Software Engineering: Software Engineering in Society (ICSE-SEIS) (pp. 71-82). IEEE.

Omanyo, J. O., & Ndiege, J. R. (2025). Knowledge management considerations in learning management systems in higher education institutions: A systematic review, synthesis and research agenda. *VINE Journal of Information and Knowledge Management Systems, 55*(3), 586–603. DOI: 10.1108/VJIKMS-09-2022-0305

Omona, K., & O'dama, M. K. (Eds.). (2024). *Global perspectives on micro-learning and micro-credentials in higher education.* IGI Global. DOI: 10.4018/979-8-3693-0343-6

Oni, M. B., & Ijov, T. M. (2022). Peace education as a catalyst for sustainable development in Nigeria. *International Journal of Peace. Education and Development, 10*(2), 63–71. DOI: 10.30954/2454-9525.02.2022.5

Osah, G., Nwakanma, N. F., & Isikalu, A. A. (2021). Nomadic education and managing violent conflicts in Northern Nigeria. In Audu, B. J., & Hamza, M. (Eds.), *Conflicts and the vulnerable in Northern Nigeria: Festschrift in honour of Dr. Nafisat Dahiru Muhammad* (pp. 599–616). Pyla-Mak Press and Publishers.

Osei, K., & Eze, N. J. (2023). Teaching peace in fragile contexts: The role of teachers in Nigeria. *African Educational Review, 18*(1), 91–108.

Óskarsdóttir, E., Donnelly, V., Turner-Cmuchal, M., & Florian, L. (2020). Inclusive school leaders – their role in raising the achievement of all learners. *Journal of Educational Administration, 58*(5), 521–537. DOI: 10.1108/JEA-10-2019-0190

Owens, T. (2021). The innovation delusion: How our obsession with the new has disrupted the work that matters most. *The American Archivist, 84*(2), 545–548. DOI: 10.17723/0360-9081-84.2.545

Owusu-Agyeman, Y. (2021). Transformational leadership and innovation in higher education: A participative process approach. *International Journal of Leadership in Education, 24*(5), 694–716. DOI: 10.1080/13603124.2019.1623919

Özcan, M. (2021). The bottleneck metaphor of leadership culture: How shared understandings about leadership develop in groups and impede diversity and effectiveness of leaders—frontiers in Psychology, 12, 635751.

Özel, D., & Sümer, Z. (2025). Adapting Peace Education Programs: A Sustainable Approach to Harmony. *Journal of Ethnic and Cultural Studies, 12*(2), 231–251. DOI: 10.29333/ejecs/2142

Paju, B., Kajamaa, A., Pirttimaa, R., & Kontu, E. (2022). Collaboration for Inclusive Practices: Teaching Staff Perspectives from Finland. *Scandinavian Journal of Educational Research, 66*(3), 427–440. DOI: 10.1080/00313831.2020.1869087

Pal, D. P., Dietzenbacher, E., & Basu, D. (2007). Economic integration: Systemic measures in an input - Output framework. *Economic Systems Research, 19*(4), 397–408. DOI: 10.1080/09535310701698464

Palmer, C. G., Fry, A., Libala, N., Ralekhetla, M., Mtati, N., Weaver, M., Mtintsilana, Z., & Scherman, P. A. (2022). Engaging society and building participatory governance in a rural landscape restoration context. *Anthropocene, 37*, 100320. DOI: 10.1016/j.ancene.2022.100320

Palmquist, A., Alves, J., Baranyi, R., Munkvold, R., Carvalho, V., & Oliveira, E. (2025). Blended Realities - Higher Education Student Reflections on Acquiring Skills for Game Creation in a Project-Based- and Blended Learning Environment. *Games: Research and Practice, 3*(1), 2–26. DOI: 10.1145/3704414

Panayotou, T. (2016). Economic Growth and the Environment. In Haenn, N., Wilk, R. R., & Harnish, A. (Eds.), *The Environment in Anthropology: A Reader in Ecology, Culture, and Sustainable Living* (2nd ed., pp. 140–148). New York University Press.

Paulsen, L., & Lindsay, E. (2024). Learning analytics dashboards are increasingly becoming about learning and not just analytics - A systematic review. *Education and Information Technologies, 29*(11), 14279–14308. DOI: 10.1007/s10639-023-12401-4

Peters, A.-K., Capilla, R., Coroamă, V. C., Heldal, R., Lago, P., Leifler, O., Moreira, A., Fernandes, J. P., Penzenstadler, B., Porras, J., & Venters, C. C. (2024). Sustainability in Computing Education: A Systematic Literature Review. *ACM Transactions on Computing Education, 24*(1), 1–53. DOI: 10.1145/3639060

Pinto, J. M. de R. (2021). *The Education System of Brazil: Financing of Education in Brazil* (pp. 265–289). DOI: 10.1007/978-3-030-41651-5_21

Polozhentseva, I., Zhilkibaeva, R., Luzina, T., & Vijaya Kumar, K. (2025). *AI Digital Learning Adaptation Challenges and Issues in Current Higher Education Field.*, DOI: 10.1007/978-981-96-1981-8_12

Ponomarev, S. V., Mirgorod, E. E., Beilina, A. F., Chudaeva, A. A., & Maksaev, A. A. (2024). Online Education in BRICS Countries: New Opportunities for Post-pandemic Development. *Advances in Science. Technology and Innovation*, (Part F2356), 373–378. DOI: 10.1007/978-3-031-49711-7_62

Poole, A. H., & Todd-Diaz, A. (2022). 'I'm not a very good visionary': Challenge and change in twenty-first century North American archival education. *Archival Science, 22*(4), 585–616. DOI: 10.1007/s10502-022-09389-0

Pozzer, M. R. O., & dos Reis Neuhold, R. (2025). Vocational education and training and regional development in Brazil. *Journal of Vocational Education and Training, 77*(1), 207–228. DOI: 10.1080/13636820.2025.2449657

Prasad, K. (2013). Building Bridges in South Asia: Regional Cooperation, Information Technologies and Opportunities for Integration. *Innovation. Technology and Knowledge Management, 28*, 99–112. DOI: 10.1007/978-1-4614-5254-6_7

Przytula, S. (2024). Expatriate academics: What have we known for four decades? A systematic literature review. *Journal of Global Mobility, 12*(1), 31–56. DOI: 10.1108/JGM-03-2023-0024

PTI. (2025). Politicization of Educational Institutions Should not be Tolerated: Kerala Governor. *Deccan Herald* (March 22, 2025). https://www.deccanherald.com/india/kerala/politicisation-of-educational-institutions-should-not-be-tolerated-kerala-governor-3458061

Putri, H. A., Pisriwati, S. A., & Siswanto, D. H. (2024). Leadership strategies in decision-making for senior high school principals. *Journal of Organizational and Human Resource Development Strategies, 1*(02), 104–111. DOI: 10.56741/ohds.v1i02.707

Qasmi, F., & Fatima, S. K. (2024). *Enhancing Education and Well-Being Through Artificial Intelligence: Opportunities and Challenges* (pp. 154–164). DOI: 10.1007/978-3-031-65996-6_13

Raffe, C. P., & Loughland, T. (2021). "We are not data analysts": Teachers' perspectives on factors impacting their use of student assessment data. *Issues in Educational Research, 31*(1), 224–240.

Rafiki, A., Mohd Subri, I., Mohiddin, M. N., Hidayat, S. E., & Mohd Salleh, M. M. (2025). Salient practices of halal management in Southeast Asia: A systematic literature review. *Journal of Islamic Marketing, 16*(7), 1821–1843. Advance online publication. DOI: 10.1108/JIMA-02-2024-0059

Rajan, S. I. (2024). Kerala Migration Survey 2023. *Kerala Economy,* 5(3), 1-13. https://www.gift.res.in/wp-content/uploads/2024/09/Kerala-Migration-Survey-Report-2023-Irudaya-Raj.pdf

Ratzinger, D., Amess, K., Greenman, A., & Mosey, S. P. (2018). The impact of digital start-up founders' higher education on reaching equity investment milestones. *The Journal of Technology Transfer, 43*(3), 760–778. DOI: 10.1007/s10961-017-9627-3 PMID: 31258242

REHAN, S. (2025). A paradigm shift in storytelling and narrative styles: a study of anime effect.

Reisz, R. D., & Stock, M. (2012). Private Higher Education and Economic Development. *European Journal of Education*, *47*(2), 198–212. https://onlinelibrary.wiley.com/doi/abs/10.1111/j.1465-3435.2012.01518.x. DOI: 10.1111/j.1465-3435.2012.01518.x

Riaz, B. K., Ali, L., Ahmad, S. A., Islam, M. Z., Ahmed, K. R., & Hossain, S. (2020). Community clinics in Bangladesh: A unique example of public-private partnership. *Heliyon*, *6*(5), e03950. DOI: 10.1016/j.heliyon.2020.e03950 PMID: 32420500

Ribeiro, J. D., Falanga, R., & Moniz, J. (2025). Assessing the Role of Democratic Innovations in Environmental Sustainability: A Systematic Literature Review. *Sustainable Development (Bradford)*, *33*(5), 7775–7790. Advance online publication. DOI: 10.1002/sd.3545

Ricart-Huguet, J. (2021). Colonial Education, Political Elites, and Regional Political Inequality in Africa. *Comparative Political Studies*, *54*(14), 2546–2580. DOI: 10.1177/0010414021997176

Rich, P. J., Mason, S. L., & O'Leary, J. (2021). Measuring the effect of continuous professional development on elementary teachers' self-efficacy to teach coding and computational thinking. *Computers & Education*, *168*, 104196. DOI: 10.1016/j.compedu.2021.104196

Riggs, L., & Landrum, T. (2023). Trauma-Informed PBIS: How Educators Can Combine Evidence-Based Practices for Behavior Management With Trauma-Informed Care. *Beyond Behavior*, *32*(3), 152–161. DOI: 10.1177/10742956231201351

Riyani, M., Brata, N. T., & Shintasiwi, F. A. (2021). Making Peace with the Past: Peace Education in Post-Conflict Aceh Societies through the Application of Cognitive Behavioural Therapy. *Journal of Social Studies Education Research*, *12*(2), 330–376.

Robinson, V. M. J., Lloyd, C. A., & Rowe, K. J. (2008). The impact of leadership on student outcomes: An analysis of the differential effects of leadership types. *Educational Administration Quarterly*, *44*(5), 635–674. DOI: 10.1177/0013161X08321509

Rodríguez-Zurita, D., Jaya-Montalvo, M., Moreira-Arboleda, J., Raya-Diez, E., & Carrión-Mero, P. (2025). Sustainable development through service learning and community engagement in higher education: A systematic literature review. *International Journal of Sustainability in Higher Education*, *26*(1), 158–201. DOI: 10.1108/IJSHE-10-2023-0461

Romer, P. M. (1986). Increasing Returns and Long-Run Growth. *Journal of Political Economy, 94*(5), 1002–1037. https://www.jstor.org/stable/1833190. DOI: 10.1086/261420

Ronksley-Pavia, M., & Neumann, M. M. (2022). Exploring educator leadership practices in gifted education to facilitate online learning experiences for (re)engaging gifted students. *Education Sciences, 12*(2), 99. Advance online publication. DOI: 10.3390/educsci12020099

Rosenberg, B. (2023). *"Whatever it is, I am against it": Resistance to change in higher education*. Harvard Education Press.

Roszkowska, P., & Melé, D. (2021). Organizational Factors in the Individual Ethical Behaviour. The Notion of the "Organizational Moral Structure.". *Humanistic Management Journal, 6*(2), 187–209. DOI: 10.1007/s41463-020-00080-z

Rutayisire, T., & Kabwete, C. (2022). Post-genocide education and social healing in Rwanda. *International Journal of Peace Education, 19*(2), 115–134.

Ryan, A. W., Kolås, L., Nilsen, A. G., & Almås, A. G. (2024). Systematic literature review as a digital collaborative research-like learning activity: A case study. *Education and Information Technologies, 29*(5), 5243–5257. DOI: 10.1007/s10639-023-11997-x

Rybnicek, R., Leitner, K. H., Baumgartner, L., & Plakolm, J. (2019). Industry and leadership experiences of the heads of departments and their impact on the performance of public universities. *Management Decision, 57*(12), 3321–3345. DOI: 10.1108/MD-10-2018-1173

Sáez, L. (2014). SAARC, the road-map for economic co-operation from a European perspective. In *The Merits of Regional Cooperation: The Case of South Asia*. Springer International Publishing., DOI: 10.1007/978-3-319-02234-5_8

Saini, M., Singh, M., Kaur, M., & Kaur, M. (2021). Analysing the Tweets to Examine the Behavioral Response of Indian Citizens over the Approval of National Education Policy 2020. *International Journal of Educational Development, 82*, 102356. DOI: 10.1016/j.ijedudev.2021.102356

Saito, A. T., Dias Fouto, N. M. M., & De Angelo, C. F. (2018). Consumption and bank credit at the BRICS countries: A new light on the financial education process. *International Journal of Education Economics and Development, 9*(4), 366–393. DOI: 10.1504/IJEED.2018.096064

Sajuyigbe, A. S., Abiodun, A., Ayeni, A., & Ineba, H. L. (2024). Organisational Citizenship Behavior, Employee Voice and Academic Staff Retention in Nigerian Universities: Mediating Role of Conflict Resolution. *Revista Colombiana de Psicología, 33*(1), 87–106. DOI: 10.15446/rcp.v33n1.100117

Salanova, M., Lorente, L., Chambel, M. J., & Martínez, I. M. (2011). Linking transformational leadership to nurses' extra-role performance: The mediating role of self-efficacy and work engagement. *Journal of Advanced Nursing, 67*(10), 2256–2266. DOI: 10.1111/j.1365-2648.2011.05652.x PMID: 21535088

Sallis, E. (2002). *Total Quality Management in Education*. Taylor & Francis.

Samaniego López, M. V., Orrego Riofrío, M. C., Barriga-Fray, S. F., & Paz Viteri, B. S. (2025). Technologies in Inclusive Education: Solution or Challenge? A Systematic Review. *Education Sciences, 15*(6), 715. DOI: 10.3390/educsci15060715

Sánchez Galera, M. D. (2020). Facing Cultural and Education Challenges at the EU Level: Fragmentation and Multiple Solutions. In *Educational and Cultural Challenges of the European Sustainability Model* (pp. 179–266). Springer International Publishing. DOI: 10.1007/978-3-030-38716-7_5

Sarachek, B. (1968). Greek concepts of leadership. *Academy of Management Journal, 11*(1), 39–48. DOI: 10.2307/255195

Sarkar, P. (2024). An Overview of Migration Study in Kerala: Analysing In-Migration and Out-Migration Trends Using Census 2011. *Journal of Migration Affairs, 6*(1-2), 1–8. https://migrationaffairs.com/wp-content/uploads/2024/03/1-pinak-sarkar-commentary-migration-affairs-march-2024.pdf. DOI: 10.36931/jma.2024.6.1-2.1-8

Sart, G., Bayar, Y., Sezgin, F. H., Danilina, M. V., & Karagöz, E. (2025). The effect of shadow economy, life expectancy, education, and income on CO2 emissions: An analysis of BRICS countries. *Frontiers in Environmental Science, 13*, 1550389. Advance online publication. DOI: 10.3389/fenvs.2025.1550389

Saxena, A., Ramaswamy, M., Beale, J., Marciniuk, D., & Smith, P. (2021). Striving for the United Nations (UN) Sustainable Development Goals (SDGs): What will it take? *Discover Sustainability, 2*(1), 20. DOI: 10.1007/s43621-021-00029-8

Sayed, W. S., Noeman, A. M., Abdellatif, A., Abdelrazek, M., Badawy, M. G., Hamed, A., & El-Tantawy, S. (2023). AI-based adaptive personalized content presentation and exercises navigation for an effective and engaging E-learning platform. *Multimedia Tools and Applications, 82*(3), 3303–3333. DOI: 10.1007/s11042-022-13076-8 PMID: 35789938

Schank, C., & Rieckmann, M. (2019). Socio-Economically Substantiated Education for Sustainable Development: Development of Competencies and Value Orientations between Individual Responsibility and Structural Transformation. *Journal of Education for Sustainable Development, 13*(1), 67–91. https://journals.sagepub.com/doi/epub/10.1177/0973408219844849. DOI: 10.1177/0973408219844849

Schaper, M.-M., Tamashiro, M. A., Smith, R. C., & Iversen, O. S. (2025). *Diversity in AI Education: Tailoring students' learning paths for inclusive learning about facial recognition.* ACM Transactions on Computing Education., DOI: 10.1145/3727985

Schilke, O., Reimann, M., & Cook, K. S. (2021). Trust in social relations. *Annual Review of Sociology, 47*(1), 239–259. DOI: 10.1146/annurev-soc-082120-082850

Schiuma, G., Schettini, E., Santarsiero, F., & Carlucci, D. (2022). The transformative leadership compass: Six competencies for digital transformation entrepreneurship. *International Journal of Entrepreneurial Behaviour & Research, 28*(5), 1273–1291. DOI: 10.1108/IJEBR-01-2021-0087

Schoemaker, P. J. H., Krupp, S., & Howland, S. (2013). *Strategic Leadership: The Essential Skills.* Harvard Business Review, January–February Issue.

Seale, O. (2019). Re-imagining leadership development for middle-level academic leaders in Africa. *Journal of Higher Education in Africa / Revue de l'enseignement supérieur en Afrique, 17*(1), 1–26.

Sebastian, C. (2024). Not Just Studies and Jobs: Why Kerala's Youth Choose to Migrate. *Centerfor Public Policy Research.* https://www.cppr.in/articles/youth-migrate

Selwyn, N. (2023). Lessons to be learnt? Education, techno-solutionism, and sustainable development. Technology and sustainable development, 71, 83.

Sercu, L., Ayana, D. K., & Mengistu, D. (2025). Intercultural Citizenship Education in Post-Conflict Contexts: The Case of Ethiopia. *African Journal of Education and Practice, 11*(2), 17–35. DOI: 10.47604/ajep.3287

Sharma, R., Bhatnagar, M., & Ozen, E. (2025). The role of intellectual capital in combatting deepfake threats to corporate reputation and trust. In *Mastering Deepfake Technology: Strategies for Ethical Management and Security.* River Publishers. https://www.scopus.com/inward/record.uri?eid=2-s2.0-105007657679&partnerID=40&md5=f313a80a3279f91fbedf7fd10c6a4f7a

Sharma, S. (2024). Kerala Among the Top in India's Youth Unemployment Chart Despite High Literacy Rate: What are the Real Culprits? *The Times of India*. https://timesofindia.indiatimes.com/education/news/kerala-among-the-top-in-indias-youth-unemployment-chart-despite-high-literacy-rate-what-are-the-real-culprits/articleshow/113673214.cms

Sharma, S. N., & Adeoye, M. A. (2024). *New perspectives on transformative leadership in education*. EduPedia Publications Pvt Ltd.

Shaw, T. M., Grant, J. A., & Cornelissen, S. (2016). The Ashgate research companion to regionalisms. In *The Ashgate Research Companion to Regionalisms*. Taylor and Francis., DOI: 10.4324/9781315613499

Shaya, N., Abukhait, R., Madani, R., & Khattak, M. N. (2023). Organizational Resilience of Higher Education Institutions: An Empirical Study during Covid-19 Pandemic. *Higher Education Policy*, *36*(3), 529–555. DOI: 10.1057/s41307-022-00272-2 PMID: 35529423

Shehu, A. B. (2023). *Culture, religion and peace education in Northern Nigeria*. Ahmadu Bello University Press.

Shuangshuang, Y., Zhu, W., Mughal, N., Aparcana, S. I. V., & Muda, I. (2023). The impact of education and digitalisation on female labour force participation in BRICS: An advanced panel data analysis. *Humanities & Social Sciences Communications*, *10*(1), 598. Advance online publication. DOI: 10.1057/s41599-023-02020-2

Silvestre, B. S. (2015). Sustainable supply chain management in emerging economies: Environmental turbulence, institutional voids and sustainability trajectories. *International Journal of Production Economics*, *167*, 156–169. DOI: 10.1016/j.ijpe.2015.05.025

Simon, S., Heck, D., Christie, M., & Farragher, Y. (2021). Leading pedagogical reform: Australian principals tell their stories. *International Journal of Leadership in Education*, *24*(2), 266–289. DOI: 10.1080/13603124.2019.1613566

Singh, D. P., Thompson, R. J., & Curran, K. A. (Eds.). (2021). *Reimagining leadership on the commons: Shifting the paradigm for a more ethical, equitable, and just world*. Emerald Publishing Limited. DOI: 10.1108/S2058-8801202101

Singh, M., Sehajpal, S., & Khati, K. S. (2025). Global branding partnerships for financial growth and SDG 17: Building sustainable and inclusive economic strategies. In *Brand Creation and Management in the Phygital Era* (pp. 307–340). IGI Global., DOI: 10.4018/979-8-3373-0948-4.ch012

Sonetti, G., Barioglio, C., & Campobenedetto, D. (2020). Education for Sustainability in Practice: A Review of Current Strategies within Italian Universities. *Sustainability (Basel)*, *12*(13), 5246. DOI: 10.3390/su12135246

Soni, V. K., & Sahoo, S. (2021). The Development Narratives in South Asia: A Case Study of Print Media. In *Development, Governance and Gender in South Asia: Perspectives, Issues and Challenges*. Springer Nature. DOI: 10.1007/978-981-16-5109-0_12

Sooryamoorthy, R. (2023). *Barriers to Self-Reliance*., DOI: 10.1007/978-981-99-5577-0_6

Sotiriou, S. A., Lazoudis, A., & Bogner, F. X. (2020). Inquiry-based learning and E-learning: How to serve high and low achievers. *Smart Learning Environments*, *7*(1), 29. DOI: 10.1186/s40561-020-00130-x

South African Institute of Chartered Accountants (SAICA). (2021). *CA2025 Competency Framework: Pathways to relevance*. Johannesburg.

South African Institute of Chartered Accountants (SAICA). (2023). *SAICA-accredited academic programmes: CA (SA) and AGA (SA).*

Sowetan. (2007). "Concerns About the Graduate Quality of the University of Venda's BCom Accounting Programme".

Sridharan, K., & Srinivasa-Raghavan, T. C. A. (2007). Regional cooperation in South Asia and Southeast Asia. In *Regional Cooperation in South Asia and Southeast Asia*. Institute of Southeast Asian Studies. https://www.scopus.com/inward/record.uri?eid=2-s2.0-84895082186&partnerID=40&md5=6a02e8b2020710393013f2e6e13e71fd

Srinivasa, K. G., Kurni, M., & Saritha, K. (2022). *Harnessing the Power of AI to Education*., DOI: 10.1007/978-981-19-6734-4_13

Srinivasan, V., Thomas, L., Peter, K. V., Remashree, A. B., & Cheriyan, H. (2024). Spices: Area, production, and export scenario. In *Handbook of Spices in India: 75 Years of Research and Development*. Springer Nature. DOI: 10.1007/978-981-19-3728-6_2

Staziaki, P. V., Santo, I. D. de O., Skobodzinski, A. A., Park, L. K., & Bedi, H. S. (2021). How to Use YouTube for Radiology Education. *Current Problems in Diagnostic Radiology*, *50*(4), 461–468. DOI: 10.1067/j.cpradiol.2020.11.007 PMID: 33261926

Steiner, E. D., Woo, A., & Doan, S. (2023). *All work and no pay—Teachers' perceptions of their pay and hours worked*. Rand Corporation.

Stephenson, L. (2011). Developing a Leadership Education Framework: A Transformative Leadership Perspective. *Counterpoints, 409*, 321–341. https://www.jstor.org/stable/42981314

Stewart, J. (2006). Transformational Leadership: An Evolving Concept Examined through the Works of Burns, Bass, Avolio, and Leithwood. *Canadian Journal of Educational Administration and Policy*, (54), 1–29.

Stolz, J., & Megerle, H. E. (2022). Geotrails as a medium for education and geotourism: Recommendations for quality improvement based on the results of a research project in the Swabian Alb UNESCO Global Geopark. *Land (Basel), 11*(9), 1422. DOI: 10.3390/land11091422

Swargiary, K. (2024). State-Wise Literacy Rates in India: Analysing Regional Disparities, Gender Gaps, and Policy Impacts. *SSRN*. https://papers.ssrn.com/sol3/papers.cfm?abstract_id=4886091

Swift, C. (2023). Lead Like No One Else.

Tähtinen, L. (2022). Exploring crisis resilience in the built environment: Institutional frameworks and crisis prioritisation in steering crisis management.

Tan, S. (2023). Exploiting Disruptive Innovation in Learning and Teaching. In *Learning Intelligence: Innovative and Digital Transformative Learning Strategies* (pp. 149–176). Springer Nature Singapore. DOI: 10.1007/978-981-19-9201-8_4

Tao, Y., He, J. X., Liu, H., & Zhang, Z. Y. (2024). Strategy configurations and competitive advantage, organisational resilience: Research based on Chinese manufacturing firms. *Guanli Gongcheng Xuebao, 38*(5), 1–21. DOI: 10.1234/jiieem.2024.38501

Terepyshchyi, S. (2021). In search of peacebuilding strategies for the global civilisation: From "education for war" to "education for peace". *Philosophy and Cosmology, 27*(27), 153–162.

Tewari, D. D., & Ilesanmi, O. A. (2022). Conflicting Goals of SAICA and South African Universities: Implications for Accounting Research. *South African Journal of Accounting Research, 36*(1), 1–15.

Thacker, N. E., & Duran, A. (2022). Operationalising intersectionality as a framework in qualitative grief research. *Death Studies, 46*(5), 1128–1138. DOI: 10.1080/07481187.2020.1795749 PMID: 32692617

Thangeda, A., Baratiseng, B., & Mompati, T. (2016). Education for Sustainability: Quality Education is a Necessity in Modern Day. How far do the Educational Institutions Facilitate Quality Education? *Journal of Education and Practice*, *7*(2), 9–17. https://files.eric.ed.gov/fulltext/EJ1089752.pdf

The Hindu Bureau. (2023). 32nd Anniversary of Total Literacy Announcement Observed. *The Hindu* (April 18, 2023). https://www.thehindu.com/news/national/kerala/32nd-anniversary-of-total-literacy-announcement-observed/article66752754.ece

Thelma, C. C., & Chitondo, L. (2024). Leadership for sustainable development in Africa: A comprehensive perspective. *International Journal of Research Publications*, *5*(2), 2395–2410.

Theoharis, G. (2024). *The school leaders our children deserve: Seven keys to equity, social justice, and school reform*. Teachers College Press.

Thryv, 2024. Small Business Index Report, available at: https://www.thryv.com/2024-smb-index/ (accessed September 20 2025).

Tian, M., & Huber, S. G. (2021). Mapping the international knowledge base of educational leadership, administration and management: A topographical perspective. *Compare: A Journal of Comparative Education*, *51*(1), 4–23. DOI: 10.1080/03057925.2019.1585757

Tilak, J. B. G. (2020). Dilemmas in Reforming Higher Education in India. *Higher Education for the Future*, 7(1), 54-66. https://journals.sagepub.com/doi/abs/10.1177/0019466221145290

Timmis, S., & Muñoz-Chereau, B. (2022). Under-represented students' university trajectories: Building alternative identities and forms of capital through digital improvisations. *Teaching in Higher Education*, *27*(1), 1–17. DOI: 10.1080/13562517.2019.1696295 PMID: 34584277

Touchton, M., Wampler, B., & Spada, P. (2019). The digital revolution and governance in Brazil: Evidence from participatory budgeting. *Journal of Information Technology & Politics*, *16*(2), 154–168. DOI: 10.1080/19331681.2019.1613281

Townsend, T. (2024). Transforming educational leadership: A historical context. *Education Sciences*, *14*(8), 890. DOI: 10.3390/educsci14080890

Trajkovski, G., & Hayes, H. (2025). *Foundations of AI in Educational Assessment.*, DOI: 10.1007/978-3-031-88252-4

Tripp, J. N., & Waight, N. (2024). Co-creating a community of belonging and presence: Multilingual learners' experiences of science and language learning at an urban, inclusive STEM-focused high school. *Science Education, 108*(1), 25–62. DOI: 10.1002/sce.21827

Tsarkos, A. (2024). *Servant Leadership and Transformative Change.*, DOI: 10.4018/979-8-3693-4119-3.ch007

Tsaurai, K. (2017). Education-economic growth nexus in BRICS countries: Does financial development matter? *International Journal of Education Economics and Development, 8*(4), 250–265. DOI: 10.1504/IJEED.2017.088817

Tsiotas, D. (2022). A 3D index for measuring economic resilience with application to the modern international and global financial crises. *arXiv*. https://doi.org//arXiv.2202.08564DOI: 10.48550

Tufa, G., Kinde, Z., & Kant, S. (2025). Strategic Leadership: Effect on Employee Performance With Mediation of Dynamic Capabilities in Case of Ethiopian Public Organizations. In *Generation Alpha and Next Generation Leadership for Greener Futures* (pp. 115-138). IGI Global Scientific Publishing. DOI: DOI: 10.4018/979-8-3693-9281-2.ch006

Udogu, E. I. (2021). Democratic governance and the neglect of peace education in Nigeria. *African Journal of Peace and Conflict Studies, 10*(1), 70–85.

Ugwueze, M. I., & Ojukwu, C. C. (2023). Secessionism and the crisis of federalism in Nigeria. *American Journal of Political Science, 27*(1), 55–70.

Ullah, M. S. (2022). *Under the Wheel of Decolonization and Recolonization: The Crossroads of Journalism Education in South Asia* (pp. 139–163). DOI: 10.1007/978-3-031-13749-5_7

UNESCO. (2021). *Reimagining our futures together: A new social contract for education.* UNESCO Publishing. https://unesdoc.unesco.org/ark:/48223/pf0000379707

UNESCO. (2023). Bringing into Focus the Future of the Right to Education. https://articles.unesco.org/sites/default/files/medias/fichiers/2023/12/Future-of-right-to-education-working-document-en.pdf

UNESCO. (2023a). *Education for peace and prevention of violence.* UNESCO Publishing.

UNESCO. (2023b). *Peace and global citizenship education: A guide for policy-makers.* UNESCO Publishing.

UNESCO. (2023c). *Transforming education for peace and sustainable futures.* UNESCO Publishing.

UNICEF. (2021). *Reimagining education: Learning in a post-COVID-19 world.* UNICEF. https://www.unicef.org/reports/reimagining-education-learning-post-covid-19-world

Universities South Africa. (2024) *Thought Leadership Series.* Available at: https://usaf.ac.za/thought-leadership-series/ (Accessed: September 27 2025).

Unnikrishnan vs. State of Andhra Pradesh (1993) 1 SCC 645.

Urhahne, D., & Wijnia, L. (2023). Theories of Motivation in Education: An Integrative Framework. *Educational Psychology Review, 35*(2), 45. DOI: 10.1007/s10648-023-09767-9

Ursavaş, Ö. F. (2022). *Conducting Technology Acceptance Research in Education.* Springer International Publishing., DOI: 10.1007/978-3-031-10846-4

Valeeva, R., Kalimullin, A., & Baklashova, T. (2024). Editorial: BRICS Countries on the Improvement of Teacher Education. *Education and Self Development, 19*(3), 6–8. DOI: 10.26907/esd.19.3.01

Valero, A. (2021). Education and Economic Growth. In McCall, B. P. (Ed.), *The Routledge Handbook of the Economics of Education* (pp. 555–582). Routledge. DOI: 10.4324/9780429202520-20

Valtonen, T., Leppänen, U., Hyypiä, M., Kokko, A., Manninen, J., Vartiainen, H., Sointu, E., & Hirsto, L. (2021). Learning environments preferred by university students: A shift toward informal and flexible learning environments. *Learning Environments Research, 24*(3), 371–388. DOI: 10.1007/s10984-020-09339-6

van der Oord, S., & Tripp, G. (2020). How to Improve Behavioral Parent and Teacher Training for Children with ADHD: Integrating Empirical Research on Learning and Motivation into Treatment. *Clinical Child and Family Psychology Review, 23*(4), 577–604. DOI: 10.1007/s10567-020-00327-z PMID: 32968886

Van Wart, M., Suino, P., & Medina, P. S. (2023). *Leadership in public and nonprofit organisations: an introduction.* Routledge. DOI: 10.4324/9781003261896

Varma, A., Patel, P., Prikshat, V., Hota, D., & Pereira, V. (2021). India's New Education Policy: A Case of Indigenous Ingenuity Contributing to the Global Knowledge Economy? *Journal of Knowledge Management, 25*(10), 2385–2395. https://www.emerald.com/insight/content/doi/10.1108/jkm-11-2020-0840/full/html. DOI: 10.1108/JKM-11-2020-0840

Venegas, C. (2024). *Flow in the office: implementing and sustaining lean improvements*. CRC Press. DOI: 10.4324/9781003576440

Verwolf, B. (2025). Stepping into Leadership: Addressing the Transition for New Heads of School (Doctoral dissertation, Baylor University).

Viter, D., & Rudenko, O. (2025). National security in the multi-domain environment: Public administration issues. *Public Administration and Law Review*, *1*(21), 40–49. DOI: 10.36690/2674-5216-2025-1-40-49

Voelkel, R. H.Jr, Fiori, C., & van Tassell, F. (2023). District leadership in redefining roles of instructional coaches to guide professional learning communities through systemic change. *Leadership and Policy in Schools*, *22*(1), 141–160. DOI: 10.1080/15700763.2021.1917622

Vogler, G. (2024). *Judging Complicity: How to Respond to Injustice and Violence*. Edinburgh University Press. DOI: 10.1515/9781399522489

Von Behren, M. T. (2025). Servants of the Times: A Phenomenological, Critical Realist, and Servant-Leadership Study of the Lived Experience of Five People Who Started New Non-Profit Organizations to Serve People in Intercultural Settings (Doctoral dissertation, Gonzaga University).

Votto, R. (2025). *Navigating Ethical Friction: From Coercion to Connection in Organizational Lifea Paired Case Study of Leadership, Trust, and Power*. Trust, and Power.

Wahyuni, A. S., Málovics, G., & Gébert, J. (2025). Critical factors influencing sustainable and impactful university–community engagement: A systematic review of top-down and bottom-up initiatives. *International Journal of Sustainability in Higher Education*. Advance online publication. DOI: 10.1108/IJSHE-02-2024-0089

Waidyaratne, S. M. (2022). Impact of transformational leadership on employee resilience during a crisis. *Sri Lanka Journal of Management Studies*, *4*(1), 147–162. DOI: 10.4038/sljms.v4i1.92

Walker, J. G. (2022). How to develop and nurture academic leaders at our universities. https://usaf.ac.za/how-to-develop-and-nurture-academic-leaders-at-our-universities

Walsh, S., Johnston, A., & Gabriel, C. L. (2024). Building resilient leadership: A study exploring leadership development during uncertainty. *Human Resource Management and Services*, *6*(2), 3474. DOI: 10.18282/hrms.v6i2.3474

Wang, R., Qamruzzaman, M., & Karim, S. (2024). Unveiling the power of education, political stability and ICT in shaping technological innovation in BRI nations. *Heliyon, 10*(9), e30142. DOI: 10.1016/j.heliyon.2024.e30142 PMID: 38707328

Waqif, A. A. (1999). Civil service capacity for regional cooperation: Some comparative aspects in the EU and SAARC regions. *South Asian Survey, 6*(1), 75–88. DOI: 10.1177/097152319900600109

Weaver, J. L., & Swank, J. M. (2020). A Case Study of the Implementation of Restorative Justice in a Middle School. *RMLE Online: Research in Middle Level Education, 43*(4), 1–9. DOI: 10.1080/19404476.2020.1733912

Weber, A. S. (2011). The Role of Education in Knowledge Economies in Developing Countries. *Procedia: Social and Behavioral Sciences, 15*, 2589–2594. DOI: 10.1016/j.sbspro.2011.04.151

Weiskittel, P. (1999). President's message: The concept of leadership. *ANNA Journal, 26*(5), 467, 536.

Western, S. (2008). An overview of the leadership discourses. In Preedy, M., Bennett, N., & Wise, C. (Eds.), *Leadership and Management in Education: Cultures, Change and Context* (pp. 11–16). SAGE Publications.

White, J. L., Chávez, A. F., & Longerbeam, S. D. (2023). *Teaching Across Cultural Strengths*. Routledge., DOI: 10.4324/9781003447344

White, R., Lowery, C., & Johnson, J. (2025). Enhancing high-quality education through systemic school leadership: A systematic review. *Quality Education for All, 2*(1), 227–244. DOI: 10.1108/QEA-09-2024-0096

Whitney, D. E. (2024). Manufacturing by design. In *Revitalizing Manufacturing* (pp. 282–292). CRC Press. DOI: 10.4324/9781003571872-24

Wilkes, J. (2022). Reconnecting with nature through good governance: Inclusive policy across scales. *Agriculture, 12*(3), 382. DOI: 10.3390/agriculture12030382

Wilkinson, J. (2021). *Educational leadership through a practice lens*. Springer Singapore. DOI: 10.1007/978-981-16-7629-1

Williams, S. S. (2020). Culturally Sustaining Leadership: Supporting the Resilience of Indigenous Students in the United States and Australia. *Journal of School Leadership, 30*(6), 565–587. DOI: 10.1177/1052684620951725

Willocks, K. E. (2023). Making leadership as practice development visible: Learning from Activity Theory. *Management Learning, 54*(5), 705–726. DOI: 10.1177/13505076221105870

Wilson, R. (2009, May–June). The color green: A "go" for peace education. *Peace Education Exchange*, 40–43. https://www.exchangepress.com/library/5018740.pdf

Woldegiorgis, E. T., & Chiramba, O. (2025). Access and success in higher education: Fostering resilience in historically disadvantaged students in South Africa. *Journal of Applied Research in Higher Education*, *17*(2), 759–776. DOI: 10.1108/JARHE-05-2023-0217

World Bank. (2020). *The World Bank education strategy 2020: Learning for all – Investing in people's knowledge and skills to promote development.* World Bank. https://www.worldbank.org/en/topic/education/publication/education-strategy-2020

World Population Review. (2025). Education Rankings by Country 2025. https://worldpopulationreview.com/country-rankings/education-rankings-by-country

Wright, C., Rolston, B., & Ní Aoláin, F. (2023). Navigating colonial debris: Structural challenges for Colombia's peace accord. *Peacebuilding*, *11*(1), 62–77. DOI: 10.1080/21647259.2022.2027153

Wu, C. (2025). Redefining concepts of nation and national security and establishing their models for the new era. *Journal of Safety and Sustainability*, *2*(1), 45–58. DOI: 10.1016/j.jsasus.2024.12.002

Xing, W., & Imran, A. (2025). Financial and Technological Drivers of Sustainable Development: The Role of Communication Technology, Financial Efficiency and Education in BRICS. *Sustainability (Basel)*, *17*(5), 2326. Advance online publication. DOI: 10.3390/su17052326

Yagboyaju, D. A., & Akinboye, S. O. (2022). *Elections and democratic consolidation in Nigeria*. University of Lagos Press.

Yakubovna, Y. B. (2024). CONDUCT OF EXACT SCIENCES IN AN INTERACTIVE WAY IN THE SYSTEM OF PROFESSIONAL EDUCATION. *PEDAGOGICAL SCIENCES AND TEACHING METHODS*, *3*(32), 118–121.

Yang, J., Qiu, H., & Yu, W. (2024). Surging currents: A systematic review of the literature on dynamic stakeholder engagements in higher education in the generative artificial intelligence era. *Journal of Asian Public Policy*. Advance online publication. DOI: 10.1080/17516234.2024.2429046

Yared, H., Grové, C., & Chapman, D. (2023). *Who Belongs in Schools?* How the Education System Fails Racially Marginalised Students., DOI: 10.1007/978-981-16-5908-9_13

Yi, H., Wang, G., & Feng, J. (2024). Gender inequality: Policy responses to employment and education in BRICS countries. *African Journal of Reproductive Health, 28*(12), 88–96. DOI: 10.29063/ajrh2024/v28i12.10 PMID: 39764841

Yukl, G. (1999). An evaluation of conceptual weaknesses in transformational and charismatic leadership theories. *The Leadership Quarterly, 10*(2), 285–305. DOI: 10.1016/S1048-9843(99)00013-2

Yulianti, K., Denessen, E., Droop, M., & Veerman, G.-J. (2022). School efforts to promote parental involvement: The contributions of school leaders and teachers. *Educational Studies, 48*(1), 98–113. DOI: 10.1080/03055698.2020.1740978

Yuliantini, T., Ramli, Y., Kuswibowo, C., Zulfikar, R. R. O., & Soelton, M. (2024). Conceptualizing Work Engagement And Knowledge Sharing To Increase Organisational Citizenship Behavior. *Jurnal Riset Bisnis dan Manajemen, 17*(2), 105-116.

Yun, J. S. (2025). To Reflect & to be Reflective: Student Experiences of Critique in Art & Design Higher Education.

Yu, Y., Appiah, D., Zulu, B., & Adu-Poku, K. A. (2024). Integrating Rural Development, Education, and Management: Challenges and Strategies. *Sustainability (Basel), 16*(15), 6474. DOI: 10.3390/su16156474

Zahid, M., Khalid, F., Ramzan, M., Haq, M. Z. U., Lee, W., Hwang, J., & Shim, J. (2021). The significance of monetary policy transmission mechanism in the sustainable development of the SAARC economic community. *Sustainability (Basel), 13*(23), 13171. Advance online publication. DOI: 10.3390/su132313171

Zaki, J. (2022). Do not let cynicism undermine your workplace. *Harvard Business Review, 100*(5), 70–78.

Zhang, H., & Huang, H. (2024). Low-Carbon Transformational Leadership: Conceptualization, Measurement, and Its Impact on Innovation Outcomes. *Sustainability (Basel), 16*(24), 10844. DOI: 10.3390/su162410844

Zhang, H., & Tian, M. (2025). Unpacking the multi-dimensional nature of teacher competencies: A systematic review. *Scandinavian Journal of Educational Research, 69*(5), 1004–1025. DOI: 10.1080/00313831.2024.2369867

Zhang, X., & Xiao, L. (2025). Eco-literate societies: The interplay of education, environmental policy stringency, and digital innovation in BRICS nations. *Frontiers in Environmental Science, 13*, 1607166. Advance online publication. DOI: 10.3389/fenvs.2025.1607166

Zhang, Y., Chen, D., & Xu, J. (2025). The relationship between faculty members' perceptions of technology leadership and their technology integration into higher education—Evidence from China. *British Educational Research Journal*, berj.4204. Advance online publication. DOI: 10.1002/berj.4204

Zhu, Y., Zafar, S. M., & Salahodjaev, R. (2022). Mitigations pathways towards sustainable development: Assessing the influence of higher education on environmental quality in BRICS economies. *Environmental Science and Pollution Research International*, *29*(57), 86851–86858. DOI: 10.1007/s11356-022-21772-z PMID: 35802318

Ziguras, C. (2023). *The Global Market for Digital Educational Content and its Impact on Institutional Strategy*. Program Design and Teaching Practice., DOI: 10.1007/978-3-031-16065-3_9

Zulfqar, A., Valcke, M., Devos, G., & Tuytens, M. (2021). Developing academic leaders: Evaluation of a leadership development intervention in higher education. *SAGE Open*, *11*(3), 1–13. DOI: 10.1177/2158244021991815

Zvereva, E. V, Belenkova, N. M., & Kruse, I. I. (2020). From the economic union to the harmonisation of higher education in the BRICS countries: The experience of RUDN University. *Space and Culture, India, 7*(5), 60 – 69.://DOI: 10.20896/saci.v7i5.671

About the Contributors

Icarbord Tshabangu (PhD), is an Associate Professor at the Institute of Childhood and Education, Leeds Trinity University, UK. He has previously worked as a Senior Lecturer and Coordinator of Educational Foundations and Management programmes, teaching postgraduate and undergraduate courses at the University of Arusha, Tanzania and at the University of Namibia, Namibia. He was also associated with the University of Liverpool Online as Honorary Senior Lecturer (doctoral programmes). He has served as an internal and external examiner at both undergraduate and postgraduate levels and continues to be a research supervisor. His teaching and research interests are largely children's rights, democratic citizenship, education policy, and qualitative methodologies. He is also a Global Citizenship and Children's Rights Network (GLOCCRIN) coordinator and non-Executive Director for Community Development and Services Alliances (CODESA), UK.

***

Nnamdi Chijindu Azubuike is a PhD candidate in Political Science, specializing in Peace and Conflict Studies at Babcock University, Nigeria. He also serves as an adjunct lecturer in the Department of Political Science and Public Administration at Babcock University. His research interests focus on peace and conflict, ethnic and transgenerational conflict, as well as the psychological and behavioural dimensions influencing conflict dynamics.

Most. Sharmin Ara Chowdhury is a research practitioner with a strong focus on key areas such as Artificial Intelligence, strategic innovation, management information systems, and sustainability. Her research explores the intersection of emerging technologies and organizational strategy. By aligning innovation with practical needs, she addresses real-world challenges through applied and impactful research. Sharmin's expertise also extends to education technology, human-computer interaction, the Internet of Things (IoT), cognitive behavior, and intelligent computing. Her work bridges academic theory and professional practice, making significant contributions to the evolving landscape of digital transformation and sustainable development.

Md Mehedi Hasan Emon is a research practitioner in Business and Management, with specialized in Supply Chain Management, Digital Transformation, Marketing, Information Systems, and Educational Technology (Edutech). His work bridges a diverse range of domains including Artificial Intelligence in Business, Human-Computer Interaction, Cognitive Behaviour, E-commerce, and Smart Logistics. His research extensively explores the integration of emerging technologies in business ecosystems focusing on AI-driven innovation, behavioral responses to technology adoption, and digital marketing strategies. He has also contributed significantly to sustainability-focused fields such as GreenTech, Green Finance, Renewable Energy, and Blockchain-enabled financial innovation. Additionally, his work in Smart Cities and IoT adoption emphasizes the importance of user trust, security, and operational efficiency. Emon has authored numerous peer-reviewed publications on topics including AI adoption intention, supply chain visibility, digital learning acceptance, and crisis-resilient supply chains. Many of his studies adopt behavioral and cognitive perspectives to understand how professionals and consumers interact with technology highlighting the psychological and user-centric aspects of digital transformation. He has participated in several research initiatives funded by the University Grants Commission of Bangladesh and the European Union. His work aligns closely with the United Nations Sustainable Development Goals (SDGs), particularly in areas such as poverty reduction, access to quality education, clean and affordable energy, inclusive economic growth, sustainable industrialization, responsible consumption, climate resilience, and ocean sustainability. His work also reflects a commitment to reducing inequalities and fostering international partnerships for sustainable development. In addition to his research contributions, he serves as a peer reviewer for several high-impact academic journals and is widely recognized for promoting academic rigor and ethical scholarship. As a prolific author, he continues to shape the discourse on sustainability, innovation, and digital advancement through his research, writing, and knowledge dissemination.

Chinedu Ekperechukwu Eti is a detail-oriented political scientist with over 5 years of teaching and experience in Political Science with research interests in security, peace and conflict resolution, public policy advocacy, human rights and environmental protection, peace and rural development, with particular interest on the Niger Delta region of Nigeria. He holds a PhD in Political Science specializing in Peace and Conflict Studies from Babcock University, Nigeria. He is also a member several academic and professional bodies locally and globally.

Mohammad Kamrul Hasan obtained a Ph.D. in Management Science and Engineering from Shijiazhuang Tiedao University, Hebei, China, in 2024. Before getting his Ph.D., he obtained 2nd Master degree in Business Administration in China. Currently, he is working in School of Business Administration and involved in teaching & research in Tongling University, Tongling, Anhui, China. His research interests mainly include logistics management, green and sustainable logistics, and qualitative and quantitative research methodologies. He has already published a few papers in WoS and SCOPUS-indexed journals.

Sanjeev Jain is armed with a Post Graduate Diploma in Management from the prestigious Indian Institute of Management Ahmedabad and a Bachelor's degree in Engineering with a Gold Medal from Swami Bikaner University, Rajasthan. He stands out as a seasoned professional with a total work experience of over 30 years of industry and teaching. He is currently serving as the Director of the Centre of Excellence for Data Analytics and Digital Transformation, as well as heading the AIT Management department at Chandigarh University. Mr. Jain has played pivotal roles in shaping academic and industry landscapes. His earlier assignment at Nirma University reflects his commitment to excellence. Mr. Jain has excelled in strategy development, target setting, and plan execution throughout his career, having held key positions in business development, sales, marketing, project management, contract administration, and operations management. His expertise extends to managing profit and loss accounts, showcasing a profound understanding of revenue and cost management. Also, he has been awarded letter of appreciation for smooth conduct of the events at various instances. He has an Excellent project management and organisational skills and is highly proficient in spoken and written English. Mr. Jain has also secured two copyrights, notably: "NEURODECISION MATRIX OF CONSUMER CHOICE (NDMCC); A structured strategic planning framework (SOSTAC). Further, he has contributed towards one case study in Taylor and Francis book entitled "Contemporary Cases in Management: Perspectives from Emerging Markets". In his distinguished career, Mr. Sanjeev Jain has contributed significantly to various fields through his research endeavors. He has written various research paper on the subject like hybrid learning, green bonds. His seminal papers include "Probabilistic Paradigms for Employee Performance Prognostication: Unveiling Influential Factors via Bayesian Networks," shedding light on innovative approaches to forecasting employee performance. Additionally, his research on "Intrusion Detection Systems for Cybersecurity using Machine Learning" addresses critical challenges in cybersecurity, demonstrating his commitment to advancing technological solutions in safeguarding digital environments. Mr. Jain's expertise extends to "IoT Smart Communication Technologies for Narrow Band IoT," where he explores the intricate realm of Internet of Things, paving the way for efficient communication technologies in IoT networks.

Jipson Joseph has a PhD in Ethics from DVK Bangalore. Currently, he is a Research Scholar at School of Law, Christ University, Bangalore, India. His research interests are in the fields of ethics, gender studies, sustainable education, constitutional law, human rights, human security, environmental justice, SDGs, developmental policies, and global poverty. He has published 6 books, co-edited one book, and contributed scholarly articles to many international and national journals and edited volumes including IGI Global Scientific Publishing's edited books.

Rishikaysh Kaakandikar is an accomplished academician, researcher, and author, currently serving as Associate Professor of Finance at SaiBalaji International Institute of Management Sciences (SBIIMS), Pune. With over 15 years of academic experience and a year in the corporate sector, he has made significant contributions to the fields of Finance, Human Resource Management, Artificial Intelligence, FinTech, Sustainability, and Digital Transformation. He has authored and published more than 100 research papers in reputed national and international journals, with over 1,200 citations and 47,000+ reads on platforms like ResearchGate. His published books, including AI-Powered HR Finance, TechHumanize: The FinTech Evolution in HR, Sustainable Tourism in the Digital Era, and The Three Pillars of Business, reflect his expertise in integrating technology with management disciplines. Widely recognized for bridging academic research with practical industry applications, Dr. Kaakandikar is also a sought-after speaker, mentor, and workshop facilitator, known for his dedication to fostering student development, promoting financial literacy, and advancing research in digital finance, ESG investing, and HR analytics.

Tahsina Khan is serving as Deputy Director (Research) at the Centre for Higher Studies and Research in Bangladesh University of Professionals (BUP). In addition, she is also serving as the Assistant Editor of the BUP Journal. She is an Academician in Business Studies with more than 14 years of teaching, research & consulting experience in Higher Education Institutions. Over the years, she has successfully supervised multilateral academic programs in collaboration with the Government, NGOs, and Corporations from the Business sector. As a Visiting Lecturer, she has taught in the MBA program of the University of Gavle, Sweden. She has worked as Director of the research projects funded by the University Grants Commission (UGC) under the Ministry of Education. Her research papers were presented in National and International Conferences in Canada, France, Malaysia and Indonesia.

As Session Chair, she presided over the conference organized by Higher Education and Innovation Group (HEAIG). She has also been invited as a resource speaker at the United Nations affiliated conference at the Yonsei University in Wonju, South Korea. She has published a number of peer-reviewed articles in reputed international journals and her policy brief paper on Rural Development has been included in the knowledge hub of the UN Task Force on SDG implementation. She is a member of International Sociological Association (ISA) which is associated with UNESCO, Economic & Social Council of the United Nations.

Goodnews Osah, PhD teaches governance, peace and strategic studies in the in the Department of Political Science and Public Administration, Babcock University, Nigeria. His teaching and research interests are demilitarisation of ethnic militias; post-conflict peacebuilding; defence and strategic studies. He holds membership with several academic and professional bodies including the Nigerian Political Science Association (NPSA), Society for Peace Studies and Practice (SPSP). He is a fellow of the Institute of Policy Management Development and The Institute of Management Consultants. He is Review Editor and on the editorial board membership of several journals.

Tejashree Soni is an Assistant Professor in Finance at Sai Balaji International Institutes of Management with over 9 years of academic and industry experience. She specialises in management accounting, financial management, personal financial planning, and management fundamentals and is currently pursuing a Ph.D. in Financial Management from Savitribai Phule Pune University. Her professional journey includes roles at Akemi Business School, NBN Sinhgad School of Management Studies, Oceanic Tecno Chem Pvt. Ltd., and the Suryadatta Group of Institutions. She has actively contributed to SPPU examination processes, student mentoring, NAAC documentation, and institutional publications, while also coordinating entrepreneurial and literacy initiatives. Her research interests lie in investment decisions, corporate frauds, and financial strategies. She has published papers in reputed journals. She has also presented at several state, national, and international conferences and participated in multiple FDPs and workshops on finance, teaching innovations, and research methodology.

Index

A

B

C

D

E

F

G

H

I

R

S

T

U

V

W

www.ingramcontent.com/pod-product-compliance
Lightning Source LLC
LaVergne TN
LVHW062338300926
849161LV00007B/1737